A SURVEY OF

United States-
Latin American
Relations

J. LLOYD MECHAM

Professor Emeritus of Government

The University of Texas

HOUGHTON MIFFLIN COMPANY

Boston · New York · Atlanta · Geneva, Ill. · Dallas · Palo Alto

UNDER THE EDITORSHIP OF

DAYTON D. MCKEAN

UNIVERSITY OF COLORADO

To John Stephen and Lois Eleanor

with parental love and pride

Contents

PART TWO

Caribbean and Country Relations

TABLES

MAPS

CHART

Preface

A bibliographical listing of titles dealing with United States-Latin American relations would reveal the interesting fact that, among the almost innumerable books that have been published, few could qualify as general surveys of relations. Virtually all are restricted to aspects of Latin-American relations, being confined to individual countries or to selected topics.

Probably the earliest broad treatise on United States relations with the Latin-American nations was that of Professor John H. Latané, published in 1900 under the title *The Diplomatic Relations of the United States and Spanish America.* In 1920 Dr. Latané revised and enlarged the original volume under the title *The United States and Latin America.* In 1922 appeared Graham H. Stuart's *Latin America and the United States,* a work destined to five editions through 1955; and in 1923 was published William Spence Robertson's *Hispanic-American Relations with the United States.* None of these works attempted to trace the evolution of the Latin-American policy of the United States from its beginning in the days of independence to the date of publication. The Latané and Robertson volumes, in particular, were little more than collections of essays on topics dealing with United States-Latin American relations. In fact, all three volumes left broad gaps in a comprehensive survey of diplomatic relations between the United States and the Latin-American countries.

In 1943 appeared Professor Samuel F. Bemis' *The Latin American Policy of the United States: An Historical Interpretation.* Although this excellent study, which was never revised, traced the evolution of policy from Latin-American independence to 1942, it omitted the important subject of country relations (i.e., United States relations with individual countries). Granting that the Latin-American policy of the United States has had a conspicuous regional basis, and thus lends itself to general survey under such topics as the Monroe Doctrine, Pan Americanism, the Doctrine of Nonintervention, the Good Neighbor Policy, and the Alliance for Progress, it is nevertheless true that many special problems with individual countries do not lend themselves to inclusion in any of these regional policies.

For a number of years there has been urgent need for a college text for courses in inter-American diplomacy and United States-Latin American relations. It is the purpose of the present survey to satisfy that need, and to give adequate attention to both the policies of general application as well as to country relations. A few countries have not been selected for special treatment for the reason that the problems of their relations are adequately handled in the section dealing with general policies.

Grateful acknowledgment is given to Mr. Frank H. Wardlaw, Director of the University of Texas Press, for his permission to draw on the author's *The United States and Inter-American Security.* Also gratefully acknowledged is the contribution of Dr. Horace V. Harrison of the University of Maryland to portions of Chapters X–XIII, and his careful reading of Chapters I–IX.

J. Lloyd Mecham

Part One

POLICIES OF GENERAL APPLICATION

The Foundations of Hemispheric Intercourse

United States-Latin American relations have been the product of many factors, but certainly among these the most important is common occupancy of a huge segment of the earth's surface, the Western Hemisphere. The mere fact of geographic contiguity has contributed greatly to the making and influencing of our policies and contacts with Latin America. For this reason, and preliminary to discussion of the origins and development of United States relations with its southern "neighbors," certain basic facts concerning the physical and social geography of the region should be noted.

1. The Physiography of Latin America

With the exception of the Guianas in South America, British Honduras (Belize) in Central America, and the Lesser Antilles in the Caribbean, the vast land mass south of the United States is Latin America. In area it is almost eight million square miles, or more than two and one-half times that of continental United States, and twice that of Europe. This portion of the Western Hemisphere where are located twenty independent republics, not too accurately called "Latin," is an area of great contrasts, topographic and climatic. It is a complex of high mountains, semi-arid plateaus, jungle, plains, and for the most part only "pockets" of arable land. The most notable exceptions to the pattern of widely distributed parcels of cultivable lands are: the Argentine pampas, vast level stretches of the deepest and richest soil in all the world; most of Uruguay and Paraguay, southern Brazil; and the rich central valley of Chile.

The dominant physical feature of the map of Latin America is the great mountain chain or cordillera which extends from the borders of the United States to the tip of the southern continent. In Mexico two widely divergent mountain ranges, the Sierra Madre Occidental and the Sierra Madre Oriental, parallel the Pacific coast and the Gulf of Mexico respectively. Between the two, the great Mexican plateau ascends from an altitude of about 3,000 feet at the United States border to about 8,000 feet at the point of convergence near Mexico City. From Mexico the cordillera backbone persists through Central America to Panama.

In South America the mountain chain known for its full length of 4,000 miles as the Andes, emerges from the shores of the Caribbean and extends along the edge of the Pacific to Cape Horn. At places, the mountains rise almost sheer from the ocean, but at most they leave only a narrow coastal plain. In width the mountain barrier varies from less than 100 miles in the south to about 400 miles in Peru and Bolivia, where they spread out in a plateau. Not only is the Andes the world's longest mountain range, but its few passes are the highest. The volcanic peak Aconcagua (Elevation 22,835 feet) is the highest mountain in the Western Hemisphere. No less than thirteen Latin-American republics repose in the folds of the great cordillera in Middle and South America. Two more of the Latin-American states, Haiti and the Dominican Republic, occupying the same Caribbean island, are also distinctly mountainous. Most of Brazil which is not Amazonian jungle is plateau occupying an area of close to a million square miles at a height varying from 2,000 to 3,000 feet. The Brazilian highlands, belonging to a geological age much older than that of the Andes, crowd close to the Atlantic coast and reach a height no greater than 9,400 feet.

Next to its mountainous terrain another natural feature of the map of Latin America is the Amazonian basin of South America, the world's largest area of tropical forest through which the Amazon River flows. The Amazon exceeds in volume of water any three of the world's other rivers combined. It carries one-fifth of all the world's running fresh water. Little wonder, since this river collects the waters that drain about 40 per cent of all South America. The only highway into impenetrable jungles, the Amazon allows ocean ships to ascend 900 miles to Manaos, and smaller vessels 1,400 miles farther to Iquitos, the Peruvian "metropolis of the Amazon." Because of the high mountain barrier which separates Iquitos from the rest of Peru, the most comfortable and convenient passage from Lima to Iquitos was, before the airplane, by way of Panama to London, thence to Manaos and finally up the river to Iquitos. Detour by way of London was necessary, since there were no scheduled sailings from Panama to Manaos.

In addition to the Amazon, South America is endowed with several more great river systems. Two of these are the Magdalena-Cauca in Colombia and the Orinoco in Venezuela. Both rivers are navigable for considerable distances upstream. But of the continent's river systems, the one of greatest commercial utility is the Paraná-Paraguay, which empties into the estuary of the Río de la Plata. The Paraná system, which drains northern Argentina,

Paraguay, Uruguay, and southern Brazil, has a total of about 2,000 miles of water navigable for large vessels. It is of first importance in all of Latin America as a highway of commerce, being indispensable to northern Argentina and Paraguay. Central America and the west coast of South America have no rivers of consequence as avenues of communication.

The geographical relationships of North and South America also call for special mention. In the first place, a rather general impression in the United States that South America is altogether south of this country, that Chile and Peru are south of California, and Rio de Janeiro and Buenos Aires south of New York, needs to be corrected. Lima, Peru, is approximately due south, not of San Francisco, but of New York City, for a line through New York City parallels the western side of South America only a few miles east of the coast line. Since Brazil extends about 2,600 miles to the east of a line passing through New York City, South America is thus brought as close to Europe as to the United States. The hump of Brazil is only 1,900 miles from Africa. Barring the countries of Middle America, it is a denial of vast distances to call the nations of South America our "neighbors."

The two continents have a certain similarity in configuration, each being widest in the north and tapering off to the south; each has high mountains on the western edges, and lower and older elevations in the east; and in the center of each are great river valleys. Here the similarities end, for the heart of the North American continent, the great Mississippi Valley, is one of the most favorably endowed regions of the world for human habitation, in soil, climate, and resources. In contrast, the great Amazonian basin is one of the least favored dwelling places for man. South America is unfortunate in shape because its widest part, or two-thirds of its total area, is located in the tropics. Its narrowest part, which tapers off into bleak Patagonia and Tierra del Fuego, is in the temperate zone. Fourteen countries are completely within the torrid zone. Six countries (Mexico, Argentina, Chile, Bolivia, Paraguay, and Brazil) lie partly in the two zones. Only Uruguay, the most progressive and democratic of all the Latin-American nations, is completely within the temperate zone. The handicap of tropical location has been reflected in Latin-American history and development.

Another erroneous impression of Latin America entertained by *Norte Americanos* is that the climate is truly torrid ascending in intensity as one approaches the equator. This is not true on two counts: neither is the heat of the tropics greater than in our own southwest, nor are the highest degrees registered at the equator. Compared with North America the southern part of the hemisphere has moderate climates, neither too cold nor too hot. Nowhere can the winters be compared with those of northern United States and Canada, and the summers are more comfortable. Very high temperatures are rare in Latin America. According to Preston James, "The only part of Latin America, outside of Mexico, where temperatures are over 110° at any time of the year is in northern Argentina." As for excessive heat at the equator, the same authority holds that the highest temperatures occur not

TABLE 1

Latin America: The Land and People (1960)

Country	Area Sq. mi.*	Population Total*	Population Per sq. mi.	Racial Composition[a] (per cent) White	Indian	Mestizo	Negro & Mulatto
Argentina	1,073	20,006	20	90	2	8	
Bolivia	424	3,462	8	13	63	24	
Brazil	3,287	65,743	20	53	3	18	26
Chile	286	7,340	26	30	5	65	
Colombia	440	14,132	32	20	15	60	5
Costa Rica	20	1,171	60	94[b]	1		5
Cuba	44	6,797	154	75			25
Dominican Republic	19	3,014	160	25			75
Ecuador	105	4,317	41	15	40	40	5
El Salvador	8	2,612	320	5	18	75	
Guatemala	42	3,765	90	5	55	40	
Haiti	11	3,505	327				100
Honduras	43	1,953	45	3	10	85	2
Mexico	761	34,988	46	11	29	59	1
Nicaragua	57	1,477	26	17	5	69	9
Panama	29	1,055	37	12	11	59	18
Paraguay	157	1,768	11	96[b]	4		
Peru	496	10,857	22	53[b]	47		
Uruguay	72	2,827	39	86	2	12	
Venezuela	352	6,709	19	10	10	70	10
Total: Lat. Am.	7,725	197,325	26				
U.S. (Continental)	3,022	180,670	60				
U.S. (with Alaska and Hawaii)	3,615		51				

Source: *Statistical Abstract of Latin America, 1962* (Center of Latin American Studies, University of California, Los Angeles, 1963).
a. There are no reliable statistics of racial composition. These figures, which are only of an approximate nature, are based on scattered estimates. b. Includes mestizos.

* in thousands

on the equator but rather between the middle and low latitudes during the summer months.[1]

For much of Latin America, that is, the mountainous areas, climate is not so much a matter of latitude as of altitude. The highlands of Middle and South America have furnished temperate settings for ancient native cultures and modern civilization. On the coastal fringes of the continent ocean currents refresh the atmosphere. For example, at Lima, only a short distance from the equator, one does not discard moderately heavy clothing, even in midsummer.

2. The People

Too many *Norte Americanos* view all south of the border as a unity, not only in ethnic composition, but in political, economic, social, and cultural development. This is an error which needs to be corrected if the real Latin America is to be understood. (See Table 1.)

In the first place, there is great lack of uniformity among the twenty Latin-American nations in area and in population. Brazil, both in size and in population outstrips all others by a wide margin. It has about 42 per cent of the surface area and 37 per cent of the population of all Latin America. El Salvador, with only 8,260 square miles, is the smallest in area; Panama is the least populous with about one million inhabitants.

Population

The population of Latin America is growing faster than that of any other major region of the world. For example, from 1920 to 1950 the rate of increase was more than 80 per cent.[2] The world increase for the same period was 33 per cent. Today the population of Latin America is pressing the 200 million mark. If the present rate of increase continues, by the end of the century it will be 600 million.[3] As in the United States, most of Latin America's population increase is urban. Argentina is the most urbanized of all of the Latin-American republics: almost two-thirds of its people live in cities and towns. One-fourth of all Argentines live in Buenos Aires, and one-third of all Uruguayans live in Montevideo. Also, most of Latin America's population increase is natural, for efforts to encourage mass immigration from Europe have not materialized, since Europe lacks the mass of peasant labor which Latin America wants. Wrote Kingsley Davis, Latin America "cannot attract the kind of immigrants it wants, and does not want the kind it can attract."[4] Latin America seeks farm labor to do what the Latins will not do.

---

[1] Preston E. James, *Latin America* (New York: The Odyssey Press, 1959, 3rd ed. rev.), 30, 32.

[2] *Ibid.*, 5.

[3] According to the Population Branch of the UN, the population of Latin America will be trebled between the years 1960 and 2,000. It is difficult merely to keep up living standards as population grows.

[4] Kingsley Davis, "Latin America's Multiplying Peoples," *Foreign Affairs*, 25, No. 4 (July, 1947), 643–645.

Latin America's huge open spaces are said to be available for mass migration from a crowded world. This myth arises from the fact that Latin America with only 6 per cent of the world's population, covers 19 per cent of the earth's inhabited continents. By contrast Asia has a population density per square mile seven times that of Latin America. Therefore, so goes the argument, Latin America is underpopulated. This is not necessarily true, for in relation to its visible potential the area cannot support a much larger population. In comparison with other continents South America is poor in resources. At best the population gains are absorbed in feeding more mouths. Can the empty Amazon basin, the vacant Patagonian plains, the unexploited Guiana and Brazilian highlands accommodate homes for millions of immigrants? These are broad areas of sparsely settled hinterlands precisely because, up to the present date, they cannot be economically exploited. The problem is not the need of people, for they are at hand, but of capital, technical skills, and new economic and social orientation, all of which may or may not be effective in bringing more inhabitants to the vacant areas of Latin America.

Ethnic and racial

The ethnic contrasts are equally marked. There is of course no typical Latin American, for ethnic diversity is one of the principal characteristics of Middle and South America. The inhabitants of the different regions and countries are white (European), Indian, or Negro, or a mixture in varying degrees of two or of all three. Thus, Argentina, Costa Rica, and Uruguay are overwhelmingly white, and Chile and Paraguay are white to a lesser extent. The Indian predominates in Guatemala, Bolivia, Ecuador, and Peru. The countries in which the mestizo, or mixed white and Indian bloods, are in the majority are Mexico, Honduras, El Salvador, Nicaragua, Colombia, and Venezuela. In the remaining countries Negro blood is an important component but in varying degrees; thus, Haiti is almost entirely Negro, the Dominican Republic is predominantly mulatto, and Cuba and Panama are mixed white, mestizo, and mulatto. The mainland fringes of the Caribbean all have substantial negroid elements in the population. Finally, Brazil presents a curious racial pattern of white, Negro, and Indian, with the whites constituting a major part of the population. Because intermarriage and concubinage have produced racial mixtures, Latin Americans have escaped a caste-like distinction between races. Color consciousness is existent but to no such pronounced degree as in the United States.

Although the independence of the Latin-American states dates in no instance farther back than 1804 for Haiti and 1810 for Argentina, and although most of them enjoyed a common colonial heritage, there has developed in every one a self-conscious spirit of unique identity known as nationalism. Thus, there are today in Latin America twenty sovereign, independent, nation-states, each one different more or less from the others. For this reason, we must exercise caution when categorizing the Latin-American states with respect to matters political, economic, and social. We look first at the political.

Political

Influenced by the examples of the United States and France, all of the emergent states subscribed to written constitutions providing for popular representative republics. Ever since their original efforts, the Latins, in seeking the ideal constitution as a cure-all for political and governmental ills, have essayed a grand total of nearly 200 constitutions, or about 10 per country. If the drafting of democratic constitutions serves as preparation for practice in the art of popular government, then, indeed, Latin Americans are well prepared. Unfortunately, as is well known, this is not true, for the future of responsible government in Latin America generally is scarcely brighter today than it was twenty-five, fifty, or one hundred years ago.

With the exception of Uruguay, and the doubtful addition of Costa Rica and Chile, democratic government does not exist in Latin America. Although lip service has always been paid to the principle of popular sovereignty, the prevailing forms of government since independence have been personalistic dictatorships and pseudo-democracies.

Paradoxically, contemporary Latin-American constitutions measure up well, compared with other world constitutions, as advanced instruments of democratic government. Their ample provisions for progressive social welfare programs are in harmony with the ideals and realities of the mid-twentieth century. But unfortunately much of this is reduced to mere verbiage because of the Latins' general attitude toward constitutional law. Whereas to the Anglo-American the constitution is the fundamental law and must be observed, to the Latin American it is in many respects merely a declaration of ideal objectives. We subscribe to the principle of a government of law; to the Latin the constitution, generally a useful and convenient guide and program, must bend to the principle of a government of men, or, as has been too often the case, government by one man.

Thus, despite the numerous and ingenious safeguards provided by the "paper constitution" against the exercise of arbitrary power by the executive, we find that in response to the strong-man tradition, the president is in fact the dominant power in the government. His supremacy derives from his dual position as constitutional chief executive and as extraconstitutional *caudillo,* or boss. From the earliest days of their independence Latin Americans have shown a strong disposition for *caudillos,* preferably those with a military background, for the magnetic attraction of the man on horseback can always be expected to reinforce the lure of demagogues. The *caudillo* embodies the program of his political partisans; he is the platform of his pseudo-party. This is what is called *personalismo* in Latin-American politics, which means placing emphasis on individuals rather than on public policies. *Caudillismo* and *personalismo* have transformed the constitutional office of the presidency beyond recognition. Also, in consequence of the dominance of the executive it is hardly necessary to indicate that the congress and the courts are almost completely amenable to the executive's pleasure. The constitutional principle of the separation of powers is a nullity.

One of the most patent facts of Latin-American government, and certainly the best known to Anglo-Americans, is recurring *revolutions.* The term is a misnomer, for it usually refers to nothing more than a *coup d'état* or *cuartelazo* (barracks revolt), the classic "substitution of bullets for ballots," the ousting of the "ins" by the "outs," or perhaps the enforcement of the principle of "alternability of public office." If we restrict the term to those deep-seated popular movements aimed at fundamental change in the political, social, and economic orders, we find that only a limited number of demonstrations of force so common to the Latin-American scene are worthy of designation as "revolutions." What Latin America needs, paradoxically, is not less but more revolutions. In fact, fundamental revolution may be the specific cure for the chronic pseudo-revolutions which bring new faces into government, but do not change the basic political and social systems.

In view of the considerable divergencies of actual practice from the constitutional norm in Latin America, a question arises: Does the fact that they are observed in the breach prove their artificiality? Not if we recall that Latin-American constitution-makers do not delude themselves that they are building upon achieved democracy, but rather are setting their nations upon the road to democratic achievement. How indeed can these so-called artificial and exotic constitutions be modified to conform to the realities of the Latin-American scene and still retain their democratic character? They already contain in profusion curbs on *caudillismo,* the *cuartelazo,* and the rigging of elections. What constitutional formulae are missing which will broaden and strengthen the bases of popular government and usher in political, social, and economic democracy?

The simple truth of the matter is that there are no constitutional formulae which, however well-suited to any practical situation or unique environment, will of themselves inaugurate a democratic regime. The road to popular and responsible government in Latin America is a long and difficult way. There are no easy shortcuts.[5]

A casual listing of certain requisites for the development of Latin-American constitutional democracy reveals the great distance that still separates most of the countries from the goal. First, the high illiteracy rate of about 50 per cent or more for most of the republics must be drastically reduced. It is obvious that an educated citizenry is essential to a democracy. Yet in Mexico, which is in the upper echelon of Latin-American nations in economic and social development, illiteracy is nearly 40 per cent, with about 1,500,000 children unable to attend school because of lack of facilities and teachers. Second, the pitifully low standards of living must be raised, for it is equally obvious that democracy cannot exist in an economic and social environment where a deep cleavage separates the very rich from the very poor. Nor can popular government survive where the masses from birth to grave struggle on the precarious margin of mere existence. Third, the vestiges of feudalism,

[5] See J. Lloyd Mecham, "Latin American Constitutions: Nominal and Real," *The Journal of Politics,* XXI (May, 1959), 258–276.

particularly in landholding, prevalent throughout Latin America, are incompatible with democracy, and so agrarian reform and land redistribution is essential. Fourth, a large middle class, an urban middle sector, to hold the balance between the traditional elite and the great mass of workers, is also a democratic must. It is quite true that in some of the countries there is emerging a middle class of professionals and independent proprietors and managers in agriculture, trade, and industry, but as yet this necessary bulwark of democracy is in its feeble beginnings. Finally, and most important, there is a lack of those inner qualities, characteristic of a democratic citizenry, which have deep roots in their historical past. These are: fair play, tolerance, self-discipline, responsibility, human dignity, majority rule but respect for the minority, a spirit of compromise, and respect for the rule of law. These qualities, which are of the inner man and so cannot be legislated into existence, unfortunately have not prospered in Latin America. Nor after 150 years of tortured experience in self-government does the present status of democratic achievement in most of the Latin-American nations augur much improvement in the foreseeable future.

According to a leading authority, force and violence are apparently institutionalized in the organization, maintenance, and changing of governments in Latin America. He held that, because the traditional institutions of Hispanic culture — such as the family, church, educational institutions, army, and economic systems — are essentially authoritarian in nature, the Latin has been conditioned "to more frequent acceptance of processes of dictatorship, including violence, than processes of democracy."[6]

Awareness of the nature of political power in Latin America and the methods of achieving authority in the state should have great relevancy to the conduct of our relations with Latin America. However, this seems to be overlooked in face of the desire of our policy makers to consider the Latin-American republics as democracies in the political sense. It is in fact a dangerous delusion based more on idealism and hope than on reality and understanding.

3. The Economy of Latin America

Resources

Failure to understand the nature of Latin-American economy and some of the limitations of its resources have contributed to survival of the old myth of *El Dorado* — that it is a land of "untold riches." Even today there are too frequently over-optimistic appraisals of the physical resources of the area. It is not a rich continent; on the contrary, it is the least favored of the major regions of the world.

Formerly the supposed wealth of the continent was measured in terms

[6] William S. Stokes, "Violence as a Power Factor in Latin American Politics," *The Western Political Quarterly*, V, No. 3 (September, 1952), 467.

of the great quantities of gold and silver produced by the mines of Mexico and Peru. Since these have not for many years been important in Latin-American production, how is the value of the mineral resources measured now? It is by the output of the base metals — lead, zinc, copper, iron,[7] manganese, bauxite, and tin — upon which the industrial machine of the world is greatly dependent. The mineral resources of Latin America, however, are limited in quantity and distribution. In fact, the value of production of metals and minerals in Latin America is approximately only one-sixth that of the United States.[8]

In energy resources Latin America has deficiencies in fuel and power. Less than one per cent of the world's estimated reserves of coal are in Latin America, and the coal is of poor quality and frequently is not located near other resources (e.g., iron). In petroleum Latin America has one-sixth of the world's supply, but variations within Latin America are great. For example, of the ten countries that produce oil, only three (Venezuela, Colombia, and Mexico) produce significant amounts, and of these Venezuela alone produces 63 per cent of Latin America's total. As for water power, Latin America is more fortunate: it possesses 14 per cent of the world's water power resources. The sites best adapted to development, however, are far removed from population centers. In fact, a feature of the "mad geography," or *geografía loca,* which characterizes much of Latin America, is the location of natural resources in isolated mountains, jungle, and desert areas.

Agriculture

Although undoubtedly Latin America's richest natural resource is land, the percentage adapted to agricultural production is less than 5 per cent of the total land area. This compares with 37 per cent for Europe, 10 per cent for North America, 6 per cent for Asia, and 3 per cent for Africa.[9] Belief that the tropical jungle is excessively fertile and adaptable to cultivation is not well founded. Concerning the Amazon basin, Fairfield Osborn wrote, "Most of the region is densely covered by tropical forests. When the tree canopy is removed the land suffers rapid leeching of the life-supporting mineral elements in the soil because of the violence of the tropical rains."[10]

In Mexico, by contrast, 94 per cent of the land is arid or semiarid. Only 11 per cent of the land was under cultivation in 1960. A little more than half the population lives off agriculture, many persons in miserable conditions. Nevertheless, despite the scarcity of truly arable lands, with few exceptions, the national economies of Latin America are essentially agrarian, for two-thirds of the population are engaged in agriculture. In most of the countries

[7] Brazil has the largest of the world's iron ore deposits at Itabira, probably one-sixth of the world's reserve. Simon G. Hanson, *Economic Development in Latin America* (Washington, D.C.: The Inter-American Affairs Press, 1951), 52.

[8] See Tables 8–9 in *ibid.,* 56.

[9] See Table 5 in *ibid.,* 38.

[10] Fairfield Osborn, *Our Plundered Planet* (Boston: Little Brown and Company, 1948), 174–175.

agricultural production is not only the most important portion of the total national production, but it contributes more than any other industry to foreign trade. Thus, for Latin America agriculture generally accounts for more than two-thirds of the total exports, and in some of the countries more than 90 per cent. (See Table 2.)

Because of the great importance of production for export the trend has been toward monoculture. Thus, in most of the countries some one agricultural product is the largest item on the export list. In seven republics this item is coffee; in some it is sugar, and in others bananas or cotton. Since the agriculture of so many of the countries is organized for the production of a single export product, the national economies are at the mercy of external market factors. Another consequence of overspecialization is that few of the countries have sufficient diversification to meet the needs of local consumption or the requirements of a healthful nutrition. It is truly anomalous that countries which are essentially agrarian find it necessary to import staple foodstuffs. To escape the risks of reliance on one or a few export products, proposed solutions are diversification of production and industrialization. Either or both have been tried, and with varying results. However, monoculture has been so profitable that there is considerable resistance to change.

Land tenure

Although Latin America's agricultural economy produces specialized commodities in exceptional quantities, this does not negate the fact that most of the agriculture is inefficient and substandard. Productivity per man-hour is less than one-fifth that of the United States. This is due to a variety of reasons, including lack of technical skills and mechanical equipment; but probably the most important reason for the agricultural lag is the system of land tenure which obstructs a healthy adjustment between population and land resources. Be that as it may, there seems to be a consensus that of the various economic impediments to political and social progress the most important is the system of land ownership.

A high degree of inequality in land ownership is the basic characteristic of the Latin-American agrarian system. In spite of the fact that in some of the countries less than 3 per cent of the land is suitable for cultivation, and 65 per cent of the population is rural, and one-half of the labor force is on the land, yet 90 per cent of the land belongs to 10 per cent of the owners. This is *latifundia,* or the large estate, the prevailing form of land ownership.

Derivatives of the large-estate system of land tenure are peonage (debt servitude), absentee landlordism, and monoculture. Instead of increasing production through greater efficiency, the landowners have been satisfied to obtain their profits by keeping their tenants and farm workers in a state of semi-servitude or peonage. The landlords' preference for the immediate gains of commercial crops for export results in overconcentration on a few cash crops. Also, the semi-feudal organization of land usually ignores any regard for the concept of the social functions of land and evades a fair share of the

TABLE 2. *Latin America: Agricultural Production*

Country	Live Stock (thousand head)			Crop Production (thousand metric tons)					
	Cattle	Hogs	Sheep	Bananas	Coffee	Corn	Cotton	Sugar	Wheat
Argentina	40,000	3,470	49,000	9		4,850	122	859	3,960
Bolivia	2,260	509	7,224		2	100			11
Brazil	72,829	46,523	18,995	4,798	2,640	8,255	483	3,500	683
Chile	2,809	902	6,129			172			
Colombia	13,390	1,455	1,126	344	480	864	70		1,187
Costa Rica	954	95	1		54	60		61	
Cuba	4,150	1,440	174		51	196		6,000	
Dominican Republic	949	1,648	70		35	101	4	1,281	
Ecuador	1,363	1,081	1,502	1,790	32	157		109	47
El Salvador	827	221	3		94	180	40	53	
Guatemala	1,142	406	841	116	97	506	21		2
Haiti	607	1,136	52	2	22	230		72	
Honduras	1,121	615	11	735	24	293	2		2
Mexico	21,561	9,423	5,788	274	117	5,500	437	1,633	1,100
Nicaragua	1,331	521	1		24	119	33	73	
Panama	661	247		390	4	77			
Paraguay	3,666	476	402		1	143	11	30	14
Peru	3,590	1,464	15,136		22	330	130	840	163
Uruguay	7,433	581	23,303			197		35	445
Venezuela	7,162	2,362	176	924	45	440	8	245	
Total	187,400	73,300	129,000	11,000	3,775	20,900	1,190	18,149	7,791
United States	101,250	58,464	33,170	3	5	110,562	3,103	2,785	36,750
World Total	823,000	485,500	967,100	15,100	4,605	222,900	10,900	55,745	249,900

Source: *Statistical Abstract of Latin America, 1962* (UCLA, 1963). Dates for production figures extend from 1951 to 1961.

14

cost of government. Since monopolization of the land has in Latin America been the chief source of political power, agrarian reform has had its political, as well as social and economic implications. Traditionally, the Church, the army, and the landowners exercised almost absolute power, and, to protect their vested interests, cooperated in blocking agricultural reform. Thus, notwithstanding a few notable examples of agrarian reform, such as have been carried out in Mexico, in most of the countries efforts under the Alliance for Progress to broaden the base of land ownership have not been successful. Agrarian reform is still Latin America's number one problem.

Mining and petroleum

Next to agriculture, the extractive industry (mining and oil production) is Latin America's most important occupation. But unlike agriculture, mining provides employment for only a very small part of the population. The countries where mining is more significant as an employment factor are Mexico, Peru, Bolivia, and Chile. In Chile mineral production employs only 5 per cent of the population, and in Bolivia 4 per cent. In all four countries fewer than 250,000 persons are employed in the organized mining industries. Mining's great importance derives from the quantity and value of the mineral products, most of which are exported. Of the four principal mining countries mentioned, which account for 80 per cent of the total mineral production of Latin America, the mineral exports range from 25 per cent for Peru to 90 per cent for Bolivia. For Latin America as a whole, the mining industry accounts for about 10 per cent of the total exports.

The importance of Latin America in mineral production is partially shown in Table 3. Illustrative of the importance of particular countries in world production, we note that: Bolivia has about 15 per cent of all tin deposits; Chile is the largest producer of natural nitrates and ranks second in copper production; Mexico is first in silver, second in lead, and third in zinc; Peru is leader in vanadium and bismuth, and ranks high in copper, lead, and zinc; and Venezuela ranks a possible second in oil production and iron ore deposits.

The mineral production of Latin America, although considerable, is not believed to be equal to its potential. This is due to a number of reasons, probably the most important being the handicaps of physical location, for usually the minerals are discovered in remote mountainous, desert, or jungle areas distant from all existent means of transportation. Therefore it becomes necessary to construct at great expense roads and railways, over which the ore is transported, also at great expense. Because of the necessities of processing and refining at distant places the expenses mount. Only to a limited degree can these costs be compensated by cheaper labor.

Because of their dependence on one or a few mineral products, some of the mining countries, notably Chile and Bolivia, are virtually on a monocultural economy, and are constantly threatened by all the perils of a one-crop or commodity production for export. Thus the foreign market for

TABLE 3

Latin America: Mining Production (1960) (thousand metric tons)

Country	Minerals, Fuels		Mineral Production						
	Coal	Oil	Iron	Lead	Copper	Zinc	Bauxite	Tin	Manganese
Argentina	217	9,146	52	30	2	40			6
Bolivia		415		22	2	3		24,195	
Brazil	2,330	3,871	4,749	9			70		421
Chile	1,741	943	4,744	2	546	1			27
Colombia	2,500	7,713	172						172
Costa Rica									
Cuba		27			9				24
Dominican Republic							771		
Ecuador		361							
El Salvador									
Guatemala				6					
Haiti							259		
Honduras				3					
Mexico	1,772	14,350	521	191	57	264			77
Nicaragua									
Panama									
Paraguay									
Peru	172	2,530	2,090	115	50	143			
Uruguay									
Venezuela	34	153,251	19,490						
Total	8,766	192,607	31,318	378	666	451	1,100	24,195	727
United States	391,070	147,976	89,039	232	748	386	1,700	41	90
World Total	1,896,300	980,600	191,400	1,910	3,180	2,710	19,560	143,000	5,100

Source: *Statistical Abstract of Latin America, 1962* (UCLA, 1963). The dates for the production figures extend from 1951 to 1961.

copper or tin controls not only the amount of the nation's foreign exchange, but also a substantial segment of the government's revenue. Internal prosperity and governmental stability are hostages to the prices for these minerals fixed in foreign exchanges.

Foreign ownership

A special feature of Latin America's mining industry is that it is heavily dominated by foreign capital. The enormous oil production of Venezuela, the copper production of Chile and Peru, the bulk of the mining and smelting operations in Mexico, are not only foreign-owned but United States-owned.

Why this predominance of foreign ownership in the mining industry? It is due largely to inadequate and reluctant domestic capital. Modern mining operations in Latin America are excessively complicated and expensive, and apparently overtax the accumulation of domestic investment capital. However, this is only a part of the explanation, for it seems that local capitalists shy away from the great risks and heavy long-term investment that the mining industry requires. They evidently prefer to put their money in land and commercial enterprises that promise quicker and richer returns. Thus it has been left to the foreigner to develop Latin America's mineral resources, as well as other "risk" enterprises.

Because the extractive nature of the mining industry causes irreplaceable depletion of the subsoil resources and because the industry is foreign-owned, it has become the special target of nationalistic pressure and discriminatory legislation. The petroleum industry especially, has felt the full weight of nationalistic pressure. The foreign oil holdings have been expropriated in Mexico and Bolivia. In Venezuela, although foreign ownership is still legal, the government's royalty on the net oil income has been progressively increased to the present 67–33 division in favor of the government. In both Argentina and Brazil policies have been adopted denying to foreign companies the right to acquire lands for exploration and drilling — all this with the expectation that domestic capital and government entities would develop the field which had been reserved from foreign entry. Since this happy development has not occurred, the restriction policy was modified in Argentina. However, in fuel-poor Brazil, the spector of "oil imperialism" has obstructed any policy change. The result is that Brazil spends precious foreign exchange for oil imports. This is illustrative of the uneconomic consequences of misguided nationalism.

Industry

Although industry is a distant third, after agriculture and mining, as a contributor to the gross national product, it nevertheless has been making remarkable progress in some of the Latin-American countries — notably, Argentina, Brazil, Chile, and Mexico, and to a lesser degree in Cuba, Colombia, Peru, and Venezuela. There is some heavy industry in the first four countries (each has one or more steel plants, a prestige symbol), but it is in the field of light industries where the greatest developments have occurred.

There are two types of light industry activity: (1) production of consumer goods for domestic consumption, and (2) the processing of raw materials, largely for export. With respect to consumer goods, Latin-American industry is producing and largely satisfying the domestic market in textiles, synthetic fibers, apparels, leather goods, cigars and cigarettes, beverages, pharmaceuticals, glass and ceramics, cement, paints and varnishes, household appliances, auto tire manufacturing, and auto assembly. Food processing is the most important of the various industrial activities. With respect to the processing of raw materials, the most important industrial activities in Latin America are sugar production, smelting of minerals, oil refining, and meat packing.

The astonishing progress of industrialization in parts of Latin America notwithstanding, those who dream of industrial development in terms of the example of the United States are probably doomed to disappointment. They ignore the fact that the whole economic, social, and physical setting is different. We have already referred to the difficult geography, unfavorable climate, deficiency of energy resources, and also lack of adequate supplies of some mineral resources. The lack of a skilled labor force and technical and managerial skills can probably be corrected in time. We must also add the lack of adequate domestic investment capital, coupled with a growing nationalistic opposition to foreign investments. All this adds up to serious doubts concerning the future of heavy industry in Latin America. It is in the field of light industry where the immediate industrial future seems to lie. But notwithstanding these encouraging developments Latin America is still a one-sided economy dependent on exports of foodstuffs and raw materials to the industrialized nations. It also depends on foreign sources of capital for investment.

Foreign trade and investments

As has been noted, Latin America produces for export. The value and distribution of the exports and imports with the United States are indicated in Table 8 (p. 196). Normally about one-half of Latin America's exports have gone to Europe, and about two-fifths to the United States. United States imports from Latin America, in 1962, represented 20.4 per cent of our total imports. Of our total exports, 14.6 per cent went to Latin America. This represented 41.2 per cent of Latin-America's exports and 41.9 per cent of Latin America's imports. The principal imports from the United States are capital goods for industries, such as tools and machinery, metal goods, electrical equipment; also wood and paper, fuels, chemicals, and textiles. Foodstuffs are also high on the list of imports; about one-half of the Latin nations, which are primarily agrarian, import large quantities of staple foods, such as flour and corn, while they concentrate on one-crop agriculture.

Not only does the economy rely heavily on foreign trade, but it also depends on foreign sources of capital for investments. This of course is a facet of the so-called "colonial economy," which relies upon foreign capital for the investment needed to produce and export primary products. Thus, when the value of the exports drops, as happened during the Great Depression, the inflow of foreign capital comes to a stop.

European bankers and private investors were first in the Latin-American investment field. It was during and after World War I that the financial relations of Latin America changed entirely, and the United States became the leading factor in the economic life of the southern neighbors. The growth of United States investments mounted until in 1929 they amounted to $5,587,494,000.[11] Following a decline during the Great Depression, United States direct investments in Latin America mounted from $2,803,000,000 in 1936 to a peak of $8,730,000,000 in 1958. The principal fields of foreign investment in Latin America are mining and smelting, petroleum, manufacturing, transportation, public utilities, and trade and distribution. (See Table 4 below and Table 5 on p. 23.)

TABLE 4

U.S. Direct Investments in Latin America, by Industry, 1962
(in millions of dollars)

Country	Total	Mining & Smelting	Petroleum	Manufacturing	Public Utilities	Trade	Other
All areas, total	37,145	3,183	12,661	13,212	2,039	3,015	3,035
Latin America	8,472	1,099	3,159	1,893	709	839	773
Argentina	797			404		33	300
Bolivia	32						32
Brazil	1,088	26	79	611	195	136	41
Chile	768	504		29		14	221
Colombia	456		257	102	27	51	19
Costa Rica	63				14	5	44
Dominican Republic	108				6	3	99
Guatemala	127		28		69	6	24
Honduras	99				23	1	75
Mexico	873	127	67	448	26	98	107
Panama	556	18	77	10	25	247	179
Peru	451	248	66	44	20	47	26
Uruguay	53			24		5	24
Venezuela	2,826		2,202	191	35	179	219
Other Countries	65		25			18	23

Source: *Survey of Current Business,* August, 1963 (U.S. Dept. of Commerce, Office of Business Economics).

[11] Max Winkler, *Investments of United States Capital in Latin America* (Boston: World Peace Foundation, 1929), 278.

These large foreign investments have been an important economic factor in influencing politics and governmental policy. They have led to charges of "economic imperialism," particularly against the United States. Rabid nationalism is prone to exaggerate the power of foreign interests and their alleged "despoliation of the resources" of the country. The result is a so-called "plural economy" of Latin America, that is, foreign and domestic economic sectors which are regarded as distinct and separate segments of the economic community. National policy distinguishes in many ways between the two sectors. Whereas the domestic enterprises are coddled by protective legislation, often exploitive of the consumers, the foreign concerns are discriminated against in many ways; for example, by highly restrictive labor and social legislation, burdensome taxation, and regulations concerning the transfer of earnings and capital. In many countries the participation of foreign capital in various kinds of businesses is either prohibited or restricted to a percentage of the shares. This is particularly true of oil production and refining, air transport, coastal shipping, and insurance. Not only are limitations imposed on the amount of shares which can be foreign-owned, but the number of aliens who can be employed in such enterprises is also severely restricted.[12]

Moreover, the trend in Latin America is toward even greater economic nationalism. The ideal of self-sufficiency and economic independence is apparently the objective of governmental policy, even though it runs counter to the fact that foreign investment capital is indispensable for future economic development. The confidence of foreign private capital has been shaken by these restrictions and discriminatory actions, not to mention the dangers of expropriation and political upheaval. Thus, the flow of investment capital has lessened. Latin America is no longer the happy hunting ground of private United States investment, a fact which no doubt has impeded and, unless the investment climate becomes more hospitable, will continue to impede the Alliance for Progress and the general economic and social development of the area.

Additional economic and sociological factors

A trend in Latin America which must be reckoned with not only by United States investors, but by the State Department as well, is the expanding role of government in the economy. This trend is two-fold: (1) government as a promoter and regulator, and (2) government as a direct participant in production. In the first category are included the various stimuli by government to the different segments of the economy. Probably the most important instrument used by many of the countries to foster economic growth is the development corporation or *fomento*. These corporations either finance existing or proposed industries, or, if private capital is reluctant, will acquire and operate agricultural and industrial enterprises. The Export-Import Bank of the United States has been a principal contributor to the *fomento* loan fund.

[12] Hanson, *op. cit.*, 14.

Although through *fomento* and other specialized financial and developmental agencies, industry appears to be most favored, agriculture is also a beneficiary of "indirect participation" by the government. For example, low-cost farm credit is supplied and price support is attempted. Also, government aids agriculture by large scale irrigation and land reclamation projects.

In Latin America, as in the United States, government undertakes to stabilize the economy by its fiscal policy (taxes and expenditures) and by its monetary policy (cost and availability of bank credit). Governmental intervention to protect the national economy from the abuses of foreign exploitation has already been discussed. Undoubtedly much of the legislation, particularly that dealing with labor-management relations, was enacted with the foreign-owned concerns in mind.

The government as a direct participant in economic production has also aroused considerable concern in the United States, not only because of the expropriation of properties, but because this seems to be a trend to socialism. Rightly or wrongly socialism appears to many Americans to be a step on the road to Communism. Thus, beyond the accepted areas of governmental activities, such as health, education, water supply and the like, Latin-American governments are expanding into areas regarded in the United States as the exclusive domain of private enterprise. Government oil monopolies exist in Argentina, Brazil, and Mexico, the three major countries of Latin America. Several of the countries own steel mills, sugar refineries, ocean shipping companies, railways, telephone and telegraph lines, electric power plants, and chemical manufacturing plants. Some operate commercial banks, insurance companies, airlines, hotels, moving picture production, and grain storage facilities. Over 10 per cent of all industrial employment in a number of the Latin-American countries is in government-owned industrial operation. The goods and services produced in these government plants bulk large in relation to private production, and even larger is the influence of governments in guiding the economic activities of the Latin-American countries.

Taxation and living level

For their revenue Latin-American governments generally place heavy reliance on the excise or consumption tax. This is regressive in application for it hits hardest the commodities in larger use among persons with lower incomes. The income tax, which is not a principal source of revenue, as in the United States, is also regressive. It is relatively low in the upper brackets, and is generally evaded except by foreign companies. Import duties, a traditional revenue producer, also impose unequal burdens, for like the other taxes they bear heaviest on the lower incomes, since the basic necessities carry higher duties than luxuries. There are exceptions of course, as for example both the use and import taxes on automobiles are excessively high. The high import taxes, however, are often the result of governmental effort to discourage purchases and conserve foreign exchange. Duties are also imposed on exports, and in some countries, such as Chile, they have been a very important revenue source. Finally, the general property tax is a minor revenue producer, for "by and large, use of the property tax has been neglected in Latin America."[13] Since the land has always been concentrated in the hands of the relatively few, the landowners have been able to control governments and block effective general property tax. In fact, with respect to the whole tax structure, the old inequities persist. A general revamping, such as the Alliance for Progress program envisages, is long overdue.

With few exceptions, the countries of Latin America are fundamentally so poor that a living standard approaching that of the United States is unattainable. The overall average per capita income is only about $300, or one-eighth that of the United States.[14] Coupled with the low per capita income level is low productivity. The productivity of the gainfully employed is reduced by a number of reasons, among them less effective equipment and conditions of labor, illiteracy, malnutrition, poor health, and poor housing. Despite some advances made in recent years, the standards of living in Latin America remain extremely low, a condition aided by the determined efforts of the oligarchs to oppose measures of reform. (For vital statistics, see Table 5.)

The economic prosperity of Latin America is spotty. Even in urban areas, where the new prosperity is largely confined, there exist unbelievable slums. Rural poverty is almost untouched. Despite strenuous efforts to provide schools, illiteracy still exceeds 50 per cent in most of the countries. With respect to problems of health, although life expectancy has been increased in recent years, it is still only one-half to three-fourths that of persons born and living in the United States.[15] The race between production and population in Latin America is ominous because of the extreme deficiencies in diet which already exist in all of the countries except Uruguay and Argentina. Some authorities contend that more than one-half of the Latin Americans are physically undernourished, and almost as many are suffering from infectious and deficiency diseases. Undoubtedly the production of the gainfully employed is reduced by malnutrition and poor health. Obviously the public health services are pitifully inadequate.

It is said that Latin America generally is in a pre-Castro state, that is, ripe for a series of revolutions. A number of maladjustments, already noted, represent inflammable tinder for revolution. Inevitably and irresistibly the countries to the south of us, in varying degrees, are undergoing social, economic, and political change. This is the greatly delayed culmination of a century and a half of tortured experience in the mysteries of self-government,

---

[13] Wendell C. Gordon, *The Economy of Latin America* (New York: Columbia University Press, 1950), 209.

[14] The range of per capita annual incomes is estimated to vary from less than $100 to $800. In large areas, for millions of people, it is less than $70.

[15] Estimated literacy rates are 11 per cent in Haiti, less than 50 per cent in eight other countries, and 50 per cent or more in eleven countries, including Argentina 87 per cent, and Costa Rica 88 per cent. "Our Southern Partners," Dept. of State Publication 7404 (November, 1962), 12–18.

TABLE 5

Latin America: Vital Statistics and Net Food Supply

| Country | Year | Birth and Death Rates | | | Net Food Supply per Person | |
		Birth rate	Death rate	Infant Mortality rate	Year	Calories per day
Argentina	1961	22.4	8.0	61.2	1950	2,950
Bolivia	1961	26.6	8.5	90.7		
Brazil	1950	43.0	20.6	170.0	1957	2,680
Chile	1961	34.5	11.7	116.2	1957	2,570
Colombia	1961	43.4	12.2	89.6	1956–58	2,200
Costa Rica	1962	50.5	8.5	71.9		
Cuba	1956	25.1	5.8		1948–49	2,730
Dominican Rep.	1960	36.7	10.4	113.2		
El Salvador	1962	45.3	10.8	71.5		
Guatemala	1961	49.9	16.3	84.8		
Honduras	1961	45.3	9.5	49.9	1954–55	2,200
Mexico	1961	44.9	10.6	70.3	1957–59	2,440
Nicaragua	1961	40.8	8.0	65.1		
Panama	1961	41.3	8.2	54.4		
Paraguay	1960	46.6	10.6	52.1	1957–59	2,500
Peru	1961	28.1	8.5	97.2	1959	2,050
Uruguay	1960	21.3	8.1	49.1	1954–56	2,960
Venezuela	1961	44.4	7.0	51.4	1960	2,490
United States	1962	22.4	9.5	25.4	1960	3,120

Source: *Statistical Abstract of the United States, 1963,* p. 910.

which brought little or no amelioration of the wretched conditions of the great mass of the populace. Today new aspects of social and economic structure are emerging. Industrialization and urbanization are giving rise to new social groups and classes. No longer does society consist only of an elite of large landholders, an insignificant fringe of professional and commercial middle class, and the mass of illiterate workers. Since World War II there have appeared new industrial magnates and small capitalists, large professional groups, and masses of literate city wage earners. A phenomenon of great importance is the emergence of various segments of the middle class. These new urban-oriented groups are bringing pressure to bear for fundamental political change.

It is truly a very different Latin America with which United States policy makers must reckon today. Not only are there changed physical conditions and altered social and economic structures, but the attitude of both governments and people toward the United States has changed. We turn now to a survey of our policies and relations with the Latin-American nations from the early days of their independence.

SUPPLEMENTARY READING

Adams, Richard N., Gillin, John P., Holmberg, Allan R., Lewis, Oscar, Patch, Richard W., and Wagley, Charles. Introd. by Bryson, Lyman, *Social Change in Latin America Today: Its Implications for United States Policy* (New York: Harper & Brothers, 1960).

American Assembly, *The United States and Latin America* (New York: Columbia University Press, 1959), Chaps. 1–4. (2nd ed., Prentice-Hall, Inc., 1963).

Dávila, Carlos, *We of the Americas* (Englewood Cliffs, N.J.: Prentice-Hall, Inc., 1949).

Davis, Harold Eugene, ed., *Government and Politics in Latin America* (New York: The Ronald Press Company, 1958).

Davis, Kingsley, "Latin America's Multiplying Peoples," *Foreign Affairs,* 25, No. 4 (July, 1947), 643–645.

Dozer, Donald Marquand, *Latin America: An Interpretive History* (New York: McGraw-Hill Book Company, Inc., 1962).

Freyre, Gilberto, *New World in the Tropics: The Culture of Modern Brazil* (New York: Alfred A. Knopf, Inc., 1959).

Gordon, Wendell C., *The Economy of Latin America* (New York: Columbia University Press, 1950).

Hanson, Simon G., *Economic Development in Latin America* (Washington, D.C.: The Inter-American Affairs Press, 1951).

James, Preston E., *Latin America* (New York: The Odyssey Press, 3rd ed., rev., 1959).

Mecham, J. Lloyd, "Latin American Constitutions: Nominal and Real," *The Journal of Politics,* XXI (May 1959), 258–276.

Schurz, William L., *This New World: The Civilization of Latin America* (New York: E. P. Dutton & Co., Inc., 1954).

Stokes, William S., *Latin American Politics* (New York: Thomas Y. Crowell Company, 1959).

Stokes, William S., "Violence as a Power Factor in Latin American Politics," *The Western Political Quarterly,* V, No. 3 (September, 1952), 445–468.

Wythe, George, *Industry in Latin America* (New York: Columbia University Press, rev. ed., 1950).

2

The Origins of Policy

[During most of the history of the United States, Latin America has commanded a special policy interest.] Ever since the early years of the nineteenth century when the Spanish colonies made their bid for independence, the United States has looked upon them in a different manner from Europe. [By 1810 when the Spanish-American wars for independence began, there was a strong determination in the United States to insulate itself from Europe. Isolation and noninvolvement in the broils of Europe was in process of crystallization as a basic principle of foreign policy. But this principle was never applied to Latin America, for almost from the beginning the security of the United States was identified with the security and welfare of the other nations of the Western Hemisphere.

The idea that the nations of the Western Hemisphere, coinhabitants of this segment of the globe, and all products of revolt against European overlords, have special relationships to each other that set them apart from the rest of the world has had almost universal acceptance. This politico-geographic concept, called the Western Hemisphere idea,[1] has been responsible for United States policies of a distinctive regional nature, such as the Monroe Doctrine, Pan Americanism, Nonintervention, Good Neighbor, and Alliance for Progress. Since the original assumption of United States-Latin American affinity was a product of the independence movement, we turn our attention now to the progressive development of policy during the course of the wars for Latin-American independence (1810–1824).[2]

[1] See Arthur P. Whitaker, *The Western Hemisphere Idea: Its Rise and Decline* (Ithaca: Cornell University Press, 1954).

[2] For historical surveys of the Latin-American wars for independence, see: A. Curtis Wilgus, ed., *Colonial Hispanic America* (Washington, D.C.: George Washington University Press, 1936), Chaps. 15–19; Donald M. Dozer, *Latin America: An Interpretive History* (New York: McGraw-Hill Book Company, Inc., 1962), Chap. X; Hubert Herring, *A History of Latin America* (New York: Alfred A. Knopf, Inc., 1955), Chaps. 13–17.

Territorial problems

Except along the borderlands where the United States came into physical contact with the sparsely settled northern margins of the Spanish Empire, the American people and those of the Spanish Indies knew as little of each other, prior to the outbreak of the independence movement, as though they lived on opposite sides of the world. It was the wars for independence, creating new situations and new problems, that led almost immediately and automatically to the "discovery" of Latin America by the United States.

Territorial questions dominated the Latin-American policy of the United States during all phases of the revolution. Since the revolt threatened further to weaken, if not liquidate, Spain's feeble authority in the borderlands, American appetites were stimulated while their apprehensions of European ambitions were aroused. Thus, in a real sense it can be said that the original Latin-American policy of the United States was inspired by territorial considerations — that is, to acquire disputed borderlands while the Spanish Empire was in process of dissolution, and to deny to European powers strategic territories threatening the security and development of the United States. American statesmen believed implicitly that the territorial integrity and independence of the United States depended on the elimination of all European controls over the Gulf Coast from Texas to Florida, and even Cuba, which was referred to as "the real mouth of the Mississippi."

The purchase of Louisiana in 1803 had saved the United States from a great danger by eliminating Europe from the Mississippi Valley. But Louisiana was not safe so long as the Floridas, East and West, remained in the hands of Spain. West Florida was acquired early and without difficulty. On September 23, 1810, settlers of American origin, who comprised nine-tenths of the population, staged a revolt against the feeble Spanish authority, proclaimed the independence of the West Florida Republic, and appealed for annexation to the American Union. On October 27 President Madison issued a secret proclamation annexing West Florida as far east as the Perdido River. But, in order to avoid conflict with small Spanish garrisons at Mobile and Pensacola, General Claiborne occupied only as far east as the Pearl River.

Aroused because of a British protest on behalf of Spain, and fearful of British occupation of the remainder of the Floridas, President Madison, on January 3, 1811, sent a special message to Congress, asking authorization "to take temporary possession" of the Spanish territories to anticipate their transfer to "any other foreign Power." The response of the Congress was the adoption, on January 15, 1811, of a joint resolution and enabling act as follows:

> Taking into view the peculiar situation of Spain and her American provinces; and considering the influence which the destiny of the territory adjoining the southern border of the United States may have upon their security, tranquility and commerce: Therefore,

> *Resolved by the Senate and House of Representatives of the United States of America, in Congress assembled,* That the United States, under the peculiar circumstances of the existing crisis, cannot without serious inquietude, see any part of the said territory pass into the hands of any foreign Power; and that a due regard to their safety compels them to provide, under certain contingencies, for the temporary occupation of the said territory; they, at the same time, declare the said territory shall, in their hands, remain subject to a future negotiation.

The enabling act authorized the President, "Under certain contingencies, to take possession of the country lying east of the river Perdido, and south of the State of Georgia and the Mississippi territory." To defray the expenses of taking possession, $100,000 were appropriated.[3]

The measures adopted by the Congress were justified not as "a claim of right," but as "inescapable self-interest dictated by geographical and economic necessity." In fact, Secretary of State Robert Smith, for the information of the British government, frankly admitted United States aspiration to the possession of the Floridas because this was "essential to its future peace and safety upon honorable and reasonable terms."[4] The famous "No-transfer Resolution of 1811," so vital to the independence, security, and continental future of the United States, is regarded by a distinguished American historian, as "the first significant landmark in the evolution of its Latin-American policy."[5] It meant that the President and the Congress were agreed that this country did not intend to remain a passive spectator while the Spanish Empire was in process of dissolution. The imposing of a caveat on the transfer of nearby Spanish possessions was a significant precursor to one of the great principles of the Monroe Doctrine. United States policy definitely was orienting in a southerly direction.

Although armed with Congressional authorization, President Madison refrained from overt force, but sought by intrigue and negotiation to win the coveted territory. By acts of Congress, on April 14, 1812, and May 14, 1812, the United States formally annexed West Florida, first to the Pearl River and then to the Perdido, under the theory that the region occupied was part of the Louisiana Purchase. By April, 1813, the whole of West Florida had been occupied and placed under the civil and military jurisdiction of the United States. Since the Spanish government refused to recognize the legality of these developments, the West Florida question remained for final settlement by subsequent negotiations.

[3] D. Hunter Miller, ed., *Secret Statutes of the United States* (Washington, D.C., Government Printing Office, 1918), 5–6; *Annals of Congress,* 11th Cong. 3rd Sess., 1810–1811, Col. 374, 375, 376.

[4] William R. Manning, ed., *Diplomatic Correspondence of the United States Concerning the Independence of the Latin American Nations* (3 vols. New York: Carnegie Endowment for International Peace, 1925), II, 222; Laurence F. Hill, *Diplomatic Relations between the United States and Brazil* (Durham: Duke University Press, 1932), 7.

[5] Samuel Flagg Bemis, *The Latin American Policy of the United States* (New York: Harcourt, Brace and Company, 1943), 30.

As for East Florida, it seems that the "expansionists of 1812," who maneuvered the United States into war with Britain, hoped to take Florida while Britain and her ally Spain were involved in conflict with Napoleon. Unfortunately the easy conquest did not materialize. On the contrary, the United States was hard put to preserve its own territorial integrity. As a result, after the war, the solution of the Florida question was left to American diplomacy, which in the end proved to be much more competent and effective than American arms. At Ghent, where the treaty terminating the War of 1812 was signed, there was only casual mention of the attempt by the United States to wrest the Floridas from Spain.

Fears that Spain would cede the Floridas to Britain continued to plague the United States. When informed by our Minister in London, John Quincy Adams, that the United States had a claim to West Florida by right, and to East Florida by necessity, and would go to war to prevent their transfer, Foreign Secretary Lord Castlereagh disavowed any aspiration to these territories. At the same time he admonished the Americans against "pursuing a system of encroachment" upon their Spanish neighbors. It is interesting to note that two years later, by late 1817, Lord Castlereagh had come to the conclusion that Spain's loss of the Floridas to the United States was inevitable. It became increasingly clear to the Spaniards therefore, during the course of their negotiations with the United States, that they could not rely on the support of Britain.

The negotiations were interrupted when, during the Seminole War early in 1818, General Andrew Jackson, with the objective of wiping out bases for hostile Indian raids into the United States, captured St. Marks and Pensacola in Florida. In the course of this invasion two British subjects were executed by Jackson for trading in munitions with the Indians. Fortunately for the United States, but not for Spain, Castlereagh was not disposed to make an issue of the affair. When it was evident to the Spaniards that neither Britain nor any other European nation would aid them, and equally evident that the Americans would not hesitate to use force to achieve their ends, they instructed their negotiator, Minister Luis de Onís to sign a treaty. Thus, on February 22, 1819, a treaty variously known as the Adams-Onís Treaty, the Florida Purchase Treaty, and the Transcontinental Treaty, was signed in Washington. It was immediately and unanimously ratified by the United States Senate two days later.

With characteristic Bourbon guile and stubbornness Ferdinand VII delayed Spanish ratification. The obvious intention was to hold the hand of the United States from giving assistance to Spain's revolted colonies and according them the recognition of their independence. When all recourse to delaying tactics was exhausted, the King finally ratified the treaty on October 24, 1820. A second ratification by the United States Senate was necessary, and following this formality, the treaty went into full force on February 22, 1821.

By the terms of the treaty Spain relinquished to the United States all her territories east of the Mississippi, that is, the Floridas. As for the western boundary, the line agreed on began at the mouth of the Sabine River and ascended the river to 32° North Latitude, then due north to the Red River, thence westward along the southern bank of that river to 100° West Longitude, then north to the south bank of the Arkansas River and westward up that river to its source, from which point the boundary line was to run either due north or due south to the 42° North Latitude, and then westerly to the Pacific Ocean. Adoption of the 42nd parallel meant that Spain was transferring to the United States all of her claims to the Oregon territory.

In exchange for these vast concessions on the part of Spain, the United States relinquished its quite shadowy claims to Texas. In addition, the United States assumed the claims of its own citizens against Spain for damages and injuries, up to $5 million. It is because of this feature that it has been called a "purchase" treaty. Actually it was a treaty of exchange — that is, American pretensions to Texas for Spanish rights in Florida and pretensions to Oregon. The winning of this treaty was one of the greatest of all American diplomatic victories.[6]

Thanks particularly to the incomparable diplomatic skill of John Quincy Adams, the United States exploited to the limit the opportunities presented by the Latin-American wars for independence to rectify its boundaries and extend its borderlands. It remained for future developments in our relations with Mexico, Spain's successor as a border neighbor, to make further additions to the territorial expansion of the United States. We turn now from territorial problems with Spain, arising from the Spanish-American wars for independence, to the problems of initiating relations with the emergent nations themselves.

1. Problems of Recognition and Neutrality

Pre-1815, first phase

Peoples struggling for liberty and independence have always evoked popular sympathies in the United States. Thus, the general lack of information about the Spanish Indies did not deter the American people, when they heard about the outbreak of the revolt, from sympathizing with their "fellow Americans" striving to break the bonds of a European despotism. There was more to this attitude than mere self-interest in territorial gain, for it was also based in the ideal of republican independence of the New World, separated from the wars and intrigues of monarchical Europe.

In his message to the Congress, November 5, 1811, President Monroe referred to an obligation on the part of the United States toward the Spanish

[6] For territorial problems and diplomacy, see: *ibid.,* Chaps. 2–3; Philip C. Brooks, *Diplomacy and the Borderlands: The Adams-Onís Treaty of 1819* (Berkeley: University of California Press, 1939); Isaac J. Cox, *The West Florida Controversy* (Baltimore: The Johns Hopkins Press, 1918); Charles C. Griffin, *The United States and the Disruption of the Spanish Empire, 1810–1822* (New York: Columbia University Press, 1937), Chaps. 1, 6; Manning, *op. cit.,* I, 5–15.

colonies; namely, an interest in their destinies. Portions of the President's message concerning South America were referred to a committee which, on December 10, 1811, offered the House a resolution of sympathy with the struggling Latin-American countries. This is said to be the first public statement by an organ of the United States government declaring sympathy with the cause of Spanish-American independence.[7] The ideas of "hemisphere solidarity" and community of republican institutions apparently inspired this declaration of sympathy. On May 4, 1812, the Congress, on receipt of reports of a terrible earthquake at Caracas, Venezuela, appropriated $50,000 to purchase provisions for the victims. This was probably the first Congressional appropriation of its kind. It was reported later that this humane gesture saved many from famine.[8]

Nor was the Executive of the United States government wanting in sympathy for the rebel cause, despite fears that either Britain or France would garner the spoils of Spain's dissolving empire. Almost immediately after the outbreak of the revolts, and prior to the arrival of rebel agents in the United States, the Madison administration sent "agents for seamen and commerce" to several of the rebel provinces. This type of representation was not diplomatic and certainly did not mean recognition of independence.

In June, 1810, Robert K. Lowry was sent as agent for seamen and commerce to the port of La Guaira in Venezuela. He was our first agent to serve in South America after the outbreak of the revolution. He was instructed to send reports to Washington of important events and to direct the attention of the rebel government to the importance of fostering commerce with the United States.

On June 28, 1810, Joel Roberts Poinsett of South Carolina was appointed special agent of the United States to South America. His instructions reveal the attitude of the United States toward the people of Spanish America at the beginning of their war for independence.

Poinsett was instructed to proceed to Buenos Aires, and there he was to make it his object

> to diffuse the impression that the United States cherish the sincerest good will towards the people of Spanish America as neighbors, as belonging to the same portion of the globe, and as having a mutual interest in cultivating friendly intercourse . . . and that, in the event of a political separation from the parent country, and of the establishment of an independent system of National Government, it will coincide with the sentiments and policy of the United States to promote the most friendly relations and the most liberal intercourse, between the inhabitants of this hemisphere, as having all a common interest, and as lying under a common obligation to maintain that system of happiness for nations. . . .

[7] Arthur P. Whitaker, *The United States and the Independence of Latin America, 1800–1830* (Baltimore: The Johns Hopkins Press, 1941), 82–83.

[8] Charles Lyon Chandler, *Inter-American Acquaintances* (Sewanee, Tenn.: The University Press of Sewanee, 1915), 48–49.

The real as well as ostensible object of your mission is to explain the mutual advantages of commerce with the United States, to promote liberal and stable relations, and to transmit seasonable information on the subject.[9]

On November 8, 1811, Poinsett was appointed consul general for the provinces of Buenos Aires, Chile, and Peru. While in Chile Poinsett disregarded the elementary canons of neutral behavior by giving military aid to the patriots and even taking part in the factional strife among the patriots.[10] Following the appointment of Poinsett, the United States sent several consular agents to the principal ports of South America to promote commerce and to act as political observers.[11] (All this showed a desire on the part of the United States to form ties with Latin America but not to become involved.) However, the sincere endeavors of the government to observe its mutual responsibilities were seriously hampered by the activities of the rebel agents who came into this country in hordes.

The first agent to represent a Latin-American nation which had asserted its independence was Telésforo de Orea, who, on July 27, 1811, was made the "extraordinary agent of the Venezuelan Confederation" to the United States.[12] He and others like him, in some instances, sought to secure acknowledgment of their independence, but in all cases to acquire supplies and arms. They also facilitated the easy commissioning of privateers to prey on Spanish commerce.

President Madison could not receive these envoys officially, but both he and his Secretary of State met them in cordial informality. In fact, the Administration facilitated the efforts of the agents in the purchase of arms, munitions, and even ships. If neutral, the government of the United States was a neutral friendly to the rebel cause. In modern parlance this status, unknown in international law, is called "nonbelligerency." South American vessels were admitted into United States ports under whatever flags they bore. There was no formal declaration according belligerent rights to the rebel provinces, although a declaration to that effect had been introduced in the Congress as early as December 10, 1811.[13] Although the United States, from the start of the revolution, seems to have regarded the revolted colonies as belligerents in a civil war, it was not until September 1, 1815, that a proclamation of neutrality was issued.

In this neutrality proclamation President Madison warned all Americans against taking part in the war against Spain, particularly by organizing

---

[9] Manning, *op. cit.*, I, 6–7.

[10] Whitaker, *Independence of Latin America,* 71–72.

[11] There is no evidence that exequaturs were issued to any of these agents, although in their despatches they speak of being favorably received. F. L. Paxson, *The Independence of the Spanish American Republics* (Philadelphia: Ferris & Leach, 1903), 111.

[12] William Spence Robertson, *Hispanic-American Relations with the United States* (New York: Oxford University Press, 1923), 27.

[13] *American State Papers, Foreign Relations* (6 vols. Washington, D.C., 1832–1859), III, 538. On November 27, 1806, President Jefferson issued a neutrality proclamation because of information concerning preparations for the Miranda expedition. All persons were warned against taking any part in it.

expeditions within the jurisdiction of the United States.[14] Thus, all officers, civil and military, were enjoined to be vigilant in searching out and bringing to punishment all persons engaged in such unlawful enterprises.

The neutrality proclamation is significant for several reasons. First, it reflected widespread violations of the neutral obligation of the United States. Second, it clarified the policy of the United States with respect to the conflict in Spanish America. Spain viewed the colonies as in a state of rebellion, and tried to get the United States to accept this view. But the United States insisted that the conflict was a civil war, in which the parties were equal, and entitled to belligerent rights. Third, it marked a modification of United States policy toward the revolutionary wars. Henceforth the government was going to be more scrupulous in meeting its neutral responsibilities, and more reliant on diplomacy and less on emotion. It was more than coincidence that this new departure in policy followed the decline of the rebel cause in most of Latin America, the welcome end of the hapless War of 1812, and the advent of John Quincy Adams as Secretary of State in the Monroe administration.

Post-1815

The War of 1812, which preoccupied American interest, naturally shunted concern with Latin-American developments into the background. Also, chastened by a series of military reverses, Americans abandoned their dreams of easy territorial conquests. The Monroe administration, coming as it did shortly after the war with England and the general European settlement at Vienna in 1815, was loath to risk a war with Spain, and so pursued a policy of strict neutrality. This contrasted with the pre-1812 benevolent neutrality. Thus, "one of the chief victims of the War of 1812 was the Latin-American policy of the United States."[15] As has been noted, the experiences of the war convinced the United States government of the desirability of diplomacy, not arms, as a means of achieving its goals. It was a happy circumstance that John Quincy Adams was called to the office of Secretary of State to implement this policy. During his long tenure under President Monroe, Secretary Adams managed with consummate skill the problems of the United States with and concerning Latin America.

Neutrality

The problems of neutrality were not settled by the proclamation of 1815. In fact, it was after the resumption of the rebellion, following a brief restoration of Spanish authority in all of the colonies except La Plata, that the activities of the Spanish-American agents became most intensive. American citizens, because of their sympathies and their commercial interests, exploited the inadequacies of the neutrality laws (1794 and 1797) to support the southern patriots. In many cases, American adventurers took part in the struggle not only for the cause of liberty but also for the opportunity afforded them to prey upon Spanish commerce. Thus, while the government of the

---

[14] *Ibid.,* IV, 1.   [15] Whitaker, *Independence of Latin America,* 95.

United States refrained scrupulously from giving aid directly to the revolting colonies, it found difficulty in preventing its citizens from taking up the cause of the rebels.

Blank commissions for privateers were issued from the South American capitals in a steady stream, and distributed at American ports by the agents. From Baltimore and New Orleans particularly, vessels equipped for privateering set forth to prey on Spanish commerce. Most of them did not even bother to put in first at a South American port, nor did they hesitate to put into a United States port to refit and recruit. All of this was in violation of neutrality, which the Spanish Minister Luis de Onís, protested. However, because of the imperfections of the neutrality laws and popular sympathy for the rebel cause, which made jury convictions impossible, the Latins were able to make United States ports virtual bases for operations.[16] John Quincy Adams noted that even some of the federal officers in Baltimore were fanatics of the South American cause and were involved in privateering. Baltimore became so well known throughout Latin America as a center for privateering and rendezvous for Spanish-American agents that some identified the city with the United States as a country.

Some of the zeal of the privateers got out of hand. They became undiscriminating in their choice of prey, and too often attacked any commerce, thus becoming pirates. They brought their prizes to Amelia Island, in Florida, Galveston, and other places just outside United States jurisdiction, for sale. In order to wipe out the privateer and pirate rendezvous at Amelia Island a United States naval force occupied it on December 23, 1817. Later, in response to numerous United States complaints of irresponsible acts of piracy by ships flying the Buenos Aires flag, that government in October, 1821, revoked the commissions of privateers.[17]

After 1817 it was no longer for want of adequate neutral legislation that these large-scale violations occurred, for in 1817 and 1818 our neutrality laws were revamped in order to close loopholes in the earlier laws.[18] In spite of the revised neutrality law, the evasions of United States' neutral obligations continued. The Spanish Minister, Luis de Onís, kept a record of these violations, and on December 30, 1818, brought to the attention of the administration facts which he said were "universally public and notorious." Unquestionably the situation was embarrassing to Secretary Adams in his treaty negotiations with Onís. But more embarrassing to Adams were the constant pressures to accord recognition to the Spanish colonies.

Recognition

The propaganda for recognition came from two sources: the Latin-American agents and sympathetic citizens of the United States. Of the many rebel agents who came to the United States after 1815, the one who was most importunate in his demands for recognition was Manuel Hermenegildo de

---

[16] Paxson, *op. cit.*, 116–117.   [17] Bemis, *op. cit.*, 45–46.
[18] Charles G. Fenwick, *The Neutrality Laws of the United States* (Washington, D.C.: Carnegie Endowment for International Peace, 1913), 39.

Aguirre representing the United Provinces of La Plata. After its declaration of independence at Tucumán on July 9, 1816, La Plata dispatched Aguirre to Washington. In a letter to President Monroe, Supreme Director Juan Martín de Pueyrredón asked that Aguirre be granted "all the protection and consideration required by his *diplomatic* rank and the present state of our relations." However, according to Adams, "He had no commission as a public minister of any rank, nor any full power to negotiate as such."[19]

At Washington on December 16, 1817, Aguirre wrote Secretary of State Adams urging acknowledgment of the sovereignty of the Province of La Plata. He said, "My Government, considering that of the United States as one of the first of whom it ought to solicit this acknowledgment, believed that the identity of political principles, the consideration of their inhabiting the same hemisphere, and the sympathy so natural to those who have experienced similar evils, would be so many additional reasons in support of its anxiety."[20]

Aguirre wrote other letters importuning recognition but he never succeeded in budging the imperturbable Adams. No more successful, of course, were the other representatives of the rebel colonies, nor for that matter were those sympathic Americans, the most outstanding of whom was Henry Clay.

When in the spring of 1817 news came from South America indicating a more hopeful turn of the war for the patriots, the President decided to learn the truth about the revolution in order to be ready for any event. Already popular pressures were being revived for recognition. Accordingly, on April 25, 1817, Joel Poinsett was asked by President Monroe to visit the coast of South America, on a public ship, as far as Buenos Aires, to acquire information helpful to public policy. But Poinsett declined on the excuse of private business. Then, on July 18, 1817, Caesar Rodney and John Graham were appointed special commissioners to go on a fact-finding mission to South America. Circumstances prevented an early departure by the two, thus later Theodorick Bland was added to the commission. A short time before this, John B. Prevost had been sent to Chile and Peru on a similar mission.[21]

The three commissioners departed from Hampton Roads on December 4, 1817, aboard the U.S. frigate *Congress*. They touched at Rio de Janeiro to deliver despatches to our minister resident there, and then proceeded to Montevideo and Buenos Aires. Bland went on to Chile. The three returned to the United States and reported to the President in early November, 1818.

Unfortunately, the commissioners could not agree on what they had seen and learned in South America. Although Bland admitted that "any kind of return to their former allegiance is utterly impossible," he confessed little confidence in the patriots. Rodney wrote an enthusiastic report, and Graham was evasive. The three reports were sent by the President to the Congress, together with a fourth solicited from Joel Poinsett, who was emphatically opposed to recognition. The President informed the Congress that, because of the continued political instability in South America and the danger of

[19] Manning, *op. cit.*, I, 59.
[20] *Am. State Papers, For. Rel.*, IV, 111–112.
[21] Manning, *op. cit.*, I, 38–39.

Spanish attack from Peru, there was no present reason why the policy of neutrality should be abandoned. All this reinforced Secretary of State John Quincy Adams in his determination to hold off recognition.

Adams had little confidence in the South Americans, and was unwilling to allow sentimental sympathy to compromise a determined policy. But not so Henry Clay, Speaker of the House of Representatives, who, according to Adams, had "mounted his South American great horse . . . to control or overthrow the Executive by swaying the House of Representatives." For ten years Clay led a continuous campaign on behalf of the South American cause, partly because of sentiment, partly because as a Westerner he was anti-Spanish, and partly because he was personally ambitious and believed it good politics. He professed to see a comity of interests between the Americas and advocated an "American system" of politics and economy distinct from that of Europe. Secretary Adams rejoined scornfully, "As to an American system, we have it; we constitute the whole of it."[22]

Henry Clay sought to secure an amendment to the General Appropriation Bill of 1818 by moving an item of $18,000 to provide for a minister "to the independent provinces of the River Plata in South America." On this, as on other occasions, Clay claimed the power of recognition for the Congress in the exercise of its constitutional power to regulate foreign commerce. "Suppose for example," he said, "we passed an act to regulate trade between the United States and Buenos Aires, the existence of the nation would be thereby recognized, as we could not regulate trade with a nation which does not exist." In this speech of March 25, 1818, counted one of his greatest, the Speaker argued eloquently for his American System in which the New World would comprise a unity in contradistinction to the Old World. "There can be no doubt," he said, "that Spanish America, once independent, whatever may be the form of government established in its several parts, these governments will be oriented by an American feeling and guided by an American policy."[23]

The debate on Clay's amendment continued for four days (March 24–28), but despite a general sympathy for the Latin rebels, most of the members opposed the amendment on the grounds of its impropriety, not only because of their conviction that the power of recognition belonged to the Executive, but because of the uncertainty of independence in the Spanish colonies. Thus, Clay's original motion was withdrawn, and even his substitute motion, which omitted the term "independent" and added that the salary was to commence, "Whenever the President shall deem it expedient to send a Minister to the said United Provinces," was lost by a decisive vote of 115 to 45.[24]

The administration was quite content not to have the matter of recognition pressed at that time. The Florida treaty negotiations were in a delicate state, and caution dictated no needless aggravation of Spain on the score of her rebel colonies. Unfortunately, the final signing of the treaty on February 22,

---

[22] Charles Francis Adams, ed., *Memoirs of John Quincy Adams* (12 vols. Philadelphia, 1874–1877), IV, 28, V, 176.

[23] Chandler, *op. cit.,* 101.

[24] John H. Latané *The United States and Latin America* (New York: Doubleday, Page & Company, 1926), 51.

1819, did not relieve the situation for Secretary Adams, for the Spanish government resorted to dilatory tactics to delay ratification. A demand that the United States pledge nonrecognition as a condition of Spanish ratification was indignantly rejected by Adams, who believed, quite correctly, that the Spanish King was legally and morally bound to ratify unconditionally.

It was at this juncture that Henry Clay, to the great vexation of Secretary Adams, mounted his "South American great horse," and reopened the question of recognition. On May 20, 1820, he introduced a motion in the House to inaugurate, when the President might deem it expedient, diplomatic relations with "any of the governments of South America which have established and are maintaining their independence of Spain." The motion carried, but of course had no effect on Secretary Adams.[25] But, persistent as always, in the next session of Congress, Clay was able, on February 6, 1821, to get the House to pass another resolution declaring sympathy with the South Americans and the readiness of the House to support the President whenever he should think it expedient to recognize those governments. With this minor success to his credit, Henry Clay retired from the Congress to private life. His was indeed a hollow victory, for it is very doubtful that Clay's persistent campaign hastened recognition by a single day. That momentous event occurred as a logical conclusion to the policy stubbornly defended by the great Secretary of State for several years.

Adams was frank to declare to Clay, as he recorded in his diary, his complete lack of faith in the Latin Americans. Although he wished them well in their struggle for independence, he believed the true policy for the United States was unequivocal neutrality. "But," he said, "I have not yet seen and do not now see any prospect that they will establish free or liberal institutions of government. . . . They have not the first elements of good or free government. . . . We shall derive no improvement to our own institutions by any communion with theirs. Nor is there any appearance of a disposition in them to take any political lesson from us."[26]

The timing of recognition had posed for Adams harsh alternatives. If he waited too long he would incur the ill-will of the Latin Americans and encourage their further orientation in the direction of Britain. On the other hand, if he acted too soon, there was danger of Spain making war over the issue, and failure of the Florida treaty negotiations. Fortunately, the date of the final ratification of the Florida treaty, February 14, 1821, coincided rather closely with developments in the wars for independence which indicated beyond reasonable doubt that the Spanish cause was hopeless. The time for recognition had arrived.

Recognition accorded

In response to a House request for information indicating the political status of the new Spanish-American governments, President Monroe, on March 8, 1822, sent to the House communications from United States agents in Latin

[25] *Ibid.,* 52.
[26] Adams, *Memoirs,* V, 324–325.

America, notably John M. Forbes at Buenos Aires and J. B. Prevost at Santiago, Chile. The papers and documents covered generally the political conditions in La Plata, Chile, Peru, Great Colombia, and Mexico. The President said that all of these five states were in full enjoyment of their independence, and recognition could not be considered by Spain as a hostile act. Moreover the neutrality of the United States would be maintained. On the other hand, if recognition were withheld any longer, "friendly relations" with the Latin-American states might suffer, and they might become the dupes of European polity. President Monroe therefore suggested Congressional appropriations to defray the expenses of recognition. On May 4, 1822, a bill was signed by the President which appropriated $100,000 for "such missions to the independent nations in the American Continent as the President might deem proper." It is significant that the bill left the President wide discretion in the matter of selecting the nations to which diplomatic missions were to be sent. But more significant was the fact that recognition came as an independent American act. No European power was consulted or had forewarning. The hope long held by Adams that Britain and France, or at least the former, would join the United States in joint recognition was abandoned. Unilateral recognition had a purely American basis, for it was intended to forestall European advantage and promote free republican governments.

On June 19, 1822, Secretary of State Adams presented Manuel Torres to President Monroe as *chargé d'affaires* from the Republic of Colombia. This was the first formal act of recognition. Torres spoke of the great importance of recognition to Colombia and the great satisfaction of Simón Bolívar. President Monroe replied with so much kindness that Torres was moved to tears. Unfortunately, the Colombian, who had the distinction of being the first Latin-American diplomat to be received by the President of the United States, was at that time a very ill man, and within a month he died at Philadelphia.[27]

After the recognition of Manuel Torres, other Latin-American states were recognized either by receiving or sending diplomatic representatives. On December 12, 1822, José Manuel Zozaya was received as minister of the Mexican Empire. On August 4, 1824, Antonio José Cañaz was received for the Central American Federation. On May 26, 1824, José Silvestre Rebello, *chargé d'affaires,* was received by President Monroe as the diplomatic representative of the Empire of Brazil. In October, 1824, General Carlos de Alvear appeared in Washington bearing credentials as minister of the United Provinces of La Plata.

The first diplomatic representative of the United States to serve his government in Hispanic America was Richard C. Anderson, appointed minister to Colombia on January 27, 1823. On that day the President also appointed Caesar A. Rodney[28] minister to Buenos Aires and Heman Allen minister to Chile; however, they did not immediately assume their posts. Later, he

---

[27] Chandler, *op. cit.,* 107.
[28] Rodney left Philadelphia on June 8, 1823, and arrived at Buenos Aires on November 16, 1823. He died at Buenos Aires on June 10, 1824. Rivadavia delivered an oration at his funeral. *Ibid.,* 77.

appointed Joel Poinsett minister to Mexico, James Cooley *chargé d'affaires* to Peru, and Condy Raguet *chargé d'affaires* to Brazil.

The recognition of their independence by the United States was hailed by the new governments. In fact, Bernardino Rivadavia, the great Buenos Aires statesman and patriot, declared that the acknowledgment of the independence of the United Provinces by the United States was "the most important event in the history of his country."[29] However, it is only fair to record that, however appreciative the Latins were because of the United States action, they were very slow in sending duly accredited diplomatic representatives to Washington. And, on its part, the United States government was equally slow in appointing ministers to the South American governments. Whereas the Latins' delay may have been the result of preoccupation with internal problems, that of the United States seems to have stemmed from a desire to provoke the European powers as little as possible by this implied condemnation of their principle of legitimacy. At first, Adams thought of sending a minister to a new government only after receiving one from it. But, because of the aggressions of the so-called Neo-Holy Alliance,[30] the Secretary of State saw that nothing could be gained by further efforts to placate them, and so decided to continue sending ministers to Latin America.

Great care was given to the drafting of the instructions for the first ministers, for the Secretary of State professed a real concern over the existence of a European threat to America. While Adams did not see immediate danger of an armed attack on Spanish America, he was nevertheless fearful of Latin-American susceptibility to European influence. Unless this strong inclination were checked, the new countries might relapse into a condition of colonial servitude to Europe. Therefore in his instructions to his ministers Secretary Adams made clear his desire that the new states should be politically and commercially independent of Europe.

Secretary Adams firmly believed that the European allies posed a threat to the security of the Americas. This belief was due to a number of factors, the most important of which was his observation that the Spanish Empire in America was in a state of dissolution. It is in this context therefore that we note the origins of the most famous and, until recently, the most enduring of United States policies, the Monroe Doctrine.

2. *The Origins of the Monroe Doctrine*

The Monroe Doctrine was, in its broad lines, a caveat by the United States against the extension of European influence and power to the Western Hemisphere. It was based on the separation of the New World from the Old — not only because of the obvious geographical separation, but because of the equally valid economic, social, and political separation. The development in

[29] Robertson, *op. cit.*, 37.

[30] The term was applied to Austria, Prussia, and Russia after the Congress of Troppau, where the principle of intervention was adopted. Whitaker, *Independence of Latin America*, 409, n.26.

the New World, even before independence, of a separate and distinct set of interests, commended to the Americans the policies of isolation and no binding political connection with any European power. The ingrained American sentiment of isolationism which crystallized a determination to stay out of Europe, also produced as a normal corollary the determination to keep European complications out of America. Thus the ideological origins of the Monroe Doctrine are complementary to the policy of isolation. The basic theme of the Monroe Doctrine, i.e., that the political system of Europe is different and that it must not extend to this hemisphere, "is in itself, a restatement of the old international doctrine that America is a new world, separate and distinct from Europe, to which the European system of politics and diplomacy does not apply."[31]

It is not surprising, therefore, that the basic ideas inherent in the Monroe Doctrine had been stated over and over again since the earliest days of the Republic — and even before independence. According to J. Reuben Clark, former Under Secretary of State and distinguished expositor of the Monroe Doctrine, "the principles cast into definite formulae in the Doctrine (in 1823) had long been the common property of the American statesmen of the time, and even of European statesmen." A discussion of the general background of the Monroe Doctrine will show, therefore, that each of its essential principles "had been understood, announced, and invoked as between ourselves and Europe, years before the framing of Monroe's declaration was contemplated."[32]

General background

Isolation, nonentanglement, and the principle of the two hemispheres — germinal ideas of the Monroe Doctrine — had their beginnings in the colonial period. A community of race and civilization might have been expected to perpetuate an attachment of the New World for the Old, but the very nature of the origins of the colonies and their subsequent development dictated otherwise.

Most of the migrants who shook the dust of Europe from their feet were consciously effecting a complete break with the lands of their origin. Whatever the burden of their discontent — religious, political, social, or economic — their dissatisfaction was so great that they turned their backs on Europe with no thought of return. The hardships and expense of the long voyage across the ocean ruled out, in the great majority of cases, any thought of a return voyage. The Massachusetts General Court in 1651 reminded Oliver Cromwell that the founders of the colony had come to America in order to escape Europe. It was not difficult, consequently, to effect almost immediately an immunity to the attachments of the Old World.

---

[31] Maxwell H. Savelle, "Colonial Origins of American Diplomatic Principles," *Pacific Historical Review,* III (1934), 337.

[32] J. Reuben Clark, *Memorandum on the Monroe Doctrine,* Dept. of State Publication 37 (Washington, D.C.: Government Printing Office, 1930), xi, xv.

The intercolonial wars not only accentuated the fact that the colonies were entities separate and distinct from Europe with their own set of interests (doctrine of two spheres), but fostered the idea of separation (isolation) and noninvolvement in the broils of Europe. It was the belief of the English colonists — a belief which was not entirely valid — that the intercolonial wars between Britain and France and Spain represented for them entries on the debit side of the ledger. They overlooked the end result of the colonial wars — i.e., the expulsion of France from the continent of North America, thereby opening the way for Anglo-American continental expansion. However, after witnessing their hard-won conquests in the wars with France bartered away in European peace settlements in exchange for advantages to Britain in other parts of the world, little wonder that the colonials became cynical and regarded themselves merely as pawns on the chessboard of European politics.

By the time of the Revolution, isolationism "was already a tradition of the American colonies, based on a deep-seated feeling of escape from Europe and a strong tendency, encouraged by European diplomacy, to avoid becoming entangled in European conflict."[33] The necessities of the war, however, forced a compromise of the principles of nonentanglement by the negotiation of a treaty of alliance with France (1778). Nevertheless the new republic did not relax its guard against the increase of European power in America, for the very treaty of alliance, which was so eagerly sought, prohibited the French from making any conquest on "any part of the continent of North America." This clearly indicated an intention on the part of the infant United States not only to oppose all increase of European power in the Western Hemisphere, but to reduce it at every convenient opportunity.

The isolationist inclinations of the new republic were evidenced by historical acts and by utterances of early American statesmen too numerous for detailed mention here.[34] A few selected examples will suffice to illustrate this view. John Adams, whose writings are replete with isolationist utterances, wrote in 1776: "We should make no treaties of alliance with any European power.... [but] we should separate ourselves, as far as possible and as long as possible, from all European politics and wars." In 1782 Adams remarked to the British peace negotiator Richard Oswald, "I do not doubt but that the nations of Europe will attempt to attract us into their political system, but it is to our interest to remain aloof from all that." In a resolution adopted by the Congress of the Confederation in 1783 it was declared to be the fundamental policy of the United States to avoid entanglements in the politics and controversies of European nations. Thomas Jefferson, quite as extreme an isolationist as John Adams, wrote in 1785 that if he could have his way the United States would adopt the policy of China and remain aloof from the world.

[33] Savelle, *op. cit.*, 337.

[34] For a compilation of acts and utterances illustrative of the developing principles of the Monroe Doctrine, see Clark, *op. cit.*, 7–40; John Bassett Moore, *A Digest of International Law* (Washington, D.C.: Government Printing Office, 1906), VI, 369–386.

Despite this apparent aberration, Jefferson was not a dreamy doctrinaire, for he was realistic enough to see the danger to the United States that would come from the transfer of American territory from one European power to another. This thought was expressed in a letter, written in March, 1793, to our minister to Spain, concerning the possibility that the Spanish possessions, Louisiana and the Floridas, would become a theatre of struggle among England, France, and Spain. This is said to be one of the earliest expressions which drew a distinction between American political interests and European political interests and thus is "the germ of the actuating motive which lay behind the Monroe Doctrine."[35]

This was followed, three years later, by the classic statement of American separation from the affairs of the Old World. In his Farewell Address of September 17, 1796, George Washington counseled his countrymen, as a "great rule of conduct," to have as little political connection with foreign nations as possible. This, he said, was desirable, because:

> Europe has a set of primary interests which to us have none or a very remote relation. Hence she must be engaged in frequent controversies, the causes of which are essentially foreign to our concerns. Hence, therefore, it must be unwise in us to implicate ourselves by artificial ties in the ordinary vicissitudes of her policies or the ordinary combinations and collisions of her friendships or enmities.

The detached and distant situation of the United States, argued Washington, invited it to pursue a different course. "Why forego," he asked, "the advantages of so peculiar a situation? Why quit our own to stand upon foreign ground? Why, by interweaving our destiny with that of any part of Europe, entangle our peace and prosperity in the toils of European ambition, rivalship, interest, humor or caprice?"

In conclusion, while advising against "permanent alliances with any portion of the foreign world," the retiring President, a true pragmatist, said, "Taking care always to keep ourselves by suitable establishments on a respectable defensive posture, we may safely trust to temporary alliances for extraordinary emergencies."[36]

Washington thus developed principles which underlay the Monroe Doctrine. His message was a clear suggestion of an America that was to be distinct from Europe.

It was in his inaugural message of March 4, 1801, that Thomas Jefferson coined the famous phrase, so greatly cherished by isolationists, "peace, commerce and honest friendship with all nations, entangling alliances with none." Yet, only slightly more than a year later, on April 18, 1802, *apropos* of the cession of Louisiana to France, Jefferson wrote, "The day that France takes possession of New Orleans . . . seals the union of two nations who, in conjunction, can maintain exclusive possession of the ocean. From that moment we

[35] Clark, *op. cit.*, 12.
[36] *Am. State Papers, For. Rel.*, I, 34–38.

must marry ourselves to the British fleet and nation." Fortunately, the easy acquisition of all Louisiana saved the United States from an unnatural alliance with Britannia.

The prospective dissolution of the Spanish Empire in America created great concern, as we have already noted, over the possible transfer of territory. Obviously such transfer from weak Spain to some strong European power would present a distinct threat to the security and development of the United States. This ominous prospect was clearly understood by American statesmen and thus evoked a number of policy declarations, several of which we have noted above. Thus there is no further need here to dwell on the statements and acts which were legitimate precursors to the no-transfer principle of the Monroe Doctrine.

The immediate background

The noncolonization clause of the Monroe Doctrine was not related in its origins, as were the other principles of the Doctrine, to the existence of war in Spanish America. It was directed against Russia, because of the Czar's extravagant pretension to sovereignty over a large part of northwestern North America and adjacent seas.

On September 4, 1821, Czar Alexander of Russia issued a ukase which provided:

> 1. The pursuits of commerce, whaling, and fishing, and all other industry on all islands, ports, and gulfs, including the whole of the north-west coast of America, beginning from Behring Straits to the 51° of northern latitude, . . . is exclusively granted to Russian subjects.
> 2. It is therefore prohibited to all foreign vessels not only to land on the coasts and islands belonging to Russia as stated above, but also, to approach them within less than 100 Italian miles. The transgressor's vessel is subject to confiscation along with the whole cargo.[37]

The imperial decree was challenged by Secretary of State Adams not only because it violated the doctrine of freedom of the seas, but because of the extravagant "assertion of a territorial claim on the part of Russia." Adams had, in fact, prior to the ukase, given some thought to the exclusion of European nations from further colonization of the Americas. By November, 1822, his thoughts had developed to the point where he declared to the British minister at Washington that "the whole system of modern colonization was an abuse of government, and it was time that it should come to an end."

Since Henry Middleton, United States minister to St. Petersburg, reported that the position taken by the Czar was not so foreboding as it seemed, and since Baron Tuyll, the Russian minister at Washington, told Adams that his government was anxious to settle differences regarding the northwestern coast by friendly negotiation, Adams agreed to furnish Middleton with powers for

[37] For correspondence between the United States and Russia, 1820–1823, see Clark, *op. cit.*, 79–89.

negotiation. Nevertheless, Adams informed Tuyll (July 17, 1823) that "we should contest the right of Russia to any territorial establishment on this continent, and that we should assume distinctly the principle that the American continents are no longer subjects for any new European colonial establishment."[38] This language was incorporated substantially in Monroe's famous message. Middleton was instructed (July 22, 1823) to admit no part of the Russian claims. Fortunately a possible diplomatic impasse was avoided, for the Czar had already decided to withdraw from his extreme position. Adams' strong language, therefore, had no influence on this decision.

It is quite beside the point to argue, as have some, that the noncolonization dictum was worthless as public law. Naturally there was reason to doubt both the ability and the willingness of the United States to support, at that time, such a policy. Nevertheless it served notice to the world of United States objections to any further extension of European territorial and political power in the Americas. Secretary Adams was tenacious in his belief in the logic of the policy. History proved him right. More important by far than the non-colonization clause were the principles of the nonextension of the European political system to this hemisphere, and the extracontinental interposition in the affairs of the Latin-American republics. The background of events which built up to President Monroe's declaration can now be surveyed.

The great powers of the Holy Alliance, dedicated to reaction, and witnessing rebellion against the Spanish king, were responsible for developments which culminated eventually in Monroe's famous message. The European allies, following the overthrow of Napoleon, renewed their association, known as the Quadruple Alliance and dedicated to the maintenance of treaty (Vienna) engagements and the preservation of peace. About the same time (September, 1815), Czar Alexander induced his brother sovereigns of Prussia and Austria to join with him in forming a "Holy Alliance," by which the three sovereigns declared their determination, in external and internal policies, "to take for their sole guide the precepts of Holy Religion, namely, the precepts of Justice, Christian Charity, and Peace." In the pursuit of these high aims, they pledged mutual aid and assistance. Almost from the outset Alexander's Holy Alliance, with its lofty idealism, was confused in the popular mind with the Quadruple Alliance, which was being transformed by Metternich into an instrument for the systematic repression of liberalism.[39]

It was at the Congress of Troppau (1820) that the Holy Allies (really the Quintuple Allies, with Great Britain abstaining) published the memorable protocol of Troppau: "States which have undergone a change of government

[38] Adams, *Memoirs*, VI, 163.

[39] After 1818, when France was admitted, it became known as the Quintuple Alliance. The original members of the Quadruple Alliance were Austria, Great Britain, Prussia, and Russia. Concerning the Holy Alliance challenge, see Clark, *op. cit.*, 59–79; Dexter Perkins, *The Monroe Doctrine, 1823–1826* (Cambridge: Harvard University Press, 1927); E. H. Tatum, *The United States and Europe, 1815–1823* (Berkeley: University of California Press, 1936); W. A. Phillips, *The Confederation of Europe* (London, 1920).

due to revolution, the results of which threaten other states, *ipso facto* cease to be members of the European Alliance and remain excluded from it until their situation gives guarantees for legal order and stability. . . . If, owing to such alterations, immediate danger threatens other states, the Powers bind themselves, by peaceful means, or if need be by arms, to bring back the guilty state into the bosom of the Great Alliance."[40] Thus they clearly declared the right of intervention in the domestic concerns of friendly states to stamp out liberal revolution.

The principles of Troppau were implemented almost immediately. At the Congress of Laibach (1821) the Allies gave a mandate to Austria to put down liberal revolutions in Naples and Piedmont. Then, at the Congress of Verona (1822), over British opposition, the Holy Allies sanctioned French military intervention in Spain to restore Ferdinand VII to his throne. The Spanish king, saved by French intervention, then appealed for aid to put down his rebellious subjects in America. Was there to be another allied congress to commission an armed intervention in South America? Both Britain and the United States became gravely concerned as to whether the Allies intended to extend the protocol of Troppau to the Western Hemisphere. This was the immediate threat which inspired the Monroe Doctrine.

With respect to the wars for Spanish-American independence, the British Ministry made honest and persistent efforts to preserve neutrality. Britain felt bound by her 1814 treaty with Spain to prevent her subjects from furnishing the rebels with arms and munitions. Neutrality proclamations were issued warning British subjects, and in 1819 a Foreign Enlistment Act was passed providing for stricter neutrality.

Realizing the increasing hopelessness of the Spanish cause, Lord Castlereagh, the British Foreign Minister, had for some time been making conscientious efforts to mediate between Spain and her revolting colonies. He hoped that Spanish concessions to the colonials would preserve at least a nominal sovereignty for the Spanish king. But Ferdinand VII, in typical Bourbon style, stubbornly declined.

A dual objective — to preserve monarchy and to garner commercial advantage in Spanish America — put a great strain on Britain's foreign policy. Fearful that Spain would turn to Russia or France for military aid, Castlereagh announced on August 28, 1817, that Great Britain would tolerate no European interference in Spain's colonial wars. We have already noted Castlereagh's vigorous denunciation of the protocol of Troppau, and his insistence that Britain's obligations extended only to holding France to the terms of the Treaty of Vienna.[41]

Nor did the attitude of the United States relieve the anxiety of the British Foreign Minister, for he feared that pending United States recognition would

[40] Lord Castlereagh, the British Foreign Minister, refused to sign the protocol. He declared that "any minister who should recommend the king to sanction such a principle would render himself liable to impeachment." Phillips, *op. cit.,* 226.

[41] C. K. Webster, "Castlereagh and the Spanish Colonies," *The English Historical Review,* XXVII (1912), 86–87.

gain for the Americans not only prestige in the new republics but also commercial advantage. As a matter of fact, United States initiative was creating great alarm in British commercial circles. The United States, well knowing Castlereagh's opposition to Allied intervention in South America, invited an understanding on the question of recognition. The overture was rejected. Nevertheless the British minister had come to the conclusion that the wars in Spanish America could only be settled on the basis of the independence of the colonies. Castlereagh no longer objected to recognition of Spain's former colonies. What he did object to was recognition of republics, or, equally bad, the establishment of monarchies under the patronage of France.

Castlereagh was preparing to fight at the Congress of Verona any project for combined armed intervention in Spanish America when he committed suicide. The Duke of Wellington, the English representative at Verona, withdrew from the Congress stating that Great Britain could not be a party to any general declaration against Spain (i.e., the liberal constitutionalists), nor to any hostile interference in her internal affairs. This was a formal warning to France not to establish a permanent military occupation of Spain or to appropriate any portion of the Spanish colonies. French determination to suppress the liberal uprising in Spain could not be shaken: the armed intervention in Spain proceeded, and Ferdinand was saved. The atmosphere nurtured rumors that the next allied step would be another congress to authorize aid to Spain in America. There was talk of placing the French fleet at the disposition of the Spanish government. Since Prussia, Russia, and Austria did not possess the means to intervene in America, France presented the only danger. This the British were determined to prevent.

The United States shared Britain's concern, but not always for the same reasons. At any rate, George Canning, Castlereagh's successor, was quite justified in his belief that the occasion called for a joint declaration by the two governments.

The Canning-Rush conversations[42]

In the months of August and September, 1823, several conversations took place in London between Foreign Minister Canning and United States Minister Richard Rush with regard to a joint pronouncement concerning the Spanish-American colonies. On August 16, 1823, Canning took the initiative by suggesting to Rush the expediency of an understanding between the United States and Great Britain. Canning's overture did not contemplate a concert of action, but he felt the knowledge that Britain and the United States held the same opinion would have a moral restraining force. Rush replied that his instructions did not authorize a commitment on his part, and he had to communicate with his government. He then asked regarding British policy

---

[42] Harold Temperley presents the whole record of the conversations in *The Cambridge History of British Foreign Policy* (London, 1922–1923), II, 633–637. Temperley also gives a summary of the conversations in *The Foreign Policy of Canning, 1822–1827* (London, 1925), 115–117.

on recognition. Canning said that Britain was considering the matter, but before taking such a step he was going to send commissioners to Latin America. So ended the first conversation.

It was during the August 20, 1823, conversation that Canning formally proposed in writing a five-point joint declaration of policy regarding Latin America:

1. That recovery of the colonies by Spain was hopeless.

2. That the question of recognition was one of time and circumstance.

3. That no obstacle was to be put in the way of an understanding between Spain and her colonies.

4. That neither of the signatories aimed at the possession of any portion of the colonies for themselves.

5. That they could not see the transfer of any portion of them to another power with indifference.

On August 23 Canning urged haste because, as he informed Rush, he had received notice that the French expected, following the achievement of their military objectives in Spain, to propose "a Congress, or some less formal concert and consultation, specially upon the affairs of Spanish America." But Rush continued to insist that his instructions were inadequate and he must await orders from Washington. However, due to continued importuning by Canning, who urged the necessity of *immediate* action, the American Minister finally conceded that, at the risk of his career, he was prepared to enter into a joint statement *provided* Britain would recognize Spanish-American independence.[43] But this Canning would not agree to, and so, as he later said, "we went on without."

Canning immediately turned to direct talks with Prince Polignac, the French ambassador at London. The Frenchman was told that Great Britain had no desire to hasten recognition of Latin-American independence, but that any foreign interference, by force or menace, would be a motive for immediate recognition. In the so-called Polignac Memorandum of October 9, 1823, inaccurately described as an "ultimatum," the French government was obliged to agree that the reduction of the colonies by Spain was hopeless, and that France "abjured, in any case, any design of acting against the colonies by force of arms."[44] The outcome of the Canning-Polignac conversations, which quite conclusively terminated the illusory threat of European intervention in the South American question, was not communicated to Rush until the latter part of November, and thus was unknown to Monroe and had no influence over the formulation of his message of December 2.

[43] J. H. Powell, *Richard Rush, Republican Diplomat, 1780–1859* (Philadelphia: University of Pennsylvania Press, 1942), 160. Rush undoubtedly would have been supported in Washington, for in Monroe's cabinet J. Q. Adams maintained that we could act with England only on the basis of the acknowledged independence of the Latin-American states. J. B. Moore, *Principles of American Diplomacy* (New York: Harper & Brothers, 1918), 242.

[44] Perkins, *Monroe Doctrine, 1823–1826,* 118.

Developments in Washington

President Monroe, before submitting to his cabinet Canning's proposal, asked the advice of ex-Presidents Jefferson and Madison. Both responded favorably. Jefferson said:

> Our first and fundamental maxim should be, never to entangle ourselves in the broils of Europe. Our second, never to suffer Europe to intermeddle with cis-Atlantic affairs. America, North and South, has a set of interests distinct from those of Europe, and peculiarly her own. She should therefore have a system of her own, separate and apart from that of Europe. While the last is laboring to become the domicile of despotism, our endeavor should surely be, to make our hemisphere that of freedom. One nation, most of all, could disturb us in this pursuit; she now offers to lead, aid, and accompany us in it. By acceding to her proposition, we detach her from the bonds, bring her mighty weight into the scale of free government, and emancipate a continent at one stroke, which might otherwise linger long in doubt and difficulty. Great Britain is the nation which can do us the most harm of any one, or all on earth; and with her on our side we need not fear the whole world.[45]

Madison also was entirely in favor of accepting the British proposal of some kind of joint pronouncement. But he would go further than Jefferson and express disapproval of the French invasion of Spain, and of any interference with the Greeks who were at that time in revolt against Turkey. President Monroe, it appears, was in strong agreement with Madison's suggestion that there be a broad declaration against the intervention of the great powers in the affairs of weaker states *in any part of the world.*

Almost the whole of November was taken up by the cabinet discussion of Canning's proposal and the problem of Russian pretentions in the northwest. In the cabinet all but Adams favored collaboration with Britain, for they feared the imminence of Allied intervention. The Secretary of State, however, was not so alarmist, nor did he take at face value Canning's professed motives. In short, Adams "smelled a rat." He believed the wily Britisher hoped to secure a public pledge from the government of the United States against any further territorial acquisitions of its own in Latin America. Over and above his opposition to a territorial self-denying pledge, Adams opposed the spectacle of the United States coming "in as a cock-boat in the wake of the British man-of-war."[46]

Not only did Secretary Adams succeed in convincing the President of the advisability of a unilateral declaration, but he also dissuaded Monroe from any reference to Greece. "The ground that I wish to take," he said, "is that of earnest remonstrance against the interference of the European powers by force with South America, but to disclaim all interference on our part with

[45] *Thomas Jefferson, The Writings of* (Monticello ed., Washington, D.C., 1903), XV, 479–480.
[46] Adams, *Memoirs,* VI, 178–179.

Europe; to make an *American cause* and adhere inflexibly to that."[47] With respect to the method of policy announcement Monroe overruled Adams. The latter wished to use the channels of diplomacy, but the President decided to inform the world in his annual message to the United States Congress.

But first it should be noted that, immediately prior to President Monroe's famous message, Secretary Adams informed both Russia and Britain of policy decisions. As for the response to Canning's proposal, this was finally indicated in an instruction to Minister Rush, dated November 29, 1823. Since the American government found it difficult to perceive much community of British and United States interests, Rush was informed that the Monroe administration was opposed to any "concurrent action of the two governments," and felt it to be "most advisable that they should act separately." Since Canning was silent and had apparently lost all interest in the matter, Rush did not convey to him the sense of his instructions. In the meantime, of course, President Monroe had made a public announcement of his fateful policy decision.

The Monroe Doctrine

The original Monroe Doctrine was incorporated in two widely separated paragraphs in the message of December 2, 1823. One related to Russian encroachments on the northwest coast and asserted the noncolonization principle in answer to the Russian ukase of 1821. It declared that "the American continents, by the free and independent condition which they have assumed and maintain, are henceforth not to be considered as subjects for future colonization by any European powers." Adams had used almost the identical language in earlier correspondence with the Russian minister. There is general concensus that to John Quincy Adams goes the credit as the formulator of the noncolonization principle.

The other paragraph relating to Spanish America and occurring near the close of the message, was the more important declaration in answer to the threat of the Holy Alliance. The language used by President Monroe was as follows:

> In the wars of the European powers in matters relating to themselves we have never taken any part, nor does it comport with our policy so to do. It is only when our rights are invaded or seriously menaced that we resent injuries or make preparation for our defense. With the movements in this hemisphere we are, of necessity, more immediately connected, and by causes which must be obvious to all enlightened and impartial observers. The political system of the allied powers is essentially different in this respect from that of America. This difference proceeds from that which exists in their respective governments. And to the defense of our own, which has been achieved by the loss of so much blood and treasure, and matured by the wisdom of these most enlightened citizens, and under which we have enjoyed unexampled felicity, this whole nation is devoted. We owe it, there-

[47] *Ibid.,* 194–195.

fore, to candor, and to the amicable relations existing between the United States and those powers, to declare that we should consider any attempt on their part to extend their system to any portion of this hemisphere as dangerous to our peace and safety. With the existing colonies or dependencies of any European power we have not interfered and shall not interfere. But with the governments who have declared their independence and maintained it, and whose independence we have, on great consideration and on just principles, acknowledged, we could not view any interposition for the purpose of oppressing them, or controlling in any other manner their destiny, by any European power, in any other light than as the manifestation of an unfriendly disposition toward the United States. In the war between these new governments and Spain we declared our neutrality at the time of their recognition, and to this we have adhered and shall continue to adhere, provided no change shall occur which, in the judgment of the competent authorities of this Government, shall make a corresponding change on the part of the United States indispensable to their security.[48]

At this point we shall present only a brief analysis of the original Monroe Doctrine, leaving for later discussion, interpretations and developments. The Doctrine reduced to its basic terms covered: (1) future colonization of the Americas by any European powers; (2) any attempt by the allied powers to extend their political control to any portion of the Western Hemisphere; (3) any interposition by any European power for the purpose of oppressing or controlling the destinies of the Latin-American governments; (4) noninterference by the United States with the existing colonies or dependencies of any European powers; and (5) the policy of leaving the Spanish-American colonies and Spain to themselves, in the hope that the other powers would pursue the same course.

Behind the Doctrine, although not expressly stated, was the principle of complete political separation of Europe and America. The nonextension of the European political system to the Western Hemisphere, and noninterposition in the affairs of the Latin-American republics were corollaries of the idea of the two spheres. Also, we may add, the exclusion of Europe from the Americas was a "hemisphere exception" to the national policy of isolation laid down by Washington. John Quincy Adams, long an isolationist, and still clinging to the "great rule" of isolation as far as Europe was concerned, made a long retreat from it in the case of Latin America. In a real sense the Western Hemisphere idea was made the basis of the policy proclaimed by Monroe in 1823.[49]

In further analysis of the original Monroe Doctrine, we note that: (1) It was policy formulated and proclaimed by the Executive. The Congress did not participate. (2) It was a unilateral declaration. Canning's proposal for a joint declaration was rejected because it was difficult to perceive the "foundation upon which the concurrent action of the two governments could

---

[48] For text of the original Monroe Doctrine, see Bemis, *op. cit.,* 63–64; Clark, *op. cit.,* 102–103.

[49] Whitaker, *Hemisphere Idea,* 37–39.

be harmonized." Nor were the new Latin-American states consulted. Since it was issued on the sole responsibility of the United States, matters of interpretation and enforcement rested exclusively with the United States. (3) It was a policy of national self-defense. The matters inhibited by the Doctrine came under the ban because they were "dangerous to our peace and safety," or were a "manifestation of an unfriendly disposition toward the United States," or were "endangering our peace and happiness." The right of self-preservation is the first law of nations. (4) Monroe did not intend to speak for future generations but for the immediate occasion only, since the warning message was intended merely to meet the threatened aggressions by the European Alliance. However, the principles, on which the policy of 1823 was based, were unlimited in time and in applicability to situations challenging our self-preservation within the terms defined by Monroe's declaration. (5) President Monroe did not pledge categorical abstinence from interference in European affairs. Only in respect to "the wars of European powers in matters relating to themselves" was Monroe promising hands off. He also said, "Our policy in regard to Europe . . . is not to interfere in the internal concerns of any of its powers."

Reaction to the Doctrine

In stating the divergence in the political ideals of Europe and the United States, President Monroe enjoyed the enthusiastic support of his countrymen. It was reported that the message "found in every bosom a chord which vibrates in strict unison with the sentiments so conveyed." The reaction of Latin America, and of Europe, to President Monroe's pronouncement did not reflect, we must admit, much awareness of the significance the Doctrine was later to attain. In Latin America it elicited little more than passing attention, although some of the newspapers and periodicals interpreted it as a shield to oppose the designs of European states against the Spanish-American nations. Several of the governments, viewing it in this light, made overtures to the United States for formal alliance. However, any possible Latin-American enthusiasm was quickly dampened when these overtures were politely declined. The "memorable promise of President Monroe" became almost immediately an illusory protection at best.

If the United States hoped by the Monroe declaration to garner advantage in Latin America over Great Britain, the effort fell far short of the goal. British prestige and preference, both political and commercial, continued on the ascendant. As early as July, 1824, in Chile, Canning was regarded as "the Redeemer of Chile."[50] The Polignac Memorandum, which was widely distributed throughout Latin America, was more valued than the doctrine of Monroe, and the navy of England more respected than the shield of the United States.

[50] J. Fred Rippy, *Latin America in World Politics* (New York: F. S. Crofts & Co., 3rd ed., 1938), 86.

Canning was taken aback, apparently, when he received news of Monroe's message. Not only did he object to the ban on the future colonization of America by European powers, but he was irritated that Rush interpreted his "sounding" as an "overture." However, the British Foreign Minister quickly adjusted to the situation and later boasted that the United States action gave him just the balance he wanted. He even assumed credit for the independence of the South American states, a credit which the Latins, as we have noted, were willing to concede.

On December 14, 1824, a year later, the British government, apprehensive "of the ambition and ascendancy of the U.S. of Am.," decided to recognize Mexico and Colombia in order to further consolidate its position in Spanish America. After recognition Canning exclaimed, "The deed is done, the nail is driven, Spanish America is free; and if we do not mismanage our affairs sadly, she is English." Still later, in December, 1826, Canning attempted to defend his position in not arresting the French invasion of Spain:

> I looked another way — I sought for compensation in another hemisphere. Contemplating Spain, such as our ancestors had known her, I resolved that, if France had Spain, it should not be Spain *with the Indies*. I called the New World into existence to redress the balance of the Old.[51]

Historical evidence does not support this claim, for the Spanish colonies had won their independence and had been recognized by the United States *two years* before Great Britain. "How do you find Mr. Canning's assertion?" indignantly wrote Lafayette to Henry Clay, December 29, 1826, "when it is known by what example, what declaration, and what feelings of jealousy the British government has been dragged into a slow, gradual, and conditional recognition of that independence."[52]

Finally, what was the reaction on the Continent to the Monroe Doctrine? Europe paid little attention to the Monroe Doctrine [53] and generally viewed it with annoyance and contempt. The Russian foreign minister declared that all the leaders of Europe "paid more heed to London than to Washington." In other words the Polignac Memorandum was far more influential than the Monroe Doctrine. Czar Alexander dismissed the President's message as meriting "only the most profound contempt." The French Minister of Foreign Affairs, Chateaubriand, referred derisively to the gulf between American pretentions and their naval power, and declared that the Doctrine "should be resisted by all the powers having commercial or territorial interests in that [American] hemisphere." Prince Metternich, Chancellor of Austria, denounced the "indecent declarations" of Monroe.

Since the European Allies had abandoned any plans they might have had to extend their intervention to America, the United States pronouncement was

---

[51] Harold Temperley, "The Latin American Policy of George Canning," *American Historical Review,* XI (1906), 781, 796.

[52] Chandler, *op. cit.,* 119.

[53] For foreign reception of the Monroe Doctrine, see Rippy, *World Politics,* 46–53.

regarded as a gratuitous and presumptuous challenge by an upstart republic. The efforts of the President to warn of a divergence in the political ideals of Europe and the United States, opposing principles of absolutism and democracy, might have been regarded a serious challenge were not the Allies aware of its feeble source. Then, as ever, the validity of a foreign commitment was measured by the power to balance it.

SUPPLEMENTARY READING

Adams, C. F., ed., *Memoirs of John Quincy Adams* (12 vols. Philadelphia: J. B. Lippincott & Co., 1874–1877), IV, V, VI.

Bailey, Thomas A., *A Diplomatic History of the American People* (New York: F. S. Crofts & Co., 3rd ed., 1946), Chaps. XI, XII.

Bemis, Samuel Flagg, *A Diplomatic History of the United States* (New York: Henry Holt and Company, 4th ed., 1955), Chaps. XI, XII.

Bemis, Samuel Flagg, *John Quincy Adams and the Foundation of American Foreign Policy* (New York: Alfred A. Knopf, Inc., 1949), XXVI.

Bemis, Samuel Flagg, *The Latin American Policy of the United States* (New York: Harcourt, Brace and Company, 1943), Chaps. II-III.

Brooks, Philip C., *Diplomacy and the Borderlands: the Adams-Onís Treaty of 1819* (Berkeley: University of California Press, 1939).

Chandler, Charles Lyon, *Inter-American Acquaintances* (Sewanee, Tenn: University Press of Sewanee, 1915).

Clark, J. Reuben, *Memorandum on the Monroe Doctrine* (Washington, D.C.: 1930. Dept. of State Publication No. 37).

Cox, Isaac J., *The West Florida Controversy; 1798–1813, A Study in American Diplomacy* (Baltimore: The Johns Hopkins Press, 1918).

Griffin, Charles Carroll, *The United States and the Disruption of the Spanish Empire, 1810–1822* (New York: Columbia University Press, 1937), Chaps. I, VI.

Manning, William R., ed., *Diplomatic Correspondence of the United States Concerning the Independence of the Latin American Nation* (3 vols. New York: Carnegie Endowment for International Peace, 1925), I, 5–15.

Perkins, Dexter, *Hands Off: A History of the Monroe Doctrine* (Boston: Little, Brown and Company, 1941. Rev. ed., 1955, under title, *A History of the Monroe Doctrine*), Chaps. I, II.

Perkins, Dexter, *The Monroe Doctrine, 1823–1826* (Cambridge: Harvard University Press, 1927).

Phillips, Walter A., *The Confederation of Europe* (London: Longmans, Green and Co., 2nd. ed., 1920).

Robertson, William Spence, *Hispanic-American Relations with the United States* (New York: Oxford University Press, 1923), 3–100.

Robertson, William Spence, "The Recognition of the Hispanic American Nations by the United States," *Hispanic American Historical Review*, I (1918), 245–250.

Tatum, E. H., Jr., *The United States and Europe, 1815–1823* (Berkeley: University of California Press, 1936).

Temperley, Harold W. V., *The Foreign Policy of Canning, 1822–1827* (London: G. Bell and Sons, 1925).

Webster, C. K., ed., *Britain and the Independence of Latin America, 1812–1830* (2 vols. London: Oxford University Press, 1938).

Webster, C. K., *The Foreign Policy of Castlereagh, 1815–1822* (London: G. Bell and Sons, 1925).

Whitaker, Arthur P., *The United States and the Independence of Latin America, 1800–1830* (Baltimore: The Johns Hopkins Press, 1941).

Whitaker, Arthur P., *The Western Hemisphere Idea: Its Rise and Decline* (Ithaca: Cornell University Press, 1954), Chaps. I, II.

3

The Monroe Doctrine: Development and Decline

For more than a century the Monroe Doctrine was an act of faith which the American people avowed with a devotion second only to their attachment to the Constitution itself.[1] Certainly, there never has been a foreign policy of the United States which endured longer and enjoyed greater popular support and understanding. This was because the meaning of the policy was so obvious — that is, "America for the Americans," and "Europe, keep hands off." So long as the doctrine of the two spheres — the Old World and the New, distinct and separate one from the other — persisted in the public mind as a real and vital principle, the Monroe Doctrine was given unquestioning support. The mere mention of the involvement of the Doctrine in any international issue was usually sufficient to commit the nation.

Today, however, the Monroe Doctrine no longer enjoys the popularity it once had; it is no longer an article of faith. There is little doubt that since the United States entered World War II, first abandoning isolationism and then initiating the atomic age, the world of the two spheres has tended to merge into a global concept. Therefore why include a chapter on the Monroe Doctrine in this volume? Because without it, a key element in a survey of United States-Latin American relations is missing.

Originally a definition of the attitude of the United States toward the relationship of European states to the American nations, in time the Monroe Doctrine became a definition of the relationship between the United States and Latin America. In the course of its long history it has taken on new

[1] Mary Baker Eddy, the founder of Christian Science, said in 1905: "I believe strictly in the Monroe doctrine, in our Constitution, and in the laws of God." (*Miscellany*, p. 282:3–4).

meanings or extensions and corollaries. This is not unusual, for, being an executive policy in origin it has always been the executive who adapted that policy to changing situations and conditions. As a living policy, it could not remain static. It is the purpose of the following discussion then to describe the evolutionary development of the Monroe Doctrine and its influence on our Latin-American relations.

The period of inaction

Two decades after their enunciation by President Monroe, his famous "principles"[2] were almost forgotten. Events seemed to indicate that the message of 1823 had been issued to meet a specific situation, and that since the threat no longer existed, the incident was closed. In fact, the United States seemed anxious to extricate itself from any commitments the message may have implied.

But the Latin Americans had taken the cautious utterances of President Monroe for much more than he intended and believed that the United States had pledged itself to resist forcibly any intervention by the allied powers in American affairs. Consequently, in 1824 and 1825, four nations appealed, one after the other, to the government of the United States for an alliance. In every instance they were politely refused. The United States was not willing to sign treaties of defensive alliance, but wished to consider each case of aggression as it arose. Of one thing we can be certain: Both President Adams and Secretary of State Clay regarded Monroe's pronouncement as unilateral and nonbinding.[3] They therefore instructed their delegates to the Panama Congress to urge the Latins to "guard *by their own means* against the establishment of any future European colony" within their borders.

Generally, President Adams was pessimistic about Latin America. He said, "I have little expectation of any beneficial result to this country from any future connection with them, political or commercial."[4] Nor, under President Jackson were Monroe's principles any incentive to closer relations with Latin America. In fact, the Jacksonian party assumed an isolationist position which excluded cooperation with Latin America. Therefore, since relations with Latin America were sporadic and never close, and since the interests of the United States were becoming more and more restricted to the domestic scene, it is no surprise that several events which challenged the principles of 1823 passed unheeded.

[2] The name "Monroe Doctrine" did not come into use until 1853. Prior to that date the policy was referred to as the "principles," "message," or "declaration" of President Monroe. This fact should be kept in mind when encountering the use of "Doctrine" prior to 1853.

[3] President Monroe himself, in 1824, made it clear that his pronouncement was not inimical to the establishment of monarchical government in the Western Hemisphere, provided it be truly democratic in origin and character; and in 1828, Secretary of State Clay declared that "President Monroe's Message" was not applicable to wars between American states.

[4] Charles Francis Adams, ed., *Memoirs of John Quincy Adams* (12 vols. Philadelphia, 1874–1877), V, 324–325.

Instances which might have been considered by later administrations as falling within the purview of the Monroe Doctrine were: (1) British encroachments in Central America, marked by extension of the boundaries of British Honduras, occupation of an island in the Bay group off Honduras, and establishment of a protectorate over the Mosquito Indians who inhabited much of the eastern shore of Central America; (2) the reoccupation by Britain of the Falkland Islands in 1833 over the protests of the United Provinces of La Plata; and (3) interventions by France and Britain in the Plata River region and by France in Vera Cruz in 1838. In none of these cases did the United States government protest violation of the Monroe principles. Perhaps the official silence was due to there being no clear appreciation of how the principles applied to these situations. Or perhaps the challenges were not regarded as sufficiently serious to warrant protest. It would have been next to impossible to marshal popular support behind any official protests. The Monroe Doctrine had not yet taken hold of the national imagination.

Revival of the Monroe Doctrine

Resentful of European interference in the Texas question and fearful of British interference and intrigue in Oregon and California, President Polk was impelled to a dramatic revival of the Monroe Doctrine. Like Monroe, Polk announced his policy in a message to Congress, on December 2, 1845:

> We must ever maintain the principle that the people of this continent alone have the right to decide their own destiny. Should any portion of them, constituting an independent state, propose to unite themselves with our Confederacy, this will be a question for them and us to determine without any foreign interposition. We can never consent that European powers shall interfere to prevent such a union because it might disturb the "balance of power" which they may desire to maintain upon this continent. Near a quarter of a century ago the principle was distinctly announced to the world, in the annual message of one of my predecessors, that — "The American continents, by the free and independent condition which they have assumed and maintain, are henceforth not to be considered as subjects for future colonization by any European powers." This principle will apply with greatly increased force should any European power attempt to establish any colony in North America. In the existing circumstances of the world the present is deemed a proper occasion to reiterate and reaffirm the principle avowed by Mr. Monroe and to state my cordial concurrence in its wisdom and sound policy. The reassertion of this principle, especially in reference to North America, is at this day but the promulgation of a policy which no European power should cherish the disposition to resist.[5]

The Polk message both contracted and expanded the scope of Monroe's principles. There was undoubted contraction in the repeated assertion that

[5] J. Reuben Clark, *Memorandum on the Monroe Doctrine,* Dept. of State Publication 37 (Washington, D.C.: Government Printing Office), 120.

the noncolonization principles applied to *North America*. While merely indicating that the United States might disapprove of interventions in South America, he made it clear that as the scenes of interventions came closer to the United States, our disposition to resist, by force if necessary, increased in ratio to their geographical proximity to our borders. This contraction has been described as a backhanded way of reducing responsibility for the enforcement of the policy in other areas. On the other hand, Polk's message was broader than that of Monroe in that it warned not only against forcible intervention, but also against European intermeddling by diplomatic intrigue in the relations of American states one with another. The Monroe noncolonization idea also seemed to be expanded by the announcement that our settled policy was that "no future European *colony or dominion* shall with our consent be planted or established upon any part of the North American continent." The word *dominion* included any kind of extension of territory whether by voluntary cession or otherwise.

Further extensions and clarifications of the Doctrine must be credited to the Polk administration. A serious Indian outbreak in Yucatán, an autonomous state in the Mexican federal union, caused the white authorities to offer transfer to the United States. A similar offer to Great Britain and to Spain alarmed President Polk; and so he, in a special message to the Congress, on April 29, 1848, called attention to the matter and declared that the United States, according to "established policy," could not consent to a transfer of Yucatán to the dominion and sovereignty of either Britain or Spain or other European powers. He specifically alluded to Monroe's declaration that "We should consider any attempt on their part to extend their system to any portion of this hemisphere as dangerous to our peace and safety." It was Polk's interpretation that the United States could prevent a Latin-American nation from accepting the dominion of a European nation, even if the Latin-American nation desired such a transfer of sovereignty.

A bill was offered in the Senate to authorize the President to occupy Yucatán "temporarily" with military forces to repel Indian attacks. This motion was withdrawn when it was learned that peace had been restored; thus ended the Yucatán affair. Nevertheless, it gave rise to an interesting question: Did Polk effect a union of the no-transfer principle and the Monroe Doctrine?

The idea that the transfer of a Spanish colony close to the United States, like the Floridas or Cuba, to another and possibly stronger European power, would be dangerous to the security of the United States, was long held by American statesmen as a cardinal principle of policy. The idea was so well expressed in the Congressional Resolution of 1811 that the no-transfer principle has been called the Madison Doctrine. Monroe did not link no-transfer with his famous Doctrine, nor on many occasions after 1823 concerning Cuba was no-transfer identified with the Monroe Doctrine. The first one to do this was Polk in his special message of 1848; in that instance the prohibition against transfer was not directed against Spain but against an American people. Although this may be regarded as a modified version of the no-transfer principle,[6] it is evident that Polk was not disposed to distinguish between the sources of the transfer, whether European or American. He was looking at the end result — that is, an extension of European dominion which he regarded as a violation of the non-colonization principle of the Monroe Doctrine. In this sense Polk extended the meaning and scope of the Doctrine: for the first time it was used as an instrument of American imperialism. In invoking the Monroe Doctrine to restrict the exercise of Latin-American sovereignty, Polk was presaging the Roosevelt Corollary of half a century later.

If there had been any doubt concerning the freedom of the United States, under the Monroe Doctrine, to acquire Latin-American territory, this doubt was removed by Polk. The taking of over half of Mexico by the Treaty of Guadalupe Hidalgo in 1848 made it very clear that the United States did not regard the Monroe Doctrine as a self-denying ordinance. The Doctrine was simply the assertion of the right of self-defense; there was no reason for the nation to impose obligations or limitations on itself.

Becomes "Doctrine"

After Polk the status of the Monroe Doctrine was uncertain, for it had not yet become popularized as national policy. Momentarily it seemed to be a partisan issue supported by the Democrats and opposed by the Whigs. Thus, in the succeeding Whig administration of President Zachary Taylor, Secretary of State John M. Clayton, who had ridiculed Polk's appeal to Monroe in 1848, was willing to enter into a treaty with Great Britain on the subject of an isthmian canal without any feeling about the Monroe Doctrine. The British, however, continued their expansion in Central America despite American efforts to interpose roadblocks, and Secretary Clayton was forced to conclude that the only wise course was compromise.[7] Thus, by the terms of the Clayton-Bulwer treaty of 1850, Great Britain and the United States agreed that they would refrain from any exclusive control over any isthmian railway or canal; that neither party would fortify the canal or its vicinity, nor occupy, colonize, or exercise dominion over any part of Central America; and that both would guard the safety and neutrality of the canal and would invite other nations to join them in doing the same.

Since the United States acquiesced in an extension of British control via joint protection over an isthmian canal, this was undoubtedly a violation of the Monroe Doctrine, a fact which cannot be erased by conceding a dilemma which confronted this country. The British expansion could only be stopped by appeasement, it is true, but concession would be at the expense of a principle which President Polk had been attempting to re-establish. If, in

[6] John A. Logan, *No Transfer, An American Security Principle* (New Haven: Yale University Press, 1961), 207.

[7] Dexter Perkins, *Hands off: A History of the Monroe Doctrine* (Boston: Little, Brown and Company, 1941), 96.

1850, Secretary Clayton, and American public opinion, did not regard an international guarantee of the projected canal as a violation of the Monroe Doctrine, it came to be so regarded in a very short time when agitation developed for the abrogation of the treaty because of British failure to withdraw from occupied territory in Central America. The return of the Democrats to power in 1853 accelerated public acceptance of the "Monroe Doctrine," as it was now called for the first time.[8] In that same year William H. Seward conceded in the United States Senate that the Doctrine had become "a *tradition* among the American people." By the end of the decade, it was so popularly accepted that it was regarded as a "national shibboleth." Lukewarm on the Monroe Doctrine in 1853, Mr. Seward, as Secretary of State in 1861 and in the years following, became its most ardent champion.

Violation and vindication

William H. Seward, a neophyte in matters of foreign policy, was hardly settled in his new office as Secretary of State, when he was confronted on March 18, 1861, by an unmistakable violation of the Monroe Doctrine: the voluntary annexation to Spain of the Dominican Republic, an island distraught by internal discord and economic collapse. On May 19 the Spanish government formally proclaimed the reincorporation of Santo Domingo. On April 2 and on June 19, Secretary Seward addressed sharp notes to the Spanish government protesting the decree of annexation.

With cavalier disregard of the fact that the American Union was at the moment embarking on a civil war, Mr. Seward, in frank, if not arrogant terms, challenged the Spanish flaunting of the Monroe Doctrine. The Spanish action, he said, manifested an "unfriendly spirit toward the United States, and to meet further prosecution of enterprises of that kind in respect to either the Dominican Republic, or any part of the American continent," the President would be obliged to adopt "a prompt, persistent, and if possible, effective resistance." Seward laid himself wide open to rebuff, and such was the nature of the Spanish response, which took little note of the great American dogma. Mr. Seward was informed by the Spanish minister "that the reincorporation of Santo Domingo with Spain, precisely because it has been unanimous and spontaneous, and on this basis accepted by Her Majesty the Queen, is a *fait accompli,* which Spain will maintain by all the means in her power."[9]

Seward's bluff had been called; nothing remained but to beat a hasty diplomatic retreat. This was a valuable experience to the new Secretary of State, and he proved his caliber by being able to profit from it. In fact, we credit this experience to the education in diplomacy of the man who was to become our second greatest Secretary of State. The Spanish, for their part, found the burden of maintaining order in the troublous island too great for their patience

---

[8] Dexter Perkins, *The Monroe Doctrine, 1826–1867* (Cambridge: Harvard University Press, 1927), 223.

[9] *Ibid.,* 287–303. See also Sumner Welles, *Naboth's Vineyard, The Dominican Republic, 1844–1924* (2 vols. New York: Payson & Clarke, Ltd., 1928), I, Chap. III.

and resources, and so they left Santo Domingo in 1865. The likelihood that the United States after the Civil War, might be disposed to defend the Monroe Doctrine with more than mere words, may have assisted the Spaniards in their decision to withdraw from the island.

The Santo Domingo experience proved to be very valuable to Mr. Seward in meeting a much more serious situation: the French intervention in Mexico. This was, by general agreement, the most flagrant violation of the Monroe Doctrine in its whole history until 1960.

Toward the end of 1861, naval vessels of England, France, and Spain sailed for Vera Cruz with the avowed intention of seizing the customhouses of two or three Mexican ports for the purpose of satisfying the claims of their respective governments.[10] Rejecting an invitation to join the expedition, the United States recognized the right of the powers to carry on hostile operations against Mexico; but it firmly objected to their possessing any port in order to control Mexico's political destiny. Secretary Seward, facing a most difficult situation, was unable to do more than protest very vigorously against the joint intervention.

Shortly after the allies had seized Vera Cruz, the British and the Spaniards, becoming dissatisfied with the attitude of the French, withdrew their forces in April, 1862, after reaching an agreement with Mexico concerning their claims. Although the Spanish withdrawal seems to have been disassociated in any way with considerations of the Monroe Doctrine, this was not true of the British, whose Foreign Secretary had declared that "it would as a matter of expediency be unwise to provoke the ill feeling of North America, unless some paramount object were in prospect and tolerably sure of attainment."[11]

After the retirement of the British and Spanish, the French discarded pretense and actively promoted *political* intervention in Mexico. They seized Mexico City, took control of the government, which was proclaimed a monarchy, and manipulated an offer of the crown to Archduke Maximilian of Austria. Maximilian entered Mexico City in June, 1864, to begin his reign as Emperor of Mexico, with the support of French arms.

These French violations of Mexican sovereignty evoked only protests on the part of Mr. Seward, who confined his notes to reminders that the permanent establishment of a foreign and monarchical government in Mexico would be neither easy nor desirable.[12] The war situation did not allow him to provoke France, whose Emperor was unquestionably sympathetic to the Southern cause. Thus, Seward had to content himself with protests for the record. But not so cautious was the Congress. On April 4, 1864, the House

[10] In July, 1861, the Mexican government decided to suspend payments on its foreign debts for two years. Some of these debts were exorbitant or fraudulent. For the French intervention in Mexico, see J. Fred Rippy, *The United States and Mexico* (New York: Alfred A. Knopf, Inc., 1926), Chap. XIV, and James Morton Callahan, *American Foreign Policy in Mexican Relations* (New York: The Macmillan Company, 1932), Chap. IX.

[11] Quoted by Perkins, *Monroe Doctrine, 1826–1867*, 371.

[12] John Bassett Moore, *A Digest of International Law* (Washington, D.C.: Government Printing Office, 1906), VI, 481.

of Representatives unanimously adopted a resolution, declaring that "it does not accord with the policy of the United States to acknowledge any monarchical government erected on the ruins of any republican government in America under the auspices of any European power." Secretary Seward's diplomatic skill was sorely taxed to reassure the aroused French that the President had not changed his policy.

With the change of the tide of war in favor of the Union, the notes of Secretary Seward took on a stronger and stronger tone. Eventually, with the close of the war, and in face of popular demands for armed intervention in Mexico, Secretary Seward increased the diplomatic pressure on France, but limited it to the extent only necessary to induce French withdrawal from Mexico. If pushed too hard and menacingly, French pride would leave no choice but armed resistance.

On November 30, 1865, John Bigelow, the United States Minister in Paris, informed the French government that the ancient friendship between the two countries would remain in jeopardy so long as France failed "to remove, as far as may depend upon her, the cause of our deep concern for the harmony of the two nations." Fortunately, at that very moment, Emperor Napoleon had decided to evacuate Mexico, and shortly after so informed the American minister. Not satisfied with the general assurance of withdrawal, and emboldened perhaps by the concentration of 25,000 troops on the Rio Grande border under General Sheridan, Seward pressed the French, on February 12, 1866, to indicate a date for the completion of the evacuation. Gradual withdrawal began in the fall of 1866 and was completed in the spring of 1867. Emperor Maximilian was left to his fate.[13]

Although this episode must be credited as a vindication of the Monroe Doctrine, it is significant that the famous policy was never mentioned by name during the whole course of the correspondence. Perhaps Mr. Seward refrained from mentioning the Doctrine because of his desire to keep emotion out of the issue. Nevertheless, there was plenty of appeal to it in the American press and by public officials. Though unmentioned by name, the strong stand taken by the United States was understood by one and all to be in defense of its established policy. And, although opinions may differ concerning the exact amount of influence which the policy of the United States had upon the French withdrawal, it seems quite certain that the Monroe Doctrine had scored a triumph.[14]

The Doctrine becomes major national policy

Emerging from the crisis of the French intervention in Mexico, the Monroe Doctrine achieved status as a major national policy. Endorsed by all political

[13] For the diplomatic exchange of notes, see Clark, *op. cit.*, 141–145, and Moore, *op. cit.*, VI, 498 ff.

[14] Several factors — a deteriorating situation in Europe, adverse developments in France, unexpected resistance from the Mexican patriots — probably would have caused Napoleon III to abandon the Mexican enterprise quite apart from United States opposition.

parties, it was indeed a true national dogma. Both the United States government and the people had become keenly sensitive to the possibility of its violation and to the necessity for its defense. Applauded in the New World, the policy won new respect in the Old World as something for which the United States would fight. Moreover, the transatlantic republic had become a force to be reckoned with. After the 1860's the Monroe Doctrine was never openly challenged by any European power until one hundred years later — by the Soviets in 1960.

Although the Mexican embroglio greatly enhanced the prestige and general recognition of the Monroe Doctrine, Secretary Seward's diplomacy wrought no significant change in the meaning of the policy. But after the 1860's, the dogma developed, not only in popular favor but also in meaning, until it reached its "apogee of pretension" in the administrations of Presidents Grover Cleveland and Theodore Roosevelt. First, we recount briefly the evolution of the Doctrine to 1896.

The first significant extension of the Doctrine — the so-called merging of the no-transfer principle into the Monroe Doctrine — occurred in the Grant administration, when Hamilton Fish was Secretary of State. In his message of May 31, 1870, to the Senate, President Grant recommended approval of the Santo Domingo annexation treaty and urged annexation of the island as a preventive measure against European intervention. "The doctrine promulgated by President Monroe," he declared, "has been adhered to by all political parties, and I now deem it proper to assert this equally important principle that hereafter *no territory* on this continent (European or American) shall be regarded as subject to transfer to a European power."[15] Secretary Fish explained to Congress that the no-transfer policy was part of the Monroe Doctrine. Henceforward it was so regarded. Although this extension, the so-called Grant Corollary, was patently a derogation of the sovereignty of both European and American nations, (and like the Polk Doctrine foreshadowed the Roosevelt Corollary), its logic has been generally recognized. Of all the extensions of the Monroe Doctrine, this one is regarded as the most defensible. It has been consistently supported and enforced by the United States with one exception — when Sweden-Norway ceded the tiny island of St. Bartholomew, in the Lesser Antilles, to France. According to a recent writer this was "the exception that proves the rule."[16]

The Monroe Doctrine had been frequently mentioned, prior to 1879, in connection with an interoceanic canal; however, because Ferdinand de Lesseps, the great French engineer, was identified with the construction project and promised its success, American concern over violation of the Doctrine mounted. Reacting to public belief that the construction of a canal by the French company under de Lesseps' direction was in violation of the Monroe Doctrine, President Rutherford B. Hayes sent a message to Congress

[15] J. D. Richardson, ed., *Messages and Papers of the Presidents*, V, 4016; Logan, *op. cit.*, 247–248.
[16] Logan, *op. cit.*, 252.

on March 8, 1880, stating, "the policy of this country is a canal under American control; . . . it will be the great ocean thoroughfare between our Atlantic and Pacific shores, and virtually a part of the coastline of the United States."[17] This statement may well have aroused fears of the Latin Americans, for it meant that their adjacent territories might come under United States control. The way was being prepared for the inauguration of United States imperialism. Although President Hayes did not mention the Monroe Doctrine, it was read into his message by his contemporaries, and when in 1881, Secretary of State James G. Blaine seized on the idea that a canal would virtually be a part of the coastline of the United States, he distinctly mentioned the Monroe Doctrine in the same breath. In apparent disregard of the Clayton-Bulwer treaty, Blaine informed the European powers, including Great Britain, that control by any one of them of an isthmian canal would be a violation of the Monroe Doctrine. Blaine was then informed by Britain that she stood on her treaty rights. Blaine's successor, Frederick Frelinghuysen, also attempted to find release from the Clayton-Bulwer treaty by injecting the Monroe Doctrine into the issue, and won for his pains sharp rebuff by the British government.

Thus, American efforts to offer the Monroe Doctrine as a barrier to European participation in any project for an interoceanic canal proved ineffectual. This is not to be regarded, however, as a setback in the history of the Doctrine. On the contrary, the constant allusions to the "traditional policy" of the United States merely served to secure for it a faster hold on the American mind. Should a President of the United States appeal to the Doctrine in a great emergency, he would not fail to receive unanimous popular support, even at the risk of war. Such a situation developed in a few short years. A new and disturbing extension of the Doctrine was at hand.

The Cleveland-Olney extension

The interpretation and application of the Monroe Doctrine with which the names of President Cleveland and Secretary of State Richard Olney are associated issued from a Venezuela-British Guiana boundary dispute concerning the Orinoco jungle. It was an old dispute which had long defied solution. During the years 1884–1887, encouraged by the discovery of gold in the disputed area, the British made extensive encroachments into territory claimed by Venezuela. Although the Venezuelans invoked the Monroe Doctrine several times, they failed to win the support of the United States until January, 1894, when they finally got a response. Warning that "the nations of the American continent . . . were not subject to colonization by any European powers," the United States proposed that this issue should be submitted to arbitration. The proposal was rejected by Britain. The Congress adopted a joint resolution, signed by President Cleveland on February 20, 1895, again urging arbitration. The interest of the public in a test of the Monroe Doctrine in the jungles of Guiana was developing apace.

[17] Richardson, *op. cit.*, VII, 585.

The culmination of the issue, which was assuming proportions unwarranted by the actual value of the territory involved, was reached on July 30, 1895, when Secretary Olney sent a trenchant note to Ambassador Bayard in London for delivery to the British Foreign Secretary. Olney argued that Great Britain, by encroaching upon Venezuelan territory, under guise of a boundary dispute, was extending European power and control over American territory and was therefore violating the Monroe Doctrine. The American Secretary of State then embarked on what has been described as "perhaps the most complete exposition of the Monroe Doctrine as applied to a concrete situation which has ever appeared in our diplomatic history."[18]

Mr. Olney declared that the Monroe Doctrine had but one purpose and object: "no European power or combination of European powers shall forcibly deprive an American state of the right and power of self-government and shaping for itself its own political fortunes and destinies." "The safety and welfare of the United States are so concerned with the maintenance of the independence of every American State," said Olney, "as to justify and require the interposition of the United States whenever that independence is endangered." In further justification of United States intervention in the Anglo-Venezuelan dispute, Mr. Olney made the statement so frequently quoted:

> Today the United States is practically sovereign on this continent, and its fiat is law upon the subjects to which it confines its interposition. Why? . . . It is because, in addition to all other grounds, its infinite resources combined with its isolated position render it master of the situation and practically invulnerable as against any and all other powers.
>
> All the advantages of this superiority are at once imperiled if the principle be admitted that European powers may convert American states into colonies or provinces of their own.

Mr. Olney concluded by observing that, since it was now clear that the United States could legitimately insist upon the merits of the boundary question being determined, it was also clear that there was but one mode of determining them, i.e., peaceful arbitration.[19]

Since it must be admitted that the tone of the Olney note was blustering and imperialistic, it should occasion no surprise that it drew a sharp, albeit delayed, rejoinder from Lord Salisbury. In his note of November 26, the British Foreign Secretary not only questioned the relevance of the Monroe Doctrine to the boundary dispute, but challenged the Monroe Doctrine itself.[20] There is little doubt that, if Mr. Olney had been undiplomatic, his more experienced British counterpart was unnecessarily irritating in his lecture on the Monroe Doctrine. The condescending attitude of Lord Salisbury, not uncommon among British statesmen of the period concerning Americans, and

---

[18] Clark, *op. cit.*, 153. For the Venezuelan question, see John B. Moore, "The Monroe Doctrine," *Political Science Quarterly*, XI (1896), 1–29.

[19] Clark, *op. cit.*, 154–163; *Foreign Relations of the United States, 1895*, Pt. I. 552–562.

[20] *For. Rel.*. 563–567.

the categorical refusal to arbitrate the boundary question, made President Cleveland "mad clear through." For the Americans there was no turning back. They would show the superior British that the Monroe Doctrine was not a "mere plaything."

On December 17, 1895, President Cleveland sent a special message to Congress recommending an appropriation for a commission to be appointed by himself, to investigate the facts and to report. After the report had been made, the United States proposed to enforce its terms. Fortunately this dangerous eventuality was never reached, for before the commission made its final report, Lord Salisbury capitulated and agreed to arbitrate with Venezuela.[21] The award of the arbitral tribunal, in 1899, was generally favorable to British claims, except for certain important territories near the mouth of the Orinoco River.

The Anglo-Venezuelan episode represented a highly significant stage in the history of the Monroe Doctrine. It has been argued that, although British occupation of the disputed territory might well have been a technical violation of the Monroe Doctrine, the extension of British control over a few thousand miles of jungle near the Orinoco could not possibly menace our safety, nor the independence of Venezuela itself. Quite true, but the crux of the matter was not the possession of this territory by Great Britain, but her acquiring it by unjust means at the expense of Venezuela. The threat to the United States would be not British possession of this small strip of territory, but the danger of this unjust acquisition forming a bad precedent for some future serious situation. This sound reasoning is what really actuated President Cleveland in his seeming quixotic role. Moreover, Cleveland seems to have been determined that South America should not become another Africa, a prey to European partition.

British acceptance of the Monroe Doctrine was also a matter of great importance. Henceforward, the world's greatest naval power was going to be most circumspect in avoiding any situation that might raise the issue of the Monroe Doctrine.[22] The critical phase of our defense of the policy had come to an end. Henceforth, with no possible threat from Great Britain, the United States should be able to cope with overseas dangers from any other source.

The role assumed by the United States in the boundary dispute between Venezuela and Great Britain evoked more approbation throughout Latin America in 1895 and 1896 than at any other time in the history of the Monroe Doctrine. Latin-American congresses adopted resolutions approving the policy of the United States, and the press joined in the chorus with a strong voice.

But well should the Latins have taken note that Olney's language presaged a new and enlarged meaning of the Monroe Doctrine. Far more important

[21] A deterioration of British position in Europe because of the South African situation and the threat of German intervention, counseled no conflict with the United States.

[22] The vulnerability of Canada to United States attack, despite Britain's sea power, undoubtedly always acted as a restraint on Britain. Truly, Canada was a "hostage" to Britain's good behavior.

than the bringing of boundary disputes under the aegis of the Monroe Doctrine, was the joining of the Doctrine and United States hegemony in what has been called the Doctrine of Paramount Interest. The assertion that, on this continent, the fiat of the United States is law in regard to those subjects upon which it has declared an interest, certainly should have alerted the Latins to United States interventions, always of course, under the guise of supporting the Monroe Doctrine. The incidence of the dogma was about to be enlarged to include the Latins themselves. The stage was being set for the famous Roosevelt Corollary.

The Roosevelt Corollary

The next, and the most extreme of all the extensions to the Monroe Doctrine was the result of another Venezuelan episode in 1902–1903. This so-called "second Venezuelan crisis" originated in the refusal by President Cipriano Castro to make payment on claims due the citizens of a number of European countries arising largely from injuries and damages suffered in civil wars. Being informed by Castro that all claimants should have recourse to a Venezuelan commission, Great Britain and Germany, characterizing this as "a frivolous attempt to avoid just obligations," served notice of intention to adopt coercive measures against Venezuela.

Quite aware of United States sensibilities, both the British and German governments, in separate notes, stated their intention to employ blockade which under no circumstances would extend to the acquisition or permanent occupation of Venezuelan territory. Secretary of State John Hay's response was that, although the United States government regretted the action, it "could not object to their taking steps to obtain redress for injuries suffered by their subjects, provided that no acquisition of territory was contemplated."[23]

A formal blockade of the Venezuelan coast was announced by England and Germany on December 20, 1902. Subsequently Italian war vessels joined the blockading squadron. On February 13, 1903, the blockade was raised when arrangements were reached by Venezuela and the blockading powers, according to which Venezuela admitted in principle to the justice of the claims, and consented to submit them to mixed commissions, that is, arbitration. In regard to the question whether the three intervening powers should enjoy priority in the settlement of claims, it was agreed to submit the matter to the Hague Court of Arbitration.

Of the blockade and its ending, and his own part in the affair, President Theodore Roosevelt said, in a public speech on April 2, 1903, that the concern of the government was "to keep an attitude of watchful vigilance and see that there was no infringement of the Monroe Doctrine, no acquirement of territorial rights by a European power at the expense of a weak sister republic. . . . Both powers assured us in explicit terms that there was not the slightest intention on their part to violate the principles of the Monroe Doctrine, and this

---

[23] William Spence Robertson, *Hispanic-American Relations with the United States* (New York: Oxford University Press, 1923), 116; Moore, *Digest of Int. Law,* VI, 592.

assurance was kept with an honorable good faith which merits acknowledgment on our part."[24]

At great variance with this statement was Roosevelt's own account, some fifteen years later when his recollection of these events must have been rather hazy, that he forced German withdrawal by threatening to use force in defense of the Monroe Doctrine. Scholarly inquiry has led to the conclusion that there was no such ultimatum, and certainly the decision by the Kaiser to retire from Venezuela was not due to any demonstration of, or threat to use, American force.[25] The American public, it is true, was very much concerned over the threat to the Monroe Doctrine. Moreover, both the President and the public were worried by German aggressiveness and the bellicosity of the Kaiser.[26] Thus, when the American people witnessed the rather hasty abandonment of the naval blockade, this was credited to the influence of the Monroe Doctrine. Perhaps President Roosevelt shared in the same public belief, and added embellishments in the remarks of his later years.

Whether, or to what extent, the Monroe Doctrine was instrumental in forcing the European powers to abandon the blockade, is not as important as the repercussions of the episode on the Doctrine itself. European interventions, even though justified, always represented a potential threat to the integrity of the Latin-American states. What should be done to prevent these possible violations of the Monroe Doctrine? Because of the easy way offered aggressive governments through financial interventions to violate the political and territorial integrity of American nations, Dr. Luis M. Drago, Foreign Minister of Argentina, on December 29, 1902, proposed to Secretary of State Hay that "the public debt cannot occasion armed intervention nor even the actual occupation of the territory of American nations by a European Power."[27]

Drago proposed his doctrine as a supplement or corollary to the Monroe Doctrine. Although the Argentine statesman accepted the Monroe Doctrine as a bulwark of Latin-American independence, his proposal really amounted to an attempt to engraft on the Doctrine a modified version of the Calvo concept of indefeasible national sovereignty. Both the Calvo and Drago Doctrines were much narrower than the Monroe Doctrine. It was for this reason, as well as his opposition to a multilateralization of the Monroe Doctrine, that Hay merely referred Drago to President Roosevelt's message of December 3, 1901, in which he declared that we do not guarantee against

[24] J. B. Moore, *Principles of American Diplomacy* (New York: Harper & Brothers, 1918), 255.

[25] Perkins, *Hands Off*, 215–220.

[26] It seems that at no time between 1870 and 1914 did Germany seriously consider territorial acquisitions in Latin America. It was true, nevertheless, that the German Navy was pressing for bases in the Caribbean. The state of world politics did not permit Germany to defy the Monroe Doctrine or to offend the United States. J. Fred Rippy, *Latin America in World Politics* (New York: F. S. Crofts & Co., 3rd ed., 1938), 149.

[27] Alejandro Alvarez, *The Monroe Doctrine* (New York: Oxford University Press, 1924), 103–104.

punishment for misconduct provided that punishment does not take the form of the acquisition of territory.

Theodore Roosevelt had been considering for some time the idea that the Monroe Doctrine implied responsibilities as well as privileges. In fact *preventive intervention,* or the unique idea that the protection of the Latin-American states by the United States justified our interference and even control over their affairs, had been evolving for many years antedating Roosevelt. The idea was present in the Polk doctrine as applied to Yucatán in 1848, and the Cleveland-Olney doctrine of paramount interest. It was also inherent in the Platt Amendment imposed on Cuba.[28] After their clash with Cleveland in 1895, British statesmen began dropping the hint that the United States perforce must assume the responsibility for keeping the troublesome Latins in order.

When the Hague Court, on February 22, 1904, ruled that the claims of the blockading powers enjoyed priority over those of other nations, this seemed to put the stamp of legality, if not a premium, on armed intervention for the collection of debts. The prospect that European creditor nations would now be inclined to make full use of their prerogatives in the Dominican Republic greatly alarmed the President, and propelled him to the making of a most important decision.

In his annual message to Congress, December 6, 1904, President Roosevelt announced a new and positive interpretation of the Monroe Doctrine, and the policy which he would apply to delinquent Latin-American republics. He said:

> If a nation shows that it knows how to act with reasonable efficiency and decency in social and political matters; if it keeps order and pays its obligations, it need fear no interference from the United States. Chronic wrongdoing, or an impotence which results in a general loosening of the ties of civilized society, may in America, as elsewhere, ultimately require intervention by some civilized nation, and in the Western Hemisphere the adherence of the United States to the Monroe Doctrine may force the United States, however reluctantly, in flagrant cases of such wrongdoing or impotence, to the exercise of an international police power. . . . It is a mere truism to say that every nation, whether in America or anywhere else, which desires to maintain its freedom, its independence, must ultimately realize that the right of such independence cannot be separated from the responsibility of making good use of it.[29]

President Roosevelt construed the Monroe Doctrine as imposing a responsibility on the United States to wield a "big stick" over the turbulent and debt-ridden Latin-American states so as to avoid any excuse for European intervention in violation of the Monroe Doctrine. This new positive interpretation,

---

[28] The Platt Amendment may properly be regarded as an implementation of the Roosevelt Corollary. Said Secretary Root, "This clause is simply an extension of the Monroe Doctrine." Benjamin H. Williams, *American Diplomacy* (New York: McGraw-Hill Book Company, Inc., 1936), 53.

[29] Richardson, *op. cit.,* (1917 ed.), XVI, 7053–7054.

which extended the incidence of the policy to the Latin-American states themselves, became known as the "Roosevelt Corollary of the Monroe Doctrine" and was destined to influence most profoundly the whole current of our Latin-American relations, because the Doctrine now became identified with interventionism.

Roosevelt's novel interpretation of the Monroe Doctrine loosed a flood of criticism, often most extreme, which never subsided until the corollary was repudiated by the State Department in 1930. It was argued, quite plausibly, that Roosevelt's interpretation was not based on the strict language of the original Monroe Doctrine, and departed from the spirit of the policy; that what Roosevelt called a corollary of the Doctrine, was not the Monroe Doctrine at all, but the American policy of hegemony operating in support of "protective imperialism."

The critics of the Roosevelt Corollary asked: Why not let the alien creditors shift for themselves? However desirable, this could not be allowed: because of the nature of the Hague award, it was not conceivable that European powers would renounce the right of intervention to secure justice, including payment of contract debts. The United States had to choose between a joint receivership with the European nations and the self-appointed role of international policeman. We must not forget that at the turn of the century the Great Powers were still pursuing aggressive colonial and imperialistic policies. Who can say that their appetites were sated by the partition of Africa? Was not Latin America desirable and easy prey? Although we know now that these fears were greatly exaggerated, the American people and their government were not then aware of this. Yes, a strong case can be made for the Roosevelt Corollary for 1903.

Implementing the Corollary

The Roosevelt Corollary was implemented not only by President Roosevelt, but also by his successors in the White House — Taft, Wilson, and Coolidge. There was acceptance and application of the principle that support of the Doctrine also included the American exercise of "police power" to remove the danger of European intervention. Thus, Latin-American countries, invariably those of the Caribbean area, which were in fiscal straits or pronounced stages of internal dissolution and chaos, accepted either voluntarily or by force, United States occupation or intervention and controls of various kinds: customs receiverships, collection of internal revenues, control over indebtedness and expenditures, arms control, supervised elections, and American-officered constabularies.

The new policy was first applied in 1905 to the Dominican Republic, which was badly in debt to certain European creditors. Since the governments of these creditors were threatening to intervene, President Roosevelt induced the Dominican government to enter into an executive agreement, or *modus vivendi,* whereby the United States assumed the responsibility of meeting the demands of the foreign creditors, but on condition that the United States assume the control of the Dominican customs. This technical infringement of the little country's sovereignty was "compensated" by a considerable improvement of its fiscal health, and by removal of the danger of European intervention. This policy was soon extended to other countries in the Caribbean area. President Taft and his Secretary of State Philander Knox not only endorsed the Roosevelt interpretation of the Monroe Doctrine, but used it as justification for governmental promotion of private American financial assistance to Latin America, called "dollar diplomacy." Said Taft, "When this helps prevent the happening of events that may prove to be an acute violation of the Monroe Doctrine by European governments, our duty in this regard is only increased and amplified."[30] The employment of American bankers' loans, at the urging of the State Department, was designed to eliminate European financial moves, and thus was a sort of Taft-Knox extension of the Monroe Doctrine.

Magdalena Bay Resolution

The next notable extension which was based on the well-recognized principle of self-defense occurred in 1912. Under the lead of Senator Henry Cabot Lodge, chairman of the Senate Foreign Relations Committee, the Senate adopted the so-called Magdalena Bay Resolution which asserted that:

> When any harbor or other place in the American continents is so situated that the occupation thereof for naval or military purposes might threaten the communications or the safety of the United States, the government of the United States could not see without grave concern the possession of such harbor or other place by any corporation or association which has such a relation to another government, not American, as to give that government practical power of control for national purposes.[31]

This resolution was evoked because of reports that a Japanese corporation was attempting to secure control of land on Magdalena Bay in Lower California, Mexico. Although it was true than an American company was attempting to sell its concessions to a Japanese concern, the facts of the matter did not seem to warrant the deep concern of the senators. Nevertheless a clarification of policy was opportune, for, due to the developing might of Japan, it was well to have it understood that for purposes of protecting the Monroe Doctrine, Japan must be grouped with the European powers. Regarded as a corollary to the Monroe Doctrine, the Magdalena Bay Resolution extended the original precept not only to an Asiatic power, but to a foreign company, as distinguished from a government. It was a veto on the transfer of property among private individuals.

It seems logical to extend the Doctrine to cases where it is thought that a "corporation or association" is really acting in behalf of a foreign government. Such a government is prevented from doing indirectly what it could not do

[30] Quoted by John M. Mathews, *American Foreign Relations* (New York: D. Appleton-Century Company, 1938), 77–78.

[31] Clark, *op. cit.*, 176.

directly. The extension to indirect encroachments, presumably of an economic nature, was simply recognition of the fact that non-American controls can be extended over the Latin-American countries by methods other than the customary military and political.

Truly the Senate resolution was based on the recognized right of nations to take measures for their defense. Support of such drastic arrogation of right, which infringes on the sovereignty of another nation, can rest only in military might. But that is sufficient. Senator Lodge did not base his resolution on the Monroe Doctrine, but he did not object when it was associated with the Doctrine in the debates. It has indeed been called the "Lodge Corollary." It might be regarded, quite logically, as an extension of the no-transfer principle.

The Lodge resolution is significant for an additional reason. The Monroe Doctrine, although purely an executive policy, received support from the Congress on many occasions. In this instance however, the Senate seems to have taken the initiative in adopting a new interpretation. The Senate's action in itself did not make policy, but since the State Department accepted the Magdalena Bay Resolution and invoked it several times later, it became incorporated into the executive policy.

Woodrow Wilson and the Doctrine

President Woodrow Wilson, the great idealist, not only continued a vigorous implementation in the Caribbean of the "big stick" interpretation of the Monroe Doctrine, but he also strongly supported the application of the Doctrine to indirect encroachments of an economic nature. With respect to the former, perhaps the most significant example was United States intervention in Haiti. Just prior to the outbreak of war in 1914, France and Germany seemed intent on obtaining some kind of customs receivership in Haiti as protection for the investments of their nationals. The United States was approached, but rejected a proposal to be included in a joint customs control. It is believed that, on the very eve of the outbreak of World War I the Germans were planning armed action in Haiti. Thus, when the United States intervened with armed force in Haiti in 1915, the action was defended as support of the Monroe Doctrine.[32]

The United States intervention, which was to continue for nineteen years, was up to that time the most thoroughgoing job of policing a Latin-American state undertaken by a United States administration. This most sweeping application of the Roosevelt Corollary was followed in 1916 by occupation of the Dominican Republic because of its refusal to accept more effective fiscal controls by the United States. The suspension of Dominican sovereignty was to last eight years.

Not only was the Wilson administration responsible for the most sweeping applications, in Haiti and the Dominican Republic, of the Roosevelt Corol-

[32] Statement by Robert Lansing, in *Congressional Record*, 62: 6487–6488 (May 8, 1922).

lary,[33] but it seriously considered the prohibition of foreign concessions in Latin America that were apt to dominate domestic affairs. Robert Lansing, Counselor of the State Department, in a memorandum, dated June 11, 1914, urged a redefinition of the Monroe Doctrine to meet the danger of foreign economic penetration of Latin America, a danger against which the Doctrine provided no answer.[34]

When early in his administration, President Wilson heard that an English company was about to receive a monopolistic oil concession in Colombia, which carried with it valuable harbor improvement rights, he declared in a public statement:

> You hear of concessions to foreign capitalists in Latin America. . . . It is an invitation, not a privilege, and the states that are obliged because their territory does not lie within the main field of modern enterprise and action, to grant concessions are in this condition, that foreign interests are apt to dominate their domestic affairs — a condition of affairs always dangerous and apt to become intolerable. . . . I rejoice in nothing so much as the prospect that they will now be emancipated from these conditions, and we ought to be the first to take part in assisting in that emancipation.[35]

President Wilson was not opposed to the legitimate investment of European capital in Latin America, but only to those forms that might be extended to political control. The British oil company, Pearson and Son, withdrew its contract with the Colombian government, giving as its reason the opposition of the United States. This was an exceptional instance, for we have no further examples of foreign concessions being frowned upon by the United States government.

The Wilson doctrine of opposition to Latin-American concessions to European capitalists might well have resulted in a closed-door policy, reserving the area to exploitation by American capitalists. Although the ever-ready chorus of Latin Yankeephobes was raised against financial imperialism, they were never able to come forward with the needed evidence. The facts are that throughout the whole history of the Monroe Doctrine, foreign financial and economic interests were able to compete with United States concerns for the Latin-American markets and investment opportunities on equal terms.[36]

In an effort to allay Latin-American fears of United States imperialism under guise of the Monroe Doctrine, President Wilson in a public address at Mobile, Alabama, on October 27, 1913, declared, "The United States will never again seek one additional foot of territory by conquest." Later, on

[33] The United States purchased the Danish West Indies (Virgin Islands) in 1916 in order to counter a possible challenge (by Germany) to the no-transfer principle.

[34] *Papers Relating to the Foreign Affairs of the United States. The Lansing Papers* (2 vols. Washington: Government Printing Office, 1942), II, 464.

[35] Quoted in John H. Latané, *The United States and Latin America* (New York: Doubleday, Page and Company, 1926), 328.

[36] Later, when Japan was promoting her "Greater Asia Co-prosperity Sphere," her claim that it was nothing more than a Monroe Doctrine of the Far East was untrue, because the Japanese policy meant the closed door, economic as well as political.

January 6, 1916, in an address to the Second Pan American Scientific Conference, President Wilson boldly proposed a Pan American pact which would amount to a continentalization of the fundamental tenets of Monroeism.

The general objective of the Wilson proposal was the negotiation of a Pan American pact by which territorial integrity and independence under the republican form of government of the nations of the New World would be severally and jointly guaranteed; also, there would be agreement to settle all boundary disputes by amicable process including arbitration. According to Colonel Edward M. House, the President's purpose was "to broaden the Monroe Doctrine so that it may be upheld by all the American Republics instead of by the United States alone as now." The same idea had been represented to the Chilean ambassador by Secretary of State William Jennings Bryan. The republics of Latin America were to have the opportunity, he said, to "join in the upholding of what is known as the Monroe Doctrine, because such a recognition of the doctrine by them would prevent for the future any misunderstanding of its purposes and any underestimating of its value."[37]

Contrary to expectation the Wilson proposal for a Pan American pact encountered opposition. Chile was the principal objector. First, there was fear that the guarantee of republican government would invite interference in the internal affairs of a country. Second, and more important, since Chile was involved in the Tacna-Arica dispute with Peru, she feared a covenant which would bind her to arbitration. Because of Chilean opposition no progress was made, and in the meantime Argentina and Brazil lost interest. President Wilson was reconciled to the failure of his proposal of an inter-American pact when he turned to the more general guarantee of "territorial integrity and existing political independence" by the famous Article 10 of the Covenant of the League of Nations.

The Doctrine and the League of Nations

Article 10 was in fact the embodiment of the idea put forth by President Wilson in an address to the Senate on January 22, 1917, when he proposed that "the nations should with one accord adopt the doctrine of President Monroe as the doctrine of the world; that no nation should seek to extend its policy over any other nation or people, but that every people should be left free to determine its own policy, its own way of development, unhindered, unthreatened, unafraid, the little along with the great and powerful." Article 10, which the President called "the very heart of the Covenant," went beyond the Monroe Doctrine in embodying a formal mutual guarantee of independence. The Monroe Doctrine only guaranteed the safety of Latin America as the safety of the United States was involved.

Because of the silence of the original draft of the League Covenant on the Monroe Doctrine, considerable pressure was put on President Wilson to insert a safeguarding clause. The result was Article 21 which provided that "nothing in this Covenant shall be deemed to affect the validity of inter-

[37] *Lansing Papers,* II, 484–488.

national engagements, such as treaties of arbitration or regional understandings like the Monroe Doctrine, for securing the maintenance of peace."

This was a most inaccurate definition of the Monroe Doctrine, for it was not an "understanding" of any sort, but a unilateral policy of the United States resting solely on its own support. Nevertheless, an interesting question arose: Did the mention of the Monroe Doctrine in Article 21 as a regional arrangement amount to recognition of its legal validity by all adherents to the Covenant of the League of Nations? Although the Legal Adviser of the Department of State maintained that "the mention of the Doctrine in an international agreement signed by all the states of the world without any dissent and with approval is *almost* a recognition of the Doctrine,"[38] there was much vigorous dissent. The question never received a definitive answer. Nor was a satisfactory clarification of the phraseology of Article 21 ever forthcoming, not that there were no urgent requests.

It was impossible for the League of Nations, with the United States not a member, to give an acceptable definition of the Monroe Doctrine. Consequently, when Mexico finally entered the League of Nations in 1931, and Argentina re-entered in 1933, both countries filed reservations declining specifically to recognize the Monroe Doctrine under Article 21 of the Covenant.

Return to the original Monroe Doctrine

Latin-American fears and suspicions of the Monroe Doctrine had been mounting ever since the turn of the century when the United States embarked on a "positive interpretation" of the Doctrine. Latent jealousies and apprehensions, born of the simple fact that Anglo-Americans were of an alien and strange culture, were nurtured by a more potent fare when the United States government became an international policeman on a Latin-American beat. Because of the many interventions, from the Dominican Republic in 1905, to Nicaragua in 1926, when the principles of 1823 were invoked to justify apparent acts of imperialism and hegemony, little wonder the belief that the Doctrine was only an instrument to fend off the imperialism of Europe from regions which the United States intended to appropriate for itself. It was a case of "hands off" to Europe and "hands on" for the United States. This became a popular theme for intellectual Yankeephobes in Latin America, such as Rubén Darío of Nicaragua, José Enrique Rodó of Uruguay, Manuel Ugarte of Argentina, Carlos Pereyra of Mexico, and Rufino Blanco-Fombona of Venezuela. Although extreme, their views gave accurate expression to Latin-American anxieties over the course of United States policy.[39]

Not only the Latins but many North Americans themselves were developing doubts concerning the validity and worth of the "new" Monroe Doctrine. In the minority were those like Hiram Bingham, professor at Yale and later

---

[38] Perkins, *Hands Off*, 297.
[39] See J. Fred Rippy, "Literary Yankeephobia in Hispanic America," *Journal of International Relations*, XII (1922), 350–371, 524–538.

Senator from Connecticut, who regarded the Doctrine as an "obsolete shibboleth" which had outlived its usefulness and should be discarded altogether.[40] The centenary of the Monroe Doctrine in 1923, marked by many speeches and publications, seemed to present an occasion for re-examination of the famous policy which still evoked the unabated support of the American people, despite the fact that they never responded with enthusiasm to the idea of tutelage of the Latin-American republics.

Because World War I resulted in the declining power of Europe and the rise of the United States, it became an open question whether it was necessary to continue the role of international policeman in the Caribbean. Certainly there was no longer any European power capable of challenging the United States, and thus this country could well afford, in the interest of better understanding with the Latin-American nations, to relax controls, and in general, liquidate imperialism in the Caribbean and Central American areas. This was the policy initiated by Secretary of State Charles E. Hughes in 1922.

In an address at Minneapolis, August 30, 1923, on an occasion commemorating the centenary of the Monroe Doctrine, Mr. Hughes defined it in narrow terms, and, although he did not mention the Roosevelt Corollary, he was in fact repudiating its radical claims for intervention. The Hughes interpretation restored the Doctrine to its original character as "solely a policy of self-defense." Each American state was urged to assume the Monroe Doctrine as its independent policy. This would give the policy the might of universal American support. Thus, there was no intent by Secretary Hughes to abandon the unilateral character of the Doctrine. While discarding any right of intervention or protection of any American republic under the Monroe Doctrine, Mr. Hughes held to the right of "temporary interposition."[41]

The initiative taken by Mr. Hughes to free the Monroe Doctrine of the Roosevelt Corollary incubus was carried to its logical conclusion when, in 1928, Secretary of State Frank B. Kellogg asked J. Reuben Clark, Under Secretary of State, to prove that the Roosevelt Corollary was not really a legitimate offspring of the original Monroe Doctrine. Mr. Clark completed his study in two months' time, and on December 7, 1928, submitted it to the Secretary. Although the memorandum became immediately a policy guide, its startling conclusions were denied the public until Secretary of State Henry L. Stimson ordered its publication in 1930.

The Clark *Memorandum on the Monroe Doctrine* undertook to restore the Monroe Doctrine to its original meaning as a policy of self-preservation. It is a case of the United States versus Europe, and not of the United States versus Latin America. Being concerned only with the peril from Europe, it "does

---

[40] Hiram Bingham, *The Monroe Doctrine, An Obsolete Shibboleth* (New Haven: Yale University Press, 1913).

[41] *American Journal of International Law*, XVII (October, 1923), 611–628. According to Sumner Welles, Secretary Hughes established beyond doubt that the Monroe Doctrine did not stand in the way of Pan American cooperation, but rather that it provided the necessary basis for inter-American security cooperation. Welles, *Naboth's Vineyard*, II, 925.

not apply to purely inter-American relations. Nor does the declaration purport to lay down any principles that are to govern the inter-relationship of the states of this Western Hemisphere as among themselves." This led Mr. Clark to the inevitable conclusion: "It is not believed that this [Roosevelt] corollary is justified by the terms of the Monroe Doctrine, however much it may be justified by the application of the doctrine of self-preservation."[42] Thus, while attempting to free the Monroe Doctrine of interventionism, the right of intervention was preserved.

Expectations by the Hoover-Stimson administration of allaying Latin-American distrust by freeing the Monroe Doctrine of the taint of intervention were not realized. In fact, the publication of the Clark *Memorandum* aroused only mild interest: since the United States had not renounced intervention, its new interpretation of the Monroe Doctrine was meaningless. So long as interventionism was practiced the Latins would continue to regard the Doctrine as a threat.

When the United States in 1933 renounced categorically its right to intervene in the internal affairs of other American states, the Monroe Doctrine ceased to be an irritant in United States-Latin American relations. Instead, the Latin-American nations manifested a willingness to enter into declarations and pacts embodying the general sense of the formerly hated policy. This so-called "Pan Americanization," or continentalizing of the Doctrine, represents the most recent, and perhaps final phase of the long history of the venerable policy.

Pan Americanizing the Doctrine[43]

We have noted President Wilson's proposal for a Pan American pact which he believed would continentalize the principles of President Monroe. We have also noted Latin-American rejection of the proposal. In 1920 a Uruguayan president, Dr. Baltázar Brum, proposed an American League of Nations based on the Pan Americanized principles of the Monroe Doctrine. Since the United States had used the Doctrine to convert Latin America into a kind of protectorate, Dr. Brum believed that by "continentalizing" the principles, the nations of Latin America would achieve moral equality with the United States. The Brum proposal was submitted to the fifth general Pan American conference at Santiago, Chile, in 1923. It was vigorously opposed by Latin delegations who seized the opportunity to condemn the American policy as contradictory and hypocritical. When the United States delegation displayed no interest in the proposal it was abandoned.

It was after 1933, with acceptance by the United States of the principle of nonintervention, that the "Pan Americanization" of the Monroe Doctrine became possible. This was by the adoption of inter-American pacts, resolu-

---

[42] Clark, *op. cit.,* xxiii-xxiv. It was not that the Roosevelt Corollary was wrong in 1905, but that it was no longer necessary in 1930.

[43] See Dexter Perkins, *A History of the Monroe Doctrine* (Boston: Little, Brown and Company, 1955. A new edition of *Hands Off*), Chap. X; and also see J. Lloyd Mecham, *The United States and Inter-American Security, 1889–1960* (Austin: University of Texas Press, 1961), 124–129.

tions, and declarations which tended to translate the principles of 1823 into international engagements binding upon all the states of the hemisphere. The process extended over a number of years. The first step was taken in 1936 at the Buenos Aires Peace Conference, where President Franklin D. Roosevelt, addressing the conference at its opening session, revealed his desire to strengthen the inter-American security system by erecting bulwarks against aggression from abroad. He declared that non-American states seeking "to commit acts of aggression against us, will find a hemisphere wholly prepared to consult together for our mutual safety and our mutual good." This was interpreted as a sweeping invitation to make the Monroe Doctrine multi-lateral.

The end result was the adoption, by the Buenos Aires conference, of a Convention for the Maintenance, Preservation and Re-establishment of Peace, popularly known as the Consultative Pact. It provided that "in the event that the peace of the American Republics is menaced" the signatory powers should "consult together for the purpose of finding and adopting methods of peaceful cooperation."

It was held by Cordell Hull and many others that the Consultative Pact clearly takes care of any situation envisioned by the Monroe Doctrine by providing for joint action on the part of the American republics. Those who make this claim miss the meaning of the venerable American policy. According to the Consultative Pact when peace is threatened there will be a consultation for the purpose of finding and adopting methods of *peaceful cooperation*. The Monroe Doctrine is a policy of national self-defense supported by the military might of the United States. It has shielded Latin America from non-American aggression. How effective would *peaceful cooperation* be in fending off non-American aggression? At best the Consultative Pact of 1936 bears only a slight resemblance to the Monroe Doctrine.

The Declaration of Lima, which issued from the Seventh International Conference of American States held in the Peruvian capital in 1938, was a longer and truer step in the continentalizing of Monroe's principles. After reaffirming continental solidarity, the American states declared that "in case the peace, security or territorial integrity of any American Republic is . . . threatened by acts of any nature that may impair them, they proclaim their common concern and their determination to make effective their solidarity, coordinating their respective sovereign wills by means of the procedure of consultation . . . using measures that in each case circumstances may make advisable." The Lima declaration differed from the Buenos Aires Consultative Pact of 1936 in that: (1) defensive cooperation was not limited to *peaceful* measures; (2) it seemed to be aimed only at non-American threats; and (3) the scope of the consultation procedure, which was to be in the meetings of the foreign ministers, was enlarged to include, in addition to "threats to the peace", also the "security and territorial integrity of any American Republic."

The declaration by the American republics of their determination to defend their sovereignty against foreign intervention has been represented incorrectly as, in effect, "the adoption of the entire principle of the Monroe Doctrine as the doctrine of two continents. . . . The twenty-one American Republics thus undertook to assume the obligation to implement the policy first stated in the Monroe Doctrine as their common cause."[44] However, the prospects for common agreement on enforcement measures were greatly diminished by the announcement that "the governments of the American republics *will* act independently in their individual capacity." This could mean no more than that the American nations recognize a collective concern over threats to their security and territorial integrity, but reserve to each individually the right to determine defensive measures; that is, common concern, but not necessarily common response. Therefore, the Declaration of Lima fell short of transforming the Monroe Doctrine into a continental doctrine. But, like the Buenos Aires Consultative Pact it marked another step "toward common international action in defense of the principles of 1823."[45]

The relation between the various consultative agreements and the Monroe Doctrine was well stated by Under Secretary of State Sumner Welles:

> It would not be correct to say that the Monroe Doctrine had been replaced or superseded by the group of inter-American agreements that has grown up in recent years. . . . The Monroe Doctrine was promulgated, in the first place, as a unilateral declaration on the part of the United States. It still stands as such a declaration. It could still be invoked, if there were occasion, unilaterally, by the United States. . . . But what has happened is this. The purposes that it sought to accomplish have become the recognized concern of all the American nations and they have declared, multilaterally, their support of its objectives. . . . Thus we may naturally expect in the future the unilateral character of the Doctrine will be pushed more and more into the background and its multilateral character emphasized. . . . What has taken place is not a change in policy but a change in emphasis. The emphasis is now on joint action rather than on single action.[46]

It was at the Panama Meeting of Foreign Ministers in 1939 that a first step was taken to Pan Americanize the no-transfer principle of the Monroe Doctrine. Because of the possibility that the war in Europe might result in the forcible transfer of sovereignty of colonial possessions in America, a resolution provided that in such a contingency a meeting of foreign ministers should be called to consult. This resolution, according to one authority, "marks the beginning of the end of the sole proprietorship of the United States over the no-transfer principle."[47] It became a fully shared responsibility of the Latin-American nations at the next meeting of the foreign ministers held in Havana only ten months later.

On June 17, 1940, the State Department warned that "the United States would not acquiesce in any attempt to transfer geographic regions of the Western Hemisphere from one non-American power to another non-American

---

[44] Robert A. Smith, *Your Foreign Policy* (New York: The Viking Press, 1941), 199.
[45] Mecham, *op. cit.*, 142–144.
[46] *Ibid.*, 144.
[47] Logan, *op. cit.*, 217–218. See also F. O. Wilcox, "The Monroe Doctrine and World War Two," *American Political Science Review*, XXXVI (1942), 433–453.

power." This warning was immediately endorsed by a Joint Congressional Resolution (June 18, 1940), which stated that in the event of such a transfer or any attempt to transfer, the United States would, "in addition to other measures, immediately consult with the other American republics to determine upon the step which should be taken to safeguard their common interests."[48] Thus the Grant Corollary on no-transfer became a part of the statutory law of the United States. Notes were sent to Berlin and Rome reminding the belligerents of the traditional American attitude toward the transfer of territories. The German reply of July 1 protested no intention to acquire American territories, but added that the Reich considered it also a corollary of the Monroe Doctrine for Americans to refrain from interfering in Europe.[49]

The United States delegates went to the Havana Meeting of Foreign Ministers in July, 1940, with the intention of seeking Latin-American adherence to the no-transfer principle of the Monroe Doctrine. They were not disappointed, for the meeting adopted both a declaration known as the Act of Havana Concerning the Provisional Administration of European Colonies or Possessions in the Americas, and a formal Convention on the Provisional Administration of European Colonies and Possessions in the Americas. The American republics refused to accept any transfer, or attempt to transfer any interest or right in the Western Hemisphere. In case of such an attempt, which would be regarded as threatening to the peace of the continent, provision was made by the convention for the taking over and the provisional administration of such a region by an Inter-American Commission of Territorial Administration, to be composed of representatives of each state that ratified the pact. The Act of Havana was a supplementary declaration which authorized the creation of an emergency committee to cover situations arising prior to the promulgation of the convention.[50] Most important, the Act provided that "should the need for emergency action be so urgent that action by the Committee cannot be awaited, any of the American republics shall have the right to act in the manner which its own defense or that of the Continent requires."

Since force was to be the principal sanction of the Act of Havana, this can be construed as a blanket authorization to the United States, the only American power with adequate force, to occupy any European possession

---

[48] In urging the resolution before the Congress, Secretary Hull indicated that the State Department favored a "Pan Americanization" of the no-transfer principle. Logan, *op. cit.*, 317.

[49] *Ibid.*, 328–329. A feature of the original Monroe Doctrine generally misunderstood is that Monroe pledged nonintervention only in the *internal* concerns of European powers. Thus the Monroe Doctrine has never been regarded as a barrier to United States participation in extra-continental affairs *which concern us.*

[50] The Convention, having been ratified by two-thirds of the American republics, became effective on January 8, 1942. Since no occasion arose to invoke the pact, the trusteeship committee never administered a European dependency. The collective trusteeship arrangement as provided by the Havana Convention is said to have been the idea of President Roosevelt. Logan, *op. cit.*, 333.

as a hemisphere danger spot. In other words, the Latin-American nations were formally endorsing the United States implementation of the no-transfer principle of the Monroe Doctrine. At the same time they were incorporating the principle into American international law.

Another act of the Havana Meeting, a further step in the continentalizing of the principles of 1823, was the Declaration of Reciprocal Assistance and Cooperation for the Defense of the Nations of the Americas. It declared:

> Any attempt on the part of a *non-American state* against the integrity or inviolability of the territory, the sovereignty or the political independence of an American state shall be considered as an act of aggression against the states which sign this declaration.

In the event of aggression by a non-American state the signatories pledged to consult in order to agree upon measures it might be advisable to take. Also, two or more of the signatory nations were to negotiate defense agreements in preparation for mutual defense in the event of aggression. This resolution, proclaiming the "all for one, one for all" principle, moved closer to the real meaning of the Monroe Doctrine. It aimed only at non-American aggression. The matter of sanctions was still left to consultation, although the resolution did recommend defense agreements among its signatories. It was not true, as many again alleged, that the Havana Resolution of Reciprocal Assistance marked the end of the Monroe Doctrine or its disappearance into a general formula of an international character. This could be true only if the American states, *by formal agreement,* should severally guarantee to one another by effective sanctions, their territorial integrity and political independence against non-American aggression. To this length they never went.

Next came the Act of Chapultepec, negotiated at the Inter-American Conference on Problems of War and Peace at Mexico City in 1945. It repeated the Havana Resolution of Reciprocal Assistance, but with two differences: first, it contemplated the use of force to meet threats of aggression *from any source,* and second, the enforcement measures to be considered in consultation ranged from the mere recall of diplomatic representatives, and the imposing of embargoes, to the use of armed force. In effect the Act of Chapultepec made all the American republics coguardians of American security even against *American aggressors.* Thus the Havana resolution of 1940 was expanded into a kind of Pan American defense doctrine, but not in every respect a multilateral Monroe Doctrine.

Since the Act of Chapultepec was a war measure, and its term was limited to World War II, it was necessary to negotiate a permanent treaty to formalize its provisions. This was the reason for the Inter-American Treaty of Reciprocal Assistance negotiated at a special conference in Rio de Janiero in 1947. Using the Act of Chapultepec as a frame of reference, the Rio treaty provided that: first, an armed attack by any state against an American state should be considered an attack against all, and each one of the contracting states undertakes (but is not bound) to assist in meeting the attack; second, each one is privileged, immediately or prior to a consultation decision, to afford the aggressed member any assistance it may wish to extend; third, the nature of assistance to be rendered collectively is to be determined by consultation; fourth, in case of acts of aggression other than armed attacks, and all threats of aggression, the parties to the treaty are bound only to consult; fifth, the measures that may be taken by the parties individually or collectively ranged from suspension or breaking of diplomatic relations and severance of economic relations, to the use of armed force. The imposing of sanctions binding on all states that have ratified the treaty will be by a two-thirds majority, with the exception that no state can be required to use armed force without its consent.

The Rio treaty, which has been formally ratified by all of the American republics, capped the evolutionary development of the so-called "Pan Americanization" of the Monroe Doctrine. By its terms the American states are bound to act together against aggression from any source. Has the objective of the Monroe Doctrine therefore become the common property of the inter-American community rather than merely a self-defense policy of the United States opposed to the extension of foreign political controls to the Western Hemisphere?

The argument that the Monroe Doctrine is "no longer an exclusively American doctrine" is at variance with the highest authority. President Eisenhower said, "I think that the Monroe Doctrine has by no means been supplanted." The same idea was inherent in President Kennedy's declaration, following the Bay of Pigs fiasco, that "if the nations of this hemisphere fail to meet their commitments against Communist penetration," the United States would act unilaterally in exercise of its right of self-defense.

Thus, the Monroe Doctrine has apparently been put on the shelf, not to be resorted to so long as the American republics mutually support the principle of continental defense in consonance with the security interests of the United States. But in weighing its interests there is a point of time and circumstance beyond which the United States might not allow its national security to await the pleasure of its Latin-American associates. Notwithstanding, it seems that, with respect to the Cuban situation, the United States, because of its futile efforts to secure an implementation of the "Pan Americanized" Monroe Doctrine, sacrificed national interests by withholding its own unilateral action.

The Monroe Doctrine and Communism

It was the threat to hemispheric security posed by the activities of international Communism which revealed the shallow and spurious content of the so-called "Pan Americanized" Monroe Doctrine. In a startling move to claim Cuba as a Communist protectorate, Nikita Khrushchev, on July 9, 1960, declared that any attack on Cuba would bring about instant retaliation against the United States by Soviet inter-continental missiles. The Monroe Doctrine, he said, is dead, and should be buried "so that it should not poison the air by its decay." President Eisenhower vehemently denied the passing of the Doctrine and warned that the United States, in conformity with its treaty obligations, would not "permit the establishment of a regime dominated by international Communism in the Western Hemisphere."

Despite the brave words of President Eisenhower, the Soviets continued to build up power in Cuba, with the eventual result that there could be little doubt the Castro regime had been gathered into the fold of "the political system of an extracontinental power" dedicated to the destruction of our way of life. For the first time in one hundred years the Monroe Doctrine was directly and openly challenged, and the United States government, fearful of the consequences, delayed over long before offering resistance.

The Soviet-American confrontation of October, 1962, which forced removal of Soviet missiles from Cuba, can hardly be called a defense of the Monroe Doctrine, since the United States' objective did not seem to include freeing Cuba of Russian armed forces or the extrusion of a political system in effect controlled by an extracontinental power.

The status of the Pan Americanized Monroe Doctrine seems to be this: the brave pledges of collective defense against the various forms of non-American aggression dissolve into mere verbiage in situations calling for the union of the wills of twenty-one American nations. It does not seem to be effective as a deterrent to subtle intrusions by the international Communist conspiracy. The Latins seem unable to mobilize collective resistance to anything short of an overt armed attack on an American republic.

The status of the unilateral Monroe Doctrine seems to be this: it is not dead, but is in a moribund state. The United States fears to invoke it, much less to mention it by name, because this might disrupt our Latin-American relations, and also because the Russians might not be bluffing. Only the future can disclose whether the advent of the atomic-ballistic missile age has outmoded the Monroe Doctrine.

SUPPLEMENTARY READING

Alvarez, Alejandro, *The Monroe Doctrine, Its Importance in the International Life of the States of the New World* (New York: Oxford University Press, 1924).

Barcía Trelles, Camilo, *La Doctrina de Monroe y La Cooperación Internacional* (Madrid: Editorial Mundo latina, 1921).

Bemis, Samuel Flagg, *A Diplomatic History of the United States* (New York: Henry Holt and Company, 4th ed., 1955), 384–404, 416–423.

Bemis, Samuel Flagg, *The Latin American Policy of the United States* (New York: Harcourt, Brace and Company, 1943), Chaps. VII, IX.

Bingham, Hiram, *The Monroe Doctrine, an Obsolete Shibboleth* (New Haven: Yale University Press, 1913).

Clark, J. Reuben, *Memorandum on the Monroe Doctrine* (*December 17, 1928*) (Washington, D.C.: 1930. Dept. of State Publication No. 37).

Fabela, Isidro, *Las Doctrinas Monroe y Drago* (Mexico, D.F.: Librería Universitaría, 1957).

Logan, John A., *No Transfer. An American Security Principle* (New Haven: Yale University Press, 1961).

Nerval, Gaston, *Autopsy of the Monroe Doctrine* (New York: The Macmillan Company, 1934).

Moore, John B., *A Digest of International Law* (8 vols. Washington, D.C.: Government Printing Office, 1906), VI, 368–604.

Papers Relating to the Foreign Relations of the United States: The Lansing Papers, 1914–1920 (2 vols. Washington, D.C.: Government Printing Office, 1939–1940. Dept. of State Pub. No. 1420), II, 459–471.

Pereyra, Carlos, *El Mito de Monroe* (Madrid: Editorial América, 1914).

Perkins, Dexter, "Bringing the Monroe Doctrine Up to Date," *Foreign Affairs,* XX (1941–1942), 253–265.

Perkins, Dexter, *Hands Off: A History of the Monroe Doctrine* (Boston: Little, Brown and Company, 1941. Rev. ed., 1955, under title, *A History of the Monroe Doctrine*).

Perkins, Dexter, *The Monroe Doctrine, 1823–1826* (Cambridge: Harvard University Press, 1927).

Perkins, Dexter, *The Monroe Doctrine, 1826–1867* (Baltimore: The Johns Hopkins Press, 1933).

Perkins, Dexter, *The Monroe Doctrine, 1867–1907* (Baltimore: The Johns Hopkins Press, 1937).

Perkins, Dexter, *A History of the Monroe Doctrine.* A new edition of *Hands Off: A History of the Monroe Doctrine* (Little, Brown and Company, 1955).

Quesada, Ernesto, *La Doctrina Monroe, Su Evolución Histórica* (Buenos Aires: Imprenta y casa editora "Coni," 1920).

Robertson, William Spence, *Hispanic-American Relations with the United States* (New York: Oxford University Press, 1923), Chap. IV.

Smith, Robert Aura, *Your Foreign Policy: How, What, and Why* (New York: The Viking Press, 1941), Chaps, VII, XIII.

Thomas, D. Y., *One Hundred Years of the Monroe Doctrine* (New York: The Macmillan Company, 1923).

Vasconcellos, José, *Bolivarismo y Monroismo* (Santiago de Chile: Editorial Ercilla, 1935).

Williams, Benjamin H., *American Diplomacy* (New York: McGraw-Hill Book Company, Inc., 1936), Chap. IV.

South America

84

4

The Pan American Policy of the United States: Origins and Development, 1826–1932

The United States policy of cooperation with the other American republics, once known as "Pan Americanism," really had its beginning in the Monroe administration, for there is much truth in the saying that "all roads of Pan Americanism lead back to the Monroe Doctrine of 1823." Belated converts to the Western Hemisphere idea of a community of neighbors sharing common interests and ideals, Secretary of State John Quincy Adams and President Monroe made it the basis of national policy in the famous message of 1823. Although the Monroe Doctrine was originally defined as a unilateral policy of the United States and therefore not an appropriate subject for inter-American action, this does not negate the fact that the mantle of United States protection was cast over Latin America because of "a community of interests."

In 1823 a new policy was adopted for the New World involving an exception to global isolationism as counseled by Washington. United States cooperation with the states of the Western Hemisphere was implicit in President Monroe's principles. The idea of community was entertained by President Adams when he accepted an invitation for the United States to take part in the first international conference of American states, the Congress of Panama, in 1826. Although fate decreed that the United States' representatives were not to participate in the deliberations at Panama, President Adams had made clear the moral presence of this country at that meeting.

The inter-American cooperative movement, of which the Panama Congress was the first meeting, has evolved through a number of phases. The first extends from the winning of Spanish-American independence to about 1888.

This phase was marked by the participation of only Spanish-American states, and these on a numerically limited scale. The primary purpose of their cooperation was security, i.e., defense of their newly won independence. The second phase, covered the years 1889 to 1932. Characteristics of this period were the all-inclusive membership of the American republics, the virtual elimination of politico-security matters from common consideration, and the domination of the movement by the United States. The third phase, extending from 1933 to 1945, was marked by significant expansion of the security aspects of inter-American cooperation and their implementation in World War II. The fourth, and present post-World War II phase, finds the perfected inter-American system, or Organization of American States, challenged by hemispheric problems of political and economic relationships, and particularly by the aggressions of international Communism. The role of the United States in the evolving conception of inter-American cooperation will be the subject of the ensuing discussions. As with the Monroe Doctrine, a survey of United States participation in the inter-American cooperative movement will bring under focus a considerable area of general United States-Latin American relations.

1. Pan Americanism, 1826–1888[1]

Bolívar's initiative

Simón Bolívar, the great Liberator, is regarded as the father of the Pan American movement. It is true that he was the greatest and most active exponent of the idea of Spanish-American solidarity and close cooperation for mutual development and protection, yet he was no more the originator of the idea than were Washington and Monroe the originators of the principles of "no entangling alliances" and the "doctrine of the two spheres." Many other Latin Americans,[2] inspired by a common feeling of continental brotherhood, supported the cause of American cooperation with proposals ranging all the way from organization of the colonies in a single state to a loose confederation. Yet it remained for Bolívar to attempt to convert this idea into a reality.

It was in his famous "Jamaica Letter," September 6, 1815, that Bolívar first gave utterance to the idea of a union of the American nations, dedicated to confederation for their common defense. The war with Spain delayed for several years the practical application of Bolívar's idea.

[1] For surveys, see J. Lloyd Mecham, *The United States and Inter-American Security, 1889–1960* (Austin: University of Texas Press, 1961), Chap. II; John P. Humphrey, *The Inter-American System* (Toronto: The Macmillan Company, 1942), Chap. 2; Francisco Cuevas Cancino, *Del Congreso de Panamá a la Conferencia de Caracas, 1826–1954* (2 vols. Caracas: Editorial "Ragon," 1955), I; José Joaquín Caicedo Castilla, *El Panamericanismo* (Buenos Aires: Roque Depalma, Editor, 1961), Chap. I.

[2] San Martín, Martínez de Rosas, Juan Egaña, Bernardo O'Higgins, and Bernardo Monteagudo advocated Latin-American union.

On December 7, 1824, as President of Peru, he invited "the American republics, formerly Spanish colonies," to send plenipotentiaries to Panama to meet with Peru in a Congress. The object of the conference was declared to be "the establishment of certain fixed principles for securing the preservation of peace between the nations of America, and the concurrence of all those nations to defend their common cause, each contributing thereto upon the basis of its population."[3]

Bolívar also extended an invitation to Great Britain, for he believed that the presence of that power was vital. He said, "If we bind ourselves to England, we shall exist; if we do not bind ourselves we shall be lost without fail." The Liberator hoped that his American amphictyonic union might be erected under the direction and with the protection of England.

Bolívar did not invite the United States because he felt that the Spanish colonies had a common enemy, Spain, and that it was vital for them to band together in defense of their independence, whereas the United States, as a neutral, could not feel the same interest. Moreover, he feared that the presence of the United States would compromise the new Spanish-American states with England, for he said, "the Americans of the United States are the only rivals of England in respect of America."[4] Nevertheless, without any objection on the part of Bolívar, the United States was invited to participate in the Panama conference by the governments of Colombia, Mexico, and Central America. The United States was assured that it would not be embarrassed by being called upon to depart from its policy of neutrality with respect to the war between Spain and her former colonies. On the other hand, the Panama meeting was represented as a wonderful opportunity "to fix some principles of international law." It was intimated that the recently enunciated Monroe Doctrine might be made the subject of an alliance.

Development of United States policy

What was the attitude of the United States toward Latin-American union and the proposed conference? For some time prior to the receipt of the formal invitation, the United States was kept informed by its agents regarding the Colombian treaties and the proposed congress of plenipotentiaries. Secretary of State John Quincy Adams bestowed upon the proposed Colombian confederacy the unqualified blessings of the United States regardless of whether its object should be to form a defensive alliance against Europe, or to create a real federation "from the wreck of the Spanish power in America."

Richard C. Anderson, our minister at Bogotá, had informed Secretary Adams that the United States might be invited to participate in a conference. Thus, the formal invitations from Colombia and Mexico in November, 1825,

---

[3] Daniel Florencio O'Leary, ed., *Memorias del General O'Leary publicadas por su hijo, Simón B. O'Leary* (32 vols. Caracas, 1879–1888), XXIV, 250–253.

[4] For Anglo-American rivalry in Latin America, see J. Fred Rippy, *Latin America in World Politics* (New York: Alfred A. Knopf, Inc., 1928), Chaps. IV-VI.

came as no surprise to the new Adams-Clay administration.[5] President Adams, viewing acceptance of the invitation as being in full harmony with the advice of Washington, decided to appeal to Congress to concur with him in his belief that the United States should be represented at the Panama conference. In a special message to Congress, December 26, 1825, he stated his policy. First, he assured Congress that the United States neither intended, nor was expected, to take part in any deliberations of a belligerent character. Our neutral status would be preserved. Next, the President urged the importance of meeting with the representatives of the Latin-American nations to advocate the adoption of "principles of a liberal commercial intercourse." In this connection the Congress was reminded of a Latin-American tendency to favor European trade over that of the United States. President Adams also mentioned the opportunity the conference would afford to discuss principles of maritime neutrality. As for the recently enunciated Monroe Doctrine, which was on the conference agenda, the President said, "It may be so developed to the new southern nations that they will all feel it as an essential appendage of their independence." Another proper subject for discussion would be the advancement of religious liberty.[6]

Since President Adams was careful to avoid any kind of security or political commitment, we may infer that the reasons he advocated for participation in the Congress of Panama were generally removed from considerations of the Western Hemisphere idea. There was little in the President's message that conveyed the sense of regional interest. Nevertheless, there was considerable opposition in the Congress to a departure, as it was viewed, from the nonintervention policy advised by President Washington. It was feared that the plan of inter-American cooperation would commit this country to a more hazardous connection with the fortunes of other countries than was desirable. Specifically, participation was opposed by representatives of the slave states because the subject of abolishing the African slave trade was on the conference agenda. Protracted partisan discussions in the Congress delayed embarrassingly the eventual decision to participate.

From the instructions of Secretary Clay to the United States delegates we learn more concerning the extent to which the administration was willing to participate in an inter-American cooperative movement. After a preliminary admonition that the conference was merely a diplomatic body without powers of ordinary legislation, the delegates were warned not to discuss matters relating to the war with Spain. But with respect to the general subject of maritime neutrality they were to advocate the traditional American principles

---

[5] William R. Manning, ed., *Diplomatic Correspondence of the United States Concerning the Independence of the Latin American Nations* (3 vols. New York: Carnegie Endowment for International Peace, 1925), I, 205. Also see J. B. Lockey, *Pan Americanism, Its Beginnings* (New York: The Macmillan Company, 1920; A. P. Whitaker, *The United States and the Independence of Latin America* (Baltimore: The Johns Hopkins Press, 1941), Chaps. 18–19.

[6] J. D. Richardson, ed., *Messages and Papers of the Presidents, 1789–1897* (10 vols. Washington, D.C.: Government Printing Office, 1899), II, 318–320.

of security for private property upon the high seas, a restricted definition of "contraband" — free ships make free goods, and enemy ships make enemy goods. With respect to commercial intercourse, the delegates were not to seek exclusive privileges, but the most-favored-nation principle. The Monroe Doctrine was to be preserved as a unilateral policy, but each American state, acting for and binding only itself, should not allow European colonies to be established within its territory. Regarding an interoceanic canal, which was also on the agenda, the United States demanded merely that the benefits of the canal ought not to be exclusively appropriated by any one nation. Since the liberation of Cuba was also scheduled to be discussed, the United States, said Clay, opposed a war for the liberation of the island. It preferred that Cuba remain in Spanish hands, for it feared that a weak independent Cuba would attract the intervention of strong European powers. Finally, concerning the forms of government and free institutions, while the United States preferred republican institutions, its policy was to refrain from any interference in matters concerning the original structure or subsequent internal changes in the governments of other independent nations.[7]

Thus, President Adams and Secretary Clay clearly indicated the conditions under which the United States was willing to participate in a Pan American conference. There was to be an avoidance of political commitments and involvements, but significantly, there was a willingness, and even desire on the part of the Adams-Clay administration to enter into agreements that might be conducive to enlarged trade relationships with Latin America. With respect to fundamentals, this earliest Pan American policy of the United States was not substantially different from the one supported for some years after 1889, that is, the fostering of trade relations, but the shunning of political commitments.

President Adams nominated, and the Senate approved, Richard C. Anderson of Kentucky and John Sergeant of Pennsylvania, to be envoys extraordinary and ministers plenipotentiary to the assembly of American nations at Panama. Mr. Anderson, who was in Bogotá as United States Minister to Colombia, died at Cartagena while en route to Panama. Mr. Sergeant was informed before he left the United States that the Panama Congress had adjourned to meet again at Tacubaya, Mexico, and he later put in an appearance there. Thus, the United States was not represented at the Panama meeting.

The Panama and subsequent conferences

During the first phase of Pan Americanism, from 1826 to 1888, there were four general political conferences and several special conferences, all adhering to the Bolivarian concept of Pan Americanism, that is, close cooperation of the former Spanish colonies for their mutual development and protection. Mutual security was its essence.

[7] J. B. Moore, *Principles of American Diplomacy* (New York: Harper & Brothers, 1918), 370–375.

The Congress of Panama,[8] the first of this series of Spanish-American conferences, met on June 22 and adjourned on July 15, 1826. Only four American states — Central America, Colombia, Mexico, and Peru — were represented, although the British and Dutch were unofficially represented by agents. The British agent had been instructed by Canning to "oppose any project for putting the United States of North America at the head of any American Confederacy." British anxieties would have been greatly relieved had they known of Adams' opposition to any such design.

Four conventions were signed at Panama. They embodied the following essential principles: (1) the contracting parties to aid one another with military and naval forces if attacked by foreign nations; (2) settlement of all disputes by friendly arbitration; (3) extension of rights of citizenship in each country to citizens of other American countries; (4) renunciation of the traffic in slaves; and (5) material guarantees of the integrity of each American state.

These provisions unfortunately were not destined to be carried into effect, for the treaties were not ratified by the contracting parties. With respect to tangible achievements, the Panama Congress was a complete failure. Yet, in the realm of the intangibles Panama gave impetus to the idea of inter-American conference for the discussion of mutual problems affecting the American republics. It was the germ from which later developed a regional arrangement for the Americas. It was not until December 1847-March 1848 that the second conference met in Lima, Peru. Only the South American countries Bolivia, Chile, Ecuador, New Granada (Colombia), and Peru were represented. The United States was informally invited by President Castilla of Peru to send representatives to the conference to exhibit the unity of all America "to oppose and put down any attempt at conquest or subversion of American institutions."[9] The conference was being assembled primarily because of fear of an invasion of Ecuador by a former president, General Juan José Flores, who was attempting to raise an armed expedition in Spain and England. President Polk, dismissing this fear as unworthy of consideration, did not send an envoy to the conference.

The principal act of the Lima Conference, a Treaty of Confederation, provided that the contracting parties should aid one another with land and naval forces in the event of attack by a foreign power. Neither this treaty nor the other ones drafted at Lima were ratified by the participating governments. Although the other American governments, *including the United States,* were invited to subscribe to the several conventions, the response was unanimously negative.

The third general conference of the series, also inspired by fear of foreign

---

[8] See Lockey, *op. cit.;* and Cuevas Cancino, *op. cit.,* I.

[9] William R. Manning, ed., *Diplomatic Correspondence of the United States: Inter-American Affairs, 1831–1860* (12 vols. Washington: Government Printing Office, 1938), X, 551. John Bassett Moore suggests (*Principles of American Diplomacy,* 381) that the invitation to the United States was probably intended as a pointed reminder to this country, then engaged in a war with Mexico, of the prime object of the conference, i.e., respect for territorial integrity.

aggression, took place in Santiago, Chile, in 1856. But this time, significantly, the threat came from the United States. The Latins looked with apprehension on the territorial acquisitions by the United States at the expense of Mexico. Moreover, the filibustering expeditions of William Walker and others in Central America and Mexico heightened their apprehension. There was good reason to fear the onward march of "manifest destiny," which, fortunately for the Latins, was brought to a halt by the occurrence of Civil War in the United States.

The Santiago conference adopted another treaty of alliance and confederation, called a "Continental Treaty," which contained, in addition to mutual aid provisions, the pledge to prevent the organizing of hostile expeditions by political émigrés within any of the allied states. The other Spanish-American states, and Brazil, were to be invited to join a union. However, it was the same old story: the Continental Treaty was never ratified. The United States was not approached.[10]

At Lima in 1865, the fourth and last of the Spanish-American conferences dedicated to political objectives consonant with the Bolivarian ideal of inter-American cooperation, was convened.[11] Since it was limited to republics which at one time belonged to Spain, the United States was not invited. Only seven of the Spanish-American nations, inspired by fear of France and Spain, attended the conference. Once more a treaty of confederation, or Treaty of Union and Defensive Alliance, was signed. The signatories were pledged to defend each other against all aggression from any source. But again none of the treaties negotiated was ever ratified.

The United States and the "old" Pan Americanism

President Adams and Secretary Clay were the first American statesmen to make it clear that it was not compatible with United States interests to enter into inter-American agreements of a security nature. At best the Latin states, because of their weakness and great instability, would only be a burden and liability to the United States, which was unwilling therefore to extend its formal cooperation much beyond matters of equitable commercial relations.

After the mild concessions to inter-American cooperation by Adams and Clay, there followed several decades of almost total uninterest in further cooperation with Latin America. Certainly from about 1830 to 1880, Latin America figured only slightly in United States foreign policy; this was a period of absorption in domestic problems. As far as Latin America was concerned, the United States was only aware of that area: (1) in connection with an interoceanic canal, and the strategic importance of the approaches to it; and

---

[10] At Washington, in 1856, the ministers of seven Latin-American countries signed a treaty designed to meet the problem of expeditions organized by political exiles. The pact was never ratified.

[11] Because of French intervention in Mexico, Spanish reoccupation of Santo Domingo, and Spanish seizure of Peru's Chincha Islands, it was European menace which motivated the calling of this conference.

(2) in connection with territorial expansion, particularly at the expense of Mexico. Trade with Latin America had not yet attained significant proportions, and, of course, the era of United States investments in Latin America was many years away. The immediate successors to President Adams and Secretary Clay were quite unaware of any logical or compelling reasons for a special kind of relationship with the Latin-American nations. The United States was not sufficiently conscious of Latin America to feel the need of a regional cooperative movement, certainly not one dominated by motives of security.

Accordingly, the first essay at inter-American association was undertaken by the Latin-American states themselves. This attempt to accomplish union and confederation along the lines advocated by the great Liberator was a complete failure, if we omit, of course, the stimulation of the habit of conference. Principally, the movement suffered from inertia and lack of leadership. There was need of new leadership directed toward a less rigid unity than that envisioned by Bolívar, one that permitted a freer course of action for each country. This need was supplied by the United States in 1889, when it inaugurated the second phase of the Pan American movement.

2. The Second Phase of Pan Americanism, 1889–1932[12]

The new Pan American movement sponsored by the United States bore only a slight resemblance to the one inaugurated by Simón Bolívar. In its first phase, the movement, exclusively Spanish American in its membership (and with meager participation at that), was mostly concerned with problems of a political nature; in its second phase, its membership included *all* the American states, and its objectives were mostly non-political. For a number of years, the United States effectively limited consideration of "political"[13] questions, and confined the conference discussions to those "safe" non-controversial subjects in the realms of economic, educational, scientific, and social relations which afforded the best prospect for friendly agreement. Although it was not a conscious intention of the United States, it seems that its original objective was to inaugurate cooperation on as workable a basis as possible, and then, as the idea took hold and confidence developed, to evolve gradually a regional security system. At least this was the history of evolving Pan

[12] For surveys covering the period 1889–1932, see Mecham, *op. cit.,* Chaps. III-IV; Humphrey, *op. cit.* Chaps. III-IV; Caicedo Castillo, *op. cit.,* 25–54; Cuevas Cancino, *op. cit.,* II, 9–97.

[13] Dr. Ricardo J. Alfaro, the distinguished Panamanian diplomat and statesman, defined "political" questions: "Those which concern the juridical equality, territorial integrity, the national independence, the international obligations, the rights of American states. In this category are such momentous questions as the codification of international law, the organization of the American League of Nations, the creation of an American Court of Justice, and all such kindred questions as the pacific settlement of international conflicts, the definition of the aggressor, and the maintenance of peace in the continent."

Americanism after the United States saw fit to enter into association with its Latin-American neighbors.

Blaine and the Washington conference

With the advent of the 1880's the United States seemed ready at last to enter into more intimate association with the other New World republics. James G. Blaine, Secretary of State in the Garfield administration, and a far-sighted statesman, was one of the first to realize the need of a policy change, for the United States was in a condition of transition from a debtor to a creditor status. The accumulation of domestic capital was stimulating the search for opportunities for foreign investment; expanding industry was building up a surplus of goods and thus creating a demand for foreign markets. Secretary Blaine envisioned Latin America as an ideal economic complement to the United States.

But, Mr. Blaine's interest in Latin America was more than economic. Indeed, his study of the speeches of Henry Clay is supposed to have inspired his belief in the Western Hemisphere idea that the inhabitants of the Americas have common interests which should be promoted by cooperation. Accordingly, because of his concern that Latin-American conflicts should not invite European intervention, on November 29, 1881, he invited the independent states of America to a conference at Washington. Although the purpose of the conference was to discuss the prevention of war, Mr. Blaine later confided that it had been his intention to follow up the peace conference with a commercial conference. He believed that any large increase in our export trade with Latin America would be dependent on stability and order in this area.[14] The assassination of President Garfield, which unfortunate event meant a new administration and a new Secretary of State, necessitated the recall of the invitations to Mr. Blaine's conference.

The idea of an inter-American conference, although opposed by both the Arthur and Cleveland administrations, found strong support in the United States Congress. Finally, in May, 1888, a resolution was adopted. Becoming effective without President Cleveland's signature, it authorized the President to arrange for a conference of American states. The invitations issued by the retiring Secretary of State, Thomas F. Bayard, set forth in the agenda:

> 1. Measures that shall tend to preserve the peace and provide for the prosperity of the several American states.
> 2. Agreement upon the recommendation for adoption to their respective governments of a definite plan of arbitration of all questions, disputes, and difficulties that may now or hereafter exist between them to the end that all difficulties and disputes between such nations may be peacefully settled and wars prevented, and
> 3. Measures for the promotion of commercial relations.[15]

[14] See A. Curtis Wilgus, "Blaine and Pan Americanism," *Hispanic American Historical Review,* V (1922), 662–708; Alice Felt Tyler, *The Foreign Policy of James G. Blaine* (Minneapolis: University of Minnesota Press, 1927), 165–190.

[15] First International Conference of American States, *Minutes, Sen. Exec. Doc.* No. 231, 51st Cong., 1st Sess. (Washington, D.C., 1890), 1–3.

The invitations contained assurances that the conference was to be merely consultative in nature and would not be competent to make any political decisions. Thus reassured, all of the Latin-American republics, except for the Dominican Republic, accepted the invitation of the United States government. This near-unanimity augured well for future all-American membership in the "new" Pan American movement.

When the conference, the first in a series of International Conferences of American States, took place in Washington in October, 1889, by strange chance it was presided over by the new Secretary of State in the Harrison administration, James G. Blaine. But, before the conference got down to the business at hand, the Latin delegates were exposed to a bit of Mr. Blaine's none too subtle propaganda. They were taken on an official tour of industrial centers as guests of the government. The object was to impress them with the industrial potential of the United States to supply their import needs should they be willing to give it preference over European nations.

Blaine's startling proposal for a Pan American *zollverein,* or customs union, failed to win much support. In the first place, it appeared to be a one-sided proposition in favor of the United States, which was in no position to make concessions to Latin America, for the principal imports were tropical products already on our free list. In the second place, according to the Argentine delegate Latin America was opposed to "belligerent tariffs," or any other action, economic or political, that would weaken traditional ties with Europe.[16]

With respect to the other items on the agenda designed to promote economic intercourse, the delegates were generally able to agree either in fact or "in principle." Several international agreements or recommendations were adopted relating to the adoption of the decimal system of weights and measures, a common system for the nomenclature of merchandise, an international monetary union and inter-American bank, consular fees, port dues, sanitary regulations, patents, copyrights, and trademarks.

Notwithstanding their importance, it was not the economic but political matters that attracted the Latins to the Washington conference. Weak, backward, emergent states in a world dominated by predatory great powers who made the rules of the game called international law, they were with good reason obsessed by one need: respect for their national sovereignty. They were quick to see therefore, in the United States-sponsored Pan American conference, a wonderful opportunity to press their demands for equal respect for the sovereignty of small and backward states. If the United States could be won over, then a long step would have been taken toward winning international recognition and acceptance of the Calvo Doctrine, so named after the great Argentine international lawyer, Carlos Calvo, who only a few years earlier had declared the doctrine of indefeasible sovereignty.[17] According to

---

[16] *Ibid.,* 323. See T. F. McGann, *Argentina, the United States, and the Inter-American System, 1880–1914* (Cambridge: Harvard University Press, 1957), 130–165.

[17] Carlos Calvo, *Le droit international* (4 vols. Paris, 1896, 5th ed.).

Calvo, sovereignty is inviolable, and *under no circumstance* does the resident alien enjoy the right to have his own government interpose in his behalf. Not even a denial of justice could warrant intervention, for it would convey a privileged status to aliens not enjoyed by the nationals. Calvo and his followers rejected the rather generally accepted principle of international law which requires states to maintain a minimum standard of treatment of foreigners no matter how they treat their own nationals.

It was at the Washington conference in 1889, therefore, that the United States became acutely aware, for the first time, of radically different views on the subject of diplomatic protection of aliens. A resolution was proposed by one of the committees that "a nation has not, nor recognizes in favor of foreigners, any other obligations or responsibilities than those which in favor of the natives are established, in like cases, by the constitution and the laws." The United States, eager to maintain high standards of international conduct, was the only country to vote against the resolution.[18] The irreconcilability of the positions of the United States and the Latin-American governments on the subjects of diplomatic protection was destined to operate as a brake on the cooperative movement inaugurated in 1889.

The item on the agenda of the Washington conference upon which the greatest interest centered was a project for international arbitration. There were so many differences of opinion on the subject of compulsory arbitration, so many objections, particularly by Chile, sensitive about her recent territorial seizures in the War of the Pacific, that a stalemate developed. In order to reconcile the discordant views, Secretary Blaine himself drafted an arbitration plan. Adopted in modified form, as a project for a so-called "general compulsory arbitration treaty," it provided that: (1) arbitration should be adopted by the American nations "as a principle of American international law" for the solution of disputes among themselves or between them and other powers; (2) arbitration should be obligatory in all controversies except those which, in the judgment of one of the states involved in the controversy, compromised her independence; and (3), the court of arbitration should consist of one or more persons selected by each of the disputants, and an umpire who should decide all questions upon which the arbitrators might disagree.[19]

In order to give special form to the project of a treaty of arbitration it was opened for signature. Only eleven states, including the United States, signed. It was to become effective as a treaty when ratified by fifteen states. However, not one state ratified. Although the United States delegation signed the plan of arbitration, and although President Benjamin Harrison urged its approval by the United States Senate, that body failed to "advise and consent." Here we have an early example of what was to become an all-too-common practice in inter-American conferences: the approval of a resolution or the signing of a treaty in a conference carried no assurance that the respective governments would later implement or ratify it. Thus, the lofty declarations in the

18 First Int. Conf. of Am. States, *Minutes,* 813–814.
19 *Ibid.,* 690, 706–718.

Washington conference in support of "arbitration as a principle of American international law," did not truly reflect the policies of the individual governments.

Although the Washington conference was not without significance because it was the first of a series of Pan American meetings which attested to a broadening sense of inter-American cooperation and solidarity,[20] almost its sole tangible achievement was the establishment of the International Union of American Republics, which was to be represented in Washington by the Commercial Bureau of American Republics. Under the supervision of the Secretary of State of the United States, this inter-American agency was to collect and distribute useful commercial information.

The Mexico City conference

More than ten years elapsed before the Second International Conference of American States met in Mexico City in 1901. If this seems to prove that the idea of conference among the American republics was slow in taking hold, it merely reflected the halting progress of hemispheric unity and solidarity. From the point of view of the United States, the time for another inter-American conference was overdue. Fortuitously a protocol of adherence to the Hague Convention of 1899 for the Pacific Settlement of International Disputes, awaited signature by the Latin-American delegates.[21] Thus, it was President McKinley who suggested to President Porfirio Díaz of Mexico that he invite the Second International Conference of American States to meet in Mexico City.

Delegations from the United States and all of the Latin-American republics convened in the Mexican capital in October, 1901. They met in no moment of crisis; no problems pressed for immediate solution. Instead, they were merely seeking cooperative measures to promote their common interests and welfare. The agenda called for further consideration of points studied at the previous conference. The delegates agreed to several conventions concerning such matters as copyrights, patents, trademarks, extradition, and the codification of international law. One of the conventions, on the rights of aliens, repeated the Calvo Doctrine that (1) states are not bound to accord to aliens privileges not enjoyed by their own citizens; (2) states are not responsible for damages sustained by aliens in civil war; and (3) claims of aliens shall be made to a competent court of the country and through diplomatic channels. The United States stood alone in its refusal to sign.

Once again it was arbitration which aroused the greatest interest at the Mexico City conference. And once again there was sharp division of opinion concerning compulsory as opposed to voluntary arbitration. After much

[20] A Mexican delegate declared that the most important result of this first Pan American conference was "the sentiment of mutual respect and consideration" which was spread among its delegates. W. S. Robertson, *Hispanic American Relations with the United States* (New York: Oxford University Press, 1923), 394.

[21] Mexico was the only Latin-American power to participate in the First Hague Peace Conference.

wrangling they agreed on a plan which provided for: (1) the adherence of the American states not already members (as were Mexico and the United States) to the Hague Convention, which provided for voluntary arbitration, and (2) a treaty of compulsory arbitration, to be signed by those republics advocating it.

Since the Hague Convention was a closed convention and could be adhered to by nonsignatory states only with the consent of the signatory powers, all that could be accomplished by the Mexico City conference was to request Mexico and the United States to sponsor the adherence of the other American republics. This was done, and in 1907, at the Second Hague Peace Conference, a protocol of adherence was approved for signature by the seventeen Latin-American countries.

Those delegations to Mexico City that could be satisfied with nothing less than compulsory arbitration, drafted such a treaty; however, because of its numerous exceptions, it was somewhat less than obligatory in nature. Nine Latin-American delegations signed it, but only six of the states ratified it later. This failure to back up brave words by binding agreement sharply reinforced the position taken by Secretary of State John Hay when instructing the American delegates. Because of the strong position taken by the United States Senate against compulsory arbitration, the Secretary of State had decided against obligatory recourse to the arbitral procedure, as well as general arbitration pacts. Therefore, the delegates were instructed to strive for a pecuniary claims convention, because it was reasoned that damage claims by individuals against the government of another country constituted the type of dispute most susceptible to arbitral settlement. Let the Latins prove their attachment to the principle of arbitration by applying it to this special type of dispute, before generalizing its application. Accordingly, a treaty providing for the arbitration of pecuniary claims was signed by seventeen of the republics, and ratified later by ten, including the United States. The pecuniary claims convention never became an effective feature of the Inter-American system, given the Latins' hearty endorsement of the Calvo Doctrine.

The Rio de Janeiro conference

The progress of inter-American cooperation under the guidance of the United States was not, by any standard of measurement, going well. Latin-American suspicions and fears of the United States developed in earnest soon after the Mexico City conference, thanks to the "big stick" wielded by President Theodore Roosevelt. Evidences of the new Yankee imperialism — the "taking" of the Panama Canal Zone, the establishment of protectorates over Cuba and Panama, the assuming of customs control in the Dominican Republic, and the self-appointed international police power known as the Roosevelt Corollary of the Monroe Doctrine — created a profound distrust of the United States. Yankeephobe intellectuals were becoming popular in Latin America.

Given this unfriendly atmosphere, the United States could not allow the next Pan American conference, due to be held in Rio de Janeiro in 1906, to be used as a forum for the denunciation of Yankee imperialism. Consequently the agenda was carefully purged of political subjects that might become controversial. Special care was taken to confine the discussions to the so-called "safe and sane" social, economic, and cultural topics. It did not augur well for an interesting or constructive conference.

The Third International Conference of American States assembled at Rio de Janeiro in 1906. Delegates from the new states of Cuba and Panama partly compensated for the temporary absence of Haiti and Venezuela. It cannot be concluded, however, that the near-unanimous attendance of the Latin-American states indicated enthusiasm for the Pan American movement. On the contrary, the atmosphere at Rio was one of suspicion, if not restrained hostility, toward the United States. In an effort to conciliate the Latin-American delegates, Secretary of State Elihu Root made this famous statement of reassurance to the conference:

> We wish for no victories but those of peace; for no territory except our own; for no sovereignty except the sovereignty over ourselves. We deem the independence and equal rights of the smallest and weakest member of the family of nations entitled to as much respect as those of the greatest empire, and we deem the observance of that respect the chief guaranty of the weak against the strong. We neither claim nor desire any rights, or privileges, or powers that we do not freely concede to every American Republic.[22]

To the credit of the American Secretary of State, his sincerity and persuasiveness rewon for the United States a considerable measure of confidence. The Rio conference proved to be much more harmonious than might have been expected.

As for the acts of the conference we might dismiss at the outset the four conventions which were adopted. The first dealt with the status of naturalized citizens who return to the country of their origin. The second reaffirmed with certain modifications conventions adopted at Mexico City dealing with patents, trademarks, and copyrights. The third extended the 1902 treaty on pecuniary claims for a period of five years. The fourth and final convention provided for the codification of public and private international law by a commission of jurists composed of one member appointed by each of the signatory nations.

Despite the care with which Mr. Root had culled contentious political subjects from the agenda, it included an item which called for the adoption of a resolution recommending that the Second Hague Conference (which was to meet the following year and to which all of the American republics had been invited) be requested "to consider whether and if at all, to what extent, the use of force for the collection of public debts is admissible." The door was opened wide for a conference endorsement of the Drago Doctrine, which,

[22] Third Int. Conf. of Am. States, *Minutes, Resolutions, and Documents* (Rio de Janeiro, 1907), 131–132.

as we have already noted, was a restatement, in a somewhat restricted sense, of the Calvo Doctrine. The Argentine Minister of Foreign Affairs, Luis María Drago, contended that because public debts are contracted by the sovereign power of the state, they constitute a special kind of obligation, and armed force should not be used for collecting them.[23]

Since Theodore Roosevelt had recently announced his corollary of the Monroe Doctrine to frustrate the use of force for the collection of contract claims, it could hardly be imagined that the United States would consent to the unqualified immunity of Latin-American governments from forcible collection. It was the strategy of the United States at Rio to induce the conference to avoid taking definite action on the question of the forcible collection of contract debts because this would arouse distrust on the part of European capitalists, and would harm the credit of certain American states. Since the United States did not object to the problem's being recommended for discussion at the Second Hague Conference, a resolution was adopted which invited the individual countries to raise the question of compulsory collection of public debts. To the great disappointment and bitterness of the Latins, the United States succeeded at the Hague Conference in 1907 in having the use of force for the collection of contract debts outlawed, but *with the proviso* that the debtor state accept arbitration and the arbitral award. Drago, following Calvo, would tolerate no intervention whatsoever.

The Buenos Aires conference

Profiting from the experience of the Rio conference, the United States was careful, when preparing the agenda for the next Pan American conference, not to leave the slightest loophole for the entry of political questions. Thus, when the Fourth International Conference of American States assembled in Buenos Aires in 1910, the delegates were faced with the unexciting prospect of discussing customs regulations, commercial statistics, sanitation and quarantine, patents, trademarks, copyrights, and steamship and railway communications. A host of resolutions and a number of conventions were adopted. The pecuniary claims convention was to be continued for an indefinite period. An effort by the Brazilian delegation to secure a conference vote of appreciation for the Monroe Doctrine died aborning, to the embarrassment of the United States delegation.

Probably the most constructive action of the Buenos Aires conference was the adoption of a resolution which created the Pan American Union.[24] Administered by a Director-General, the control of the Union was vested in a Governing Board composed of the diplomatic representatives of the American republics accredited to the government of the United States, with the Secretary of State as the permanent chairman. Understandably, since the Pan American

[23] Luis María Drago, "State Loans in their Relation to International Policy," in Alejandro Alvarez, *The Monroe Doctrine* (New York: Oxford University Press), 244–257.
[24] *Cuarta conferencia internacional americana*, II, 545–554.

Union was to be housed shortly in a million-dollar palace — thanks to the generosity of Andrew Carnegie — adjacent to the State Department and the White House, it came to be regarded as a creature of the United States.

The success of the United States in excluding all controversial matters from the agenda of the Buenos Aires conference, at the very time when our motives and methods in the Caribbean were the subjects of bitter criticism, virtually killed all enthusiasm in Latin America for Pan Americanism. "There is no Pan Americanism in South America," said an Argentine diplomat; "it exists only in Washington." "We reject Pan Americanism," cried a leading Buenos Aires newspaper, "which is but a hollow mockery for us South Americans." Although the Latins were disappointed by the failure of the movement to measure up to the Bolivarian ideal of inter-American cooperation, they found manifest indications of progress too promising to risk abandoning the "new" Pan Americanism. This conclusion is supported by the modest evidences of unity and solidarity revealed by the outbreak of World War I.

World War I

In their four general conferences up to World War I the American republics had not considered the need or advantages of collaboration to preserve their neutrality in the event of a foreign war, or to defend themselves against possible aggression. Thus the outbreak of war in 1914 found the American nations without any plan of action; consequently whatever measures of cooperation were undertaken had to be on a completely *ad hoc* basis.

The one instance of effective cooperation during the neutral phase of the war was the meeting of the financial ministers in Washington in May, 1915. This meeting, the First Pan American Financial Conference, was initiated by Secretary of the Treasury William G. McAdoo, who had noted the economic and financial dislocations in Latin-American countries brought about by the severance of their European connections. Secretary McAdoo saw an opportunity for the United States to supply the needs of Latin America, and, as he said, "to develop the spirit at least of continental solidarity."[25] The acts of the conference covered the categories of finance, commerce, and transportation. A continuing agency, an International High Commission, was created to study commercial and financial problems. The First Pan American Financial Conference was historic in that it marked the transition of Latin America's financial and economic dependence from Europe to the United States.

With the exception of the Financial Conference and its creature, the International High Commission, the record of Pan American cooperation during the period of neutrality (August, 1914–April, 1917) was most disappointing. For the Latins the essential compulsion for security cooperation was absent, since there was insufficient apprehension of danger. They persisted in a belief that the issues of the war were none of their business. The United States should have been more aware of the dangerous potentialities inherent in the

[25] *Actas del Primer Congreso Financiero Pan Americano* (Washington, D.C.: 1915), 116–117.

world conflict, but the Wilson administration was without sufficient foresight to recommend some kind of defensive agreement.

Fortunately there were clear evidences of inter-American unity following the United States declaration of war on April 6, 1917.[26] One day later both Cuba and Panama declared war. Eventually eight Latin-American republics — Brazil, Cuba, Costa Rica, Guatemala, Haiti, Honduras, Nicaragua, and Panama — declared war on Germany, and five — Bolivia, the Dominican Republic, Ecuador, Peru, and Uruguay — broke diplomatic relations. Seven remained neutral: Argentina, Chile, Colombia, Mexico, Paraguay, El Salvador, and Venezuela.

The seeming remarkable demonstration of solidarity by the eight countries that declared war is tempered somewhat by the fact that both Cuba and Panama were treaty protectorates of the United States, and Haiti and Nicaragua were *de facto* protectorates. Thus it would be rather difficult to conceive of any of the four pursuing independent foreign policies. However, the decision by the remaining four countries to declare war was their own and was not induced by any United States pressure. In their declarations, more than one made reference to "continental solidarity." Brazil declared that an attack on one member of the American community was tantamount to an attack on all the rest, and thus called for common defense.

Insofar as there were military defense agreements among the hemisphere belligerents, these were all on a bilateral basis with the United States. There was no multilateral inter-American security cooperation.

Demonstrations of solidarity were not confined to the belligerents. Those that broke relations with Germany assumed a status of nonbelligerency or "friendly neutrality" toward the United States and the other Latin-American belligerents, thus incurring the risks of German displeasure. International law does not protect the "friendly neutral" who concedes favors in violation of his neutral responsibilities. The following decree, therefore, by Uruguay made that country liable to German reprisal: "No American country, which in defense of its own rights should find itself in a state of war with nations of other continents, will be treated as a belligerent." Even little El Salvador, which remained technically a neutral, declared a policy of benevolent neutrality toward the United States.

It is a matter of record that the American belligerents, and those that severed diplomatic relations with Germany, did not see fit to consult or act cooperatively on a multilateral basis. There were a number of suggestions but no action. However unfortunate this failure to implement by collective action the principles of continental solidarity, it must be conceded that the absence of three of the most important countries — Argentina, Chile, and Mexico — hampered collective agreement and action. Moreover, because

26 See Percy A. Martin, *Latin America and the War* (Baltimore: The Johns Hopkins Press, 1925); Dana G. Munro, *Pan America and the War* (New York: World Peace Foundation, 1934); and Peter N. Goldsmith, *South American Opinions on the War* (New York: Carnegie Endowment for International Peace, 1918).

of the importance of these countries, the noncooperative and even obstructionist behavior of Argentina and Mexico tended to obscure the demonstrations of solidarity on the part of most of the other Latin-American countries.

Both President Hipólito Irigoyen of Argentina and President Venustiano Carranza of Mexico, pursued policies of neutrality that, if not pro-German as was generally believed at the time, were apparently anti-United States. They have both been defended as distinctly nationalistic. Be that as it may, President Irigoyen tried to take advantage of United States preoccupation in the war to organize a conference of the Latin-American states. Ostensibly, Argentina sought the position of leadership. This effort failed. The attitude of most of the Latin-American nations was expressed by Peru: "The government of Peru considers that the policy on this continent should be one with the policies of the United States; . . . . that the defense of the United States and all other American nations against German imperialism requires, as an essential condition, a uniform policy throughout the entire continent."[27]

President Carranza of Mexico was responsible for a number of suspect pro-German actions, the most notorious of these being a phony cooperative proposal for neutrals. He proposed that all neutrals, particularly those of America, seek to end the war by mediation, but that if this failed they should impose an economic boycott on all belligerents.[28] Superficially this proposal seemed to be impartial, but actually it would have operated entirely in favor of Germany, who did not have access to the food products and raw materials of Latin America because of the Allied blockade. Britain and her allies enjoyed this privilege as a belligerent right; to deny it would have been a violation of the responsibility of neutrals. Obviously the Carranza proposal found no takers.

How well did the Pan American states meet the test of World War I? Despite the failure of seven states to cooperate, they measured up surprisingly well by their demonstrations of solidarity. The spontaneity with which most of them supported the United States proved without question the existence and recognition of a continental community of interest.

Peace and the League of Nations

The Latin-American nations that had declared war on Germany or broken off relations with her were invited to the Paris Peace Conference, where, however, they were little more than onlookers. Being denied a voice in arranging the peace settlement, they threw their support behind President Wilson's "grand project" of a League of Nations. Ten Latin-American states became charter members, and six others were invited to accede to the League Covenant. Eventually all of the Latin-American states became members of the League of Nations — at least for a time.[29] The United States never joined,

[27] *Foreign Relations of the United States, 1917,* 368, 382, 388–389.
[28] *Ibid.,* 45–46.
[29] Warren H. Kelchner, *Latin American Relations with the League of Nations* (Boston: World Peace Foundation, 1929), 6, 14–15.

and that abstention posed problems for the Latin-American nations and for the inter-American system.

Initially the Latin-American republics were attracted to the League of Nations not only because of idealism and considerations of prestige, but also because the League was expected to be a counterpoise to the United States. Article X of the Covenant, which guaranteed the political and territorial integrity of its members, made a strong appeal to the Latins, concerned as they were with United States interventionism.

The failure of the United States to join the League altered the whole situation. To the Latins it meant that the United States as a nonmember was free of the controls and limitations which they had hoped would be imposed on their powerful neighbor. But the League, aware of its own weaknesses and the imprudence of provoking the United States by interfering in American disputes, adopted a hands-off policy. Therefore, in balancing American regionalism against Geneva universalism the Latin Americans found the latter wanting.[30] The situation was one which seemed to call for strengthening of the regional concept. An opportunity to do so presented itself at the long-delayed Fifth International Conference of American States, which convened in Santiago, Chile, in 1923.

The Santiago conference

After the Buenos Aires conference of 1910, much had happened in United States-Latin American relations to add fuel to the fires of Yankeephobia. The Taft-Knox policy of "dollar diplomacy" had become an unpalatable fact in the politics of Central America and the Caribbean. Then under President Wilson interventionism had been extended to unprecedented limits. As a result, United States unpopularity was as great as it had ever been when the Santiago conference met in 1923. Under the circumstances, how and to what extent should the agenda subjects be restricted?

It was apparent that the Latin Americans would no longer be willing to confine their discussions to the innocuous "safe and sane" subjects. Their experiences during World War I and as members of the League of Nations had developed a consciousness of their positions as independent American states and of their rights, which they were determined to support even against the United States itself.

Wisely, the State Department did not impose its veto on topics close to the hearts of the Latin-American members. Its evident intention was to indulge the Latins in their protestations of "sovereign" prerogatives, but to apply the brakes as needed. As a result, an exceptional number of political subjects appeared on the conference agenda, such as: wider application of the principle of judicial and arbitral settlement of disputes, reduction and limitation of armaments, rights of aliens resident in any of the American republics, ques-

[30] In fact, at League meetings, they irritated the other members by upholding the inter-American system as a model, and repeatedly referred to inter-American cooperation. *Ibid.*, 5, n. 3.

tions arising out of an encroachment by a non-American power on the rights of an American nation, and organization of the Pan American Union.

Unwisely, the United States, using its great influence and control over many of the small states, and exploiting the disunity and nationalistic suspicions among the Latin-American states themselves, was able to defend its conception of Pan Americanism.

The only significant action of the conference was adoption of the Treaty to Avoid or Prevent Conflicts Between the American States, popularly known as the Gondra treaty, after its sponsor, Dr. Manuel Gondra of Paraguay. This treaty provided for submitting to a commission of inquiry all controversies not settled through diplomatic channels. Under its terms, the disputants were not to make war preparations from the time the commission was convened until six months after the report, thus providing time for passions to cool. Gondra frankly acknowledged the Bryan "cooling off" treaties as the inspiration for his proposal.[31] The Gondra treaty is significant as the first of several multilateral treaties destined to become basic elements of the inter-American security structure.

The other actions of the Santiago conference can be dismissed summarily. There was first the problem of reorganization of the Pan American Union because of the preponderant position occupied by the United States: the seat of the Union was in Washington; membership on the Governing Board was confined to diplomatic representatives to the United States government in Washington; the United States was represented by the Secretary of State, who outranked diplomatically all other members; the Secretary of State was the permanent Chairman of the Board; and the Director-General of the Union was an American.

To prevent a country having no diplomatic representative at Washington from being deprived of its membership on the Governing Board of the Union, it was agreed that a special representative could be designated to serve as a member. It was also agreed that the Secretary of State should not be designated as permanent chairman, but that the board chairman should be elected. However, the practice of electing the Secretary of State board chairman continued. The acts of the Santiago conference did not alter the preponderant position of the United States in the Pan American Union.

Since there appeared to be no disposition to examine military expenditures, the problem of "the reduction and limitation of military and naval expenditures was virtually confined to the three principal naval powers: Argentina, Brazil, and Chile. On the matter of future naval expenditures, however, the negotiations were wrecked by opposing points of view.

The discussions on the other subjects of the conference agenda were equally fruitless. A convenient device was to refer certain matters — for

---

[31] Secretary of State William J. Bryan had negotiated treaties of inquiry, known as the Bryan "cooling off" treaties, because of the provision for delay in resort to arms pending the inquiry, which could last as long as a year. Eleven Latin-American states had entered into these pacts with the United States.

example, the rights of aliens — to the Rio de Janeiro Commission of Jurists. A novel proposal by President Baltázar Brum of Uruguay for an American League of Nations was sent to the Governing Board of the Pan American Union for further study. Brum proposed that each American state make a declaration similar to the Monroe Doctrine, i.e., bind itself to support any American state if attacked by a non-American country. This proposal was unique up to that time, because it called for inter-American security against non-American aggression.

In view of its repudiation of the League of Nations, the failure of the United States to indicate the slightest interest in transforming the Pan American system into an effective regional-security arrangement was disappointing, although understandable. This lack of interest was due to (1) resurgent isolationism and opposition to so-called "entangling alliances," and (2) the belief that the crushing of Germany eliminated all threats to the Western Hemisphere. Secure behind the oceans and our great fleet, there existed no power anywhere having either the disposition or the capacity to challenge the hegemony of the United States in the Americas. Believing regional defensive arrangements unnecessary and bothersome, and addicted to isolationism and "normalcy," the Harding and Coolidge administrations, therefore, resisted change in the original United States conception of Pan Americanism.

Thus, at Santiago the lines were held, but at considerable cost. Press comments on the conference throughout Latin America were generally unfriendly to the United States. Despite Latin-American criticism and distrust, which continued to mount during the next five years, the United States government was not yet ready to revamp its Pan American policy.

The Havana conference

The United States attended the Sixth International Conference of American States in Havana in 1928 under the most unfavorable circumstances conceivable. Its intervention in Nicaragua and a "war scare" with Mexico provided ample ammunition for Latin-American snipers at its policy. It was clear that the Latins, resentful because of their frustrated hopes at Santiago, were coming to Havana prepared for a showdown.

Because of the seriousness of the situation, an exceptionally strong United States delegation was appointed, headed by Charles Evans Hughes. President Coolidge himself went to Havana to address the conference. Ignoring unfortunate precedent, the American government imposed its usual restrictions on controversial political questions. As a result, only two political questions — reorganization of the Pan American Union (with a view to limiting United States control) and the report of the Rio Commission of Jurists — were on the agenda. But despite the efforts of the United States these two topics opened wide the floodgates, giving the Latins ample opportunity to vent their criticism of the Anglo-American version of an inter-American system.

Recalling their failure at Santiago, once again the Latin Americans attempted at the Havana conference to reduce the influence of the United States in the

Pan American Union. It was agreed that the member-nations have the fullest liberty in appointing their representatives on the Governing Board, but a proposal to rotate the office of Chairman was rejected in favor of retaining the principle of free election. A proposal to rotate the office of the Director-General annually was also rejected.

Evidently concluding that it was impossible to curb United States control of the Pan American Union, the Mexican delegation proposed that the Union not exercise functions of a political character. The proposal was adopted by resolution. A draft convention on the organization of the Pan American Union was then submitted for consideration. Since it merely formalized the existent *de facto* organization as provided by resolutions of prior conferences, it was not the source of disagreement. The preamble, however, occasioned one of the critical debates of the conference.

Dr. Honorio Pueyrredón, head of the Argentine delegation, insisted that, to the statement that the moral union of the American republics "rests on the juridical equality of the Republics of the Continent and in the mutual respect of the right inherent in their complete independence," there be added a declaration against excessive barriers to inter-American trade. He held that obstacles to the free circulation of agricultural products and the arbitrary use of sanitary policy regulations were incompatible with American solidarity. This was Argentina's reaction to the exclusion of her beef from the United States on the ground that Argentine cattle were infected with the hoof-and-mouth disease. Dr. Pueyrredón threatened to withdraw from the conference unless his proposals were accepted.

Tantamount to an American *zollverein,* the Argentine proposal held little appeal to the United States delegates as well as to those from Latin America, who had to consider the heavy dependence of their governments on customs revenues. True to his word, Dr. Pueyrredón withdrew from the conference and resigned as ambassador to the United States.[32] President Irigoyen manifested no interest in appointing a successor to the Washington post. As for the Pan American Union convention, since it was never ratified by more than sixteen states it never went into effect, and so the Union continued, without inconvenience, on a resolution basis.

It was one of a dozen projects prepared by the Rio Commission of Jurists, and submitted to the Havana conference in the form of draft treaties, that released a barrage against the United States on the subject of intervention. The draft treaty, entitled "States: Existence, Equality, Recognition," contained the clause "no state may intervene in the internal affairs of another." The most critical issue in United States-Latin American relations, the subject which had been carefully barred from prior conferences, was now before this Sixth Pan American Conference. The debate was extremely bitter. Most of the Latin-American delegations, true to Calvo's principles, made strong

---

[32] This was the same Argentine diplomat who withdrew from the First League of Nations Assembly when that body rejected an Argentine ultimatum on amendment of the League Covenant.

declarations in favor of nonintervention. A true Pan Americanism, it was asserted, was futile as long as the right of intervention was exercised.

Although the situation was a difficult one for the United States, Hughes measured up to the occasion. In a forceful defense of American intervention policy, he told the conference:

> We do not wish to intervene in the affairs of any American Republic. We simply wish peace and order and stability and recognition of honest rights properly acquired so that this hemisphere may not only be the hemisphere of peace but the hemisphere of international justice. . . . Now what is the real difficulty? Let us face the facts. The difficulty, if there is any, in any one of the American Republics, is not of any external aggression. It is an internal difficulty, if it exists at all. From time to time there arises a situation most deplorable and regrettable in which sovereignty is not at work, in which for a time in certain areas there is no government at all. . . . What are we to do when government breaks down and American citizens are in danger of their lives? Are we to stand by and see them killed because a government in circumstances which it cannot control and for which it may not be responsible can no longer afford reasonable protection? . . . Now it is the principle of international law that in such a case a government is fully justified in taking action — I would call it interposition of a temporary character — for the purpose of protecting the lives and property of its nationals. I could say that that is not intervention. . . . Of course the United States cannot forego its right to protect its citizens. International law cannot be changed by the resolutions of this Conference.[33]

When it became apparent that a resolution without the concurrence of the United States would be meaningless, it was agreed to postpone further consideration of the problem until the next general Pan American conference. Since Hughes did not regard intervention, even by force, as an act of aggression, he saw no contradiction in giving his approval to a resolution which condemned acts of aggression. The resolution made no attempt to define "aggression," nor did it consider any sanctions against aggressors.[34]

In addition to the convention on the Pan American Union, the Havana conference adopted treaties submitted by the Rio Commission of Jurists, dealing with: aliens, asylum, consular agents, diplomatic officers, maritime neutrality, private international law, rights and duties of states in event of civil strife, and treaties. Nothing was done to strengthen the inter-American peace machinery, but because of the technical problems involved in the drafting of arbitration and conciliation treaties, the delegates agreed to convene a special conference on arbitration and conciliation in Washington within a year.

The Washington arbitration and conciliation conference

Because of the technical problems involved in the drafting of arbitration and conciliation treaties, it had been decided at Havana to convene a special

[33] *New York Times,* February 19, 1928.
[34] Sixth Int. Conf. of Am. States, *Final Act,* 175, 179.

conference for this purpose. Accordingly the Conference of American States on Conciliation and Arbitration took place in Washington from December 10, 1928, to January 5, 1929. This conference produced two significant contributions to the inter-American security structure: a general treaty of arbitration and a general convention on conciliation.

The General Convention of Inter-American Conciliation was intended to supplement the Gondra treaty. It accepted the permanent diplomatic commissions and the *ad hoc* special commissions of inquiry, as provided by the Gondra treaty, but invested both kinds of commissions with conciliatory functions. Since the whole procedure of inquiry as well as conciliation was on a purely voluntary basis, the delay of some states to sign or ratify the treaty is difficult to understand,[35] except in terms of utter lack of interest.

The General Treaty of Inter-American Arbitration signed at the Washington special conference bound the contracting parties to submit to arbitration any dispute of an international character arising from a claim of right that is susceptible of decision by application of legal principles. Only excluded from the operation of the treaty were domestic issues and issues referring to the interests of states not bound by the treaty. Also there were the usual exceptions in favor of independence or national honor.

A majority of the American nations signed and ratified the treaty, but with reservations.[36] The United States reservation was one of the most radical. In keeping with an established policy, the United States Senate agreed to ratification *provided* that "no special agreement would be made on behalf of the United States except with the advice and consent of the Senate." This meant that the *compromis* itself would be subject to Senate approval, giving that body a veto on each individual arbitration. In other words, the United States obligated itself, when a dispute arose, to consider whether it wished to arbitrate.

The Gondra treaty and the Washington conciliation and arbitration treaties represented the most important components of the burgeoning inter-American peace system devised to that time. Numerous inter-American bilateral treaties of arbitration were in effect. The United States was a party to five of these, known as the Root treaties. There were also numerous bilateral treaties of inquiry and conciliation in force among the American republics, and the United States entered into these so-called Bryan "cooling-off" treaties with eleven of the Latin-American countries.

[35] After ten years, on the eve of World War II, the Conciliation Convention had not been ratified by Argentina, Bolivia, Costa Rica, and Paraguay.

[36] By 1939 the Arbitration Treaty had not been ratified by Argentina, Bolivia, Costa Rica, Paraguay, and Uruguay. For the reservations, see Pan American Union, *Improvement and Coordination of Inter-American Peace Instruments* (5 vols. Washington, 1941–1943), II, 37–39.

SUPPLEMENTARY READING

Belaunde, Víctor Andrés, *Bolívar and the Political Thought of the Spanish American Revolution* (Baltimore: The Johns Hopkins Press, 1938), 259–271.

Caicedo Castilla, José Joaquín, *El Panamericanismo* (Buenos Aires: Roque Depalma Editor, 1961), 3–54.

Cuevas Cancino, Francisco, *Del Congreso de Panamá a la Conferencia de Caracas, 1826–1954* (2 vols. Caracas: Editorial "Ragon," C.A., 1955), I, 3–105; II, 9–97.

Goldsmith, Peter N., *South American Opinions on the War* (New York: Carnegie Endowment for International Peace, 1918).

Humphrey, John P. *The Inter-American System, A Canadian View* (Toronto: The Macmillan Company, 1942), 21–111.

Inman, Samuel Guy, *Problems in Pan Americanism* (New York: George H. Doran Company, 1925).

Kelchner, Warren H., *Latin American Relations with the League of Nations* (Boston: World Peace Foundation, 1929).

Lockey, J. B., *Pan Americanism, Its Beginnings* (New York: The Macmillan Company, 1920).

McGann, T. F., *Argentina, the United States and the Inter-American System, 1880–1914* (Cambridge: Harvard University Press, 1957).

Martin, Percy A., *Latin America and the War* (Baltimore: The Johns Hopkins Press, 1925).

Mecham, J. Lloyd, *The United States and Inter-American Security, 1889–1960* (Austin: University of Texas Press, 1961), 28–112.

Munro, Dana G., *Pan America and the War* (New York: World Peace Foundation, 1934).

Rippy, J. Fred, "Literary Yankeephobia in Hispanic America," *Journal of International Relations,* XII (1922), 350–371, 524–538.

Scott, J. B., ed., *The International Conferences of American States, 1889–1928* (Washington, D.C.: Carnegie Endowment for International Peace, 1931).

Whitaker, Arthur P., *The United States and the Independence of Latin America, 1800–1830* (Baltimore: The Johns Hopkins Press, 1941), 564–603.

Wilgus, A. C., "Blaine and Pan Americanism," *Hispanic American Historical Review,* V (1922), 662–708.

5

The Pan American Policy of the United States: The Good Neighbor, 1933–1939

The Good Neighbor phase of the inter-American cooperation movement[1] was marked by the most significant developments in the history of Pan Americanism up to that time. The more or less designed efforts of the United States, in the decade following the end of World War I, to abandon imperialism in Latin America and make concessions in the interest of confidence and good will, culminated in 1933 with the renunciation of the right of intervention. This, more than anything else, contributed to the allaying of long-standing Latin-American fears, suspicions, and distrust of the motives of the dominant member of the inter-American system. It was then possible for the Latin-American states, for the first time, to regard Pan Americanism as a truly cooperative movement for mutual advantage, and not merely a "made in the U.S.A." instrument to serve selfish United States interests.

It is no exaggeration to assert that the keystone in the arch of the inter-American system, elaborated after 1933, was the principle of nonintervention. The Latins manifested a new confidence and trust in the United States, and even came to cherish their regional association of nations as a prized possession. The United States, on its part, discovered that a policy of good neighborliness removed barriers to continental solidarity and paid rich dividends in reciprocal security cooperation.

[1] See Samuel Flagg Bemis, *Latin American Policy of the United States* (New York: Harcourt, Brace and Company, 1943), 256–367; John P. Humphrey, *The Inter-American System* (Toronto: The Macmillan Company, 1942), 112–168; J. Lloyd Mecham, *The United States and Inter-American Security, 1889–1960* (Austin: University of Texas Press, 1961), Chap. IV.

Precursors of the Good Neighbor

It is widely held that the Good Neighbor policy, which was carried to its much-publicized heights by the New Deal, really originated in the Hoover administration.[2] There are some who would advance the date of the policy's origin even earlier than that. On the other hand, there are others who hold that the Roosevelt administration was solely responsible for the changes in policy that became associated with the idea of the Good Neighbor.

Without becoming involved in the technicalities of the policy's paternity, it can surely be agreed that its origins can be detected in the various modifications of official and unofficial attitude toward Latin America in the decade preceding the advent of the Roosevelt administration.

Although there does not seem to have been any specific and conscious determination by the State Department after World War I to reorient Latin-American policy, there were many indications of a new attitude if not a new policy. There was a trend toward the abandonment of American imperialism in Latin America. The new power position of the United States was too real to be ignored. It had become all too apparent that it was no longer necessary to extend an unwelcome protection over the Caribbean and Central American countries in support of "Monroeism" and the security of the Panama Canal. Thanks to its great strength and the nonexistence of any overseas threat, the United States could now be more indulgent about those comic-opera political demonstrations which in the past provoked an energetic wielding of the "Big Stick."

Besides the altered world situation, American public opinion provided a powerful stimulus toward a modification of United States policy in Latin America. The American conscience has always imposed restraint on the policy makers. Although ardent supporters of the Monroe Doctrine, the American people reacted with self-conscious uneasiness to the various implementations of the Roosevelt Corollary. They were particularly disturbed about the occupations of Haiti and the Dominican Republic, and later the increasing involvement of United States Marines in Nicaragua.

It was Secretary of State Hughes who, in the Harding and Coolidge administrations, took the first steps in seeking to relieve the pressures of American hegemony on Latin America without necessarily abandoning traditional policy objectives.[3] Well aware that the Latins equated the Monroe Doctrine with interventionism, Mr. Hughes, while not repudiating the Roosevelt Corollary, did in fact repudiate its radical claims for intervention. He attempted to allay Latin-American suspicions and distrust by restoring the Monroe Doctrine to its original meaning.

It also was Secretary Hughes who, probably with modified views on the subject of intervention, undertook successfully to eliminate American inter-

[2] Bryce Wood, *The Making of the Good Neighbor Policy* (New York: Columbia University Press, 1961), 123–128.

[3] Merlo J. Pusey, *Charles Evans Hughes* (New York: The Macmillan Company, 1951), II. See Chaps. 51, 53, for "Latin-American Policy."

vention in the Dominican Republic. In 1924 the Marines were withdrawn under terms of a treaty which restored full sovereignty to the Caribbean republic. The United States ceased to enjoy any political rights as a "protector."[4] Furthermore, Hughes announced the removal of a symbol of United States control in Nicaragua: the Marine legation guard at Managua.

Unfortunately the withdrawal of the Marines in August, 1925, was followed almost immediately by a *coup d'état,* which necessitated another United States intervention. A peaceful and honorable solution of the Nicaragua question was found by applying to it the spirit of tolerance and justice, the spirit of the good neighbor. The Stimson-Moncada agreement of 1927 is also generally regarded as a precursor of the Good Neighbor policy, as is the Dwight Morrow mission to Mexico in 1927, which healed a crisis in relations by adjusting "outstanding questions with that dignity and mutual respect which should mark the international relationships of two sovereign and independent states."[5]

Hoover-Stimson "Good Neighborliness"

The eleventh hour efforts of the Coolidge-Kellogg administration to inject a new spirit into United States-Latin American relations were too recent when the next administration took over to account for much change in Latin-American attitude toward the United States. The greater significance of these initiatives was the plotting of a new course in Latin-American relations for the succeeding administrations.

Seeking better understanding with the Latin Americans, Herbert Hoover made a trip to the principal countries of South America between his election and inauguration. Both he and Secretary of State Stimson, while not prepared to renounce formally the right of intervention, were determined to remove, so far as possible, this barrier to better relations. As a logical consequence, therefore, Secretary Stimson ordered the publication of the Clark *Memorandum on the Monroe Doctrine,* thus proclaiming the official repudiation of the Roosevelt Corollary.

The Hoover-Stimson administration undertook to implement its nonintervention policy in many ways.[6] First, it was necessary to remove the last trace of United States imperialism in Nicaragua and Haiti. The Nicaraguan experience of electoral supervision and bandit fighting increased Secretary Stimson's distaste for intervention, interposition, or interference in the internal affairs of other peoples. He therefore arranged for the evacuation of Nica-

---

[4] Sumner Welles, *Naboth's Vineyard, The Dominican Republic, 1844–1924* (2 vols. New York: Payson & Clarke, 1928), II, 934–935.

[5] Harold Nicholson, *Dwight Morrow* (New York: Harcourt, Brace and Company, 1935), 313–314; Howard F. Cline, *The United States and Mexico* (Cambridge: Harvard University Press, 1953), 210–213.

[6] *The Memoirs of Herbert Hoover: the Cabinet and the Presidency, 1920–1933* (New York: The Macmillan Company, 1952), 333. For the Latin-American policies of President Hoover and Secretary of State Stimson, see Alexander DeConde, *Herbert Hoover's Latin American Policy* (Stanford: Stanford University Press, 1951), and Henry L. Stimson and McGeorge Bundy, *On Active Service in Peace and War* (New York: Harper & Brothers, 1947).

ragua by the American forces. On January 2, 1933, shortly before the end of the Hoover administration, the last contingent of United States Marines left Nicaragua.

Steps were also taken to withdraw from Haiti. After investigation and recommendation by a special commission (Forbes Commission, February, 1930) a treaty was finally concluded on September 3, 1932, which provided, among other things, that the withdrawal of the Marines should start no later than December 31, 1934. President Roosevelt advanced the date of the withdrawal to October 1, 1934.

A difficult Cuban situation put to the test Secretary Stimson's determination to avoid intervention, although in this instance it would have borne the stamp of legality because of the Platt Amendment. The administration of President Gerardo Machado, which had started in 1924 as eminently liberal and respectable, degenerated later into one of the harshest of Latin-American dictatorships. Popular resistance was met by cruel repressive measures. Americans and other foreigners were caught in the crossfire. It was a situation which, under the Platt Amendment, warranted United States intervention. But Secretary Stimson resisted pressures and declared, "the situation in Cuba is an internal political situation in a sovereign state, and it would be intermeddling imperialism of the most flagrant sort to intervene therein."[7] He had a growing conviction that interventions in general were more costly and difficult than they were worth.

Since *de jure* recognition (the nonrecognition of new governments set up by revolution until they had been legitimatized by free election) was condemned as "indirect intervention," Mr. Stimson also sought to free the United States from the burden of this unwelcome policy. On June 6, 1932, he formally announced that the United States would return to its traditional Jeffersonian *de facto* recognition policy, although he pledged continued adherence to the Central American treaty of 1923, which applied *de jure* recognition. When this treaty was abandoned in 1934, the last vestige of the Woodrow Wilson nonrecognition policy disappeared.

Secretary Stimson was also successful in inducing the American republics to apply to the Chaco War the "Stimson Doctrine" of nonrecognition of territorial gains brought about by force. On August 3, 1932, nineteen American republics (excepting only Paraguay and Bolivia) entered into a declaration announcing their refusal to recognize "any territorial arrangements of this controversy which have not been obtained by peaceful means."

Finally, in April, 1931, Stimson announced a new limited protection policy for United States citizens in Nicaragua as well as in other Latin-American countries. His announcement was prompted by disturbed conditions in Nicaragua: clashes between the Sandino rebels and the *Guardia Nacional* were causing American citizens throughout the country to appeal for protection. Stimson, however, declared that the United States could not undertake their protection, because this would lead to difficulties and involve commitments which it was not prepared to assume. Americans were advised, therefore,

[7] Quoted in Wood, *op. cit.,* 57.

if they did not feel sufficiently protected by the *Guardia Nacional,* to go to the coastal towns where they could be protected or evacuated.

About this same time American investors in certain Latin-American countries were notified that they must exhaust local legal remedies before appealing for diplomatic protection. Furthermore, the State Department refused to press for full and punctual settlement of financial obligations due American citizens. This new protection policy meant that interposition to protect private property might not be undertaken if it clashed with broader national policies. American citizens could no longer accept as a matter of course that they had the right to call for troops or diplomatic interposition whenever or wherever danger apprehended.[8]

We submit that the Hoover-Stimson Latin-American policy contained all of the components of the Roosevelt Good Neighbor policy with one exception: the *formal* renunciation of intervention. The overt abandonment of intervention by the Hoover administration, and its other acts of conciliation and good will, created unfortunately only a mildly favorable and hopeful response in Latin America.

Skeptical of professions of good neighborliness coming from a Republican administration — for all Republicans were regarded as capitalists, isolationists, and imperialists — Latin-American statesmen and publicists demanded deeds in addition to words as evidence of good faith on the part of the United States. They also insisted that the policy of nonintervention be elevated to the level of a legally binding pledge.

President Hoover labored under several serious handicaps in trying to develop a new policy. In the first place, United States intervention in Nicaragua and the Coolidge administration's mishandling of our Mexican relations engendered intense bitterness throughout Latin America that could not be quickly erased. Second, the four-year term of President Hoover was too short for policy development. For example, it was not until the end of his term, or after, that the Marine withdrawals could be carried out. Finally, the passage of the Smoot-Hawley Act of 1930, which raised the tariff wall to unprecedented heights, stirred up talk of trade reprisals against the United States, especially by Argentina.

Nevertheless, despite their failure to bridge effectively the chasm of hostility and misunderstanding which separated the United States and Latin America, President Hoover and Secretary Stimson deserve great credit, because they showed themselves responsive to popular demands for a new policy in the Americas. They completed the foundations for Franklin D. Roosevelt's Good Neighbor policy.

The Good Neighbor policy

Prior to his election Franklin Roosevelt had seriously thought about revamping our Latin-American policy. In 1928, when he was governor of New York, he wrote an article for *Foreign Affairs* in which he harshly crit-

[8] Stimson and Bundy, *op. cit.,* 182.

icized American interventionism in Latin America. He called for a renunciation of the practice of "arbitrary intervention in the home affairs of our neighbors." He said, "Single-handed intervention by us in the internal affairs of other nations must end; with the cooperation of others we shall have more order in this hemisphere and less dislike."[9] It is to be noted that Mr. Roosevelt was only protesting *single-handed* intervention. Sumner Welles, an outstanding expert on Latin-American relations, and intimate adviser of the president-elect, had urged that the keystone of our foreign policy should be the abandonment of armed intervention.

In his inaugural address of March 4, 1933, President Roosevelt set forth the principle that was to govern the foreign policy of his administration: "In the field of world policy I would dedicate this nation to the policy of the good neighbor — the neighbor who resolutely respects himself, and, because he does so, respects the rights of others — the neighbor who respects his obligations and respects the sanctity of his agreements in and with a world of neighbors."

The good neighbor principle was specifically applied by the President to Latin America in his Pan American Day address on April 12, 1933:

> The essential qualities of a true Pan Americanism must be the same as those which constitute a good neighbor, namely, mutual understanding, and through such understanding, a sympathetic appreciation of the others' point of view. It is only in this manner that we can hope to build up a system of which confidence, friendship and good will are the cornerstones.

Only a month later the President indicated his willingness to forego the practice of armed intervention, in the countries of the Caribbean and elsewhere.[10]

The way was cleared for the grand renunciation at Montevideo. In December, 1933, the delegates of the American republics assembled in the Uruguayan capital for the Seventh International Conference of American States. The atmosphere of the conference presented quite a contrast to that of Havana in 1928 when Latin-American ill will was at an all-time high. Encouraged by Roosevelt's election, which was acclaimed as a "beautiful episode" in democracy,[11] by his good neighbor promises, and by the promise of the Democratic platform of 1932, which called for "no interference in the internal affairs of other nations," the Latins confidently expected that the long-sought outlawry of intervention was at hand. A proposed Convention on the Rights and Duties of States embodied most of the political objectives toward which the Latin Americans had been striving since the very inception of the Pan American movement. The more pertinent articles of the Convention were the following:

[9] *Foreign Affairs,* VI (1928), 573–586.
[10] New York *Herald-Tribune,* May 17, 1933.
[11] For Latin-American opinion regarding President Roosevelt and the Good Neighbor policy, see Donald M. Dozer, *Are We Good Neighbors?* (Gainesville: University of Florida Press, 1959), 1–188.

Article IV. States are juridically equal, enjoy the same rights, and have equal capacity in their exercise. The rights of each do not depend upon the power which it possesses to assure its exercise, but upon the simple fact of its existence as a person under international law.

Article VI. The recognition of a state merely signifies that the state which recognizes it accepts the personality of the other with all the rights and duties determined by international law. Recognition is unconditional and irrevocable.

Article VIII. No state has the right to intervene in the internal or external affairs of another.

Article IX. The jurisdiction of states within the limits of national territory applies to all the inhabitants.

Nationals and foreigners are under the same protection of the law and the national authorities, and the foreigners may not claim rights other or more extensive than those of the nationals.

Article X. The primary interest of states is the conservation of peace. Differences of any nature between them should be settled by recognized pacific methods.

Article XI. The contracting parties definitely establish as the rule of their conduct the precise obligation not to recognize territorial acquisitions or special advantages which have been obtained by force whether this consists in the employment of arms, or in any other effective coercive measures. The territory of a state is inviolable and may not be the object of military occupation nor of other measures of force imposed by another state directly or indirectly or for any motive whatever, even temporarily.[12]

The title of this convention was a misnomer because it neglected almost entirely the *duties* and *responsibilities* of states. In this respect it reflected unhappily an all-too-prevalent disregard for the core idea of the Good Neighbor, "a two-way street" of reciprocal privileges and obligations. This was not the reason, however, which caused Secretary Hull to hesitate when the delegations were asked to vote on the convention. Like Secretary Hughes,[13] Hull felt that a nonintervention project should incorporate interpretations and definitions; unlike Hughes, he decided to sign anyway, but with a reservation that the United States reserved its rights "by the law of nations as generally recognized." This withholding of unqualified renunciation was disappointing to the Latin Americans.

The Hull reservation left open such fundamental questions as: What is intervention? Does it include diplomatic protection? Is it restricted to armed interference? Does the formula mean that collective intervention is also il-

[12] For the acts of the conferences and meetings for the period 1933–1940, see *The International Conferences of American States, First Supplement, 1933–1940* (Washington, D.C.: Carnegie Endowment for International Peace, 1940). For the Montevideo Conference, see pp. 3–124.

[13] Mr. Hughes said in Havana on February 18, 1928: "If I should subscribe to a formula which others thought might prevent action which a nation is entitled to take in these circumstances, there might come later the charge of bad faith because of acceptance of a formula with one interpretation in my mind while another interpretation of it is in the minds of those proposing the formula." Foreign Policy Association, *Information Service*, IV, No. 4 (April 27, 1928), 66, n. 86.

legal? Did Mr. Hull understand it to mean the unqualified abandonment of all rights of intervention, which certainly was the Latin-American understanding of the formula? Evidently the Latins' struggle for nonintervention had not yet come to a conclusion. They returned to the attack at the Buenos Aires Peace Conference in 1936.

The Montevideo conference also dealt with the problem of strengthening the inter-American security structure. Not yet aware of any necessity to provide security against non-American dangers or aggressions, the additional safeguards reflected only a concern with threats to the peace of the Americas from within the hemisphere. One of these was the Anti-War Treaty of Non-aggression and Conciliation which had been drafted by the Argentine Foreign Minister Carlos Saavedra Lamas. The Argentine government, a consistent nonratifier of Pan American treaties and conventions, was apparently presenting its own substitute for the Gondra and Washington treaties of 1923 and 1929. Moreover, it was the evident intention of Saavedra Lamas to assume the role of leader of the Pan American movement.

The situation called for adroit handling by Secretary Hull, but he proved equal to the occasion. According a larger measure of praise to the Argentine's treaty than it really deserved, for it was quite innocuous, Mr. Hull promised to adhere to the pact if Saavedra Lamas would lead a movement to secure the missing signatures to the earlier Pan American peace treaties. Succumbing to this flattery, Saavedra Lamas put his treaty before the conference, and, to facilitate adherence, he proposed a resolution urging those countries that had not already done so to sign and ratify the Gondra treaty, the two Washington treaties, the Kellogg-Briand Pact of Paris, and his own Anti-War treaty.[14]

As might have been expected, Argentina ratified its own Anti-War Pact. The other Pan American peace pacts were not ratified, and in fact remained unratified until after the fall of Perón in 1955.

On the motion of Secretary Hull, the Montevideo conference adopted a resolution which recommended that the American republics adopt liberal trade principles, particularly lower tariffs. Reversing the position taken by Mr. Hughes at Havana in 1928, Mr. Hull actually introduced tariff discussion into the realm of international politics by proposing the negotiation of liberal reciprocity agreements based upon mutual concessions. The United States Secretary of State was proposing economic disarmament not only because of the economic objective *per se,* but also because he believed that the relieving of economic tensions among nations was essential to world peace. His most cherished peace formula was the return of nations to liberal trade principles. It must be recorded here that, whereas the Latin-American delegations were willing to sign Mr. Hull's resolution, local economic factors prevented revision of policy by their own governments.

It is generally agreed that the Montevideo conference went further toward creating genuine good will than any preceding Pan American conference.

[14] Bemis, *op. cit.,* 271–272.

In fact, it represented a turning point in the history of the movement. The Roosevelt administration was prompt in proving to Latin America that the "good neighbor" was more than a catchy phrase, and that renunciation of intervention was more than lip service. The implementation of the policy was undertaken almost immediately.

Implementing nonintervention

Since our original treaties with Cuba and Panama were incompatible with the new doctrine of nonintervention, it obviously was necessary to negotiate new treaties abolishing the protectorates. With Cuba a treaty of relations was negotiated eliminating the Platt Amendment, which gave to the United States the right to intervene in Cuban affairs. The treaty, signed on May 29, 1934, and ratified by the Senate in record time, on May 31, abrogated the right of intervention and removed all restrictions on Cuban sovereignty. The United States only retained its lease to the naval base at Guantánamo. The island republic had regained its full national sovereignty.

Similarly, on March 2, 1936, a treaty was signed with Panama abolishing the protectorate over that country provided by the old Hay-Bunau Varilla treaty of 1903. This new treaty, however, did not find such easy sailing through the United States Senate as did the Cuba treaty because of the vital relationship of the Panama Canal to the defense of the United States. Finally, in 1939, the Senate consented to ratification when it was assured that the rights of the United States to defend the Canal were adequately secured. Notwithstanding, the new treaty with Panama, like the Cuban treaty, abolished the protectorate over the country.

The Roosevelt administration implemented the nonintervention and Good Neighbor policies not only by treaties but also by concrete acts. The military occupation of Haiti was terminated in August, 1934. In Cuba, economically distressed and convulsed by a desperate struggle for freedom from the Machado dictatorship, President Roosevelt and Secretary Hull were reluctant to exercise the right of intervention accorded by the Platt Amendment. Instead, they sent Summer Welles to Havana, with the title of Ambassador, to bring about a "truce" between the contending factions.[15]

Welles' plan frankly was to "ease out" Machado, and although he said his purpose was to make intervention unnecessary, the pressures he brought to bear on Machado contributed to the overthrow of the dictator. Later Welles' refusal to recognize the government of Dr. Ramón Grau San Martín contributed to the fall of that administration. By pursuing the objectives of political reform in Cuba, the United States was led to the verge of armed intervention. In fact Mr. Welles repeatedly called for naval demonstrations, "limited intervention," and even the landing of the Marines. Secretary Hull disagreed, and he was able to convince the President and the Cabinet.[16]

[15] See Sumner Welles, *Time for Decision* (New York: Harper & Brothers, 1944), 193–200, for this mission to Cuba.
[16] Wood, *op. cit.,* 80–98.

Thus the New Deal administration, after a false start, soon adjusted itself to a policy of complete noninterference in the internal affairs of Cuba.

The South American republic of Bolivia soon presented the Roosevelt administration with an unwelcome opportunity to test its adherence to the new doctrine of nonintervention. Before discussing the Bolivian problem, however, it should be noted that at the Buenos Aires Peace Conference of 1936, an Additional Protocol Relative to Nonintervention was adopted which declared intervention inadmissible "directly or indirectly, and for whatever reason, in the internal or external affairs of any other of the Parties." To the United States, the term "intervention" meant the use of armed forces, and "directly or indirectly" meant the landing of troops or the threat to use them.[17] But to some of the Latin-American governments, it appears that these terms meant limitations on customary protective measures by the United States. In other words, the Latins felt that there were several kinds of interventions, now all prohibited by the Buenos Aires protocol; the United States, on the other hand, held that only the exercise of armed force constituted intervention, and only this was now "inadmissible." Although the United States ratification of the Additional Protocol was without reservation, the scope of the renunciation of "intervention" was still unclear. In the end this worked to the advantage of the Latins.

On March 13, 1937, the Bolivian government by decree annulled the petroleum concession of the Standard Oil Company and confiscated its properties.[18] The company was charged with defrauding the Bolivian government by avoiding the payment of taxes, and also with being noncooperative during the Chaco War.

In Bolivia, as in Mexico and some other Latin-American countries, where there were powerful foreign-owned corporations, the renunciation of intervention did not, in their view, remove the menace of imperialism. It still existed by the very presence of the great companies. Thus, Bolivia and other countries in her position, could not feel free until they had achieved economic independence of the great international oil octopus. The pledge of nonintervention by the United States offered security for the achievement of this objective. There is no doubt that expropriation in Bolivia was a calculated move by a government which was fully confident that, as the Bolivian Foreign Minister confessed, "the American Government will never lift a finger in defense of the Standard Oil Company."[19]

In fact, the Bolivians were not disappointed in their expectations of noninterference by the State Department which, unlike the oil company, accepted the expropriation as legal, and therefore did not express an opinion on the expropriation decree. In its cautious approach to the problem, the Department limited itself to the hope that Bolivia would take early steps to offer compensation, or arbitration, or adjudication as a means of settlement. The Department also seemed to agree with the company that it was entitled to some kind of

---

[17] *Ibid.*, 164.   [18] For the Bolivian issue, see *ibid.*, 168–203.
[19] *Ibid.*, 171.

compensation for the refineries and other installations confiscated. The company was urged to exhaust all remedies and continue conversations with the Bolivian government. The Department's technique was one of friendly representation, but not formal protests.

This approach won nothing for the oil company. Later the State Department adopted a slightly altered, but still amicable, position. First, it refused to recommend the extension of governmental loans or technical assistance until the Bolivian government came to terms with the Standard Oil Company. Later, when this carrot, or "reward technique," proved also to be ineffectual, the Department began to ask itself, because of the developing war scare, whether it was wise to refuse economic aid to Bolivia. In time of crisis the national interest may necessitate the sacrifice of the legitimate rights of corporations. In August, 1941, the United States entered into a plan for economic assistance to Bolivia. In January, 1942, the Bolivian government, induced by desires for fuller economic collaboration with the United States, entered into an agreement with the Standard Oil Company providing for the modest payment of $1,500,000 "for the sale of all its rights, interests, and properties in Bolivia."[20]

Hopes earlier entertained by the State Department that its moderation and self-restraint would evoke general good will and a spirit of reciprocity in Bolivia had not materialized. In the end, it was simply the desire to enjoy more of the economic manna dispensed by the United States that caused La Paz to reach a settlement with the Standard Oil Company.

The trend of the expropriation issue in Bolivia did not pass unnoticed in Mexico where there was also confidence among government leaders that the nonintervention protocol and the "personal sentiments" of President Roosevelt offered reasonable assurance of noninterference by the United States. Confident of United States adherence to the Good Neighbor policy, the Lázaro Cárdenas government in Mexico, in pursuance of its program to recover the resources of the nation and distribute land to the landless, expropriated agricultural and petroleum lands owned by United States citizens.

At no time did the Mexican government betray any fear of official interference by the Roosevelt administration. The anticipated self-restraint by the United States toward the oil expropriation decree of March 18, 1938, was hailed by President Cárdenas as a new proof of friendship, the result of "a policy which is winning" for the United States "the affection of many peoples of the world."[21] Regarding United States intervention, the Mexican Ambassador Castillo Nájera said, on March 30, 1938: "Roosevelt would not commit such an attack, both because of his personal sentiments, and because of the international pledge of the Non-Intervention Protocol."[22] As in the Bolivian matter, the Department of State did not recognize the expropriations as violations of international law.

---

[20] *Ibid.,* 190, 194, 197.
[21] U.S. Dept. of State, *Press Releases,* XVIII (April 2, 1938), 435–436.
[22] Quoted by Wood, *op. cit.,* 221.

Convinced that the avoidance of intervention required noninterference in the oil expropriation issue, Secretary Hull assured Mexico that the Roosevelt government did not question their right to expropriate properties within their jurisdiction. But he insisted that, in accordance with international law, the owners of these expropriated properties were entitled to prompt, adequate, and effective compensation. Accordingly, the State Department concerned itself solely with the amount of compensation and the arrangements for its satisfactory payment.[23]

In order to accomplish this objective several types of action were tried out by the State Department, but all were regarded as "unneighborly" by Mexico, and so were abandoned. On March 26, 1938, Hull sent a note to Ambassador Josephus Daniels for delivery to the Mexican Foreign Minister. In his note he referred to the increasing disregard by Mexico of the rights held by American citizens in agricultural and oil properties and inquired:

> in the event that the Mexican government persists in this expropriation, . . . what specific action with respect to payment for the properties in question is contemplated by the Mexican government, what assurances will be given that payment will be made, and when such payment may be expected.[24]

Secretary Hull regarded his policy as firm but friendly and in keeping with the spirit of the Good Neighbor. But Ambassador Daniels thought otherwise, and, fearing that the Mexicans would regard it as an "ultimatum," arranged with Foreign Minister Eduardo Hay that the note be regarded as "not received," this unbeknown to Secretary Hull. When President Cárdenas announced, on March 31, that "Mexico will know how to honor its obligations of today and its obligations of yesterday," and Daniels was assured that Mexico was able to pay compensation and would discuss indemnities with the oil companies, both Roosevelt and Hull were satisfied. The whole episode proved that an ultimatum was not the way of a Good Neighbor.

Nor were coercive economic measures compatible with the Good Neighbor policy, not that the United States actually applied them in the Mexican situation. Nevertheless it was publicly announced on March 27, 1938, that the silver purchase agreement with Mexico would be suspended. This was popularly accepted as a boycott to coerce Mexico, in spite of the fact that, without the agreement, the purchases continued on a day-to-day basis. There is no evidence that Mexico was hurt by the spurious "boycott," which indeed was *not a reprisal measure.*

As if testing the protective measures not prohibited by the Good Neighbor policy, the Department of State then cautiously suggested to the Mexican government the propriety of arbitration. The Mexicans were emphatic in their rejection, declaring in March, 1940, that neither the right of expropria-

[23] For the Mexican oil expropriation issue, see *ibid.*, 203–260; Cline, *op. cit.*, 229–251; Edward O. Guerrant, *Roosevelt's Good Neighbor Policy* (Albuquerque: University of New Mexico Press, 1950), 106–114; Josephus Daniels, *Shirt-Sleeve Diplomat* (Chapel Hill: University of North Carolina Press, 1947), Chaps. XVIII-XXIV.
[24] Wood, *op. cit.*, 210; Daniels, *op. cit.*, 232–235.

tion nor the amount of compensation were issues ripe for arbitration. In the end, however, the United States and Mexico came to an understanding and on November 19, 1941, agreed to appoint a joint commission of experts to determine the just compensation due American oil companies. This, it seemed to both countries, was a good neighborly way to settle their differences. The application of the policies of nonintervention and noninterference in the internal affairs of Mexico revealed unexpected limitations on the protective recourses of the State Department.[25]

The passage of the Reciprocal Trade Agreements Act of 1934 and the negotiation of trade agreements with Latin-American countries must also be included as evidences of the implementation of the Good Neighbor policy. The Roosevelt-Hull administration came into power on the heels of Latin-American resentments against the highly protectionist Smoot-Hawley Tariff Act of 1930. It was Secretary Hull's hope that by negotiating reciprocal trade agreements our declining Latin-American trade could be reinvigorated. Under powers granted by the Congress in the Trade Agreements Act, it was now possible to arrange for mutual tariff reductions through a process of clearly defined reciprocity.

Trade agreements were negotiated with several of the Latin-American countries, starting with Cuba, but it must be recorded that, although they exerted some remedial influence, they failed to break down artificial trade barriers which clogged the channels of foreign trade. Nor were Latin-American resentments alleviated, for the United States market continued to be highly protectionist.

Most bitter of all was Argentina, whose beef was excluded under unfair quarantine restrictions as being infected with hoof-and-mouth disease. In an attempt to appease the Argentines, a Sanitary Convention was signed in 1935 which would have allowed the importation of properly inspected animal and plant products from portions of a country declared to be free of the disease. Although President Roosevelt, when visiting Buenos Aires in 1936, promised early ratification of the treaty, the cattlemen's lobby proved to be too strong. The treaty never won the advice and consent of the Senate.

The establishment of the Export-Import Bank in 1934 to encourage American foreign trade was not originally concerned with economic assistance to Latin Americans. Its important role as a provider of credits to Latin-American governments came after the outbreak of war in 1939. It was then that the Exim Bank was oriented toward strengthening the economies of the Latin-American republics as a means of assisting the defense of the Western Hemisphere.

Finally, in further evidence of a new United States policy toward Latin America, we note that the United States government took no direct action to assist its bondholders to recover their losses in the defaulted Latin-American government bond issues. In the decade of the 1920's there had been an orgy of borrowing by Latin-American governments. The banks and invest-

[25] Daniels, *op. cit.,* 236.

ment houses were in many instances irresponsible to their clients, the investing public, in ignoring the poor credit resources of the borrowing countries. Between 1921 and 1931 almost two billion dollars of Latin-American government bond issues were floated in the United States. After 1929, because of the Great Depression, these governments — national, state, and local — defaulted or repudiated their bonds. The policy of the State Department was to keep hands off: it took no direct action to assist the bondholders to recover their losses. Instead, the Department, in December, 1933, launched and sponsored an unofficial Foreign Bondholders' Protective Council to negotiate on its own. This medium for the representation of the creditors was partially successful in working out a number of adjustments, although there is no disguising the fact that the United States private investor took a terrific beating. Samuel F. Bemis called this "dollar diplomacy in reverse."[26]

What is the Good Neighbor?

The Good Neighbor policy evolved during the Roosevelt administrations. There can be little doubt that it eventually took on new meanings of scope and content that were not anticipated in the early days of its enunciation. We are here concerned only with the pre-1939, or "old" Good Neighbor, characterized by the practices of mutual respect and restraint. It was largely negative in the sense that the unfolding policy revealed the implications of nonintervention. We leave for later discussion the post-1939 Good Neighbor, which, because of the war, became a policy of mutual assistance or positive collaboration.

According to Under Secretary of State Sumner Welles, the policy of the "good neighbor" rested

> upon the belief of this government that there should exist an inter-American political relationship based on a recognition of actual and not theoretical equality between the American Republics; on a complete forbearance from interference by any republic in the domestic concerns of any other; on economic cooperation; and finally, on the common realization that in the world at large all the American Republics confront the same international problems, and that in their relations with non-American powers, the welfare and security of any one of them cannot be a matter of indifference to the others.[27]

When the Roosevelt administration renounced intervention, there was confident expectation that the putting aside of the "Big Stick" would evoke among the American nations a collective responsibility for peace and order in the Hemisphere. President Roosevelt emphasized the *obligations* as well as the *rights* of states. He also believed, as we have indicated, that nonintervention only meant the illegality of *unilateral forcible* interposition. In fact, he expected multilateral action in the future. Not only were the Latin-Amer-

[26] Bemis, *op. cit.,* 340.
[27] *Christian Science Monitor,* February 4, 1936.

ican states expected to meet their collective responsibilities, but the individual states were expected to *reciprocate* for our renunciation of intervention. The Good Neighbor policy was a "two-way street" in the sense that, if the United States did certain things wanted by the Latins — specifically, renunciation of intervention — then those states should respond by doing things desired by the United States — specifically, equitable treatment of aliens. In short, the New Deal expected that the sacrifice of intervention for the protection of the lives and property of its citizens and the advancement of democracy in Latin America would be compensated by the Latins' acceptance of the idea of reciprocity. It was assumed that each nation would play a responsible mature role in the inter-American community. According to President Roosevelt, the Good Neighbor policy "can never be unilateral. In stressing it the American republics appreciate, I am confident, that it is bilateral and multilateral and that the fair dealing which it implies must be reciprocated."[28]

The Latin Americans, however, did not take kindly to the "two-way" idea. Without minimizing in any way their sincere and legitimate desires to gain freedom from outside interference in the conduct of their domestic political affairs, it was also apparent from their own admissions, that the freedom from intervention meant freedom to treat foreign enterprises and corporations as they thought fit. Certainly the expropriation of the oil properties in Bolivia was carefully calculated, and Mexico counted absolutely on United States acquiescence.

The failure of the Latins to "reciprocate," as expected, forced the State Department to feel its way on a course midway between diplomatic representation and total abstinence from involvement. To the outsider it looked like complete abandonment of the American companies. Instead, the State Department was endeavoring earnestly to support the companies but without appearing to do so. The policy of noninterference seemed to leave little room in which to operate.

As the gathering war clouds in Europe were becoming darker, the State Department was more and more disposed to give higher value to Latin-American collaboration in the event of war. Thus, since considerations of national interests as a whole far outweighed those of the petroleum companies, the State Department negotiated accommodations with Bolivia and Mexico at the expense of the business enterprises. The property losses of corporations and individuals were expendable; they were the unavoidable price of the policy of nonintervention.

This raises a question concerning the limits of the renunciation of the use of force. Events proved that not only the use of force but even diplomatic interposition would not be used for the protection of the property rights of American citizens in Latin America. But in a situation threatening to the Monroe Doctrine, for example, would the United States be restrained by the nonintervention protocol?

---

[28] Franklin D. Roosevelt, *Public Papers and Addresses* (New York: The Macmillan Company, 1941), 1938 vol., 412.

President Roosevelt, in 1938, at a press conference, made it clear, using Mexico as a hypothetical case, what he would do if European governments were to do in Mexico what they did in Spain. He said, "Do you think that the United States could stand idly by and have this European menace right on our own borders? Of course not. You could not stand for it."[29] According to Roosevelt the nonintervention pledge was not absolute.

As might be expected, Latin-American public opinion responded favorably to the Good Neighbor policy. There was a predisposition to believe the words of Franklin Roosevelt and his colleagues, and the many acts of policy implementation persuaded the Latins to accept the United States as a trustworthy friend. It has been asserted, with some degree of truth, that "greater progress had been made toward the attainment of inter-American harmony in this brief period of Roosevelt's Good Neighbor Policy than during the entire previous century of inter-American relations."[30]

Not only did Latin America respond favorably to the Good Neighbor policy, but it actually succeeded in making the United States a "prisoner" of its own good neighborliness. On many occasions before and after 1939 the State Department was criticized by the Latins for failing to live up to the Good Neighbor policy. It was put on the defensive in supporting its own definition of the policy as opposed to that of the Latins. Since the good neighbors could make persuasive claim that they had an interest in a policy initiated by the United States, the State Department had no choice but to accept their interpretation. Thus, President Roosevelt opened the way for other countries to impose on the United States their understanding of the sacrifices that should be required of this country.

The Buenos Aires peace conference

Since an objective of the Good Neighbor policy, according to Sumner Welles, was the common realization that "all the American Republics confront the same international problems, and that in their relations with non-American powers, the welfare and security of any one of them cannot be a matter of indifference to the others," we note now the progress of inter-American security collaboration to 1939.

The Latin-American policy of the Roosevelt administration gradually assumed the character of a security policy intended to protect the United States and Latin America from overseas aggressors. On January 30, 1936, President Roosevelt sent personal letters to the presidents of the other American republics suggesting that an extraordinary inter-American conference be summoned to meet in Buenos Aires

> to determine how the maintenance of peace among the American republics
> may best be safeguarded — whether perhaps through the prompt ratification
> of all of the inter-American peace instruments already negotiated; whether
> through the amendment of existing peace instruments in such manner as

[29] Wood, *op. cit.,* 349.
[30] Dozer, *op. cit.,* 36.

experience has demonstrated to be most necessary; or perhaps through the creation, by common accord, of new instruments of peace, additional to those already formulated.[31]

Termination of hostilities in the Chaco afforded the occasion for a conference to revamp the inter-American peace machinery. But President Roosevelt had in mind more than the safeguarding of security from inter-American wars alone. He wanted the American nations to organize a common neutrality front in the event of a general war in Europe. This both President Roosevelt and Secretary Hull regarded as the most important problem to be met by the conference.

The Inter-American Conference for the Maintenance of Peace, a special conference, met in Buenos Aires on December 1–23, 1936. President Roosevelt, a guest of the Argentine nation, addressed the opening session of the conference. Extolling the "glories of interdependence," he urged the strengthening of the inter-American system by erecting bulwarks against aggression from abroad. Secretary Hull also endeavored to arouse the delegates to the dangerous realities of the world situation. For the first time since the inauguration of the Pan American movement in 1889 a conference was being asked to consider security measures against a non-American aggressor. It was also significant that the United States now urged these measures, in view of its blindness to their need in the past.

The agreement to consult, the greatest achievement of the Buenos Aires conference, was contained in the Convention for the Maintenance, Preservation and Re-establishment of Peace, popularly known as the Consultative Pact. It provided for consultation among the American republics for the purpose of finding and adopting methods of cooperation in three sets of circumstances: (1) in the event that the peace of the Americas is menaced from any source; (2) in the event of war or virtual state of war between American states; and (3) in the event of a war outside of America which might menace the peace of the American republics. There was no obligation to do more than consult, and no machinery was set up to invoke consultation. However, recognition of an obligation to consult was an achievement, for it indicated the collective concern and common interest of each American republic in the security of all. The Consultative Pact was also significant in that it was the first inter-American agreement, after 1889, concerned with security against an extra-continental threat. The base of the inter-American security system was being extended.

An Additional Protocol Relative to Non-Intervention, adopted by the 1936 conference, reaffirmed more emphatically the nonintervention doctrine adopted at Montevideo in 1933. It declared "inadmissible the intervention of any of them [the High Contracting Parties], directly or indirectly, and for whatever reason, in the internal or external affairs of any other of the parties;" it also declared that in cases of violation there should be "mutual consultation,

---

[31] Inter-American Conference for the Maintenance of Peace, *Special Handbook for the Use of the Delegates* (Washington: Pan American Union, 1936), 1.

with the object of exchanging views and seeking methods of peaceful adjustment." Thus, the consultation formula was also attached to nonintervention. Without fully realizing the far-ranging implications of unqualified nonintervention, Secretary Hull signed the protocol. Later, the United States ratified the Additional Protocol without reservation. Among the resolutions adopted by the conference was one endorsing Hull's liberal trade principles. It proved to be meaningless, for, although approved by the conference, governmental policies remained the same.

Although President Roosevelt and Secretary Hull did not secure at Buenos Aires the kind of positive measures for defense against the dangers of foreign wars which they preferred, the Consultative Pact proved to be a fairly effective substitute. It represented a move by all of the American nations toward greater responsibility for their common security. Opposition to any aggression from overseas was now recognized as a *collective* right and responsibility. Yet, too many Latin Americans, like Saavedra Lamas, scoffed at the suggestion of a European attack as an "imaginative hypothesis." But throughout the next two years, until the general conference at Lima in 1938, the acts of totalitarian aggression in Austria, Czechoslovakia, Spain, and China were too shocking to be ignored. Like the United States, the Latin-American nations were beginning to realize that their own interests were affected by what was happening in Europe and Asia.

The Lima conference

Following the Munich crisis, President Roosevelt proposed, on November 15, 1938, a defensive alliance of the American nations against external aggression. Although the President believed that the problem of national defense had now become a problem of continental defense, he also declared that it "does not rest solely on our shoulders."[32]

In his opening address to the Eighth International Conference of American States, which met in Lima, Peru, December 9 to 27, 1938, Secretary Hull said that the policy of the United States was to strengthen the inter-American system of consultation and common action in order to resist the invasion of this hemisphere by the armed forces of any power or combination of powers. He hoped that the Latin-American republics would agree to resist collectively any threats to their peace, security, or territorial integrity from a non-American source.[33]

The United States proposal for a hemisphere front against possible totalitarian aggression was rejected largely because of Argentine opposition to any pact that might entangle them in future non-American conflicts, and their denial of the existence of "aggressive perils." Instead, the conference adopted a devitalized resolution, called the "Declaration of Lima."

[32] *New York Times,* November 16, 1938.
[33] Samuel Guy Inman, "Lima Conference and the Totalitarian Issue," *Annals* of the American Academy of Political and Social Science, 204 (July, 1939), 9–17; David Elfron, "Latin America and the Fascist 'Holy Alliance,'" *ibid.,* 17–26.

The Declaration, after reaffirming the principle of continental solidarity, declared the intention of the American republics to consult whenever the peace, security, or territorial integrity of any American republic should be threatened from a foreign source. Beyond the provision that the meetings of the foreign ministers should implement the procedure of consultation, the Declaration of Lima added little to the Buenos Aires Consultative Pact.

Other acts[34] of the Lima conference need only be accounted for in a summary fashion. Another liberal-trade resolution offered by Secretary Hull received unanimous approval by the delegations, but there was continued violation by the respective governments. Unfortunately for Mr. Hull's trade program, which he regarded as an essential feature of the Good Neighbor policy and a means for the preservation of world peace, the Latin-American nations were moving almost in a body to barter practices, bilateralism, and exchange controls.

Nazi-Fascist propaganda in the Americas, and their efforts to obtain economic and political advantage by subversive activity, were responsible for some additional resolutions voted by the Lima conference. The adoption of the anti-Axis resolutions was quite an achievement considering the fact that at the conference the agents of the totalitarian powers resorted to every device possible to create division. An unseemly feature was the lavish display of the banners of Germany, Italy, and Japan, among the national banners displayed along the flag-bedecked streets of Lima, meeting place of an exclusively American conference.[35] In such an environment it was not easy for the American delegations to demonstrate solidarity against potential foreign aggressors.

Since the Lima conference had assembled in the shadow of Munich to develop more effective inter-American cooperation against political and cultural penetration and possible armed aggression by the totalitarian states, how shall we appraise its results?

On his return from Lima, Mr. Hull said, "The American republics made it clear to all the world that they stand united to maintain and defend the peace of this hemisphere. . . . I return from the Conference with the conviction that its results will be of real and permanent value . . . as time goes on."[36] Events soon proved he was correct. In evidence of this fact note the record, in the following chapter, of inter-American collaboration in World War II.

Cultural relations

It was natural that the Roosevelt administration should supplement its Good Neighbor policy with the promotion of cultural relations with Latin America. Good neighbors become better neighbors when there is sympathetic cultural contact and exchange. Foreigners are usually viewed with suspicion, for those we do not understand we mistrust, fear, or disparage. It seems to

[34] For the Lima Conference, see *Int. Conf. of Am. States, First Suppl.,* 1933–1940, 215–315.
[35] *Christian Science Monitor,* December 21, 1938.
[36] U.S. Dept. of State, *Press Release,* January 7, 1939.

be a commonplace, therefore, that cultural understanding among nations eases the way to political solidarity. This is not always true, for cultural divergences usually do not stand in the way of international cooperation when two nations have enough common interests. Nor, on the other hand, have cultural similarities or understanding been sufficient to create solidarity in the face of divergent national interests. It can hardly be denied, however, that measures to promote intellectual and cultural relations between nations can at least assist understanding and soften enmity. Certainly no harm can result, and much good may be accomplished.

Prior to 1936 the United States government had never regarded the promotion of cultural exchange as a proper governmental function. Insofar as there were efforts to promote such an exchange, this was undertaken by unofficial entities — American Protestant missionaries, universities, and foundations, particularly the Rockefeller and Carnegie Foundations.

It was only when the governments of aggressive totalitarian states began to promote cultural exchange with Latin America on an extravagant scale as an instrument to undermine the Good Neighbor policy and soften political resistance that the United States government was stimulated into action. At the Buenos Aires conference of 1936 the United States introduced a Convention for the Promotion of Inter-American Cultural Relations which provided for a system of government-supported exchange of university professors and students. This convention was signed by all of the countries and eventually ratified by seventeen. The United States, excusing itself on the ground that our federal government lacked constitutional authority, did not sign the Convention Concerning Peaceful Orientation of Public Instruction and the Convention Concerning Facilities for Educational and Publicity Films. However, no constitutional impediment prevented the United States from signing and ratifying two additional conventions in the cultural exchange area negotiated at the Buenos Aires conference. These were the Convention on the Interchange of Publications and the Convention Concerning Artistic Exhibitions. In addition to these conventions the Buenos Aires conference of 1936 adopted a number of resolutions and recommendations dealing with the promotion of intellectual and cultural relations among the American republics. It was not until 1940 that the first exchange of professors and students took place under the Cultural Relations Convention.

In the meantime, in 1938, the Division of Cultural Relations was organized in the Department of State to take general charge of the cultural relations activities of the Department and to assist private agencies in their related activities. Originally cultural relations were restricted almost exclusively to Latin America. In a short time the United States progressed from a position of almost complete indifference toward inter-American cultural exchange to an aggressive policy of varied activities.[37] Soon the purely cultural and

---

[37] For the inauguration of cultural relations, see *The Program of the Department of State in Cultural Relations,* Dept. of State, Inter-American Series, No. 79 (Washington, D.C., 1941); Guerrant, *op. cit.,* 115–119.

humanitarian aspects of the policy gave way, due to the threat and outbreak of war, to measures of defense against antidemocratic forces. These developments will be discussed in the next chapter.

SUPPLEMENTARY READING

Bemis, Samuel Flagg, *The Latin American Policy of the United States* (New York: Harcourt, Brace and Company, 1943), 256–367.

Cuevas Cancino, Francisco, *Del Congreso de Panamá a la Conferencia de Caracas, 1826–1954,* II, Chap. 3.

Cuevas Cancino, Francisco, *Roosevelt y la Buena Vecindad* (Mexico, D.F.: Fondo de Cultura Económica, 1954).

Daniels, Josephus, *Shirt-Sleeve Diplomat* (Chapel Hill: University of North Carolina Press, 1947), Chaps. XXIII, XXIV.

DeConde, Alexander, *Herbert Hoover's Latin-American Policy* (Stanford: Stanford University Press, 1951).

Dozer, Donald M., *Are We Good Neighbors?* (Gainesville: University of Florida Press, 1959), 1–69.

Guerrant, Edward O., *Roosevelt's Good Neighbor Policy* (Albuquerque: University of New Mexico Press, 1950), Chaps. I, VI.

Hull, Cordell, *The Memoirs of Cordell Hull* (2 vols. New York: The Macmillan Company, 1948).

Humphrey, John P., *The Inter-American System, A Canadian View* (Toronto: The Macmillan Co., 1942), 112–168.

The International Conferences of American States, First Supplement, 1933–1940 (Washington, D.C.: Carnegie Endowment for International Peace, 1940).

Mecham, J. Lloyd, *The United States and Inter-American Security, 1889–1960* (Austin: University of Texas Press, 1961), Chap. IV.

Pusey, Merlo J., *Charles Evans Hughes* (New York: The Macmillan Company, 1951), II, Chaps. 51, 53.

Quintanilla, Luis, *A Latin American Speaks* (New York: The Macmillan Company, 1943), 89–172.

Stimson, Henry L., *American Policy in Nicaragua* (New York: Charles Scribner's Sons, 1927).

Stimson, Henry L., and Bundy, McGeorge, *On Active Service in Peace and War* (New York: Harper & Brothers, 1947).

Welles, Sumner, *Time for Decision* (New York: Harper & Brothers, 1944), 193–200.

Wood, Bryce, *The Making of the Good Neighbor Policy* (New York: Columbia University Press, 1961).

6

The United States and Latin America in World War II

The outbreak of World War II, on September 1, 1939, presented the American community with the greatest challenge to that date of its vaunted "solidarity." How the hemisphere nations cooperated with the United States to meet the challenge, first as neutrals, and then later as belligerents, is the subject of the following discussion.

In view of the portents of impending world conflict, the Latin-American republics had been blind in rejecting urgent prodding by the United States, as early as 1936, for cooperative defense plans. Not until war had actually come would they agree on the nature and extent of their cooperative action. This, fortunately, they were able to do in a succession of consultative meetings of their foreign ministers. Moreover, the foundations for concerted action had already been laid, thanks to the Good Neighbor policy which contributed much to confirming the principles of inter-American solidarity.

The United States government and the American people were agreed that the defense of Central and South America was essential to national security and that everything possible had to be done to provide for the stability, the economic welfare, and the military protection of the hemisphere. Programs of economic assistance were laid down, and initial steps were taken to arrange for military collaboration against aggressors from overseas. Plans for defense collaboration were both multilateral (among all of the American nations) and bilateral (principally between the United States and individual Latin-American nations). When war came to the Americas, it was necessary to do little more than seek the implementation of these multilateral and bilateral engagements. The American states, that is, most of them, were able to glide

131

smoothly and naturally into their predetermined roles as cobelligerents. Inter-American collaboration in World War II contrasted sharply with its almost complete absence in World War I.

1. Neutral America, 1939–1941[1]

Pre-1939 preparations

On November 15, 1938, President Roosevelt enunciated a new national policy of hemisphere defense: the continental United States could not be successfully threatened by air or sea unless a hostile power first secured a lodgment within the Western Hemisphere. In announcing his immediate goal to be an aircraft production capacity of 10,000 planes a year, the President declared that the United States had to protect any part of North or South America, and that its air force had to be capable of deterring anyone from landing in either North or South America. The problem of national defense, said the President, had become a problem of continental defense which "does not rest solely on our shoulders."[2] There was need of the friendly and active support of the other American nations. At the Lima conference, in December, 1938, the American nations unanimously adhered to a declaration that "affirmed the intention of the American Republics to help one another in case of a foreign attack, either direct or indirect, on any one of them." This became the basis for later negotiations to insure the political, economic, and military cooperation of the Latin-American nations.

To meet the President's formal announcement of a new national policy of hemisphere defense, a Joint Planning Committee of the Army and Navy made a thorough study of the practicable courses of action open to the military and naval forces of the United States should the Monroe Doctrine be violated by one or more of the Fascist powers. These were called the "Rainbow Plans." In general they allotted to the United States Army and Navy the primary task of defending the Western Hemisphere against military attack from the Old World; then, when the successful accomplishment of that task had been concluded or assured, American forces would engage in offensive operations. Because they lacked military potential, the Latin-American nations were assigned only a secondary supporting role in the plans. There should be maximum use of Latin-American military strength for defensive roles; the threat of Nazi subversion in the Western Hemisphere should be eliminated; the United States should be given the use of naval and air-base sites on Latin-American soil; and the United States should enjoy full access

---

[1] See Donald M. Dozer, *Are We Good Neighbors?* (Gainesville: University of Florida Press, 1959), Chap. 3; Edward O. Guerrant, *Roosevelt's Good Neighbor Policy* (Albuquerque: University of New Mexico Press, 1950), 135–170; J. Lloyd Mecham, *The United States and Inter-American Security 1889–1960* (Austin: University of Texas Press, 1961), Chap. VII.

[2] Franklin D. Roosevelt, *Public Papers and Addresses* (13 vols. New York: Random House, The Macmillan Company, Harper & Brothers, 1938–1950), Vol. VII, 598–600.

to Latin America's strategic raw materials. The Rainbow Plans, reported to the Joint Board on April 21, 1939, and approved in August, served as a basis for the detailed strategic planning that followed.[3]

The Panama meeting of foreign ministers

President Roosevelt had decided, in consultation with the State Department, that as soon as war broke out in Europe, the United States would call a meeting of the foreign ministers of the American republics to confirm the front of "continental solidarity" agreed on at Lima. Thus, as soon as news of the German attack on Poland, September 1, 1939, was received, the United States asked for a consultative meeting of the foreign ministers at Panama. The meeting, held from September 23 to October 3, was the first of an important series of inter-American consultations as provided by the Declaration of Lima. The principal objectives of the Panama consultation were to keep the American republics out of war, and to consider economic problems that would arise as a result of the war.

With respect to its first objective, the meeting undertook, in a General Declaration of Neutrality, to clarify the rights and duties of the American republics in their capacity as neutrals. To study and formulate recommendations concerning the problems of neutrality, an Inter-American Neutrality Committee of seven experts in international law was to sit at Rio de Janeiro for the duration of the war.

As a measure of continental self-defense and insulation against involvement in the war, the Declaration of Panama proclaimed a neutrality zone or safety belt around the shores of the Americas averaging 300 miles in width. This warning to European belligerents to keep their warships on the other side of the Atlantic was President Roosevelt's own idea.

As for its enforcement, the Declaration merely provided that the American republics would consult when necessary to determine upon measures. They should be free in the meantime to patrol the zone individually and collectively as they willed. The Declaration of Panama had no precedent in international law and therefore could be validly objected to by the belligerents — as indeed was the case.

With respect to economic difficulties brought on by the war, the First Meeting of Foreign Ministers adopted a Resolution on Economic Cooperation which provided for the creation of an Inter-American Financial and Economic Advisory Committee consisting of twenty-one experts on economic problems, one for each of the American republics. This committee, installed in Washington, was to study and propose solutions to the economic problems with

---

[3] Stetson Conn and Byron Fairchild, *The Framework of Hemisphere Defense*. The United States Army in World War II: The Western Hemisphere (Washington, D.C.: Government Printing Office, 1960), 7–10; Maurice Matloff and Edwin M. Snell, *Strategic Planning for Coalition Warfare, 1941–1942. The United States Army in World War II* (Washington, D.C. Government Printing Office 1953), 5–8; William L. Langer and E. Everett Gleason, *The Challenge to Isolation* (New York: Harper & Brothers, 1952), 40–41.

which the American nations would be confronted as a result of the war. It proved to be one of the most active and valuable of the several inter-American war agencies.

The acts[4] of the Panama meeting reflected the attitude of the American republics toward the war in its first phase, that is, the so-called "phony phase" of comparative calm from September, 1939, to April, 1940. The problem of the Americas was merely to ensure noninvolvement by preserving a scrupulous neutrality. In view of subsequent developments this was a naive hope. Although it was crystal clear that this European war was different from any in the past, and that a Nazi victory would adversely affect the rights and liberties of all states, even in the Western Hemisphere, the American nations did not acknowledge any difference between the war objectives of the respective belligerents.

The crisis of 1940

The first American country to give evidence by its acts of an awakening consciousness of its real interests was the United States. The elimination from the Neutrality Act of 1937 of the arms embargo provision was the first significant move toward the scrapping of United States neutrality. It was the first step along the road to nonbelligerency and the undeclared war. Prior to the outbreak of the war, the Congress, in June, 1939, appropriated funds to permit the Army to embark on an air-expansion program to be completed in mid-1941. This was our first "hemisphere defense" air program.

It was not until after the "blitzkriegs" of April and May, 1940, however, that there was a complete reorientation of fundamental attitudes and policy on the part of the American republics, including the United States, with respect to the war. The illusion that the Western Hemisphere was immune to economic and political developments in other parts of the world was completely destroyed. The efficacy of a perfect neutrality, as a shield of defense, was now revealed by the fate of the Low Countries for what it was worth. To meet the challenge inter-American cooperation, multilateral and bilateral, had to be shifted from preserving neutrality and insulating against the effects of the European war, to actual defense of this hemisphere. We take note first of collective action.

On July 21, 1940, the foreign ministers of the American republics met in Havana in a Second Consultative Meeting. Of the various problems raised by the overrunning of the Low Countries and France by the German armies, and the threatened invasion of Great Britain, the most urgent was the fate of the European colonies in this hemisphere. At the Panama meeting it had been resolved that the transfer of colonial possessions in America would occasion a consultation of the foreign ministers. Since the ground had been prepared for a common inter-American policy, the Havana meeting adopted

[4] Carnegie Endowment for International Peace, *The International Conferences of American States: First Supplement, 1933–1940*, 315–342.

a declaration known as the Act of Havana Concerning the Provisional Administration of European Colonies or Possessions in the Americas. It provided that, when there was danger of colonies changing hands, the American republics, collectively or individually, could take them over, subject to the eventual restoration of their previous status or their being made independent.[5]

A convention containing the essential features of the Act of Havana and designed to formalize the provisional administration of European colonies in America was signed by the delegates. It called for the establishing of an Inter-American Commission for Territorial Administration. Although the convention received the necessary ratifications and became effective on January 8, 1942, it never became necessary to invoke either it or the Act of Panama. Since it was obvious that the principal sanction of the Act of Havana would be employment of military force by the United States, this amounted to tacit endorsement by the Latin Americans of the no-transfer principle of the Monroe Doctrine.

Another action of the Havana meeting, equally as important as the Act of Havana, was the Declaration of Reciprocal Assistance and Cooperation for the Defense of the Nations of the Americas. It declared that aggression by non-American powers against an American republic should be considered as aggression against all, that consultation should then be in order, and that consequently the American republics should enter into agreements to insure cooperation in defense. The real importance of the declaration lay in the fact that it afforded a basis for the numerous agreements that were soon to be negotiated for reciprocal assistance in the event of an overseas aggression. It was also significant as the first inter-American security instrument aimed specifically at non-American powers.

The American governments, in another resolution adopted at Havana, expressed a determination to take all necessary measures to combat fifth-column activities. Thus, moral support was promised any Latin-American nation that was serious in its resistance to totalitarian propaganda. Other resolutions sought to defend the Americas against subversive techniques practiced by the Nazis.

The Havana meeting was also concerned with economic matters. It expanded the functions of the Inter-American Financial and Economic Advisory Committee, created at Panama in 1939, and endorsed programs concerned with the creation of facilities for the orderly marketing of accumulated surpluses and the development of commodity agreements. Adherence to liberal principles of international trade meant that if Germany wished to trade with the American nations it had to be on their terms or not at all.

Thanks to the acts of the Panama and Havana Meetings of Foreign Ministers, the way was prepared for the United States to enter into a number of politico-military and economic hemisphere defense measures and agreements, which were based generally on declared principles of hemispheric solidarity.

[5] For the acts of the Havana Meeting, see *ibid.,* 348–377.

The United States prepares for hemisphere defense

The Declaration of Panama, which provided for a neutrality zone girding the Americas, clearly implied inter-American military cooperation. By its terms a security zone was to be patrolled, but, since most of the states, parties to the declaration, had no means by which they could patrol their coastal waters, they were willing to put their facilities at the disposal of the United States. Thus, agreements and understandings were entered into which opened the harbors, bays, and territorial waters to United States patrol vessels. In some instances conversations paved the way for joint patrolling of territorial waters.

With no more than token assistance from the Latin-American states, the United States carried on a neutrality patrol in the Gulf of Mexico, the Caribbean, and the western fringes of the Atlantic from Newfoundland to the Guianas.[6] In 1941, after the acquisition of British bases by the exchange of destroyers, the Navy was able to extend the patrol to the mid-Atlantic. This did not mean, however, that belligerent operations were excluded from the zone. There were many violations, the most notable being the engagement of British warships with the German "pocket" battleship *Graf von Spee,* off the coast of Uruguay.

After the conclusion of the Rainbow Plans, prior to the outbreak of war in September, 1939, the problem of acquiring base facilities in Latin America had been explored, but no progress had been made. Nor did the Army make any progress in supplying Latin America with munitions. The situation was changed, however, after the blitz in the spring of 1940. Because of the fateful turn of the war tide the United States felt a greater urgency in seeking Latin-American defense collaboration, and the Latins, on their part, were now more aware of the need of collaboration.

On May 16, 1940, following the fall of France, President Roosevelt asked his military advisers to prepare plans at once for developing closer military relations with Latin America. This was the initiative which led to staff conversations with the military authorities of the Latin-American governments. Beginning in June, 1940, and extending to the end of October, United States military officers carried on detailed conversations in the capitals of all the Latin-American countries except Bolivia, Paraguay, Panama, and Mexico. The latter country preferred to carry on the negotiations in Washington.[7] The conversations dealt with the use of naval, land, and air bases in Latin America, transit rights through their air spaces by United States aircraft, and the supplying of Latin America's military needs. It was made clear to the Latins that the United States was not planning to use their forces as effective allies

[6] Samuel Eliot Morison, *History of the United States Naval Operations in World War II: The Battle of the Atlantic, September 1939–May 1943* (14 vols. Boston: Little, Brown and Company, 1947), I, 13–16.

[7] Since both Paraguay and Bolivia were landlocked, they presented no immediate defense problems. Panama was a special problem and was handled on an individual basis.

in the war. Instead, they would be supplied with enough arms to ward off an external attack until United States forces could arrive. Their land, air, and sea base facilities should be available to United States forces when they did arrive.

All of the nations approached, except Argentina,[8] indicated general willingness to cooperate with the United States in military measures for hemisphere defense. By the terms of the Staff Agreements, each Latin-American nation, in return for pledges of United States defense assistance, was itself expected:

1. To call on the United States for armed assistance in event of actual or threatened attack.

2. To report to the United States any non-American attack.

3. To explain, via radio, to the rest of the world, and especially to Latin America, the reason for its request of United States assistance.

4. To permit the transit of United States forces going to the aid of a neighbor.

5. To develop and maintain an effective and complete interchange of intelligence relating to continental security.

6. To develop and maintain an adequate and efficient secret service in order to keep under surveillance aliens and subversive groups.

7. To eliminate anti-United States propaganda in times of emergency.

The commitment by the United States, through the Staff Agreements, to defend the whole Western Hemisphere was a new departure in policy. For the first time in its history it was seeking to enter into close military relations with the other Western Hemisphere nations. But whatever it did for hemisphere defense, it did obviously to safeguard its own national security and interests. And the Latin-American nations, on their own part, had become sufficiently aware of the Nazi-Fascist menace to be ready to collaborate with their powerful northern neighbor.

The acquisition of base facilities in Latin America, contemplated by both the Rainbow Plans and the Staff Agreements, engaged the early and earnest attention of the United States. Since the war plans of the United States assumed that its forces would be required to defend Latin America against overseas attack, it naturally followed that access to base facilities should be assured. Despite the fact that there was no real opposition or disapproval of the United States program, the base sites negotiations encountered hard going, largely because of considerations of national pride.

The United States defense departments wanted leaseholds modeled after the recent acquisitions from Great Britain in the destroyer-base deal, that is, long-time leases and full jurisdiction. The Latins soon made it clear that they were not willing to concede these requests. There was considerable fear that the United States, if granted the bases, would not be willing later to leave

[8] For the staff conversations and agreements of 1940, see Conn and Fairchild, *op. cit.*, 175–183. Argentina refused, not only to engage in staff conversations, but opposed the grant of base facilities by Uruguay to the United States. Argentina aimed to reserve to itself the dominant role in its own vicinity.

them. Some even accused the United States of exaggerating imaginary perils in order to take possession of their territory. In some instances the subject was made a partisan domestic issue in which the "outs" did their best to sabotage the negotiations.

A satisfactory formula to resolve the base issue emerged from our negotiations with Uruguay. In November, 1940, it was announced that Uruguay, with financial assistance from the United States, would construct air and naval bases for continental defense. The bases would remain under Uruguayan sovereignty and would be manned by Uruguayans, but with technical help from the United States. The bases were available to all American nations engaged in the common defense. Despite political opposition internally, and Argentine opposition externally, Uruguayan Foreign Minister Dr. Alberto Guani emerged victor in his determination to pursue a cooperative hemisphere policy.[9]

The Uruguay base formula served to clarify United States policy, for it revealed that the United States did not seek concessions that would in any way affect the sovereignty of any Latin-American nation. Washington was willing to help finance the development of Latin-American bases and certainly desired to use them in case of emergency, but jurisdiction was to remain with the home country. Sixteen Latin-American nations sanctioned the development in their territory of air and naval bases available to the forces of the United States. Of these the most important were those that guarded the Panama Canal and its approaches and the "bulge" of Brazil.[10]

Early in 1939 the United States initiated conversations with Panama concerning the enlargement of defense facilities in the Canal area, consisting largely of a number of sites outside the Canal Zone for the installation of air bases, searchlights, and aircraft detectors. Because of excessive demands by the Army for exclusive jurisdiction and long-term tenure of the bases, the negotiations lagged. Then in October, 1940, Arnulfo Arias succeeded to the presidency of the isthmian republic. Arias, suspected of pro-Nazi sympathies, made several financial and economic demands as conditions for further base rights. Although the State Department was prepared to pay an unreasonable price to preserve good will and cordial relations, the American military authorities objected and held that the request for base sites was legitimate under the terms of the treaty of 1936. The negotiations dragged on month after month. In the meantime, the State Department, under pressure of the military, and with the approval of President Roosevelt, secured permission for the United States military personnel to enter the desired base areas — seventy-one sites — the terms of occupancy to be determined later.

Fortunately for the United States, in October, 1941, President Arias was ousted and replaced by Ricardo Adolfo de la Guardia. Although the new Panama administration was more favorably disposed toward the United States, it was politically inexpedient to retreat from the position taken by the Arias

[9] William L. Langer and S. Everett Gleason, *The Undeclared War, 1940–1941* (New York: Harper & Brothers, 1953), 155–157.
[10] Conn and Fairchild, *op. cit.,* 237.

government. The bases agreements were finally signed on May 18, 1942, though not ratified by Panama until May 11, 1943. Fortunately, United States forces had been in occupation of the essential base sites since April, 1941.[11]

Next to Panama the most vital region to be defended in Latin America was the "bulge," or Natal, region of Brazil. Because it was only 1,900 miles from Africa, it was regarded as the one point of the hemisphere vulnerable to overseas attack or invasion. It was, in the view of the United States military, the pivotal point for hemisphere defense. But, despite the priority of Natal on the list of desired bases, it took nearly three years of delicate negotiations to secure Brazilian permission to station United States forces in the area.

Because of the known sensitivity of the Brazilian government on the matter of granting base rights to a foreign government, even though it be good friend and neighbor, a novel alternative was adopted. In June, 1940, President Roosevelt authorized the Army to use the Pan American Airways as a cover for the expansion of existing airfields and the construction of new ones in northern and northeastern Brazil. But when the airfields were nearing completion the Brazilian government was reluctant to allow United States military personnel to occupy them. For a while General Marshall, Chief of Staff, was seriously concerned that the partially developed and virtually unprotected airfields in Brazil would afford the Nazis a ready-made route to the Caribbean for an air invasion from Africa.

In July, 1941, a Joint United States-Brazilian Staff Conference worked out details of military collaboration. It was agreed that: (1) only Brazilian troops should be used on Brazilian territory; (2) in the event of a positive threat to its territory, Brazil might request aid of the United States; (3) Brazil would retain control of all bases, although they might be occupied by United States forces at Brazil's request; and (4) a Joint Planning Group should determine the nature and amount of aid to be given by the United States for the construction of bases. Brazilian national self-respect demanded that permission for the United States troops to enter the country should be withheld until an attack was actually impending.

Nevertheless, Brazil stood squarely on Pan American solidarity and cooperation with the United States. Foreign Minister Oswaldo Aranha declared that Brazil proposed to cooperate 100 per cent with the United States. In November, 1941, he said, "We were, are, and desire to be Pan Americans. We go along with America and will follow the destiny of America. We will not remain neutral if an American nation takes part in the war."[12]

In June, 1941, Brazil forbade the export of strategic materials to the Axis countries. On November 26, 1941, following the sinking of Brazilian ships by German submarines, the United States Navy was given permission to use Brazilian ports for patrol purposes. American aid was accepted to develop

[11] For the Panama base sites problem, see Almon R. Wright, "Defense Sites Negotiations Between the United States and Panama, 1936–1948," Dept. of State *Bulletin,* XXVII (August 11, 1952), 212–217. Also, see Langer and Gleason, *Undeclared War,* 610–615.

[12] For Brazil and defense of the "bulge," see *ibid.,* 515 ff., 600–605.

Natal and Maceió as bases for both countries. In order to give protection to the Surinam (Dutch Guiana) bauxite mines, so important to the United States aluminum industry, Brazil collaborated with the United States in the occupation of the Dutch colony in November, 1941.[13] This joint action was in pursuance of the no-transfer principle sanctioned by the Havana Meeting of Foreign Ministers in 1940.

The United States was not able to make base agreements with Mexico until after Pearl Harbor. Mexico had expressed a willingness to construct the necessary naval bases, particularly on the Pacific coast, and make them available cooperatively for continental defense, but only on condition that the United States assume the financial burden of such construction and that the Mexican flag continue to fly over the installations. This was not satisfactory to the United States Navy. The American government therefore decided, because of acute Mexican nationalism stimulated by the foreign petroleum properties expropriations, to let the matter rest until a more propitious time. On this, as on several other occasions, we note conflict between the extreme demands of the defense departments of the United States and restraint imposed by the State Department, always mindful of the Good Neighbor policy. However, on April 2, 1941, it was announced that a reciprocal air-transit agreement had been signed. This opened an overland air route to United States planes en route from the United States to Panama.[14]

The United States-Latin American military defense agreements contemplated rearmament programs supported by the American government. Although United States military planning assigned to Latin America only a limited role, it was necessary to furnish those nations with enough arms to maintain internal security and hold off external attacks until relief forces could arrive. Unfortunately it was impossible for the United States to fulfill these limited obligations. Not only were there inadequate arms reserves, but there was a legal problem which restricted the sales to surplus arms. On several occasions the Latins rejected offers of arms and equipment because they were not sufficiently attractive in type or price to justify purchase.[15]

The thorny problem of financing arms purchases by Latin America was solved by including the Latin-American nations under the terms of the Lend-Lease Act, approved on March 21, 1941. The Act permitted the release of any type of weapon, and thus ended the legal limitations on the arms supply to Latin America. On April 22, 1941, the Secretaries of State, War, and Navy recommended to the President that matériel be furnished the Latin-American states to the value of $400 million and that such matériel be provided by lend-lease. The President approved, and by the end of June the basic text of a lend-lease agreement with Latin America had been approved. Prior to Pearl Harbor the United States had negotiated lend-lease agreements with seven Latin-American governments (Bolivia, Brazil, Cuba, Dominican

[13] *Ibid.*, 602; Dozer, *op. cit.*, 80.
[14] Langer and Gleason, *Undeclared War,* 158–159, 605–607.
[15] Conn and Fairchild, *op. cit.*, 211.

Republic, Haiti, Nicaragua, and Paraguay), but relatively little equipment had been supplied because of acute shortages. In general, the record of arms supply to Latin America, from the summer of 1940 to December, 1941, was a story of good intentions, extensive planning, and refinement of policy by Army staff officers, but of almost no performance on the part of the United States; and on the part of the Latin Americans it is a story of exaggerated and frustrated hopes and of understandable irritation.[16] It was not until early 1943 that the United States could supply Latin America with an adequate amount of modern arms. But by that time the dangers of hemisphere invasion by the Nazis had ended.

A United States military-missions program in Latin America was vigorously promoted after 1939 to counter the Axis subversive threat and promote the consolidation and unification of continental defenses. Whereas the Latin-American states had been accustomed to draw heavily on Germany and Italy for their army and navy advisers, the trend after 1939 was the increase of United States missions and dismissal of the Axis missions. By Pearl Harbor all of the Axis missions had been eliminated.

Coupled with its missions program the United States opened its own training facilities to selected Latin-American service personnel. Also, Latin-American personnel participated in or observed military, air, and naval maneuvers; and high-ranking officers were brought to the United States on inspection tours.

On May 27, 1941, President Roosevelt proclaimed an unlimited national emergency and called for hemispheric solidarity and cooperation. Although there was a developing conviction in Latin America that a Hitler victory would be equivalent to an American defeat, public opinion was divided, as in the United States, into the "interventionists" and the "isolationists." Many favored a studiously neutral position. Others were skeptical of the wisdom of the United States policy of "undeclared war." The progressive abandonment of neutrality caused great apprehension. Some even charged that "what the United States calls an American interest is merely a United States interest."

Thus the call for a united front and solidary hemisphere resistance to Axis propaganda and subversion was challenged by Latin-American nationalism, regionalism, and neutralism. Pro-United States sentiment was strongest in Central America and the Caribbean where the countries were more likely to share the military consequences of United States policy. Several of the presidents of the Central American republics sent official messages of support and approval to President Roosevelt.

Believing that the fate of America seemed to be linked with that of the United States, Uruguayan Foreign Minister Alberto Guani, in June, 1941, proposed that all American governments adopt the policy of "friendly neutrality," that is, no American country which in defense of its own rights should find itself in a state of war with nations of other continents, would be treated as a belligerent. The United States and Brazil lent active support to

---

[16] *Ibid.,* 214; Langer and Gleason, *Undeclared War,* 517; Dozer, *op. cit.,* 81.

this proposal. But the general response was disappointing. The end result was that individual negotiations were necessary to secure port uses.[17] Thus, in the course of 1941, discussions and negotiations were conducted on this point, as has been indicated.

On July 17, 1941, President Roosevelt authorized the publication of "The Proclaimed List of Certain Blocked Neutrals." This "black list" denied the benefits of inter-American trade to individuals and companies who were undermining the peace and independence of the Western Hemisphere by serving Axis interests. It was primarily the responsibility of the Office of the Coordinator of Inter-American Affairs to compile the "black list" of Axis controlled firms and agencies and to persuade American firms not to trade with them.[18]

Economic defense[19]

Integral and essential features of the hemisphere economic defense structure were multilateral measures of economic defense and bilateral arrangements and activities initiated by the United States.

In the first category we note the creation, by the Panama Meeting of Foreign Ministers, of the Inter-American Financial and Economic Advisory Committee. The purpose of the Committee was "to establish a close and sincere cooperation between the American Republics in order that they may protect their economic and financial structure, maintain their fiscal equilibrium, safeguard the stability of their currencies, promote and expand their industries, intensify their agriculture, and develop their commerce." The Committee was authorized to provide for the interchange of information on financial and commercial problems. The functions of the Committee were extended and strengthened by the Havana Meeting of Foreign Ministers.

One of the projects inaugurated by the Inter-American Financial and Economic Advisory Committee (FEAC) was the establishment, in June, 1940, of the Inter-American Development Commission to aid, with mixed United States and Latin-American capital, the establishment of new lines of Latin-American production. In each of the American republics, affiliated National Development (*fomento*) Commissions were established.

The FEAC was also responsible for the creation of the Inter-American Maritime Technical Commission to assist in the more efficient use of merchant vessels in the Latin-American trade and other problems of shipping that assumed serious proportions after the outbreak of hostilities.

Finally, the FEAC undertook the study of commodities of which the American republics were important producers, in order to stabilize the market in a manner equitable to both producers and consumers. These efforts resulted in only one commodity agreement, the Inter-American Coffee Agreement of

[17] Langer and Gleason, *Undeclared War*, 598–599.
[18] Conn and Fairchild, *op. cit.*, 196.
[19] See Percy W. Bidwell, "Self-Containment and Hemisphere Defense," *The Annals* (November, 1941) 175–185; Guerrant, *op. cit.*, 160–170.

November 28, 1940. The coffee market of the United States was divided, and annual quotas were assigned to the fourteen coffee-producing American republics. An Inter-American Coffee Board was set up to administer the agreement.

Although the measures of inter-American economic cooperation for hemisphere defense were not without significance and importance, the United States economic program was far more important in bulwarking defense. In a speech at the Pan American Union, on April 14, 1939, President Roosevelt said that the United States would "give economic support, so that no American nation need surrender any fraction of its sovereign freedom to maintain its economic welfare." This meant that the President "realized that all hope of political solidarity would be illusory unless supported by adequate financial and trade arrangements."[20]

At the Panama Meeting of Foreign Ministers, which convened shortly after, Sumner Welles announced that the United States, in order to prevent economic dislocations, would expand shipping facilities and assist the Latin-American nations financially to develop new fields of production. President Roosevelt regarded economic assistance as merely supplementary to the measures of collaboration provided by other and earlier policies. He therefore secured an enlargement of the function of the Export-Import Bank to become a lender to Latin-American governments as well as to United States exporters.

The United States now began to offer loans[21] and other forms of economic aid. This was a transformation of the concept of reciprocity as a central idea of the Good Neighbor policy. It was changed from vague generalizations about a "two-way street" to concrete grants of economic assistance to accompany and support political collaboration; that is, the use of specific financial inducements to gain policy objectives. The Good Neighbor was taking on more and more the character of a security policy.[22] President Roosevelt believed that the kind of Latin-American collaboration that the United States sought for national defense could not be expected solely in response to the earlier Good Neighbor policy. Thus, it was not until late 1939 and early 1940 that economic assistance and support of Latin-American welfare became a feature of the Good Neighbor. At a press conference on January 12, 1940, President Roosevelt indicated a "new approach" to Latin-American problems, that is, a concern for the well-being of the people of Latin America.[23]

The policy of strengthening the economic base of the hemisphere followed a course generally similar to that of military cooperation. Even as the United States faced embarrassments in fulfilling its promises to arm Latin America,

---

[20] Langer and Gleason, *Undeclared War,* 208.

[21] As of December, 1941, the Exim Bank had loans or active undisbursed commitments in Latin America amounting to more than $300 million. Credits exceeding $130 million went to twelve Latin-American governments for the purchase of industrial and agricultural equipment and other purposes.

[22] Bryce Wood, *The Making of the Good Neighbor Policy* (New York: Columbia University Press, 1961), 312, 354.

[23] *Ibid.,* 359.

so it faced difficulties in translating into a concrete program of assistance the generous promises of President Roosevelt that the Latin Americans should suffer no economic privations because of their support of hemisphere solidarity. Although the United States accepted the obligation to replace the former overseas suppliers of Latin America, the adjustments and necessities of rearmament put much of what the Latins wanted in short supply. Nevertheless, in 1939–1940, the export trade of the United States with Latin America increased 50 per cent.

It was United States imports from Latin America that really boomed. Because of our defense program needs, the Latin Americans had no difficulty in disposing of most of their raw materials. In fact, various United States war agencies entered into agreements both to facilitate increased production, and by "preclusive contracts," to purchase the entire exportable surplus. For example, by the end of 1941, the Metals Reserve Company had acquired a virtual monopoly of strategic metal exports of Latin America. The United States government instructed its purchasing agents to give priority to Latin America when purchasing strategic and critical materials. In September, 1940, the lending authority of the Exim Bank was increased from $200 million to $700 million to enable it to assist in the development of the resources, the stabilization of the economies, and the orderly marketing of the products of the countries of the Western Hemisphere.[24]

Accompanying and supporting its hemisphere policies of military and economic defense, the United States promoted cultural relations with Latin America. To the activities of the State Department's Division of Cultural Relations was added the more elaborate program of the Office for the Coordination of Commercial and Cultural Relations between the American Republics. By executive order, on August 16, 1940, the agency, which was later known as the Office of the Coordinator of Inter-American Affairs, was created, with Nelson Rockefeller named as "Coordinator." The President directed the CIAA to promote "hemisphere defense, with particular reference to the commercial and cultural aspects of the problem."

In the purely cultural area the CIAA sent to Latin America archaeological expeditions, art exhibits, ballet, college glee clubs, and movie stars. It facilitated the exchange of "creative workers," and aided exhibits of Latin-American arts and crafts in the United States. It also stimulated the teaching of Latin-American studies in United States colleges and universities.

To combat the influence of German news services, radio broadcasts, moving pictures, and propaganda literature, the CIAA undertook the systematic dissemination by various media of communication of the truth about the hemisphere defense efforts of the United States.

In the economic area the Office of the Coordinator was primarily responsible, as we have already mentioned, for the compiling of the "black list." It joined hands with the Board of Economic Warfare to bolster the economies of the Latin-American countries, as well as to insure that the Axis did not get

[24] Mecham, *op. cit.,* 206; Dozer, *op. cit.,* 76.

any vital raw materials from Latin America. In November, 1941, the Rocke-feller agency was proposing to undertake $100 million in public works pro-grams in Latin America, including hospitals, housing, sanitation, water sys-tems, transportation, and communications facilities. Although CIAA was created as an emergency war agency, the Coordinator and his associates seemed to manifest as much interest in long-range projects looking toward improvement of conditions in the hemisphere as they were in those connected with the war effort. The Coordinator's Office was the principal agency of the Roosevelt administration which implemented the revised objective of the Good Neighbor policy to promote the *general welfare* of Latin America.[25]

2. The War Comes to the Americas, 1941–1945[26]

Pearl Harbor and the Rio meeting

Although war came to the Americas under shocking circumstances, its coming was not unexpected. The status of the United States as a "nonbel-ligerent" in an undeclared war was too delicate and precarious to be continued for long. Fortunately, war involvement found the American republics gen-erally prepared by political, military, and economic agreements to mount a common defense. But, probably even more important was the psychological factor of shock which, because of the perfidy of the Japanese attack on Pearl Harbor, awakened the Latin Americans to the terrible reality of the war and their own peril. Most of their earlier objections to defense understandings with the United States were soon dismissed in favor of a true continental solidarity.

The immediate Latin-American reaction to Pearl Harbor was impressive. By December 12 all nine of the Central American and island republics of the Caribbean had declared war on Japan, and before the end of December they had also declared war on Germany and Italy. On January 1, 1942, these same nine signed the United Nations Declaration. It is significant that, despite the condition of relative defenselessness of the United States following the Pearl Harbor attack, these countries followed the wounded giant into the war. They certainly were not fair-weather friends. Moreover, let us note that, in contrast to World War I, their decision now was one of their own making. They were no longer protectorates of the United States. These were remarkable demonstrations of sincere attachment to the principle of continen-tal solidarity.

By December 31, Colombia, Mexico, and Venezuela had severed diplo-matic relations with the Axis powers. Brazil, Ecuador, Paraguay, and Peru

---

[25] For cultural relations, see Dozer, *op. cit.*, 81–82; Guerrant, *op. cit.*, 115–128; *The Program of the Department of State in Cultural Relations*, Dept. of State Inter-American Series No. 19 (Washington, D.C., 1941); Donald W. Rowland, *History of the Office of the Coordinator of Inter-American Affairs: Historical Report on War Admin-istration* (Washington, D.C.: Government Printing Office, 1946), 3–10, 11 ff.

[26] See Mecham, *op. cit.*, Chap. VIII; Dozer, *op. cit.*, Chap. 4.

declared their solidarity with the United States, and Argentina, Bolivia, Chile, and Ecuador offered to regard the United States as a nonbelligerent, exempting it from the limitations that would otherwise be imposed upon it within their territories by their international obligations as neutrals.[27]

Responding to the initiative of the Chilean government, the Pan American Union called a Third Meeting of Ministers of Foreign Affairs of the American Republics which convened in Rio de Janeiro from January 15–28, 1942. In pursuance of the Havana Declaration of Reciprocal Assistance and Cooperation, which declared that aggression against one American state should be considered aggression against all, the consultative meeting was called to consider the situation and adopt suitable measures for continental defense.

The principal objective sought by the United States at this meeting was a resolution calling on all of the American governments to break diplomatic relations with the Axis powers. Declaration of war was not desired. In fact the United States feared that if these countries went ahead and declared war it might be difficult to defend them. Our interest was to deprive the Axis of opportunities to carry on their propaganda and subversive activities through their diplomatic missions. Under Secretary of State Sumner Welles, head of the United States delegation, urged a severing of relations by those countries that had not already taken such action so that "those republics engaged in war shall not be dealt a deadly thrust by the agents of the Axis ensconced upon the soil and enjoying the hospitality of others of the American republics."[28]

Although most of the delegations were agreeable to a strong resolution, Argentina and Chile held out for a mild formula which would not commit their governments to immediate action. The Chileans seemed to be concerned that a break in diplomatic relations with the Axis powers would expose their long and undefended coastline to Japanese attack.

The refusal of the Argentines to support a resolution that *required* a severance of diplomatic relations with the Axis was quite in keeping with their habitual attitude of indifference or even opposition to inter-American cooperation, that is, under United States leadership. On many occasions, in inter-American conferences, it had been necessary, because of the rule of unanimity, to water down resolutions and actions in order to secure Argentine consent. At Rio, however, it was more than the customary jealousy and resentment of the United States which was responsible for the refusal of the Argentine government to support a strong resolution calling for an immediate break in diplomatic relations with the Axis countries. The truth of the matter was that the Castillo government in Buenos Aires was actually pro-Nazi, and, as was later revealed by documentary evidence in the German archives, "pursued a policy of positive aid to the enemy."[29]

[27] Dozer, *op. cit.*, 115.

[28] U.S. Dept. of State *Bulletin*, VI, No. 134 (January 17, 1942), 60.

[29] U.S. Dept. of State, *Consultation Among the American Republics with Respect to the Argentine Situation,* Publication 2473 (Washington, D.C.: Government Printing Office, 1946), 1. (Cited hereinafter as the *Blue Book.*)

Since Sumner Welles insisted that no resolution on breaking diplomatic relations should be adopted without the concurrence of Argentina and Chile, a diluted resolution was finally adopted which merely "recommended" a break.

American public opinion greatly exaggerated the rift in continental solidarity because of the intransigence of Argentina and Chile at the Rio meeting; indeed, this consultative meeting resulted in a number of measures necessary for the defense of the hemisphere.[30] First, it created the Inter-American Defense Board, located in Washington, and composed of military personnel from each American republic to study and recommend measures for the defense of the Americas. Second, it established at Montevideo the Emergency Advisory Committee for Political Defense, composed of seven members, to study and coordinate defensive measures against Axis espionage, sabotage, and subversion. This committee, designed to combat the activities of non-American elements that were harmful to American security, proved to be probably the most active and valuable of the special inter-American war agencies. Third, the Inter-American Neutrality Committee, now that neutrality and its problems had been thrown into the discard, was converted into the Inter-American Juridical Committee. The revised committee was charged with the study of juridical problems relating to the war and the postwar settlement. Like its predecessor, the Juridical Committee was composed of seven members and had its permanent seat at Rio de Janeiro. Finally, the Rio meeting adopted a resolution which declared that an American state involved in war with a non-American state should not be considered a belligerent. These surely were encouraging evidences of a degree of inter-American solidarity, which, although somewhat short of the "one for all and all for one" principle as declared at Havana in 1940, nevertheless reassured the United States. The defense of the Americas became a relatively easy matter.

All of the Latin-American governments, except Argentina and Chile, in pursuance of the Rio resolution, immediately severed relations with Germany, Italy, and Japan. Then followed declarations of war: by Mexico and Brazil in May and August of 1942 respectively; and by Bolivia and Colombia in 1943. Chile severed relations with the Axis in 1943, and Argentina in 1944.

Secretary Hull took the position that the Rio recommendation really imposed an obligation on all American governments to sever relations with the Axis, and that those nations failing to comply were remiss in the observance of their inter-American obligations. He was particularly concerned that the Germans were making use of their embassies to operate a network of espionage, sabotage, and subversion. United States ships were being sunk by German submarines on information supplied by agents enjoying diplomatic immunity.

[30] *Final Act of the Third Meeting of Ministers of Foreign Affairs of the American Republics, Rio de Janeiro January 28, 1942,* in Dept. of State *Bulletin,* VI, No. 137 (February 7, 1942), 118–134.

Responding to United States pressure, Chile closed the Axis embassies and broke off relations on January 29, 1943, exactly one year after the Rio meeting. Another year elapsed before Argentina broke off diplomatic relations. The pro-Nazi Castillo government was overthrown in June, 1943, but contrary to general belief at the time, the military *coup d'état* which ushered in "the government of the Colonels" was no expression of disapproval of the pro-Nazi orientation of the Castillo government. Quite to the contrary, for the new military regime of General Pedro Ramírez reassured the Germans of its intention not to break relations and of its need of military equipment to support this position.[31] Of course Germany was prevented by the Allied blockade from giving any aid to the fascist-minded military leaders of the country. Eventually President Ramírez had to bend to United States pressure and, on January 26, 1944, broke relations with the Axis. This action proved to be more nominal than real, for Argentina continued to afford facilities for Axis espionage and subversion. This was because Ramírez himself was ousted by the more rabid pro-Nazi elements in the army who rendered the diplomatic break meaningless. The members of the Axis missions continued to enjoy ample opportunity to carry on activities injurious to Argentina's own neighbors. For this reason, all of the American governments except Bolivia, Chile, and Paraguay, seized advantage of the change in government in Buenos Aires to withhold recognition of General Edelmiro Farrell as president and Colonel Juan Perón as vice-president. Diplomatic quarantine proved to be unavailing in forcing any change in Argentine policy.

Inter-American defense cooperation

The inter-American system, originally formed to advance the peacetime collaboration of the American republics, was, after 1941, transformed into a war-making system for common defense. We note first collective actions of hemisphere defense in which the United States participated, then the measures and actions of the United States acting alone or on a bilateral basis.

The principal agency of military cooperation by the American republics acting collectively was the Inter-American Defense Board. The Board was created by the Rio de Janeiro Meeting of Foreign Ministers to study and recommend to the American governments the measures necessary for the defense of the continent. The proposal for the establishment of an inter-American defense board originated in the State Department, which believed that it was important from the political point of view to afford the American republics a channel through which they could voice their views and recommendations.[32]

The idea had been opposed by the defense departments, and particularly by Chief of Staff General George C. Marshall. Among the objections raised by the Army to a defense board were the following: it would be too large and unwieldly for effective action; the establishment of a board would be too

---

[31] *Blue Book,* 12.
[32] Conn and Fairchild, *op. cit.,* 194–200.

time-consuming in face of the need of immediate action; it would not be possible to discuss secret plans before so large a body; the board would lack authority to carry out its adopted measures; the board would absorb the time of high-caliber men needed for more pressing duties. The War Department feared that the Latin Americans would try to use the board to press their demands for United States arms.

The State Department countered with the argument that the existence of the defense board would impress upon the inter-American community the unitary character of its defense problems and thus would contribute to a strengthening of the spirit of cooperation. In the end the President decided with the State Department that the proposal should be submitted to the Rio meeting.

During the war most of the Latin-American nations were represented on the Board by their military, naval, and air attachés in Washington. A United States general officer served as Chairman of the Board.

Although the war contributions of the Inter-American Defense Board were limited because its actions were purely advisory and because the United States withheld from it so many of the cooperative measures, nevertheless the fact of its existence served a valuable purpose as a symbol of inter-American solidarity and military cooperation. It was important that the nonactive belligerents should feel that they too were concerned with the military decisions of the war.

Defense against subversion

Equally important as the inter-American reaction to the threats of Axis armed aggression was the defensive reaction against insidious propaganda, espionage, sabotage, and other forms of subversive activities. In the Panama meeting of 1939 a resolution was adopted which recommended that the respective governments take steps to eradicate the spread of doctrines dangerous to the inter-American democratic ideal. At the Havana meeting of 1940 several resolutions were adopted concerning subversive activities, and measures were recommended for their control. All of this culminated in the creating, by the Rio Meeting of Foreign Ministers in 1942, of the Emergency Advisory Committee for Political Defense (CPD).

The CPD, composed of seven members named by the governments of Argentina, Brazil, Chile, Mexico, the United States, Uruguay, and Venezuela, was permanently located at Montevideo under the chairmanship of the Uruguayan Minister of Foreign Affairs, Dr. Alberto Guani. Dr. Guani, a powerful personality, moulded the committee into one of the most active and valuable of the inter-American emergency war agencies.

It was the purpose and function of the CPD to study and recommend to the governments measures of political defense against the subversive activities of Axis agents. The numerous resolutions adopted by the CPD covered the following broad categories of subjects: registration, detention, and expulsion of dangerous aliens; control of the grant of citizenship to Axis nationals; the clandestine crossing of national boundaries; and propaganda, espionage, and sabotage.

Thanks to the efforts of the Committee for Political Defense, substantial progress was made by the American republics in uncovering and stamping out enemy activities at a time when the continent was believed to be threatened with invasion. To encourage the roundup of dangerous enemy aliens the United States agreed to remove them to this country for safekeeping.

Collective economic defense[33]

Finally, in our consideration of evidences of inter-American defense on a multilateral basis, we turn to economic collaboration. The Inter-American Financial and Economic Advisory Committee (FEAC), created by the Panama Meeting of Foreign Ministers in 1939, had been quite active, as we have noted, in strengthening the inter-American economic front in the pre-Pearl Harbor period. After Pearl Harbor it continued to be the principal agency for economic cooperation on the multilateral plane. New tasks were assigned the Committee by the Rio de Janeiro Meeting of Foreign Ministers. These included: production of strategic materials; support of the economy of the American republics; strengthening the Inter-American Development Commission; encouragement of capital investments in the American republics; organization and improvement of transportation facilities; and the severance of economic relations with the Axis countries.

The FEAC, a collective economic weapon, proved to be an effective instrument for the mobilization and development of the economic resources of the Americas. Secretary Hull declared that the activities of the Committee were an indispensable supplement to the war effort of the United States.

United States-Latin American bilateral cooperation

However important collective inter-American cooperation was to the successful prosecution of the war, of vastly greater importance were the bilateral undertakings by the United States with individual Latin-American countries. We discuss these not necessarily in order of their importance.

Immediately following the Pearl Harbor attack, the Army and Navy put the Rainbow 5 War Plan into operation. It provided, first, for the defense of the Western Hemisphere against military attack from the Old World; then, when the successful accomplishment of that task had been assured, American forces might engage in offensive operations against the aggressor nations. In the early weeks, military operations in Latin America loomed as a distinct possibility, but soon after early 1942 it became clear that no large-scale army expeditionary forces would be necessary to help defend Latin America from overseas attack. The United States was hopeful that, with our assistance, the Latins could assume the major burden of their own defense. Our assistance in various forms was generally directed to this end.

[33] Guerrant, *op. cit.,* 195–206; Mecham, *op. cit.,* 235–242.

Reciprocal defense pacts,[34] entailing all phases of military cooperation from joint operations by armed forces to the use of base sites, were concluded between the United States and the more strategically important nations, i.e., Mexico, Cuba, Panama, and Brazil. Less comprehensive agreements, many of which conveyed the use of base sites to the United States, were negotiated with other nations.

The United States-Mexican defense agreements not only provided for a Joint Mexican-United States Defense Commission to study problems relating to the defense of the two countries, but also opened up the territory and facilities of each nation to military use by the other. In addition, with small craft obtained from the United States, Mexico assisted in the submarine patrol of the Gulf of Mexico.

Cuba also granted the use of facilities to the United States, and with United States assistance participated in the antisubmarine patrol. By formal agreement, Cuba was brought into full cooperation with the United States under virtually the same conditions as those made with Mexico.

The agreements with Panama were, for obvious reasons, of the utmost importance. Immediately following Pearl Harbor, Panama generously offered the United States full military cooperation. Accordingly, agreements were entered into which greatly increased the amount of territory, granted in 1941, for various kinds of installations for the defense of the Canal. By the end of the war no less than 130 sites were being utilized for anti-aircraft gun implacements, searchlights and airplane detector stations, and auxiliary airfields.

Almost as important as our Panamanian agreements were cooperative military measures with Brazil. The strategic importance of the Brazilian "bulge" gave the South American giant a vital role in joint military planning and operations. The use of airfields on Brazilian territory to fly lend-lease planes from the United States to Africa and Europe was of incalculable value to the Allied cause. When the United States mounted its own African and Italian campaigns the Brazilian ferry route took on added importance.

In August, 1942, following Brazil's formal entry into the war, the Joint Brazil-United States Defense Commission was created to supervise their numerous cooperative military measures. One of the earliest and most pressing was the antisubmarine campaign and naval convoying. Brazil was assisted in meeting these responsibilities with United States arms, equipment, and small ships.

Except for Mexico, which sent an air squadron to the Pacific war theater, Brazil was the only Latin-American country whose forces participated in offensive combat operations overseas. An expeditionary force of division strength, trained, equipped, and transported by the United States, landed in Naples, Italy, in July, 1944. It saw combat under General Mark Clark until September. This was the first appearance of Latin-American combat troops in any overseas campaign.

In addition to the military agreements mentioned with Mexico, Cuba,

34 See Mecham, *op. cit.,* 218–222; Langer and Gleason, *op. cit.,* 596–617.

Panama, and Brazil, several minor agreements provided additional operational air and naval bases for use by the United States. Some were intended to support antisubmarine patrols; others to protect oil fields and refineries, particularly the oil-refining installations on the islands of Curaçao and Aruba; and others to protect both the Caribbean and Pacific approaches to the Panama Canal. A major addition to the defense perimeter was the acquisition from Ecuador of base rights in the Galápagos Islands.

In order to build up a defense pattern for the hemisphere, the United States continued in operation the system of armament assistance through lend-lease aid and Export-Import Bank loans, programs inaugurated before Pearl Harbor. Ostensibly the purpose of this assistance was to help the various nations arm and maintain forces to defend against aggression and protect vital installations. It must be conceded, however, that the United States hoped, through lend-lease, to bolster governments in power — including dictators — and thus diminish the likelihood of Axis-inspired revolutionary movements. Stability and order were prime necessities for the prosecution of the war.

During the first year of our active participation in the war, there was not a great deal that the United States could do about meeting the importunate demands of the Latin-American governments for more modern military equipment. Nevertheless the United States planned for future deliveries. Between August, 1941, and March, 1943, the Department of State negotiated basic lend-lease agreements with eighteen Latin-American countries, granting credits of more than $425 million. Optimistically the agreements contained clauses providing for immediate delivery. This proved to be impossible for about twelve months. The United States made no attempt to bargain reciprocal aid from Latin America. When in 1943, the arms production of the United States had attained a level that permitted larger deliveries to Latin America, the war outlook had so changed that the armament needs were no longer urgent. Consequently, in 1944, lend-lease aid was greatly reduced to all nations except the two active belligerents, Mexico and Brazil. The military cooperation of these two countries qualified them for special consideration in lend-lease aid.[35]

The total dollar value of lend-lease aid to Latin America during the war amounted to $459,422,000. Of this almost 75 per cent ($348 million) went to Brazil, principally to outfit an expeditionary force. The next largest sharers in lend-lease grants were Mexico ($38 million), Chile ($22 million), and Peru ($18 million).[36] Out of a total lend-lease disbursement of $42 billion, the Latin-American share was 1.1 per cent. It was United States policy to grant lend-lease aid to Latin America only in the form of military equipment and services. No civilian supplies of any kind were furnished under lend-lease. Nevertheless Latin America was the recipient of considerable economic assistance from the United States through other agencies, notably the Recon-

---

[35] Conn and Fairchild, *op. cit.,* 233, 236.
[36] U.S. Dept. of State, *Twenty-Third Report to Congress on Lend-Lease Operations,* Publication 2707 (Washington, 1946), 27.

struction Finance Corporation, the Export-Import Bank, and the Institute of Inter-American Affairs.

Economic defense: bilateral[37]

Subsidiaries of the Reconstruction Finance Corporation, i.e., the Metals Reserve Company, the Rubber Reserve Company, and Defense Supplies Corporation, organized in 1940 to procure and finance production of strategic materials in Latin America, continued after Pearl Harbor to negotiate procurement and other agreements with the important producing countries. The Commodities Credit Corporation, the Defense Surplus Corporation, and the Foreign Economic Administration also contracted procurement agreements.

These agreements, which covered a wide range of subjects, facilitated the supply to the United States of needed commodities and materials, and, in some instances, the entire production of strategic metals. Indeed, the United States depended heavily on Latin America for certain strategic materials and for other products in short supply. The effort put forth by the Latins in meeting these urgent demands was a considerable contribution to the war effort. From 1941 to 1945 Latin America sent over 50 per cent of its exports to the United States, and received from the United States more than 60 per cent of their imports. Whereas Latin-American trade with the United States was, in a technical sense, extraordinarily favorable, they could not cash in on it during the war. Economically they seemed to be losing much more to the United States than they were gaining.

By the end of the war the Latin-Americans had accumulated a vast reserve of unexpendable dollars, which unfortunately lost much of their value due to postwar inflation in the United States. This should not obscure the fact, however, that the United States during the war pursued a policy of economic assistance far beyond the normal and temporary needs of wartime allies. In short, the United States assistance program represented an extention of the general welfare idea which had been engrafted on the Good Neighbor policy.

Three weeks after Pearl Harbor the United States announced it would support the economic stability of the Latin-American republics by providing for their essential civilian needs "on the basis of equal and proportionate consideration with our own." This principle was actually applied to the allocation of scarce civilian materials. Nor did the United States shirk the obligation imposed by a resolution adopted by the Rio Meeting of Foreign Ministers which pledged the American nations to cooperative measures for the maintenance of their internal economies. At Rio de Janeiro Under Secretary Sumner Welles declared that the United States stood ready "to render financial and technical assistance, where needed, to alleviate injury to the domestic economy of any of the American republics."

A year later in January, 1943, Mr. Welles, reviewing the last ten years of the Good Neighbor policy, said that "this government reflects in its foreign policy the objective of its domestic policy, namely, improvement in

[37] Mecham, *op. cit.,* 237–242.

the *standard of living* in which all elements will participate, particularly those heretofore ill-clothed, badly housed, and poorly fed."[38]

In pursuance of this philosophy, the procurement agreements and contracts contained "labor clauses" which provided that contractors should be required to abide by all local laws for the benefit of labor. The agency most active in promoting the welfare aspects of the Good Neighbor policy was the Office of the Coordinator of Inter-American Affairs. The operations of the CIAA, too elaborate for detailed description here, represented both short-term and temporary projects directly connected with the war, and long-term development and welfare promotion quite unrelated to the war. Activities belonging to either or both of these categories included the following: commercial, financial, and economic development activities; transportation; press and publications; radio and motion picture operations; information services; and cultural and educational activities. Not only did the Office of the Coordinator of Inter-American Affairs virtually pre-empt the cultural relations activities formerly belonging to the Division of Cultural Relations of the State Department, but the Coordinator himself became a sort of Secretary of State for Latin America.

A subsidiary of the CIAA, the Institute of Inter-American Affairs was created in March, 1942, to promote technical programs and projects for health, sanitation, and food supply. These operations, carried out under cooperative agreements with the other American republics, set up agencies called *servicios* within the appropriate ministries of the host country. The *servicio* represented both the Institute of Inter-American Affairs and the home government. The specific programs were carried out by field parties of the Institute working through the *servicio*. Technical assistance in Latin America antedated by several years the famous "Point Four" program of President Truman.[39]

In addition to the agencies and procedures already mentioned for aiding the essential needs of the Latin-American nations, there were general agreements for cooperation in a wide range of activities. One with Brazil provided for "a program for the mobilization of the productive resources of Brazil" and for a line of credit of $100 million to be made available by the Exim Bank. Probably the most important of these cooperative agreements was the one with Mexico, dated April 30, 1943. It created a Joint Mexican-American Commission for Economic Cooperation to study and make recommendations for joint action by the two countries on pressing economic problems. Probably Mexico's most pressing problem was an unbalanced economy, which of course was typical of most of Latin America. But due to the activities of the Commission, and a special interest of the United States government in maintaining the Mexican economy on an even keel, practically all materials and equipment required by projects recommended by the Commission were given clearance and made available by the United

[38] U.S. Dept. of State *Bulletin,* VIII (January 2, 1943), 6.
[39] See Rowland, *op. cit.,* 234–235.

States. According to President Roosevelt (February 20, 1944), "Although in 1943 and 1944 the industry of the United States, through conversion and expansion, was primarily engaged in the production of war materials, it was nevertheless possible to make available and supply to Mexico for its consumption needs and the maintenance of its economy more products in those years than during any similar period of time in the trade between the two countries."[40] There certainly can be little doubt that the United States responded to the limits of its ability to maintain the internal economies of its Latin-American allies.

[40] Mecham, *op. cit.,* 240.

SUPPLEMENTARY READING

Bemis, Samuel Flagg, *The Latin American Policy of the United States* (New York: Harcourt, Brace and Company, 1943), 362–382.

Conn, Stetson, and Fairchild, Byron, *The Framework of Hemisphere Defense. The United States Army in World War II: The Western Hemisphere* (Washington, D.C.: Government Printing Office, 1960).

Dozer, Donald M., *Are We Good Neighbors?* (Gainesville: University of Florida Press, 1959), Chaps. III, IV.

Guerrant, Edward O., *Roosevelt's Good Neighbor Policy* (Albuquerque: University of New Mexico Press, 1950), 135–213.

Langer, William L., and Gleason, S. Everett, *The Undeclared War, 1940–1941* (New York: Harper & Brothers, 1953), 147–175.

Lieuwen, Edwin, *Arms and Politics in Latin America* (New York: Frederick A. Praeger, rev. ed., 1961), 188–195.

Logan, John A., *No Transfer. An American Security Principle* (New Haven: Yale University Press, 1961), Chaps. X–XIV.

Manger, William, *The War and the Americas* (Washington, D.C., Pan American Union, 1944).

Mecham, J. Lloyd, *The United States and Inter-American Security, 1889–1960* (Austin: University of Texas Press, 1961), Chaps. VII, VIII.

Rowland, Donald W., *History of the Office of the Coordinator of Inter-American Affairs.* (Historical Report on War Administration, Washington, D.C.: Government Printing Office, 1946).

Wood, Bryce, *The Making of the Good Neighbor Policy* (New York: Columbia University Press, 1961), 285–363.

7

Perfecting the Inter-American System, 1945–1948

1. Integration of the Inter-American Security System into the United Nations[1]

Latin-American discontent

The fact that after the meeting of the Foreign Ministers at Rio de Janeiro in January, 1942, the American republics were not assembled again in any general conference until the ebb days of the war in 1945, occasioned great and justifiable concern to the Latin members of the inter-American system, for they feared that the United States was growing lukewarm in its support of hemispheric regionalism. The failure to convene a conference was due not to the absence of problems vital to the inter-American community, but rather to the opposition of the United States itself. In the State Department were strong divergencies of opinion, represented respectively by Sumner Welles and Cordell Hull, concerning the postwar status of the inter-American system in a new global organization which was abuilding. Secretary Hull, who inclined to the concept of a general international security organization, preferred to remain free of further inter-American commitments which might compromise the effectiveness of the global organization. It was largely for this reason, therefore, that the State Department turned a deaf ear to repeated suggestions by the Latins that the time for the next inter-American conference was long overdue.

[1] See J. Lloyd Mecham, *The United States and Inter-American Security, 1889–1960* (Austin: University of Texas Press, 1961), Chap. IX.

156

Uppermost in the minds of the Latin Americans was the prospective status of regional arrangements, such as the inter-American system, in the future general international organization. It is an interesting fact that, immediately after the outbreak of World War II, and even before our own entry into the war, serious studies were undertaken under both official and private auspices, of an international security organization to succeed the defunct League of Nations. After Pearl Harbor a Division of Political Studies was set up in the State Department to draft a model project for a global organization of united nations. In view of these preparations the Latins were eager for an opportunity to confer and express collectively their ideas concerning the nature of the future world organization and particularly the safeguarding of the autonomous character of their own regional system. Enough information concerning the apparent ascendancy of the global concept had trickled from the State Department to warrant Latin-American concern.

That Latin America, after 1943, became the champion of hemispheric regionalism, in apparent opposition to the position of the United States government itself, is a historical phenomenon worth noting. In earlier years, especially in the 1920's, it was the Latin-American countries who had dragged their feet in the development of a really effective hemisphere organization; they had branded the existing system as merely an artifical association "made in the U.S.A." to serve the purposes of that country only. But in the intervening years, with the liquidation of American imperialism in the Caribbean and Central America, the renunciation of the right of intervention, and the adoption of the Good Neighbor policy, the inter-American system became a cherished possession belonging to all of the American nations. Not only did the hemispheric security arrangement enjoy the enthusiastic support of its Latin-American members, but, as the world's oldest and most advanced regional system, it had acquired status and respect in the international community. It was logical therefore to expect that a way would be found to reconcile regionalism and globalism within the new organization of United Nations. Sumner Welles expressed this expectation, when, in a speech on May 30, 1942, he said of the inter-American system, "It should constitute a cornerstone in the world structure of the future."[2]

On this, as on many other matters relating to Latin America, Secretary Hull differed from Mr. Welles. Not only did the Secretary of State strongly favor the powerful global international organization, with regional arrangements distinctly subordinated to it, but he insisted that a conference with the Latin Americans on this subject be delayed until after the great powers had agreed on the general blueprint of a world organization. Accordingly, consent to an inter-American conference was withheld until after the Moscow meeting of the Big Four Foreign Ministers in November, 1943, and the Dumbarton Oaks conference in August-October, 1944.

Following their meeting in Moscow, the Foreign Ministers of the United States, the United Kingdom, the Soviet Union, and China, issued on October

[2] *Vital Speeches of the Day* (New York: City News Publishing Co., 1942), VIII, No. 17, 514–516.

30, 1943, a Declaration on General Security. They jointly declared that "they recognize the necessity of establishing at the earliest practicable date a general international organization, based on the principle of the sovereign equality of all peace-loving states, and open to membership by all such states, large and small, for the maintenance of international peace and security." Nothing was said about regional security organizations in the declaration, and, according to Mr. Hull in his *Memoirs,* he strongly argued against them in the discussions at Moscow.[3]

Cordell Hull's opposition to regionalism was kept secret, even though his inadvertence put him in an equivocal position. Following his return from Moscow he said in a speech before the United States Congress: "There will no longer be need for spheres of influence, for alliances, for balance of power, or any other of the special arrangements through which, in the unhappy past, the nations strove to safeguard their security or to promote their interests."[4] Clearly the inter-American system fell in the category of "special arrangements" indicted by the Secretary; at least this was the belief of Latin-American diplomats and many others who analyzed his speech. In view of his later admission in the matter, Mr. Hull was less than frank when he denied, in November, 1943, that he intended to include the inter-American system in his remarks.

Although there were feeble attempts by high officials of the State Department to reassure the Latin-American diplomats in Washington who were concerned over the prospective fate of the inter-American system, there was no weakening of opposition by the United States government to a consultative meeting of the Foreign Ministers of the American republics. Mr. Hull felt himself bound by the Moscow Declaration to withhold discussion of an international organization with the smaller powers until after the big powers had agreed on a draft project.

Eventually representatives of the Big Four — the United States, Great Britain, the Soviet Union, and China — joined later by France — met at Dumbarton Oaks in Washington on August 21, 1944, to draw up a project of a world organization. On October 7 they signed the Dumbarton Oaks Proposals for the Establishment of a General International Organization, a document which embodied the basic features of the kind of international organization which the Big Five had agreed to sponsor.

At the Dumbarton Oaks Conference, the United States took the initiative in proposing that regional arrangements be subordinated to the general security organization, and the other four powers supported that position; this idea was formalized in the Dumbarton Oaks *Proposals.*[5] The section which dealt with regional arrangements provided that, although regional security arrangements are consistent with the purposes and principles of the international organization, no enforcement action should be taken by the regional

[3] Cordell Hull, *The Memoirs of Cordell Hull* (2 vols. New York: The Macmillan Company, 1948), II, 1647.

[4] *New York Times,* November 19, 1943.

[5] See Durward V. Sandifer, "Regional Aspects of the Dumbarton Oaks Proposals," Dept. of State *Bulletin,* XII, No. 292 (January 28, 1945), 145–147.

agency unless authorized by the Security Council of the general organization. In short, no enforcement action could be taken by a regional agency without authorization by the global body. This would mean the end of the inter-⮪ American system's autonomy.

Mr. Hull and Under Secretary of State Edward R. Stettinius, Jr., failed to convince the Latin Americans that the position and responsibilities of the inter-American system would actually be enhanced by the Dumbarton Oaks *Proposals*. Believing that their purposes could be better achieved through concerted action, the Latins once more urged that a consultative meeting of their foreign ministers be called to consider the participation of the Americas in the future world organization. An additional reason for an immediate conference, they felt, was the urgency of dealing with postwar economic problems.

The Latin Americans were fearful of the economic consequences of the peace. As the end of the war approached, reconversion to peacetime economic relations presented serious problems of readjustment. Two questions that beset both governments and businessmen were: What will be done with the millions of men who lose their jobs with the advent of peace? and, How will readjustment of raw materials be made upon termination of the requirements of war industries? The end of the war would bring not only a drastic reduction and eventual termination of war-created demand for raw materials, but the revival of foreign industrial competition as well. Latin America believed that an inter-American conference could not meet too soon to attack these postwar economic problems, which, incidentally, depended largely for their solution on the United States.

But, even after the State Department had acquiesced in the demands for an inter-American conference, the attitude of Argentina contributed to further delay. The Farrell-Perón regime, although denied recognition by the inter-American community, continued by word and action to manifest sympathy with the Axis nations. It not only afforded facilities for enemy espionage and subversion, but openly adhered to the totalitarian philosophy of government. The Argentine government left little doubt that it had repudiated the principles upon which the inter-American system was based. Said Secretary Hull, "The whole moral foundation and splendid structure of hemispheric cooperation had been undermined and seriously impaired by Argentina's desertion."[6] Under these circumstances Argentina's participation in an inter-American conference on the problems of war and peace was too disagreeable for Mr. Hull to stomach.

The Mexico City conference

Eventually an escape from the dilemma was contrived by limiting the proposed conference to those American nations that had cooperated in the war effort, and so had earned the right to consider American problems arising out of the war as well as the proposed United Nations organization. With Argentina excluded by this procedural device, the Inter-American Conference

[6] Hull, *Memoirs,* II, 1404.

on the Problems of War and Peace convened in Mexico City from February 21
to March 8, 1945.

Since the war was in its final phase at the time of the Mexico City conference there were no "war" measures of any great importance to be considered.
There were, however, other important items on the conference agenda: international organization, postwar economic cooperation, and the Argentine
question.[7]

With respect to the Dumbarton Oaks *Proposals,* the Latin-American delegation sought a declaration favoring autonomous status for the inter-American
system. Since the new Secretary of State Stettinius objected, it was decided
that there would be no resolution on regional arrangements, but that individual countries might make their own "observations" to be submitted in a
comprehensive report to the San Francisco conference. It was clear from
these "observations" that the Latin-American countries were unalterably committed to their regional security system and insisted that it be given priority
in the settlement of hemisphere disputes.

The Latin-American delegations well understood, however, that merely
to oppose the Dumbarton Oaks *Proposals* on regional arrangements was not
enough; they had to demonstrate that the inter-American security system was
fully competent in organization and functions to meet the responsibilities of an
effective autonomous regional agency. Therefore, the conference adopted a
resolution entitled "Reorganization, Consolidation, and Strengthening of the
Inter-American System."[8] Changes to be effective immediately included
annual meetings of the Foreign Ministers, quadrennial general conferences,
annual election of the Chairman of the Governing Board, a ten-year term for
the Director-General, and, most significantly, enlarged functions and broader
powers to the Pan American Union and the Governing Board. The Governing
Board was now to take action "on every matter that affects the effective
functioning of the inter-American system and the solidarity and general welfare of the American Republics." This specific validation of political functions
by the Union and its Governing Board, which reversed the action by the
Havana conference in 1928, was extremely significant in that, while seeming
to banish old-time fears of United States dominance of the Pan American
Union, it opened up for that agency new opportunities to serve the Americas
in a security capacity.[9]

---

[7] See Dana G. Munro, "The Mexico City Conference and the Inter-American System,"
Dept. of State *Bulletin,* XII, No. 301 (April 1, 1945), 525–530; Manuel S. Canyes,
"The Inter-American System and the Conference of Chapultepec," *American Journal of
International Law,* XXXIX, No. 3 (July, 1945), 504–517.

[8] For acts of the Mexico City Conference, see *Report Submitted to the Governing
Board of the Pan American Union by the Director General, Inter-American Conference
on Problems of War and Peace, Mexico City, February 21–March 8, 1945* (Washington, D.C.: Pan American Union, 1945); U.S. Dept. of State, *Report of the Delegation
of the United States of America to the Inter-American Conference on Problems of War
and Peace, Mexico City, Mexico, February 21–March 8, 1945* (Washington, D.C.:
Government Printing Office, 1945).

[9] According to our former Ambassador to the OAS, John C. Dreier in *The Organiza-*

In order to provide a comprehensive charter for the inter-American system, the Governing Board of the Pan American Union was instructed to prepare a draft to be submitted to the next general conference to be held at Bogotá in 1946. It was felt that the time had arrived to put the regional system on a permanent treaty basis. The added strength and dignity that this would bring would enhance the claims to regional autonomy under the aegis of a general international organization.

It was, however, the adoption of the Act of Chapultepec by the Mexico City conference, that contributed most to the strengthening of the inter-American security system. The Act declared that "every attack of a State against the integrity or the inviolability of the territory, or against the sovereignty or political independence of an American State, shall . . . be considered an act of aggression against the other states," and in case of an act of aggression "the States signatory to this Act will consult among themselves in order to agree upon measures" ranging from the breaking of diplomatic and economic relations to the actual use of armed force to stop the aggression. This was the first time an inter-American agreement provided for the use of armed force as a sanction. The Act was to be effective however, only during World War II. A permanent treaty incorporating its general principles was to be negotiated immediately following the establishment of peace.

In order to reconcile the very apparent conflict between the Act of Chapultepec and the Dumbarton Oaks *Proposals* on regionalism, Secretary Stettinius insisted on a clause which declared that the Act was in harmony with the general international organization-to-be. He seemed to feel bound by agreements reached at Dumbarton Oaks and Yalta, which meant plainly that no security action could be taken by a regional agency without approval by the Security Council, and this approval could be denied by the vote of one of the Great Powers.[10]

It is most surprising how far the State Department was willing to go in order to secure the "cooperation" of Premier Joseph Stalin. As a result, the strange conflict between the United States and the Latin-American governments concerning the future of their regional arrangement had to await the San Francisco conference for solution.

To the Latin-American delegations at the Mexico City conference, important as were the problems of postwar security organization, equally important were those of postwar economic cooperation. Their greatest concern was the economic consequences of an abrupt termination by the United States, with the advent of peace, of its procurement contracts for strategic materials. To allay these fears the United States supported a resolution which provided in general for a "tapering off" of continued buying of strategic raw materials. Adequate notice of curtailment or termination of procurement

---

tion of American States (New York: Harper & Row, 1962), 122–123, the political functions of the Council derive principally from the Rio treaty. The member governments are timid toward the assumption of authority by the Council.

[10] *Inter-American Conference on Problems of War and Peace,* 6.

contracts was pledged. Thanks in part to this pledge by the United States there was no serious economic dislocation in Latin America caused by change from a war to a peacetime economy.

But, with respect to meeting Latin America's need for long-range economic development, we can only record that, at the Mexico City conference the United States lent its voice to glowing generalities, but withheld its support of concrete programs. It cannot be said therefore, that from the Latin American's point of view, the economic actions of the conference were encouraging. The seeds of discontent were being planted.

Before adjournment the Mexico City conference had to take notice of the Argentine problem. Indeed, a solution had been prearranged. Accordingly, a resolution was adopted which provided that if Argentina accepted the acts of the Mexico City conference, all would be forgiven. Since the American republics, even including the United States, seemed to be self-conscious about Argentina's absence from the conference, and were solicitous of her return, it is not surprising that the wayward nation consented to return to the fold. Thus, on March 27 the Argentine government announced its adherence to the actions of the Mexico City conference, and, in order to qualify for participation in the United Nations conference at San Francisco, declared war on the Axis countries. Needless to say, Argentine compliance with the Mexico City resolution was purely opportunistic, a fact which was soon proved by subsequent developments.

The San Francisco conference[11]

The United Nations Conference on International Organization met in San Francisco from April 25 to June 26, 1945, "to prepare a charter for a general international organization for the maintenance of international peace and security." The basis for the discussions was the Dumbarton Oaks *Proposals*. Invitations to the conference were extended only to those countries that had declared war on the Axis by March 1, 1945. Of the seven Latin-American countries that had not yet declared war, six qualified by the end of February. This left the seventh, Argentina, which declared war on March 27, nearly four weeks after the March 1st deadline. Argentina's admission was now contingent on Soviet approval. Since the United States had pledged itself, at Mexico City, to support Argentina's membership in the United Nations conference, and since at Yalta it had pledged two additional seats to Russia in the General Assembly, Mr. Stettinius marshalled Latin-American support to secure Russian consent to Argentina's admission in return for their consent to the admission of White Russia and the Ukraine.

The unpalatable position occupied by the United States delegation at San Francisco, arguing and bargaining on the one hand in behalf of a pro-Nazi

[11] See *The United Nations in the Making: Basic Documents* (Boston: World Peace Foundation, 1945); *The United Nations Conference on International Organization, San Francisco, April 25 to June 26, 1945: Selected Documents*, Dept. of State Publication 2490 (Washington, D.C.: Government Printing Office, 1946).

and obstructionist dictatorial regime in Buenos Aires, and on the other, for unequal representation for the Soviet totalitarian colossus, represented American diplomacy at its nadir. These maneuvers, however, were only preliminary to the real issue — the position of the inter-American system in the world organization.

The principal discussions at the conference on regional arrangements took place in a subcommittee of which Dr. Alberto Lleras Camargo of Colombia was chairman, and on which Senator Arthur Vandenberg was the United States member. The fact that the Senator was sympathetic to the principle of regional autonomy was significant. Thus, when an impasse developed between the regionalists and the universalists, it was Senator Vandenberg who offered a compromise plan which broke the logjam. The Vandenberg formula was, simply, that nations have an inherent right of self-defense, and in the event of an attack on any one of a group having a tradition of mutual assistance, then the states may take concerted action against an attack on any one of them. This does not, however, deny to the Security Council the right to take any action it deems necessary to preserve peace and security.[12]

The Vandenberg compromise plan became the basis of Article 51 of the UN Charter, which provided:

> Nothing in the present Charter shall impair the inherent right of individual or collective self-defense if an armed attack occurs against a member of the United Nations, until the Security Council has taken the measures necessary to maintain international peace and security. Measures taken by members in the exercise of this right of self-defense shall be immediately reported to the Security Council and shall not in any way affect the authority and responsibility of the Security Council under the present Charter to take any action as it deems necessary in order to maintain or restore international peace and security.

The chapter on regional arrangements in the Charter followed substantially the general terms of the Dumbarton Oaks *Proposals,* although there were certain modifications to reconcile them with the sense of Article 51. We are now in position to note the nature and extent of the so-called integration of regional arrangements, including the inter-American system, into the United Nations.[13]

Regional arrangements are recognized not only as being compatible with the UN, but as being peculiarly appropriate for regional action in the settlement of local disputes. But, although regional systems have primary respon-

---

[12] Arthur H. Vandenberg, Jr., ed., *The Private Papers of Senator Vandenberg* (Boston: Houghton Mifflin Company, 1952), 188–189.

[13] See Josef L. Kunz, "The Inter-American System and the United Nations Organization," *American Journal of International Law,* XXXIX, No. 46 (October, 1945), 758–767; J. Lloyd Mecham, "The Integration of the Inter-American Security System into the United Nations," *The Journal of Politics,* IX, No. 2 (May, 1947), 193–196; Manuel Canyes, *The Organization of American States and the United Nations* (Washington, D.C.: Pan American Union, 1960).

sibility to seek pacific settlement of disputes among their members, and every opportunity should be given to them to settle local disputes, the Security Council reserves the right to step in at any time. Also, any member of a regional system has the right to bypass its own agency and carry its dispute to the Security Council itself. However, with respect to the inter-American system, there seems to have been an understanding at San Francisco, from which a body of precedent has developed, that the UN will defer to inter-American action pending proof of the regional system's inability to act.

As for the right of the American states to take collective measures of self-defense in the event of overseas attack, under the Act of Chapultepec and the Rio Treaty of Reciprocal Assistance (1947), the contracting states are free to meet their mutual security obligations, provided only that their action is reported to the Security Council. Thus, the threat that a veto in the Security Council could prevent regional action against aggression was removed. It was by such understandings and their interpretation that the autonomous nature of the inter-American system was preserved, and its integration into the United Nations was accomplished.

2. Strengthening the Security Structure[14]

The Rio de Janeiro conference

When the Act of Chapultepec was signed in 1945 it was understood that it was to be effective only during World War II, and that immediately after the peace a treaty should be negotiated formalizing its principles. At San Francisco Secretary of State Stettinius, in order to get Latin-American support for the Vandenberg formula, agreed to the calling of an inter-American conference at the earliest possible date in order to conclude a regional defense treaty which would include the basic principles of the Act of Chapultepec, and be integrated into the security framework of the United Nations.

It developed that, despite the sincere intentions of the United States, the conference which was originally scheduled to meet at Rio de Janeiro in October, 1945, was postponed several times over a period of two years. Question: Why the delay? Answer: The perennial Argentine problem.

Although Argentina had, at the eleventh hour plus, declared war on the Axis powers in order to qualify for the San Francisco conference, it soon became evident that her belligerency status was purely *pro forma,* for she failed to fulfill the obligations assumed by her adherence to the acts of the Mexico City conference. This fact, plus the evidence that the Buenos Aires regime was operating in frank repudiation or violation of the principles on which the inter-American system was founded, made Argentine participation in the negotiation of a mutual security pact a travesty. It was for these reasons that the United States government urged delay of the conference. Unfortunately the Latins did not share the American point of view and

[14] Mecham, *The United States and Inter-American Security,* Chap. X.

revealed a strong inclination to accept the Perón regime as compatible with continental peace and solidarity. To them, since unity was impossible without Argentina, it was certainly worth the sacrifice of democratic principles. On this issue, as on so many similar ones, like the later problem of Castro's Cuba, the Latins preferred to view United States opposition to the Perón regime as a purely two-sided quarrel in which the other countries were not involved.

The United States finally decided that the urgency of a hemisphere defense pact outweighed the issue of Argentine participation and consented to the calling of a conference at Rio de Janeiro in August, 1947. This belated decision to forego further opposition to the Argentine dictator, with whom in fact "good relations" were restored, was due to the heightening of East-West tensions into what became known as the "Cold War."

Mutual security pacts usually have specific objectives in that they respond to more or less clearly defined threats. As far as the United States was concerned, meeting the threat of international Communism was the more immediate and specific objective of a hemisphere mutual security pact. As for the Latin-American nations, fear of the U.S.S.R. was hardly present in their desire to formalize in a treaty the principles of the Act of Chapultepec. They were desirous simply of strengthening the inter-American system so as to enable it to discharge more efficiently its responsibilities as a regional arrangement under the United Nations.

The Inter-American Conference for the Maintenance of Continental Peace and Security met on August 15, 1947, at Quitandinha, a resort hotel near Petropolis in the state of Rio de Janeiro. Since the sole purpose of the conference was "to give permanent form to the principles embodied in the Act of Chapultepec," it was able to act with expedition, and on September 2, 1947, the Inter-American Treaty of Reciprocal Assistance, or Rio treaty, was signed.[15]

The Rio treaty is, in a very real sense, the capstone of the inter-American security structure. A pact of mutual assistance, it formalizes the obligation of continental solidarity in face of aggression and threats to the peace. It also reconciles a regional pact of self-defense with the obligations assumed by the American nations under the United Nations Charter. Because of its great importance in inter-American relations, since the date of its ratification in 1948, a detailed analysis of the Rio de Janeiro Inter-American Treaty of Reciprocal Assistance seems to be in order.

First, in case of an *armed attack* by any state (continental or extraconti-

[15] For acts of the Rio de Janeiro Conference, see Pan American Union, *Inter-American Conference for the Maintenance of Continental Peace and Security, Rio de Janeiro, August 15–September 2, 1947; Report on the Results of the Conference by the Director General* (Washington, D.C.: Pan American Union, 1947); U.S. Dept. of State, *Report of the Delegation of the United States of America, Inter-American Conference for the Maintenance of Continental Peace and Security, Quitandinha, Brazil, August 15–September 2, 1947*, Publication No. 3016 (Washington, D.C.: Government Printing Office, 1948).

nental) against an American state, each one of the contracting states undertakes voluntarily to assist individually in meeting the attack. The nature of the assistance to be rendered collectively — including recall of chiefs of diplomatic missions, breaking of diplomatic and/or consular relations, economic sanctions, and armed force — is to be determined by consultation. The Governing Board of the Pan American Union, converted into the Council of the OAS in 1948, may act in an emergency as a provisional Organ of Consultation, and the Meeting of Ministers of Foreign Affairs acts as the regular Organ of Consultation.

Second, the degree of obligation to assist the victim of armed aggression is conditioned by the locality of the attack. If the attack takes place on the overseas possessions or forces of an American state outside the Western Hemisphere as defined in Article 4 by lines of latitude and longitude, assistance by individual states will be withheld until the Organ of Consultation can meet. Otherwise the obligation to assist the victim of attack by collective measures determined in consultation remains the same without reference to the locale of the attack.

Third, in the event of other forms of aggression that are not armed attack, or any other fact or situation that might endanger the peace of America, the Organ of Consultation shall meet to agree on measures to be taken.

Fourth, the decisions of the Organ of Consultation shall be by two-thirds vote of the ratifying states. This includes the imposing of sanctions, with the sole exception that no state shall be required to use armed force without its own consent. The treaty establishes no form of military cooperation or organization of military forces under collective command.[16]

Fifth, the Rio treaty, in a number of references to the United Nations, sought to leave no doubt that this regional security arrangement was fully compatible with the Charter of the United Nations. It declared that the obligation to assist the victim of aggression was an exercise of the inherent right of self-defense recognized by Article 51 of the Charter. These measures of self-defense "may be taken until the Security Council of the United Nations has taken the measures necessary to maintain international peace and security." Complete reports on these activities, in exercise of the right of self-defense, shall be sent to the Security Council.

The Rio treaty was the first treaty of collective self-defense to be concluded under Article 51 of the United Nations Charter. In reconciling defensive alliance with the obligations of United Nations membership, the Rio treaty was destined to serve as a model for the North Atlantic Treaty (NATO) and similar pacts. Viewed as a regional arrangement, it represented inter-American security cooperation at the highest level of practical achievement. It added inestimable strength to the hemisphere security structure. Also, from the point of view of the United States, the Rio treaty served our policy objectives well in that: (1) it made it possible, as will be indicated later, to confine

---

[16] This is in marked contrast to both the United Nations and NATO. For analysis of the Rio treaty, see Dreier, *op. cit.,* 23–30.

the solution of intra-American conflicts to the nations of the hemisphere, and thus avoid any pretext for UN or non-American intervention, and (2) it organized inter-American resistance to the aggressions of international Communism.

The Bogotá conference[17]

In order to meet the responsibilities of a regional security arrangement under the United Nations, the American republics decided at the Mexico City conference that the inter-American system would be finally and permanently founded on three great acts: (1) a treaty of reciprocal assistance; (2) a charter of the organization of American states; and (3) a comprehensive treaty on pacific settlement. The adoption of the Rio Inter-American Treaty of Reciprocal Assistance discharged the first responsibility. A principal objective of the Ninth International Conference of American States, which met at Bogotá, Colombia, March 30, 1948, was to adopt the other two treaties: the Charter of the Organization of American States, and the Treaty on Pacific Settlement, otherwise known as the Pact of Bogotá.[18]

The Charter of the OAS put the organization of the inter-American system on a formal treaty basis giving it security and permanence. Formerly it existed only by virtue of resolutions adopted by the several Pan American conferences. Part I of the Charter contains a reaffirmation of the basic principles of inter-American solidarity and cooperation. It lays the foundation, in principles and purposes, for the organization.

The essence of many past resolutions and declarations are here assembled in an enumeration of the fundamental rights and duties of states, and the obligations of peaceful settlement and reciprocal assistance. Of course, the obligation of nonintervention is repeated, this time more forcibly than ever: "The foregoing principle prohibits not only armed force but also any other form of interference or attempted threat against the personality of the State." Economic sanctions are prohibited, for, "No state may use or encourage the use of coercive measures of an economic or political character in order to force the sovereign will of another state and obtain from it advantages of any kind." And finally, according to the Charter of the OAS, the member states, including the United States, agree to cooperate for "the common welfare and prosperity of the peoples of the continent." The Good Neighbor policy in support of the general welfare of Latin America thus became a treaty obligation under the Charter of the OAS.

Part II of the Charter deals with the instrumentalities through which the OAS operates. Generally, most of the old basic features of the inter-American

[17] See Alberto Lleras, "Report on the Ninth International Conference of American States," *Annals* of the Organization of American States, I, No. 1 (1949), 1–76. For texts of Inter-American Treaty of Reciprocal Assistance, the Charter of the OAS, and the American Treaty of Pacific Settlement, see *ibid.*, 76–109.

[18] For analysis of the Charter of the OAS and the Pact of Bogotá, see William Sanders, "Bogotá Conference," *International Conciliation,* No. 442 (June, 1948), 385–405.

system were retained, for while the Charter introduced changes, it did not seek to throw out the old and replace it with something entirely new.

The principal organs of the OAS are: the Inter-American Conference, the Meeting of Consultation of Ministers of Foreign Affairs, Specialized Conferences, Council of the Organization, Pan American Union, Specialized Organizations, and Dependent Technical Organs. (See Chart, p. 169).

The Inter-American Conference, a continuation of the International Conference of American States first held in Washington in 1889, is according to the Charter "the supreme organ" of the OAS which decides "the general action and policy of the Organization," and "has the authority to consider any matter relating to the friendly relations among the American States." It is supposed to meet every five years.[19] The Meeting of Consultation of the Ministers of Foreign Affairs is to convene when called "to consider problems of an urgent nature and of common interest . . . and to serve as Organ of Consultation." The Council of the Organization is made up of representatives of all the American republics and meets in permanent session. In addition to its supervision of the Pan American Union, which is the secretariat of the OAS, the Council from the Rio treaty derives an outstanding grant of political power in that it can act provisionally as Organ of Consultation.

The Charter, like the Rio treaty, stressed the fact that this regional arrangement was completely integrated into the United Nations. Of the several regional arrangements within the United Nations, the Organization of American States is the most elaborate in its organization and function.

Although the Bogotá conference succeeded in adopting a Treaty on Pacific Settlement, hopes for a single instrument coordinating and unifying all the measures of peaceful settlement scattered among treaties, conventions, and declarations previously adopted were vitiated by the addition to the pact of new and unacceptable features. The most important and controversial of these related to the obligatory resort to peaceful settlement. In addition, the United States found unacceptable the article which would deny the right of diplomatic protection, "when the said nationals have had available the means to place their case before competent domestic courts of the respective state." Because its "bold" and "progressive" innovations were impractical, the Pact of Bogotá received no more than nine ratifications. The United States never ratified it.

Generally, the Bogotá conference was quite successful in formalizing and strengthening the inter-American system. To these efforts the United States lent its full cooperation, for the State Department realized that in inter-American association rested our best hopes for the peace and security of the hemisphere. Its former depreciation of regionalism at the Moscow Foreign Ministers Conference and at Dumbarton Oaks proved to be only a momentary aberration. Both logic and expediency dictated support of the OAS as a cardinal principle of United States foreign policy.

---

[19] There has been no general Inter-American Conference since the Tenth Conference, which met in Caracas in 1954. The Eleventh Conference, which was to meet at Quito, Ecuador, has been successively and indefinitely postponed.

ORGANIZATION OF AMERICAN STATES

Source: Organization of American States. Reprinted by permission.

Less successful was the Bogotá conference in providing practical means for effective inter-American economic cooperation. Before the end of World War II the Latin Americans insisted that cooperation included not only political and military, but also economic assistance — that is by the United States. After the war, economic cooperation assumed first-place importance ✓ in the opinion of the Latin-American states.

It cannot be recorded that much progress was made at Bogotá in assuring the Latins of the type of "economic cooperation" which they demanded. The presidents of the Exim Bank and the World Bank were on hand to assure the availability of capital for "sound productive projects," and together with Secretary of State George C. Marshall, stressed the fact that private capital✓ must play the major role in the area's economic development. It was Mr. Marshall's delicate task to disabuse the Latins of any expectation of aid on the Marshall Plan scale. He urged them to put their need of United States help second to the European Recovery Program. Unfortunately the Latins ✓ remained unconvinced.

The sum total of the Bogotá discussions was an innocuous Economic Agreement. It did little more than recite general principles of economic cooperation, leaving the details of practical application to be worked out later at a special economic conference. Later developments seemed to prove that, because of the magnitude of the problem and the unwillingness of the Latin Americans to be satisfied with palliatives, it was not within the power or the disposition of the United States to extend effective assistance. Meanwhile, however, economic discontent was destined to develop, to the point where it threatened all other considerations of cooperation.

3. Defense Cooperation and Pro-Democratic Policy

Postwar defense cooperation

In addition to the strengthening of the structure of the inter-American security system, the United States, in the postwar years 1945–1948, lent its support to the perfecting of defense cooperation and the strengthening of the democratic basis of inter-American cooperation.

As the result of actions taken by the Mexico City conference, the Inter-American Defense Board adopted a number of resolutions relating to military cooperation, including: standardization of matériel, utilization of manpower, and standardization of organization and training of the armed forces. In accord with these resolutions the United States undertook to maintain or strengthen the military defense structure of the Americas.

The matter of the bases was a primary problem. Although it was clear that most of them were no longer needed and should be returned to their original owners, the defense departments of the United States were desirous of entering into negotiations for the retention of certain key bases in Ecuador, Brazil, and Panama.[20] In no instance were the negotiations successful.

[20] Mecham, *The United States and Inter-American Security,* 295–298.

The Ecuadorean government, influenced by violent public opposition to an extension of United States base rights in the Galápagos Islands, only agreed to operational use by the United States in an emergency. This was the same kind of agreement concluded with the Cuban and Brazilian governments. For special reasons relating to the protection of the Panama Canal, the United States government was particularly anxious to retain a number of the bases and defense sites it had occupied during the war. On December 10, 1947, an agreement was signed providing for United States use of thirteen sites for technical installations and a military air base at Rio Hato.

When news of the agreement became public there was violent protest in Panama which induced the national assembly to reject the agreement. Accordingly, the State Department announced the immediate evacuation of all the sites outside the Canal Zone.

Although base agreements were considered by the Inter-American Defense Board to be within the accepted framework of the inter-American security system, in view of the opposition encountered the United States was willing to let the matter rest. Outside of Puerto Rico it retained no bases in Latin America other than Guantánamo in Cuba, and those in the Canal Zone. Should an emergency arise, there was confident expectation that facilities wherever needed in Latin America would be made immediately available to the United States.

The recommendation by the Inter-American Defense Board, in October, 1945, that the governments of the American republics proceed immediately to the standardization of the organization and training of their armed forces appealed strongly to President Truman. Accordingly, in May, 1946, the President sent to Congress the text of a proposed bill entitled "The Inter-American Military Cooperation Act," which he believed would standardize military organization, training, and equipment as had been recommended by the Inter-American Defense Board and authorized by the Act of Chapultepec.

Administration representatives argued strongly for the bill in Congressional committee hearings. It was represented as an effort to counter European military influence in Latin America: Unless the Latins were supplied with the most modern weapons, they would seek arms and training elsewhere. Thus, the success, if not the very existence, of the United States military missions program was involved. The objection that this plan would contribute to an arms race was countered by the claim that there would be no arms increase, but merely the exchange of old for new arms.

Despite strong administration support, the proposed bill failed to pass Congress in both the 1946 and 1947 sessions. Perhaps that body was not unmindful of the fears and criticisms of this legislation by the Latin Americans, who held that it would load them down with costly armaments and would buttress dictatorial governments instead of strengthening democracy in their countries. The defeat of the arms-standardization bill was only a momentary setback to the military defense program, for soon, means were provided to pursue this objective.[21]

[21] *Ibid.,* 298–300.

Dictators and Democracy

Efforts to strengthen inter-American solidarity and cooperation were made not only by security pacts and military assistance. In the postwar years the issue of democracy versus dictatorship proved to be one of the most troublesome and delicate problems of United States-Latin American relations. It concerned both the recognition of governments under dictators and the conduct of friendly and even cooperative relations with such regimes.[22]

It is an interesting fact that this had not been an issue in the prewar years. Formerly the establishment of normal, friendly, official relations with whatever kind of government existed was taken as a matter of course. Except for deviations into *de jure* recognition during the years 1913 to 1932, the United States adhered to the Jeffersonian *de facto* recognition policy, which meant that a government was recognized on the fact of its existence and its ability and willingness to meet its international responsibilities. According to this policy, the recognizing power should not concern itself with the circumstances and methods whereby a government came into existence, for this would be intervention in the internal affairs of a sovereign state. The United States had been bitterly assailed on many occasions in the past when it put recognition on a *de jure* basis.

A project was submitted to the Mexico City conference by Guatemala to prevent the establishment of "antidemocratic regimes" in the Americas, such regimes being considered dangerous to the solidarity, peace, and defense of the continent. The project called for the American republics to refrain from recognizing or maintaining relations with such regimes, particularly those "that may originate from *coup d'état* against governments of a legally established democratic structure."

The Inter-American Juridical Committee, to which the Guatemala resolution was referred, reported against the proposal, saying that the phrase "antidemocratic regimes" was too vague, and that because the resolution allowed individual states to decide what constituted a democratic or antidemocratic regime, the principle of nonintervention would be placed in jeopardy. Also the Juridical Committee, clearly recognizing the provocation of rotating governments by revolutionary action, held that the withholding of recognition from governments originating in *coup d'état,* "might be unsuitable to the democratic future of America." Thus, nothing tangible came of the Guatemalan initiative.

About the same time Uruguay came forward with a proposal for nothing less than multilateral intervention in support of democratic principles and human rights. Her foreign minister, Dr. Eduardo Rodríguez Larreta, on November 22, 1945, sent notes to the American republics, stating that the

---

[22] See Russell H. Fitzgibbon, "Dictatorship and Democracy in Latin America," *International Affairs,* Vol. 36, No. 1 (January, 1960), 48–57; J. Lloyd Mecham, "Democracy and Dictatorship in Latin America," *The Southwestern Social Science Quarterly,* Vol. 41, No. 3 (December, 1960), 294–303.

"parallelism between democracy and peace must constitute a strict rule of action in inter-American policy." Peace is safe, he said, only where democratic principles of government prevail. The basic rights of man are an essential part of these principles. Thus, in case of their violation in any American republic, the other members of the community should take collective multilateral action to restore democracy. Conceding that his proposal was in conflict with the accepted principle of collective nonintervention, Dr. Rodríguez Larreta said, "Nonintervention cannot be converted into a right to invoke one principle in order to be able to violate all other principles with impunity."

The United States gave its quick and unqualified approval to the policy recommendation of the Foreign Minister of Uruguay. On November 27, 1945, Secretary of State James F. Byrnes announced: "Violations of the elementary rights of man by a government of force and the nonfulfillment of obligations by such a government is a matter of common concern to all the republics. As such, it justifies collective multilateral action after full consultation among the republics in accordance with established procedures."[23] Mr. Byrnes felt, as did Dr. Rodríguez Larreta, that the principle of nonintervention should not shield the notorious violation of the elementary rights of man.

This quick approval by the State Department was in pursuance of a new "enlarged formula" of the Good Neighbor to espouse in Latin America "a greater affinity and a warmer friendship for those governments which rest upon the periodically and freely expressed consent of the governed." This so-called Braden Corollary of the Good Neighbor policy, named after Ambassador and later Assistant Secretary of State Spruille Braden, meant the cold-shouldering of dictators and disreputable regimes in Latin America as enemies of democracy and liberty. Braden declared that the United States must distinguish between "legitimate" governments and those usurping powers from the people.[24] This meant that the United States would use at least its moral force to secure honest elections and observance of civil and human rights. Braden held that, because of its great power and influence, the United States could not escape its responsibilities. Thus, he warned against intervention by inaction. Secretary of State Byrnes supported the Braden idea and therefore gave his unqualified approval of the Rodríguez Larreta proposal.

As should have been anticipated, Latin-American opposition to the Uruguayan proposal was overwhelming. There was a firm resolve to prevent any weakening of the principle of nonintervention, even though intervention might be necessary in the interests of inter-American peace. The United States certainly was incautious in giving such unreserved and hasty endorsement of a procedure which might compromise the nonintervention principle. It was surprising that the State Department should subscribe to the belief that democratic regimes could be instituted by multilateral intervention, and even

---

[23] "U.S. Adherence to Principle Opposing Oppressive Regimes Among American Republics," Dept. of State *Bulletin*, XIII (December 2, 1945), 892.

[24] Donald M. Dozer, *Are We Good Neighbors?* (Gainesville: University of Florida Press, 1959), 213–220.

more surprising that the State Department was so naive as to believe that the Latin Americans would accept multilateral intervention *for any reason*.

Notwithstanding a decisive rejection of Dr. Rodríguez Larreta's thesis by a majority of the American governments, the United States did not abandon support of a positive prodemocratic policy for the Americas. Spruille Braden, as Assistant Secretary of State, continued the anti-dictator attack on Perón which he had initiated as ambassador to Argentina, for during his brief mission at Buenos Aires in July and August of 1945, he had waged a vigorous and undiplomatic campaign against the Farrell-Perón regime's suppression of civil liberties and its friendship with the Axis powers.

Two weeks before the Argentine presidential election in February, 1946, Mr. Braden was responsible for the publication of the State Department's *Blue Book* on Argentina, with the obvious intention of influencing the votes against Perón. The booklet, based on "incontrovertible evidence" drawn from captured German archives, showed that high officials of the Argentine government, including Perón, "were so seriously compromised with the (Nazi-Fascist) enemy that trust and confidence could not be reposed in that government."[25]

Despite the long campaign waged against him by the State Department, climaxed by the publication of the *Blue Book* on the eve of the election, Perón won the election. The unilateral campaign waged by the United States against dictatorship failed. Throughout Latin America the Braden policy was generally condemned as just another attempt to return to interventionism, this time under the pretext of safeguarding democracy. The Latins seemed not as concerned about fascism in Argentina as fearful of giving the United States an entering wedge for intervention. This is a bogy that apparently will never die.

Perón's election and general Latin-American disapproval of the Braden anti-dictatorship policy were responsible for an about-face by the State Department. First, only two days after the election, Perón's victory received a measure of recognition, when, after a lapse of several months, ambassadorial representation was resumed at Buenos Aires. Since the new ambassador, George Messersmith, was well known to be out of sympathy with Braden's "tough" policy, his appointment meant a return to "business as usual" with Perón. Braden's resignation as Assistant Secretary of State in June, 1947, was hailed in Latin America as a return to the policy of nonintervention, and failure by the United States to impose its type of democracy on Latin America. It is true that democracy cannot be imposed; nor, indeed, as so many Latin-American "liberals" seem to believe, will the ousting of dictators automatically usher in democratic regimes.[26]

[25] U.S. Dept. of State, *Consultation Among the American Republics with Respect to the Argentine Situation,* Publication 2473 (Washington, D.C.: Government Printing Office, 1946), 4. (Cited hereinafter as *Blue Book.*)

[26] Arthur P. Whitaker, *The United States and Argentina* (Cambridge: Harvard University Press, 1954), 213–219; Robert J. Alexander, *The Perón Era* (New York: Columbia University Press, 1951), 203–208. For a defense of the Braden policy, see Thomas

Since the Latin-American nations registered an emphatic veto on proposals by Uruguay and the United States to employ collective intervention in support of democratic principles, nonrecognition was resorted to once more as an alternative instrument. When in May, 1947, Anastacio Somoza seized the Nicaraguan government by armed revolt and imprisoned President Arguello, his hand-picked successor who refused to be a rubber stamp, an occasion presented itself for the use of nonrecognition as an instrument in support of democratic procedures. The Somoza *coup* was studied by the various American governments to determine whether the Chapultepec Act could be invoked against the resurgent dictator. The consultations resulted in a decision to abstain from relations with Nicaragua until after the elections, at which time the matter could be taken up for further review. Following a pseudo-election in Nicaragua, President Somoza was eventually recognized. Certainly the democratic cause was not aided by this brief withholding of recognition.

The Nicaragua incident seemed to prove that there was no general disposition to favor use of recognition as an instrument of policy. For example, a negative vote resulted from a consultation solicited by the State Department, following the seizure of the Venezuelan government by the military on November 25, 1948. Consequently the United States recognized the military *junta* January 21, 1949. The same attitude prevailed in connection with a *coup d'état* that occurred in Panama in November, 1949. Following the *coup,* Assistant Secretary of State Miller announced that the United States would consult with the other American republics. The consultation favored recognition of the usurper government in Panama, and the United States granted its recognition immediately. Although there seemed to be a willingness to consult on the subject of recognition, there definitely was slight disposition to use nonrecognition as an instrument in defense of democratic practices and principles.

Nevertheless the State Department persisted in its efforts to enlist the collective support of the other American republics to strengthen the democratic and constitutional framework of the governments of this hemisphere. On December 21, 1948, the Department made known to a number of American republics its concern because of recent instances in which popularly elected governments had been overthrown by military forces. It solicited comments on appropriate action that the inter-American organization might take in view of the principle proclaimed in the Charter of the Organization of American States that "the solidarity of the American States and the high aims which are sought through it requires the political organization of those states on the basis of the effective exercise of representative democracy."

Since it was hardly conceivable that any effective inter-American program to discourage dictatorship in Latin America was possible without the employment of some form of collective intervention, it is not surprising that the

---

F. McGann, "The Ambassador and the Dictator. The Braden Mission to Argentina and its Significance for United States Relations with Latin America," *The Centennial Review* VI, No. 3 (Summer, 1962), 343–357.

response to the State Department's note was unenthusiastic and devoid of constructive suggestions.[27] A fair inference drawn by the Department from this and other failures to mobilize some kind of cooperative action against nondemocratic regimes was that in the opinion of the Latin Americans the evils of dictatorship did not counterbalance the dangers inherent in compromising the nonintervention principle.

Accordingly, the United States, preoccupied with the cold war, and supercautious not to violate the nonintervention principle, abandoned further efforts to initiate collective sanctions against the dictators. Not only was there a resumption of normal official and business accommodations with those regimes, but there were instances when it appeared that the United States government was lending support to the dictators, thus earning for itself the bitter criticism of Latin-American "liberals."

In view of the widespread criticism of the United States as a befriender of dictators, it is well to recall — merely to keep the record straight — the instances herein cited in which the Latins themselves rejected proposals by this country to discourage antidemocratic regimes. In presenting these instances of United States efforts to curb dictatorship in Latin America, it is not our intention to uphold those proposals as effective and desirable. In fact, it should be clear beyond any question that collective measures against Latin-American dictators would be both ineffectual and dangerous; ineffectual because democracy must be an internal development and cannot be imposed from the outside, and dangerous because of the patent abuses that would arise from applying the sanction of so-called "legitimate intervention." It was the opinion of the Inter-American Juridical Committee that "in the provisions of the Bogotá Charter there is no place for collective action in defense of or for the restoration of democracy under that heading alone."[28]

Thus, in the immediate postwar period there was practically no disposition by the Latin-American community to assume responsibility for policing the hemisphere insofar as the promotion of democracy was concerned. The day may come when the Latin-American governments will be willing to take positive collective measures against dictatorial regimes, but that time has not yet arrived.

[27] *Ibid.,* U.S. Dept. of State *Bulletin,* XX (January 2, 1949), 30.
[28] Inter-American Juridical Committee, *Study on the Juridical Relationship Between Respect for Human Rights and the Exercise of Democracy* (Washington, D.C.: Pan American Union, May, 1960), 12–13.

SUPPLEMENTARY READING

Bebr, Gerhard, "Regional Organizations: A United Nations Problem," *American Journal of International Law, XXIX,* No. 2 (April, 1955), 166–184.

Canyes, Manuel S., "The Inter-American System and the Conference of Chapultepec," *American Journal of International Law,* XXXIX, No. 3 (July, 1945), 504–517.

Canyes, Manuel S., *The Organization of American States and the United Nations* (Washington, D.C.: Pan American Union, 5th ed., 1960).

Cuevas Cancino, Francisco, "The Bogotá Conference and Recent Developments in Pan-American Relations: A Mexican View," *International Affairs,* XXIV, No. 4 (October, 1948), 524–533.

Dozer, Donald M., *Are We Good Neighbors?* (Gainesville: University of Florida Press, 1959), 188–273.

Duggan, Laurence, *The Americas* (New York: Henry Holt and Company, 1948), 101–122.

Furniss, Edgar S., Jr., "The United States, the Inter-American System and the United Nations," *Political Science Quarterly,* LXV, No. 3 (September, 1950), 415–430.

Houston, John A., *Latin America in the United Nations* (New York: Carnegie Endowment for International Peace, 1956), Chap. I.

Hull, Cordell, *Memoirs* (2 vols. New York: The Macmillan Company, 1948), II, *passim.*

Kunz, Josef L., "The Inter-American System and the United Nations Organization," *American Journal of International Law,* XXXIX, No. 4 (October, 1945), 758–767.

Mecham, J. Lloyd, "The Integration of the Inter-American Security System into the United Nations," *The Journal of Politics,* IX, No. 2 (May, 1947), 178–196.

Mecham, J. Lloyd, *The United States and Inter-American Security, 1889–1960* (Austin: University of Texas Press, 1961), Chaps. IX, X.

Munro, Dana G., "The Mexico City Conference and the Inter-American System," U.S. Dept. of State *Bulletin,* XII, No. 301 (April 1, 1945), 525–530.

Sandifer, Durward V., "Regional Aspects of the Dumbarton Oaks Proposals," U.S. Dept. of State *Bulletin,* XII, No. 292 (January 28, 1945), 145–147.

The United Nations in the Making: Basic Documents (Boston: World Peace Foundation, 1945).

Thomas, Ann Van Wynen, and Thomas, A. J., Jr., *The Organization of American States* (Dallas: Southern Methodist University Press, 1963).

8

Problems of Political and Economic Relations Since 1948

Following the Bogotá conference, in many respects a landmark in the historical development of the inter-American system, new forces and factors were destined to alter profoundly the bases and objectives of inter-American cooperation. There were mounting criticism of the United States and rabid anti-Yankee demonstrations; in short, a deterioration of United States-Latin American relations. It seemed at times that the validity of oft-declared principles of inter-American solidarity were called into question.

1. Problems of Political Relations[1]

Strengthening security

Immediately following the Bogotá conference the United States collaborated with the Latin-American nations in further strengthening the mechanism of continental security, in perfecting the military defenses of the hemisphere, and in lending its support to the OAS in keeping the peace in the Caribbean area.

A significant addition to the inter-American security structure was the Inter-American Peace Committee. Although the Committee had a paper existence dating back to 1940, it never functioned, and in fact was forgotten when the OAS was formally organized by the Charter in 1948. It was the Dominican Republic that in July, 1948, rescued from oblivion the Inter-American Peace Committee, created by a resolution of the Havana Meeting of Foreign Ministers in 1940.

[1] See J. Lloyd Mecham, *The United States and Inter-American Security, 1889–1960* (Austin: University of Texas Press, 1961), Chap. XI; William Manger, *Pan America in Crisis. The Future of the OAS* (Washington, D.C.: Public Affairs Press, 1901), Chap. V.

The Committee, composed of representatives of five governments chosen by the Council, has the duty of "keeping constant vigilance to insure that states between which any dispute exists or may arise . . . may solve it as quickly as possible . . . and of suggesting the measures and steps that may be conducive to a settlement." As a security instrument the Inter-American Peace Committee has achieved a status in the inter-American system second only to the Rio treaty. With the exception of a brief interval the United States has always been represented on the Committee.

Post-Bogotá planning for the military defense of the continent was accomplished both by multilateral action through the instrumentality of the Inter-American Defense Board, and through bilateral agreements between the United States and individual Latin-American countries. These activities were clearly based on the commitments of the Rio treaty, which established the responsibility of each American republic to cooperate for the defense of the continent.

Although the Inter-American Defense Board had been originally created as an emergency war agency of the Inter-American system, at the Bogotá conference it was retained "to act as the organ of preparation and recommendation for the collective self-defense of the American Continent against aggression."

The Defense Board is only a technical advisory and consultation body. It has no legislative or treaty-making power, nor has it armed forces under its direct control, for its mission is defense planning only. Its duty is to recommend measures for the common defense to the member governments. It is exclusively concerned with hemisphere defense and thus cannot be called upon in inter-American disputes. It is not concerned with the touchy problems of attacks by one American state on another. The member states have been reluctant to grant a larger role to the Board because of considerations of national sovereignties and fear of the United States.[2]

Following the outbreak of the Korean War, the Washington Meeting of Foreign Ministers in 1951 directed the Inter-American Defense Board to carry forward its military plans for continental defense. Accordingly, on November 15 the Board approved and forwarded to the respective governments a "General Military Plan for the Defense of the American Continent." Annexes to the plan were forthcoming later. In July, 1957, a new military plan was approved in order to make further accommodations of hemisphere defense plans to a clearer delineation of global defense. Since a direct attack by Communist forces on South America was not seriously anticipated, Latin America's chief responsibility would be that of maintaining order, preventing subversive activities, defending vital military and economic installations,[3]

---

[2] Edwin Lieuwen, *Arms and Politics in Latin America* (New York: Frederick A. Praeger, rev. ed., 1962), 214–215; John C. Dreier, *The Organization of American States* (New York: Harper & Row, 1962), 43–48.

[3] In World War II more than 100,000 United States troops were tied down in Latin America. "Military Assistance to Latin America," Dept. of State *Bulletin*, XXVIII, No. 718 (March 30, 1953), 466. The inter-American defense plans sought to make it unnecessary to repeat this action in any future war.

keeping air and sea communications open, and producing strategic and critical raw materials.

Because of the limitations under which the Inter-American Defense Board operates, the United States has had to rely almost exclusively on the bilateral approach to promote its continental defense objectives. Nevertheless, to a considerable degree, it was on the basis of plans devised by the Defense Board, and on its general recommendations, that the United States entered upon a military assistance program.

Under authorization of the Mutual Security Act of 1951, which specified that "military assistance may be furnished to the other American republics . . . to participate in missions important to the defense of the Hemisphere," negotiations for bilateral military assistance agreements were initiated with several Latin-American countries. Eventually agreements were formalized with the following: Brazil, Chile, Colombia, Cuba, Dominican Republic, Ecuador, Guatemala, Haiti, Honduras, Nicaragua, Peru, and Uruguay.

According to the provisions of the agreements,[4] the United States undertakes to make available to each party to the agreement "equipment, materials, services, or other military assistance . . . to promote the defense of the Western Hemisphere." The Latin-American nation on its part agrees to make effective use of the assistance received and to employ it solely for carrying out specific defense plans agreed on by both governments.[5] Also, each Latin-American government agrees "to facilitate the production and transfer to the Government of the United States of America . . . raw and semi-processed materials."

In addition to direct grants of equipment and other assistance to countries with whom we have contracted military assistance agreements, the United States under the terms of the Mutual Security Act supplied arms and military equipment both on a cash sale and reimbursable basis. By the end of fiscal 1959 the twelve countries with whom the United States had contracted MDA pacts had received $317 million in grants for military aid. These and seven other Latin-American countries obtained about $140 million worth of military equipment under the reimbursable provisions of the Mutual Security Act. Over the period 1951–1959 United States military assistance grants and reimbursable aid averaged only $65 million annually for nineteen Latin-American nations.[6] Despite this, United States military assistance has been unfairly criticized as promoting an arms race and fixing militarism on Latin America.

The military missions in Latin America continue to be a virtual United States monopoly. In 1961 between 500 and 600 United States officers and

---

[4] See Lieuwen, *op. cit.* (Appendix B, 308–313), for a copy of the agreement between the United States and Honduras.

[5] In 1958, by the Moore Amendment to the Mutual Security Act, arms and equipment must not be used in civil strife. This of course proved to be a feeble restraint.

[6] Eventually all the Latin-American countries except Mexico made formal request for military aid. The amount received from the United States averaged annually: $45 million MDA grants and $20 million reimbursable aid. Lieuwen, *op. cit.,* 216. The total military budget of the twelve countries with which the United States concluded military assistance pacts was about $1 billion annually.

men were attached to the Army, Navy and Air missions. The mission system is a key component of both United States and Inter-American Defense Board planning for continental defense. Ideally it promotes standardization of arms, equipment, training, tactics, and methods, but it is charged that the program in Latin America falls short of these achievements. The training is not extensive enough, the amount of equipment supplied is not adequate, and the arms supplied are often either obsolete or discontinued items. Thus, the Latins are forced to shop elsewhere, to the detriment of standardization.[7]

Keeping peace in the Caribbean[8]

In the postwar years ample opportunities arose, particularly in the Caribbean area, to test the recently strengthened inter-American security procedures. In fact, the greatest achievement of the OAS has been the maintenance of peace among its own members. To these endeavors the United States has lent its full support, for it welcomes the principle of collective responsibility for the peace and security of the continent. This was the hope and expectation of the United States government when it renounced the right of intervention. Strangely, most of the controversies of the post-Bogotá years which were responsible for the invoking of the Rio treaty or recourse to the Inter-American Peace Committee resulted from interventionism — not by the United States, but by the Central American and Caribbean governments in the affairs of their own neighboring states.

At the risk of oversimplifying the general situation we note that the heads of the liberal and dictatorial regimes in the area, in seeking to bring about the overthrow of each other, did not hesitate to resort to tactics ranging from propaganda, subversion, and sabotage, to attempted assassination and armed invasion. Prominent on the liberal side, with its elusive "Caribbean Legion," were José Figueres of Costa Rica, joined later by Rómulo Betancourt of Venezuela. The dictators, who seemed to feel an urge to cooperate, were Rafael Leonidas Trujillo of the Dominican Republic, Marcos Pérez Jiménez of Venezuela, and Anastacio Somoza of Nicaragua, all since removed from power by violent death or deposition. Fidel Castro of Cuba was briefly associated with the liberals, but soon embarked on his own to carry his Communist revolution to the neighboring countries, whatever might be the nature of their regimes.

In general therefore, in the period 1948–1965, the situation in the smaller Latin-American countries located in the Caribbean region was one of chronic international disturbances and friction. It was a situation to which the Rio treaty[9] was applied a number of times, and on some occasions there was resort to the Inter-American Peace Committee.

[7] *Ibid.*, 206–215.
[8] See Mecham, *op. cit.*, Chap. XIII.
[9] Dr. Manger (*op. cit.*, 49–55) criticizes the excessive use of the Rio treaty in strictly inter-American cases. He believes it should be reserved for extra-continental threats. For the Rio treaty and its application, see Robert J. Redington, *The Organization of American States as a Collective Security System* (Washington, D.C.: Industrial College

The Rio treaty was brought into play in the following disputes between American states:

1. In 1948 Costa Rica called upon the OAS for help in repelling an armed attack originating in Nicaragua. The OAS Council convoked the Organ of Consultation, but itself acted provisionally as that organ. It was never necessary actually to convene the Meeting of Consultation of Foreign Ministers. An investigating committee went to the scene of the conflict, collected information in both Nicaragua and Costa Rica, and then reported to the Provisional Organ of Consultation. On the basis of the report, the Council prevailed on the governments involved to sign agreements for improving their mutual relations. These procedures, the first under the Rio treaty, became precedent for subsequent invocations of the pact.

2. In 1955 Costa Rica again called on the OAS to deal with another invasion of its territory by armed elements from Nicaragua. Acting as Provisional Organ of Consultation the Council was able to induce the two governments to sign agreements terminating the issue between them.

3. In 1957, a flare-up resulting from a longstanding boundary dispute between Nicaragua and Honduras was terminated by OAS action and a final settlement was arranged.

4. In April, 1959, the Panamanian government requested Rio treaty assistance because of an "invasion" of Panama by a band of Cubans. Prompt action by the OAS Council acting as Provisional Organ of Consultation was instrumental in resolving an apparently trivial problem which nevertheless had a serious potential.

5. In June, 1959, Nicaragua requested application of the Rio treaty to the situation created by an attack on the Somoza regime by a group of exiles coming from Costa Rica. Although there was reluctance on the part of many of the members to invoke the Rio treaty for the protection of a dictatorship, the Council finally voted to constitute itself a Provisional Organ of Consultation. No government was formally charged with responsibility or complicity in the case. The United States argued that to disregard interventions against dictators would jeopardize the principle of nonintervention. The cogency of the argument was recognized by all of the Council members except Cuba and Venezuela.

6. In 1960, the Sixth Meeting of Consultation of Ministers of Foreign Affairs (serving as Organ of Consultation in application of the Inter-American Treaty of Reciprocal Assistance) held at San José, Costa Rica, applied the sanctions of the Rio treaty for the first time in the "aggression" (i.e., attempted assassination of President Betancourt) by the Dominican Republic against Venezuela.

7. In January, 1962, the Eighth Meeting of Consultation of Ministers of Foreign Affairs (serving as Organ of Consultation in application of the Inter-

---

of the Armed Forces, 1961–1962), 8–25; Pan American Union, *Aplicaciones del Tratado Interamericano de Asistencia Reciproca, 1948–1960* (Washington, D.C.: Pan American Union, 1960, 3rd ed.).

American Treaty of Reciprocal Assistance) held at Punta del Este, Uruguay, decided to exclude the Cuban regime of Fidel Castro from the Inter-American system, and to apply limited sanctions against Cuba.[10]

8. On October 23, 1962, the Council of the OAS, acting provisionally as Organ of Consultation in application of the Inter-American Treaty of Reciprocal Assistance, followed President Kennedy's proclamation of a quarantine of Cuba, by adopting measures intended to preserve the peace and security of the Continent. Both actions were prompted by Soviet installation in Cuba of ballistic missiles and other arms of an offensive capability. A resolution called for "the immediate dismantling and withdrawal from Cuba of all missiles and other weapons with any offensive capability," and the members were recommended, in accordance with Articles 6 and 8 of the Rio treaty, to "take all measures, individually and collectively including the use of armed force."[11]

9. Because of a flare-up between the Dominican Republic and Haiti, due to violations of the Dominican embassy in Port-au-Prince, the OAS was called into action on April 28, 1963. Invoking the Rio treaty, the Council, acting provisionally as the Organ of Consultation, was able temporarily to alleviate the situation.

10. In July, 1964, the Ninth Meeting of the Ministers of Foreign Affairs, serving as Organ of Consultation in application of the Rio treaty, adopted a resolution (with Bolivia, Chile, Mexico and Uruguay dissenting) imposing diplomatic and economic sanctions against the Cuban government. Notwithstanding the mandatory nature of the resolution, Mexico refused to suspend relations with Fidel Castro.

The Inter-American Peace Committee was also brought into play in the following situations in the Caribbean area:

1. In 1948 the Peace Committee was requested by the Dominican government to lend its services in a dispute with Cuba because of activities on Cuban territory by Dominican exiles and others against the government of Dictator Rafael Trujillo. The Committee investigated and paved the way for amicable negotiations between the two governments.

2. In 1949 the Peace Committee took cognizance of a Haitian request for an investigation of a conspiracy with the knowledge and approval of the Dominican government, to overthrow the constitutional government of Haiti. After making an on-the-ground investigation, the Committee was able to induce the two governments to sign a joint declaration professing "good neighbor sentiments based in the lofty principles of nonintervention, mutual respect, and American solidarity."

3. In 1949, the United States, disturbed because of the activites of the

---

[10] On at least four occasions the Rio treaty was invoked unsuccessfully by countries seeking OAS action. In each instance the Council decided that the situation did not warrant application of the treaty. Realizing that an appeal would be futile, Trujillo refrained on one occasion from seeking the protection of the Rio treaty.

[11] *The Council of the Organization of American States Acting Provisionally as Organ of Consultation* (Minutes), Council Series, October 23, 1962.

Caribbean Legion and its dictatorial antagonists, called for a meeting of the Inter-American Peace Committee. After a careful consideration of the situation, the Committee decided that its competence was limited to the simple affirmation of certain standards and principles basic to American peace and solidarity. The governments were cautioned to be vigilant to prevent conspiracies against neighboring regimes. All this seemed to prove that nothing short of some form of collective action by the American nations could bring order to the Caribbean.

4. In 1953 the Colombian government tried to secure the Committee's help in its dispute with Peru over the long-continued asylum of Víctor Haya de la Torre in the Colombian Embassy in Lima. Peru declined the Committee's offer of its services in the case.

This was the last resort to the Inter-American Peace Committee until 1959. In 1956 the OAS Council, when approving new statutes of the Peace Committee, limited the Committee's freedom of action by providing that only a state directly concerned in a dispute could request the Committee to take action, and that the Committee could take up the case only with the prior consent of the other party or parties to the dispute. Formerly the Committee could take action in a dispute at the request of any American state. Apparently as a result of the restrictions imposed in 1956 no case came before the Peace Committee for three years. Rescued from oblivion in 1948, it seemed to be returning to oblivion, but it was saved from this fate by action of the Fifth Meeting of Consultation of Foreign Ministers.[12] The subsequent activities of the Peace Committee have been merged in our discussion of Caribbean problems since 1959.

The Fifth and Sixth Consultative Meetings

The emergence of Fidel Castro, coupled with the perennial nuisance factor of the Trujillo dictatorship, compounded turmoil in the Caribbean. In 1959 the peace was again broken by a series of interventions and uprisings, inspired by the Castro revolution in Cuba, and aimed at overthrowing dictatorial governments. The long-time hatred of Castro for Trujillo, because of Trujillo's support of Batista during the Castro rebellion, now accentuated by Trujillo's grant of asylum to the fallen Cuban dictator, threatened an explosion. Because of alleged Cuban and Venezuelan participation in two abortive "invasions" of the Dominican Republic, and their intention to initiate new invasions, the Dominican government appealed in July, 1959, to the Council of the OAS for action under the Rio treaty. The request for protective action was soon withdrawn, however, when the Dominican representative saw that his government was not going to receive support from the other Latin-American governments. It seemed that the protective shield of the Rio treaty was to be denied to dictators.

This was a dangerous development, for if the principle of nonintervention was permitted to be violated in the present situation, it would be violated

[12] For activities of the Peace Committee, see Redington, *op. cit.*, 26–31.

increasingly in the future. Moreover, the principle of collective security set forth in the Rio treaty and the Charter of the OAS applied equally to all members, without reference to the nature of their governments. This was the position taken by the United States when it proposed a Meeting of Foreign Ministers under Article 39 of the Charter of the OAS, instead of the Rio treaty, to consider the whole problem of turmoil in the Caribbean. Such a meeting would afford the opportunity for consultation without limiting the meeting to specific charges. Because of the popularity of Castro and the Cuban revolution, it was well to avoid any thought or implication of coercive settlement.

The Fifth Meeting of Consultation of Ministers of Foreign Affairs met in Santiago, Chile, in August of 1959.[13] The primary issue was whether the remaining Latin-American dictatorships in the Dominican Republic, Nicaragua, and Paraguay should be eliminated by some form of international action, or whether they should be shielded by the sacred principle of nonintervention. Secretary of State Christian Herter stood foursquare on the principle of nonintervention. The delegates of Cuba and Venezuela did not believe, however, that nonintervention should block the way to the overthrow of dictators.

Since the majority agreed with Secretary Herter, a Declaration of Santiago was adopted which condemned dictators, reasserted the principle of nonintervention, approved democratic systems, held that democracy cannot be imposed from without but must develop from within, and delegated to the Inter-American Peace Committee watch-dog supervision of Caribbean peace until it should report to the pending eleventh inter-American conference to be held in Quito, Ecuador.

To enable the Peace Committee to carry out its assignment to study existing international tensions in the Caribbean area, it was given temporarily broadened powers to act at the request of a government or on its own initiative. In pursuance of its assignment the Inter-American Peace Committee visited the countries of the Caribbean area, with the exception of Cuba, whose government refused to grant permission.

On request of the Venezuelan government the Peace Committee investigated violations of human rights in the Dominican Republic which were aggravating tensions in the Caribbean. Although not permitted to visit the Dominican Republic, the Peace Committe issued a stinging report on flagrant and widespread violations by the Trujillo dictatorship. Furthermore, in April, 1960, the Peace Committee issued a special report showing how the existence of dictatorial governments and their violation of human rights aggravate international relations. Measures to assure greater respect for human rights and the exercise of democracy were recommended.

In June, 1960, the State Department submitted to the Inter-American Peace Committee a memorandum of provocative actions by the Cuban govern-

[13] See Dreier, *op. cit.*, 70–73. For acts of the Santiago Meeting, see *Fifth Meeting of Consultation of Ministers of Foreign Affairs, Final Act* (Washington, D.C.: Pan American Union, 1960).

ment. It described Cuba's systematic campaign of "distortions, half-truths, and outright falsehoods" against the United States. The United States did not call for action by the Peace Committee, for, given the general Latin-American enthusiasm for Castro and the Cuban revolution, it realized the futility of pressing for any kind of collective action at that time. The memorandum submitted to the Peace Committee was merely a formal list of Castro's excesses for the record. Despite the evidence of growing communization of Cuba and its subversive activities against other governments, the Committee seemed to find it easier to put blame for Caribbean tensions on Trujillo than on Castro.

When it became plain that Dictator Trujillo was behind an assassination attempt on the life of Venezuela's President Betancourt, the OAS Council found the evidence conclusive enough to vote for a Consultative Meeting of the Foreign Ministers to meet at San José, Costa Rica, on August 16, 1960. A committee appointed by the Council to investigate the charges of aggression and intervention brought by Venezuela against the Dominican Republic, seemed to prove beyond much doubt that Trujillo had indeed plotted the murder of Betancourt.

The San José Meeting, serving as Organ of Consultation in application of the Rio Treaty of Reciprocal Assistance, adopted a resolution condemning the government of the Dominican Republic for acts of aggression and intervention against Venezuela. In addition, two sanctions were provided: the suspension of diplomatic relations with the Dominican Republic, and the immediate cessation of trade in arms and implements of war of every kind.[14]

The San José resolution was significant on at least two counts: (1) this was the first time sanctions provided by the Rio treaty were voted; and (2) this was the first time the Latin-American members of the OAS agreed to qualify absolute nonintervention. In essence the OAS seemed to be saying that an act of aggression upon the sovereignty of a member relieves the other members from the obligation of nonintervention. They apparently decided to be noninterventionist only toward those members who practice nonintervention themselves. Protection of human rights was only secondary.

The sanctions imposed on the Dominican government did not accomplish the overthrow of Trujillo. In fact the United States government found itself in the embarrassing position of actually aiding the dictator whom it had pledged to overthrow, for President Eisenhower's plea for Congressional authorization to withhold an extra sugar allotment to the Dominican Republic was ignored. Finally, in mid-1960, one of Latin America's most ruthless tyrannies was terminated, not by action of the United States or of the OAS, but by assassins' bullets.

[14] "OAS condemns Government of Dominican Republic," Dept. of State *Bulletin,* XLIII, No. 1106 (September 5, 1960), 355–360. Dr. Manger (*op. cit.,* 53–54) questions whether the Rio treaty was applied to the Dominican question on the basis of principle or politics. For the Sixth Meeting, see also *Inter-American Efforts to Relieve International Tensions in the Western Hemisphere.* Dept. of State Publication 7409, Inter-American Series No. 79 (Washington, D.C.: Government Printing Office, 1962), 65–70. Hereinafter cited as *Inter-American Efforts, 1959–1960.*

The United States had been constrained at the San José meeting to go along with the Latin-American countries in their demands for sanctions against Trujillo, because it hoped for similar collective action against Castro. We shall see later, when we discuss the Seventh Meeting of Ministers of Foreign Affairs, also held at San José, Costa Rica, in August, 1960, that the Latin-American membership did not believe that the transgressions of the Castro regime warranted another compromise of the principle of nonintervention. Moreover, in this instance, unlike the Trujillo case, many of the Latin-American governments resisted any kind of anti-Castro action because of their fear of popular or radical reaction in their own countries.

Weakened solidarity

Tensions in United States-Latin American relations, which had been intensifying since World War II, finally erupted in 1958 and 1959 in shocking demonstrations of anti-United States hostility. Since the effectiveness of inter-American defense cooperation must be equated with the degree of solidarity existent among the American nations, the mounting jealousies, resentments, suspicions, envy, and downright anti-Yankee hostility must be viewed in light of their relation to inter-American security.

It was the mob assaults on Vice-President Richard Nixon, on his South American tour in 1958, which shocked the American public into a belated realization that all was not well in Latin America. Too many had allowed themselves to be lulled into the belief that the southern flank was secure because of our continued adherence to the Good Neighbor policy. But, as we have already noted, the Latins accused the Truman and Eisenhower administrations of abandoning the Good Neighbor, of taking them too much for granted, and of giving other areas of the world priority in American assistance. It was a situation which called for inquiry into the basic causes of anti-Yankeeism and a re-examination of United States policy. Since policy modifications were principally economic, these will be discussed in the next section of this chapter. At the moment let us consider other causes of Latin-American hostility toward the United States.[15]

The anti-United States attitude so largely prevalent in Latin America is principally psychological. It springs from racial and cultural differences of the two peoples. The Latins are no strangers to the anti-foreign complex: those that you do not know or understand you fear or suspect. There is little doubt that the stimulation of hostility toward the United Sates has been made easier by playing on nationalistic and racial prejudices. The contrasts in cultures, the different ways of doing things, the different attitudes of mind, set the people of the United States and of Latin America far apart. When to these factors we add the retarded development of the Latin-American countries as contrasted with the rapid growth of a powerful and progressive

---

[15] For a discussion which throws light on "incompatibilities," see Donald M. Dozer, *Are We Good Neighbors?* (Gainesville: University of Florida Press, 1959), Chap. 10, *passim*. For excellent studies dealing with Latin-American hostility toward the United States, see Dept. of State, *External Research Papers* (Brazil, No. 126, February 24, 1956; Chile No. 126.1, August 28, 1956; Argentina, No. 126.2, May 27, 1957).

United States, the result is envy and even dislike of this country. It is an interesting fact that anti-Yankeeism is prevalent among Latin-American intellectuals. Probably it is because those who are better educated and have travelled, realize more acutely the disparities between the United States and their own countries, and seek to compensate a feeling of nationalistic frustration by criticizing the United States. Moreover, the intellectuals regard themselves as defenders of Latin-American culture, which they believe is being threatened by the invasion of Yankee "materialism."

In addition to the psychological factor, the Latin's hostility for the United States is often a reaction to the behavior of individuals whom he observes. It can hardly be denied that great damage to inter-American understanding is chargeable to private individuals — businessmen and tourists — who have not, in the foreign environment, successfully presented a true image of the average United States citizen.

Much of the Latin-American hostility manifested in 1958 was attributed to an alleged pro-dictator policy of the United States. Vice-President Nixon reported, after his ill-fated tour, that the question most frequently directed at him was why the United States supported, and even honored, dictators. The fact that the United States was adhering meticulously to the doctrine of non-intervention was not accepted as a satisfactory excuse for its being "soft" on dictators. Thus, the United States found itself suspect as a champion of freedom and democratic government in Latin America. In response to this criticism the United States at the Santiago Meeting of Foreign Ministers in 1959 began to adopt a more positive attitude toward dictatorships of all kinds.

Finally, in accounting for anti-United States hostility in Latin America the Communists played a most important role. With great skill and pertinacity they seized on more or less latent Latin-American fears, jealousies, and resentments of their Yankee neighbor and inflated these into explosive proportions. Frequently, legitimate and restrained discontent with United States policy has been whipped up by Communist agitators into mob demonstrations which unfortunately exaggerate greatly the picture of weakening solidarity.

Cultural relations

Recognizing that inter-American solidarity can be strengthened by the cultivation of better understanding between the neighbors of the hemisphere, the United States has ever since 1938 promoted a vigorous cultural exchange program with Latin America. Up to about twenty-five years ago Latin-American cultural relations were oriented primarily toward Europe. Since then there has been a steady flow of students, teachers, lecturers, and specialists between the United States and the Latin-American nations.

Today some three-fourths of the Latin-American students who go abroad to study come to the United States. In the 1959–1960 academic year there were 9,000 such students. Since 1940 more than 5,000 Latin Americans have come to the United States under State Department-administered educational and cultural exchange programs, and during the same period, about 650

United States specialists were sent to Latin America. In addition, under the President's Special International Program for Cultural Presentations, many individuals and groups in the fields of the fine arts and sports have made appearances in Latin America.

In the field of information a variety of media are employed by the USIA (United States Information Agency), which, while furthering United States foreign policy objectives in Latin America, contribute generally to the promotion of cultural understanding. These media include press releases, books, radio and television, and documentary films. In nineteen of the Latin-American republics there are more than fifty binational cultural centers staffed by United States grantee personnel under the control of binational boards of directors. Their activities include the teaching of English, lectures, exhibits, and library services. The teaching of English has received the greatest popular response. Finally, information libraries and reading rooms have been established in many Latin-American cities.[16]

Although the cultural relations program of the United States is based on presumably sound premises, and has been intelligently administered, its effectiveness can easily be exaggerated. It does not necessarily follow that an understanding of cultural distinctions will pave the way to more harmonious national relationships. It has not been want of acquaintance by Latin-American intellectuals with the culture of the United States that has been responsible for their anti-United States attitude. Nevertheless, we hold to the belief that, over the years and on the general average, cultural exchange will effect an ameliorating influence over our relations with our Latin-American neighbors.

2. *Problems of Economic Cooperation*[17]

Divergent points of view

Ever since the end of World War II the economic aspects of inter-American cooperation and solidarity have challenged the political ones for primacy in Pan American deliberations. This is because the Latin neighbors insist that the rule of "all for one, one for all" includes economic cooperation as well as political and military. Since inter-American economic cooperation, to which the American governments have been formally committed by the Charter of the OAS, really means assistance by the United States, our discussion of the economic factor in continental relationships becomes perforce a description of the position of the United States vis-à-vis the Latin-American countries.

[16] Edward O. Guerrant, *Roosevelt's Good Neighbor Policy* (Albuquerque: University of New Mexico Press, 1950), Chap. V; Dept. of State, *Our Southern Partners*, Publication 7040 (Washington, D.C.: Government Printing Office, 1962), 34–35, 40–44.

[17] Mecham, *op. cit.*, Chap. XII. Also see *United States-Latin American Relations*. *Sen. Doc.* No. 125, 86th Cong., 2nd Sess. (Washington: Government Printing Office, 1960), Studies Nos. 4, 5, 6; *Economic Developments in South America*, Hearings before the subcommittee in Inter-American Economic Relationships of the Joint Economic Committee of the Congress of the United States, 87th Cong., 2nd Sess., May 10 and 11, 1962.

There is little doubt that the OAS was intended to play a constructive role in the promotion of inter-American economic and social development. This was certainly the preference of the Latin-American members who appreciated the advantages of conducting economic relations with the United States on a multilateral basis. While sincerely disavowing any desire to "gang up" on the United States, they appreciated that it would be much harder for the United States in an international conference to oppose a desired collective action than it would be to oppose each one of them separately. In pursuance of this idea the Latin-American countries repeatedly tried to get the United States to sign a treaty committing the members of the OAS to policies of economic cooperation, including an inter-American bank.

While the United States categorically rejected the idea of a bank, it was willing to lend lip service to innocuous economic agreements. Such a one was the Economic Agreement of Bogotá (1948) which only three governments eventually ratified.

It will be recalled that the Bogotá conference also recommended that a special inter-American economic conference be convened at an early date in Buenos Aires in order to attack the vital issues of economic cooperation. Since the United States preferred bilateral negotiations, it forced several postponements of the conference. Eventually a meeting of the ministers of finance met at Rio de Janeiro in 1954. It is not possible to record that the Rio Economic Conference made much constructive progress, for the United States refused to budge from its established policy: (1) foreign private-investment capital should be given priority in the Latin-American development program, and (2) the lending agencies of the United States government and of the United Nations were believed adequately financed to meet all requests for "sound" loans.

History repeated itself at the long-delayed "Economic Conference of the OAS" in Buenos Aires in 1957. Not only were the Latins told that they must rely first on private loans, and that existing public lending agencies were adequate to meet their needs; they were also informed that an inter-American bank or loan fund was out of the question.

The efforts of the Latins to work out, with the United States in the OAS, a cooperative program of so-called "economic defense," failed because the United States did not favor the multilateral approach which apparently put this country at a disadvantage.[18] We turn therefore to our own preferred bilateral procedure.

The encouragement of private investments

On economic, as on political issues, the Truman and Eisenhower administrations pursued almost identical policies, i.e., the encouragement of private capital investments[19] and United States assistance to Latin America on a restricted public loan basis. Although the United States government believed

18 Manger, *op. cit.*, 55–58; Dreier, *op. cit.*, 77–79.
19 The long-term economic development of Latin America, said Secretary of State Marshall at Quitandinha in 1947, required "a type of collaboration in which a much

that private capital could meet the larger needs of Latin-American economic development, it soon realized that the political climate was not necessarily inviting to foreign investors. Accordingly, assurances to investors against loss by expropriation, currency inconvertibility, and other disabilities burdening foreign operations were needed. Both the State Department and the United States Congress set about encouraging the private investor.

The State Department negotiated treaties which sought to reduce the risks of private capital investment by assuring nondiscriminatory and equitable treatment. But of the four treaties signed, only the one with Nicaragua went into force. Thus the treaty approach to reassure private investors was a failure.

Congressional initiative was somewhat more successful. Under authority of the Mutual Security Act of 1951, guarantees were extended to *new* United States investors in Latin America upon the conclusion of guarantee agreements between the United States and the country involved. A number of such agreements have been entered into providing insurance to investors against currency inconvertibility and loss by expropriation.[20]

The efforts of the United States government to stimulate private investments rather than to expand public credit facilities left the Latin Americans cold. This was viewed as a diluting of the Good Neighbor policy, for the United States government seemed to be retiring from the capital loan market in favor of Wall Street bankers. The Latin Americans held tenaciously to the conviction that they had been victimized and were still exploited by foreign private capital. Nevertheless, since the need of foreign capital was realized — for as one put it, "We need, ask for, and hate foreign capital at the same time" — the general attitude was that of willingness to accept the investment of private capital provided it came not as émigré capital but as resident capital. Foreign capital should be creative as well as profitable, but not exploitive. And, most important, it must submit to the laws of the country.[21]

In 1962 United States private direct investments in Latin America totaled more than $8 billion. (See Table 6.) This almost equalled one-fourth of the United States world total. Their importance to Latin America is indicated by the following facts and figures: (1) Latin-American governments collect 15 per cent of all their revenues from U.S. companies; (2) profit remittances by U.S. companies are only about one-half as large as their tax payments in

---

greater role *falls to private citizens and groups* than is the case in a program designed to aid European countries from the destruction of war." Dept. of State *Bulletin,* XVII (September 14, 1947), 500. For private direct investment abroad, see J. Fred Rippy, *Globe and Hemisphere* (Chicago: Henry Regnery Company, 1958), Chap. IV.

[20] In 1962 AID's investment guarantee program provided insurance protection at low cost against the special nonbusiness risks of doing business in developing countries, i.e., inconvertibility, expropriation and confiscation, war, revolution, and insurrection. For investment guarantees proper in Latin America, see *United States-Latin American Relations (Sen. Doc.* 125, 86th Cong., 2nd Sess.), 518, Appendix VIII. At the end of 1962 investment guarantee agreements were in force with all Latin-American countries except Brazil, Cuba, Mexico, Uruguay, and Venezuela.

[21] There is conflict of U.S. and Latin-American views regarding dependence on private capital. Manger, *op. cit.,* 62–63.

Latin America; (3) about three-quarters of the gross revenues of U.S. companies is paid out in Latin America to cover local tax, wage, and material costs; (4) U.S. companies provide jobs for 625,000 persons, less than 9,000 coming from the United States; and (5) United States companies, from their existing investments, are contributing to Latin-America up to $1 billion annually.[22]

TABLE 6

Value of U.S. Direct Investments in Latin America
(in millions of dollars)

Country	1950	1957	1960	1961	1962
All areas, total	11,788	25,394	32,778	34,664	37,145
Latin America	4,445	7,434	8,387	8,255	8,472
Argentina	356	333	472	656	797
Bolivia	11	16	33	43	32
Brazil	644	835	953	1,008	1,008
Chile	540	666	738	748	768
Colombia	193	396	424	425	456
Costa Rica	60	62	62	63	63
Dominican Republic	106	88	105	107	108
Guatemala	106	106	131	127	127
Honduras	62	108	100	95	99
Mexico	415	739	795	826	873
Panama	58	201	405	498	556
Peru	145	383	446	436	451
Uruguay	55	57	47	49	53
Venezuela	993	2,465	2,569	3,012	2,836
Other Countries	701	978	1,107	162	174

Source: *Survey of Current Business,* August, 1963 (U.S. Dept. of Commerce, Office of Business Economics).

Economic assistance

While urging on the Latin Americans the importance of foreign private investments, the United States government, ever since the end of World War II, continued to provide economic assistance to Latin America. This assistance took various forms: grants, technical assistance, and capital loans by United States governmental agencies.[23] (See Table 7 on p. 194.)

Outright grants, that is gifts, have been very limited, with the exception, of course, of military assistance, which has been almost completely on the grant basis. But with reference to economic aid, with the exception of the expenditures for the eradication of the hoof-and-mouth disease in Mexico,

[22] U.S. Dept. of State, *Our Southern Partners,* Publication 7404 (Washington, D.C.: Government Printing Office, 1962), 47.
[23] Rippy, *op. cit.,* 81–95.

and for technical assistance, virtually the only recipients of grant aid in Latin America have been Bolivia, Haiti, and Guatemala. After the overthrow of the Arbenz regime, Guatemala for a time received generous grant assistance from the United States, which was particularly concerned that the restoration of popular government in the Central American republic be attended by a return to economic stability. As for Bolivia and Haiti, a continuous flow of grants was necessary to save these countries from economic collapse and political chaos. Bolivia, in fact, has been the recipient of the largest per capita grant economic aid given by the United States to any country in the world.

Of the various forms of economic aid, technical assistance, or the export of United States know-how to underdeveloped areas, has been generally the most satisfactory, and certainly the most palatable to the United States Congress, because it is the least expensive. As we have noted, the technical assistance or Point Four program of President Truman really had its beginning during World War II in the programs of the Institute of Inter-American Affairs in the areas of education, health, sanitation, and agriculture.

Under the terms of the Mutual Security Act of 1951, Point Four General Agreements were signed with every Latin-American country except Argentina by June, 1953. These general agreements with individual countries define the basic terms of cooperation. Specific agreements are then drawn up, usually with a given ministry of the host country. This second agreement is for the purpose of carrying out a program in the field for which that ministry is responsible. The program agreements generally provide that the United States will furnish and pay for the technical specialists sent to the host country. A conspicuous feature of most program agreements is the establishment of a *servicio,* or special bureau set up by the sponsoring ministry of the host country. The *servicio* then becomes the administrative agency for all projects developed under the program agreement. It is jointly administered by the United States and the host country, and is jointly financed. Although the majority of the *servicios* operate in the fields of agriculture, health, and education, the projects include housing, transportation, communications, development of natural resources, and public administration.

Although the United States usually assumes initially a large part of the expenses of a project, the host country gradually assumes more and more of the responsibility until eventually it carries two-thirds or three-quarters of the financial burden. Generally, for every United States dollar spent for technical assistance in Latin America the host nation contributes more than two dollars.[24] The United States technical cooperation program in Latin America represented a total expenditure for the period 1950–1960 of $267.8 million.

[24] For example, in 1955 the United States contributed $20 million, and the Latin-American host countries contributed $72.10 million. U.S. Congress, Senate, *Technical Assistance Programs.* Hearings before a subcommittee of the Committee on Foreign Relations, 84th Cong., 1st Sess., 1955, 31.

By all odds the principal form of economic aid extended directly to Latin America by the United States government has been the public loan or credit. (See Table 7.) The principal agency serving the government in this capacity is the Export-Import Bank. Other lending agencies of the United States, such as the Development Loan Fund, have played a minor role in the economic development of Latin America.

TABLE 7

U.S. Government Grants and Credits to Latin America
July 1, 1945–June 30, 1963
(in millions of dollars)

Country	Total (Net)	Military Supplies	Economic and Technical Assistance			By Country FY 1962
			Total	Grants	Credits	
American Republics	5,095	802	4,293	1,228	2,757	1,365.7
Argentina	421	40	381	5	364	110.6
Bolivia	266	6	261	204	50	39.5
Brazil	1,511	225	1,285	138	943	244.6
Chile	590	92	497	99	378	244.6
Colombia	370	62	308	61	227	81.8
Costa Rica	71	1	70	51	19	10.4
Cuba	57	16	40	4	36	
Dominican Republic	55	8	47	17	29	36.8
Ecuador	116	35	80	35	42	36.8
El Salvador	30	1	28	17	11	23.8
Guatemala	137	6	131	123	8	10.6
Haiti	91	5	87	63	23	8.0
Honduras	44	4	40	29	11	4.6
Mexico	447	1	446	130	312	142.4
Nicaragua	54	5	50	36	13	14.7
Panama	74	1	73	47	25	25.5
Paraguay	53	2	51	27	18	8.2
Peru	288	84	204	66	128	91.9
Uruguay	89	34	56	4	32	10.1
Venezuela	137	8	128	8	120	76.0

Source: *Survey of Current Business,* August, 1963, and April, 1964 (U.S. Dept. of Commerce, Office of Business Economics).

Although originally designed to finance directly export and import transactions, the Export-Import Bank has for many years been indirectly promoting United States foreign trade by assisting in the development of the resources of the Latin-American countries. It is a general rule of the Bank to extend credits only to finance purchases of materials and equipment produced or manufactured in the United States.

While assistance for general economic development has never ceased to be considered a prime purpose of Exim Bank loans, the rearmament program during and following the Korean War made it necessary to increase the resources and broaden the lending powers of the Bank. Thus the Bank was empowered to extend loans for the development of new sources of strategic materials. These loans involved risks that would normally preclude a loan.

Since the Export-Import Bank operated like a bank, always scrutinizing loan requests to be certain that they were "sound," numerous worthy projects were rejected because they could not qualify under the high standards set by the Bank. Thus, the apparent adequacy of Exim Bank funds to meet Latin America's loan requests was quite beside the point because of the hard-boiled banker's insistence on financing only "sound" projects. Not only did the Latins complain about the high standards set by the Bank, but they objected to the requirement that loans had to be used for the purchase of equipment manufactured in the United States. Since machinery and equipment of identical or even superior quality could be bought at considerably lower prices in Europe and Japan, the Latin Americans began to develop a disinclination to negotiate United States credits. These complaints added to Latin America's demands for larger and easier credit through the agency of an inter-American bank or loan fund.

The net total of grants and credits by the United States to the American republics for military and economic assistance from July 1, 1945, through September 30, 1961, amounted to $3,743 million. Of this total sum, $675 million were military grants, leaving a total net of $3,068 million for economic and technical assistance, and farm products sales through a net accumulation of foreign claims. Of the total net economic assistance, $937 million were grants, $1,928 million were credits, and $303 million were farm products sales.[25]

For the period July 1, 1945, to June 30, 1951, the net economic assistance to Latin America was $437 million, of which $139 million was in the form of grants and $298 million in credits. This means that, from 1951 to 1961 Latin America received from the United States in grants and credits for economic assistance, $2,631 million. In other words, over the period of ten years preceding the Alliance for Progress, the average annual grants and credits to Latin America for economic aid amounted to $263,100,000. This did not include United States contributions to OAS and UN technical assistance programs, and those contributions by the United States to the World Bank which were used for economic assistance to the Latin-American republics.[26] These facts and figures serve as an answer to Latin-American complaints, voiced throughout the Truman and Eisenhower administrations, that the United States was neglecting their economic necessities.

[25] The above figures have been drawn from *Foreign Grants and Credits by the U.S. Government.* U.S. Dept. of Commerce, Office of Business Economics; and International Cooperation Administration, Office of Statistics and Reports, *Operations Reports.* For other items which might reasonably be considered as direct contributions by the United States to promote the welfare of Latin America, see J. Fred Rippy, "U.S. Postwar Aid to Latin America: An Exhibit of Incomplete Official Accounting," *Inter-American Economic Affairs,* Vol. 14, No. 4 (Spring, 1961), 57–65.

[26] The United States has contributed $1,500,000 annually to OAS technical assistance and $15,500,000 to the UN technical assistance program of which more than $5 million annually has gone to Latin America.

Latin America's economic troubles, which they hoped to solve with United States assistance, extended into the area of trade relations. The burden of their complaint, which contributed greatly to anti-United States feeling, was, "We must sell to you at prices you dictate." It is well-nigh impossible to correct the impression that it is the United States that fixes the prices of their raw commodities and not the competitive markets of the world, of which the United States is only a part. Moreover, under existing policy, the United States cannot accommodate Latin America's demands for an adequate market at fair prices in terms of production costs, for it is opposed in principle to stabilization agreements, though more recently it has retreated on this point to some extent, as demonstrated by our ratification of the International Coffee Agreement in 1963.[27] (See Table 8.)

In order to meet the demand for a stabilization of the coffee market, an

TABLE 8

U.S. Trade with Latin America
(in millions of dollars)

Country	Exports			Imports		
	1960	1961	1962	1960	1961	1962
Grand Total	30,550	20,962	21,628	14,654	14,713	16,387
Latin America	3,478	3,407	3,162	3,536	3,215	3,357
Argentina	350	424	375	98	102	106
Bolivia	25	26	32	9	10	12
Brazil	430	494	425	570	562	541
Chile	195	229	171	193	184	191
Colombia	246	245	226	299	276	275
Costa Rica	44	42	50	35	40	40
Cuba	224	14	13	357	35	7
Dominican Republic	41	29	71	110	90	153
Ecuador	55	50	45	65	54	71
El Salvador	42	35	41	32	37	44
Guatemala	63	60	61	59	63	63
Haiti	25	26	24	18	19	24
Honduras	34	37	43	34	33	33
Mexico	820	813	790	443	538	578
Nicaragua	30	72	46	21	25	27
Panama	89	107	105	24	23	23
Paraguay	9	13	8	8	9	7
Peru	143	173	184	183	194	191
Uruguay	62	48	44	21	23	24
Venezuela	551	515	468	948	898	976

Source: *Statistical Abstract of the United States, 1963; Commodity Trade Statistics, 1963.* U.N. Dept. of Economic and Social Affairs, Statistical Office of the United Nations. Statistical Papers, Series D. Vol. XII, No. 1–15.

[27] See "United States and Latin American Policies Affecting their Economic Relations," in *United States-Latin American Relations, op. cit.,* 399–539; Rippy, *Globe and Hemisphere,* 149–165.

inter-American agreement was entered into during World War II, only to be abandoned later. But, at Punta del Este, in 1961, the United States announced its decision to join the International Coffee Agreement, and in mid-1963 the American Congress approved our adherence to it. As for sugar, the United States has allocated among the various supply areas, domestic and foreign (i.e., Latin America), specific shares of the United States market at considerably reduced tariff rates. The Cuban quota, the largest by far, was in 1960 distributed among the other countries, because of the reprehensible conduct of the Castro government. At Punta del Este the United States also announced its willingness to study an international system of compensatory financing to cushion Latin America against price fluctuations in raw materials.

Tariff restrictions and quotas imposed on nonferrous metals are bitterly resented and branded as incompatible with inter-American solidarity. Undoubtedly the hostile demonstrations against Vice-President Nixon were inspired by resentments against actual or prospective restrictive trade practices of the United States affecting certain products of countries visited, especially Peru and Venezuela.

To point up the economic truism that one must buy if he wishes to sell, we cite the case of Venezuela in 1957. In that year Venezuela's imports from the United States totaled $998 million, and exports to the United States, principally petroleum, amounted to $902 million. The importation of Venezuelan petroleum was harmful to the Texas economy, but beneficial to the industrial North. Resentful of import restrictions imposed on their products entering the United States, the Latin Americans are all too prone to overlook the important fact that economic nationalism is also operative in the United States, a fact of life which the President and the Congress must reckon with.

In 1960, while the total value of world exports doubled, Latin America's relative share of world trade declined from 11.1 per cent in 1950 to 6.7 per cent in 1960. President Felipe Herrera of the IADB (Inter-American Development Bank) said, "The economic development of Latin America has slowed down more and more, and in the last five years has scarcely managed to keep pace with an accelerated population growth."[28] Latin America's hopeful answer to this trade stagnation was the establishment of free trade areas. By the Treaty of Montevideo (February, 1960), Argentina, Brazil, Chile, Mexico, Paraguay, Peru, and Uruguay created a Latin-American Free Trade Association. As a starter they agreed on a list of nearly 400 products which were multilaterally listed as preferential with an average discount of about 20 per cent. Also the Central American republics signed a Treaty of Economic Association creating a Central American common market "to foster the orderly growth of their foreign trade." These self-help efforts by Latin-American nations have received the blessings of the United States government.[29]

[28] *Américas,* December, 1962, 42.
[29] U.S. Dept. of State, *Our Southern Partners,* Publication 7404 (Washington, D.C.: Government Printing Office), 26–27.

The United States bends to the inevitable

The ill-fated Nixon tour of Latin America in 1958 marked a turning point in United States policy towards Latin America. It impressed upon the American nation the vital urgency of Latin America's economic situation, and the need of a large program to meet a large problem.

Following the Nixon episode President Eisenhower commissioned his brother, Dr. Milton Eisenhower, to make a fact-finding trip to Central America. Earlier, in 1953, Dr. Eisenhower had made a trip to South America. On his return he reported his observations and accompanied them with pertinent recommendations to ameliorate the economic ills of the area. His report contained no surprises. He believed that public loans should be forthcoming only when private financing was not available. He frowned on the demand for an inter-American bank. Although in his report on his Central American trip, Dr. Eisenhower reaffirmed essentially all that he had said in his earlier report, he added a note of urgency to his general recommendation that the United States re-examine its Latin-American policies. As if to guide the new thinking, he declared his concurrence in the subsequent announcement of the willingness of the United States government to consider in principle the establishment of an inter-American bank.[30]

Another result of the anti-Nixon demonstrations was a communication by President Juscelino Kubitschek of Brazil to President Eisenhower, May 28, 1958, suggesting a "thorough review of the policy of mutual understanding in this hemisphere." In the exchange of correspondence between the two presidents, the Brazilian president elaborated his idea which became known as "Operation Pan America," or "the battle against the festering sore of underdevelopment."[31] What was necessary to effect a cure was a bolder and more ambitious approach than had ever been tried before — no more palliatives and half measures, but a wholly new and reoriented program of inter-American economic and social cooperation.

At an informal meeting of the Foreign Ministers, held in Washington in September, 1958, it was decided that the programs of economic and social development in Operation Pan America should be entrusted to the OAS.[32] Accordingly, a special committee of the Council of the OAS, popularly known as the Committee of Twenty-one, was set up to formulate new measures of economic cooperation.

Another action by the informal meeting of Foreign Ministers, when informed that the United States would support the establishment of an inter-

[30] For the Milton Eisenhower reports, see Dept. of State *Bulletin,* XXIX (November 23, 1953), and XL (January 19, 1959).

[31] The plan suggested seven areas of study: (1) increased private investment; (2) inflation control; (3) increase of U.S. loans and establishment of an inter-American bank; (4) stabilization of export prices for Latin America's raw materials; (5) establishment of a Latin-American common market; (6) the impact of the European Common Market on Latin America; and (7) increased technical assistance. Dept. of State *Bulletin,* XXXVII (June 30, 1958), 1090–1091.

[32] Brazil had preferred that Operation Pan America be "free from the procedural and bureaucratic handicaps of the existing organs." Dreier, *op. cit.,* 83.

American lending institution, was to authorize the drafting of articles of agreement for such a bank. The articles were duly drawn up by a specialized committee of the IA-ECOSOC (Inter-American Economic and Social Council), and signed on April 8, 1959. In October, 1960, the Inter-American Development Bank began operations.

The charter of the new bank provided for a capitalization of $1 billion, of which the United States was to put up $450 million, the balance to come from Latin-American countries, rated according to their ability to subscribe. Decisions are reached by weighted voting according to the respective contributions to the total capital subscribed.

The charter also provides for two complementary agencies: the Inter-American Development Bank (IADB) with an authorized capital stock of $850 million for loans for wealth-producing projects on terms like those of regular commercial banks, and the Special Operations Fund of $150 million, for "soft loans" (repayable in local currencies), that would normally be regarded as unacceptable bank risks. Normally the IADB will not lend more than 50 per cent of the total cost of the project to be financed.

The Inter-American Development Bank is located in Washington, where it maintains an office to help the applicant republics with technical advice in preparing loan projects. Unlike the United States lending agencies, the Bank does not tie the borrower to buying within the hemisphere. But, most important, here is an agency of the OAS which can be expected to understand and be sympathetic with the development problems of the Latin-American countries.[33] By the end of 1963 the Bank had authorized loans totaling $875 million.

Act of Bogotá

The Eisenhower administration's reversal on the issue of an inter-American bank presaged a fundamentally changed attitude on general economic assistance to Latin America. Developments in Cuba — the orientation of Communism and the threat of the export of the Cuban revolution to other parts of Latin America — convinced President Eisenhower, in the very last months of his administration, that the United States should immediately redouble its efforts to meet the socio-economic needs of the Good Neighbors. It seems that there was need of a threat such as that presented by Fidel Castro to drive home the point that restricted, or even moderate, assistance would no longer suffice.

Accordingly, President Eisenhower, on July 11, 1960, announced that the United States, in accord with the concept known as Operation Pan America, would cooperate in promoting a socio-economic program in Latin America. Without delay the President recommended, and the Congress authorized, an appropriation of $500 million to establish a special inter-American social·

[33] *Agreement Establishing the Inter-American Development Bank.* Treaty Series No. 14 (Washington, D.C.: Pan American Union, 1959). For a description of the Bank, see *Américas,* II (June 4, 1959), 2, 32. The bank members had, by the end of 1963, agreed to increase the total capital to $2.1 billion.

development fund. To a meeting of the Committee of Twenty-one, held in Bogotá in September, 1960, Under Secretary of State Douglas Dillon presented a draft agreement, prepared by the United States, for the establishment of an inter-American program of social development.[34]

The deliberations of the meeting culminated in the Act of Bogotá, a cooperative project based on a United States draft, of "measures for social improvement and economic development within the framework of Operation Pan America." The Act was unprecedented in inter-American affairs in that Latin Americans accepted, as a condition of receiving foreign aid, the necessity of following sound economic policies, and of eliminating obstructions to economic and social progress, a concept that was to be developed more fully in the Alliance for Progress.[35]

Alliance for Progress

President John F. Kennedy, shortly after taking office, not only requested the appropriation of the authorized $500 million for Latin-American development, but he also called for a comprehensive cooperative program of economic and social development to accelerate the rate of progress in the Latin-American countries. It was on March 13, 1961, that the President, speaking to the assembled representatives of the Latin-American republics and members of the United States Congress, proposed that the American republics join in an *Alliance for Progress,* "to satisfy the basic needs of the American people for homes, work and land, health and schools." The President called for a ten-year plan, and as a starter he pledged $1 billion in United States aid during the first year of the program. But, he warned the Latin-American nations, "they and they alone can mobilize their resources, enlist the energies of their people, and modify their social patterns so that all, and not just a privileged few share in the fruit of growth."[36]

A Special Meeting of the Inter-American Economic and Social Council at the Ministerial Level was held at Punta del Este, Uruguay, in August, 1961, to draft concrete plans for carrying out President Kennedy's Alliance for Progress. Douglas Dillon, who was Secretary of the Treasury in the Kennedy administration, headed the United States delegation. Supplementing the Act of Bogotá, the special meeting was asked to approve a general blueprint for cooperative action. Mr. Dillon promised development loans to Latin America on a long-time basis "at a very low or zero rate of interest." He predicted that Latin-American efforts would be matched by an inflow, principally from the United States, during the next ten years of at least $20 billion.

[34] U.S. Dept. of State *Bulletin,* XLIII, No. 1110 (October 3, 1960), 536.
[35] For text of the Act of Bogotá, see *ibid.,* 537–540; also *Act of Bogotá, Measures for Social Improvement and Economic Development within the Framework of Operation Pan America* (Washington, D.C.: Pan American Union, 1961).
[36] *Alianza Para Progreso.* Address by President Kennedy and Text of Message to Congress. Dept. of State *Bulletin,* XLIV, No. 1136 (April 3, 1961), 471–478.

The delegations at Punta del Este approved the Alliance for Progress with a Declaration of the Peoples of America and the Charter of Punta del Este.[37] The Declaration was in effect a summary of the Charter which spells out in detail the great purposes of the Alliance for Progress and the proposed measures for insuring that its promises will become realities.

The American nations agreed to work toward the following goals: (1) improve and strengthen democratic institutions; (2) accelerate economic and social development; (3) carry out urban and rural housing programs; (4) encourage agrarian reform; (5) wipe out illiteracy; (6) carry out programs of health and sanitation; (7) assure fair wages and satisfactory working conditions for all workers; (8) reform tax laws; (9) maintain monetary and fiscal policies which will check inflation; (10) stimulate private enterprise; (11) find a solution to the problem created by excessive price fluctuations in the basic exports of Latin America; and (12) accelerate the economic integration of Latin America.

The United States, for its part, agreed to "provide a major part of the minimum of twenty billion dollars, principally in public funds, which Latin America will require over the next ten years from all external sources[38] in order to supplement its own efforts." The United States development loans on a long-term basis (up to fifty years) would be "at very low or zero rates of interest." For the year which began on March 13, 1961, when the Alliance for Progress was announced, the United States would immediately contribute to the economic and social progress of Latin America more than one billion dollars, most of this to be credited to a trust fund in the Inter-American Development Bank.

Latin America's role in the Alliance for Progress is twofold: first, to devote an increasing share of its own resources to economic and social development; and second, to make the reforms necessary to assure that all the people share fully in the fruits of the program. Self-help and basic socio-economic reform are the key to the solution of hemisphere economic and social problems as envisaged in the Alliance concept. United States assistance is designed not to accomplish this task, but rather to make it much easier for the Latin Americans to accomplish. Of the $100 billion in capital required, $80 billion was to be generated within the Latin-American countries themselves. Untold Latin-American billions that sought investment security or repose abroad should be induced to return and share in internal development. The goal set by the Alliance for Progress was 2.5 per cent annual rate of growth per capita for each of the next ten years.

---

[37] *Alliance for Progress.* Official Documents Emanating from the Special Meeting of the Inter-American Economic and Social Council at the Ministerial Level. Held in Punta del Este, Uruguay, from August 5 to 17, 1961 (Washington, D.C.: Pan American Union, 1961). All of the Latin-American countries were represented at the Punta del Este meeting. Cuba was denied participation in the Alliance for Progress. Her representative "Che" Guevara indulged in obstructionist tactics.

[38] It was anticipated that Western Europe and Japan would participate in providing capital investments in Latin America.

The Latin-American countries agreed, not only that the largest part of the financial support of the national programs of economic and social development must come from themselves, but they also agreed to make certain basic changes, such as: correct unjust systems of land tenure and land use, reform defective tax laws, and establish a fair tax structure. These changes in socio-economic patterns, if carried out, would be truly revolutionary. In fact the objective was to hasten a bloodless social revolution in order to obviate a Communist revolution — that is, to channel revolutionary ferment into evolutionary development.

The Charter of Punta del Este spelled out in detail the organization and administration of the vast concerted enterprise to be carried out under the aegis of the OAS. The Inter-American Development Bank was made administrator of the Inter-American Fund for Social Progress to be applied to loans on flexible terms and low interest rates, primarily for land purchases and use, housing, water supply, sanitation, and technical assistance. Each country-plan was to be analyzed by a committee of experts before being submitted to the lending institution. So that each recipient nation should live up to the principles of self-help and domestic reform, funds would not be allocated until the lending agency received assurances that the necessary measures had been taken or projected.

The Alliance in operation

The United States supported the Alliance for Progress program not only by its appropriations to the UN (World Bank)[39] and OAS (IADB), but through agencies of its own: the Export-Import Bank and the Agency for International Development (AID).[40] By the end of the first year after President Kennedy launched the Alliance for Progress, the United States had committed $1.03 billion in loans and grants to the program, thus fulfilling its own pledge. This sum, comprising 87 per cent in loans and 13 per cent in grants, was distributed as follows: AID, $401,599,000; Export-Import Bank, $360,604,000; Social Progress Trust Fund (administered by the Inter-American Development Bank), $129,682,000; Food for Peace Program, $135,790,000; and other aid, including the Peace Corps, $1,896,000. The Exim Bank loans were generally used for projects that would increase productivity directly, or for

---

[39] The World Bank (International Bank of Reconstruction and Development) makes a valuable contribution toward the Latin-American countries' goals in the Alliance for Progress. As of March 31, 1962, seventeen countries had received loans, since 1948, amounting to $1,440,870,000. The total of loans to Latin America was about ten times greater than the total subscription paid into the Bank by the Latin-American members. *Américas* (June, 1962), 10. Two affiliates of the World Bank, The International Finance Corporation and the International Development Association, also engage in lending operations in Latin America.

[40] AID was created in 1961, incorporating activities previously carried out by ICA, the Development Loan Fund (which was abolished), and other units. This single agency within the Department of State, has responsibility and authority for the formulation and execution of the foreign development aid program. The Exim Bank provides commercial loans that enable developing countries to purchase U.S.-made equipment for their development programs.

economic infrastructure investments that would lead to increased productivity.[41]

The United States government support of the Alliance for Progress programs is illustrated by Table 9:

TABLE 9

Alliance for Progress Programs Fiscal Years 1962, 1963, 1964
(in millions of dollars)

	Fiscal Year		
	1962 Actual	1963 Estimated	1964 Proposed
Development loans	$190	$400	$602
Development grants	22	90	105
Supporting Assistance	107	57	18
Inter-American Program for Social Progress:			
Social Progress Trust Fund	224	170	196
Chile reconstruction	100		
IAPSP grants	64	34	4
Total	$707	$751	$925

Source: Proposed Mutual Defense and Assistance Programs FY 1964, Agency for International Development and Department of Defense, April, 1963.

The Alliance program got $690.7 million in AID funds for fiscal 1963 which ended June 30, 1963. For fiscal 1964 Latin America was allotted from $665.7 million to $717.7 million, the exact amount to depend on how some proposed projects measured up to Washington's standards.[42] The funds of AID were applied mainly on a grant basis to promote progress in activities generally not self-liquidating and therefore not appropriate for loan financing such as: education and training, public health, and public administration in fields related to economic and social development. It later became the policy of AID to concentrate on key points in the hemisphere. When satisfactory performance by a country was not forthcoming, United States aid was discontinued. Thus, aid to Haiti was curtailed because the dictator there had refused to cooperate with the self-help precepts of the Alliance. Nearly two-

[41] See *Américas,* 14 (June, 1962), 4, for a country-by-country summary of AID and Exim Bank loans distributed during the first year of the Alliance.

[42] For reports on progress of the Alliance for Progress, see *Proposed Mutual Defense and Assistance Programs FY, 1964* (Agency for International Development and Department of Defense, April, 1963), 43–53, 60, and *ibid., FY, 1965,* 47–81. Also see: Inter-American Economic and Social Council, *The Alliance for Progress: Its Second Year, 1962–1963* (Washington, D.C.: Pan American Union, 1964); and The Government of the United States of America, *Report to the Inter-American Economic and Social Council,* for the Second Annual Meetings of the Inter-American Economic and Social Council at the Expert and Ministerial Levels, São Paulo, Brazil, October-November, 1963 (Washington, D.C.: September, 1963).

thirds of the total development lending for the fiscal 1964 was confined to Brazil, Colombia, Chile, and Central American countries.[43]

Although the amount of United States government appropriations did not fall far short of what had been pledged, the status of the program three years after its inception by President Kennedy was not encouraging. This fact was noted at the two meetings of the Inter-American Economic and Social Council at the ministerial level, as provided by the Charter of Punta del Este to review annually the progress of the Alliance. The ministers at the first meeting, which occurred in Mexico City in October, 1962, recognized the need to stimulate the confidence and cooperation of all classes in each country in support of the Alliance. They adopted a resolution recommending "that the member states instill in their peoples the conviction that their own national efforts, both public and private, in the field of economic and social development, constitute an essential aspect of the Alliance for Progress." This resolution was frank acknowledgment that general lassitude in Latin America was a challenge to the program. The IA-ECOSOC adopted another resolution instructing the OAS Council to appoint Juscelino Kubitschek and Alberto Lleras Camargo, former presidents of Brazil and Colombia, to report on how to infuse new life into the faltering Alliance.[44]

The reports of the two ex-presidents were presented to the Council of the OAS in June, 1963, and were considered at the second annual meeting of the IA-ECOSOC in São Paulo, Brazil, October 29 to November 16, 1963.[45] The reports represented divergent points of view concerning the failure of the Alliance for Progress. Dr. Kubitschek blamed the United States and believed that "progress of disbursements under the Alliance [should] not be impeded by rigorous observance of requirements for the presentation of *technically perfect* over-all plans for completed reforms." Dr. Lleras, on the other hand, admitted that the countries of Latin America "made a very poor showing of their ability to organize administratively the coordination of the gigantic efforts to which they had committed themselves." Both statesmen agreed however, that the Alliance for Progress was less an alliance than a series of bilateral agreements between the United States and nineteen hemisphere nations. No single inter-American organization was available to give unified direction to the program. They recommended therefore, the reshaping of the Alliance into a multilateral organization in order to give the Latin Americans a greater sense of involvement in the program.

The São Paulo meeting accordingly created a new Inter-American Committee for the Alliance for Progress (CIAP) to act as a clearing house between

[43] Statement of Teodoro Moscoso, U.S. Coordinator of the Alliance for Progress, before the House Foreign Affairs Committee, May 15, 1963 (mimeo).

[44] An estimate of the first year's achievements are set forth in an article by Wilson Velloso, "Whither the Alliance?" in *Américas* (December, 1962), 6–10. See also "The First Year of the Alliance for Progress," Dept. of State *Bulletin* XLVII (December 10, 1962), 887–890.

[45] See *Second Annual Meeting of the Inter-American Economic and Social Council at the Ministerial Level, São Paulo, Brazil, November 11–16, 1963* (Washington, D.C.: Pan American Union, 1964).

the United States and its Alliance partners. The eight-man executive committee was ready by January, 1964, to assume the difficult task of determining aid needs, channeling requests, and making recommendations on how funds should be spent. As some put it, the *Alianza* was "Latinized," but the true measure of this effort to convert the Alliance into a more cooperative program must be left for the future to gauge.

There can be no denying the great disappointment both in Washington and in Latin America that the Alliance for Progress has not achieved the momentum expected. Performance is uneven. Some nations have pitched in with vigor, and what has been accomplished is beyond reasonable expectations. But other nations, and among them the most important in Latin America — Brazil and Argentina — move only at a snail's pace. In fact the performance of the two giants of South America is disillusioning. By November, 1963, of a total $2.5 billion in Alliance aid committed, Argentina and Brazil got nearly a third, or $841.8 million between them. But since neither country had drawn up effective development plans, the result was that Alliance money was sopped up by economic chaos and unplanned spending.

Obstacles to the success of the Alliance, and various criticisms of it, may be enumerated as follows:

1. The program was oversold at the beginning, thereby causing too much to be expected of it in a few short years. Although an urgent necessity, the Alliance for Progress is a short-term impossibility. It set itself unrealistic goals, for it sought to accomplish in a decade what no nation has ever accomplished in less than a generation. Most important, it failed to take into account Latin America's most basic problem: the population explosion. The present population of 200 millions is expected in 1970, at the end of the Alliance for Progress, to total 300 million.

2. The first three years of the Alliance were marked by an exceptional number of political upheavals in Latin America. Without political stability — the thing Latin America needs most — how can any economic program succeed?

3. The flow of private capital, foreign and domestic into Latin-American investments fell far below expectations. It was estimated that if the Alliance were to succeed, private capital investments from the United States should be at the rate of at least $300 million annually. Lack of confidence, due to political instability, inflation, and fear of expropriation, greatly retarded the inflow of American capital.

Latin-American private investors also seemed to lack confidence in their own countries, for annually more than $700 million of Latin-American capital sought security outside the area. The amount of Latin-American capital invested abroad or deposited in United States or Swiss banks was believed to exceed $11 billion. If the Alliance were to stay afloat, certainly investors' confidence had to be restored.

4. Probably the most important reason for the halting progress of the Alliance was the oligarchic reaction in most of the countries. The landowning

aristocracy and conservative class, the traditional monopolizers of political and economic power, viewed the Alliance for Progress with a kind of "psychotic fear," for it proposed to reform the socio-economic structure of their countries. Businessmen and landowners were asked — so it seemed to them — to underwrite a "socialist" scheme to expropriate them. Moreover, they regarded the reformist threat of the Alliance as unwarranted interference by the United States in their internal affairs. Thus, since the Alliance program antagonized the very groups and classes whose help it needed most, the program stalled in most of the countries. Since it is highly improbable that the oligarchic reaction can indefinitely hold back the tide of reform, can it be anticipated that those privileged few will eventually realize the wisdom of accepting a peaceful revolution, or will they continue to resist reform and risk losing all? The future of the Alliance for Progress will be greatly influenced by this decision.

The dependence of the Alliance on the Latins themselves was emphasized in the report to President Kennedy, on March 22, 1963, by a special committee headed by General Lucius Clay to investigate operations of the foreign aid program:

> No matter what the amount of outside assistance, nothing will avail to promote rapid progress if Latin-American leaders do not stimulate the will for development, mobilize internal savings, encourage the massive flow of private investment, and promote other economic, social and administrative changes.[46]

[46] *Christian Science Monitor,* March 25, 1963.

SUPPLEMENTARY READING

Dozer, Donald M., *Are We Good Neighbors?* (Gainesville: University of Florida Press, 1959), 188–310.

Dreier, John C., ed., *The Alliance for Progress, Problems and Perspectives* (Baltimore: The John Hopkins Press, 1962).

Dreier, John C., *The Organization of American States* (New York: Harper & Row, 1962), 42–137.

Gordon, Lincoln, *A New Deal for Latin America: the Alliance for Progress* (Cambridge: Harvard University Press, 1963).

Lieuwen, Edwin, *Arms and Politics in Latin America* (New York: Frederick A. Praeger, rev. ed. 1961), 203–262.

Manger, William, *Pan America in Crisis: The Future of the OAS* (Washington, D.C.: Public Affairs Press, 1961), 48–67.

Manger, William, ed., *The Alliance for Progress — A Critical Appraisal* (Washington, D.C.: Public Affairs Press, 1963).

Mecham, J. Lloyd, *The United States and Inter-American Security, 1889–1960* (Austin: University of Texas Press, 1961), Chaps. XI, XII, XIII.

Redington, Robert J., *The Organization of American States as a Collective Security System* (Washington, D.C.: Industrial College of the Armed Forces, February 15, 1962).

Rippy, J. Fred, *Globe and Hemisphere. Latin America's Place in the Postwar Foreign Relations of the United States* (Chicago: Henry Regnery Company, 1958), 71–243.

Rippy, J. Fred, "U.S. Postwar Aid to Latin America: An Exhibit of Incomplete Official Accounting," *Inter-American Economic Affairs*, Vol. 14, No. 4 (Spring, 1961), 57–65.

Tomasek, Robert D., "Defense of the Western Hemisphere: A Need for Re-examination of United States Policy," *Midwest Journal of Political Science*, III, No. 4 (November, 1959), 374–401.

Unión Panamericana, *Aplicaciones del Tratado Interamericano de Asistencia Recíproca, 1948–1960* (Washington, D.C.,: Unión Panamericana, Secretaría General, 3rd ed., 1960).

U.S. Department of State, *The Story of Inter-American Cooperation. Our Southern Partners*. Dept. of State Publication 7404, Inter-American Series 78. November, 1962.

U.S. Department of State, *Inter-American Efforts to Relieve International Tensions in the Western Hemisphere, 1959-1960*. Publication 7409 (Washington, D.C.: Government Printing Office, 1962).

U.S. Senate Subcommittee on American Republic Affairs of the Committee on Foreign Relations, 86th Cong., 2nd Sess. Doc. 125, *United States-Latin American Relations: Compilation of Studies* (Washington, D.C.: Government Printing Office, 1960).

Washington, S. Walter, *A Study of the Causes of Hostility Toward the United States in Latin America* (Dept. of State, External Research Staff, Office of Intelligence Research).

a. External Research Paper No. 126 (Brazil) February 24, 1956.
b. External Research Paper No. 126.1 (Chile) August 28, 1956.
c. External Research Paper No. 126.2 (Argentina) May 27, 1957.

9

The United States, the OAS, and Communism[1]

By all odds the problem of greatest concern to the United States in its relations with its Latin-American neighbors since World War II has been the threat posed by international Communism. This threat greatly preoccupied the United States, but for the Latin Americans it apparently occasioned only mild concern. It was not until the Cuban government was communized under Fidel Castro that the Latin Americans seemed willing to recognize the stark reality of the Communist menace.

We have noted the efforts of the United States, acting bilaterally with individual Latin-American countries, and collectively in the inter-American system, to shore up the defenses of the Americas against the threatening Communist tide. These measures consisted not only of treaties and agreements of defensive alliance and collaboration; equally important, they sought to strengthen the political, social, and economic structure of the countries in order to neutralize the wiles and guiles of Communist attraction.

We turn now to the actual confrontation of the international Communist conspiracy when it revealed itself as an active and very present danger. Here is a supreme challenge to the genius of United States leadership, for, although the cold war cannot be won in the Americas, there it can probably be lost.

1. Communism in Latin America[2]

In broad terms the Communists' objective is to capture the "Revolution of Rising Expectations." They are ready to exploit the discontent and frus-

[1] See J. Lloyd Mecham, *The United States and Inter-American Security, 1889–1960* (Austin: University of Texas Press, 1961), Chap. XIV.

208

tration resulting from the slowness of economic growth and social reform. They believe that Communism is a magnet that will attract and draw unhappy people as long as the ruling elite obstruct reform.

Because of their small party membership, Latin-American Communists do not delude themselves that they can attain political power by their own efforts. For the present and for the indefinite future they are reconciled to working with other parties for more limited objectives. In fact, in 1957 they were put under strict injunction from Moscow to avoid "sectarian" policy, that is, going it alone. They thus identify themselves with popular and national aspirations, and seek through alliances with non-Communist forces to infiltrate the so-called "democratic governments of national liberation."

In order to achieve their objectives the Communists: (1) endeavor to reduce the political and economic influence of the United States in Latin America, (2) encourage "neutralism" on the part of Latin America in the cold war, and (3) strive to create a favorable image of the U.S.S.R. in Latin America.

It is the intent of Communism in Latin America to destroy whatever basis there may be for mutual trust between the United States and the Latin-American countries. They exploit real or fancied grievances. They play on nationalist and anti-foreign sentiment. They repeatedly charge that the United States is trying to drag Latin America into an imperialistic war; that it is bent on maintaining the Latin-American republics in a semi-colonial status. There can be little doubt that the postwar rekindling of anti-Yankeeism in Latin America has been fed by the Communist conspiracy.

By playing up the idea that Latin America is simply a pawn of the United States, Communists hope to encourage Latin-American "neutralism" in the great East-West cold war confrontation. A visible weakening of, or actual dissolution of the former Latin-American bloc which the United States could always count on in the United Nations, seems to betoken a rising neutralism in Latin America. This is a fact, but it would be difficult to prove that it is the result of Soviet or Chinese propaganda.

It is also difficult to appraise the results of the Communist efforts to enhance the prestige of the U.S.S.R. in Latin America. This aspect of the propaganda campaign seeks to extol the power, progress, and benevolence of the Soviet Union as a shining example of the superiority of Communism over decadent capitalism. There can be little doubt that Latin Americans, like other people of the free world, have been impressed by certain spectacular Soviet scientific achievements, but whether this has won for the U.S.S.R. the

---

[2] The best references for this subject are: Robert J. Alexander, *Communism in Latin America* (New Brunswick: Rutgers University Press, 1957); U.S. Senate, *United States-Latin American Relations: Soviet Bloc Latin American Activities and their Implications for United States Foreign Policy,* a study prepared by the Corporation for Economic and Industrial Research for the Subcommittee on American Republics Affairs of the Committee on Foreign Relations, Report No. 7 (Washington, D.C.: Government Printing Office, February, 1960), 685–828; and Dorothy Dillon, *International Communism and Latin America* (Gainesville: University of Florida Press, 1962).

sought-after position of influence and respectability in Latin America is another matter.

It is a cardinal error to equate Communist influence and threat with the small membership of the Communist parties in Latin America. In terms of numerical strength the Communists are only a splinter force, but they work ceaselessly in their attempt to exploit whatever breaks come their way. Through skillful maneuvering into political coalitions they have at times gained considerable political influence. Their infiltration tactics have led to the control or influencing of labor organizations, student and teacher groups, professional associations, mass communications groups, and peace and friendship groups. Rarely do Communists create their own organizations; they prefer, rather, to infiltrate established and accepted groups, and then divert their programs into channels compatible with Communistic objectives.

In testimony of the great success of their infiltration tactics, the Communists have strength in Latin-American trade unions far beyond their numbers. The Communist labor leaders are trained, indoctrinated, controlled, and financed by the international apparatus headed up by the Soviet Union. It is not necessarily their purpose to get a mass following among union members or to establish Communist unions, but to dominate the organizations with strategically located activists from the top federated groups down to the locals. Although the extent of Communist influence in the Latin-American labor movement is hard to measure, it can be accepted as widespread and dangerous. ORIT (Inter-American Regional Organization of Workers, an affiliate of the International Confederation of Free Trade Unions) considers the fight against the Communist menace one of its most vital objectives.[3]

Finally, we note the considerable success of Communism in infiltrating the the ranks of intellectuals and educational groups. The influence of the highly volatile and potentially rebellious university students is amply attested by their significant participation in political upheavals throughout Latin America. The attachment to Communism, either in fact or in sympathy, of so many of the so-called "better informed," poses for the United States a difficult problem of counter-propaganda.

The Americas react to the threat

Although, until the Cuban crisis of October, 1962, the United States had not been able to convince the Latin Americans of the gravity of the threat posed by Sino-Soviet political and military power in the Western Hemisphere, on various occasions the inter-American system took an encouraging anti-Communist stand. While not dismissing their belief that the United States was too nervous about Communism, Latin-American willingness to join in OAS condemnation of international Communism was due probably more to a desire to please the United States than to an acute awareness of the Communist threat.

There is no evidence that fear of the Soviet Union was responsible for any of the acts of the Mexico City conference of 1945, including the Act of

[3] *Soviet Bloc Latin American Activities*, 731–739.

Chapultepec itself. Shortly thereafter, however, the menacing clouds of international Communism began to cast a shadow over the free world. Then in 1947 at Rio de Janeiro, the Inter-American Treaty of Reciprocal Assistance was negotiated. For the United States it meant the bulwarking of American defenses against any possible Soviet aggression. But for the Latin Americans it had no particular objective other than the perfecting of the inter-American system as a regional arrangement under the United Nations.

The echoes of the Communist challenge were dramatically and ominously heard at Bogotá in 1948. At the opening session of the Ninth International Conference of American States, Secretary of State George C. Marshall referred to Communist opposition to world peace and recovery, and emphasized the need of inter-American cooperation in meeting the new totalitarian threat. This was on the eve of the tragic events of April 9 which resulted in great loss of lives and unbelievable destruction of property in the heart of Bogotá.

The assassination of Jorge Eliécer Gaitán, leader of the Liberal party, so outraged his devoted followers that a violent reaction set in immediately. Although the riots in their initial stage were sparked by a purely local political factor, the Communists rushed to the scene to fan the flames. For just such a break, many Communists from other countries, including Fidel Castro of Cuba, had foregathered to discredit or disrupt the conference. The delegations to the conference, however, stubbornly refused to concede a Communist victory, even though its meeting place was badly wrecked.

The fact of Communist involvement in the riots was accepted by the conference which, with unanimous approval, adopted a strong anti-Communist resolution. This resolution, entitled "The Preservation and Defense of Democracy in America," declared the anti-democratic nature, interventionist tendency, and political activity of international Communism to be incompatible with the concept of American freedom. Its "tendency to suppress political and civil rights and liberties" was condemned. The governments of the respective states were urged to adopt measures to control Communist activities.[4] Under the circumstances this was perhaps the extent of collective action that could be reasonably expected. Then followed the Korean situation which provided another test, although unfortunately, not a clear-cut one, because this was a case of Communist aggression outside the Western Hemisphere.

Korea

When the Republic of Korea was invaded by the North Korean forces, the two Latin-American members of the Security Council of the United Nations, Cuba and Ecuador, joined the United States in support of the resolution of June 25, 1950, which called for withdrawal of the invaders to the thirty-eighth parallel. A second resolution, introduced by the United States, recommending that members of the UN give assistance to the Republic of Korea, mustered the necessary seven-member majority for passage, thanks to the votes of Cuba and Ecuador. That the actions of these two representatives of

[4] Resol. XXXII, Final Act of the Ninth Conference, in *Annals* of the Organization of American States, I, No. 1 (1949), 133–134.

the American republics in the United Nations were induced by a feeling of continental solidarity and mutual interest with the United States was attested by a resolution adopted by the Council of the OAS on June 28, 1950.[5] On that date, at a special session, a resolution was adopted which declared adherence of the American republics to the decisions of the United Nations, and an equally firm adherence to the pledges of continental solidarity.

It was not until March, 1951, that the representatives of the American republics foregathered "to consider problems of an urgent nature and of common interest" brought about by the aggressive policy of international Communism. At the request of the United States a Fourth Meeting of Consultation of Ministers of Foreign Affairs met in Washington from March 26 to April 7.

The most important action of the meeting was the "Declaration of Washington," a pledge of unity against international Communism. It reaffirmed continental solidarity and registered firm support of the UN in the Korean crisis. Another resolution declared the necessity for positive support by the American republics of continental defense through the OAS, and of cooperation within the UN to prevent and suppress aggression in other parts of the world. But with respect to positive measures of inter-American military cooperation for continental defense, a third resolution recommended that, in accord with the Rio de Janeiro Treaty of Reciprocal Assistance, the American republics orient their military preparations in such a way as to give increased emphasis to the principle of collective defense. This called for armed forces to be available for the defense of the continent, and cooperation among the American republics in military matters, "in order to develop the collective strength of the continent necessary to combat aggression against any of them." The Inter-American Defense Board was charged with preparing military plans for common defense, to be submitted to the governments for their consideration and decision.[6]

The United States, in asking for the consultative meeting, hoped that the American republics would support the war effort with their combined military strength, and that they would plan a common program for resistance to the Communist threat. President Truman, in addressing the meeting, urged the Latin-American nations to "establish the principle of sharing our burdens fairly." But, so remote did the Latin Americans regard themselves from the Communist threat, that they felt little sense of obligation to resist until it reached the Americas.[7] Only Colombia responded to the United States' expectation of military cooperation in fighting the Communists in Korea. The

[5] See John A. Houston, *Latin America and the United Nations* (New York: Carnegie Endowment for International Peace, 1956), 118–132.

[6] Pan American Union, *Fourth Meeting of Consultation of Ministers of Foreign Affairs held in Washington, D.C., March 26-April 7, 1951, Proceedings* (Washington, D.C.: Pan American Union, 1951).

[7] See Joseph F. Thorning, "Latin American Reaction to the Korean Situation," *World Affairs*, CXIV, No. 1 (Spring, 1951), 14–16; Edwin Lieuwen, *Arms and Politics in Latin America* (New York: Frederick A. Praeger, 1962, rev. ed.), 209.

provisions of the Rio treaty, as correctly interpreted by the Latins, did not specifically cover such a situation.

A fair judgment of inter-American action vis-à-vis the aggression of international Communism in Korea is that it convincingly demonstrated moral solidarity on the ideological issue. The small contributions of food, medical supplies, and miscellaneous materials, had a token significance far beyond the quantity and value involved. As for Latin failure to supply troops to the United Nations forces in Korea, it was unrealistic to expect contributions of this nature, for it was not practicable to create an armed force made up of small contingents by the various countries. The United States indicated that it would not welcome contingents of less than 1,000 men. It is doubtful that the failure to send battalions to Korea was the result of Communist agitation against the sending of "cannon fodder for Yanqui imperialists."

The rise of Communism in Guatemala

The virtual take-over of the government of Guatemala by the Communists was a significant preview of what occurred later in Cuba. The Guatemalan episode is particularly interesting because it shows what could happen in other Latin-American countries which, like Guatemala, contain large masses of people fervently seeking reform, and in which democracy suddenly appears without the background of tradition and experience to make it succeed. The Guatemalan experience is also enlightening in that it disproves the myth that Latin America is relatively invulnerable to Communist penetration for any of these reasons — stubborn individualism, the strength of Catholicism, low industrialization, the political importance of the army, and the large Indian populations which cling to their traditional way of life. The dramatic incidents attending the rise and fall of Communism in Guatemala in the ten-year period 1944–1954,[8] are here presented therefore, as a case study of Communist take-over in a Latin-American republic.

General Jorge Ubico, conservative militarist, was the last in a long line of Guatemalan strong men. When his thirteen-year dictatorship was terminated by revolution in 1944, he left his country a legacy of political immaturity, archaic social structure, and economic backwardness. After the destruction of the old regime there was no organized group to inherit power or furnish leadership. It was a situation — a political vacuum — inviting to the Communists, who were, however, not able at first to profit from it. Ubico had

---

[8] The best work for this period is Ronald M. Schneider, *Communism in Guatemala, 1944–1954* (New York: Frederick A. Praeger, 1959). Also see Daniel James, *Red Design for the Americas: Guatemalan Prelude* (New York: The John Day Company, 1954); J. D. Martz, *Communist Infiltration in Guatemala* (New York: Vintage Press, 1956). Publications of the Department of State on the subject include: *A Case History of Communist Penetration: Guatemala*. Dept. of State Publication 6465, Inter-American Series No. 52 (1957); *Intervention of International Communism in Guatemala*, Dept. of State Publication 5556, Inter-American Series No. 48 (1954); *Penetration of the Political Institutions of Guatemala by the International Communist Movement* (Washington, D.C.: Government Printing Office, 1954).

suppressed all Communist activities and driven the leaders into exile. Thus, following the overthrow of the dictator, the returned leaders and the rank and file — only a handful in all — quickly mobilized their limited resources for the take-over of the Revolution.

Dr. Juan Arévalo, a left-of-center intellectual, was the revolutionaries' choice for president. Elected as the candidate of the National Renovation party (RN), Arévalo assumed office on March 15, 1945. It was the role of the new president, who had been living in Argentina as a university professor, to promote a fundamental social revolution in Guatemala. The new administration quickly passed reform legislation dealing with the expansion of education, protection of organized labor, social welfare, industrialization, and agrarian reform.

During the Arévalo administration the Communists made considerable headway in gaining control over organized labor and becoming entrenched in the government. Posing as ardent nationalists and adherents of the revolutionary objectives, they provided skilled political leadership in an administration in which this was sadly missing. It was undeniably true that Arévalo numbered some of the Communist leaders among his close friends and political collaborators, but it would be an error to say that he was a Communist or actively supported Communism. Because of a dearth of trained officials with democratic traditions, Arévalo came to lean more and more heavily, out of necessity, on his Communist supporters. He felt that they were useful to him and that he could control them.

Arévalo's attitude toward Communism was ambiguous. He was tolerant toward Communists as individuals and accepted their help. But he was opposed to the formation of an organized Communist party. He held that the constitutional ban on parties of "a foreign or international character" applied to organized Communism. Although the Communist party of Guatemala was secretly organized in 1949, it did not come into the open during Arévalo's government. While Communist influence in Arévalo's administration never became dominant, the end result of his tolerance toward the Communists was that they were in a position to make a virtual take-over in the next administration.[9]

Colonel Jacobo Arbenz Guzmán, candidate of the pro-Communist wing of the National Renovation party, was an easy victor in the 1950 presidential campaign, thanks greatly to the elimination by assassination of his principal rival, Colonel Francisco Javier Araña, leader of the moderate faction of the RN. Soon after the inauguration of President Arbenz, in March, 1951, the revolution took a decided leftward turn. That the energetic Communist minority influenced the new president and rapidly took over control of the movement there is no longer any doubt. Furthermore, the serious apprehensions of the United States that the government of Guatemala had fallen into the control of the international Communist movement proved to be fully justified.

[9] Schneider, *op. cit.*, 20–34.

Under the Arbenz regime we note a classic pattern of Communist operations. With great skill and subtlety they supported a revolutionary theory and program of action with a superior organization and unparalleled discipline. Having successfully identified themselves with the aspirations and demands for change unleashed by the socio-economic revolution of 1944, they won acceptance as spokesman for the depressed and inarticulate masses. Their first great success was gaining control of a unified labor movement. Then, being accepted by the president as spokesman for the peasant masses, they were given control of the administration of the agrarian reform program. Skillful infiltration tactics led to effective penetration of sensitive areas of the bureaucracy. A characteristic of Communist penetration of the Guatemala government was the principle of indirect control. Communists held key positions in certain strategic agencies which administered vital governmental programs and shaped public opinion. None of the cabinet ministers were Communists, and only four were members of the congress. Nevertheless, the Communists, through their own party, the PGT (Partido Guatemalteco del Trabajo), and the labor and *campesino* confederations, enjoyed disproportionate influence in the National Democratic Front, a government coalition of five groups which served as chief policy-making body. It was presided over by the president. Thus, by the time the Arbenz government was three years old, the Communists were in position to shape government policies. Their success was due, among other things, to the good will of the president.

The most distinctive feature of the Arbenz regime was the close relationship between the Communists and the president. He numbered Communist leaders among his most intimate friends and advisors, and turned over to them the implementation of the major social and economic programs of his administration. Whether Arbenz was a Communist or not made little difference, for he was unflagging in his support and loyalty to his Communist friends.

Near the beginning of his administration in 1952 Arbenz indicated his acceptance of the Communists by granting the PGT full legal status. According to Arbenz, the preservation of democracy required equality of opportunity for the PGT with the other parties. Were the rights of one Communist interfered with, Guatemala could no longer call itself a democracy. The inevitable next step was the branding of anti-Communism as anti-revolutionary. Communism was only an idea, said Arbenz, and no threat to Guatemala, but anti-Communism was a tool of a foreign power (the United States) and a threat to the nation.

Denials by Arbenz to the contrary, Communism in Guatemala was not solely a domestic affair, for most assuredly it played a definite and significant role in the plans of the Soviet Union. Guatemalan Communist leaders made frequent trips to the U.S.S.R. and satellite countries for training and instruction. Fundamental tasks to be undertaken by the Communist party in Guatemala were assigned to it by Moscow. Task number one was to fight Yankee imperialism. The United Fruit Company, the largest United States economic enterprise in the country, was a natural target for anti-imperialist nationalistic propaganda. Thus, the efforts of the United States government to support the company in opposition to the expropriation of its lands without "just compensation," evoked a bitter attack. Task number two was to penetrate and subvert the neighboring Central American states, using Guatemala as a base. There was a flow of propaganda materials and trained agitators into El Salvador, Honduras, and Nicaragua. Strikes and various forms of violence were planned and directed from Guatemala.[10]

The United States government was greatly alarmed over developments in Guatemala: the Communist infiltration of the Arbenz administration, the unquestioned tie-up between Guatemalan and Soviet Communism, and the intervention of international Communism in the other countries of Central America. Surely this represented a challenge to the principles of the Monroe Doctrine, and undoubtedly at an earlier date would have evoked immediate and vigorous action in support of the venerable policy. In 1954, however, unilateral action was ruled out because of nonintervention pledges. As for collective inter-American action, neither the Rio treaty nor the other pacts seemed to fit the peculiar problem presented by Guatemala. Since the Tenth Inter-American Conference was to meet in Caracas, Venezuela, the United States decided to refer the problem of Guatemala to the conference.

Communism and the Caracas conference

In response to informal inquiries by the State Department prior to the conference, a number of Latin-American governments warned against a direct showdown over Guatemala. It was the general Latin-American view that the United States overemphasized the Communist issue; furthermore, they believed that Guatemala's revolution was a good thing and should be allowed to develop without interference. They also contended that the solution of economic problems was the key to hemispheric solidarity, and that the Communist issue, if pressed too far, might be a divisive force. At the most, the United States delegation should confine the discussion of Communism to the more general question of Red intervention and measures to strengthen internal security — *but no mention of Guatemala.*

The delegates of the United States and the Latin-American republics convened in Caracas on March 1, 1954, with markedly divergent preoccupations. The United States wanted strong action on Communism. The Latin Americans minimized the threat of international Communism in the Americas and sought massive economic assistance. Over and above the Latins' apparent apathy on the Communist issue, the problem which Secretary John Foster Dulles faced at Caracas was that of seeking collective action within the confines of noninterventionism. That he succeeded in resolving the dilemma is doubtful.

There had been general resolutions at Bogotá in 1948 and Washington in 1951 that international Communism was incompatible with the concept of American freedom and was a danger to the American states. Secretary Dulles

10 *Ibid.,* 35–301.

at Caracas wanted more than mere reaffirmations of the earlier resolutions; he proposed a further resolution that "domination or control of the political institutions of an American state by the international Communist movement constitutes a threat to the sovereignty and independence of the American states, endangers the peace, and calls for the adoption of appropriate action in accordance with existing treaties."[11] The clear implication of the draft resolution presented by the United States was that the establishment of Communist political control over any American state would call for decisive collective action under the Rio de Janeiro Treaty of Reciprocal Assistance, which provides that in case of an aggression which is not an armed attack, a meeting of consultation shall be called to agree on measures to be taken for the common defense and the peace and security of the continent.

The United States draft resolution, in phrases reminiscent of the Monroe Doctrine, laid the basis for united inter-American action against the international Communist movement as a non-American political and conspiratorial system. Mr. Dulles, recalling the dictum of the Monroe Doctrine which opposes the extension of the European political system to any portion of the American continents, said:

> Those sentiments have long since ceased to be unilateral. They have become the accepted principle of this hemisphere. That is why it seems to us, we would be false to our past unless we again proclaimed that the extension to this hemisphere of alien despotism would be a danger to us all, which we unitedly oppose.

The debate on the draft resolution was spirited, and, on the part of Guatemala's Foreign Minister, Guillermo Toriello, acrimonious. The skill with which the representative of little Guatemala cast darts of sarcasm at the imperialistic United States aroused great secret amusement and admiration among the assembled Latin delegates. At the start it seemed that only six countries, all under dictatorships, gave Secretary Dulles unqualified support. In the end, however, the United States resolution, modified only slightly, was approved by a vote of 17–1 (Guatemala), with Mexico and Argentina abstaining. Many of those who voted in favor of the anti-Communist resolution (Declaration of Solidarity for the Preservation of the Political Integrity of the American States against the Intervention of International Communism)[12] charged bitterly that they felt pressured by the United States, for they did not wish to jeopardize economic assistance.

The approval of the anti-Communist resolution has been called a Pyrrhic victory for the United States. At the cost of resentments created by its pressures, the United States won a declaration of dubious value. To say that it amended the Charter of the OAS which disallowed collective intervention

[11] Statement by Secretary Dulles at Caracas, March 8, 1954. Dept. of State *Bulletin*, XXXI, No. 769 (March 22, 1954), 422–423.

[12] Resol. XCIII, *Tenth Inter-American Conference, Caracas, Venezuela, March 1–28, 1954, Report of the Pan American Union on the Conference*, in *Annals* of the Organization of American States, VI (Special Number, 1954), 114–115.

would not be true, for treaties cannot be amended by mere resolutions. This was the correct legalistic position taken by Mexico at Caracas. The atmosphere of the Caracas conference strongly suggested that the Latin-American representatives did not intend to reverse the rule against intervention. They merely expressed willingness to consult on measures that did not amount to intervention. Later, in dealing with the problem of Communism in Cuba, the Caracas declaration was never invoked; thus, it has apparently served no useful purpose.

Also, the contention that the Caracas declaration "Pan Americanized" the Monroe Doctrine is limited both in meaning and in value. The United States did not commit its unilateral political doctrine to group decision. If we accept the Latin-American argument that the Caracas declaration imposed on them no binding obligation with respect to collective intervention, it likewise imposed no restraint on unilateral action by the United States. The Monroe Doctrine still belonged to the United States for ultimate resort in self-defense.

It must be recorded also, that at the Caracas conference the Guatemalan Communists achieved their goal of using the conference as a propaganda platform. Their claims gained a sympathetic hearing from many Latin-American nationalists who bore a deep suspicion of the United States. All too many were eager to believe that Communism was a purely internal concern of Guatemala, and that the Central American country was the victim of a plot to overthrow her government and replace it with one subservient to the United Fruit Company. At any rate a situation soon developed in Guatemala to test the results of Caracas.

The fall of Communism in Guatemala[13]

The Guatemalan government, correctly interpreting the Caracas declaration as a United States effort at intimidation, reacted rather violently in order to consolidate its power. The secret police, employing the brutal tactics generally associated with Communism, instituted a reign of terror in their efforts to break up plots. There were mass arrests, suspension of constitutional guarantees, and opposition party leaders were killed. President Arbenz rejected a United States diplomatic note demanding fair compensation for the expropriated banana lands of the United Fruit Company. Then the congress of Guatemala withdrew its ratification of the Rio treaty to further heighten the tensions in external relations. Little wonder that, in the United States, Congressional and popular pressures were put on the State Department to "do something" about Communism in Guatemala.

When it was disclosed on May 17, 1954, that a shipment of Soviet-bloc arms was en route to Guatemala, action was forthcoming on several sides. The United States was provoked to counter by sending arms and airplanes to Nicaragua and Honduras to defend against Communist aggression from Guatemala. Some of these armaments apparently found their way into the hands of Guatemalan rebel-exiles led by Colonel Carlos Castillo Armas.

13 See Schneider, *op. cit.,* 302–322.

In June, Castillo Armas, with a small rebel force of only a few hundred men invaded Guatemala from Honduras. Virtually no opposition was encountered. When the country had been penetrated scarcely twenty miles, the Arbenz government toppled because of army defection in Guatemala City. An effort by Arbenz and his Communist supporters to use the recently received Soviet-bloc armaments to arm the populace was frustrated by the army leaders. On June 27 representatives of the officer corps met with President Arbenz and demanded his resignation. Despite strong opposition of the Communist leaders who wished to organize a popular defense, Arbenz resigned and fled the country, leaving the Communist-dominated government in collapse. After an interim officers' *junta,* Castillo Armas became president of Guatemala in September, 1954.

United States involvement in these developments was not confined to the alleged giving of indirect aid to the rebels (which aid, incidentally, did not prove to be necessary), but more important perhaps were the issues brought before the UN and the OAS.[14] The Castillo Armas invasion prompted Guatemalan appeals to both international bodies. On June 19, 1954, Guatemala referred to the Inter-American Peace Committee the matter of the attack from Honduras. But after that body had been immediately convened, it was told by Guatemala that it should suspend action, for the matter had already been referred on the same date to the Security Council. This development was disappointing to the members of the hemisphere community for they strongly believed that this was a matter that should be handled by the OAS. This was the first time that an issue was raised whether the regional organization or the Security Council should act.

In the Security Council a Brazilian-Colombian resolution that the case of Guatemala should be referred to the OAS was defeated by a Soviet veto. This act drew from Ambassador Lodge the bitter warning that the U.S.S.R. should "stay out of the hemisphere." After passing (unanimously) a "let there be no further bloodshed" resolution, the Security Council defeated a motion for United Nations discussion of the Guatemala case. This was the end of UN involvement in the issue, for the Security Council decided to withdraw in favor of the Inter-American Peace Committee, which had begun to investigate the facts. Guatemala, now that Soviet support in the UN had been checkmated, was willing to accept OAS jurisdiction in the affair.

On June 26 the United States and nine Latin-American countries, resorting directly to the Rio treaty, asked that a meeting of the Ministers of Foreign Affairs be convoked to consider the situation created by the intervention of international Communism in Guatemala. The Council convoked a consultation to meet at Rio de Janeiro on July 7, 1954. It is an interesting fact that the Caracas anti-Communism resolution was not invoked, thus avoiding the

---

[14] For the Guatemalan complaint before the Security Council, see Dept. of State *Bulletin,* XXXI, No. 784 (July 5, 1954), 26–31; Houston, *op. cit.,* 105–172. For the Guatemalan problem before the OAS Council, see Dept. of State *Bulletin,* XXX, No. 785 (July 12, 1954), 45–47.

necessity of proving the "domination or control" of the political institutions of Guatemala by the international Communist movement.

In the meantime, the plaintiff, the Arbenz government, fell while the Inter-American Peace Committee was making plans for an on-site investigation. Nevertheless, a subcommittee started its trip on June 29, but got no farther than Mexico City, where it was informed by the new government of Guatemala, and also by Honduras and Nicaragua, that the controversy between them, which had occasioned the committee's trip in the first place, had ceased to exist.[15] Thus, politico-military developments in Guatemala made unnecessary any further action by the peace agencies of the OAS. The proposed consultative meeting was called off. This, we may speculate, was a fortunate circumstance for the United States, since it was very doubtful that the Latin-American nations were in a mood to sanction collective intervention in Guatemala. They clung to the view that Guatemala's revolution was "legitimate" and there should be no outside interference.

The overthrow of the Arbenz regime created no enthusiasm in Latin America, but instead there was much criticism of the United States, which was credited with brutal and arrogant intervention against a popular democratic government. The avalanche of reproach loosed by Latins of all kinds of beliefs, illustrated their reluctance to recognize the vital issue of international Communist intervention in America. Here truly was an illustration of Latin America's concern over intervention by the United States far outweighing any possible fears of Communist aggression. Undoubtedly the prestige of the United States was hurt by these reactions. Later, however, when the truth of United States charges against the Arbenz government was supported by captured documents and by subsequent developments, much of the criticism abated. This all tended to prove that, among the Latin Americans, there was great disinterest and misinformation on the subject of the Communist threat. How greatly was this confirmed by the Cuban crisis!

2. The Cuban Problem

The Communist problem returned, after the Guatemalan episode, to plague the United States and the OAS in far more serious dimensions, with the policies and actions of the Cuban government under Fidel Castro. After its seizure of power on January 1, 1959, the revolutionary government of Cuba soon became a major disruptive force creating international tensions in the Caribbean area. Because of its Communist-dictatorial orientation, alignment with the Sino-Soviet bloc, calculated efforts to infiltrate its brand of revolution into other Latin-American countries, and virulent attacks on the OAS and the United States, the Castro regime not only put a strain on American solidarity

---

[15] For the *Meeting of Consultation of Ministers of Foreign Affairs*, and *Report of the Inter-American Peace Committee on the Controversy between Guatemala, Honduras, and Nicaragua*, see *Annals* of the Organization of American States, VI, No. 3 (1954), 159–162, 239–245.

unmatched by any situation in the past, but more important, jeopardized the national security and even the very existence of all American republics by introducing into their midst the atomic might of the Soviet Union.

The emergence of Castroism[16]

Originally, the initial acts and pronouncements of the leaders of the 26th of July Movement seemed to indicate dedication to a program of democracy and socio-economic reform. Thus, Castro became the idol of the masses, not only in Cuba, but throughout Latin America. He was a symbol of hope for millions of underfed, undereducated, and underprivileged people. But, in the course of a few short months the perversion of the original Cuban revolution became more and more apparent.

Employing totalitarian techniques, Fidel Castro, with the cooperation of his Communist colleagues in a triumvirate of absolute political power — his brother Raúl, minister of the armed forces, and Ernesto "Che" Guevara, economic czar — converted Cuba by the end of 1960, into a full-fledged police state.

First, Castro consolidated his military power by destroying the entire organization of the Batista army. In the process, more than 500 officers were executed, a shocking departure from the rather mild treatment of the defeated opposition which was traditional in Latin-American revolutions. The old army was replaced by loyal Castro forces and secret police. The size of the revolutionary army and militia, with armaments secured first from Western Europe and later from the Communist bloc, converted Cuba into a highly militarized state.

Further evidences of Communist-totalitarian trend were: seizures of private property, diverting agrarian reform into a community of goods rather than a reparcelling of the lands, and a drive for state control of the entire economy; suppression of democratic trade unions, abolition of collective bargaining, abolition of freedom of the press by suppression of independent newspapers, and suspension of habeas corpus. The regime frankly stated that it had no intention to submit to free elections, and prevented the functioning of democratic parties by banning any critical opinion as counter-revolutionary — the Communists meanwhile being given free rein. On May 1, 1961, it was formally announced that Cuba was "a socialist state" and that there would be no more elections. In the following December, Fidel Castro openly avowed himself a "Marxist-Leninist until the last day of my life." Castro frankly declared that if he had heralded his revolution sooner, while in the Sierra Maestra, as

---

[16] From the flood of books on Castro's Cuba, those selected for special mention are: Theodore Draper, *Castro's Revolution: Myths and Realities* (New York: Frederick A. Praeger, 1962); Daniel James, *Cuba, The First Soviet Satellite in the Americas* (New York: Avon Book Division, 1961); Wyatt MacGaffey and Clifford R. Barnett, *Cuba, its people, its society, its culture* (New Haven, Conn.: HRAF Press, 1962). See also Lieuwen, *op. cit.*, 263–287; *Cuba* ("White Paper"), Dept. of State Publication 7171, Inter-American Series No. 66, April, 1961 (Washington, D.C.: Government Printing Office, 1961).

being "Marxist-Leninist" he and his guerrilla army "possibly could not have descended to the plains."[17]

Cuba's drift into Communism was accompanied by an increasing orientation toward the Sino-Soviet bloc. Ostensibly to free herself of economic dependence on the United States, Cuba negotiated a commercial agreement with the U.S.S.R. in February, 1960. The Soviet Union agreed to buy over the next five years five million tons of Cuban sugar, and to supply in exchange petroleum, iron and steel, and machinery, plus $100 million in credits. When Cuba's normal oil supply from Venezuela was cut off, following Castro's confiscation of the British and American oil refineries because of their refusal to process Soviet oil, the U.S.S.R. hastened to supply the island republic's petroleum needs. Then, when President Eisenhower cancelled Cuba's sugar quota, Communist China negotiated a five-year trade pact, signed July 25, 1960, providing for the annual purchase of 500,000 tons of Cuban sugar to be paid for almost entirely in Chinese goods. By the end of 1960 most of Cuba's sugar production had been contracted for by the Communist bloc on a barter basis. Castro had become dependent on the Sino-Soviet bloc for his survival.

The course of Cuban foreign policy became critical when, on July 9, 1960, following Cuban claims that the United States was planning an invasion, Soviet Chairman Nikita S. Khrushchev offered to support Cuba with Soviet rockets if it should be attacked by the United States. A few days later in the UN Security Council, the Soviet delegate warned that the U.S.S.R. would not remain indifferent if an armed intervention were undertaken against Cuba. In addition to Cuba, he extended an unsolicited blanket of Soviet protection over all the Latin-American countries. The Soviet Union was moving into the American community in frankly expressed disregard for the Monroe Doctrine, which the United States seemed fearful to defend.

The Cubans of course welcomed the threat of Soviet military intervention in the Americas. It was declared to be a "solid guarantee" that the military and economic superiority of the United States could no longer "impose political and economic policies contrary to our interests . . . and perpetuate the misery of our peoples." The rest of the Americas, however, viewed with concern this acceptance of Khrushchev's offer as a grave betrayal of the peace and security of the hemisphere.[18] We turn now to a consideration of the attitudes and policies of the United States, the Latin-American nations, and the OAS toward the Cuban problem.

The United States views the Castro revolution

The overthrow of the increasingly unpopular Batista by the forces of Fidel Castro and his 26th of July Movement was at first generally popular in the United States, and without hesitation the United States government, on Jan-

---

[17] *New York Times,* December 2, 3, 1961.

[18] *Inter-American Efforts to Relieve International Tensions in the Western Hemisphere, 1959–1960.* Dept. of State Publication 7409 (Washington, D.C.: Government Printing Office, July, 1962), 72–73. Hereinafter cited as *Inter-American Efforts.*

uary 7, 1959, recognized the new revolutionary government of Cuba. Shortly after, with an obvious gesture of good will and sincere desire for harmonious relations, the American government designated as its new ambassador to Cuba Philip W. Bonsal, a career officer well known and well liked in Latin America because of his sympathetic understanding of its problems. The United States, wishing to see democratic government restored in Cuba, indicated its willingness to give financial aid to the Cuban government. But Premier Castro would have none of this; indeed, he appeared to go out of his way to exacerbate relations. It has been suggested quite plausibly that "Castro well knew that his greatest defense was to proclaim and provoke the opposition, both real and imagined, of the United States to his revolution, thus gaining sympathy and friendship throughout Latin America."[19] At any rate, the spectacle of the brave leader of a small country openly defying the greatest power on earth, met with an emotionally sympathetic response throughout Latin America.

Castro had made it clear earlier that he resented the military assistance the United States had given to Batista and would welcome the withdrawal of United States military missions to Cuba. After he came into power he tore up the Military Assistance Pact and dismissed the missions. Almost at its outset the Cuban government began to wage an intense campaign of hostile propaganda against the United States. A whole series of discriminatory and confiscatory actions against United States trade and investments took place. Steps were taken by the Cuban government to divert its import trade to the Soviet bloc. United States citizens were dispossessed of properties valued at over $850 million — without assurances of adequate compensation. Cuba seemed to be deliberately seeking to sever economic ties with the United States without regard for equity or international law and practice. The former rich tourist revenue dried up.

All efforts of Ambassador Bonsal to carry on even brief and restrained conversations with either Premier Castro or "Che" Guevara, were rebuffed. In many ways the Ambassador was subjected to calculated insult. Despite these provocative circumstances, the United States government felt constrained to adopt the policy of wait and see, for it did not dare to act unilaterally because of its nonintervention commitments, nor could it count on the support of the "good neighbors" in multilateral OAS action. Thus, merely for the record, the State Department, on June 21, 1960, sent a memorandum to the Inter-American Peace Committee describing Cuba's systematic campaign of "distortions, half-truths, and outright falsehoods" against the United States.[20]

Because of further deterioration of relations, President Eisenhower, on July 6, 1960, cancelled all United States imports of Cuban sugar under the existent quota, which provided a premium considerably above the world

[19] John C. Dreier, *The Organization of American States* (New York: Harper & Row, 1962), 91.
[20] U.S. Dept. of State *Bulletin*, XLIII (July 18, 1960), 79–88.

price.[21] This act, a heavy blow at Cuba's economy, provoked anguished cries of "economic aggression," which, in a sense, it was. In further efforts to hasten the expected economic collapse of Cuba, the United States government progressively cut imports from Cuba and our own exports to the island almost to the vanishing point, the principal export exceptions being foods and medical supplies.

Contrary to some expectations, these measures of economic pressure did not result in the collapse of the Castro regime. Quite to the contrary, they brought about Cuba's more intimate identification with the Communist bloc. The Soviet Union, Communist China, and the satellites all rushed to Castro's assistance. Frightening evidence of Cuba's incorporation into the Communist camp was Nikita Khrushchev's startling move of July 9, 1960, claiming Cuba as a Communist protectorate. His threat to use missiles in defense of Cuba, and his disdainful remark about the Monroe Doctrine drew from President Eisenhower the immediate rejoinder that the United States would not be deterred from meeting its responsibilities, nor would it, in conformity with its treaty obligations (OAS Charter and Rio treaty), permit the establishment in the Western Hemisphere of a regime dominated by international Communism. President Eisenhower declared that Khrushchev's promise of support of the Castro regime revealed not only close ties between the U.S.S.R. and Cuba, but also clear intention of the Soviet Union to make Cuba a satellite in the Western Hemisphere.[22]

In view of the Khrushchev threat, following other evidences of Cuba's alignment with the Communist bloc, such as the arms buildup and subversive activities against other Latin-American governments, the United States believed that the Cuban situation warranted collective action under the Rio treaty. But, before a consultative meeting could be convened the Cuban government itself preferred its own charges against the United States to the United Nations Security Council. These charges, repeated on numerous occasions and rejected by the United States, included the following: threats and aggressive acts against Cuba, protection granted Cuban "war criminals," violation of Cuban air space, exercise of undue diplomatic pressure, economic aggression, and abetting counterrevolutionary activities against the Cuban government.

The Security Council met July 18–19, 1960, to consider the Cuban complaint. Since this was a patent disregard by Cuba of her obligations under the OAS Charter and the Rio treaty to resort first to established inter-American procedures for the settlement of disputes, Ambassador Henry Cabot Lodge urged the Security Council to take no action until the OAS had an opportunity to deal with the problem. The United States viewpoint was accepted by the Security Council, which voted 9 to 0, with the U.S.S.R. and Poland abstain-

---

[21] Cuba, under the terms of the Sugar Act enjoyed a quota of 3,129,000 tons, or one-third of total U.S. requirements.

[22] *Inter-American Efforts,* 215–218.

ing, to adjourn consideration of the question pending receipt of a report from the OAS.[23]

Castro's attempt to short-circuit the OAS by direct appeal to the UN was only further evidence of his scorn for the inter-American organization which he contemptuously labeled a "colonial office" of the United States. His policies seemed designed to undermine and discredit the regional system.

The OAS and the Cuban problem[24]

A number of the Latin-American governments preferred to regard the Cuban problem as an essentially bilateral matter between Cuba and the United States in which they did not wish to share a collective responsibility. The United States, however, in demanding a consultation meeting, emphasized that the problem was one for all the American republics, since it involved Communist subversion which threatened governments individually and the security of the hemisphere in general. According to Secretary of State Christian Herter, the real issue was one that affected all the American republics, because (1) Cuba had shown its willingness to permit the penetration of Soviet influence in the hemisphere, and (2) Cuba had refused to accept its responsibilities and obligations as a member of the inter-American system. The OAS Council decided to convoke a Seventh Meeting of Consultation of Foreign Ministers in San José, Costa Rica, on August 22, to consider the threat of extracontinental intervention in hemisphere affairs.

The Seventh Meeting of Consultation met in San José immediately after the closing of the Sixth Meeting in the Costa Rican capital. At the Sixth Meeting the American republics, in unprecedented action, imposed heavy sanctions on the Dominican government, but at the Seventh Meeting they were reluctant even to mention Cuba in any of its acts. Was this because Dictator Trujillo was regarded as a greater threat to the peace and security of the Americas than the alignment of Castro with the missile-brandishing Khrushchev?

Secretary Herter hoped to get the Foreign Ministers gathered at San José to join in a specific denunciation not only of Sino-Soviet Communist intervention, but also of Cuba for inviting it. Since, however, the Latins were not willing to identify the Cuban government as a party to the critical situation, a compromise resolution was adopted which condemned Communism but not Cuba. Specifically, the Declaration of San José: (1) condemned the intervention or threat of intervention by an extracontinental power in the affairs of the American republics, and declared that the acceptance by any American state of such intervention or its threat, endangers American solidarity and security; (2) rejected the attempts of the Sino-Soviet powers to exploit the political, economic, or social situation in any American state as threatening to hemisphere unity, peace, and security; (3) reaffirmed the principle of non-intervention by any American state in the internal or external affairs of the

[23] *Ibid.,* 53–54.   [24] *Ibid.,* 54–64, 71–89.

other American states, and declared that the inter-American system was "incompatible with any form of totalitarianism"; and (4) proclaimed the obligation of all member states to submit to the discipline of that system and to comply with the provisions of the Charter of the OAS.[25]

Although the Declaration of San José contained no specific reference to Cuba, its applicability was manifest, and in recognition of this fact the Cuban delegation withdrew from the meeting.

It cannot be recorded that the Seventh Meeting marked any progress on the part of the OAS in confronting the Cuban situation. It was paralyzed when faced with the difficulties created by the presence of Communism in Cuba. Manuel Tello, the Mexican Foreign Minister, expressed a general attitude when he advised patience with the Cuban revolution and expressed the view that "our task is to make Cuba feel that her destiny is in America." While rejecting any threats of extracontinental intervention, he declared that collective action could endanger the principle of nonintervention unless it was limited to cases where peace and security were clearly threatened.[26] The Latins evidently wanted more proof that the hemisphere was really in danger.

Unilateral action

Failing to influence effective cooperation within the inter-American system, the United States turned to its own unilateral action. Because of alleged Cuban-inspired revolts in Costa Rica, Guatemala, and Nicaragua, in November, 1960, the United States, without consulting the OAS, sent a naval task force to patrol the coasts of the Central American countries against rumored invasion from Cuba. The patrol was withdrawn only a few days later when the emergency ended.

In answer to the urging of Cuban exiles that the United States assist the arming and training of a landing force of anti-Castro shock troops, President Eisenhower finally gave his go-ahead signal. For several months prior to the expiration of the Eisenhower administration, United States agencies, in collusion with the governments of Guatemala and Nicaragua, supported the training and equipping of Cuban exile groups in preparation for an assault on Cuba.

The inevitable break of relations between the United States and Cuba came on January 3, 1961. When the Cuban government arbitrarily limited the personnel of the United States embassy at Havana to only eleven persons, President Eisenhower, interpreting this as having no other purpose than to render impossible the conduct of normal relations, formally terminated diplomatic and consular relations.

After President Kennedy came to power, the preparations for an invasion of Cuba continued. Soon, because of the arms buildup in Cuba, the new President was told that time was running out. The operation must be

[25] See *Final Act, Seventh Meeting of Consultation of Ministers of Foreign Affairs, San José, Costa Rica, August 22–29, 1960* (Washington, D.C.: Pan American Union, 1960).
[26] *Inter-American Efforts*, 73.

launched immediately, or abandoned. The fateful decision to go ahead was influenced by the President's military advisers and CIA intelligence; the latter however, proved to be incorrect in its expectation of a popular Cuban uprising. When President Kennedy gave the green light to the operation, it was with the proviso that American forces would never be used.

On April 19 the invasion took place on the southern coast of Cuba at the Bay of Pigs. The invaders, about 1,500 strong, were met by Castro's far superior forces, and, lacking indispensable air cover, were utterly crushed. Over 1,200 were taken prisoner. The anticipated popular uprising never took place, not only because there had been failure to coordinate the invasion with the Cuban underground leaders, but because Castro, warned of the invasion, had plenty of time to round up and jail or detain tens of thousands of suspects.[27]

That the United States government was heavily involved in the invasion fiasco President Kennedy was frank to acknowledge when he assumed personal responsibility. That this was a flagrant violation of the nonintervention principle to which the United States was bound by numerous inter-American declarations and treaties, the President was not willing to concede. He said, "While we could not be expected to hide our sympathies, we made it repeatedly clear that the armed forces of this country would not intervene in any way. Any unilateral American intervention, in the absence of an external attack upon ourselves or an ally, would have been contrary to our traditions and to our international obligations." According to the President intervention is limited to the employment of our own armed forces.

In the same statement, made on April 20, 1961, President Kennedy warned:

> But let the record show that our restraint is not inexhaustible. Should it ever appear that the inter-American doctrine of noninterference merely conceals or excuses a policy of inaction — if the nations of this hemisphere should fail to meet their commitments against outside Communist penetration — then I want it clearly understood that this government will not hesitate in meeting its primary obligations, which are the security of our nation.[28]

The Bay of Pigs debacle opened the floodgates wider for anti-United States criticism throughout Latin America, and of course, behind the Iron Curtain. The new President of the United States was cast in the image of Teddy Roosevelt, brandishing a big stick in support of American imperialism. Also, not only did the intervention damage the integrity and prestige of the United States, but the incredible military fiasco reflected on its qualities of leadership. United States participation was too limited and restricted to assure success, but sufficient to constitute intervention. In addition, the sad outcome of the feeble enterprise seemed to discourage further willingness on the part of the

[27] See Stewart Alsop, "The Lesson of the Cuban Disaster," *Saturday Evening Post,* June 24, 1961, 26–27, 68–70; and Tad Szulc and Karl E. Meyer, *The Cuban Invasion, The Chronicle of a Disaster* (New York: Ballantine Books, 1962).
[28] U.S. Dept. of State *Bulletin,* XLIV, No. 1141 (May 8, 1961), 658–661.

President and his advisers to chance further bold and positive action against the Communists. They became "gun-shy." Since the detention of the captured invaders weighed on his conscience, President Kennedy facilitated an "unofficial" ransom arrangement with Premier Castro. In exchange for about $63 million worth of pharmaceuticals and infant foods, publicly subscribed, the 1,200 prisoners were released in December, 1962.

Return to multilateralism

The return of the United States to a multilateral approach to the Cuban problem finally resulted in another meeting of consultation. To enlist support for action against Castro the State Department published on April 3, 1961, a "White Paper" depicting Cuba as a Communist-bloc appendage, and on December 6, it submitted to the Inter-American Peace Committee a lengthy paper pointing out the "serious threat" of the Castro regime and its Communist connections to the "individual and collective security of the American Republics."

The OAS Council, on December 4, convoked a meeting of consultation, to be held in January, 1962, at Punta del Este in Uruguay. The call for the meeting had been opposed by six countries, including the three largest, Mexico, Brazil, and Argentina, a fact disquieting to the United States, but not sufficient to deter it from its objective.

The Eighth Meeting of Consultation of Foreign Ministers, acting as Organ of Consultation under the Rio treaty, met at Punta del Este, January 22–31, 1962.[29] It produced some notable results, but not without travail, for there were serious disagreements among the delegations.

Secretary of State Dean Rusk warned that the Castro regime "has extended the global battle to Latin America. It has supplied Communism with a bridgehead in the Americas." The Secretary urged sanctions in the form of a collective break of diplomatic relations and an embargo on all trade with Cuba.[30] But the countries that had opposed the meeting in the first place opposed any sanctions, for this amounted to interference with the "self-determination of the Cuban people." Brazil, the former reliable supporter of the United States in Pan American actions, played a leading role in opposing United States hopes for the adoption of hemisphere economic and diplomatic sanctions against Communist Cuba. Brazil favored a coexistence plan for Cuba — that is, leave the door open and don't drive Cuba into the Communist camp. The Punta del Este meeting revealed the deep difference of viewpoint that had developed among members of the inter-American system. Under the circumstances, credit for the limited successes of the meeting was due to Secretary Rusk for his patience and persistence in seeking agreement on more fully acceptable measures.

[29] *Final Act, Eighth Meeting of Consultation of Ministers of Foreign Affairs, Punta del Este, Uruguay, January 22–31, 1962* (Washington, D.C.: Pan American Union, 1962).

[30] Statement by Secretary Rusk, January 25, 1962, Dept. of State *Bulletin,* XLVI (February 19, 1962), 270–277.

All twenty countries unanimously agreed on identifying the Castro government as a Communist regime aligned with the Soviet bloc.[31] They then declared that the principles of Communism were incompatible with the principles of the inter-American system. It would then follow that by the same vote of twenty, the Cuban government should be excluded from the inter-American system. But not so, for six countries — Argentina, Bolivia, Brazil, Chile, Ecuador and Mexico — were not willing to take the drastic step, holding that the exclusion of a member state is not juridically possible unless the Charter of the OAS were first amended. By the bare majority of two-thirds, as required by the Rio treaty, the Eighth Meeting voted to exclude the *present government* of Cuba from participation in the inter-American system. This action meant that while the meeting could not legally expel Cuba as a member state, it could suspend Cuba so long as it maintained its present Communist incompatibility with the inter-American system.

The meeting, by a vote of sixteen (with Brazil, Chile, Ecuador, and Mexico abstaining) voted to "suspend immediately trade with Cuba in arms and implements of war of every kind." Then by the same vote the Council was instructed to study the feasibility and desirability of extending the suspension of trade to other items, with special attention to items of strategic importance. All of the governments voted to exclude Cuba from the Inter-American Defense Board. Finally, the member states were urged to take appropriate steps of individual and collective self-defense against subversion and intervention by the Sino-Soviet powers.

The Punta del Este meeting, like the OAS on previous occasions, laid the greatest fault for the Cuban situation at the door of the Sino-Soviet powers rather than on the Cubans themselves. The Cuban government was not specifically identified by the meeting as a threat to the peace and security of the hemisphere. The only actual delinquency attributed to Cuba was that of being "incompatible" with the inter-American system, a new basis for Rio treaty action against a state.[32]

Shortly after the Punta del Este meeting the Argentine government of President Frondizi was forced, because of military pressures, to break diplomatic relations with Cuba, thereby reversing its position at the consultative meeting. The United States thus gained a powerful adherent to its anti-Castro front. Bolivia, Brazil, Chile, Mexico, and Uruguay were the only Latin-American countries still maintaining diplomatic relations with Cuba.

The acts of Punta del Este, and the subsequent tightening of economic pressures on Cuba by the United States, were all equally ineffectual in has-

[31] It is an interesting fact that the Inter-American Peace Committee, in its report to the Eighth Meeting (*Report of the Inter-American Peace Committee to the Eighth Meeting of Consultation of Ministers of Foreign Affairs, 1962,* Pan American Union, Washington, D.C.) abandoned its earlier reticence, and now described fully and frankly Cuba's integration into the Sino-Soviet bloc.

[32] See Robert J. Redington, *The Organization of American States as a Collective Security System* (Washington, D.C.: Industrial College of the Armed Forces, 1961–1962), 48–53.

tening a solution to the Cuban problem. In fact the Communist threat centered in the island continued to mount, until, on October 22, 1962, it culminated in a great world crisis.

The Cuban missile crisis

By the late summer of 1962 the increasing movement of Soviet technical and military personnel and equipment into Cuba was attaining such proportions as to alarm many American citizens and members of Congress. At his press conference on September 4 President Kennedy tried to inject a reassuring note. He said, "There is no evidence of any organized combat force in Cuba from any Soviet bloc country; . . . of the presence of offensive ground-to-ground missiles, or of other significant offensive capability either in Cuban hands or under Soviet direction and guidance." At his next press conference on September 13, President Kennedy, in reply to the continuing alarm over Soviet armaments in Cuba, said, "But I will repeat the conclusion that I reported last week, that these new shipments do not constitute a serious threat to any part of this hemisphere." The President promised that if and when the Communist buildup in Cuba attained an offensive capacity threatening our security, then "this country will do whatever must be done to protect its own security and that of its allies."

The administration undoubtedly was strongly influenced by an official Soviet statement of September 11, 1962, that "The armaments and military equipment sent to Cuba are designed exclusively for defensive purposes." Nevertheless, Congressional concern over the Cuban situation resulted in the adoption of a joint resolution on October 3, 1962, which declared that the United States is determined to prevent by whatever means, including the use of arms, the Communist regime in Cuba from extending its aggression and subversion activities to any part of this hemisphere, and to prevent in Cuba the creation or use of an externally supported military capability endangering the security of the United States.[33]

At Secretary Rusk's suggestion, an informal meeting of the OAS Foreign Ministers was held at Washington, October 2–3, 1962, to discuss "the situation in Cuba and other subjects of mutual interest." In their communiqué the ministers unanimously characterized the Sino-Soviet intervention in Cuba as "an attempt to convert the island into an armed base for Communist penetration of the Americas and subversion of the democratic institutions of the Hemisphere." They called for consideration of further limitations upon trade with Cuba, with special attention to items of strategic importance. They voiced deep sympathy for the victims of the "present" Cuban regime.[34] A Soviet threat, based in Cuba, had thus become too apparent for further dis-

---

[33] U.S. Dept. of State *Bulletin*, XLVII (September 24, 1962), 450; (October 1, 1962), 481; (October 22, 1962), 597. For the missile crisis in Cuba, see Daniel James and John G. Hubbell, *Strike in the West: The Complete Story of the Cuban Crisis* (New York: Holt, Rinehart and Winston, 1963), and David L. Larson, ed., *The "Cuban Crisis" of 1962* (Boston: Houghton Mifflin Company, 1963).

[34] U.S. Dept. of State *Bulletin*, XLVII (October 22, 1962), 598.

regard by the more purblind members of the inter-American community. The most unexpected proportions of this threat were soon brought home to the Kennedy administration and to the American people.

That the Soviet arms buildup in Cuba was more than *defensive*, was belatedly recognized by the United States government as an ominous fact — this after a number of categorical denials. According to President Kennedy, in a radio and television address on October 22, it was not until after October 16 that unmistakable evidence established the fact that a number of offensive missile sites were being prepared on the island. The sites, completed and not yet completed, appeared to be designed for both medium-range and intermediate-range ballistic missiles capable of carrying nuclear warheads to most of the major cities of the Western Hemisphere. In addition, said the President, jet bombers capable of carrying nuclear weapons were being uncrated and assembled in Cuba. "This urgent transformation of Cuba into an important strategic base by the presence of these large, long-range, and clearly offensive weapons of sudden mass destruction, constitutes an explicit threat to the peace and security of all the Americas."

Therefore, in defense of our own security and of the entire Western Hemisphere, the President directed that: (1) a strict quarantine be placed on all offensive military equipment under shipment to Cuba from whatever nation or port; (2) a close surveillance of Cuba and its military buildup be kept; (3) any nuclear missile launched from Cuba be regarded as an attack by the Soviet Union on the United States, requiring a full retaliatory response upon the Soviet Union; (4) our base at Guantánamo be reinforced; (5) an immediate meeting of the Organ of Consultation, under the OAS be called for, to consider this threat to hemispheric security and to invoke Articles 6 and 8 of the Rio treaty in support of all necessary action. He also asked for (6) an emergency meeting of the Security Council to take action against this latest Soviet threat to world peace, and (7) called upon Chairman Khrushchev to halt and eliminate this clandestine, reckless, and provocative threat to world peace.[35]

On October 23, following President Kennedy's "quarantine" address, the Council of the OAS, meeting as the Provisional Organ of Consultation, resolved: (1) to call for the immediate dismantling and withdrawal from Cuba of all missiles and other weapons with an offensive capability; (2) to recommend that the member states, in accordance with Articles 6 and 8 of the Rio treaty, take all measures, individually and collectively, to prevent further shipment of military matériel to Cuba and to prevent the offensive missiles in Cuba from ever becoming an active threat to the peace and security of the continent.[36]

---

[35] "The Soviet Threat to the Americas." Address by President Kennedy, October 22, 1962, Dept. of State *Bulletin*, XLVII (November 12, 1962), 715–719.

[36] The Council of the Organization of American States Acting Provisionally as Organ of Consultation. Resolution adopted at the meeting held on October 23, 1962. Council Series, OEA/Ser. G/V, C-d·1024 (Washington, D.C.: Pan American Union, October 23, 1962). For text of the OAS resolution, see also Dept. of State *Bulletin*, XLVII, No. 1220 (November 12, 1962), 722–723.

When President Kennedy, on October 23, issued a proclamation interdicting the delivery of offensive weapons to Cuba, he cited as authority for his action not only the Constitution and statutes of the United States, but also the Joint Resolution of the U.S. Congress of October 3, and the resolution of the Organ of Consultation of the American Republics of October 23. The Secretary of Defense was ordered to take appropriate measures to prevent the delivery of the prohibited material to Cuba by employing the land, sea, and air forces of the United States in cooperation with any forces made available by the other American States. The quarantine went into effect on October 24. Some of the American republics took immediate steps to contribute units to the blockading forces.

On October 23, while the OAS Council was meeting as Provisional Organ of Consultation, the Security Council of the United Nations also met in emergency session. Ambassador Adlai E. Stevenson presented the United States charges of Soviet military buildup in Cuba as a grave threat to the peace of the world. He said, "It should be the purpose of Security Council action to bring about the immediate dismantling and withdrawal of the Soviet missiles and other offensive weapons in Cuba, under the supervision of United Nations observers, to make it possible to lift the quarantine which is being put into effect."

Because of the refusal of the Soviet representative, Ambassador Valerian A. Zorin, to admit the presence of long-range missiles in Cuba, Mr. Stevenson resorted to the presentation (October 25) of photographic evidence. Even then the representative of the Soviet Union preferred to regard as the official answer of the U.S.S.R. the Tass statement that they "don't need to locate missiles in Cuba." Mr. Stevenson's question remained unanswered — until Chairman Khrushchev, on October 28, tacitly acknowledged the presence of long-range missiles in Cuba.[37]

The Security Council discussions did not result in any action. They did contribute, however, to exposing to world public view, the cynical duplicity of the Soviet government. The Council adjourned late on October 25 to give Secretary-General U Thant an opportunity to hold discussions with interested parties and report back. In pursuance of this instruction the Secretary-General proposed a voluntary suspension of all arms shipments to Cuba, and also the voluntary suspension of the quarantine for a period of two or three weeks. President Kennedy replied, on October 25, that Ambassador Stevenson was ready to enter into preliminary talks to determine whether satisfactory arrangements could be assured. The next day the White House announced that there seemed to be no evidence of any Soviet intention to dismantle or discontinue work on the missile sites. Because of this fact, the White House declared, on October 27, "that as an urgent preliminary to consideration of any proposals work on the Cuban bases must stop; offensive weapons must be

---

[37] "U.N. Security Council Hears U.S. Charges of Soviet Military Buildup in Cuba," Statements by Ambassador Adlai E. Stevenson. Dept. of State *Bulletin,* XLVII, No. 1220 (November 12, 1962), 723–740.

rendered inoperative; and further shipment of offensive weapons to Cuba must cease — all *under effective international verification.*"

We note now the exchange of messages between President Kennedy and Chairman Khrushchev, on October 27 and 28,[38] which resulted in a formula for the ending of what proved eventually to be only a phase of the Cuban crisis:

1. Chairman Khrushchev's message of October 27. "We agree to remove those weapons from Cuba which you regard as offensive weapons," but on condition that the United States "will evacuate its analogous weapons from Turkey." Mr. Khrushchev insisted that the Soviet had as much right to station rockets in Cuba as the United States in Turkey. He also insisted that the United States pledge no invasion of Cuba, and, to balance matters he would make the same pledge regarding Turkey.

2. President Kennedy's message of October 27.[39] The key elements of the Soviet leader's proposals were declared "generally acceptable," as follows: "(1) You would agree to remove these weapons systems from Cuba under appropriate United Nations observation and supervision; and undertake, with suitable safeguards, to halt the further introduction of such weapons systems into Cuba; (2) We, on our part, would agree — upon the establishment of adequate arrangements through the United Nations to ensure the carrying out and continuation of these commitments — (a) to remove promptly the quarantine measures now in effect and (b) to give assurances against an invasion of Cuba." But, the President emphasized, there first must be a "cessation of work on the missile sites in Cuba and measures to render such weapons inoperable, under effective international guarantees."

3. Chairman Khrushchev's message of October 28. The President was informed that "the Soviet Government, in addition to earlier instructions on the discontinuation of further work on weapons constructions sites, has given a new order to dismantle the arms *which you described as offensive,* and to crate and return them to the Soviet Union." Mr. Khrushchev assured President Kennedy that he was "prepared to reach agreement to enable UN representatives to verify the dismantling of these means." He then reminded the President of the pledge of no attack, no invasion of Cuba.

4. President Kennedy's message of October 28. The President replied to the Premier as follows: "I consider my letter to you of October twenty-seventh and your reply of today as firm undertakings on the part of both our governments which should be promptly carried out. I hope that the necessary measures can at once be taken through the United Nations, as your message says, so that the United States in turn will be able to remove the quarantine measures now in effect."

The White House immediately announced to an anxiously waiting world "Chairman Khrushchev's statesmanlike decision to stop building bases in Cuba, dismantling offensive weapons and returning them to the Soviet Union

38 *Ibid.,* 740–746.
39 This was in reply to Khrushchev's letter of October 26, which was not released.

under United Nations verification." But since Premier Fidel Castro would not permit any international inspection and verification in Cuba, the United States had to rely solely on its own air reconnaissance. Aerial photography, and inspection at sea of departing ships, seemed to confirm Soviet reports that all nuclear weapons had been withdrawn from Cuba. Therefore, when on November 20, Chairman Khrushchev informed President Kennedy that all of the IL-28 bombers would be withdrawn within thirty days, and that the Soviet ground combat units would also be withdrawn "in due course," the Secretary of Defense was instructed to lift the naval blockade. At the same time the President made it clear that, until there were adequate international arrangements for inspection in Cuba, the United States would not be bound by a noninvasion pledge.[40]

The successful confrontation of the Soviet Union on the issue of ballistic missiles in Cuba proved to be only a moment of glory for the United States. It soon became apparent that just a phase of the problem had been met, for the Cuban issue lingered ominously. The removal of so-called "offensive" weapons was not followed by any significant pull-out of Soviet troops, as had been promised "in due course." Instead, there was apparently a progressive buildup of both armed personnel and elaborate "defensive" equipment.

The continued presence in Cuba of considerable numbers of Soviet military elements caused great concern in the United States. There were loud demands that the government "do something about Cuba." But the Kennedy administration was unwilling to risk nuclear war once again and thus was unable to do more than tighten economic pressures on Cuba. These pressures generally were not effective, for they were cancelled out by the assistance given Castro by his Communist allies and by the refusal of some members of the Western Alliance to observe the embargo.

In the meantime the *Fidelistas* continued their efforts to subvert other Latin-American governments, Venezuela being the principal target at the time of its presidential election of 1963. The discovery of several tons of Cuban arms cached on the coast of Venezuela for use by Communist terrorists precipitated a demand by the Venezuelan government for OAS investigation.[41]

It seemed that the American public was being conditioned to accept Castro Communism in Cuba, with Soviet support, on a more or less permanent

---

[40] The legality of President Kennedy's "quarantine" has been raised. A matter at issue is whether the United States, in the absence of an "armed attack," could plead the right of self-defense as defined in Article 51 of the UN Charter. The conclusion seems to be that, if there is a threat of *imminent danger,* the right of self-defense can be asserted. Certainly the presence of Soviet middle-range ballistic missiles in Cuba was an *imminent danger* to the United States. See Abram Chayes (Legal Adviser), "The Legal Case for U.S. Action in Cuba," Dept. of State *Bulletin,* XLVII, No. 1221 (November 19, 1962), 763–765; "Law and the Quarantine of Cuba," *Foreign Affairs,* 41, No. 3 (April, 1963), 550–557; Philip W. Thayer, "Signals to Moscow," *SAIS Review,* 7, No. 2 (Winter, 1963), 3–10.

[41] This resulted in the convoking of the Ninth Meeting of Foreign Ministers in July, 1964, in application of the Rio treaty. Although mandatory economic sanctions were voted against Cuba, Mexico continued relations with Castro.

basis.[42] As for the Soviet presence in Cuba, President Lyndon B. Johnson, in April, 1964, assured the American people that most of the Soviet troops had been withdrawn from Cuba, leaving the operation of their highly specialized "defensive" equipment to the uncertain charge of Fidel Castro and his trigger-happy Cubans. The United States persisted in its air reconnaisance over Cuba despite Castro's threats to shoot down the American planes.

In early February, 1964, Castro cut off the water supply to the United States naval base at Guantánamo. Washington was not unprepared for the Cuban action and so was able to take immediate steps to make Guantánamo self-sustaining in its water needs. Undoubtedly it was Castro's strategy to lay the basis for future renegotiation of the treaty between the United States and Cuba concerning the naval base. Although Guantánamo will surely revert to Cuba eventually, it is highly improbable that Fidel Castro will still be in power at that time.

[42] In a notable speech of March 25, 1964, Senator J. W. Fulbright, Chairman of the Senate Foreign Relations Committee, recommended acceptance of Castro not as a danger to the United States but more as a nuisance.

SUPPLEMENTARY READING

Alexander, Robert J., *Communism in Latin America* (New Brunswick: Rutgers University Press, 1957).

De Madariaga, Salvador, *Latin America Between the Eagle and the Bear* (New York: Frederick A. Praeger, 1962).

Dillon, Dorothy, *International Communism and Latin America, Perspectives and Prospects* (Gainesville: University of Florida Press, 1962).

Draper, Theodore, *Castro's Revolution: Myths and Realities* (New York: Frederick A. Praeger, 1962).

James, Daniel, *Red Design for the Americas: Guatemalan Prelude* (New York: The John Day Company, 1954).

James, Daniel, *Cuba. The First Soviet Satellite in the Americas* (New York: Avon Book Division, 1961).

Lieuwen, Edwin, *Arms and Politics in Latin America* (New York: Frederick A. Praeger, rev. ed., 1961), 263–298.

MacGaffey, Wyatt, and Barnett, Clifford R., *Cuba, its people, its society, its culture* (New Haven: HRAF Press, 1962).

Martin, Edwin M., "Communist Subversion in the Western Hemisphere," Dept. of State *Bulletin*, XLVIII, No. 237 (March 11, 1963), 347-356; No. 238 (March 18, 1963), 404-412.

Martz, J. D., *Communist Infiltration in Guatemala* (New York: Vintage Press, 1956).

Matthews, Herbert L., *The Cuban Story* (New York: George Braziller, 1961).

Mecham, J. Lloyd, *The United States and Inter-American Security, 1889-1960* (Austin: University of Texas Press, 1961), Chap. XIV.

Pflaum, Irving Peter, *Tragic Island: How Communism Came to Cuba* (Englewood Cliffs, N.J.: Prentice-Hall, Inc., 1961).

Schneider, Ronald M., *Communism in Guatemala, 1944–1954* (New York: Frederick A. Praeger, 1958).

Szulc, Tad, and Meyer, Karl E., *The Cuban Invasion. The Chronicle of a Disaster* (New York: Ballantine Books, 1962).

U.S. Department of State, *A Case History of Communist Penetration: Guatemala,* Publication 6465, Inter-American Series 52 (Washington, D.C.: Government Printing Office, 1957).

U.S. Department of State, *Cuba,* Publication 7171, Inter-American Series 66, (Washington, D.C.: Government Printing Office, April, 1961).

U.S. Department of State, *Inter-American Efforts to Relieve International Tensions in the Western Hemisphere, 1959-1960.* Publication 7409, Inter-American Series 79 (Washington, D.C.: Government Printing Office, July, 1962), *passim.*

U.S. Senate, 86th Cong., 2nd Sess. Doc. 125, *United States-Latin American Relations: Soviet Bloc Latin American Activities and their Implications for United States Foreign Policy,* a study prepared by the Corporation for Economic and Industrial Research for the Subcommittee on Foreign Relations, Report No. 7 (Washington, D.C.: Government Printing Office, February, 1960), 685-828.

🙠 *Part Two*

CARIBBEAN AND COUNTRY RELATIONS

10

The General Caribbean Policies
of the United States

1. The Development of a Caribbean Consciousness

The Caribbean area[1] has been regarded by the United States as a regional unit to which it applied a distinctive set of policies. It is obvious that, because of the geographical adjacency of this region to the continental United States, and to the Panama Canal, it possessed great strategic importance. In view of this fact, American diplomacy has been so much concerned with the countries of the area that it is hardly an exaggeration to say that most of its major policy decisions and actions relating to Latin America originated in this region.

The Caribbean in early American policy

The United States developed a policy program applicable to the Caribbean area when it became aware of its importance as a regional unit. This Caribbean consciousness, which was not fully awakened until the latter part of the nineteenth century, was the product of many years of development of American national interests in the region: economic, political, and strategic.

Although the economic interest is here mentioned first, it is only because it came first in time, for it was strictly secondary as a determinant of policy. For a long time Americans had been interested in trading in the West Indies. A lively trade had been carried on between New England and the British West Indies during the colonial period. With the winning of independence by the Anglo-American colonies this trade was virtually prohibited, but the Amer-

[1] By "Caribbean" we mean not only the island republics, but also the republics of Central America, including Panama, and Colombia and Venezuela.

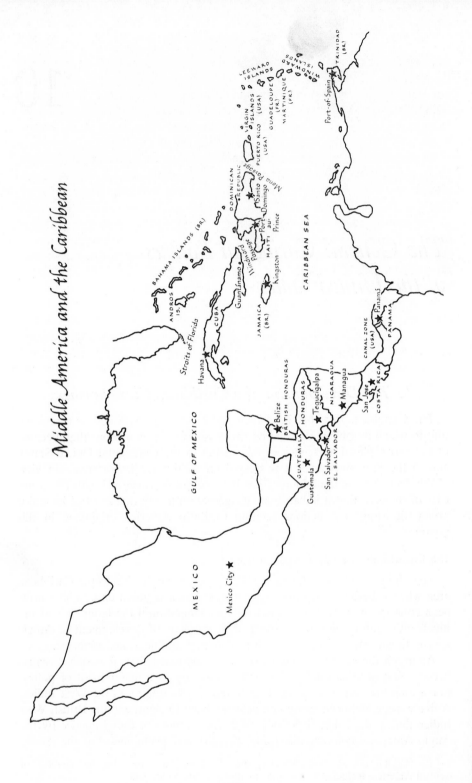

Middle America and the Caribbean

MEXICO

Mexico City ★

GULF OF MEXICO

Straits of Florida

Havana ★

CUBA

ANDROS IS.

BAHAMA ISLANDS (BR.)

Guantánamo

Windward Passage

JAMAICA (BR.)

Kingston

HAITI

Port-au-Prince

DOMINICAN REPUBLIC

Santo Domingo

Mona Passage

PUERTO RICO (USA)

VIRGIN ISLANDS (USA)

LEEWARD ISLANDS

GUADELOUPE (FR.)

MARTINIQUE (FR.)

WINDWARD ISLANDS

TRINIDAD (BR.)

Port-of-Spain

CARIBBEAN SEA

Belize

BRITISH HONDURAS

GUATEMALA

Guatemala ★

San Salvador ★

EL SALVADOR

HONDURAS

Tegucigalpa ★

NICARAGUA

Managua ★

COSTA RICA

San José ★

CANAL ZONE (USA)

Panamá ★

PANAMA

icans found some compensation when Spain opened the trade of Cuba and Puerto Rico. Commerce with Cuba averaged annually about 6 per cent of our total foreign trade.[2] Notwithstanding, the minor increase of American trade in the whole Caribbean area in the nineteenth century, compared most unfavorably with our surging foreign trade with other parts of the world. Trade was not a prime factor in the development of Caribbean consciousness in the United States.[3] And less important were American investments, despite the fact that President Cleveland, in December, 1896, justified United States interest in the current Cuban revolution by citing not only the nearness of Cuba to the United States, but also an American investment of from thirty to fifty millions in the island, and a trade volume of $96 million.[4] American trade and investments in the other countries of the Caribbean did not even approximate these figures. To locate the more influential factors responsible for a developing awareness of the importance of the region to the United States we must take note of the political and strategic considerations.

So predominant has been the security factor in our dealings with the Caribbean countries, that the United States evolved, albeit somewhat empirically, a pattern of methods and techniques possessing such a high degree of coherence, consistency, and singleness of purpose as to constitute a general policy posture. While some variations and even inconsistencies can be observed in our relations with individual countries, the essentials of our general Caribbean policy can be found in our dealings with all of the states of this area.

Beginning with the imminent collapse of the Spanish empire in the Americas and the possibility that some of Spain's possessions might fall into the hands of stronger European powers, the United States was not a little concerned by this ominous prospect, particularly with respect to Cuba and Florida. The problem of Florida was settled by the Adams-Onís treaty, but the precarious possession of Cuba by Spain forced the island to the forefront of the Caribbean issues for the balance of the century. Spanish ownership of the "Pearl of the Antilles" was consistently supported by the United States, except on those occasions when annexation was advocated. American concern was not limited to Cuba during this period; the vulnerability of Santo Domingo and Haiti,

[2] Based on tabulation compiled by Samuel Flagg Bemis, *A Diplomatic History of the United States* (New York: Henry Holt and Company, 1955, 4th ed.), 307–308. From 1876 to 1891, U.S. $ imports from Cuba amounted to $924 million, and U.S. exports totaled only $189 million because of the restrictive Spanish tariff laws. When tariff schedules were relaxed in 1891, American commerce took a jump to a total of $105 million in 1894. See also C. E. Chapman, *A History of the Cuban Republic* (New York: The Macmillan Company, 1927), 70–71.

[3] "Prior to 1895 United States trade with the Caribbean countries was so small that the figures for the five Central American countries were published as one item; Haiti and Santo Domingo were regarded as one trade area; and Panama was then a part of Colombia." Charles P. Howland, *Survey of American Foreign Relations* (New Haven: Yale University Press, 1929), 280. Also, see C. L. Jones, *Caribbean Backgrounds and Prospects* (New York: D. Appleton and Company, 1931), 221–223.

[4] Jones, *op. cit.,* 86.

neighboring island republics, also caused the United States to adopt counter-measures in support of the no-transfer principle of the Monroe Doctrine.

The substitution of steam for sailing vessels during the middle of the nine-teenth century was one of the most important factors contributing to the development of a Caribbean awareness by the United States. The need of coaling stations, which resulted in one of the earliest (1854) but unsuccessful negotiations with Santo Domingo for a base on strategic Samaná Peninsula,[5] was dramatically emphasized during the Civil War. The lack of bases in the area had seriously handicapped the Union navy in its pursuit of Confederate sea raiders.

With these experiences in mind, plus his own well-known "Arctic to the Isthmus" expansionist ideas, Secretary of State Seward, in 1867, negotiated with Denmark a treaty for the purchase of the Danish West Indies, strategically located eastward of Puerto Rico on the Anegada Passage. The treaty was never ratified by the United States.[6] The House, still harboring doubts raised by the purchase of Seward's Alaska "ice box," adopted a resolution declaring "any further purchase of territory" to be "inexpedient." Mr. Seward then sounded out Spain concerning acquisition of the small islands, Culebra and Vieques, adjacent to Puerto Rico. The soundings failed to evoke favorable response.

Although President Cabral of the Dominican Republic had failed to interest Secretary Seward by his offer, in 1866, of a leasehold on the Samaná Peninsula, his successor, President Buenaventura Baez, initiated negotiations for the annexation of the entire republic by the United States. President Grant was responsive, for, in addition to his aspiration to become known as a nation-builder, he appreciated the strategic importance of the island of Santo Domingo. Furthermore, he reasoned that United States annexation would put an end to European moves threatening to the Monroe Doctrine. As a result of negotiations, on November 29, 1869, alternate agreements were signed for a lease on Samaná Bay and for annexation of the republic. Both treaties failed of acceptance by the United States Senate which was motivated both by partisan and personal motives, and also by conscientious opposition to extra-continental expansion.[7]

The failure of President Grant's efforts to annex Santo Domingo put an end for more than a quarter of a century to further aspirations by the United States to acquire strategic territorial sites in the Caribbean. It was not, in fact, until 1898, that the United States made its first territorial acquisitions in the area, as a result of the Spanish-American War. In the meantime, however,

[5] General William L. Caznau, special agent for President Franklin Pierce, negotiated by treaty "the acquisition of a strategic tract as a coaling depot" on the Samaná Peninsula. The treaty failed because of pressures on the Dominican government by Britain and France.

[6] See Charles C. Tansill, *The Purchase of the Danish West Indies* (Baltimore: The Johns Hopkins Press, 1932), Chaps. I, II.

[7] For a more detailed discussion of General Grant's annexation *debacle*, see Sumner Welles, *Naboth's Vineyard, The Dominican Republic, 1848–1924* (2 vols. New York: Payson & Clarke, 1928), I, Chaps. V, VI.

American interest in the region was developing apace because of its relation to an isthmian interoceanic canal which inevitably would soon be constructed, and which would be vitally important to the defense and future development of the United States. For these reasons, and in this context, we turn to a discussion of canal diplomacy in the nineteenth century.

Canal diplomacy to 1898

In the early nineteenth century the United States seemed determined to prevent the appropriation of an interoceanic canal by a European power for its exclusive purposes, but actually showed little concern for a canal of its own. Later, when the United States came to realize, as it did clearly by 1880, that, for both strategic and commercial reasons, it had a predominant interest in the Caribbean which required a canal all its own, it left nothing undone in its attempt to secure the exclusive right to construct and control its own canal, and to establish an effective screen of defensive outposts along its approaches.[8]

Although the United States government was a party to almost endless negotiations in regard to an interoceanic canal, only three treaties of any practical importance were successfully concluded before 1900, and none of these cleared the way diplomatically for this country to proceed with the construction and control of a canal. In fact, one of them had just the opposite effect as far as unilateral control by the United States was concerned. Chronologically, these treaties were: (1) the Bidlack treaty with New Granada (Colombia) in 1846; (2) the Clayton-Bulwer treaty with Great Britain in 1850; and (3) the Dickinson-Ayon treaty with Nicaragua in 1867.[9]

The question of the construction of a ship canal across the isthmus engaged the attention of both the United States and the newly independent Latin-American countries as early as the first inter-American conference held at Panama itself in 1826. In the first announcement of American policy, Secretary of State Henry Clay instructed our delegates to that conference to feel free to discuss the canal subject, but he insisted that should such a project ever be executed its benefits should not be exclusively appropriated to any one nation.

Oddly enough, the first canal treaty contracted by the United States was concluded on the initiative of the other party. The government of New Granada, apprehensive that the continuing encroachments of the British along

[8] For the evolution of the canal policy of the United States, see Dwight Carroll Miner, *The Fight for the Panama Route* (New York: Columbia University Press, 1940), Chap. I; also Willis Fletcher Johnson, *Four Centuries of the Panama Canal* (New York: Henry Holt and Company, 1906); and Mary W. Williams, *Anglo-American Isthmian Diplomacy, 1815–1915* (Washington, D.C.: Government Printing Office, 1916).

[9] For texts of all treaties entered into by the United States relating to an isthmian canal, see William M. Malloy, comp., *Treaties, Conventions, International Acts, Protocols and Agreements between the United States of America and Other Powers* (3 vols. Washington, D.C.: Government Printing Office, 1910–1923). The first two volumes are for the years 1776–1909; Vol. 3 is for 1910–1923. Also, see *Treaties and Acts of Congress Relating to the Panama Canal* (Washington, D.C.: Government Printing Office, 1917).

the eastern (Mosquito) coast of Central America might involve her own territory at the Isthmus of Panama, sought the protection of the United States. The so-called Bidlack treaty, concluded in December, 1846, and ratified by both governments in 1848, gave the United States the right of transit across Panama by any means of communication that then existed or might be constructed thereafter, under the same terms as enjoyed by the citizens of New Granada. The United States was not granted, nor did it seek, exclusive possession of an isthmian canal. In return, it agreed to protect the neutrality of the isthmus and to guarantee the sovereignty of New Granada over it. This treaty was the first instance in which the United States formally committed itself to come to the aid of a Latin-American state when its sovereignty was in danger of impairment.

Only four years after the signing of the Bidlack treaty, and two years after its ratification, the United States entered into its second — and most important — canal treaty in the nineteenth century, the Clayton-Bulwer treaty with Great Britain. For many years Great Britain had been extending her dominion over the eastern, or Mosquito, coast of Central America and its offshore islands. Because of the continuing British encroachment in the area, especially at the expense of Nicaragua, the United States became apprehensive that Britain would appropriate an isthmian canal route for its exclusive purposes.[10]

In an attempt to counter these aggressive designs of Great Britain, Elijah Hise, United States *chargé d'affaires* in Central America, in June, 1849, negotiated, without the authorization or knowledge of his government, a treaty with Nicaragua which gave the United States the exclusive right to construct a canal through the territory of that state, in return for the guarantee of the sovereignty of Nicaragua. Only a few months later, in September, 1849, Ephraim G. Squier, also without authorization of his government, signed a treaty with Honduras which ceded to the United States Tigre Island, in the Gulf of Fonseca, key to the Pacific terminus of the Nicaragua route. The occupation of Tigre Island by the British immediately thereafter cooled American enthusiasm for these transactions and thus neither of the treaties was ever submitted to the United States Senate for approval. Nonetheless, they were used as levers to secure Britain's signature on a far more important treaty by which she would deny herself the exclusive right to construct and control a canal across the isthmus.

Faced with a virtual standoff between them, and desirous of preventing any further aggravation of the Anglo-American rivalry which was building up dangerously in Central America, the United States and Great Britain, after considerable negotiation, concluded, in April, 1850, the famous Clayton-Bulwer treaty.[11] The most important feature of this treaty was its self-denying provision by which both parties bound themselves never to obtain or maintain

---

[10] For the Anglo-American contest in Central America, see J. Fred Rippy, *Latin America in World Politics* (New York: F. S. Crofts and Co., 1938, 3rd ed.), 99–101; Graham H. Stuart, *Latin America and the United States* (New York: Appleton-Century-Crofts, Inc., 1955, 5th ed.), 296–298; and Williams, *op. cit.*, 46–66.

[11] *Sen. Exec. Doc.* No. 194, 47th Cong., 1st Sess., 55–82.

any exclusive control over the proposed Nicaragua canal; nor to erect or maintain any fortifications commanding the canal or its vicinity; nor to occupy, colonize, or exercise dominion over Nicaragua, Costa Rica, the Mosquito coast, or any part of Central America; and never to influence any of these states to obtain unequal advantage in regard to commerce or navigation through the said canal. The treaty also provided for the neutralization of such a canal under international guarantee, and a mutual guarantee of protection for the persons and property of any parties that might undertake the construction of a canal anywhere across the isthmus.

The Clayton-Bulwer treaty remained in force until 1901 and restrained both the United States and Great Britain from engaging in any unilateral canal action in Central America throughout that period. Because of its self-denying character, this convention was destined to become perhaps the most controversial treaty entered into by the United States. In later years, seemingly unmindful that the treaty had been negotiated by the United States principally to checkmate Britain's expansionist designs in Central America, which might have resulted in her exclusive control of a canal, many Americans condemned the treaty on the ground that it was an unnecessary concession on our part, and, moreover, was a violation of the Monroe Doctrine!

The conclusion of the Clayton-Bulwer treaty failed, however, to bring the expected tranquillity in Anglo-American relations over Central America. On the contrary, almost as soon as the treaty was signed, a difference of opinion developed over the interpretation of some of its provisions.[12] This disagreement revolved about two major questions: (1) Were the abrogatory clauses respecting the exercise of political dominion over Central America to have retroactive effect, in which case Great Britain would be obliged to abandon her protectorate over the Mosquito coast, or were they directed only against future acquisitions in Central America? (2) Did the Bay Islands, located off the Honduran coast and occupied by Great Britain in the early 1840's, come within the purview of the treaty? The answer to the latter question, depended on whether the Bay Islands were to be considered as belonging to Honduras, or to Belize (British Honduras), the latter of which was expressly excluded from the treaty. The British provided their own answer in 1852 by formally proclaiming the Bay Islands as part of Belize and hence outside the pale of the treaty of 1850, though not without protest from the United States.

Attempts to resolve the difficulties arising from the conflicting interpretations of the treaty resulted in the conclusion of the Dallas-Clarendon treaty of 1856. By its terms the British would have abandoned their protectorate over the Mosquito Indians, negotiated a compromise settlement respecting the boundaries of Belize, and ceded the Bay Islands to Honduras. The United States Senate found the treaty unacceptable, and thus the United States and Britain were back where they started with the Clayton-Bulwer treaty.

[12] For difficulties concerning interpretation of the Clayton-Bulwer treaty, see Williams, *op. cit.*, 106–107.

In December, 1857, when negotiations were at a virtual standstill, President Buchanan proposed abrogation of the treaty of 1850 by mutual consent, but nothing came of his proposal. Although failing to reach agreement directly with the United States, Great Britain had, by 1860, concluded treaties with Guatemala, Nicaragua, and Honduras by which she relinquished all of her territorial claims to Central America except British Honduras, over which she exercises sovereignty to this day, though under almost constant protest from Guatemala. These concessions by Great Britain placated even the expansionist-minded Buchanan, who in 1860 publicly declared his satisfaction with this settlement of the question.

With the coming of the Civil War, the project of an isthmian canal was laid aside because of more absorbing domestic matters. Then, following this conflict, the energies of the United States were directed to the reconstruction of the Union and matters of internal development, with the result that American interest in a canal remained temporarily largely dormant. Moreover, the completion of the first transcontinental railroad, the Union Pacific in 1869, linking the Atlantic with the Pacific, took some of the pressure off the demand for a canal, which had mounted considerably with the acquisition of California and by the gold rush which followed soon after. Nonetheless, the United States government continued to evince interest in an isthmian waterway; this interest, however, took a new direction. Whereas the principal objective of our canal policy before the Civil War had been to prevent the exclusive construction and control of a canal by another power, something largely realized in the Clayton-Bulwer treaty, the objective of our policy after the war became that of securing a free hand for the unilateral control of a canal.

The third of our significant canal treaties during the nineteenth century was that signed with Nicaragua in 1867, known as the Dickinson-Ayon treaty. Under it the United States obtained the right of transit across the isthmus by whatever means of communication then existed or might be constructed in the future on equal terms with the Nicaraguans. In return, the United States pledged its protection of all such routes of communication and guaranteed the neutrality and innocent passage of the same. The United States further agreed to use its influence to induce other nations to guarantee such neutrality and protection. Like the treaties with Colombia in 1846 and with Great Britain in 1850, this convention also contemplated the neutralization of the canal. It in no way infringed the commitments of the United States under the Clayton-Bulwer treaty, and in fact was strictly in accordance with the provisions of that agreement.

To the end of the century dissatisfaction with the Clayton-Bulwer treaty mounted in the United States because of the growing conviction that the self-denying character of the treaty was a major roadblock to the realization of a canal objective more consonant with the national interest, that is, a canal under exclusive United States control. One event especially stimulated the United States to free itself from the incubus imposed by the treaty of 1850 —

the award of a concession by Colombia to a privately financed French company under the direction of Ferdinand de Lesseps, the promoter of the recently completed Suez Canal. When it appeared that this company might well complete its project for a canal which would probably be controlled by the French government, American anxiety was aroused.

The French company began to dig the canal in 1878. Despite the magic of the name of de Lesseps, which seemed to insure success for the undertaking, the project turned out to be a miserable failure, due largely to the embezzlement and mismanagement of company funds and the ravages of yet unconquered yellow fever. The company went bankrupt in 1889, with only one-third of the canal completed.

In a message to Congress in March, 1880, President Rutherford B. Hayes announced, for the first time, that the policy of the United States was a canal under exclusive American jurisdiction.[13] Hayes further asserted that he considered such a canal "virtually a part of the coastline of the United States," a portentous omen of our future actions throughout the Caribbean area.

President James Garfield, in his inaugural address in 1881, reiterated the policy of his predecessor on the canal question. Shortly thereafter, in November, 1881, Secretary of State James G. Blaine made overtures to the British government for a modification of the Clayton-Bulwer treaty which would have amounted to a complete abrogation of the treaty and given the United States a free hand to proceed with the construction and control of a canal. The British government was unimpressed by Blaine's arguments that a change in circumstances warranted revision of the treaty.[14] The position taken by the British was that "the Clayton-Bulwer treaty was designed at the time of its execution to establish a permanent principle of control over interoceanic communication in Central America," and was not intended to serve merely as a momentary accommodation of interests between the two countries. Hence the treaty was just as valid and applicable in 1880 as when it was consumated in 1850.

When Grover Cleveland became President in 1885, he reverted to the policy of a canal under international control.[15] More than ten years later, President Cleveland's Secretary of State, Richard Olney, declared that the only remedy for our canal difficulties was to be found not in resorting to "ingenious attempts to deny the existence of the treaty or to explain away its provisions, but in a direct and straightforward application to Great Britain for a reconsideration of the whole matter."[16] This is where matters stood when war with Spain intervened to create a new urgency for the construction and control of a canal by the United States.

[13] J. D. Richardson, *Messages and Papers of the Presidents* (10 vols. Washington, D.C.: Government Printing Office, 1897), VII, 515–586.

[14] *Sen. Exec. Doc.* No. 237, 56th Cong., 1st Sess., 380–396.

[15] Richardson, *op. cit.,* VIII, 327.

[16] John Bassett Moore, *A Digest of International Law* (Washington, D.C.: Government Printing Office), III, 209.

2. Implementing a Caribbean Policy

The achievement of our canal objective

The Spanish-American War was an epochal event in the historical development of a Caribbean policy. As a result of the war the United States achieved status not only as a world power but as the dominant political and military force in the Caribbean. With the annexation of Puerto Rico and the acquisition of a permanent base in Cuba, the United States finally achieved a territorial foothold in the area. It was inevitable that a Caribbean consciousness, now fully awakened in the United States, would manifest itself by implementing a policy peculiarly identified with the region.

In the first place there was the achievement of our canal objectives. The Spanish-American War transformed what had been a desirability into a necessity, that is, a transisthmian canal constructed and controlled by the United States. The difficulties encountered in waging war on two widely separated fronts, in the Caribbean and the Far East, and the dramatic sixty-six day voyage of the *U.S.S. Oregon* around Cape Horn to join the Atlantic battle fleet off Cuba, aroused public opinion to the need of an interoceanic canal for the national defense.

This in fact was what Admiral Alfred T. Mahan, the great naval historian, had been trying to teach for many years. Admiral Mahan, who greatly influenced the thinking of neo-expansionists and big-navy men such as Theodore Roosevelt, Albert Beveridge, and Henry Cabot Lodge, argued that no nation had the same interest in an isthmian canal as did the United States. Mahan and his disciples believed that a large two-ocean navy was necessary to defend the continental homeland and that in order for this navy to fight at maximum strength in either ocean an isthmian canal was also necessary. In 1897 Mahan predicted that the isthmus of Central America, which separated the two oceans, would one day unite them, and that "entrance to the Caribbean and transit across the Caribbean to the isthmus are two prime essentials to the enjoyment of the advantages of the latter. Therefore, in case of war, control of these two things becomes a material object not second to the isthmus itself, access to which depends on them."[17] Admiral Mahan foresaw the extension of United States control over a "Greater Panama Canal Zone" in order to guarantee access through the far-flung Caribbean to the canal itself.

Fortified by the increasingly popular doctrines of United States preeminence in Western Hemisphere affairs, and its manifest destiny to construct and control a canal through the isthmus of Central America, Secretary of State John Hay undertook in 1899 to negotiate a new treaty with Great Britain. The result, known as the first Hay-Pauncefote treaty of February, 1900, authorized the United States to construct and operate an isthmian canal,

---

[17] A. T. Mahan, *The Interest of American Sea Power, Present and Future* (Boston: Little, Brown and Company, 1898), 299.

either directly or through a company, provided it was neutralized in accordance with the Clayton-Bulwer treaty. The United States Senate objected to some of the provisions of the new treaty, and particularly to the fact that it neglected to include an express abrogation of the treaty of 1850. Accordingly, negotiations had to be renewed.

The British government at first refused to accept amendments insisted on by the United States, but eventually it had to acquiesce because of broader considerations of foreign policy. The increasing power and aggressiveness of Germany, plus the unpopularity of the Boer War in Europe, impelled the British to cultivate the good will of the United States, now a world power in its own right. In fact, the well-known determination of the United States to have a canal of its own, and its ability to brush aside opposition, caused the British to make the best of the situation by acquiescing in good grace.

Accordingly, in November, 1901, a second Hay-Pauncefote treaty incorporating the desired American amendments was signed and promptly approved by the Senate. The treaty expressly abrogated the Clayton-Bulwer convention and provided that a canal might be constructed, directly or indirectly under the auspices of the United States government and under its exclusive regulation and management. Provision was also made for the neutralization of the canal under substantially the same rules as those governing the Suez Canal, the most important of which guaranteed the right of vessels of all nations to transit the canal at reasonable cost on a strictly equal basis. Finally, the clause of the first treaty forbidding fortifications was omitted.[18]

With the removal of the principal diplomatic obstacle to the construction of a canal by the United States, there remained the task of choosing the most practical route and of securing the permission of the country in whose territory it would be built. While the Hay-Pauncefote negotiations were in progress, the Walker Commission was appointed to investigate all available canal routes.

In November, 1901, the Commission, after a thorough investigation of both the Nicaragua and Panama routes, made its report.[19] It estimated the cost of the construction of a Nicaragua canal at $190 million, and the cost of completing the Panama canal, begun by the now defunct French company, at $144 million. To the latter sum, however, had to be added the cost of acquiring the rights and property of the French company, estimated by the Commission to be worth $40 million, but for which the company was asking $109 million. Therefore, unless the French company scaled down to $40 million the price for its Panama interests, the Commission recommended the Nicaragua route.

Inspired by the Walker Commission recommendation, the House almost immediately, in January, 1902, adopted the Hepburn Bill which authorized the President to proceed with the construction of a canal through Nicaragua. Panic-stricken by the prospect of suffering a total loss of its canal investment

[18] *Diplomatic History of the Panama Canal, Sen. Exec. Doc.* No. 474, 63rd Cong., 2nd Sess., 1 ff.

[19] *Isthmian Canal Commission (Walker), Report, 1899–1901* (Washington, D.C.: Government Printing Office, 1901); also, see Miner, *op. cit.,* 91–116.

the French Panama Canal Company hastily offered to sell for $40 million, the price fixed by the Commission. Fortunately for the French company the Hepburn Bill had not yet reached the Senate. Therefore, thanks to a vigorous campaign waged by proponents of the Panama route, particularly Philippe Bunau-Varilla,[20] former chief engineer of the French company, the Senate was won over to the Panama site. The Senate under the Spooner Amendment, altered the Hepburn Bill so as to authorize the President to purchase the rights and property of the French company for a sum not to exceed $40 million, and to secure from Colombia the necessary rights for the construction of the canal through Panama. If, however, a satisfactory arrangement could not be reached with both the French company and Colombia within a reasonable time, the President was to proceed with the construction of a canal through Nicaragua. The House concurred with the amendment, and, on June 28, 1902, President Theodore Roosevelt signed it into law.[21]

Negotiations with Colombia and Panama

Title to the property of the French company was acquired with virtually no difficulty, but negotiations with Colombia presented formidable and unexpected difficulties.[22] Secretary of State John Hay lost no time in negotiating with Colombia the Hay-Herrán treaty, signed on January 22, 1903, whereby the United States agreed to pay Colombia $10 million in cash and a yearly rental of $250,000, beginning nine years thereafter, in return for Colombia's rights and properties, and for perpetual control and jurisdiction over a six-mile-wide zone across the isthmus on which to build the canal. In March, 1903, the treaty was approved by the United States Senate, but the Colombian senate, reacting to a strong surge of public opinion, unanimously rejected it. The chief complaint was that, since Panama was the country's greatest asset, it should bring a substantially better price than the United States was offering. Specifically, Colombia wanted ten of the forty million dollars paid to the French company, and a raising of the $10 million cash payment to $15 million. Colombia also felt that under the Hay-Herrán treaty it would be forced to surrender too much of its authority over the canal zone.[23]

The Colombian rejection of the treaty evoked screams of anguish and displeasure from the United States. President Roosevelt, vehement in his denunciation of the Colombian action, attributed the rejection to the cupidity of government leaders who merely wished to wait until the charter of the French

---

[20] See Philippe Bunau-Varilla, *Panama: Creation, Destruction, and Resurrection* (New York: Robert M. McBride and Co., 1914).

[21] For the "battle of the routes" and the Spooner Act, see Miner, *op. cit.*, Chaps. III, IV. For an exhaustive inquiry into all of the steps attending the selection of the Panama route, see *The Story of Panama:* Hearings on the Rainey Resolution before the Committee on Foreign Affairs of the House of Representatives (Washington, D.C.: Government Printing Office, 1913).

[22] For the Colombian side of the Panama question, see Antonio José Uribe, *Colombia y los Estados Unidos de América* (Bogotá: Imprenta Nacional, 1931).

[23] E. J. Parks, *Colombia and the United States, 1765–1934* (Durham: Duke University Press, 1935), 396–397.

company expired so that the Colombian government could confiscate its property and then sell it to the United States. Whatever its motive, the Colombian government was playing a dangerous game in attempting to drive a hard bargain with the United States. Though the Panama route had been decided on, there still remained the alternative Nicaragua route. Moreover, the Colombian authorities were well aware that the Panamanians felt very strongly about the matter and would probably revolt against Colombian rule if this became necessary to insure a canal through their territory. Nonetheless, however politically foolish the Colombian government may have been, however unreasonable its demands, and however much its rejection of the Hay-Herrán treaty might have held up the progress of civilization, as Roosevelt warned, the legal right of Colombia as a sovereign and independent nation to reject the treaty cannot be disputed.[24]

When it became apparent that a canal treaty with Colombia would not be approved, this came as a great disappointment to most of the Panamanians who believed that their economic status would be vastly improved if a canal were constructed in their territory. Moreover, the French company, and particularly its chief agent Bunau-Varilla, became alarmed for fear that it would lose the $40 million salvage on its investment in Panama. Consequently there developed popular agitation in the isthmus, aided and abetted by Philippe Bunau-Varilla, for an independent Panama. The idea of a revolt appealed to President Roosevelt, because it would be much easier to deal with the new and tiny republic than with proud and stubborn Colombia, which was trying to "high-jack" the United States.

To further their independence aspirations the Panamanians sent an agent, a Dr. Amador, to Washington to secure a promise of assistance from the United States; but no definite pledge of aid was obtained, either by him or by Bunau-Varilla, who even broached the subject to President Roosevelt. Although there is no evidence that the President was directly involved in the revolt plot, it seems Bunau-Varilla was justified in implying from what he learned in Washington that, in the event of an insurrection, the United States would intervene to prevent interruption of free transit across the isthmus.[25] Thus, when the *U.S.S. Nashville* arrived in the harbor of Colón, those Panamanians who were poised for revolt, believed, as they had been assured by Bunau-Varilla, that the *Nashville* was there to help them in their revolt. In this expectation they were not disappointed, for, following the outbreak of the bloodless revolt on November 3, 1903, United States Marines landed to protect the railway across the isthmus and refused to permit Colombian troops the use of the railroad from Colón to Panama City to get at the center of the revolt and suppress it. The United States interpreted, against Colombia itself, its rights under the treaty of 1846 to bar passage of Colombian troops across

[24] For a good discussion of negotiations with Colombia concerning the canal, see Miner, *op. cit.*, 157–335. For texts of the Hay-Herrán and Root-Cortes-Arosemena treaties, see *Diplomatic History of the Panama Canal*, Sen. Exec. Doc. No. 474, 63rd Cong., 2nd Sess.

[25] Bunau-Varilla, *op. cit.*, 327–331.

the isthmus on the ground that such passage would precipitate civil war and disrupt the free transit which the United States was pledged to protect. Since the United States forbade the further landing of Colombian troops the success of the independence movement was assured.[26] By novel treaty interpretation the United States had prevented a state with which it was on friendly terms from attempting to suppress an outbreak of revolution within its own territory.

Only three days after the start of the revolt, the Roosevelt administration recognized the independence of Panama in what has been described as "indecent haste." A reason for Roosevelt's hasty recognition was to make the Panama canal route an accomplished fact before Congress, which was inclined toward the Nicaragua route anyway, could convene and change his plans.

No time was lost in negotiating with the new republic a treaty under which the United States could finally proceed with the construction of the great waterway. On November 18, 1903, Secretary of State Hay and Panamanian representative Philippe Bunau-Varilla signed a treaty which removed the last diplomatic hurdle to the construction of a canal. The treaty was quickly ratified by both governments, ratifications being exchanged on February 26, 1904.[27]

Since the Hay-Bunau-Varilla treaty became the basis of United States relations with the Republic of Panama up to the present time, the provisions of the convention warrant a full summarization. After providing a guarantee that the United States would maintain the independence of Panama, the treaty granted to the United States in perpetuity the use, occupation and control of a zone of land, and land under water, for the construction, maintenance, operation, sanitation and protection of a canal. The zone was to be ten miles in width extending across the isthmus from Colón to Panama, though those cities and their harbors were to be excluded from the zone. The United States was also granted the right to acquire, by purchase or by the exercise of the right of eminent domain, any lands and waters outside the zone deemed necessary and convenient for the construction, operation, and protection of the canal and other incidental enterprises. The treaty further granted to the United States

> . . . all the rights, powers and authority within the Zone . . . and within the limits of all auxiliary lands and waters . . . which the United States would possess and exercise if it were the sovereign of the territory within which said lands and waters are located, to the entire exclusion of the Republic of Panama of any such sovereign rights, power and authority.

The canal was to be "neutral in perpetuity," and the Republic of Panama was to have the right to transport its vessels, troops, and munitions of war through the canal "at all times without paying charges of any kind." The United States was permitted to employ whatever troops and construct what-

[26] *Dipl. Hist. of the Panama Canal*, 353–354; 362–367.
[27] For text, see Malloy, *op. cit.*, II, 1349.

ever fortifications it deemed necessary to protect and defend the canal. Panama was not to levy taxes, duties, or other charges upon vessels of the United States connected with the canal enterprise except when such cargo was destined for consumption in the Republic outside the zone or in the cities of Panama and Colón. Nor was Panama to tax any property or employees of the canal. The United States was permitted to import duty free into the areas under its control anything for use or consumption in connection with the canal operation. In return for the rights and powers acquired under the treaty, the United States was to pay Panama $10 million upon ratification, and $250,000 annually beginning nine years thereafter.

Diplomacy had done its part; the rest belonged to the engineers. The construction of the canal began at once and was successfully carried through, despite engineering difficulties, problems of sanitation and disease, and a scarcity of labor which was met largely by the importation of Negro workers from the West Indies. Particular credit for the success of the enterprise must go to General George W. Goethals, the chief construction engineer, and to Dr. William C. Gorgas, who headed the sanitation program and kept disease to a minimum by eradicating the dreaded yellow fever. The canal was opened to traffic on August 15, 1914, at a most timely moment, for with the outbreak of World War I the new waterway acquired immediately a commercial and strategic importance to the United States as well as to the other Allied countries. The canal decreased by 7,873 miles the sea distance between New York and San Francisco.

The total cost of the canal, approximately $500 million, if fortification costs are included, far exceeded the original estimate, but it was well worth the expense and effort. If the subsequent "conscience" payment made to Colombia in 1921 is included, the total cost was somewhat more. Some would add to this the cost of the Virgin Islands, purchased from Denmark in 1917 for $25 million for the protection of the Atlantic approaches to the canal. However one reckons the cost, the Panama Canal has been of incalculable value to the United States from the standpoint of both commerce and security. Of greatest significance for the purposes of this study is the fact that the canal became the key to the hemispheric defenses of the United States and the principal focus of our policy in the entire Caribbean area, which unfolded in dramatic fashion in the early years of the twentieth century.[28]

Diplomatic problems with Colombia and Great Britain

The cost of the Panama Canal in terms of international good will was another matter. The methods used by President Roosevelt in the acquisition of the Canal Zone caused indignation and alarm throughout Latin America and created strained relations with Colombia, which deeply resented the intervention of the United States in the Panama revolution. The Colombian government refused to recognize the independence of Panama and demanded

[28] See Norman J. Padelford, *The Panama Canal in Peace and War* (New York: The Macmillan Company, 1942).

that her claim to the province, as well as her interests in the canal, be submitted to international arbitration. But both Secretary Hay and his successor,
Elihu Root, rejected the demand for arbitration on the ground that the questions involved were of a political nature and hence were not justiciable.

After emotions had calmed somewhat, the United States began to realize
that it had committed a serious diplomatic blunder which should be corrected.
Secretary Root, in 1907, attempted to set aright our relations with Colombia
by negotiating a series of three treaties between the United States, Panama,
and Colombia. Known as the Root-Cortes-Arosemena treaties, they assigned
to Colombia preferential rights in the use of the canal and a payment of $2.4
million, the latter to consist of the first ten installments of the annuity promised
Panama. Colombia, in return, was to recognize the independence of Panama.
Although ratified by the United States and Panama, this arrangement was
indignantly rejected by the Colombian congress.[29] Subsequent and similar
efforts of the Taft administration to reach a settlement were also rejected.

The United States persisted, however, in attempting to pacify Colombia.
In 1914, Secretary of State William Jennings Bryan succeeded in negotiating
a settlement satisfactory to the offended nation. Under its terms the United
States agreed to extend an expression of regret to Colombia for the part it
played in the Panama episode, to make payment of $25 million to that
nation, and to grant it preferential rights in the use of the canal. Colombia
was to recognize the independence of Panama. This arrangement pacified the
Colombian government, but the United States Senate, influenced by former
President Theodore Roosevelt, who was indignant over the American concessions, refused to be a party to an admission of guilt accompanied with a
payment of "conscience" money.[30] The "regret clause" was subsequently
eliminated from the treaty, but the Senate still refused to approve it. Because
of preoccupations with World War I, the United States did not pursue the
matter any further during the Wilson administration.

Pressure continued to build up to make a settlement satisfactory to
Colombia and finally, on April 20, 1921, during the Harding administration,
and after the death of Roosevelt, a treaty with Colombia was approved by the
Senate with amendments which differed slightly from the earlier version. The
principal change was elimination of the so-called "regret" or "apology" clause.
Otherwise the treaty provided that, to compensate for the damages suffered by
Colombia in Panama, the United States would pay to Colombia $25 million.
Colombia was also to have equal rights with the United States in the use of
the canal. Treaty ratifications were exchanged in March, 1922, and on May
15, 1924, the Colombian government formally recognized the independence
of Panama. Aside from the death of Roosevelt, which removed the principal
opponent of any *rapprochement* with Colombia, a factor of considerable
significance in bringing about a satisfactory settlement between the two
estranged countries was the desire of American business interests to acquire

29 *Dipl. Hist. of the Panama Canal,* 314–325.
30 Theodore Roosevelt, *Fear God and Take Your Own Part* (New York: George H.
Doran Co., 1916), 305–342.

oil concessions in Colombia. The treaty of 1921 brought to an end the unhappy chapter of our relations with Colombia — and facilitated the acquisition of the oil concessions.[31]

Another dispute, a heritage of canal diplomacy, was the Panama Canal tolls controversy with Great Britain. In anticipation of the opening of the canal the United States Congress, in 1912, passed the Panama Canal Act which established the toll rates to be charged the users of the canal, but in so doing exempted American ships engaged in coastwise trade from the payment of tolls. This action was immediately protested by the British government, which claimed that this exemption was in violation of the Hay-Pauncefote treaty, which stated that any such canal should be open to all nations on terms of equality.

President Taft and Secretary Knox, both excellent lawyers who should have known better, argued that "all nations" meant all nations except the United States, and that the United States was within its rights in giving preference to its own citizens. The best legal opinion in the country, including that of Elihu Root, who helped to negotiate the treaty of 1901 with Great Britain, held that the Taft-Knox interpretation was wrong. The British government took a very serious view of the controversy, and was particularly aroused when the Taft administration refused to submit the dispute to arbitration.

When Woodrow Wilson became President in March, 1913, he re-examined the American position, though the Democratic platform on which he was elected in 1912 upheld the tolls-exemption principle. Convinced of the legal and political error of the preceding administration, and desirous of closing the breach with Great Britain, especially since he needed British support for his policy in the controversy with Mexico, Wilson requested Congressional repeal of the exemption clause. Although the President's appeal precipitated a stormy debate in Congress, especially in the Senate, a bill repealing the exemption clause was finally passed on June 15, 1914. Thereupon Britain withdrew her recognition of Victoriano Huerta as president of Mexico. It is interesting that a few years earlier, Great Britain, in apparent acknowledgement of the fact that the Caribbean had become for the United States a "mare nostrum," had withdrawn her naval squadron which long had been based at Kingston, Jamaica.

Strategic expansion

As Admiral Mahan had foreseen, the adequate defense of the Panama Canal required United States control of its Caribbean approaches. In other words the acquisition of the Panama Canal Zone dictated control over a "Greater Panama Canal Zone." Thus the basis was laid for a policy of strategic expansion in the Caribbean.[32]

---

[31] Watt Stewart, "The Ratification of the Thomson-Urrutia Treaty," *Southwestern Political and Social Science Quarterly,* X, No. 4 (March, 1930), 416–428.

[32] W. V. Judson, "Strategic Value of the West Indian Possessions to the United States," *Annals* of the American Academy of Political and Social Science, XIX, No. 3, 383–391.

The acquisition of Puerto Rico at the end of the Spanish-American War in 1898, with its adjacent Culebra and Vieques islands, secured for the United States its first territorial footholds in the Caribbean and assured a commanding position on the strategic Culebra Passage eastward of Puerto Rico, and on the Mona Channel separating the island from the Dominican Republic to the west.

Probably the most important of all the seaways through the Antilles leading into the Caribbean is the Windward Passage between Cuba and Haiti. Conscious of its significance the United States, as early as 1891, sought to obtain as a coaling station the Mole St. Nicolas which commanded the Haitian or eastern side of the Passage. Frustrated in its efforts to acquire a leasehold the United States seemed to be satisfied thereafter with a pledge by Haiti not to grant any rights or privileges to any foreign government concerning the occupation of the Mole St. Nicolas.[33]

The United States could well afford to abandon aspirations for a base in Haiti when its command of the Windward Passage was established by the acquisition of base rights from Cuba at Guantánamo Bay. Originally, after the Spanish-American War, and during the occupation of Cuba, the United States contemplated the retention of bases following withdrawal from the island. The Isle of Pines and four different sites in Cuba were tentatively considered, but in 1904 a treaty was negotiated providing for the return to Cuba of the Isle of Pines,[34] and by the treaty of 1903 the United States abandoned claims to base sites on the bays of Cienfuegos and Nipe, but retained rights on Guantánamo Bay and Bahía Honda. In 1912 the United States gave up its rights to Bahía Honda in return for greater concessions at Guantánamo.[35]

United States rights at Guantánamo were established by the treaty of 1903 (amended in 1912 and 1934), which granted virtually complete control over the bay of Guantánamo and a tract of land at Caimanera. Under the original lease agreement the United States paid a yearly token rental of $2,000 in gold, but in 1934 this was raised to $3,300 annually. The lease, a perpetual one, could be revoked only by mutual consent. The United States soon converted "Gitmo" into a major naval base. The installations at the base were valued at many millions of dollars, but in terms of United States strategic interests, military and diplomatic estimates of its value were much higher.

Although the Danish West Indies occupied an important strategic position in relation to the seaways at the junction of the Greater and Lesser Antilles, and the harbor of St. Thomas was reputed one of the finest in the Caribbean, the islands were sought not only for base purposes but also to prevent their falling from the weak hands of Denmark into the control of a strong European power. The effort to secure the islands by purchase in 1867 was rejected by

[33] Article XI of the treaty of 1915 (ratified, May, 1916).

[34] The Isle of Pines treaty was not ratified by the Senate until 1925; thus it was in that house for twenty-one years, a record.

[35] Charles E. Chapman, *A History of the Cuban Republic* (New York: The Macmillan Company, 1927), 156–157.

the United States Senate as another case of "Seward's Folly." A second treaty of purchase was negotiated upon President Roosevelt's initiative in 1902, but it was rejected by the Danish Parliament. Finally, in 1915, when it was feared that a victorious Germany in World War I might acquire the islands by purchase or by conquest of Denmark, the United States decided to purchase them, "price no object."

While discounting the need of the islands by the United States for base purposes, Admiral Dewey, acting on behalf of the General Board of the Navy, in December, 1915, advised the Secretary of the Navy:

> In a military sense, that of forestalling a possible enemy rather than that of endeavoring to gain a favorable position for ourselves, it is advisable that the Danish Islands should come under our flag by peaceful measures before war. The Caribbean is within the peculiar sphere of influence of the United States, and if any of the islands now under foreign jurisdiction should change their nationality, the General Board believes that for military reasons the United States should not tolerate any change other than to the United States itself.[36]

By treaty, signed on August 4, 1916, the United States purchased the Virgin Islands, (originally the Danish West Indies) for $25 million. Since the purchase price was five times greater than what was asked in 1902, the Danish government profited greatly because of the delay; as for the United States, it was satisfied to acquire islands occupying a most strategic spot. It little mattered, perhaps, that the islands became a financial burden, "a poorhouse surrounded by salt water." Early plans to construct a base at St. Thomas were abandoned in favor of greater improvements at San Juan, Puerto Rico.

The negotiation of the Bryan-Chamorro treaty of 1916 must also be considered in the context of Caribbean expansion and creation of a "Greater Panama Canal Zone." The treaty, signed in 1914 but not ratified until 1916, conveyed to the United States, for a payment of $3 million, the grant in perpetuity of the monopoly on a canal route across Nicaragua, and the cession of naval bases on the Great and Little Corn Islands in the Caribbean, and in the Gulf of Fonseca.[37]

The United States never undertook to construct a Nicaraguan Canal or occupy the naval base sites conveyed by the Bryan-Chamorro treaty, nor for that matter were these the principal or sole purposes of the treaty. An equally important objective, as stated in the preamble to the treaty, read as follows: "and the government of Nicaragua wishing to facilitate in every way possible the successful maintenance and operation of the Panama Canal, the two governments have resolved to conclude a convention to these ends." Thus, it was a prime purpose of the Bryan-Chamorro treaty to protect the

---

[36] Quoted in Tansill, *op. cit.*, 481–482.
[37] See "The United States and the Nicaraguan Canal," Foreign Policy Association, *Information Service*, IV, No. 6 (May 25, 1928), 112–126.

Panama Canal by perfecting the defenses and promoting the order and stability of Nicaragua. Competition for the ownership or control of a Nicaraguan canal was now eliminated in favor of the United States. Moreover, the expenditure of the $3 million paid by the United States was "to be applied by Nicaragua upon its indebtedness or other public purposes for the advancement of the welfare of Nicaragua in a manner to be determined by the two High Contracting Parties, all such disbursements to be made by orders drawn by the Minister of Finances of the Republic of Nicaragua and approved by the Secretary of State of the United States or by such person as he may designate." All this was designed to protect the Nicaraguan flank of the Panama Canal.

The acquisition by the United States of base leases in the British West Indies may be regarded as the culmination of strategic expansion in the Caribbean. By the Destroyer-Bases Agreement of September 2, 1940, the United States acquired 99-year leases for naval bases in British Guiana, Trinidad, Antigua, Santa Lucia, and Jamaica in the Caribbean as well as in the Bahamas, Bermuda, and Newfoundland. In 1964 the United States still retained rights in all the Caribbean sites except Jamaica.

Interventionism in the Caribbean

When the Caribbean became a recognized American sphere of influence, the United States applied to the underdeveloped countries of the region a set of policies peculiarly applicable to their retarded development and to the requirements of United States defense.[38] The specific objective was support of Latin-American order and stability, for politically this would help to eliminate excuse for foreign interventions potentially violative of the Monroe Doctrine, and economically this would help improve trade and investment prospects with the United States.

The United States supported stability and order in the Caribbean countries in many ways, some of these amounting to intervention — direct and indirect, forcible and nonforcible. In fact, the interventionist practices of the United States, which earned for it such universal and persistent condemnation throughout Latin America, were generally restricted in application to the Caribbean and to Mexico. We now examine the various uses to which American interventionism was put.[39]

[38] For surveys of Caribbean policy, see Wilfred Hardy Callcott, *The Caribbean Policy of the United States, 1890–1920* (Baltimore: The Johns Hopkins Press, 1942); C. P. Howland, *Survey of American Foreign Relations* (New Haven: Yale University Press, 1929); Chester Lloyd Jones, *The Caribbean Since 1900* (New York: Prentice-Hall, Inc., 1936); Dana G. Munro, *The United States and the Caribbean Area* (Boston: World Peace Foundation, 1934); Dexter Perkins, *The United States and the Caribbean* (Cambridge: Harvard University Press, 1947); and J. Fred Rippy, *The Caribbean Danger Zone* (New York: G. P. Putnam's Sons, 1940).

[39] There is a vast bibliography on the theory and practice of intervention. A few titles more applicable to the present study are: J. Reuben Clark, *Right to Protect Citizens in Foreign Countries by Landing Forces* (Washington, D.C.: Government Printing Office, 1929, 2nd rev. ed.); Luis Guillén Atienzo, *El Principio Internacional de No Intervención y las Doctrinas Americanas* (Santiago de Chile, 1949); D. A. Graber,

The United States' ideal of national political order was adherence to constitutionalism. All of the republics had adopted constitutions providing for democratic, representative governments. Believing that constitutionalism was the only political order which would benefit all people, the United States intervened in the internal affairs of the Latin countries to encourage respect for national constitutions. There were many facets to the American policy of constitutionalism applied to the Caribbean countries.[40]

Generally, the support of constitutionalism called for the denial of recognition to a government that came into existence by unconstitutional means, at least until an election could confirm the results of a revolution. Thus, *coups d'état, cuartelazos* (barracks revolts), and other kinds of rebellions, all violative of the constitutional order, should be discouraged by the denial of recognition.[41] This was the rule adopted by the Central American republics at a conference which met in Washington in 1907. President Wilson applied this principle to Victoriano Huerta of Mexico, whom he refused to recognize because his violent succession to the Mexican presidency was "unconstitutional." In announcing his policy of *de jure* recognition President Wilson declared his intention to instruct the Latins in the virtues of constitutionalism.

President Wilson applied his policy of *de jure* recognition to the usurper Tinoco of Costa Rica in 1918.[42] At the second Central American conference which met in Washington in 1923, another convention was adopted pledging the five republics to the application of *de jure* recognition among themselves. The United States agreed to conform to the same rule in its relations with the Central American republics. It applied the policy on a number of occasions.[43]

The use of recognition was also manipulated, it must be conceded, for less noble purposes than support of constitutionalism. On many occasions recognition was used as an instrument of policy — that is, recognition would be accorded a government not as a matter of right but conditioned by its willingness to make concessions or pledges to the grantor nation. For example, in 1922–1923, the United States tried to condition its recognition of President Álvaro Obregón of Mexico by his pledge not to enforce Article 27 of the Mexican Constitution retroactively to the disadvantage of American oil in-

---

Crisis Diplomacy, A History of U.S. Intervention Policies and Practices (Washington, D.C.: Public Affairs Press, 1959); Henry G. Hodges, *The Doctrine of Intervention* (Princeton: The Banner Press, 1915); Sara Gómez Valle, *La No Intervención de los Estados Americanos* (Mexico, D.F., 1949); C. Neale Ronning, *Law and Politics in Inter-American Diplomacy* (New York: John Wiley and Sons, 1963), 63–89; and Dana G. Munro, *Intervention and Dollar Diplomacy in the Caribbean, 1900–1920* (Princeton: Princeton University Press, 1964).

[40] See Raymond Leslie Buell, "The United States and Central American Stability," *Foreign Policy Reports*, VII, No. 9 (July 8, 1931), 177–186.

[41] For this nonrecognition policy, see Munro, *United States and the Caribbean*, 211–216; R. L. Buell, "The United States and Central American Revolutions," *For. Pol. Rep.*, VII, No. 10 (July 22, 1931), 190–201; Julius Goebel, Jr., *Recognition Policy of the United States* (New York: Columbia University Press, 1915); and Ronning, *op. cit.*, 6–33.

[42] *For. Pol. Rep.*, VII, No. 9, 180–184.

[43] *Ibid.*, VII, No. 10, 193–201.

terests in Mexico. Obregón successfully resisted conditioned recognition. With Nicaragua in 1911, the Dominican Republic in 1914 and 1916, and Haiti in 1915, the United States exchanged its recognition for economic and political concessions.

Recognition by the United States was so vital to the life of Latin-American governments — particularly if they were to contract foreign loans — that to grant or withhold it amounted to very real intervention by the United States in the internal affairs of countries not only in the Caribbean area but in other parts of Latin America as well. Indeed, manipulating recognition was undoubtedly the most generally applied form of United States intervention.

Like its use of recognition, the United States applied arms control[44] both for the support of constitutionalism and for other objectives. Because of the dependence of Latin-American rebels, and governments also, on arms supplies from abroad, particularly from the United States, the embargo of these shipments gave the President of the United States considerable control over the success of revolutions and the fate of governments. Dating back to March, 1912, when the Congress by joint resolution authorized the President to impose embargoes on arms shipments to Mexico, the use of arms control became an important instrument of American policy to promote Latin-American stability and order. The President imposed arms embargoes to reinforce United States policy in the Dominican Republic in 1905, in Cuba in 1924, in Nicaragua in 1926, and in Mexico in 1912, 1915, 1919, and 1924. There were sales of arms to governments, but denials to rebels, as in Cuba in 1917, and in Mexico in 1924 and 1929. In 1928 the United States signed, and later ratified, a Pan American pact regulating the sale of arms during civil war. The terms of the pact invalidated further manipulation of the arms embargo as an instrument of intervention.

Internal disorder, corrupt elections and fiscal irresponsibility, so characteristic of the republics of the Caribbean, were responsible for interventionist measures by the United States such as the organization of native constabularies, the supervision of elections, and the establishment of financial controls.[45] These rather specialized forms of intervention were restricted, in Latin America, with few exceptions, to the Caribbean area.

The United States supported the building up of native police forces and elimination of the regular army because of its desire to free those small poor countries of the financial burden and the political threat of militarism. Moreover, the constabularies, when sufficiently organized, were expected to maintain order and protect property, thus obviating the necessity of maintaining an army of occupation. In Haiti an American-officered constabulary was provided by the treaty of 1915. After years of organization, training, and leadership by the United States Marine Corps, the *Garde d'Haiti*[46] was

[44] B. H. Williams, *Economic Foreign Policy of the United States* (New York: McGraw-Hill Book Company, 1929), 145–150.

[45] *Ibid.,* Chaps. IX-XI *passim.*

[46] See James H. McCrocklin, *Garde D'Haiti, 1915–1934* (Annapolis: The United States Naval Institute, 1956).

taken over by native Haitians in 1934. In the Dominican Republic, as in Haiti, the United States, taking advantage of its position as an occupying power, organized a native constabulary or *Policía Nacional Dominicana.* The *Policía,* until 1924, was trained and supervised by American officers. Upon the withdrawal of the Americans in 1924, the Dominicans assumed full control of the constabulary. When the United States prepared to withdraw its legation guard from Nicaragua, it offered to help organize a native constabulary. Nicaragua agreed, and in May, 1925, the first steps were taken to develop such a force. However, the outbreak of civil war in which the United States was deeply involved interrupted the program. When the conflict was settled by the Stimson-Moncada Agreement of 1927, one of the items of the agreement was the organization of a constabulary. Thus, in 1928, President Moncada created a *Guardia Nacional* in place of a national army. At the start the *Guardia* was organized and trained by American Marine officers. When the United States Marine forces were finally withdrawn from Nicaragua in January, 1933, the *Guardia Nacional* was on its own. It was not long before its commander, Anastacio Somoza, seized control of the Nicaraguan government, thus embarking on a long dictatorship. It is interesting to note that in Haiti and in the Dominican Republic, future dictators of the two countries, Paul Eugene Magloire and Rafael Leonidas Trujillo, stepped into the national presidency from command of their respective constabularies.

Since elections in most of the republics of the Caribbean area were notoriously corrupt, the United States lent its services, both with and without solicitation or pressure, to the formulation of electoral codes and the supervision of elections. General Enoch Crowder drafted two electoral codes for Cuba (1908 and 1919), and Dr. Harold W. Dodds one for Nicaragua (1923). On several occasions — in Cuba, Panama, the Dominican Republic, Haiti, and notably in Nicaragua in 1928 and 1932 — the United States assumed the supervision of elections.[47] Not surprisingly, these instances produced that rarity in the Caribbean scene — honest elections.

Imposition by the United States of different kinds of financial controls,[48] because of fiscal irresponsibility in the Caribbean countries, is our final example of intervention for the support of policy. To understand United States concern for the stabilization of Central American and Caribbean finances, we must recall that default on foreign bonded indebtedness was chronic, and hence the threat of foreign intervention was ever present. It was because of this potential danger that the United States believed itself obliged to pursue a policy of "preventive intervention."

The earliest type of financial control was the customs receivership. The first customs receivership assumed by the United States was in the Dominican Republic as originally provided by executive agreement in 1905, and later

---

[47] D. W. Dodds, "American Supervision in the Nicaraguan Election," *Foreign Affairs,* VII (1929), 488–497.

[48] See Williams, *Econ. For. Pol.,* Chaps. X, XI.

by convention in 1907. The treaty of 1915 with Haiti also provided for customs control. The general purpose of the customs receiverships was to insure that the customs would be efficiently and honestly administered, and the revenues allocated to their proper destinations, including service on the foreign indebtedness. These objectives were achieved, and in fact were so successful that the United States was encouraged to extend the scope of its fiscal controls.

The next step, therefore, was to extend control over the collection of internal revenues. Refusal of the Dominican government to accept United States tax collection and the appointment of an American financial adviser provoked the armed intervention and occupation of 1916–1924. When the United States withdrew from the island in 1924 the administration of the internal revenue service was turned back to the Dominican government, but a modified customs control continued for a few years longer.

In Haiti, United States insistence on supervision of the internal revenue service was resisted at first, but eventually in 1924 the Haitian government agreed to the creating of an Internal Revenue Bureau operating under the supervision and control of the American Receiver General of Customs.

In Nicaragua the State Department was satisfied to lend its support to agreements between American bankers and the Nicaraguan government concerning customs and internal revenue collections.

Finally, another kind of financial control imposed by the United States on the Caribbean republics was the limiting of their indebtedness and expenditures. In short, the United States was prepared to force the Caribbean governments to live within their means. They were to be saved, even against their will, from fiscal irresponsibility.

In the case of Cuba, Article II of the Platt Amendment restrained that government from contracting any public debt "to pay the interest upon which, and to make reasonable sinking-fund provision for the ultimate discharge of which, the ordinary revenues of the island, after defraying the current expenses of Government shall be inadequate." There were many instances of American interventions to control Cuba's public debt and expenditures. Probably the most important of these was the "Crowder memoranda" of 1922, in which General Crowder set forth fifteen conditions of reform which the Cuban government had to meet before receiving permission to contract a $50 million loan.

The Dominican Republic, by Article III of the treaty of 1907, pledged that until it "has paid the whole amount of the bonds of the debt, its public debt shall not be increased except by previous agreement" with the United States. In 1913 the United States approved a $1.5 million loan to take care of outstanding accounts, but this proved to be insufficient. The refusal of the Dominicans to live within their budget prompted the United States to propose an American financial advisership. After the rejection of this proposal, there followed military occupation, and, of course, complete financial control.

Haiti, also, was limited by the treaty of 1915 not to increase its public debt without United States agreement, nor to assume financial obligations beyond the capacity of its ordinary revenues. The office of the Financial Adviser was utilized by the United States to hold Haiti to its treaty obligations. This official's powers included approval of the budget as well as expenditures.

The fact that the financial delinquency of the Caribbean republics provided immediate occasion for American interventions, and the further fact that American banking interests became heavily involved because of the loans which they extended to the governments to correct their financial problems, led to exaggerated charges of "dollar diplomacy"[49] against the United States which were not substantiated by the facts. Since the repayment of bank loans was usually guaranteed by the United States government in the form of American-controlled customs collections, the American bankers naturally realized a profit, though not a usurious one. The patronage of American banking interests was, however, quite incidental to the State Department's concern for the stabilization of Caribbean finances. American banking interests were, in fact, often quite reluctant to become involved in the financial affairs of these countries, and did so only on the initiative, and sometimes at the direct request of the State Department, which believed that American financial control was necessary to prevent European financial intervention, possibly followed by political control. The fundamental objective of financial control by the United States was, therefore, political — political in the sense of satisfying the strategical requirements of continental security.

The interventionist policies and practices of the United States in the early decades of the present century — whether they be those of Roosevelt, Taft, or Wilson — must be explained primarily in terms of fulfilling the security requirements of the United States, and not as a means of accommodating the selfish desire of a handful of American commercial and financial interests to enrich themselves. The phrase "dollar diplomacy" was more a slogan seized upon by anti-American propagandists than an accurate characterization of the Caribbean policy of the United States.

The incidental effects of American interventionism is a matter which need not detain us here, except to say that the secondary objective of promoting stable, democratic, and responsible governments went largely unrealized, since in most instances the intervened countries of the Caribbean lapsed back into their old errant ways as soon as American authority was withdrawn. Worst of all, despite the generally good intentions of the United States to help those countries forward in their political, economic, and social development, these efforts were not only frustrated by an unresponsive populace, but were rewarded negatively with an upsurge of anti-Americanism throughout Latin America. This legacy of ill will has yet to be overcome.

---

[49] See Munro, *op. cit.*, 216–222; *For. Pol. Rep.*, VII, No. 9, 174–176; Bemis, *Latin American Policy*, Chap. IX; and Rippy, *op. cit.*, Chap. VII. Scott Nearing and Joseph Freeman, *Dollar Diplomacy* (New York: The Viking Press, 1928), is strongly anti-imperialist.

SUPPLEMENTARY READING

Bemis, Samuel Flagg, *The Latin-American Policy of the United States* (New York: Harcourt, Brace and Company, 1943).

Bonsal, Stephen, *The American Caribbean* (New York: Moffat, Yard and Co., 1913).

Borchard, Edwin M., *The Diplomatic Protection of Citizens Abroad* (New York: The Banks Law Publishing Co., 1915).

Bunau-Varilla, Philippe, *Panama: The Creation, Destruction, and Resurrection* (New York: McBride, Nast & Co., 1914).

Callcott, Wilfred Hardy, *The Caribbean Policy of the United States, 1890-1920* (Baltimore: The Johns Hopkins Press, 1942).

Clark, J. Reuben, *Right to Protect Citizens in Foreign Countries by Landing Forces* (Washington, D.C.: Government Printing Office, 2nd rev. ed. 1929).

Diplomatic History of the Panama Canal, Sen. Exec. Doc. No. 474, 63rd Cong., 2nd Sess.

Goebel, Julius, Jr., *Recognition Policy of the United States* (New York: Columbia University Press, 1915).

Gómez Valle, Sara, *La No Intervención de los Estados Americanos* (Mexico, D.F.: 1949).

Graber, D. A., *Crisis Diplomacy, A History of U.S. Intervention Policies and Practices* (Washington, D.C.: Public Affairs Press, 1959).

Guillén Atienza, Luis, *El Principio Internacional de no Intervención y las Doctrinas Americanas* (Santiago de Chile: 1949).

Hodges, Henry G., *The Doctrine of Intervention* (Princeton: The Banner Press, 1915).

Howland, Charles P., *Survey of American Foreign Relations* (New Haven: Yale University Press, 1929. Published for the Council on Foreign Relations), Chap. 11.

Johnson, W. F., *Four Centuries of the Panama Canal* (New York: Henry Holt and Company, 1907).

Jones, Chester Lloyd, *The Caribbean Since 1900* (New York: Prentice-Hall, Inc., 1936).

Judson, W. V., "Strategic Value of Her West Indian Possessions to the United States," *Annals* of the American Academy of Political and Social Science, XIX, No. 3, 383-391.

Mecham, J. Lloyd, "Intervention in Latin America", in *The Southwest in International Affairs,* Proceedings of the Third Annual Conference, Institute of Public Affairs (Dallas, Texas, March 10-14, 1936), 75-89.

Miner, Dwight Carroll, *The Fight for the Panama Route: The Story of the Spooner Act and the Hay-Herrán Treaty* (New York: Columbia University Press, 1940).

Munro, Dana G., *The Five Republics of Central America* (New York: Oxford University Press, 1918), Chaps. X-XIV.

Munro, Dana G., *The United States and the Caribbean Area* (Boston: World Peace Foundation, 1934).

Nearing, Scott, and Freeman, Joseph, *Dollar Diplomacy* (New York: The Viking Press, 1925).

Offut, Milton, *The Protection of Citizens Abroad by the Armed Forces of the United States* (Baltimore: The Johns Hopkins Press, 1928).

Padelford, N. J., *The Panama Canal in Peace and War* (New York: The Macmillan Company, 1942).

Perkins, Dexter, *The United States and the Caribbean* (Cambridge: Harvard University Press, 1947).

Pratt, Julius W., *America's Colonial Experiment* (New York: Prentice-Hall, Inc., 1950), Chaps. 1–4.

Rippy, J. Fred, *The Caribbean Danger Zone* (New York: G. P. Putnam's Sons, 1940).

Stuart, Graham H., *Latin America and the United States* (New York: Appleton-Century-Crofts, Inc., 5th ed. 1955), Chaps. V, VI.

Thomas, Ann Van Wynen, and Thomas, A. J., Jr., *Non-Intervention: The Law and its Import in the Americas* (Dallas: Southern Methodist University Press, 1956).

Uribe, Antonio José, *Colombia y los Estados Unidos de América* (Bogotá: Imprenta Nacional, 1931).

Walker Commission Report, *Sen. Exec. Doc.,* Nos. 54 and 123, 57th Cong., 1st Sess.

Wilgus, A. Curtis, ed., *The Caribbean: Contemporary International Relations* (Gainesville: University of Florida Press, 1957).

Williams, Mary W., *Anglo-American Isthmian Diplomacy* (Washington, D.C.: Government Printing Office, 1916).

11

Relations with the Island Republics of the Caribbean[1]

Because of their strategic location, the islands of Cuba and Hispaniola have long commanded the special attention of the United States. Since the early nineteenth century, Cuba has been regarded as the "Key to the Americas," because, situated between Florida and Yucatán, it controlled the two entrances to the Gulf of Mexico and one of the chief passages to the Caribbean Sea. It thus was in position to bottle up the Gulf ports of the United States and hamper American control of interoceanic canal routes. In spite of the fact that United States trade and investments in Cuba attained great proportions after Cuban independence, few regions of the world have given the United States more concern than the "Pearl of the Antilles" in the politico-strategic sphere.

Between Cuba and Puerto Rico lies Hispaniola, at another important gateway to the Caribbean; the eastern two-thirds of the island is occupied by the Dominican Republic, the western third by Haiti. Haiti is one of the most densely populated areas of the world, and in social, economic, and political development it occupies undisputed last place among all of the Latin-Amer-

[1] For general works on relations with the Caribbean republics, see Wilfrid H. Callcott, *The Caribbean Policy of the United States, 1890–1920* (Baltimore: The Johns Hopkins Press, 1942): Charles P. Howland, ed., *Survey of American Foreign Relations* (New Haven: Yale University Press, 1929), 1–167; Chester Lloyd Jones, *The Caribbean Since 1900* (New York: Prentice-Hall, Inc., 1936), 1–353; Dana G. Munro, *The United States and the Caribbean Area* (Boston: World Peace Foundation, 1934) 1–194; Dexter Perkins, *The United States and the Caribbean* (Cambridge: Harvard University Press, 1947); and J. Fred Rippy, *The Caribbean Danger Zone* (New York: G. P. Putnam's Sons, 1940).

ican republics. Its inhabitants number about 3.5 million and are almost exclusively pure black. Illiteracy is estimated at almost 95 per cent, and the per capita income is scarcely more than $50 per year. Ever since the winning of their independence, more than 150 years ago, Haitians have never enjoyed even a brief respite from political violence and staggering poverty.

The population of the Dominican Republic, estimated at about 3 million, is mostly mulatto, the balance being evenly divided between the pure blacks and near-whites. Although considerably higher than Haiti in the scale of literacy, standards of living, and political development, the Dominican Republic ranks among the lowest of all the Latin-American countries.

United States trade with and investments in Haiti and the Dominican Republic never attained proportions sufficient to influence policy. It was the strategic location of Hispaniola, and particularly the value of the Mole St. Nicolas on the northwestern extremity of Haiti, and the Samaná Bay in northeast Santo Domingo, which gave to the two island republics an importance in United States foreign policy vastly disproportionate to their resources and population.

To the three island republics of the Caribbean the United States applied policies — described in the preceding chapter — peculiar to the region. Although the pattern of relations was remarkably similar in all of the republics, any attempt to merge these into a composite discussion is here avoided, for generally the flow of relations followed divergent courses, this being particularly true of Cuba. Nevertheless, in all three cases, our surveys of country relations are largely confined to the period when the United States actively supported a clearly defined Caribbean policy. But after its virtual liquidation by application of the policy of nonintervention, detailed surveys of country relations seem no longer necessary, since the countries of the Caribbean, particularly the two on the island of Hispaniola, lost much of their former importance to the United States. As for Cuba, its new and paramount importance derives from the introduction of an alien element, i.e., its domination by international Communism. This is why the Cuban problem, after the advent of Fidel Castro, is discussed in the chapter on Communism in Latin America.

1. Haiti[2]

The island of Santo Domingo, or Hispaniola, was the original seat of Spanish empire in America, and remained under the unchallenged domination of Spain until the end of the seventeenth century. By the Treaty of Ryswick in 1697 the western part of the island was ceded to France. Saint-Domingue was soon converted by France into one of its richest colonial

[2] For general works descriptive of Haiti, see H. P. Davis, *Black Democracy, the Story of Haiti* (New York: Dodge Publishing Company, 1936); James G. Leyburn, *The Haitian People* (New Haven: Yale University Press, 1941); and Blair Niles, *Black Haiti* (New York: G. P. Putnam's Sons, 1926).

possessions. For employment in the culture of sugar, cotton, tobacco, and coffee, over 500,000 Negro slaves were introduced from Africa.

The French Revolution set in motion a train of developments which extended even to the island slave colony in the West Indies. There the promises of the "Rights of Man" were taken so seriously that open rebellion developed — slaves rose against their masters and indiscriminately massacred white men, women, and children. It was one of the world's most horrible servile revolts. An ex-slave, Toussaint L'Ouverture, emerged as brilliant leader of the revolt, and by 1800 had gained control of virtually the entire island, including the Spanish part which had been ceded to France by the Treaty of Basle in 1795. Then his fortunes suffered an eclipse when French reinforcements under General Leclerc were sent to the island by Napoleon. Treacherously arrested and deported to France, the great Negro leader soon died in a French prison. The revolt, however, continued, and by the end of 1803, the pitiful remnants of a once-magnificent French army of about 50,000 men, decimated by yellow fever, was forced to capitulate. On January 1, 1804, the independence of Haiti was proclaimed.

Control of the Spanish part of the island remained in contention for a number of years. In 1809 the Spanish inhabitants revolted and re-established Spanish rule. In 1821 Dominican patriots rebelled against Spanish rule and attempted to proclaim independence, but a Haitian army marched in, and in 1822, declared the union of the whole island under the rule of Port-au-Prince. It was not until 1844 that the Dominicans were able to win their definitive, albeit precarious, independence of brutal Haitian rule.

Early relations with the United States

United States recognition of the Negro republic was withheld for many years, even longer than Britain's recognition in 1826, and French recognition in 1838. The real reason for United States delay was, of course, the slavery question. Pro-slavery sentiment was strong enough to prevent recognition until after the outbreak of the Civil War. Then, with the removal of Southern influence from the Congress, Haiti was recognized in 1862. A treaty of amity and commerce was ratified in 1865.[3]

The only matters of any significance in United States-Haitian relations during the remaining years of the nineteenth century related to (1) base sites aspirations by the United States, and (2) mounting fiscal troubles of the Haitian government. Haiti's Mole St. Nicolas was the site most attractive to United States strategists for a coaling station. The United States was eventually satisfied to secure a Haitian pledge never to alienate the site to a foreign power.[4]

In the meantime, however, the fiscal involvements of the Haitian government with foreign interests were developing dangerous aspects which became

---

[3] For the recognition question, see Ludwell Lee Montague, *Haiti and the United States, 1714–1938* (Durham: Duke University Press, 1940), Chaps. III-V.

[4] See *ibid.*, Chap. 14, for the Mole affair.

increasingly difficult for the United States to ignore, given the disposition of European governments, particularly France and Germany, to defend and promote the enterprises of their nationals in Haiti. Undoubtedly the chaotic political conditions in the Negro republic were attractive to foreign speculators and adventurers, who often helped to finance revolutions and expected rich profits in return. The inevitable result was a mounting and unmanageable public debt. Refunding loans were frequent. A suggestion from Paris that Haitian finances be placed under the tripartite control of France, Germany, and the United States, came to naught but increased anxieties in Washington. In 1910, a loan of 65 million francs was contracted with American, French, and German bankers for the purpose of funding the internal debt and retiring depreciated currency. In addition to its external obligations, Haiti also owed a large internal debt due to the increasing costs of combating revolutions, which occurred almost annually after 1912. To meet these costs several bond issues were necessary, most of which went into the hands of local German merchants.[5] In 1915 the Haitian public debt amounted to $32 million.

American intervention

Although American economic interests in Haiti were relatively unimportant, this was not necessarily true of France and Germany, for there were a considerable number of French and German merchants in the island, and the Republic was heavily in debt to European creditors. When we add to these facts the approach of virtual anarchy in Haiti we have all the necessary conditions for application of the "big stick." On account of the utter collapse of government in a land where our strategic interests could not permit such a condition to exist, the United States was forced to exercise an "international police power." In 1914, the United States urged Haiti to accept controls such as had been imposed on the Dominican Republic in 1905 and 1907, which are described later. This failing, armed intervention was the alternative.

In 1914 a controversy developed between the Haitian government and the Banque Nationale when the government, in serious financial straits, circulated a large amount of new paper money and attempted to obtain possession of the large fund held by the bank under the 1910 loan contract for retiring the paper currency issued in earlier years. Although the Haitian government did seize some of the cash from the bank, most of the fund ($500,000) escaped its clutches by being shipped to New York on an American warship, at the request of the bank and under arrangement with the United States Department of State.[6]

Further aggravating the situation was the development of a dispute between the Haitian government and the National Railroad Company, an American

[5] Munro, *op. cit.*, 147.
[6] For the details of the controversy between the bank and the Haitian government, see *Foreign Relations of the United States*, 1914, 334–382; *ibid.*, 1915, 496–521.

corporation which had received a new concession in 1910 to build a railroad from Port-au-Prince to Cap Haitian. Seizure of the railroad was averted by the intercession of Secretary of State Bryan.[7]

Although agitation for American intervention on behalf of the bank and the railroad no doubt influenced the final decision of the United States government to take forceful measures in Haiti, the principal motivation behind American action was much broader than the special interests of a few bankers and railroad builders. As in the case of the Dominican Republic, President Woodrow Wilson adopted a deliberate policy of attempting to eliminate revolutionary activities in Haiti as a part of a general program of promoting orderly and constitutional governments throughout the Caribbean area. The President believed that the establishment of a stable and democratic government in Haiti would be the most effective way of preventing those conditions which might lead to intervention by European powers, some of which had already threatened to intervene. For example, early in 1914 several foreign powers, notably Germany, had landed troops in Haiti to protect their nationals during disturbances on the island; German shipping interests had made attempts to establish coaling stations at the strategically located Mole St. Nicolas; and both the French and German governments had notified the United States that they had special interests in Haiti which entitled them to participate in any outside financial control which might be established over the country.

The United States itself was no longer interested in obtaining a lease or cession of Mole St. Nicolas or any other Haitian territory, nor did it aspire to specific concessions or exclusive economic privileges in Haiti; but it was determined not to permit any other power to gain such advantages either. Its professed aim was to promote political and financial stability, preferably under a democratic government, and it was convinced that this could be achieved only by the direct intervention of the United States in at least Haiti's fiscal affairs.[8] Since ordinary diplomatic methods had failed to achieve these objectives it was now necessary to turn to the extraordinary.

The United States government in July, 1914, stated its opposition to a German and French proposal which would have established international control of Haitian affairs; it instructed its minister to Haiti to approach the Haitian government regarding its willingness to enter into a treaty whereby the United States would assume sole control over Haitian customs, in much the same manner as was provided in the agreement of 1905 with the Dominican Republic. The apparent success of the experiment in customs control in the Dominican Republic no doubt encouraged the United States government to attempt a similar undertaking in neighboring Haiti, whose problems were substantially the same. Hardly had treaty negotiations begun, however, when the government of President Oreste Zamor was overthrown.

---

[7] *Ibid.*, 1915, 538–548; *ibid.*, 1916, 377; Rippy, *op. cit.*, 185.

[8] Arthur C. Millspaugh, *Haiti Under American Control, 1915–1930* (Boston: World Peace Foundation, 1931), 32–33.

On November 12, 1914, immediately after the inauguration of President Davilmar Théodore, the United States informed him that it would recognize his regime only if he agreed to negotiate conventions providing for the establishment of American customs controls, a settlement of the bank and railroad controversies, guarantee of full protection to all foreign interests in Haiti, a pledge that no Haitian territory would be leased to any European government for use as a naval or coaling station, and, finally, a settlement by arbitration of all American claims against Haiti.[9] The United States' objective, apparently, was to bind Haiti by a modified Platt Amendment. President Théodore rejected the American proposal and the United States government, not desirous of assuming the responsibility of administering Haiti's fiscal affairs without the consent of her government, decided not to press the matter.

Nonetheless, Secretary Bryan continued his efforts to apply in Haiti the same policy that had been instituted earlier in the Dominican Republic. In March, 1915, commissioners were sent to Haiti to obtain a similar arrangement with that republic; however, they failed to negotiate a customs receivership. Two months later another commissioner, Paul Fuller, also failed (1) to secure the right of armed intervention by the United States to protect the Republic from outside attack; (2) to aid the government to suppress rebellion from within; (3) to secure a pledge from Haiti not to alienate Mole St. Nicolas; and (4) to arbitrate all foreign claims.[10] By July, 1915, it was obvious that no Haitian government would enter into an agreement by which the management of its fiscal affairs would be turned over to the American government.

American intervention: the first stage, 1915–1922

The internal situation in Haiti worsened when Guillaume Sam became president in March, 1915. Revolution began almost immediately, resulting in the imprisonment of a large number of suspected revolutionaries, many from prominent Haitian families. On July 27, when an uprising broke out in the capital, 167 of these prisoners were massacred by prison officials apparently by order of the president. The next day, an aroused mob forcibly entered the French Legation, where Sam had taken refuge, dragged him out and literally tore his body to pieces. With Haitian authority in a state of complete collapse, American Marines under Admiral William B. Caperton landed within twenty-four hours, assumed control of the custom houses and impounded the revenues, disarmed the Haitian forces, and gradually established order. The commanders of arriving British and French war vessels were asked not to land their troops. President Wilson was resolved to make the whole affair a unilateral action of the United States.

Shortly thereafter, when the Haitian Congress was assembled under the protection of the American Marines, the United States government declared

---

[9] *For. Rel.,* 1914, 359–360.
[10] Millspaugh, *op. cit.,* 30–32.

its intention to suppress factional disorder, to assume control over the customs and whatever other financial matters would be necessary for an efficient administration of Haitian affairs, to assist in the conduct of a new presidential election, and to use its authority to insure the establishment and continuance of constitutional government. At the same time, the United States disclaimed any designs on the political or territorial integrity of Haiti.[11]

Following the election by the Haitian Congress of Philippe Sudre Dartiguenave to the presidency on August 12, 1915, negotiations for a treaty began, despite continuing disorders in the interior and opposition to the American intervention in the Haitian capital itself. After slight modifications to meet objections raised by the Haitian government, the treaty as proposed by the United States, was signed on September 16, 1915, and shortly thereafter ratified by the Haitian government, though only after it was made clear to the Haitians that the sole alternative to accepting the treaty was submission to military government by the United States.[12] This treaty surpassed both the Platt Amendment treaty with Cuba and the Dominican treaty of 1907, in the degree to which it established American control and supervision. What had begun as a mere interposition for the protection of American lives and property in Haiti had quickly become a political intervention and a military occupation designed to create stability in a country notorious for its instability.

Since United States-Haitian relations for the next nineteen years hinged on the treaty of 1915, some attention should be given to its principal provisions. It provided that: (1) the Haitian president, upon nomination by the President of the United States, was to appoint a general receiver of customs and a financial adviser to be attached to the Ministry of Finance; (2) Haiti was not to increase its public debt or to reduce its customs duties without the consent of the president of the United States, and was not to assume any financial obligations which could not be met by ordinary government revenues; (3) Haiti was not to alienate any of its territory to any foreign government, or to enter into any treaty or arrangement with any power that would impair or tend to impair its independence; (4) the Haitian government was to agree to the arbitration of all foreign claims against Haiti, including those of the bank and railroad; (5) Haiti was to undertake whatever measures the United States deemed necessary for sanitation and public improvement; (6) a Haitian constabulary officered by Americans was to be established; and (7) the United States was to have authority to take whatever actions it deemed necessary to preserve Haitian independence and to maintain "a government adequate for the protection of life, property, and individual liberty."[13]

An executive agreement, or *modus vivendi,* signed on November 29, 1915, provided that the treaty would go into effect provisionally, pending its approval by the two governments. The treaty was to be in force originally for ten years, but provision was made for its extension for another ten years if for

---

[11] *For. Rel.,* 1915, 479–480.   [12] Montague, *op. cit.,* 215–217.
[13] For text of the treaty, see Millspaugh, *op. cit.,* 211–215, and Munro, *op. cit.,* 295–299.

any reason either party felt the purposes of the treaty had not been fully accomplished. Upon the signing of the *modus vivendi,* naval officers were appointed to the various positions named in the treaty; but on May 3, 1916, at which time the treaty went fully into effect, civilians were appointed as general receiver, deputy general receiver, and financial adviser, though Navy and Marine officers were placed at the head of the other treaty services. It soon became apparent that the attainment of the objectives of the treaty would require more than ten years of American control of Haiti's finances, so on March 28, 1917, the treaty was extended to twenty years.[14]

The new relationships which the treaty established between the United States and Haiti required a modification of the Haitian constitution to bring the constitutional system into conformity with the new situation and requirements. After much discussion between American authorities and the Haitian president, as well as careful consideration by the State and Navy Departments in Washington, the draft of a new constitution was hammered out in 1918.[15] Among its provisions were the removal of the prohibition against foreign land ownership contained in the old constitution, and the validation of all acts of the military occupation. The Haitian Congress refused to approve the new constitution, whereupon President Dartiguenave dissolved the Congress and, on June 12, 1918, secured its approval by popular plebiscite that merely echoed the influence of the American authorities.

Under this constitution, President Dartiguenave and his successor, Louis Borno, governed the country for the next twelve years "without the assistance of an elected Congress." A Council of State, whose members were appointed by the president, served as the republic's legislative body. In reality it was the American naval commander and the Marine officers, vested with the so-called treaty services, who ruled Haiti by ruling the Haitian president.

Despite some resistance by the Haitian government, effective American control had been established over Haitian finances. All funds, those derived from the internal revenue as well as from the customs, were deposited to the credit of the general receiver; and by an agreement reached on December 3, 1918, the American financial adviser was not only to advise the Haitian government on all budgetary matters but his approval was required for every order of payment issued by the Minister of Finance before being honored by the bank. Furthermore, by another agreement, every law relating in any way to the purposes of the treaty had to be approved by the United States government, before being submitted to the Haitian legislative body.

In an attempt to stabilize Haiti's financial situation a protocol[16] provided that all foreign claims against the Haitian government should be adjudicated by a three-man commission. To pay the awards of the commission, and in general to establish Haitian finances on a sound basis, there was to be a 30-year

[14] Munro, *op. cit.,* 299–300.

[15] Franklin D. Roosevelt, Assistant Secretary of the Navy at that time, claimed authorship of this constitution.

[16] For text of the protocol, see Millspaugh, *op. cit.,* 225–229, and Munro, *op. cit.,* 300–304.

loan of $40 million, secured by a first charge on the internal revenues of Haiti, and a second charge on the customs receipts. In order to afford full protection to the bondholders during the life of the loan after the expiration of the treaty, it was agreed that the collection and allocation of the hypothe-cated revenues would be under the control of an officer or officers appointed by the Haitian president and nominated by the President of the United States.

Further progress was made toward the rehabilitation of Haiti's finances when the differences between the Haitian government and the National Bank were settled.[17] A currency reform measure was put into effect in 1919 by which the Haitian *gourde* was stabilized, and in 1920 the National City Bank of New York purchased complete control of the National Bank of Haiti.

While these fiscal reforms were proceeding, the tranquillity of the country was interrupted by a *caco* revolt, which though fomented and supported by disgruntled Haitian politicians, was more directly caused by the revival and abuse of the *corveé,* an obsolete Haitian law which required every inhabi-tant to work for a given period on the roads. Although the resistance was eventually overcome, some 1,500 Haitians were killed in the process, re-sulting in charges of mistreatment and cruelty against the American troops who suppressed the uprising. These charges, which intensified the criticism of certain elements in the United States opposed to the occupation of Haiti — as well as the concurrent occupation of the Dominican Republic — inspired a Senatorial investigation. Concluding its investigation in April, 1922, the Senate committee absolved the American authorities of any serious wrongs in the suppression of the *caco* revolt, and even commended constructive ac-complishments of the occupation regime. On matters of general policy, the committee acknowledged the objectives of the occupation but deplored tardiness in achieving these ends. It felt that a "definite and constructive policy" was lacking and that a greater effort should be made to promote the social, economic, and intellectual advancement of the Haitian masses. Specific measures toward this end were recommended.[18]

American intervention: the second stage, 1922–1929

The Senate investigation led to significant changes in the United States administration in Haiti. Authority was centralized in a High Commissioner, a personal representative of the United States President, who was to replace the American minister and to rank over all treaty officials, as well as the commandant of the Marine brigade. His approval was required for the enactment of any law or the granting of any important contract by the Haitian government. Greater administrative efficiency was also achieved by the consolidation, in January, 1924, of the offices of financial adviser and general receiver. The appointment of a High Commissioner greatly enhanced the

17 *For. Rel.,* 1916, 359.
18 For Senate Committee report, see Millspaugh, *op. cit.,* 229–232.

effectiveness of the treaty services by increasing coordination among them and eliminating duplication of activities.[19]

From 1922 to 1929, General John H. Russell, United States Marine Corps, served efficiently as High Commissioner with the collaboration of Louis Borno, elected president in 1922. Considerable progress was made toward the realization of the objectives of the American occupation. A complete reform of Haiti's financial administration was effected; customs receipts increased to such an extent that the Haitian government was able to maintain essential public services and make public improvements, as well as to continue payments on the foreign debt even during the depression of the 1930's; and peace and tranquility prevailed throughout the period, despite increasing Haitian annoyance with American control. United States Marines remained in the country on a stand-by basis, but they participated in neither the maintenance of order nor political matters. The function of keeping law and order was assumed by the Haitian constabulary,[20] to whose officer ranks Haitians were constantly added. Particularly notable progress was made in public works and sanitation. To improve the technical skills and general productivity of the natives, a special effort was made to promote agricultural and industrial education, notably the establishment of vocational schools.[21]

Although during the period from 1922 to 1929, the United States succeeded in correcting many of its earlier mistakes in the occupation of Haiti, and brought some material benefits to the people, the Haitians grew increasingly restless as foreign control continued.

American withdrawal and restoration of Haitian rule[22]

The general discontent with American control was responsible for protest strikes, student demonstrations, and eventually, in December, 1929, for an attack on the Marines at Cayes by a mob of some 1,500 infuriated Haitians in which several natives were killed or wounded. Upon learning of the Cayes incident, President Hoover sent a special message to Congress, requesting authorization to dispatch a commission to Haiti to investigate the entire situation. Congress approved his request and, on February 7, 1930, the President appointed a commission headed by W. Cameron Forbes, a former Governor-General of the Philippines, to conduct an on-the-spot investigation of the American administration, and to make recommendations regarding how and when withdrawal could be effected. Beginning February 28, 1930, the commission spent sixteen days on the island, where it gave the Haitian

---

[19] Munro, *op. cit.*, 169.

[20] See James H. McCrocklin, *Garde D'Haiti, 1915–1934* (Annapolis: The United States Naval Institute, 1956).

[21] For a discussion of these accomplishments, see Millspaugh, *op. cit.*, 135–137. For an anti-imperialist view, see Emily Balch, *et al., Occupied Haiti* (New York: Writers Publication Company, 1927).

[22] See Donald B. Cooper, "The Withdrawal of the United States from Haiti, 1928–1934," *Journal of Inter-American Studies,* V (January, 1963), 83–101.

opponents of the occupation a full hearing and conducted a thorough study of the various treaty services.[23]

The Forbes Commission, in its official report to President Hoover, applauded the American administration in Haiti for its accomplishment in such fields as fiscal management, health and sanitation, and public works, and commended the personal leadership of High Commissioner Russell. It deplored, however, the fact that the political and administrative training of Haitians for the responsibilities of government had been inadequate, and the apparent assumption of the American authorities in Haiti that the occupation would continue indefinitely. In its more important specific recommendations, subsequently approved by President Hoover, the commission proposed: (1) an accelerated Haitianization of the administrative services (i.e., replacement of Americans by Haitians), with the object of having experienced Haitians prepared to take over all aspects of the country's public administration at the expiration of the treaty in 1936; (2) the abolition of the office of High Commissioner at the expiration of General Russell's term and the appointment of a civilian minister to assume his duties as well as those of diplomatic representation; (3) the gradual withdrawal of the Marines in accordance with arrangements to be made by the two governments; and (4) modification of the existing treaty and agreements providing for reduced United States intervention in Haitian domestic affairs. These proposals became the basis for negotiations that looked toward the ultimate termination of the American intervention. It is noteworthy, however, that the commission did not recommend the immediate withdrawal of the Marines, for fear that general chaos would set in.

With the election of Stenio Vincent to the presidency in November, 1930, Haiti's civil government, at least in its outward form, was restored. General Russell resigned as High Commissioner, thereby terminating nearly eight years of devoted and effective service, which was far from appreciated by the Haitians; and Dr. Dana G. Munro, then chief of the Latin-American Division of the State Department, was appointed minister to Haiti. It was under his direction that agreements were to be negotiated with the Haitian Government "providing for as rapid a withdrawal as might be practicable of all American control in Haiti's internal affairs."[24] The negotiation of the necessary agreements was difficult and time-consuming, especially since the United States was now dealing with an anti-occupation regime bent on ending the occupation under terms unacceptable to the United States government.

Although the United States strongly desired to terminate its intervention in Haiti as soon as feasible, it insisted that the withdrawal be gradual so that the governmental services established by the occupation authorities should be continued with the least possible interruption. The United States balked, therefore, at hasty termination of American financial control, especially since

[23] For the Forbes Commission and its report, see Montague, *op. cit.*, 270–271; also, Millspaugh, *op. cit.*, 242–245.

[24] Munro, *op. cit.*, 182.

it felt an obligation not to accept any arrangement under which the United States would not be able to guarantee full payment to Haiti's creditors.

On September 3, 1932, after thirteen months of discussion, a treaty was concluded which was intended to be a final settlement of practically all issues arising out of the American occupation. The treaty met vigorous opposition in the Haitian Congress and was promptly and decisively rejected by it, chiefly because of the provisions continuing American financial control. The task of completing American withdrawal, for which plans were drawn up by the Hoover administration, passed to President Franklin D. Roosevelt when he took office in March, 1933. The Haitians distrusted Roosevelt because of his reputed authorship of the obnoxious constitution of 1918, but shortly after his administration began he demonstrated a conciliatory attitude toward Haiti and set out vigorously to liquidate the American intervention.

Negotiations were therefore resumed on the basic matters of Haitianization of the *Garde,* financial arrangements, and the withdrawal of the Marines. The responsibility of negotiating new agreements fell to Norman Armour, who had replaced Dr. Munro as United States minister; but after some efforts in this direction the new minister realized the impossibility of reaching agreements satisfactory to both the United States government and the intensely nationalistic Haitian Congress. Since President Vincent was, for reasons of political expediency, much more amenable to American demands, it was agreed that a final settlement of all outstanding issues would take the form of an executive agreement between the two presidents, thus bypassing the uncooperative Haitian legislature.

An executive agreement was signed on August 7, 1933, which embodied essentially the same provisions as the rejected treaty, though the United States did make a few concessions.[25] The date for final Haitianization of the *Garde* was set for October 1, 1934, with the last Marines scheduled to depart in thirty days. On the touchy financial issue, the United States agreed to employ only Haitians in the custom houses, though the American-appointed fiscal representative was authorized, until the complete repayment of the American loan, to collect all customs duties and to prohibit the modification of taxes or tariffs.

Although there were protracted negotiations to work out a compromise arrangement whereby United States financial supervision could be ended prior to final amortization of the loan, no acceptable solution could be found, and so the fiscal representative and his staff remained in Haiti until 1941, when a new financial agreement was reached. By this agreement the office of fiscal representative was abolished and all funds were transferred to the National Bank of Haiti as sole depository for the Haitian government. It was to remain in effect until the loan was paid off.

[25] *For. Rel.,* 1933, V, 691–761. For the termination of the occupation, see R. L. Buell, "The Caribbean Situation: Cuba and Haiti," *Foreign Policy Reports,* IX, No. 8, 90–92.

On August 15, 1934, shortly ahead of schedule, the final complement of the Marine brigade was withdrawn from Haiti. Now, with the exception of a greatly modified supervision of Haitian finances, which was to continue for only a few years longer, the United States' protectorate over Haiti was terminated. To the Negro republic was restored its full sovereignty. This was one of the milestones in the implementation of nonintervention and the Good Neighbor policy.

The withdrawal from Haiti was also an important step in the liquidation of the Caribbean policy of the United States. No longer was it necessary for the United States — at least acting alone — to jealously guard against foreign intrusions into the Caribbean. Therefore, after 1934, and particularly after World War II, the problems of Haiti ceased to be problems of exclusive concern to the United States, but were shared presumably by the hemisphere community. In this connection we note recent controversies between Haiti and her neighbors, particularly the Dominican Republic, which were occasions for OAS investigation in which the United States was only a cooperating member. A serious dispute with the Dominican Republic resulting from the massacre, in 1937, of several thousand Haitian laborers seeking employment in Dominican territory, was settled within a year by application of the conciliatory procedures of the Gondra treaty. The Dominican Republic paid an indemnity of $750,000 to Haiti. In 1949, a Haitian charge of a conspiracy plotted within the territory of the Dominican Republic to overthrow the government of Haiti was investigated and peacefully resolved by the Inter-American Peace Committee on which the United States enjoyed membership. Again, in 1950, the Rio treaty was invoked to conduct investigations in four of the Caribbean republics, including Haiti, where situations existed "that threatened the peace of the continent."[26]

In the meantime, a special relationship between the United States and Haiti had by no means ceased to exist. On December 12, 1941, Haiti joined all of the other eight republics of the Caribbean and Central America in declaring war on the Axis Powers. This free and independent action by Haiti, and its sister republics, within one week after Pearl Harbor, was a remarkable demonstration of inter-American solidarity and confidence in the United States. On April 6, 1942, Haiti allowed the United States to establish a naval patrol base in western Haiti to strengthen the vital Windward Passage.

After the war, with the threat of Soviet aggression in mind, the United States negotiated with Haiti a Military Assistance Agreement, one of twelve with Latin-American states. Also, with the Communist threat in mind, and in order to save Haiti from economic collapse and political chaos, the United States maintained a continual flow of economic grants to the Negro republic. From 1957 through 1961, military and economic assistance was extended to the Haitian government in the amount of approximately $81 million. The generosity of the United States accomplished little, however, in rehabilitating

[26] J. Lloyd Mecham, *The United States and Inter-American Security, 1889–1960* (Austin: University of Texas Press, 1961), 175–176, 396, 399.

the country, due chiefly to the repressive and corrupt rule of Dr. Francois Duvalier who had come into power in late 1957. Duvalier's despotic rule and highhanded procedures were responsible for sharply worsened relations with the United States.

In April, 1961, because of Duvalier's unconstitutional maneuvers to perpetuate his own dictatorship, the State Department adopted a "cool but correct" policy toward his regime, though economic and military assistance was continued for fear that its withdrawal would cause a collapse and general chaos worse than Duvalier's despotic rule. Nevertheless, Duvalier became so violently abusive of the United States government that, in September, 1961, economic aid to Haiti was suspended. But when Haiti, in the Meeting of Foreign Ministers held at Punta del Este in January, 1962, reversed its original position, and, siding with the United States, cast the deciding vote in favor of excluding Cuba from participation in the OAS, aid was resumed in June, 1962.[27]

In the spring of 1963 the situation in Haiti reached a critical stage. On April 27, Haitian police invaded the Dominican embassy in Port-au-Prince in search of political refugees who had found asylum there. This violation of its sovereign rights evoked an immediate and angry demand by the Dominican government for withdrawal of Haitian police within twenty-four hours. Also, the Dominican army was deployed along the Haitian border with the apparent intention to invade the country if its demands were not met. Diplomatic relations were promptly broken.

As the danger of war between the Dominican Republic and Haiti increased, and Duvalier stepped up his campaign of violence against his political enemies at home, the United States government ordered the withdrawal of all American official personnel and advised the evacuation of other Americans. Diplomatic relations were temporarily suspended; the American ambassador was recalled to Washington; and American war vessels were kept on the alert just off the Haitian coast.[28]

A war between Haiti and the Dominican Republic was averted, thanks to the intercession of both the OAS and the United States. Satisfactory assurances were received from both parties that peace would be kept. Although the Bosch government of the Dominican Republic seemed bent on going to war with Haiti, or perhaps forcing the United States into armed intervention against President Duvalier, it had no choice but to accept the Haitian compliance with its demands as a solution of the controversy.[29]

After the passing of the crisis United States-Haitian relations did not improve. Diplomatic relations were maintained, but only by a thin thread. Before the end of the summer of 1963 the United States Air Force and Navy missions were withdrawn (the Marine training mission had been pulled out

27 *Hispanic American Report*, XV, No. 4 (June, 1962), 321.
28 *Ibid.*, XVI (June, 1963), 356–358.
29 See *Américas*, 15, No. 6 (June, 1963), 44; Dept. of State *Bulletin*, XLVIII (June 17, 1963), 958–959.

earlier at Haiti's request), and all economic and military aid was stopped. The termination of assistance and the maintenance of only limited diplomatic contacts with the Haitian government, although designed to emphasize United States opposition to President Duvalier, and, hopefully, to force him to respect the rights and interests of the United States and its citizens, seemed to accomplish little if anything toward this end. In fact, after the crisis with the Dominican Republic had passed, Duvalier, decreed president for life, showed no disposition whatever to assume a conciliatory attitude toward other nations, including the United States, or to relax his harsh control over his own people.

2. *The Dominican Republic*

Early relations

The Dominican Republic seemed to vie with its neighbor-occupant of the island of Hispaniola for last place among the Latin-American nations in political, economic, and social development.[30] Its history was quite as tragic, being marked by dictatorships, revolutions, counterrevolutions, and other forms of political violence. The economic and social problems that beset the nation appeared almost insoluble. To compound her difficulties, the Dominican Republic lived for many years in constant fear — and with a great deal of justification — that she would be reconquered, or at least dominated, by Haiti, from whom independence had been won after such difficulty in 1844.[31]

The repeated threats of Haitian invasion prompted the Dominican government to appeal frantically, and rather indiscriminately, to the United States, Spain, France, and Great Britain for their protection, both individually and collectively. In 1854 President Santana initiated negotiations with General William L. Cazneau, special agent of the United States, for a treaty conveying to the United States the Samaná Bay for a naval base. When the British and French got wind of what was going on, they protested vigorously, and the negotiations were dropped.[32] Soon, however, the Dominican government turned once more to Spain, and this time an offer of annexation to the former mother country was favorably received in Madrid. On May 19, 1861, the island republic was formally incorporated into the Spanish empire.[33]

The United States protested Spain's occupation as a violation of the Monroe Doctrine, but was not able to follow its protest with effective action because of its own internal conflict. By 1863, however, Spain began to lose interest in her Dominican venture because of a native uprising, occupation costs, and

---

[30] See Russell H. Fitzgibbon and Kenneth F. Johnson, "Measurement of Latin American Political Change," *American Political Science Review*, LIV, No. 3 (September, 1960), 515–526.

[31] For a sympathetic survey of Dominican history to 1924, see Sumner Welles, *Naboth's Vineyard, The Dominican Republic, 1844–1924* (2 vols. New York: Payson & Clarke, 1928).

[32] *Ibid.*, I, 172–212.

[33] For the Spanish occupation, see Welles, *op. cit.*, I, 217–299.

the decimation of the Spanish army by yellow fever. In 1865 she withdrew her troops and abandoned the enterprise, no doubt suspecting that once the American Civil War was over the United States would force her withdrawal.

The extension of Spanish control to the Dominican Republic, though short-lived, aroused a greater determination by the United States that the island should never again be dominated by a foreign power. President Andrew Johnson and Secretary of State Seward were both inclined to favor annexation, but it was left to President U. S. Grant and Secretary of State Hamilton Fish to undertake serious negotiations with Dominican President Buenaventura Baez to this end.[34] In November, 1869, two treaties were signed: one providing for annexation of the republic as a territory of the United States, and the other providing for the immediate lease to the United States of the Samaná Peninsula and Bay. Both were rejected by the United States Senate in 1870. President Grant continued his efforts to annex but never succeeded in getting sufficient popular and Congressional support to consummate the deal. A mixture of motives prompted the attitude of the Senate: honest reluctance to annex "possessions disconnected from the main continent," the revelation of unsavory financial operations connected with the project, and bitter personal and partisan opposition to the President.

After the ill-favored efforts of Grant and Fish, the United States lost interest in the annexation of the Dominican Republic. This did not indicate by any means any lessening of United States interest in the republics of Hispaniola, for with the full awakening of its Caribbean consciousness by 1900, Haiti and the Dominican Republic assumed a new and heightened importance. It was the hopeless financial delinquency of the Dominican Republic which made it the first object for application of President Theodore Roosevelt's new intervention policy, or corollary of the Monroe Doctrine.

Fiscal intervention

A financial crisis in the Dominican Republic shortly after the turn of the century prompted certain European governments to consider taking over the collection of the customs, since the Dominican Republic had failed to carry out agreements with its European creditors.[35]

To forestall any action which might lead to permanent European intervention President Roosevelt in December, 1904, promulgated his corollary of the Monroe Doctrine by which he asserted the right of the United States to act as international policeman in those countries which habitually failed to meet their international obligations. The President's pronouncement served both as a warning to Caribbean countries which failed to keep their own finances in order, and as a conciliatory gesture to those European governments poised to assist their citizens in debt collections, since he proposed to assume responsibility for the collection of Dominican revenues and their application to that

---

[34] For negotiation for annexation, see Welles, *op. cit.*, I, 359–409; and Tansill, *op. cit.*, Chaps. IX, X.

[35] Welles, *op. cit.*, II, 104–106.

country's foreign debt. In a further elaboration of his position, Roosevelt stated, in his annual message to Congress in 1905, that the Dominican Republic had been in "imminent danger of foreign intervention," and declared that only American assurance of assistance and the opening of negotiations with the Caribbean nation had prevented at least one European power from stepping in and seizing Dominican territory.

These negotiations culminated on February 7, 1905, with the signing of a treaty authorizing the United States to adjust all of the republic's financial obligations and collect all the customs revenue. The failure of the Senate to act on the treaty left European intervention a serious possibility, since, as Roosevelt himself emphasized, the United States had no moral or legal right to deny European creditors the only alternative available for the satisfaction of their claims.[36] To preclude this, Roosevelt and Dominican President Carlos Morales, contracted an executive agreement which bypassed the legislative bodies of both countries.

Under this *modus vivendi,* which became effective on April 1, 1905, United States agents assumed the responsibilities of collecting customs, making financial settlements with bondholders and claimants, and directing the flotation of loans. To insure the satisfactory adjustment of the nation's foreign indebtedness, 55 per cent of all customs revenues was to be set aside for the payment of the Dominican debt, the balance being reserved for meeting the current expenses of the government. Under American management of the customs receivership the Dominican treasury received more revenue from its 45 per cent share of the customs receipts than it had previously received from the entire collection.

The executive agreement was replaced by a treaty, in 1907, which incorporated essentially the same financial arrangements, and prohibited the Dominican government from increasing its public debt until the full amount of its foreign obligations had been paid.[37] The new treaty went into effect on July 8, 1907. Besides eliminating the possibility of foreign intervention, the United States hoped that the new arrangement would have a stabilizing influence. The belief that political stability had at last come to Dominica was destroyed, however, in 1911, with the assassination of President Cáceres. His death created a situation which convinced the United States government that the remedies provided by the treaty of 1907, though they contributed to stabilizing the country's financial condition, were not sufficient to cure its political ills.

This was the state of affairs when Woodrow Wilson took office in March, 1913. The new American President, determined to settle the Dominican problem by establishing a constitutional democracy, proposed a plan whereby rival Dominican politicians would agree on a provisional president who would then arrange for elections for both the presidency and congress. Once this constitutional government took office, no further revolutions would be per-

---

[36] *For. Rel.,* 1905, 334 ff.
[37] For the text of the treaty, see Munro, *op. cit.,* 284–287.

mitted by the United States.[38] According to Sumner Welles, "President Wilson implied that the government of the United States possessed the right to assure itself of the continuance of orderly constitutional government in the Dominican Republic, and would 'feel at liberty' to prevent all changes in the government of the Dominican Republic other than those by the 'peaceful processes' provided in the Dominican Constitution."[39]

Secretary of State Bryan advised the two commissioners sent to the Dominican Republic to execute the President's plan that "no opportunity for argument should be given to any person or faction. It is desired that you present the plan and see that it is complied with." Accordingly, agreements were worked out between the principal political leaders, and in an election "observed" by members of the commission, Juan Isidro Jiménez was elected president. On December 5, 1914, the "constitutional" president assumed office. The United States hoped that the new president would accept the reforms which it advocated for the political and financial stabilization of the country, but such was not the case.[40]

United States military intervention

In early 1915 the United States sought to increase its control over Dominican finances by securing the appointment of an American financial comptroller empowered to draw up a budget and control expenditures. This extension of American control, a modified Platt Amendment, was deemed necessary to insure that expenditures by the Dominican government would not exceed its revenues. Such controls were not sanctioned by the 1907 treaty and therefore would have required the approval of both Jiménez and his congress. But the Dominican congress refused to surrender the power of the purse, and the president was equally reluctant to accept the new restrictions. Another series of revolts caused the United States to increase its pressure and to add the requirement that a constabulary, under American officers, be organized to replace the army as the preserver of domestic order. Negotiations aimed at extending American control over Dominican finances dragged on for over a year.

The Dominican congress was violently opposed to the expansion of American controls over the nation's financial affairs, and Jiménez, fearing impeachment if he entered into an agreement with the United States without congressional approval, also resisted American demands. On the other hand, the United States would not approve additional loans without assuming the financial control needed to insure their eventual repayment.[41]

The long-expected crisis arrived in April, 1916.[42] Faced by a new insurrection and overwhelming odds, President Jiménez declined an offer of United

[38] For the text of the "Wilson Plan," see Munro, *op. cit.*, 116–118.
[39] Welles, *op. cit.*, II, 738.
[40] *Ibid.*, 740.
[41] Rippy, *op. cit.*, 197
[42] For the American intervention, see Welles, *op. cit.*, II, Chap. XIII; Howland, *op. cit.*, 89–91; and *For. Rel.*, 1916, 221–246.

States military support. Nevertheless, on May 4, the Marines were landed ostensibly to protect the legation, although they were soon operating through-out the country in pursuit of the rebels. Rather than continue the struggle, Jiménez resigned on May 7 and left the country. The Dominican cabinet took over the executive power pending the election of a new president by the congress. The actual power, however, was held by the rebel leader Minister of War Desidero Arias, whose forces had occupied the capital city, Santo Domingo.

On May 13, 1916, Rear Admiral William B. Caperton, commander of American forces in the area, delivered an ultimatum to Arias warning him that Santo Domingo City would be occupied and his forces disarmed if he did not surrender and turn in all arms and ammunition. When the deadline for the ultimatum, May 15, had passed, the Marines entered the city only to find that Arias had withdrawn into the interior with his army. With the arrival of Marine reinforcements, totaling eventually about 1,800 men, all organized resistance was eliminated by the middle of June.

On July 25, 1916, the Dominican congress elected Dr. Francisco Henríquez y Carvajal provisional president until a general election could be held. In the meantime the United States had re-established the customs receivership, and in addition, assumed control of the internal revenue collections. In effect, it put into operation a system of financial administration such as it had sought to obtain by agreement with preceding Dominican regimes.

The United States declared that its recognition of the Henríquez govern-ment would not be forthcoming until it had accepted a treaty providing for enlarged financial controls and the establishment of a native constabulary under American officers. The position taken by the United States was that it could not discharge its obligations assumed by the treaty of 1907 without additional controls. It is important to note that United States interventions in the Dominican Republic were justified on the ground that the terms of the treaty of 1907 had been repeatedly violated by the Dominican authorities.

Although President Henríquez accepted most of the American demands, his refusal to go all the way caused the American authorities to suspend nego-tiations and stop payment of any of the revenues to the Dominican govern-ment. This resulted in the suspension of all government salaries. The stalemate continued until November, 1916, when the Dominican president pre-cipitated a new crisis by calling for congressional elections. It was obvious to American observers that elections at that time would give Arias complete control of the government, which was unacceptable to the United States.

This new development, coupled with the threat of revolution and economic disaster, convinced Secretary of State Robert Lansing that formal American military occupation was the only solution. Consequently, on November 29, 1916, on orders by President Wilson, Captain Harry S. Knapp, in command of United States naval forces, proclaimed a state of military occupation and made the Dominican Republic subject to military government.[43] The reasons

43 *For. Rel.,* 1916, 241–243.

given for this action were: the continuing increase of indebtedness by the Dominican government in disregard of the treaty of 1907, which pledged that government to keep expenditures within revenue, the refusal of Dominican authorities to accept the reforms which the United States considered essential, and the continuance of internal disorder in the country. The United States government disclaimed any intention of destroying the sovereignty of the Dominican Republic.

The occupation[44]

The intent of the United States was to leave most of the Dominican cabinet ministers at their posts and to exercise only general supervision over the existing administrative organization. This proved impossible, however, for the cabinet members refused to serve, and American efforts to persuade other qualified Dominicans to take the portfolios fell on deaf ears. This forced the military governor, Rear-Admiral Knapp, to put members of his military staff in charge of the executive departments. Since it was considered inadvisable to hold new elections to fill the empty seats in congress, Knapp suspended the Dominican congress indefinitely, thereby throwing into the hands of the military government the legislative as well as the executive responsibilities of the country.[45]

In assuming these responsibilities, the military government's conduct of affairs was based from the beginning on the doctrine that it was administering the government of the Dominican Republic in trust for the Dominican people. The general policy of administration was established by the Department of State, represented by a minister acting through the Navy Department.

Although the American military government had to operate under many handicaps, being forced to introduce many new ideas and build new programs from the ground, it took seriously the responsibility of stabilizing the economic, financial, and political life of the country. Among its principal accomplishments were: (1) the maintenance of internal order; (2) the expansion and improvement of educational facilities; (3) the levying of a badly needed tax on land; (4) the taking of a census; (5) an extensive road building program; and (6) the efficient and honest administration of governmental affairs, a new experience for the Dominicans.[46] The maintenance of order promoted both economic growth and a higher standard of living; and the efficiency and honesty brought to fiscal management led to an immediate increase in public revenues, permitting the payment of debts and salaries of government employees, as well as providing substantial funds for education, public health, public works projects, and other programs for the benefit of the populace. By 1919 the increase in economic activity in the Dominican Republic under

---

[44] For the American occupation, see Welles, *op. cit.*, II, Chap. XIV. For a critical, anti-imperialist view, see Melvin M. Knight, *The Americans in Santo Domingo* (New York: Vanguard Press, 1938).

[45] *For. Rel.*, 1916, 707–708.

[46] Carl Kelsey, *The American Intervention in Haiti and the Dominican Republic* (Philadelphia: American Academy of Political and Social Science, 1922), 187.

American administration was reflected by a favorable balance of trade in the amount of $17.5 million, nearly double that of 1916 when the military occupation began.

American withdrawal

The political and economic stability produced by the military government, plus developing dissatisfaction in the United States, led President Wilson, as early as December, 1920, to propose the inauguration of procedures whereby the United States would withdraw from the Dominican Republic. This task did not prove an easy one, however, for three attempts were made before terms acceptable to both the Dominicans and the American government were reached. The first two proposals were ineffectual because of the "machinations of the Dominican politicians, who convinced the Dominican people that the terms proposed by the United States for the dissolution of the military government represented the imposition of American imperialism," and hence were intolerable. The Dominicans objected especially to the American demand for the continuance of the customs receivership and an American military mission to complete the training of the Dominican constabulary. The Dominican proposals, which called for "an immediate and unconditional withdrawal," were equally unacceptable to the United States.[47]

The failure of the Dominicans to accept terms providing for gradual withdrawal, and designed to insure continued political stability, prompted a United States Senatorial investigating commission to declare, in 1921, that American forces should not be removed. In the spring of 1922, a series of conferences produced the "Hughes-Peynado Plan," which had the approval of the United States government and was subsequently accepted by the Dominicans.[48]

Salient provisions of the withdrawal plan, final agreement on which was reached on June 30, 1922, included Dominican acceptance of a convention ratifying all contracts made by the military government and all its executive orders and administrative acts. The plan also stipulated that the bond issues of 1918 and 1922 be recognized, and that the treaty of 1907 remain in force until these obligations had been paid off.[49] The United States, in turn, agreed that elections for a constitutional government could be held under a provisional Dominican government rather than under the military, and that all American military forces would be withdrawn when the constitutional government took office. On October 21, 1922, the transition from American to Dominican control was completed with the inauguration of the provisional government under President Juan Bautista Vicini Burgos.[50]

Despite intense rivalry between opposing political factions, which delayed the national election, the Dominicans voted for a constitutional government

[47] Charles J. Miller, "Diplomatic Spurs: Our experiences in Santo Domingo," *Marine Corps Gazette,* XIX (August, 1935), 44.

[48] *Ibid.,* 45.

[49] This agreement was incorporated in a convention signed on June 12, 1924, and proclaimed on December 8, 1925. For the text, see Munro, *op. cit.,* 287–290.

[50] Welles presents a full account of the negotiations leading to United States withdrawal, in his *Naboth's Vineyard,* II, 836–900.

on March 15, 1924, and elected General Horacio Vásquez president. With
his inauguration on July 12, the American military government officially
ended. The last Marines withdrew within the next two months.

Although the chapter on military intervention was closed, the United States under a new treaty, signed in December, 1924, retained the rights of a protectorate through fiscal controls.[51] A general receiver, appointed by the President of the United States, was to collect the customs duties, apply them to the service of the bond issues, and pay the balance to the Dominican government. Until the whole amount of the bonds should be paid, the Dominican government promised not to increase the public debt except by agreement with the United States. At the outset the Dominican government was authorized to borrow a maximum amount of $25 million.

The treaty of 1924 was abrogated by a new treaty signed at Washington on September 24, 1940, and ratified on March 10, 1941. This new treaty abolished the general receivership of Dominican customs and returned the collection of customs duties to the Dominican government. It also provided for the arbitration, if necessary, of any dispute arising over service of the bonds. After 1940 it could no longer be said that the sovereign powers of the Dominican Republic were limited by United States fiscal controls. The island republic had ceased to be an American protectorate.

It is a significant fact that there was nothing in the withdrawal agreements concerning Samaná Bay; neither did the United States acquire any rights to a potential naval base, nor did it secure a pledge from the Dominican Republic that the strategic point should not be transferred to a third power. Samaná — indeed, Hispaniola itself — had lost much of its old strategic importance to the United States.

Although the interventions of the United States in the Dominican Republic, and also in Haiti, were generally well intentioned, it is difficult to argue that they accomplished much of a constructive nature except possibly that of averting European intervention in some form. It was hoped in Washington — rather naively — that the American occupations would help to promote democracy and stable government that would endure after the United States withdrew. Judging, however, from the state of political affairs in both of the republics after the American withdrawals, the interventions were futile undertakings in this respect. On the other hand, if intervention by an unfriendly European power was averted by the anticipatory action of the United States, then it might well be argued that the interests of the United States were well served — and those of Haiti and the Dominican Republic as well.

The "Era of Trujillo"

It soon became apparent that the American occupation and tutelage had effected no change in the political habits of the Dominicans. When President Horacio Vásquez, infected by the common Latin-American malady known

[51] See C. L. Jones, *The Caribbean Since 1900* (New York: Prentice-Hall, Inc., 1936), 121–125.

as *continuismo,* sought illegal re-election, dissatisfied army officers and politicians rose in revolt. Out of the melee emerged a new president of the republic, General Rafael Leonidas Trujillo Molina, head of the American-trained constabulary.[52] That was in 1930. It marked the beginning of the "era of Trujillo," which was to continue until 1961, one of the longest and most oppressive of all Latin-American tyrannies.[53]

Despite the general absence of democratic practices and individual liberty, which after all are the internal concerns of a country, the period of Trujillo's ascendancy was generally devoid of serious problems or spectacular occurrences in his relations with the United States. In fact, the political and economic stability which Trujillo maintained in his country evoked admiration and praise from many quarters in the United States, as did his uncompromising stand, first against Fascism, and then against Communism at home and abroad. One of the most consistent supporters of the United States, in World War II, the OAS, and the UN, was Generalísimo Rafael Trujillo. By virtue of these facts it would have been both illogical and unneutral for the United States to oppose the dictatorship.

Even before Pearl Harbor, Trujillo entered into an agreement, in 1940, putting harbor and other port facilities at the disposal of the United States for use by its patrol ships. Immediately after the Pearl Harbor attack the Dominican Republic was one of the earliest of the Latin-American countries to declare war on the Axis Powers. This was followed by the grant to the United States of base rights near the Bay of Samaná.

After the war, Trujillo was equally cooperative in supporting the United States in the cold war against international Communism. The Dominican Republic was one of the twelve Latin-American countries which entered into military assistance agreements with the United States stemming from the Rio treaty. Finally, the United States was granted the privilege of establishing a missile tracking station in the territory of the republic.

Because of the tenacity and harsh effectiveness of the Trujillo dictatorship, the Generalísimo became the chief target of anti-dictatorship propaganda campaigns organized in neighboring republics. Trujillo counterattacked occasionally with the collaboration of brother dictators, notably Somoza of Nicaragua. Words often resolved into action, and thus were created a number of incidents disturbing to the peace of the Caribbean. Disputes with Cuba in 1948, and with Haiti in 1949 and 1950, brought about OAS peace-making activities in which the United States, of course, was a party.[54]

The peace-making tasks of the OAS became more difficult after Fidel Castro put his oar in the muddy waters. A Meeting of the Foreign Ministers was

---

[52] Marvin Goldwert, *The Constabulary in the Dominican Republic and Nicaragua.* Latin American Monograph Series, No. 17 (Gainesville: University of Florida Press, 1962), 5–21.

[53] See Albert E. Hicks, *Blood in the Streets; the Life and Rule of Trujillo* (New York, 1946), for a lurid description of the dictatorship. For an opposite view, see Stanley Walker, *Generalísimo Doctor Rafael Leonidas Trujillo Molina* (New York: The Caribbean Library of New York, 1956).

[54] See Mecham, *op. cit.,* Chap. XIII.

convened in Santiago, Chile, in July, 1959, ostensibly to examine the turbulent Caribbean situation of chronic intervention, but more particularly to find means to overthrow the dictators, the number one culprit being Rafael Trujillo. Cuba and Venezuela were particularly insistent on collective action, and did not think that the principle of nonintervention should block the way to the use of forcible sanctions. Secretary of State Christian Herter, however, while deploring the absence of representative democracy and respect for human rights in the Dominican Republic, opposed any action that smacked of interference in Dominican internal affairs. Since he feared that the overthrow of Trujillo would more likely promote chaos and disorder in the republic than democracy, and possibly open the door to Communist penetration, he chose to defend the principle of nonintervention. Regarding their sacred principle as more important than the overthrow of dictators, the majority of the delegations satisfied themselves with only a general condemnation of dictatorships in principle.[55]

Despite the implied condemnation of the Trujillo regime, the Santiago meeting brought no improvement in the internal or external behavior of the Dominican government and hence no diminution in Caribbean tensions. On the contrary, the area became more turbulent, chiefly because of the obnoxious conduct of both Cuba and the Dominican Republic. During 1960 inter-American attention focused more sharply on the Dominican Republic than on Cuba, since the Communist character that the Castro government was soon to acquire was not yet so apparent, at least to the Latin Americans, most of whom still regarded Castro as a great social and economic reformer. While the suppression of human rights within the Dominican Republic itself caused some revulsion on the part of the inter-American community, it was not until Trujillo engaged in aggressive actions (i.e., intervened) against neighboring states, principally Venezuela, that the OAS enforcement machinery was set in motion.

Upon the presentation of incontestable evidence of the complicity of Dominican officials in an assassination attempt against Venezuelan President Rómulo Betancourt in June, 1960, another Meeting of the Foreign Ministers was held at San José, Costa Rica, August 16–21. Although the United States favored the adoption of mild measures, such as OAS supervision of free Dominican elections, the majority of the Latin delegations pressed for sanctions strong enough to overthrow Trujillo.

In the hope that its Latin-American neighbors would reciprocate by supporting the vigorous measures which the United States intended to propose against Castro Cuba in the next Meeting of the Foreign Ministers, scheduled for the following week, the United States abandoned Trujillo and supported a resolution which called upon all members of the OAS to sever diplomatic relations and suspend trade in arms and munitions with the Dominican government. Immediately thereafter the United States broke off diplomatic relations with the Dominican Republic and imposed the other sanctions mentioned in the OAS resolution.

[55] *Ibid.*, 418.

The pressures exerted by the United States and by the inter-American community, did not accomplish the overthrow of Trujillo. This desired objective was served by the assassination of the dictator on May 30, 1961. Now would be forthcoming the answer to the question so frequently asked in the past: "After Trujillo, what?"

Post-Trujillo

Vice-President Joaquín Balaguer, who succeeded to the presidency, restored a degree of democracy and respect for human rights, promised a full return to democratic and constitutional government, invited political exiles to return, and apparently averted a Communist intrusion from Cuba. When two brothers of the late Generalísimo attempted, in November, 1961, to return to the island to oust President Balaguer, the United States staged a naval demonstration to convince the brothers that the return of Trujilloism would not be tolerated.[56]

Following the departure of the Trujillos, an arrangement was worked out whereby a seven-man Council of State was established, on January 1, 1962, as the provisional government. The Council was entrusted with making preparations for a presidential election in December of that year. Impressed by the apparent sincerity and democratic inclinations of the provisional government, and confident that the Dominican Republic was no longer a threat to the peace and security of the hemisphere, the Council of the OAS, on January 4, 1962, lifted the diplomatic and economic sanctions it had imposed on the country seventeen months before. On January 6, the United States resumed diplomatic relations and sent a special mission to study the country's needs for economic assistance. It was determined to give every support, moral and financial, to the restoration of stability and constitutionalism, and thus counter threats of Communist intrusion. To this end the United States established a "Special Economic Readjustment Fund," providing $20 million annual aid for three years to assist the Dominican government in readjusting its economy. Then in December, 1962, the United States, through AID, pledged a grant of $22,750,000 to the Dominican Republic under the Alliance for Progress. If economic assistance was the answer, the United States was determined to make the Dominican Republic a "showcase for democracy" in the Caribbean. Developments proved that more than money is necessary to achieve democracy.[57]

Nevertheless the outcome of the presidential election, on December 20, 1962, seemed to augur well for the future of the country. Juan D. Bosch, a reform-minded and longtime foe of the late Trujillo who had spent many years in exile, emerged the overwhelming victor in the first democratic election in the country for a generation. Despite the material and moral support given

---

[56] *Hisp. Am. Rep.*, XIV (January, 1962), 992.

[57] *Ibid.*, XV (September, 1962), 609–610, 667–668; *ibid.*, February, 1963, 1115; Dept. of State *Bulletin*, XVII (December 24, 1962), 958–959.

President Bosch by the United States, his government came increasingly under attack by domestic elements, chiefly the military and other rightist groups. To the great consternation and apparent surprise of the United States government, Bosch, after only seven months in office, was deposed on September 25, 1963, by a bloodless military *coup d'état*.[58]

The military leaders of the *coup* established a civilian *junta* which gave the new government a façade of civilian rule though actually under military control. The United States, unimpressed by the charges against Bosch — that his administration was inefficient, that he had plunged the country into chaos and almost into war with Haiti, and that he was leading it toward Communism — was not disposed to view lightly the armed overthrow of a democratic government which it had embraced so enthusiastically and aided so generously as a counterpoise to Cuban Communism. It expressed its displeasure therefore, by immediately breaking off diplomatic relations with the revolutionary regime, and suspending all military and economic assistance, including some $50 million in loan and grant aid earmarked for the Dominican Republic under earlier commitments.[59]

Eight days after President Bosch's overthrow, a *coup* by the military in Honduras toppled the constitutional government in that country. This seemed part of an unfortunate trend in Latin America, for earlier in 1963, the military had overthrown the constitutional governments of Guatemala and Ecuador, and in 1962 that of Argentina, and that of Peru the year before. The United States was fearful therefore, that the military *coups* in the Dominican Republic and Honduras would trigger an outbreak of armed revolts in the neighboring countries across the Caribbean.

The Kennedy administration went on record, therefore, as being wholly opposed to military *coups* in Latin America and refused to resume diplomatic relations with the new Dominican regime (or that of Honduras) until it had received adequate guarantees that constitutional government would be reestablished as soon as possible, but it shunned any form of armed intervention to reverse the outcome of the military *coup* and restore Bosch to power.[60] Specifically, the United States demanded guarantees of civil liberties and a concrete schedule of elections by which constitutional government would be restored within a reasonable period of time, preferably eighteen months.

Following assurances by the Dominican revolutionary government that there would be elections and a full restoration of democratic rule by August, 1965, the United States government on December 14, 1963, and after consultation with the other hemisphere nations, extended recognition to the military-installed regime in the Dominican Republic.[61] Recognition, albeit qualified, represented acceptance of the facts of political life in the island republic.

[58] *Hisp. Am. Rep.*, XVII (November, 1963), 871–874.

[59] *Washington Post*, September 26, 1963.

[60] *Ibid.*, October 10, 1963.

[61] Dept. of State *Bulletin*, XLIX (December 30, 1963), 997–998. The military-installed Honduran government was recognized on the same day.

"After Trujillo, what?" The "showcase for democracy," carefully prepared by the United States, did not go on public view. In May, 1965, the Marines were back in the Dominican Republic.

3. The Republic of Cuba to 1959

Early American interest in Cuba

United States concerns over Cuba long antedated the winning of Cuban independence. Since our interest here is restricted to relations with the Cuban republic, a discussion of those antecedents which extended over the whole span of the nineteenth century, need not detain us long.[62] A brief summary must suffice.

We have on many occasions alluded to the strategic importance of Cuba to the United States. American interest in Cuba was keen at intervals throughout the nineteenth century, during which time the policy of the United States toward the island passed through three distinct phases. From the outbreak of the Spanish-American wars for independence until the 1840's, the major concern of the United States was to prevent the transfer of control of the island by Spain to any other European power.

Beginning in the early 1840's, by which time the United States was swept up in its first tide of "manifest destiny," a desire to purchase or even conquer the island developed, particularly on the part of the slave-holding South, which saw Cuba as a potential slave state in the American Union.[63]

Then, with the conclusion of the American Civil War in 1865, the passing of the slavery issue from domestic politics, and the nation's preoccupation with its own internal development, United States interest in Cuba, although considerably lessened, assumed new form: an American concern for order and stability in the island. There was ample reason for this, since Cuban history from 1865 to 1898 was "primarily a chronicle of political woes interspersed by rebellion." The situation caused considerable anxiety in the United States, not only because of possible security considerations, but primarily because it was bad for developing commercial relations with the island.

The outbreak of a revolution in Cuba, in 1868 (it lasted until 1878 and was known as the "Ten Years' War"), which was carried on by both sides in a most barbarous fashion, strained the patience of American administrations to the breaking point. Early in the war the United States offered mediation, and proposed terms as a basis thereof: (1) acknowledgment of Cuban inde-

---

[62] For early American interests in Cuba, see J. M. Callahan, *Cuba and International Relations* (Baltimore: The Johns Hopkins Press, 1899); F. E. Chadwick, *The Relations of the United States and Spain, Diplomacy* (New York: Charles Scribner's Sons, 1909); and G. H. Stuart, *Latin America and the United States* (New York: Appleton-Century-Crofts, 1955, 5th ed.), Chap. 9. For a survey of relations with the United States, written from a critical Cuban point of view, see Hermonio Portell Vilá, *Historia de Cuba en relaciones con los Estados Unidos* (3 vols. Havana, 1938–1939).

[63] See Albert K. Weinberg, *Manifest Destiny* (Baltimore: The Johns Hopkins Press, 1935), 205–210.

pendence, (2) payment of an indemnity to Spain by Cuba, and (3) abolition of slavery. Spain rejected the offer, for Spanish public opinion was opposed to independence, and in fact preferred the transfer of Cuba to the United States.[64] The Cuban revolution lingered on until 1878, when, with both sides exhausted, the conflict came to an end.

With the return of peace, a considerable amount of American investment capital flowed into the island, particularly into the sugar industry. By 1894 the production reached 1,000,000 tons a year, the largest part being exported to the United States. It is illustrative of the importance of United States economic relations with Cuba that, as early as 1881, an American consul reported, "Cuba has become commercially a dependency of the United States, while still remaining a political dependency of Spain."[65]

Without doubt the United States would have preferred that Cuba remain a Spanish dependency, provided, however, there was a liberal grant of autonomy to the colony. This in fact was the preference of most Cubans themselves up to the time when Spanish dalliance and perfidy terminated any desire to continue even a nominal political connection with the mother country.

The Spanish-American War

The uneasy and oppressive peace imposed on Cuba at the end of the Ten Years' War was ended by the outbreak of a new revolt in February, 1895. The Cuban uprising soon reached a high pitch of viciousness on both sides. The insurrectionists carried on a destructive type of guerrilla warfare and a "scorched earth" policy against their Spanish opponents, who, under the brutal General Weyler, the new governor and captain-general, employed the cruelest measures in attempting to crush the revolt. Cubans were rounded up in droves — men, women, and children — and thrown into concentration camps, where disease, starvation, and brutality took thousands of lives.

The severity with which the Spanish authorities dealt with the revolutionists, added to the injurious effects which the destructive struggle had on American economic interests both in and out of the island, caused widespread protest in the United States, and a clamor for intervention on behalf of the beleaguered Cubans. President Cleveland chose, however, to keep out of the conflict, and refused, despite strong urging, to recognize a state of belligerency. At the same time he proclaimed the official neutrality of the United States, and warned all persons within the country of punishment for violation of the American neutrality laws.[66] The American Congress, however, was less cautious and circumspect. That body, many of whose members favored outright intervention to free Cuba, passed overwhelmingly, in February, 1896, a concurrent resolution recognizing Cuban belligerency and offering to Spain the good offices of the United States in establishing Cuban independence. Cleveland ignored this attempt to push him to stronger action against Spain.

---

[64] Charles E. Chapman, *A History of the Cuban Republic* (New York: The Macmillan Company, 1927), 67.

[65] Howland, *op. cit.*, 7.   [66] *For. Rel.*, 1895, 1195.

Then, in April, 1896, Secretary of State Richard Olney offered to Spain the services of the United States in mediating between her and the insurgents for the restoration of peace on the basis of Cuban autonomy, but Spain rejected the overture.

In the meantime, the "yellow press" in the United States, particularly the Hearst newspapers, popularized the Cuban revolt by grossly exaggerating Spanish atrocities and brutalities but making no mention of patriot irregularities. American sympathy for the Cuban insurrectionists was naturally aroused, resulting in a popular outcry for recognition of Cuba's independence, and, if necessary, American military intervention in her behalf.

By the end of 1897, Spain belatedly moderated her policy by introducing more lenient measures in dealing with the insurrectionists. The ruthless General Weyler was recalled, and the Spanish government offered autonomy to the Cubans. President McKinley announced in December, 1897, that he would allow a reasonable time for the new policy to be tested. This Spanish gesture came too late, however, for by this time the Cubans rejected anything short of complete independence. On the other hand, the die-hard pro-Spanish party members in Cuba, who opposed any concessions, and most particularly autonomy, organized demonstrations against home rule, and even against the United States and Americans in Cuba. It was this situation which prompted the American consul-general at Havana to request that a war vessel be sent to protect American citizens. The *U.S.S. Maine* was sent to Havana in January, 1898. On February 15, while anchored in Havana harbor, the ship was blown up by a mysterious explosion with the loss of 260 lives.

An American court of inquiry was set up immediately to investigate the *Maine* affair. While indicating that it was impossible to place responsibility for the explosion, the court reported that the evidence pointed to an external blast, probably by a submarine mine. Spanish investigators, on the other hand, claimed that an internal explosion in the forward magazine of the vessel was responsible.[67] The cause has, in fact, never been conclusively determined. Perhaps the ship was blown up, not by Spaniards, but by Cuban radicals who wanted to involve the United States in the war on their side. In any case the sinking of the *Maine* seems to have accomplished that purpose. "Remember the *Maine*" became the battle cry of the war-hungry American public.

President McKinley, however, resisted the pressure of the public and the Congress, and made strenuous efforts to avoid a military showdown with Spain. On March 27, 1898, the President made his final attempt at a diplomatic settlement by presenting a virtual ultimatum to the Spanish government demanding: (1) the arrangement of a six-month armistice between Spain and the insurgents; (2) the acceptance of mediation or arbitration of the dispute by the United States; and (3) the revocation of the reconcentration order. In return, the United States would disavow any intention to obtain Cuba for itself. The Spanish government accepted some of the American demands, but

[67] *Sen. Doc.* No. 207, 55th Cong., 2nd Sess.; *Sen. Report* No. 885, 55th Cong., 2nd Sess.

made counterproposals of its own, and stipulated that the insurgents should ask for an armistice and agree to disarm. Since this was tantamount to inviting the insurgents to put themselves at the mercy of Spain while she deliberated on Cuba's fate, McKinley considered the Spanish reply as a rejection of his proposal and decided to turn the whole matter over to Congress.[68] In the meantime, several European powers, and the Pope, seeing that war was imminent, made representations to the American and Spanish governments to reconcile their differences in a peaceful manner, but to no avail.

Finally, on April 9, Spain announced her willingness to accede to every demand which McKinley had previously made, but the time had passed when the United States, much less the Cubans, would accept anything but complete independence, and this Spain was still not prepared to grant. Accordingly, under the pressure of public and Congressional opinion, McKinley, on April 11, 1898, sent a special message to Congress requesting authority to take measures to terminate the hostilities in Cuba and establish a stable government there.[69] On April 20, Congress, after considerable debate, passed a joint resolution which: (1) recognized the independence of Cuba; (2) demanded the relinquishment of Spanish political authority on the island and the withdrawal of its land and naval forces from Cuba; (3) directed and empowered the President to employ whatever military forces would be necessary to accomplish these purposes; and (4) disclaimed any intention of the United States to annex Cuba, and declared that American authority would be withdrawn from the island as soon as its independence had been assured (Teller Amendment). The combination of Spanish procrastination and American impatience was too much to overcome. The war was on.

The armed conflict could hardly be called a contest. The Spanish forces in both the Caribbean and the far Pacific were quickly routed by American military might, not because the United States was so powerful but because Spain was so feeble. Pressure soon built up to bring an end to the one-sided contest, and in July, 1898, after only about three months of fighting, Spain sued for peace on terms dictated by the United States. In the Treaty of Paris, concluded on December 10, 1898, Spain agreed: (1) to evacuate Cuba immediately, relinquish all sovereignty over it, and recognize its independence; (2) to cede Puerto Rico and Guam to the United States; and (3) to sell the Philippines to the United States for $20 million.[70]

The promise of the United States to withdraw from Cuba came as a shock to those European cynics who confidently expected that Cuba would be annexed to the United States. Spain, in fact, preferred such a settlement, for then her subjects remaining in Cuba would enjoy greater protection of life and property than under Cuban rule. It was to reassure the Spanish government that the United States agreed, in the treaty, to give guarantees to Spanish citizens and interests in Cuba.

[68] *For. Rel.,* 1898, 712, 731.   [69] *Ibid.,* 750.
[70] For text of the treaty, see *For. Rel.,* 1898, 831.

Establishment of the Cuban protectorate: the Platt Amendment

The Spanish-American War, while liberating Cuba from Spanish rule, neither brought complete independence to the island, nor ended the "Cuban problem" for the United States. Following the evacuation of Havana by Spanish troops on January 1, 1899, the United States established a military government under General John R. Brooke. He was succeeded in December, 1899, by General Leonard Wood, who served as governor-general in a highly efficient manner.[71] Although the first tasks of the American regime were to establish law and order, set up the necessary administrative machinery, and improve sanitary conditions, the main object of the American administration was to establish a constitutional government for an independent Cuba.

Accordingly, in July, 1900, General Wood ordered elections to be held in September to choose delegates to a convention to draft and adopt a constitution for the new Cuban state. Although they had been specifically instructed to make provision for the relations that should exist between the United States and Cuba after the American withdrawal, this the Cuban delegates objected to rather strenuously. They rejected the idea of a qualified independence.[72]

The United States Congress, therefore, upon the urging of Secretary of War Elihu Root, approved on March 2, 1901, a proviso attached to the army appropriation bill, since known as the "Platt Amendment," after Senator Platt, Chairman of the Committee on Foreign Relations of the Senate. This famous amendment which became the basis of relations between Cuba and the United States until 1934, authorized the President

> . . . to leave the government and control of the island of Cuba to its people so soon as a government shall have been established in said island under a constitution which, either as a part thereof or in an ordinance appended thereto, shall define the future relations of the United States with Cuba, substantially as follows:
>
> I.   That the government of Cuba shall never enter into any treaty or other compact with any foreign power or powers which will impair or tend to impair the independence of Cuba, nor in any manner authorize or permit any foreign Power or Powers to obtain by colonization or for military or naval purposes, or otherwise, lodgment in or control over any portion of said Island.
>
> II. That said Government shall not assume or contract any public debt to pay the interest upon which, and to make reasonable sinking-fund provision for discharge of which, the ordinary revenues of the Island, after defraying the current expenses of the Government shall be inadequate.
>
> III. That the Government of Cuba consents that the United States may exercise the right to intervene for the preservation of Cuban independence, the maintenance of a government adequate for the protection of life, property, and individual liberty, and for discharging the obligations with respect

---

[71] For the United States occupation of Cuba, see David F. Healy, *The United States in Cuba, 1898–1902* (Madison; University of Wisconsin Press, 1963).

[72] For the genesis of the Platt Amendment, see Munro, *op. cit.*, 9–15.

to Cuba imposed by the Treaty of Paris on the United States, now to be assumed and undertaken by the Government of Cuba.

IV. That all acts of the United States in Cuba during its military occupation thereof are ratified and validated, and all lawful right acquired thereunder shall be maintained and protected.

V. That the Government of Cuba will execute, and as far as necessary extend, the plans already devised or other plans to be mutually agreed upon, for the sanitation of the cities of the Island to the end that a recurrence of epidemic and infectious diseases may be prevented, thereby assuring protection to the people and commerce of Cuba, as well as to the commerce of the Southern ports of the United States and the people residing therein.

VI. That the Isle of Pines shall be omitted from the proposed constitutional boundaries of Cuba, the title thereto left to future adjustments by treaty.

VII. That to enable the United States to maintain the independence of Cuba, and to protect the people thereof, as well as for its own defense, the Government of Cuba will sell or lease to the United States lands necessary for coaling or naval stations at certain specified points, to be agreed upon with the President of the United States.

VIII. That by way of further assurance the Government of Cuba will embody the foregoing provisions in a permanent treaty with the United States.

The Cubans were displeased, quite understandably, with restrictions imposed on their national sovereignty. But since acceptance of American demands was prerequisite to the termination of the military occupation, they seemed to have no choice in the matter. In June, 1901, the Constitutional Convention approved the Platt Amendment, but by a very close vote. As required it was affixed to the Cuban Constitution as an "appendix." Also, as required, the first seven articles of the Amendment were incorporated in a Permanent Treaty which was signed at Havana on May 22, 1903.

The Platt Amendment was condemned not only by the Cubans, but by Latin Americans generally. Without question the position of the United States was vulnerable and regrettable, but still highly defensible. Without the Platt Amendment the intervention in the war with Spain and the liberation of Cuba would have served no national interest. Secretary Root stated the case of the United States:

It would be a most lame and impotent conclusion if, after all the expenditure of blood and treasure by the people of the United States for the freedom of Cuba and by the people of Cuba for the same object, we should, through the constitution of the new government, by inadventure or otherwise, be placed in a worse condition in regard to our own vital interests than we were while Spain was in possession, and the people of Cuba should be deprived of that protection and aid from the United States which is necessary for the maintenance of their independence.[73]

73 *Ibid.*, 10.

The nature of the relationship between Cuba and the United States having been determined by formal agreement, the elections were held in December, 1901. Tomás Estrada Palma became the new republic's first president, and on May 20, 1902, the military government formally transferred the administration of the island's affairs to the Cubans, after over three years of American rule. During the period of American occupation, internal order was restored; the legal system was reformed; an extensive program of highway construction was undertaken; the public education system was completely revamped; and, in what was perhaps the most significant achievement of all, a far-reaching sanitation program was launched which practically eliminated the plague of yellow fever.

Relations between the Estrada Palma administration and the United States were generally cordial. In accordance with the Platt Amendment, agreements were concluded in February and July, 1903, by which the Cuban government leased specified areas at Guantánamo and Bahía Honda to the United States for the establishment of American coaling and naval stations, though in a subsequent agreement in 1912 the United States relinquished its rights at Bahía Honda in return for an enlargement of the area at Guantánamo. Also, in accordance with the Platt Amendment, a treaty was signed on March 2, 1904, whereby the United States gave up to Cuba sovereignty over the Isle of Pines. Because of political pressure exerted by American landowners on the island, the treaty was not ratified by the United States Senate until 1925. In the meantime the Isle of Pines was under Cuban jurisdiction. But by far the most important agreement with the United States was a reciprocity treaty, signed December 11, 1902, which provided in general for a 20 per cent reduction in tariff duties on all importations from Cuba into the United States, and for reductions from 20 to 40 per cent upon importations from the United States to Cuba.[74]

This departure by the United States from a policy opposed to reciprocity in principle, was strongly advocated by President Roosevelt since he was concerned over the problem of Cuba's economic rehabilitation, and felt that "in the case of Cuba, . . . there are weighty reasons of morality and national interest why the policy should be held to have a peculiar application."[75] Reciprocity would be beneficial to the peace and health of Cuba and of the United States as well. Unfortunately, because of the great benefits inuring to the sugar economy, it tended to make Cuba a one-crop country.

The advantages of reciprocity to Cuba became noticeable almost immediately, particularly in the Cuban sugar industry which expanded rapidly being assured a privileged position in the American market. Cuba was also a magnet for American capital investments, increasing from $50 million in 1895 to $220 million in 1913, and $1,525 million in 1929.[76] We mention

---

[74] For text of the reciprocity convention, see Philip G. Wright, *The Cuban Situation and Our Treaty Relations* (Washington, D.C.: The Brookings Institution, 1931), 193–199.

[75] *Ibid.*, 25.   [76] *Ibid., passim.*

this increasing economic stake of the United States in Cuba to point up an interesting fact, i.e., to the traditional political and strategic reasons for United States interest in Cuba, is now added an economic one.

Interventions under the Platt Amendment

When President Estrada Palma was re-elected in December, 1905, the opposition Liberals abstained from voting and prepared to gain their ends through recourse to arms. In August, 1906, they rose in revolt, whereupon Estrada Palma, unable to quell the rebellion, sought the intervention of the United States to sustain him in power. President Theodore Roosevelt hesitated to interfere in Cuba's internal affairs. When the Cuban president threatened to resign, Roosevelt dispatched Secretary of War William Howard Taft and the Assistant Secretary of State, Robert Bacon, to Havana to try to patch up the differences. Palma refused to consider any proposal which meant compromise with the rebels while they were under arms. He seemed to prefer intervention, and finally made this inevitable by tendering his resignation. Since the vice-president also resigned Cuba was without a government. The United States had no alternative but to act. Here was a situation in which American intervention under the Platt Amendment was fully justified.[77]

On September 29, 1906, a provisional government was established under the authority of the President of the United States. Mr. Taft assumed the governorship of the island at first, but promptly, on October 13, turned it over to Charles E. Magoon, who served as head of the provisional government for the next three years. His administration has been severely criticized by Cuban writers for the harshness of his policies and methods, and he was even charged, without foundation, with reckless and corrupt expenditure of public funds. Magoon was, however, a man of high integrity and was successful in securing the enactment of badly needed electoral reform laws drafted by Colonel Enoch Crowder, and in preparing the way for an orderly and peaceful presidential election in 1908 by which the control of the island's public affairs could be returned to the Cubans.

In the election of 1908, José Miguel Gómez, the Liberal standard bearer who had been defeated in 1906, was chosen president over General Mario García Menocal, the candidate of a newly organized Conservative party, in a fair and honest election. The provisional government of Magoon thereupon convoked the Cuban Congress, and on January 28, 1909, the reins of government were turned over to President Gómez, thereby ending the first — and the only full-fledged — intervention of the United States in Cuban affairs under the authority of the Platt Amendment.[78]

Under the Gómez administration conditions developed which might have brought about another intervention. Although Secretary of State Philander

[77] Chapman, *op. cit.*, Chaps. VII-IX, *passim*.
[78] For details of the Magoon administration, see D. A. Lockwood, *Magoon in Cuba* (Chapel Hill: University of North Carolina Press, 1938); Charles E. Magoon, *Republic of Cuba, Report of the Provisional Administration, 1907–1908* (Havana, 1908–1909), II; and Chapman, *op. cit.*, Chap. X.

Knox warned the Cuban government that American intervention might be forthcoming if disorder was allowed to develop, he preferred to apply what has been called a "preventive policy," that is, to make the Cuban government prevent the development of conditions conducive to intervention.[79] For example, to protect Cuban credit, the United States, in 1911, intervened to bring about a modification of a contract between the Cuban government and the Cuban Ports Company as being "wasteful and against the best interests of Cuba." Also, in the interest of Cuban credit, the American minister, in 1912, informed the Cuban government of the "emphatic disapproval" of the American government of the Zapata Swamp Concession. This reclamation project, which involved rich timber resources, was characterized as ill advised, and a reckless waste of natural resources. Although President Gómez was obdurate, he was compelled to revoke the concession. Finally, toward the end of the Gómez administration, in 1913, the Cuban congress passed a general amnesty bill, which aroused American protests. The United States minister intervened to prevent President Gómez from promulgating the bill. The American argument was that an amnesty, which was tantamount to a general jail delivery, would create doubt concerning respect for life and property in Cuba. In these instances the United States was acting, presumably under authorization of the Platt Amendment, to impose a greater sense of responsibility on the Cuban government, and thus avoid more serious interventions.

There was no further intervention by the United States until the next election in 1916.[80] Although Menocal won at the polls, his election was disputed by the opposition Liberals. Despite warnings from the United States government that it would not recognize a revolutionary regime, the Liberals, under the leadership of ex-President Gómez, revolted in February, 1917. American Marines sent into the country did not have to employ arms in defense of the Cuban administration, but the mere fact of their presence at strategic locations on the island to protect American-owned properties convinced the rebels that they could not hope to win with the United States taking sides actively against them. The revolt was short-lived. On March 7 Gómez was captured, and by June the revolution was crushed.

Cuba declared war on Germany on April 7, 1917, one day after the United States' declaration. As an expression of solidarity it is difficult to determine to what extent this action reflected the free will of the Cuban people, bound as was their government by treaty obligations to the United States. Immediately after the war declaration the Cuban government seized a number of German ships and turned them over to the United States. Cuba's military participation in the war was restricted to antisubmarine naval patrol. Cuba's greatest contribution to the war effort of the United States and the Allies was "the turning over during two successive years of her great sugar crop under

[79] For application of the "preventive policy," see Munro, *op. cit.*, 32–38.
[80] For the elections of 1916 and the revolt of 1917, see Chapman, *op. cit.*, Chaps. XV, XVI.

conditions which assured its equitable distribution and its sale at a reasonable price."[81]

The great sugar yield was not without United States pressure. For example, on May 15, 1917, Secretary of State Lansing issued a warning to the rebels still in arms:

> . . . as the Allied Powers and the United States must depend to a large extent upon the sugar production of Cuba, all disturbances which interfere with this production must be considered as hostile acts, and the United States government is forced to issue this warning that unless all those under arms against the government of Cuba return immediately to their allegiance it may become necessary for the United States to regard them as its enemies and deal with them accordingly.[82]

This remarkable ultimatum served its purpose. Cuban revolutionary proclivities were restrained until the approach of the next presidential election.

During Menocal's second administration Cuba enjoyed a period of unprecedented prosperity, commonly referred to as "the dance of the millions," the good times resulting from high sugar prices. After the war, continued demands for sugar caused prices to soar to a peak, in May, 1920, of 22.5 cents per pound at Cuban ports. Then, with other world sugar sources coming into production, the bottom fell out of the Cuban sugar market. By December, 1920, the price of sugar declined to about four cents per pound. Economic prosperity was quickly followed by disastrous collapse. These were unfortunate conditions under which to hold the presidential election, scheduled for November 1, 1920.

Well realizing the exceptional skill of Cuban voters in finding loopholes in the electoral laws, and in an effort to prevent a repetition of the electoral frauds of prior years, the Conservatives and Liberals concurred in inviting General Enoch Crowder to come to Cuba to draft a new election law. Accordingly, in March, 1919, Crowder drafted a new law as fraud-proof as a skilled hand could provide. But evidence that Cubans could not be restrained by legality was soon forthcoming in the campaign and election. The polling resulted in the election of Alfredo Zayas over ex-President José Miguel Gómez: the Conservatives had manipulated the election to obtain a favorable verdict, despite the presence of American observers. General Gómez refused to accept the election results, and since the country was in a state of economic collapse, the threat of civil war prompted the United States to act. On January 6, 1921, General Crowder arrived at Havana as the special representative of President Wilson; his mission proved to be one of the most interesting American interventions in Cuba.[83]

---

[81] P. A. Martin, *Latin America and the War* (Baltimore: The Johns Hopkins Press, 1925), 164.
[82] *For. Rel.*, 1918, 407.
[83] Chapman, *op. cit.*, 419–426.

General Crowder, acting as a kind of American pro-consul, was instrumental in having the electoral results in a number of districts annulled and new elections held. The Liberals, however, refused to participate, and thus the victory went to Zayas by default. The threat of a revolt evaporated. General Crowder remained in Havana to investigate the critical condition of the Cuban government's finances and to suggest remedies.

He found the government's economic difficulties were occasioned not only by a dropping off of revenues due to the collapse of the sugar market, but also because of administrative evils and corruption. President Zayas needed United States approval to float a loan of $50 million, and Crowder saw an opportunity to impose a program of fiscal and internal reform. The Crowder recommendations, incorporated in fifteen specific proposals or memoranda, covered such subjects as reduction of the budget, revision or cancelling of contracts, and the elimination of graft and corruption from the national administration.

The Zayas government obediently adopted reform measures designed to minimize waste and corruption in the government and, in general, to establish fiscal responsibility on the part of public officials. An "Honest Cabinet" was appointed to carry out the anticipated reforms. As a result of these measures the United States gave its approval to the Cuban government to float a large foreign loan. Now freed of financial embarrassments, the Zayas government, early in 1923, dismissed several members of the "Honest Cabinet," and relapsed into its errant ways of robbing the public purse.[84] Thus ended the last American intervention in Cuba under authorization of the Platt Amendment. Cuba was soon to become a beneficiary of a new policy adopted by the United States shortly after World War I, known as "the liquidation of American imperialism."

The abandonment of interventionism

It is an interesting fact that General Crowder, who was appointed ambassador in January, 1923, was much less effective in Cuban affairs than he had been as the President's personal representative. For example, the Zayas administration ignored with impunity the ambassador's protests concerning the abandonment of promised reforms. His efforts led only to the passage of a resolution by the Cuban congress condemning the United States for interference in Cuban affairs.[85]

In the face of provocations which in former years would have invited effective interposition, the American government, after 1923, had apparently decided on a hands-off policy. No longer fearful of foreign aggressors, the United States felt that it could now afford to ignore irresponsible, corrupt, and tyrannical governments in Cuba so long as the consequences of their evil rule were confined to Cubans.

In 1924, the Liberal candidate, Gerardo Machado y Morales, was elected president of Cuba. Machado, truly a Liberal at first, enjoyed the support and confidence of the United States government. But when he manipulated his

[84] *Ibid.,* 426–444.   [85] *Ibid.,* 444–449.

own re-election in 1928 by suppressing all political opposition, the ardor of ✓ his supporters in Washington began to cool. As reports of his arbitrary and ✓ brutal rule mounted, demands for American intervention to end his dictatorship swelled.

The State Department declared that it was keeping a close watch on the Cuban situation and had no intention to intervene unless "a state of anarchy" developed. Despite the brutally oppressive character of the Machado regime, and his exploitation of a strong anti-American sentiment in Cuba, the United States government steadfastly refused to be provoked into armed intervention.[86] Secretary of State Henry Stimson was unalterably opposed to intervention. His policy has been regarded as a precursor to the Good Neighbor credited to Franklin D. Roosevelt.

The problem of relations with Machado was passed on by the Hoover-Stimson administration to that of Roosevelt-Hull. By that time "Cuba was a country economically prostrate, ruled by a tyrannical dictatorship to which 95 per cent of the people were fanatically opposed, a country . . . in which bombings, terrorism, and murder were daily occurrences."[87] The Machado administration and the revolutionary organizations seemed to vie in outdoing each other by murder and destruction. A veritable reign of terror existed in Cuba. Had a "state of anarchy" developed which warranted United States intervention? Unconvinced that intervention was the only answer, President Roosevelt sent to Cuba his Assistant Secretary of State Sumner Welles to offer his mediatory services in putting an end to the troubled political situation.

Quite independent of Mr. Welles' efforts "to ease out Machado," the dictator was swept from power on August 12, 1933, by a tidal wave of popular opposition.[88] The United States, because of the disorder and destruction attending the overthrow of Machado, took precautionary measures to protect American interests by stationing several warships off the Cuban coast.

A provisional government headed by Dr. Carlos Manuel de Céspedes was immediately recognized by the United States. The new regime lasted for only a few weeks; apparently it was unsatisfactory to the more radical revolutionary elements. On September 4, de Céspedes was overthrown by a *coup d'état* of army sergeants, headed by Fulgencio Batista, a sergeant-stenographer, working in concert with student leaders, a few professors, and intellectuals. On September 10, 1933, Dr. Ramón Grau San Martín, a professor in the medical faculty of the National University, became provisional president. The new regime, which found its chief support in the surging nationalist enthusiasm, was denied recognition by the United States, which was not yet convinced either that the new government represented the will of the people of the Re-

[86] For the Machado dictatorship, see Buell, *op. cit.*, 83–88; also Wright, *op. cit.*, 45–47; and Jones, *op. cit.*, 67–69.

[87] Sumner Welles, *Relations Between the United States and Cuba.* Dept. of State, Latin American Series No. 7 (Washington, D.C.: Government Printing Office, 1934), 6.

[88] For the Welles mission and the fall of Machado, see Charles A. Thomson, "The Cuban Revolution: Fall of Machado," *For. Pol. Rep.*, XI, No. 21 (December 18, 1935), 251–258.

public or that it was capable of maintaining law and order. Presumably when these qualifications were met it would be recognized.[89]

The refusal of United States recognition, and charges of interference in Cuba's internal affairs aroused a wave of anti-American feelings which threatened the lives and property of American citizens in Cuba. Although Mr. Welles, who was principally responsible for the policy of nonrecognition, repeatedly called for naval demonstrations and even the landing of Marines, his urgings went unheeded in Washington. President Roosevelt, strongly supported by Secretary Hull, reiterated his strong determination to stay out of Cuba.[90] The Cuban revolution was allowed to run its course without forcible intervention, but not without the attempted application of diplomatic pressures.

The pressure of nonrecognition was supported by Ambassador Welles to the point where he became *persona non grata* to President Grau San Martín. But, even though Mr. Welles was replaced in Havana by Jefferson Caffery as the President's personal representative, the Roosevelt administration still withheld recognition of the Grau regime. In the end, which was not long in coming, the policy of nonrecognition paid off, for apparently Colonel Batista, the army leader, was ready to sacrifice Grau to win recognition. When Batista transferred his support to Colonel Carlos Mendieta, who had both army and United States support, President Grau resigned. The next day, January 16, 1934, Mendieta took the oath as provisional president. On January 23 President Roosevelt announced recognition of the Mendieta government. Immediately, Secretary Hull announced the withdrawal of United States war vessels then in Cuban waters. This was but the first of several actions by the Roosevelt administration to convince the Cubans that a "new deal" had really been inaugurated in the relations between the two countries.[91]

President Roosevelt signed, on May 29, 1934, a new treaty of relations with Cuba which provided specifically for the abrogation of the treaty of 1903. Two days later — in record time — the United States Senate approved the treaty. It went into full effect on June 9.[92]

This formal abrogation of the Platt Amendment was the first of several actions by the Roosevelt-Hull administration to implement the nonintervention pledge signed at Montevideo in December, 1933. Unquestionably the abandonment by the United States of its protectorate rights over Cuba contributed greatly to Cuban satisfaction and improved understanding between the two countries. That it would have been handy, many years later, to have the Platt Amendment in reserve when Fidel Castro imposed Communism on Cuba, can hardly be denied.

[89] For relations with the Grau regime, see Charles A. Thomson, "The Cuban Revolution: Reform and Reaction," *For. Pol. Rep.*, XI, No. 22 (January 1, 1936), 263–269.

[90] Cordell Hull, *The Memoirs of Cordell Hull* (2 vols. New York: The Macmillan Company, 1948), I, 315–317. See also Bryce Wood, *The Making of the Good Neighbor Policy* (New York: Columbia University Press, 1961), 80–98.

[91] *For. Pol. Rep.* (January 1, 1936), 269.

[92] For text of the treaty, see Dept. of State, *Treaty Information*, Bulletin No. 56 (May 31, 1934).

A new deal in United States relations with Cuba was also evidenced by the adoption of measures for the economic rehabilitation and development of the country. The financial and economic condition of Cuba had sadly deteriorated. Cuban exports which in 1924 were about $434 million had fallen to about $80 million in 1932. Government revenues dropped almost one-half. This deterioration was due to the fact that Cuba was a one-crop country, depending on sugar exports to the United States. Therefore, when the Smoot-Hawley Tariff Act of 1930 sharply increased the duty on sugar, the price of Cuban sugar dropped because of a world overproduction. To help to solve Cuba's sugar problem the United States Congress enacted, in May, 1934, the Jones-Costigan Act, which assigned to Cuba a larger annual quota in the United States market. At the same time the import duty on Cuban sugar was reduced from 2 to 1.5 cents a pound. Far more important as an economic aid to Cuba was the new preferential trade agreement of August 24, 1934, which revised the reciprocity treaty in force since 1902.[93] By the terms of the trade agreement the duty on Cuban sugar was further reduced to 0.9 cents per pound. There were other reductions on Cuban rum, tobacco, fruits, and vegetables. In return the United States received concessions on a large array of its own exports. The trade agreement was largely responsible for a dramatic increase in the totals of United States-Cuba trade.[94] The very success of the program indicated to what extent Cuban independence, even without the Platt Amendment, was limited by economic dependence on the United States.

Economic assistance to Cuba was also extended by the United States through the agency of the Export-Import Bank, which was established in March, 1934, for the express purpose of lending money to Cuba, thereby promoting United States exports. The bank lost no time in extending financial credit to Cuba. There was an almost immediate response to these trade stimulants. United States exports to Cuba advanced from $22.7 million in 1933, to $147 million in 1941, $539.8 million in 1951, and $617.9 million in 1957. In 1955 the United States supplied 73.4 per cent of all Cuban imports, and purchased 68.9 per cent of all Cuban exports. United States direct investments in Cuba had already reached their height; they amounted to $919 million in 1929, and $850 million in 1957.[95]

From 1934 to 1959 there was a steady rise of Cuba's standard of living to one of the highest in Latin America. The fact that the United States enjoyed a favorable balance of trade in 1957, for example, indicated that the Cubans bought more goods in dollars from the United States than the United States bought from Cuba, even though the United States purchased annually approximately 3,000,000 tons of sugar from Cuba — about one-half of Cuba's entire sugar production.

[93] *For. Pol. Rep.* (January 1, 1936), 272–273.
[94] U.S. Dept. of State, *Analysis of Cuban-American Trade During the First Two Years Under the Reciprocal Agreement* (Washington, D.C.: Government Printing Office, 1937).
[95] Robert F. Smith, *The United States and Cuba, Business and Diplomacy, 1917–1960* (New York: Bookman Associates, 1960), 163–170, *passim*.

"Cuba Libre": 1934–1959

For almost twenty-five years after the release of Cuba from all political restraint by the United States, relations between the two countries unfolded normally in the sense that there were no untoward events.[96] During this period from 1934 to 1959, Cuba experienced several different administrations, though Fulgencio Batista usually figured directly or indirectly as the real political power in the country. When he was not making or unmaking presidents, he himself was in personal power. Since Batista, as a matter of calculated policy, was generally on cordial terms and cooperative with the United States, this helps to explain the smooth current of relations. Batista was one of several Latin-American dictators with whom the State Department at the time found it profitable and congenial to do business.

Under Batista's guidance, after he became president in 1940, Cuba cooperated fully, economically and militarily, with the United States in World War II.[97] Cuba was one of the nine Caribbean nations which, by December 12, 1941, had declared war on the Axis powers. On June 15 Cuba entered into an agreement with the United States granting facilities for operations against enemy submarines. The agreement was later extended to provide for a coordination of all military and naval measures taken by the two countries. This brought Cuba into full cooperation with the United States. Cuba's active military participation in the war was largely confined to the antisubmarine campaign. For these operations, and for its general defense, the country was liberally supplied with war materials by lend-lease grants. Cuba was also the recipient of Export-Import Bank loans to diversify production and improve its sugar-refining facilities. As in World War I, Cuba's principal contribution to the United Nations cause was its sugar production, which was doubled.

After the expiration of Batista's term of office in 1944, the United States relations with his successors Grau San Martín and Carlos Prío Socarrás were without serious incident, although the United States witnessed uneasily the large and active Soviet embassy in Havana, which was apparently channeling Communist influence and propaganda throughout Latin America. When Fulgencio Batista returned to power by means of a bloodless *cuartelazo,* or barracks *coup,* on March 10, 1952, he was recognized by the United States in only a few days despite his crude disregard for constitutionalism. Factors that weighed heavily in his favor were his ability to insure stability and order, his long record of cooperation with the United States, and his promise to promote a strong anti-Communist policy.

Because two Soviet couriers were searched at a Cuban airport in violation of their diplomatic immunity, on April 3, the U.S.S.R. broke diplomatic relations with Cuba. In October, 1953, Batista declared illegal the Cuban Communist party, the Partido Socialista Popular. Most of the PSP leaders were

---

[96] For the problem of defaulted public works bonds, and its final settlement in 1940 under State Department pressure, see *ibid.,* 171–173.

[97] See Mecham, *op. cit.,* Chap. VIII, *passim.*

either arrested or went into exile. There were no embassies of Communist countries in Cuba during Batista's presidency. Batista set up a Bureau for the Suppression of Communist Activities. This agency, with United States aid, was in operation for years, but its effectiveness was spotty. At times it was necessary for the American ambassador to appeal for more vigorous action, for it seemed that Batista had entered into some kind of deal with the Communists.[98]

To strengthen the defensive position of Cuba, and to make Communist subversion more difficult, the regime was bolstered by a Mutual Defense Assistance Agreement with the United States. The agreement, contracted in 1952, paved the way for grants to the Batista government of about $1 million per year in military aid, and nonmilitary grants that mounted from $40,000 in 1950 to $176,000 in 1953, and $561,000 in 1958.[99]

The Castro revolution against Batista was not generated because of the nature of his dictatorship, so it serves no purpose to mention the constructive achievements of his administration, nor its many abuses. It was the *fact* of a dictatorship, established by one of the most cynical floutings of legality in the history of the republic, which incited impatient and politically motivated young men to action. It was on July 26, 1953, that Fidel Castro and 170 followers launched a revolution against the Batista regime. The attack on the Moncada barracks at Santiago de Cuba was a disastrous failure. Captured and sentenced to a long prison term, Castro was released in May, 1955, in a general political amnesty. Soon he turned up in Mexico where he continued his revolutionary activities. On December 2, 1956, Fidel Castro, his brother Raúl and Ernesto (Ché) Guevara, and companions, numbering eighty-two men in all, landed from an old yacht on the shore of Oriente province. They were immediately discovered by the military, who attacked. Only twelve men survived to reach the nearby high and rugged Sierra Maestra. There it was that Fidel, Raúl, and Ché organized their remarkable guerrilla war against the tyrant Fulgencio Batista. Up to mid-1958 the rebels in the mountains numbered fewer than 1,000 men.[100]

It was not until early 1957 that Castro was able to make much headway. An improvement in his fortunes was due in no small measure to the publication by the *New York Times* of a series of articles by its reporter Herbert Matthews, who had secured an exclusive interview with Castro in his mountain hideout. The articles attracted wide attention to the Cuban "Robin Hood" and facilitated a flow of funds and recruits for the 26th of July Movement.

In the meantime a much larger urban resistance movement was being organized which employed terrorist tactics against the army and police. Dangerous disaffection made its appearance in Batista's armed forces. In Septem-

[98] R. Hart Phillips, *Cuba, Island of Paradox* (New York: McDowell, Obolensky, 1959), 350–351.

[99] Wyatt MacGaffey and Clifford R. Barnett, *Cuba, its people, its society, its culture* (New Haven: HRAF Press, 1962), 315.

[100] *Ibid.*, 240.

ber, 1957, there was a revolt at the naval base of Cienfuegos. It failed, but it made Batista realize that he could no longer count on the blind support of the armed forces.[101]

Faced by these developments, Batista was guilty of a fatal error of judgment. Instead of instituting even moderate changes in his government he adopted the policy of suppressing all opposition by brutal police terrorism. Obviously these developments were viewed with concern by the United States. But, did Washington have a Cuban policy?

The American Ambassador, Arthur Gardner, who resigned on May 14, 1957, "had been so pro-Batista that he had actually embarrassed the President."[102] The State Department was also embarrassed by his partisanship. Thus the new ambassador, Earl E. T. Smith, who presented his credentials to Batista on July 23, 1957, was specifically instructed "to alter the prevailing notion in Cuba that the American Ambassador was intervening on behalf of the government of Cuba to perpetuate the Batista dictatorship." According to Ambassador Smith, "my first mission (was that) of establishing the Embassy's position of impartiality in the political affairs of Cuba." His second mission was to persuade Batista to restore constitutional guarantees and lift the press censorship. The Ambassador was not successful in achieving either objective.[103]

In connection with the first objective, the observance of impartiality by an American envoy in the political affairs of Cuba was completely unrealistic, for in the view of Cubans there is no political middle ground — the United States is either for or against. And since it was clear from the record that the United States was not against Batista, it was idle to talk about impartiality. Also, it was a contradiction of fact to protest loyalty to the nonintervention principle, as did the State Department, meanwhile exerting pressures on the Batista government. "The United States was so important in the minds of the Cuban people," wrote ex-Ambassador Earl Smith, "that the American Ambassador was, to repeat, regarded as the second most important personage in Cuba." His official acts or words were usually magnified far beyond their importance, and often regarded as intervention. Such was the case, for example, when Ambassador Smith, on witnessing acts of police brutality in Santiago remarked, "Any form of excessive police action is abhorrent to me." Batista objected to this statement as intervention, but Castro regarded it as indicative of a change in United States policy.[104]

In fact, a change of policy was apparently taking form in the State Department because of mounting pressures of public opinion against the practice of "doing business with dictators." Indicative of a desire by the policy makers to demonstrate United States impartiality in the Cuban conflict was the sus-

101 Earl E. T. Smith, *The Fourth Floor, An Account of the Castro Communist Revolution* (New York: Random House, 1962), 31.
102 Phillips, *op. cit.*, 324.
103 Smith, *op. cit.*, 20, 28.
104 *Ibid.*, 23.

pension of arms shipments to the Cuban government. As justification for this action of March 14, 1958, the State Department cited a clause in the Mutual Defense Assistance Agreement with Cuba which by implication prohibited the supply of arms to a government which used them against its own people.[105]

This effort by the United States to be "neutral and impartial" was probably the most effective step taken to bring about the downfall of Batista. Not only did the denial of arms by the United States impair his military strength, but, far more important, it undermined the morale of the armed forces and other adherents of the regime. The United States action was generally interpreted, not as neutral and impartial, but as anti-Batista. "I cannot understand," the dictator complained to Ambassador Smith, "why your government refuses to sell arms to my government which is friendly to you and an enemy of Communism."[106]

If the United States expected to gain the confidence of Castro it was disappointed, for the rebel leader never abandoned his charges that American arms were being used by Batista against his revolutionaries. Castro chose to ignore the fact that his agents in the United States, and particularly the Cuban ex-President Prío Socarrás, were very successful in securing arms for the rebels in violation of United States neutrality laws.

Probably in an effort to attract attention to his revolt, Castro was responsible for a number of anti-United States incidents. First, there were a number of kidnappings of American citizens, the most notorious of these being the seizure of Marines and sailors outside the base of Guantánamo. Second, American planes were hijacked and forced to land in Cuba. And finally, from July to November, 1958, the rebels harassed the Guantánamo base by turning the water supply on and off intermittently. From July 28 to July 31 a detachment of Marines took over control of the plant at Yateras, with Batista's consent, but Castro raised the cry of "intervention," and so the State Department hastened to oblige by withdrawing the troops.[107]

Finally, in an eleventh hour response to State Department pressure for an electoral rather than a military, decision, Batista perpetrated another electoral fraud by having a puppet president elected on November 3, 1958. The gesture came too late: Batista was doomed because of the disintegration of his defenses. Also, the time had passed when it might have been possible, with effective State Department cooperation, to set up a provisional government without Castro, whose unacceptability should have been apparent at that date. It seems however, that the responsible policy makers preferred to hide behind the principle of nonintervention, that convenient alibi for inaction.

On January 1, 1959, the fallen dictator Fulgencio Batista fled into exile with a fortunate few of his associates. On January 7, 1959, Castro's designate, President Manuel Urrutia y Lleo, was recognized by the United States.

[105] Phillips, *op. cit.,* 351.
[106] Smith, *op. cit.,* 55.
[107] *Ibid.,* 109.

SUPPLEMENTARY READING

Callcott, Wilfred Hardy, *The Caribbean Policy of the United States, 1890-1920* (Baltimore: The Johns Hopkins Press, 1942).

Chapman, Charles E., *A History of the Cuban Republic* (New York: The Macmillan Company, 1927).

Davis, H. P., *Black Democracy: The Story of Haiti* (New York: Dodge Publishing Company, 1936).

Ferguson, Erna, *Cuba* (New York: Alfred A. Knopf, Inc., 1946).

Fitzgibbon, Russell H., *Cuba and the United States, 1900-1935* (Menosha, Wis.: George Banta Publishing Company, 1935).

Howland, Charles P., ed., *Survey of American Foreign Relations* (New Haven: Yale University Press, 1929).

Jones, Chester Lloyd, *The Caribbean Since 1900* (New York: Prentice-Hall, Inc., 1936).

Kelsey, Carl, *The American Intervention in Haiti and the Dominican Republic* (Philadelphia: American Academy of Political and Social Science, 1922).

Knight, Melvin M., *The Americans in Santo Domingo* (New York: Vanguard Press, 1928).

Leyburn, James G., *The Haitian People* (New Haven: Yale University Press, 1941).

McCrocklin, James H., *Garde D'Haiti, 1915-1934* (Annapolis, Md.: The United States Naval Institute, 1956).

MacGaffey, Wyatt, and Barnett, Clifford R., *Cuba, its people, its society, its culture* (New Haven: HRAF Press, 1962).

Millspaugh, Arthur C., *Haiti Under American Control* (Boston: World Peace Foundation, 1931).

Montague, Ludwell Lee, *Haiti and the United States, 1714-1938* (Durham: Duke University Press, 1940).

Munro, Dana G., *The United States and the Caribbean Area* (Boston: World Peace Foundation, 1934).

Perkins, Dexter, *The United States and the Caribbean* (Cambridge: Harvard University Press, 1947).

Phillips, R. Hart, *Cuba, Island of Paradox* (New York: McDowell, Obolensky, 1959).

Portell Vilá, Hermonio, *Historia de Cuba en sus relaciones con los Estados Unidos* (4 vols. Havana: J. Montero, 1938-1941).

Rippy, J. Fred, *The Caribbean Danger Zone* (New York: G. P. Putnam's Sons, 1940).

Smith, Earl E. T., *The Fourth Floor, An Account of the Castro Communist Revolution* (New York: Random House, 1962).

Smith, Robert F., *The United States and Cuba: Business and Diplomacy, 1917-1960* (New York: Bookman Associates, 1961).

Thomson, Charles A. "The Cuban Revolution: Reform and Reaction," *Foreign Policy Reports,* XI, No. 22 (January 1, 1936), 262-276.

Welles, Sumner, *Naboth's Vineyard: The Dominican Republic, 1844-1924* (2 vols. New York: Payson and Clarke, 1928).

Wright, P. G., *The Cuban Situation and Our Treaty Relations* (Washington, D.C.: The Brookings Institution, 1931).

12

The United States and Central America

Since Central America is a part of the region which we know as the Caribbean, United States relations with the countries of the area conformed largely to the general policy design described in the preceding two chapters. This being the case, the relationship between the United States and Central America became more intense during the period 1900-1930, when the American government aggressively promoted its Caribbean interests. Potential canal routes as well as its proximity to the United States and the Panama Canal made Central America strategically important to the United States. In addition, it was a region which harbored conditions that seemed to impose on the United States the role of an international policeman armed with a "big stick": all of the countries, with the possible exception of Costa Rica, were excessively retarded in political and economic development.

Relations with each of the countries of Central America were not, however, of equal importance to the United States. This was because two of them, Panama and Nicaragua, possessed the most feasible canal routes. But outside of this, all of the countries were rather equal in their economic unimportance, for certainly there was insufficient United States trade and investments in the area to influence government policy seriously.

Therefore this chapter will illustrate principally the thoroughness with which the United States implemented its general Caribbean policy in Panama and Nicaragua. Problems with the other countries have either been treated elsewhere in this survey or are discussed here in connection with United States efforts to promote unity and stability in Central America.

1. Relations with Panama

A survey of United States-Panama relations is concerned almost exclusively with problems arising out of the basic treaty of 1903, the Convention for the Construction of a Ship Canal, better known as the Hay-Bunau-Varilla treaty.

By the terms of this treaty Panama conveyed to the United States two sets of rights relating to the construction, operation, and protection of a canal: (1) the rights of protection and intervention by the United States in Panama, and (2) the rights of the United States within the Canal Zone.[1] A discussion of the problems of treaty relations, at least until 1936, can be simplified if considered under these two headings.

The rights of the United States in Panama[2]

It was obvious that the control and peaceful operation by the United States of a canal cut athwart the Republic of Panama, would be conditioned by the nature of political and administrative conditions prevailing within the Republic itself. Therefore, in order to ward against the possibility of Panama's being unable or unwilling to respect the administrative autonomy of the Canal, and to keep the country from falling prey to internal disorder, the United States was granted, by Articles I and VII of the treaty, rights of protection and intervention in Panama.

According to Article I, "The United States guarantees and will maintain the independence of the Republic of Panama." Article VII of the treaty provides in part:

> The Republic of Panama agrees that the cities of Panama and Colón shall comply in perpetuity with the sanitary ordinances whether of a preventive or curative character prescribed by the United States and in case the government of Panama is unable or fails in its duty to enforce this compliance by the cities of Panama and Colón with the sanitary ordinances of the United States the Republic of Panama grants to the United States the right and authority to enforce the same.
>
> The same right and authority are granted to the United States for the maintenance of public order in the cities of Panama and Colón and the territories and harbors adjacent thereto in case the Republic of Panama should not be, in the judgment of the United States, able to maintain such order.[3]

Occasions arose for the United States to intervene in Panamanian affairs by authority of its own interpretation of Articles I and VII of the treaty of 1903.

One such occasion was a boundary dispute between Panama and Costa Rica, which in 1921 threatened to cause war. The dispute dated from long before the independence of Panama when the republic was still a part of Colombia.[4] Many efforts before and after 1903 to determine the boundary

[1] For text of treaty, see William M. Mallory, comp., *Treaties, Conventions, International Acts, Protocols and Agreements between the United States of America and Other Powers, 1776–1909* (2 vols. Washington, D.C.: Government Printing Office, 1910), II, 1349; also in Dana G. Munro, *The United States and the Caribbean Area* (Boston: World Peace Foundation, 1934), 275–284.

[2] See Raymond Leslie Buell, "Panama and the United States," *Foreign Policy Reports,* VII, No. 23 (January 20, 1932), 410–418.

[3] Both Panama City and Colón lie outside the Canal Zone.

[4] See Gordon Ireland, *Boundaries, Possessions, and Conflicts in Central and North America and the Caribbean* (Cambridge: Harvard University Press, 1941), 33–42.

and the possession of the Coto district on the Pacific side of the isthmus were all unsuccessful. Finally, as a result of the good offices of the United States, Panama and Costa Rica agreed in 1910 to submit the problem to the arbitral judgment of the Chief Justice of the Supreme Court of the United States. In September, 1914, Chief Justice White announced his decision, but Panama rejected the award on the grounds that the arbitrator had exceeded his powers. So the matter rested until 1921 when Costa Rica sent troops to occupy the Coto region awarded by the Chief Justice, but were ejected by the Panamanians. With both countries preparing for war the United States, in March, 1921, intervened to enforce the White award.

Secretary Hughes justified intervention in Panama's boundary controversy by appealing to Article I of the Hay-Bunau-Varilla treaty which gave to the United States the right to guarantee the independence of Panama.[5] Said the Secretary: "The Government of Panama cannot fail to realize that in order that the Government of the United States may fully perform its obligations under the treaty it must advise itself as to the extent of the sovereignty of the Republic of Panama and hence of the territorial limits of Panama. It follows that the government of the United States deems it necessary to inquire fully into the merits of a controversy which relates to the boundary of the Republic of Panama."

Continued resistance by Panama resulted finally in an ultimatum by Secretary Hughes, on August 18, that the United States would not tolerate a resumption of hostilities and that Panama must withdraw. On August 23 Panama withdrew declaring bitterly that she was a victim of an American effort to appear impartial in the dispute.[6]

Not only did the United States claim the right as guarantor of Panama's independence to intervene in Panama's boundary disputes, but it indicated at times that it might control the foreign policy of Panama in order to obviate the necessity of defending that country from outside attack. For example, in 1909 Secretary of State Philander Knox claimed that the United States had a "moral right to prevent Panama from getting into a controversy with any government which might eventually require the United States to take part in the controversy and support Panama."[7]

Finally, in applying the guarantee of Article I of the treaty, the United States government opposed the grant of railway and harbor concessions on the ground that this would increase the difficulties of defending the Canal. By the same token the United States insisted on assuming the control of radio and civil aviation in Panama.

With respect to interventionist rights under Article VII of the treaty, no difficulties developed concerning American sanitary supervision. The administrative responsibility for the sanitation of Panama City and Colón was assumed by the United States, which also paid most of the costs. But with

[5] *Foreign Relations of the United States*, 1921, I, 184–188.

[6] "Unsettled Boundary Disputes in Latin America," Foreign Policy Association, *Information Service*, V, No. 26 (March 5, 1930), 493–496.

[7] *For. Rel.*, 1909, 469.

respect to grant of authority to maintain "public order in the cities of Panama and Colón and the territories and harbors adjacent thereto," this was so liberally and broadly interpreted by the United States as to cause considerable Panamanian resentment. In the exercise of the right of police protection American troops were sent on three different occasions (1918, 1921, and 1925) into the two cities to cope with mobs. On other occasions American threats to take over the policing sufficed to stimulate action by the local police.[8]

Under the guise of maintaining order in Panama the United States early adopted an antirevolutionary policy. Its attitude toward revolution depended upon whether such revolt imperiled Panama's independence or disturbed public order and interfered with canal construction. This asserted right was never exercised overtly. In pursuit of the same objective, however, the United States supervised elections in 1908, 1912, and 1918, but only at the formal request of the Panamanian government. There were no more supervised elections after 1918. In 1928 the State Department was asked to intervene in order to guarantee a free election, but Secretary Frank B. Kellogg refused.[9]

Rights of the United States in the Zone[10]

However important were the intervention rights of the United States in the Republic of Panama, a much more serious and lasting bone of contention was the treaty status of the United States in the Canal Zone itself. By the terms of the 1903 treaty Panama granted to the United States in perpetuity a zone ten miles wide "for the construction, maintenance, operation, sanitation and protection" of the Canal (Article II); and also "all the rights, power and authority within the zone mentioned . . . which the United States would possess and exercise if it were the sovereign of the territory . . . to the entire exclusion of the exercise by the Republic of Panama of any such sovereign rights, power or authority" (Article III). Also the treaty conveyed to the United States the right to take any lands and waters outside the Canal Zone "necessary and convenient for the construction, maintenance, operation, sanitation and protection" of the Canal.

From the time of the conclusion of the treaty of 1903 until the present, the United States and Panama have disagreed on the exact nature of the rights acquired by the former in the Canal Zone. The chief disagreement has been the true meaning of the provision of the original treaty regarding sovereignty over the Zone. The United States has insisted that it has full rights of jurisdiction within the area, while Panama, though conceding to the United States the exercise of those rights of sovereignty which are necessary for the construction and maintenance of the Canal, has always insisted that the two countries exercise jointly the sovereignty over the territory of the Canal Zone.

---

[8] *For. Rel.*, 1915, 1229.   [9] *New York Times,* July 28, 1928.
[10] See Buell, *op. cit.*, 418–424.

Hardly had the treaty of 1903 been signed before a serious controversy arose concerning the extent of the rights of the United States. By executive order issued by President Theodore Roosevelt on June 24, 1904, which opened the Canal Zone to commerce, provision was made for the establishment of American customs houses at Ancon and Cristóbal, the ports at either end of the Canal, and the Governor of the Canal Zone was authorized to arrange for reciprocal trade relations and uniform tariff rates with Panama. The Panamanian government objected to the establishment of ports, customs houses, and tariffs by the United States, arguing that such concessions would ruin Panama's commerce and, moreover, would infringe Panama's sovereignty over the Canal Zone. Secretary of State Hay took the position that the treaty of 1903, which granted the United States "all the rights which it would have if it were the sovereign of the Zone," established the right of the United States to regulate trade therein.[11]

In an attempt to resolve the differences between the two governments, Secretary of War Taft was sent to Panama where, following a series of conferences with Panamanian authorities and those of the Canal Zone, the so-called Taft Agreement was concluded in December, 1904. It permitted the importation into the Canal Zone of goods to be sold only by the Isthmian Canal Commission to Zone employees, except upon payment of proper duties to Panama. It also provided for the free passage of goods and persons between Panama and the Zone, the reciprocal use of harbors, and the regulation of the postal service between the two areas.[12] Although this agreement was intended to serve only as a *modus operandi* while the Canal was under construction, it remained in effect until formally abrogated in 1924.

The Taft Agreement met many of Panama's demands, but it failed to resolve other points of difference such as the status of the American commissaries, the standing threat of the United States to occupy other lands and waters outside the Zone, the right to issue consular exequaturs, the right of extradition, and the unequal standards of employment and pay in the Zone.

The problem of the commissaries was probably the most serious of these differences because it was the one most directly related to Panama's expectations of economic gain from the construction of the Canal. Since the early days of canal construction, commissaries were operated in the Zone by the United States government for the benefit of Canal employees. Although Panama sought to have the goods limited to "necessities," the commissaries carried elaborate stocks of so-called "luxury" items. In general, Panama merchants opposed the unfair competition of vast United States government department stores, and argued that if only a part of the commissary trade were diverted to Panama the prosperity of the country would be assured. The right to trade with ships in passage through the Canal was no particular advantage to Panamanians, since the same unfair competition applied.[13]

---

11 Munro, *op. cit.*, 73–75.
12 Buell, *op. cit.*, 419
13 *Ibid.*, 419–424.

Treaty revision

Panamanian efforts to have many of these differences arbitrated failed. Nevertheless, in order to clear the way for the negotiation of a new treaty, the Congress authorized, and President Coolidge announced in May, 1924, the abrogation of the Taft Agreement. It was the belief of the State Department that the agreement was outmoded, since it had been negotiated only for the construction period of the Canal. A new treaty to replace the Taft Agreement and presumably to settle outstanding differences was signed on July 28, 1926.

This treaty never went into effect, for it was rejected by the Panamanian National Assembly in January, 1927. Thus, it is not necessary to consider it here in detail, except to note that instead of restricting the rights of the United States in the Zone it confirmed them, and virtually restored the Taft Agreement. In addition, the new treaty would have provided that Panama join the United States automatically in any war. It was this last provision, which was regarded as violative of Panama's obligations as a member of the League of Nations, plus the belief that the treaty gave more to the United States than to Panama, that caused the Panama Assembly to reject it.[14]

Following the rejection of the treaty of 1926 by its National Assembly, Panama continued its efforts to obtain more favorable canal treaty terms, but without success for the next ten years. In the meantime the Zone authorities indicated their intention to follow the rules of the Taft Agreement. Finally, Panama became the beneficiary of the new nonintervention policy pledged by Cordell Hull at Montevideo in 1933, for it was then necessary to delete from the 1903 treaty those provisions conveying interventionist rights to the United States. Also the devalued American dollar reduced the actual annual rental paid to Panama, and so raised the issue of increasing the amount of the payment. Although the negotiations were begun in 1934, it was not until March 2, 1936, that a General Treaty of Friendship and Cooperation was signed, and not until July 27, 1939, that it went into force.[15]

The General Treaty of 1936 dropped the guarantee by the United States of Panamanian independence. This, plus the renunciation of the right to intervene in Panama, removed the isthmian republic from classification as a virtual protectorate of the United States. The United States also renounced its right to expropriate additional lands and waters outside the Zone necessary for the support of the Canal, a privilege which the Panamanians felt had been abused in the past. Residence and commerce in the Zone were limited to certain specified classes of persons having employment there. The United States renounced its right to intervene in the cities of Colón and Panama and their surrounding territories to preserve order, as well as the right of eminent

[14] For the 1926 treaty negotiations, see *ibid.,* 424–426; also see S. Shepard Jones and Denys P. Myers, eds., *Documents on American Foreign Relations, July 1939-June 1940* (Boston: World Peace Foundation, 1940), II, 198.
[15] For text, see Jones and Myers, *Documents on American Foreign Relations,* II, 199–216.

domain. Panama was granted a corridor through the Zone to the city of Colón, legally accessible only by sea under the 1903 treaty. The annuity payment was increased from $250,000 to $430,000.

The new treaty also omitted United States guarantee of Panamanian independence as provided in the original treaty of 1903, but it stipulated that, in the event of a threat to the security of Panama or the Canal, both governments would consult together concerning measures that might be necessary to protect their common interests. Although the treaty of 1936 revoked many of the rights and obligations conveyed to the United States by the treaty of 1903, it was understood to be an amendment rather than a replacement of the old treaty.[16]

In contrast to the reception of the 1926 treaty, the Panamanian Assembly, on December 24, 1936, gave the new general treaty its prompt approval, while the United States Senate delayed its consent to ratification until July 25, 1939. The Senate particularly feared that, under this treaty, the United States might find its hands tied, in the event of a sudden emergency, by the necessity of obtaining Panama's consent for military measures. Senatorial fears were laid aside, however, when it was agreed by an exchange of diplomatic notes between the two governments in February, 1939, that the United States need not in the event of an emergency await the results of consultation before taking military action. This assurance that the United States could act first and consult afterward, plus the increasingly dangerous European situation, induced the Senate, on July 25, 1939, to approve ratification. Exchange of ratifications two days later put the treaty in force and established the United States on a friendlier basis with Panama just when the security of the Canal was to be subjected to its severest test.

A comparison of the treaty of 1936 with that of 1903 indicates that the protectorate status was ended, the right of eminent domain was terminated, the right to conduct business and to establish residence in the Canal Zone was more strictly limited, and the right to acquire territory outside the Zone was given up by the United States. Joint consultation was substituted for unilateral action in military emergencies, and measures were adopted to facilitate strengthening the Panamanian economy through paying a more equitable annuity, abolishing the free ports, and clarifying economic privileges of personnel connected with the Canal.

World War II and the base sites

The advent of World War II aroused the anxieties of the War and Navy Departments for the security of the Canal and prompted the United States to seek additional suitable sites outside the Zone from which to improve its defenses.[17] As a result of difficult and protracted negotiations, described

---

16 *U.S. Treaty Series,* Nos. 945 and 946.

17 For an excellent summary of these negotiations, see Almon R. Wright, "Defense Site Negotiations Between the United States and Panama, 1936–1948," Dept. of State *Bulletin,* XXVII (August 11, 1952), 212–219.

elsewhere in this volume,[18] an agreement was finally signed on May 18, 1942. By its terms the United States acquired jurisdiction over 134 sites ranging from small radar outposts to the 19,000 acre Rio Hato Air Base, about eighty miles southwest of Panama City. They were to be evacuated one year after the signing of a definitive treaty of peace. The rental fee was fixed at fifty dollars per hectare per year, excepting the Rio Hato site, for which the United States was to pay a flat rate of $10,000 per year. Concurrently, the United States agreed to a number of concessions desired by Panama, which included the transfer to Panama, at no cost, of the waterworks and sewage systems of Panama City and Colón, and the properties of the Panama Railroad Company in those cities not essential to the operation and protection of the Canal and the railroad.[19]

Despite its hard bargaining concerning the defense sites, the Panama government followed faithfully the lead of the United States in defense preparations both before and after December 7, 1941. When the United States government strained the traditional concepts of "neutrality" in the Canal and adjacent waters, the Republic of Panama obligingly acquiesced. In those prewar days the Panamanian merchant marine, largely American-owned, was able to ply belligerent waters from which United States ships were restrained by the Neutrality Act of 1937. After Pearl Harbor, Panama collaborated in many ways in assisting the United States to assure the security of Canal installations and in reducing the threat of the German U-Boat campaign in the Caribbean.[20]

After the war, the United States had, by May, 1947, returned to Panama most of the defense sites but sought to negotiate the retention of a few of them. On December 10 an agreement was signed granting to the United States the use of thirteen sites for technical installations for a period of five years, and the Rio Hato base for ten years. Since the agreement neglected to give Panama any kind of joint control over the sites, violent public protest developed marked by student demonstrations. As a result, the national assembly on December 23 rejected the agreement. The United States thereupon, probably with too precipitate haste, proceeded to abandon the sites, the last withdrawal being completed by mid-February, 1948.[21] Panamanian nationalism and resentment of United States policies toward Panama, associated with the vagaries of partisan politics, contributed to the defeat of the defense-sites agreements.

Panamanian dissatisfaction with the terms of the General Treaty of 1936 continued to mount to the point where the United States had to heed the

<hr>

[18] *Supra*, 138–139.

[19] For a discussion of the proposals and counterproposals of the United States and Panama, see Wright, *op. cit.*, 216–217.

[20] For the Panama Canal in time of war, see Norman J. Padelford, *The Panama Canal in Peace and War* (New York: The Macmillan Company, 1942), 124–180; also see Laurence D. Ealy, *The Republic of Panama in World Affairs, 1903–1950* (Philadelphia: University of Pennsylvania Press, 1951), 39–53, 105–124.

[21] Wright, *op. cit.*, 216–219.

demand for another treaty revision. As American expenditures, which had induced a wartime prosperity, progressively decreased in the postwar period and Panama began to encounter economic difficulties, requests for greater commercial advantages were revived. Panama also demanded a greater share of the Canal income in the form of increased annuity payments.[22]

After several exchanges of views and protracted and difficult negotiations, a new treaty was worked out and signed by both governments on January 25, 1955.[23] The United States was unwilling to accede to some of Panama's requests, especially those which, if accepted, might have weakened the jurisdictional position of the United States in the Canal Zone. It did, however, make a number of concessions which, taken together, contributed to strengthening Panama's economy and to improving the economic and social status of its subjects in connection with Canal Zone activities.

This treaty, like the 1936 convention, did not replace the 1903 treaty but merely altered it. The most important change in the existing arrangement was an increase in the annuity paid to Panama from $430,000 to $1,930,000, a concession made on the condition that the rights and jurisdictional position of the United States in the Zone be fully safeguarded. Further concessions to Panama included: (1) the right to tax the income of Canal Zone employees, with exception of United States citizens and armed forces personnel, and Zone residents not citizens of Panama; (2) transfer to Panama of certain lands under American jurisdiction, when no longer needed; (3) relinquishment by the United States of its right to prescribe and enforce sanitation measures in the cities of Panama and Colón; (4) alterations in the boundary between the city of Colón and the Canal Zone; (5) restrictions of commissary and import privileges of non-United States citizen employees of Canal Zone agencies who did not reside in the Zone; (6) relinquishment by the United States of its monopoly right to construct trans-Isthmian railroads and highways, though the status of the existing Panama Railroad was to remain unchanged; (7) authorization of Panama to impose import duties on certain goods entering the Zone; and (8) giving the Panamanian economy an increased share in the business of supplying the Zone market. For her part, Panama agreed to grant a renewable fifteen-year lease of some 19,000 acres in the Rio Hato region for the exclusive use of the United States in conducting maneuvers and military training.

By the "Memorandum of Understandings Reached," which accompanied the treaty, it was agreed that legislation by the United States Congress would be sought authorizing the establishment of a single basic wage level for all employees in a given category regardless of citizenship, though United States citizens could receive an overseas differential, an income tax allowance, and greater annual leave benefits. Equality of employment opportunities for Panamanian citizens was also promised, except where security considerations required the employment of United States citizens only, and the United

22 U.S. Dept. of State *Bulletin,* XXIII (August 1, 1955), 185.
23 For text, see *ibid.* (February 7, 1955), 238–243.

States government was to "evaluate, classify, and title" all positions in the Canal Zone without regard to nationality.[24]

The sovereignty issue

The terms of the treaty were probably equal to, if they did not exceed, the expectations of the Panamanian government, a fact attested by the prompt approval of the treaty, on March 9, 1955, by the National Assembly. Apparent Panamanian satisfaction with the new canal treaty, however, soon proved to be illusory when new tensions developed. The seizure of the Suez Canal by Egypt's Gamal Abdul Nasser, on July 26, 1956, stimulated ardent nationalists in the isthmian republic to claim similar rights of sovereignty over the Panama Canal. Expressions of dissatisfaction with the recently concluded treaty soon became commonplace. The successful efforts of the United States to exclude Panama from the 22-nation conference of maritime powers to discuss at London the Suez question only served to affront Panamanians whose president issued an angry denunciation of the United States government.[25] Also the failure of the United States to correct its discriminatory wage policy in the Zone, due to the failure of the Congress to enact the enabling legislation, acerbated relations.

The issue of sovereignty came to sharp focus in the fall of 1959. The Panamanians had for several years demanded that "the residual sovereignty" of Panama be recognized by the flying of the Panamanian flag alongside that of the United States in the Canal Zone. On November 3, 1959, the fifty-sixth anniversary of Panama's independence from Colombia, a student demonstration started as a peaceful march into the Zone to plant Panamanian flags as evidence of Panama's sovereignty. The students, considerably rein-forced, forced their way into the Zone where they were repulsed by Zone police. Then followed attacks on the American embassy, the consulate in Colón, and other United States-owned or occupied property. No lives were lost but there was some property damage. Another attempt, on November 28, to invade the Zone was checked handily by the combined forces of the United States and the Panamanian National Guard. These events were fol-lowed by a heated exchange of protests between the United States and Panama; the former claimed that the Panamanian authorities had failed to control the demonstrators, while Panama countered with complaints against police brutality.[26]

As a result of these demonstrations, in June, 1960, President Eisenhower approved a nine-point program for the Canal Zone designed to improve wages and job opportunities for Panamanians employed in the Zone, as well as housing and other living conditions for zonal workers. Later President Eisenhower ignored Congressional and Defense Department objections and

[24] *Ibid.*, XXIII (August 1, 1955), 186. The matter of wage differentials and employ-ment opportunities continued to be a source of Panamanian complaint.

[25] John D. Martz, *Central America: the Crisis and the Challenge* (Chapel Hill: Uni-versity of North Carolina Press, 1959), 311–313.

[26] U.S. Dept. of State *Bulletin,* XLI (November 23, 1959), 759–760.

ordered a limited display of Panama's flag within the Canal Zone. This gesture proved to be only a temporary palliative, for it was clear that the government of Panama would continue to agitate for "increased sovereignty." The Panamanians insisted that their flag fly alongside that of the United States *any time* and *anywhere* in the Zone, as well as on ships transiting the Canal.[27]

Negotiations toward further treaty revision

The subject of a general revision of the Canal treaty of 1955 was officially introduced by President Chiari in October, 1961. On November 2, President Kennedy responded to Chiari's proposal for treaty revision by indicating that he had ordered a "new and complete" examination "of the present and future needs of the United States with respect to the Panama Canal." Kennedy expressed the hope that, following the completion of this examination, actual negotiations between the two governments would begin early in 1962.

In June, 1962, President Chiari and President Kennedy entered into an agreement to appoint two representatives each to hold high-level talks concerning points of dissatisfaction with the existing Canal treaty. No reference was made to a new treaty or the basic issue of sovereignty of the Zone, the principal Panamanian concerns. Nor was any mention made of a larger annuity payment to Panama.[28]

The Joint Panama-United States Commission was composed of American Ambassador Joseph S. Farland and the Canal Zone Governor, Major General Robert J. Fleming, Jr., for the United States, and, for Panama, Foreign Minister Galileo Solís and former Foreign Minister Octavio Fábrega; it held periodic meetings to discuss points of friction between the two countries. On October 12, 1962, Under Secretary of State George W. Ball reported that, at the Joint Commission's suggestion arrangements had been made for flying the Panamanian flag in the Canal Zone. Shortly thereafter, on October 29, President Chiari and Major General Fleming participated in a brief flag-raising ceremony at which the flags of both countries were hoisted on the Canal Administration Building in Balboa. On October 12, 1962, the $20 million bridge over the Canal, built with United States funds under provision of the 1955 treaty, was dedicated. Disjointed Panama was at long last united.[29]

On January 10, 1963, the Joint Commission issued a communiqué announcing the status of its discussions. It was agreed that (1) the flag of Panama should be flown with the flag of the United States on land in the Canal Zone where the United States flag is flown officially by civilian authorities, and (2) foreign consuls holding Panamanian exequaturs should be permitted to function in the Zone. This was the extent of the Commission's agreements.

[27] *Hispanic American Report*, XIII (June, 1960), 236; *ibid* (November, 1960), 603.
[28] *Ibid.*, XV (August, 1962), 506. For text of the joint Chiari-Kennedy communiqué of June 13, 1962, see Dept. of State *Bulletin*, XLVII (July 9, 1962), 81–82.
[29] *Ibid.*, XLVII (October 29, 1962), 648; *Hisp. Am. Rep.*, XV (December, 1962), 900

The Panama government, by April, 1963, began to manifest considerable dissatisfaction with the slow progress of the Joint Commission which had been holding meetings since June, 1962. After nearly a year of negotiations only token agreements had been reached. In July, 1963, the Commission was dissolved by Acting President Chiari of Panama.[30] Considering the smouldering Panamanian resentments against the United States because of its alleged stalling tactics in consenting to a revision of the treaty, the explosive events of January, 1964, should not have been unexpected.

Panama crisis

It was another flag incident, quite similar to that of November 3, 1959, which sparked the explosion of January 9, 1964. American students, in willful disregard of the order of the Canal Zone Governor, on January 7, 1964, raised the American flag in front of the Balboa High School. Violence erupted on January 9 after Panamanian students tried unsuccessfully to raise Panama's flag in front of the high school. Quickly an angry mob, including Castroites and ultra-nationalists, armed with guns and Molotov cocktails, tried to force its way into the Zone but were held off by the Zone police and United States troops. The mob then vented its fury on American government and business offices in Panama City and Colón, and even threatened menacingly the American embassy building. In the rioting twenty-four persons, including four Americans, were killed and more than 200 were injured. The damage to American property was considerable. At no time did United States troops move into Panama territory. Most of the Panamanian casualties were the victims of their own rioting.

President Chiari characterized the use of firearms by the police and United States troops inside the Zone (to protect the lives and property of American citizens against an onrushing crowd of several thousand, and against snipers), as "acts of aggression," and immediately appealed to the OAS and the UN.

On January 10 the Inter-American Peace Committee of the OAS met pursuant to requests of Panama and the United States to consider the situation. By midnight of the same day the members of the committee were on their way to Panama to ascertain the facts. Because of the action already taken by the OAS, the UN Security Council merely addressed an appeal to the governments of the United States and Panama "to impose the utmost restraint upon the military forces and civilians of both countries in order to bring an end to the disorder and violence."[31]

When the OAS mediation commission, and a special United States mission headed by Assistant Secretary of State Thomas Mann, arrived in Panama, they found that President Chiari had suspended diplomatic relations with the United States because of its "unprovoked armed attack" against the territory and people of Panama, and had denounced the 1903 canal treaty.

[30] *Hisp. Am. Rep.*, XVI (June, 1963), 343.
[31] See "The Situation in Panama," Dept. of State *Bulletin*, L (February 3, 1964), 152–157.

Nothing less than a complete revision of the treaty would lead Panama to resume diplomatic relations.

The report of the Inter-American Peace Committee finding Panama's charges of aggression by the United States to be baseless did not alter Panamanian insistence on agreement by the United States to treaty revision. President Johnson, on the other hand, agreed to "review" all outstanding problems between the two countries, but objected to treaty revision under duress. Since the issue had become enmeshed in partisan politics in both countries a solution was long delayed.

The riots of January 9, 1964, and the ensuing brief period of suspended diplomatic relations were followed by a resumption of negotiations on United States treaty rights in Panama. The American people discovered — or at least were so informed by the experts — that the Canal was not so vital to United States defense as they had been led to believe and that since its importance was now more commercial than military the United States could well afford to make concessions to Panama. Moreover, the day had arrived to consider the construction of a sea-level canal on a site not necessarily in Panama.

2. *Relations with Nicaragua*

Next to Panama, the Central American country with which United States relations have been most intensive has been Nicaragua. This is attributable also to a canal factor — not a canal in being, but the fact that Nicaragua possesses one of the most desirable canal routes. That Nicaragua is situated geographically in the neighborhood of Panama would not alone call special attention to that country, and certainly the economic interests of American citizens there were not exceptional. This is not to deny, however, that diplomatic and armed protection were often employed. Nicaragua, more so than other Central American republics, has felt the brunt of the Caribbean policy of the United States.

Nineteenth-century relations

In the 1850's relations between the United States and Central America were jeopardized by the filibustering activities of the American soldier-of-fortune, William Walker, who invaded Nicaragua with a small force of adventurers and soon manipulated his "election" as president.[32] The United States denounced Walker's activities (1855-1860) as contrary to official American policy and disclaimed all connection with them. Meanwhile it continued its efforts to obtain transit rights across Nicaragua. In 1857 a treaty to this effect was concluded, but the Nicaraguan government refused to ratify it. In 1867, however, a treaty did become effective which granted the United States the right of transit, though not exclusive canal rights, since this was forbidden by the Clayton-Bulwer treaty.

[32] For an excellent account of Walker's expeditions, see W. O. Scroggs, *Filibusters and Financiers* (New York: The Macmillan Company, 1916).

Although the United States' interest in Nicaragua in the nineteenth century had been largely confined to the furtherance of its canal objectives, it also was a consistent supporter of Central American union, a policy which vitally affected Nicaragua. It refrained, however, from meddling in their affairs to bring this about. At the end of the century the Central American republics were no more united than before.[33]

The beginning of American intervention[34]

The advent of the twentieth century found the United States fully conscious of its special interests in the Caribbean — including Nicaragua — and willing to employ strong measures to enforce its hegemony. As for Nicaragua, political developments there were of such a nature as not to spare the Central American republic from energetic application of the "big stick."

Nicaragua was in the midst of one of the most tyrannical rules in its long history of political violence, fiscal corruption, and military dictatorship. General José Santos Zelaya, ostensibly a Liberal, governed the nation from 1893 to 1909 capriciously and arbitrarily; he also became involved in the internal affairs of neighboring states, which were kept in almost constant turmoil because of his efforts to create a Central American union by force and under his domination. Furthermore, he arbitrarily interfered with foreign trade and investments, flouted the rights of foreigners in the country, and was completely irresponsible with respect to his financial obligations abroad. Although he entertained no scruples against intervening himself in Central American affairs, he strenuously opposed the interference of the United States, which, while favorably disposed toward political cooperation and unity in Central America, would not countenance any attempt by Zelaya to bring about union by force.

When Zelaya persisted in disturbing the entire Central American area, his Conservative opponents, with financial assistance from Americans and other foreign business interests in the country, and with no little encouragement from the United States government, revolted in October, 1909. The United States remained neutral, but when Zelaya ordered the execution of two Americans who were serving as officers in the revolutionary army, it severed diplomatic relations and denounced him in no uncertain terms.[35] Upon Zelaya's resignation, one of his confederates assumed the presidency, but his tenure was short-lived because of the refusal of the commander of American naval forces to permit the bombardment of Bluefields, an unfortified port city.

Despite the overthrow of Zelaya and his puppet, stability and order in Nicaragua were still far-distant. Liberals and Conservatives, traditionally

[33] For Central American union, see Thomas L. Karnes, *The Failure of Union: Central America, 1824–1960* (Chapel Hill: University of North Carolina Press, 1961).

[34] The best general surveys of United States-Nicaraguan relations during the period of the American intervention are: *The United States and Nicaragua: A Survey of the Relations from 1909 to 1932.* Dept. of State Latin-American Series No. 6 (Washington, D.C., Government Printing Office, 1932); and Isaac J. Cox, *Nicaragua and the United States, 1909–1927* (Boston: World Peace Foundation, 1927).

[35] *For. Rel.*, 1909, 446–459; *ibid.*, 1910, 739–767; Harold N. Denny, *Dollars for Bullets* (New York: The Dial Press, 1929), 79–83; Cox, *op. cit.*, 708.

bitter political rivals, each had their aspirants to the presidency. General Juan J. Estrada, a Liberal and former Zelaya partisan, was awarded the provisional presidency because of his role in overthrowing Zelaya, but the Conservatives, who constituted a majority of the victorious forces, strongly opposed his continuance in office.

In an attempt to resolve the question of determining a permanent president for Nicaragua, the United States proffered its good offices through Thomas C. Dawson, who had negotiated the financial arrangement with the Dominican Republic in 1905. On October 27, 1910, he signed a series of agreements with Estrada, Díaz, General Luis Mena, and General Emiliano Chamorro, the principal pretenders to the presidency. The Dawson Agreement provided for the election of a constituent assembly which would subsequently elect Estrada as president and Díaz as vice-president for a two-year term, at the expiration of which Estrada would be ineligible for re-election.[36] On December 31, 1910, the constituent assembly elected Estrada and Díaz president and vice-president, respectively, for a term of two years beginning on January 1, 1911, and this government was immediately recognized by the United States.

Observance of the Dawson Agreement soon broke down. Cabinet dissensions developed, and President Estrada, following a dispute with his Minister of War, General Mena, resigned on May 9, 1911. Adolfo Díaz became president and was recognized by the United States, but the real head of the government was General Mena.[37] In October, 1911, in contravention of the Dawson Agreement, which provided for free election by the people, the Nicaraguan assembly, completely under Mena's control, elected him president to succeed Díaz on January 1, 1913.

President Díaz reacted to Mena's irregular election by demanding his resignation as Minister of War, to which position General Emiliano Chamorro, a Conservative leader, was appointed. Mena fled the capital city, Managua, to launch a new revolt. Faced with formidable opposition from Mena, President Díaz requested intervention by the United States to keep himself in power and to protect the lives and property of Americans and other foreigners. Following the landing of American Marines at strategic points in the country, most of the revolutionaries abandoned the movement; General Mena surrendered in September, 1912. The Liberals once again had been defeated, thanks largely to the policy of the United States "to take the necessary measures for an adequate legation guard at Managua, to keep open communications, and to protect American life and property."[38] It seems that the United States had not only repudiated the tyrant Zelaya, but also the Liberals, who were in the majority.

Although order was restored, a detachment of 100 American Marines was retained in Managua to insure continuing stability.[39] With the military and

---

[36] *For. Rel.,* 1911, 652–653, 625–627; Cox, *op. cit.,* 710–713.
[37] *For. Rel.,* 1911, 650–661.   [38] *Ibid.,* 1912, 1043, 1052–1057.
[39] *Ibid.,* 1912, 1061–1064. For the "first" military intervention, see Cox, *op. cit.,* 716–719; also, see Clyde H. Metcalf, *A History of the United States Marine Corps*

diplomatic support of the United States, Díaz was able to get himself re-elected for a four-year term and to continue in the presidency until 1917. Thus began a period of American intervention in Nicaraguan affairs which turned the country into a virtual protectorate of the United States.

Efforts at financial rehabilitation

Having stabilized the political situation in Nicaragua, the United States government proceeded to try to correct the country's financial difficulties, which were particularly acute. By 1911 the Nicaraguan government had accumulated a foreign debt far beyond its capacity to liquidate, resulting in its falling into arrears to its creditors, most of whom were Europeans. As the foreign bondholders pressed their demands for diplomatic intervention to their claims, the United States became concerned, and on June 6, 1911, signed the Knox-Castrillo treaty relating to financial rehabilitation. Under this treaty Nicaragua was to refund her existing debt by obtaining a loan secured by her customs revenues, and to place the administration of the customs in the hands of an official approved by the President of the United States. Although the convention was promptly ratified by the Nicaraguan government, it was rejected by the United States Senate, despite strong approval by President Taft.[40]

Despite the failure to secure a large loan from American bankers because of the Senate's refusal to approve the Knox-Castrillo treaty, the Nicaraguan government succeeded in obtaining a short-term loan of $1 million from United States bankers for the establishment of a national bank, currency reform, and the organization of a claims commission. To insure repayment, an American, appointed by the Nicaraguan government on the nomination of the bankers and the approval of the State Department, was to be placed in charge of the customs collection.[41]

Since it appeared that the United States Senate would never approve the Knox-Castrillo treaty, both the Nicaraguan government and its foreign creditors looked to the United States for relief. In an effort to secure additional funds, Nicaragua proposed, in December, 1912, to sell to the United States, for the sum of $3 million, the exclusive right to construct a canal across its territory. A treaty including provisions similar to the Platt Amendment with Cuba, was signed in February, 1913, but it failed of ratification in the United States Senate.

A new treaty, the Bryan-Chamorro treaty, was signed on August 5, 1914, omitting the right of American intervention. Its principal provisions were: a grant to the United States of exclusive rights necessary for the construction

---

(New York: G. T. Putnam's Sons, 1939), 410–416; and United States Marine Corps, *The United States Marines in Nicaragua,* Historical Series No. 21 (Prepared by Historical Branch, G-3 Div., Hq., U.S.M.C. Washington, D.C., 1961, rev. ed., mimeo), 8–15.

[40] *For. Rel.,* 1912, 1071–1078.

[41] *Ibid.,* 1911, 625–647; Dept. of State, *A Brief History of the Relations Between the United States and Nicaragua,* 1909–1928 (Washington, D.C., Government Printing Office, 1921), 14–15.

of an interoceanic canal through Nicaraguan territory; a 99-year lease to the United States of the Great and Little Corn Islands; a 99-year lease to the site for a naval base on Nicaraguan territory bordering upon the Gulf of Fonseca; payment by the United States of the sum of $3 million to be applied upon the Nicaraguan Republic's indebtedness in a manner to be determined by the two high contracting parties; and the added amendment that nothing in the convention was intended to affect any existing right of Costa Rica, El Salvador, or Honduras. The amending clause had been added to allay the complaints of the three Central American republics.[42]

El Salvador and Honduras claimed equal rights with Nicaragua in the Gulf of Fonseca and protested that the establishment of a naval base on the Nicaraguan shore would violate their rights of condominium in the gulf. Further, it was held that the treaty would violate the Washington treaties of 1907 which proclaimed the neutrality of Honduras, including its rights in the Gulf of Fonseca. Likewise, Costa Rica protested the canal convention because it infringed her rights in the San Juan River which would be part of the canal route. While not opposed to a canal treaty with the United States, Costa Rica was offended by the fact that it had not been considered in the secret negotiations. Both Costa Rica and El Salvador indicated willingness to enter into separate treaties with the United States, but, though the American ministers were instructed to initiate negotiations, no progress was recorded. The case of the canal treaty which was submitted to the Central American Court of Justice is considered later in this present chapter.

The Bryan-Chamorro treaty encountered stiff opposition in the United States Senate, which delayed its ratification for about two years. Costa Rican claims against Nicaragua were given a hearing, and accusations of unfair and fraudulent dealings were made against the New York bankers. Also, it was charged, with a considerable basis of fact, that the United States was dealing with a puppet government which it had placed in power and which did not truly represent a majority of the Nicaraguan people.[43] On the other hand, the Wilson administration defended the treaty as a means of ending the constant disorder in Nicaragua which endangered American lives and property, and which posed a threat to the Monroe Doctrine.

The State Department, despite its earlier commitment to the bankers, opposed payment to them of the entire $3 million provided by the treaty, since numerous claimants, chiefly American and British, were also demanding payment. The Department finally prevailed on the bankers to agree to postponement of a part of the amounts due if the Nicaraguan government would adopt a general program for the adjustment of its debts. After lengthy negotiations a general plan of financial control was worked out. Under this program, known as the "financial plan of 1917,"[44] the American bankers agreed to a further extension by accepting treasury bills to cover half of this

[42] Cox, *op. cit.*, 722–724.
[43] *Ibid.*, 725–728. Also, see Ireland, *op. cit.*, 200–209.
[44] Munro, *op. cit.*, 236–238.

loan, and British bondholders also agreed to extention upon receiving the accrued interest on their bonds.

The financial plan of 1917 also provided for a High Commission composed of two Americans designated by the State Department and one Nicaraguan appointed by his government, to assist in preparing the Nicaraguan budget, act as fiscal agent, and arbitrate cases of disagreement between the collector-general of customs and the Nicaraguan government. The collector-general was to continue to administer the customs until both the treasury bills and the British bonds, as well as the new bonds to be issued in payment of claims, were paid off. The plan also provided for the adjustment of the floating debt by a new claims commission, composed of a Nicaraguan member, a resident American member, and an American umpire. This commission adjudicated all claims against the government, awarding a total of $5,304,386 out of a claimed $13,500,000.[45]

During the next three years (1917-1920), Nicaragua's financial situation improved remarkably. By mid-1920 all of the principal of the treasury bills and the arrears due on the British bonds had been paid. In 1920 a new financial plan was drawn up, though it did not materially change the system of financial control established in 1917. Under this plan the Nicaraguan government, by repurchasing from the bankers the stock which they had purchased in 1913, regained full ownership of the Pacific Railroad and the National Bank. These transactions removed the American bankers from any direct financial interest in Nicaragua, though the customs collectorship and the High Commission established under contract with them, were continued to insure payment to the bondholders.[46]

Efforts at political stabilization: first stage

General Emiliano Chamorro, a Conservative, who as minister to the United States had negotiated the canal treaty in 1914, was elected president in 1916. With continuing American support, he remained in the presidency until 1920.

The United States again played a significant if not decisive role in the presidential election of 1920 to determine Chamorro's successor. The presence of the American Marines in the Nicaraguan capital left the impression that the United States government was determined to insure the continuance of a Conservative administration, with the result that the opposition Liberals became convinced they could not expect to gain control of the government by election. In an attempt to reassure the Liberals of this impression, the State Department urged the Nicaraguan government to reform the electoral system before the next election. This the outgoing President Chamorro failed to do. Amid violent protests from the Liberals that the election in 1920 was not honest, President Chamorro's uncle, Diego Manuel Chamorro, was chosen as his successor and the Conservatives stayed in power.[47]

[45] Howland, *op. cit.*, 184.
[46] Munro, *op. cit.*, 238–239; *Relations Between the United States and Nicaragua,* 19–21.
[47] *Ibid.*, 21–22.

Although accepting the outcome of this election, the United States government renewed its "suggestions" for reform of the electoral laws and machinery. This time the Nicaraguan government responded by accepting the services of an American, Dr. Harold W. Dodds, in drafting a new electoral law which was approved by the Nicaraguan congress in March, 1923. The prospects for a fair election at the end of President Diego Chamorro's term in 1924 induced the United States to consider withdrawal of the Marines. The State Department felt, however, that withdrawal should be contingent upon the effective administration of the new electoral law in the forthcoming election in 1924, and the Nicaraguan government accepted this proposal.

In the meantime, however, President Diego Chamarro died on October 12, 1923, and was succeeded by Vice-President Bartolomé Martínez to serve out his unexpired term. When Martínez declared his candidacy for election in 1924 for the next full term, the United States protested on the ground that the Nicaraguan constitution forbade self-succesion to the presidency. Martínez withdrew and threw his support to a Liberal-Conservative coalition offering Carlos Solórzano, a Conservative of Managua, for president, and Dr. Juan B. Sacasa, a Liberal from León, for vice-president. In an election replete with fraud perpetrated by the outgoing Martínez, who refused a United States offer to supervise a fair election, Solórzano was elected over his Conservative opponent, General Emiliano Chamorro. Because of "patent election frauds" the United States at first refused to recognize Solórzano, but when he promised to conduct free elections in 1928, and made other pledges requested by the United States, his government was recognized. The legation guard was withdrawn in August, 1925.[48]

The need for the return of the Marines was not long delayed, for within less than a month after their withdrawal a new revolution headed by General Chamorro broke out. Despite warnings by the United States that it would not recognize a government established by revolution, Chamorro proceeded to oust Solórzano and put himself in the presidency. In accordance with a 1923 treaty providing for nonrecognition of revolutionary governments, the United States and the other Central American countries refused to recognize the new Nicaraguan regime. The refusal of the United States to recognize Chamorro encouraged Vice-President Juan Sacasa, who had fled the country, to claim the presidency and seek the intercession of the American government. The United States responded, however, by informing him that, although it would never recognize Chamorro, it was under no obligation under the 1923 treaty to establish a constitutional government in Nicaragua, and would view with disfavor any attempt by Sacasa or anyone else to restore the constitutional regime by armed force.[49]

Despite this warning, the Liberals, led by Dr. Sacasa and General José María Moncada, revolted in mid-1926 but with indecisive results. In October, upon the insistence of the United States, President Chamorro entered into

---

[48] *Ibid.*, 22–28; Cox, *op. cit.*, 773–776.
[49] Howland, *op. cit.*, 188.

negotiations with the revolting Liberals in the Corinto conference; but when no agreement could be reached on the question of succession to the presi-· dency, hostilities were resumed. Realizing his inability to stay in power, Chamorro resigned the presidency. A reconstructed congress, on November 11, elected ex-President Adolfo Díaz, a Conservative, to the presidency, to fill out the unexpired term of Solórzano. Despite claims by the Liberals that the election of Díaz was unconstitutional and that Sacasa was entitled to the presidency, the United States supported the constitutionality of Díaz' election, and, on November 17, recognized his government when he promised to grant amnesty to his opponents and to invite them to participate in his administration. Unable to suppress the Liberals with his own resources, President Díaz appealed to the United States for assistance in preserving order and in protecting American lives and property, attributing his inability to do so to Mexican support of the revolutionists.[50] The United States did not immediately respond to this request.

Repeating his claim that he was legally entitled to the presidency, and with Mexican support, Dr. Sacasa landed at Puerto Cabezas on December 1, 1926, and set up what he declared to be the constitutional government of Nicaragua. As Sacasa's successes continued, it became evident that the Liberals were receiving substantial aid in arms and ammunition from Mexican sources, some from the Mexican government itself. Mexico recognized Sacasa as the rightful president of Nicaragua, the only country to do so.

The involvement of Mexico in Nicaragua's civil war was viewed with great concern by the United States government, for this was regarded as an attempt to extend Mexican influence over not only Nicaragua but the entire Central American area. It was imperative, therefore, that American Marines be employed to forestall a Mexican-supported Liberal victory. Friction between the United States and Mexico arising from the Nicaraguan affair was aggravated by the anti-foreign land and petroleum legislation in Mexico.

Efforts at political stabilization: second stage

Although the United States rejected a proposal by Díaz in February, 1927, calling for a treaty by which "the territorial integrity and internal stability" of Nicaragua would be guaranteed, the United States government continued to take measures for the protection of American lives and property in the strife-torn country. American warships were sent to several Nicaraguan ports; neutral zones were established at the principal towns on the east coast and along the railroad from the coast to the capital, thus restricting Liberal operations, and the legation guard of Marines was re-established in Managua.[51]

---

[50] *Relations Between the United States and Nicaragua*, 28–37. Vice-President Sacasa probably lost any prospect of U.S. support when he sought Mexican aid. President Calles deliberately harassed Washington by extending moral and military support to Sacasa. The amount of Mexican aid has never been ascertained.

[51] For the "second" military intervention in Nicaragua (from the Marine angle), see Metcalf, *op. cit.*, 416 ff; and U.S.M.C., *Marines in Nicaragua*, 17 ff. Also see Cox, *op. cit.*, 783–809.

By March 15, 1927, some 2,000 American troops were ashore in Nicaragua, and a full-scale military intervention was under way. The United States also took other measures to assist the Díaz government. The embargo on the export of American arms to Nicaragua, imposed by President Coolidge in September, 1926, was relaxed so as to permit the sale of arms by private concerns to the government, a measure taken principally to offset the large quantities of military equipment reaching the Liberals from Mexico and other outside sources. In February, 1927, the United States government itself sold surplus arms and ammunition to Díaz.

It soon became apparent, however, that American involvement in Nicaragua was becoming very unpopular in the United States.[52] Moreover, the intervention in Nicaragua was causing increasing resentment throughout Latin America, severely damaging to United States prestige in the hemisphere.

Despite the unpopularity of its actions, the United States government felt that it had no choice but to sustain the Díaz government in power, in the meantime making every effort toward reconciling the opposing political groups. Convinced of the correctness of his administration's policy, and of the necessity to defend it against the avalanche of public and Congressional criticism, President Coolidge, in a special message to Congress on January 10, 1927, went to great pains to justify the steps which his government had taken in Nicaragua. After reviewing the situation in considerable detail, and referring especially to Mexican assistance to the revolutionists, Coolidge indicated that he would take whatever measures were necessary to protect American lives and property, maintain stability and constitutional government in Nicaragua, protect the canal interests and rights of the United States in both Panama and Nicaragua, and protect American interests which were jeopardized by outside influences or foreign powers.[53]

President Coolidge, in April, 1927, sent Henry L. Stimson to Nicaragua as his personal representative to negotiate a settlement if possible.[54] Mr. Stimson, after a thorough study of the situation, concluded that the only practicable solution was for Díaz to continue in office until a new constitutional government could be selected in an honestly conducted election supervised by the United States. Supervised elections would also require the maintenance of American Marines in the country until an effective Nicaraguan constabulary could be organized and trained to maintain order. On the basis of Stimson's suggestions, President Díaz agreed to make peace with the Liberal revolutionists on the following terms: (1) immediate cessation of hostilities and surrender of all arms into American custody; (2) general amnesty and return

---

[52] For criticism of the Nicaraguan intervention, see Bryce Wood, *The Making of the Good Neighbor Policy* (New York: Columbia University Press, 1961), 14–18.

[53] *For. Rel.*, 1927, III, 288–298.

[54] For Mr. Stimson's account of his mission, see his *American Policy in Nicaragua* (New York: Charles Scribner's Sons, 1927). For efforts to organize a native constabulary, see Marvin Goldwert, *The Constabulary in the Dominican Republic and Nicaragua*. Latin American Monograph Series No. 17 (Gainesville: University of Florida Press, 1962), 22–47.

of exiles and restitution of confiscated property; (3) participation of the Liberals in the Díaz government; (4) organization of a nonpartisan constabulary under American officers; (5) completion of Diaz' term of office, whereupon the 1928 and subsequent elections would be supervised by American authorities; and (6) temporary continuance of a sufficient force of Marines to insure the enforcement of the peace terms.[55]

Convinced of the determination of the United States to enforce the terms thus proposed, and of the futility of continued resistance against the Americans, General Moncada, the commander of the revolting Liberals, held a conference with Mr. Stimson at Tipitapa on May 4, 1927, which resulted in the so-called Stimson-Moncada Agreement calling for the implementation of Díaz' proposals. When Stimson insisted that the United States would not tolerate continued efforts to overthrow Díaz, Moncada had little difficulty in persuading his troops to lay down their arms.[56] Díaz for his part carried out the peace terms as promised with a minimum of difficulty. The troops on both sides were disarmed; the organization and training of the native constabulary, the *Guardia Nacional,* by American officers was begun; American Marines took charge of maintaining order until the organization of the constabulary was completed; the congress, courts, and local governments were reconstituted to accommodate Liberals; and a claims commission with an American chairman was set up to adjudicate all claims against the Nicaraguan government arising out of the civil war. The only serious difficulty encountered in the pacification of the country came from one of the Liberal generals, César Augusto Sandino, who refused to accept the peace settlement, and withdrew his forces into the interior to harass the constitutional government. Since his operations were confined to a remote part of the country, all efforts to capture him or to persuade him to surrender were unsuccessful. In fact, his resistance aroused great admiration in other parts of Latin America, where he was regarded not as a bandit, but as the great champion of Nicaraguan independence against the "North American imperialists."

In preparing for the election of 1928, the United States agreed to a proposal by President Díaz to establish an electoral commission with an American chairman to supervise the election, and to retain the Marines in the country to insure electoral supervision. The Marines, in the performance of their assigned task of policing the country prior to the 1928 elections, were engaged in a number of brushes with Sandino rebels. The most serious clash occurred at Ocotal on July 15, 1927, between a force of 500 to 600 men under Sandino and a small detachment of Marines. Thanks to the opportune arrival of Marine bombing planes the detachment was rescued with only one killed and four wounded.[57] In the election held on November 4, 1928, General Moncada, the Liberal war hero, was an overwhelming victor and was

[55] *Relations Between the United States and Nicaragua,* 46–53.
[56] Stimson, *op. cit.,* Chap. II.
[57] Metcalf, *op. cit.,* 424–427; Cox, *op. cit.,* 803–805.

inaugurated on January 1, 1929. In an effort to assure peaceful elections in the future, the leaders of the two political parties agreed that the United States should supervise the presidential election of 1932, as well as the congressional elections in 1930.[58]

Because of Sandino's continuing insurgent activities, with which the newly created *Guardia Nacional* was not yet sufficiently organized and trained to deal, the American Marines were retained though sharply reduced in number. When the *Guardia* was believed strong enough to deal with Sandino, and other possible internal disturbances, on February 13, 1931, the United States government announced its intention to withdraw by June of that year all Marines except officers instructing the *Guardia,* the latter to be removed after the 1932 election.

In April, 1931, when all available *Guardia* and Marine forces were engaged in relief work necessitated by a highly destructive earthquake in Managua, Sandino renewed his military activities, killing several civilians, including nine Americans. Despite criticism by the American press and Congress for its inaction, the United States government refused to provide special military protection to Americans living in the interior of the country. Instead, Secretary Stimson informed our nationals that if they felt endangered, they should withdraw from the country, or at least go to the coastal towns where they could be protected or evacuated.[59] This was quite a reversal from the policy pursued in Nicaragua only a few years before (1927), when President Coolidge showed no reluctance whatever to intervene to protect American lives and property. It reflected the Hoover-Stimson policy of liquidating American intervention in general, and the Nicaraguan venture in particular.

The efforts of the Hoover administration to bring American involvement in Nicaragua to an end were aided by the new spirit of cooperation displayed by the Nicaraguans themselves. As promised before his election in 1928, President Moncada requested and received the assistance of the United States in the supervision of the congressional election of 1930, and the presidential election of 1932 in which Dr. Sacasa was the candidate of the Liberals and Adolfo Díaz the Conservative standard bearer. In the election, which was accepted by both parties as an honest one, Dr. Sacasa emerged the winner by a substantial margin. The United States then took steps toward completing its withdrawal from Nicaragua; and on January 2, 1933, the day after Sacasa's inauguration, the last contingent of Marines was withdrawn.

Immediately after his inauguration, President Sacasa initiated negotiations with General Sandino, which resulted in an agreement to lay down his arms. Trouble still persisted, however, and in January, 1934, following a clash between *Sandinistas* and the *Guardia,* Sacasa demanded total disarmament of Sandino's forces. Subsequently, on February 21, 1934, Sandino met with Sacasa at the presidential palace to discuss the matter, but upon departing he and his aides were murdered by palace guardsmen. No serious effort was

[58] *Relations Between the United States and Nicaragua,* 80–89.
[59] *For. Rel.,* 1931, II, 808.

made to apprehend Sandino's murderers, though General Anastasio Somoza, commander of the *Guardia,* was accused of complicity in the assassination.

The American intervention in Nicaragua was unfortunate because of all the major interventions in the Caribbean it was the most difficult to justify. Consequently there was good reason for its universal condemnation in Latin America, and whole-hearted regret in the United States. Although it may have contributed in small measure to stability and order in Nicaragua for a few years, it certainly did not promote the development of democratic principles. That the twenty-year domination of the tiny republic averted European intervention was highly improbable. Nor did the relatively meager economic interests of American citizens in the republic warrant such drastic protective measures. In short, one would be hard put to prove that the national interests of the United States were served by the whole sorry business. Perhaps, unfortunately, the most tangible of United States contributions was the *Guardia Nacional,* trained by the Marines. When the Americans left in 1933, Nicaragua was at the mercy of the *Guardia* and its adroit leader, General Anastasio Somoza, who, in 1936, forced himself into the presidency of the country, a post which he held with an iron grip until his assassination by a palace guard in 1956. Since "Tacho" Somoza was generally friendly toward, and cooperative with, the United States, relations were remarkably devoid of serious incidents. If friendly relations with a dictator can be justified, Somoza supplied the State Department with substantial reasons for its support.

3. The Promotion of Central American Unity and Stability

It was after the turn of the century, when the Caribbean became a focal point of American diplomacy, that the American government adopted a policy of active participation in the promotion of Central American peace and stability, a policy which inevitably increased the influence of the United States in the internal affairs of those countries. This new policy was best reflected by the participation of the United States in the building of peace machinery for the settlement of Central American disputes, and in the promotion of stable and constitutional government in each country. To achieve these ends, the United States at first offered to act as friendly mediator but, when this failed to bring results, it assumed the role of an active interventer.

The United States and efforts at Central American unity, 1900–1920

After 1900 Central American regionalism continued to manifest itself in many ways, but obstacles to political union seemed too great to overcome. The republics nevertheless entered into a series of treaties that provided a practical form of collaboration. The United States contributed materially to the success of this effort.

With all of the Central American republics in attendance, a conference convened in Washington in November, 1907, to discuss the problems of their mutual relations. A number of treaties were signed, the most important of these being the General Treaty of Peace and Amity, which provided for: maintenance of peace and compulsory juridical settlement of all disputes; the neutralization of Honduras, "the cockpit" of Central America; prohibiting the organizing of revolutions against the government of another Central American state; constitutional reform prohibiting presidential re-election; no intervention in favor of either party contending in a civil war; and nonrecognition of any government that came into existence by revolution.[60]

Another treaty provided for the establishment of a Central American Court of Justice, composed of one judge each for the five Central American States. This Court — installed in Cartago, Costa Rica, on May 25, 1908 — was to decide all cases of every kind arising between the contracting members. The creation of the Court, regarded as the first of its kind anywhere in the world, was applauded as an historic step toward the establishment of peace and stability in Central America. The Court failed, and it was unfortunate that the United States was an indirect contributor to its demise.[61]

The Court seemed doomed to failure from the beginning, since the judges, rather than voting impartially as was the intent of its founders, voted strictly as the interests of their own governments dictated. Not only did the judges act politically, but the Court's prestige suffered because of rejections of some of its verdicts. Although its reputation was already tarnished, the event which precipitated its final collapse was the rejection by Nicaragua, with United States support, of its rulings on the Bryan-Chamorro treaty.

In 1916 Costa Rica and El Salvador complained to the Court that their rights had been violated by the Bryan-Chamorro treaty entered into by Nicaragua and the United States. Despite Nicaragua's refusal to admit the Court's jurisdiction it handed down decisions that went against Nicaragua in both cases; that is, the Court ruled that (1) the rights of Costa Rica in the San Juan River boundary had been violated, and (2) the establishment of an American naval base in the Gulf of Fonseca would menace the security of El Salvador and would violate her rights of condominium in the Gulf.

Nicaragua, with the support of the United States, refused to accept the Court's decision.[62] The cases involving the Bryan-Chamorro treaty were the last to come before the Central American Court. On March 9, 1917, Nicaragua gave the required year's notice of intention to abrogate the treaty which had established the Court. On March 12, 1918, the tribunal was formally dissolved. Obviously the behavior of the United States was damaging to its

---

[60] For an account of the Conference, see *For. Rel.*, 1907, Pt. II, 665–727. Also, see R. L. Buell, "The United States and Central American Stability," *For. Pol. Rep.*, VII, No. 9 (July 8, 1931), 166–169.

[61] For a complete history of the court, see Manly O. Hudson, "The Central American Court of Justice," *American Journal of International Law*, XXVI (October, 1932), 759–786.

[62] *For. Rel.*, 1916, 832.

prestige in Central America, for it seemed that judicial settlement of international disputes, which it had strongly advocated, was not intended for itself.

The United States and Central American unity, 1920–1933

Although the collapse of the Central American Court of Justice seemed to remove the most important prop of the treaty structure erected in 1907, the ideal of Central American union persisted. In 1920 all five of the republics drew up a pact of union, but the project, although endorsed by the United States, collapsed because of revolution in Guatemala.

The general political situation in Central America deteriorated so badly in 1922 and 1923 that the United States urged a meeting of the five Central American governments to promote closer and more amicable cooperation. Their representatives met in Washington from December 4, 1922, to February 7, 1923, under the chairmanship of Secretary of State Charles E. Hughes, and produced a number of agreements which in general reaffirmed the principles laid down in the treaties of 1907.[63] Among these contributions to the formal inter-American pattern of cooperation and security was the International Central American Tribunal. The Tribunal, unlike the ill-fated Central American Court, was not intended to be either permanent or compulsory, but, like the Hague Court, was merely a panel from which judges could be selected.

One of the most important provisions of the new General Treaty of Peace and Amity obligated the contracting parties to refrain from interfering in another's internal affairs. It also provided that revolutionary administrations should not be recognized until after a free election.

Although these and other measures taken at the Washington conference of 1923 fell far short of creating a political union, they did provide a strong basis for regional cooperation. For several years thereafter the Central American scene was relatively quiet insofar as international conflicts were concerned, though this tranquillity was doubtless due more to the determination of the United States to keep peace in the area than to the peace instruments themselves.

Since one of the major purposes of the Washington conference was to devise means to discourage the revolutionary overthrow of constitutional governments in Central America, the United States announced that it would adopt as its own the same policy adopted by the Central American states — that of denying diplomatic recognition to revolutionary regimes. An early test of the new *de jure* recognition policy came in Honduras when, in 1923, following a civil war and an agreement to hold new elections, the United States forced the withdrawal of the candidacy of General Tiburcio Carías by declaring that it would not recognize a government established by him because of his participation in the revolution. Another test of the policy occurred in 1930 when General Manuel Orellana led a military revolt which overthrew the

[63] For the conference of 1923, see R. L. Buell, "The United States and Central American Revolutions," *For. Pol. Rep.*, VII, No. 10 (July 22, 1931), 190–193.

Guatemalan president. The threat of the United States not to recognize his revolutionary government forced Orellana's retirement.[64]

The propriety of the nonrecognition policy of the United States soon came to be questioned, however, since it was viewed by many Central Americans as a form of interference in the internal affairs of the country whose government was overthrown. Moreover, it was felt that the policy discouraged justifiable revolts against repressive and unpopular regimes. On the other hand, since no Central American government could expect to exist very long if it failed of diplomatic support by the United States, the nonrecognition policy no doubt discouraged many potential revolutionists from starting revolts which had no purpose other than personal gratification. However effective the American policy of nonrecognition was in promoting stable and constitutional governments in Central America, it came to be regarded more as an instrument to insure governments friendly to the United States than as a device to foster governments responsive to the popular will.

Not only did nonrecognition as practiced by the United States raise objections in Central America, but the device of withholding recognition of revolutionary governments became increasingly unpopular among the Central Americans themselves. When a military *coup* led by General Hernández Martínez forced the resignation of President Arujo of El Salvador in December, 1931, a serious split developed among the five republics which led to the complete collapse of the policy. At first the United States, as well as the four other Central American governments, refused to recognize the Martínez regime because of its revolutionary origin. Costa Rica soon reversed its policy, however, extending recognition to the Martínez government, and denouncing the treaty of 1923. When El Salvador also denounced the treaty, the United States in January, 1934, proposed to the remaining states that they join it in extending recognition. This marked the end of the nonrecognition policy of the United States in its Central American relations. Thereafter it returned to its traditional *de facto* policy.[65]

Other United States involvements in Central American affairs, 1900–1933

Since the predominant interest of the United States in Central America during the early decades of the twentieth century was the prevention of international conflict and the promotion of stable government, it naturally followed that American diplomacy was particularly concerned with the problem of public finance which plagued all of the countries in the area. This problem became especially acute between 1910 and 1920, when the financial situation of certain governments threatened to create international complications. In order to forestall European intervention for the collection of public debts, the United States, as already noted in the cases of Haiti, the Dominion Republic,

[64] *Ibid.*, 193–197.
[65] *For. Rel.*, 1934, V, 216–256. For the problem of Tinoco, see Buell, "The United States and Central American Revolutions," *For. Pol. Rep.*, VII, No. 10 (July 22, 1931), 180–183; also *For. Rel.*, 1917, 306–308.

and Nicaragua, undertook to lend its assistance in the financial rehabilitation of delinquent governments. This policy, often identified as "dollar diplomacy," was given its most vigorous application by President Taft's Secretary of State, Philander Knox.

By 1910, all five of the Central American republics were delinquent in all or part of their foreign indebtedness, the most critical situation existing in Nicaragua and Honduras. Since the Nicaraguan question has already been discussed, attention will focus here on the efforts of the United States to remedy Honduras' chaotic financial condition. By 1908 the country owed no less than $124 million. In that year a group of British bondholders, known as the Council of Foreign Bondholders, and diplomatically supported by the British government, proposed an arrangement for refunding the Honduran debt. When the United States government objected to the scheme because it failed to safeguard properly the interests of Honduras' American creditors, the Honduran government, in April, 1909, turned to the United States for assistance in arranging a loan from American bankers. The bankers consented to float a loan of $7.5 million, but as in Nicaragua, the grant of such a loan was made contingent on the execution of a loan convention between the United States and Honduran governments guaranteeing repayment to the bondholders.

On January 10, 1911, the Knox-Paredes treaty was signed; it provided for a loan secured by Honduran customs, to be collected by a collector of customs appointed by the government of Honduras from a list of three names submitted by the fiscal agent of the loan and approved by the President of the United States. The treaty was immediately submitted to the United States Senate and the Honduran congress, but the latter overwhelmingly rejected it on the ground that it was unconstitutional and violated Honduran sovereignty. The United States Senate also failed to give its consent to the loan convention.

The United States Senate having failed to approve the treaty, the American bankers engaged in earlier negotiations withdrew from the scene. The Honduran public debt remained in default until 1926, when the British bondholders, with the approval of the Honduran congress, agreed to accept a sum of $6 million in full payment, payable at the rate of $200,000 a year for thirty years.[66]

If Secretary Knox planned, as was believed, to enter into agreements with the other three Central American governments providing for the refunding and readjustment of their foreign debts, the refusal of the United States Senate to approve the Nicaraguan and Honduran treaties, coupled with general opposition in Central America itself, caused abandonment of any further attempts to establish customs collectorships under the control of the United States.

Central American relations since 1933

Under the authority of the Reciprocal Trade Agreements Act of 1934, the United States entered into agreements with all of the Central American republics — Honduras in 1935, Nicaragua, Guatemala, and Costa Rica in 1936,

[66] *For. Rel.,* 1912, 549–595, *passim;* also see Munro, *op. cit.,* 217–219.

and El Salvador in 1937. By 1940, mainly as a result of these reciprocal trade agreements, our trade with Central America showed a substantial increase with all five countries.

The involvement of the United States in World War II brought it into even closer relationship with its Central American neighbors. Following Pearl Harbor, all five republics declared war on the Axis Powers and cooperated faithfully with the United States in the war effort. All received lend-lease aid from the United States, and with the exception of Honduras, all were recipients of military, naval, and air missions. Agreements were also reached with each of the countries whereby the United States purchased all of their rubber production not needed for domestic purposes for a five-year period. Construction on the Inter-American Highway across Central America was accelerated when, in December, 1941, the United States Congress authorized expenditures to cover a large portion of the costs.

Following World War II, Central American rivalries and animosities again asserted themselves, seriously threatening the peace of the area. Beginning in December, 1948, with a controversy between Nicaragua and Costa Rica, a series of disputes involving various Central American states took place over the next few years. Although the United States took a keen interest in these controversies, it did not return to the unilateral measures employed in earlier years to restore peace and stability, but rather cooperated with the Latin-American governments as a group, operating through the Organization of Americans states, in attempts to reach satisfactory solutions and restore peaceful cooperation.[67]

---

[67] For a discussion of these disputes, see J. Lloyd Mecham, *The United States and Inter-American Security, 1889–1960* (Austin: University of Texas Press, 1961), Chap. XIII.

SUPPLEMENTARY READING

Biesánz, John and Mavis, *The People of Panama* (New York: Columbia University Press, 1955), 167–201.

Cox, Issac J., *Nicaragua and the United States, 1909–1927* (Boston: World Peace Foundation, 1929).

Denny, Harold H., *Dollars for Bullets, the Story of American Rule in Nicaragua* (New York: Dial, 1929).

Ealy, Laurence O., *The Republic of Panama in World Affairs, 1907–1950* (Philadelphia: University of Pennsylvania Press, 1951).

Jones, Chester Lloyd, *The Caribbean Since 1900* (New York: Prentice-Hall, Inc., 1936).

Karnes, Thomas L., *The Failure of Union: Central America, 1824–1960* (Chapel Hill: University of North Carolina Press, 1961).

Mack, Gustle, *The Land Divided: A History of the Panama and Other Isthmian Canal Projects* (New York: Alfred A. Knopf, Inc., 1944).

Martz, John D., *Central America: the Crisis and the Challenge,* (Chapel Hill: University of North Carolina Press, 1959).

Munro, Dana G. *The United States and the Caribbean Area* (Boston: World Peace Foundation, 1934), Chaps. II, V–VI.

Padelford, Norman J., *The Panama Canal in Peace and War* (New York: The Macmillan Company, 1942).

Rippy, J. Fred, *The Caribbean Danger Zone* (New York: G. P. Putnam's Sons, 1940).

Stimson, Henry L., *American Policy in Nicaragua* (New York: Charles Scribner's Sons, 1927).

Stuart, Graham H., *Latin America and the United States* (New York: Appleton-Century-Crofts, Inc., 5th ed., 1955), Chaps. XIV–XV.

The United States and Nicaragua — A Survey of the Relations from 1909 to 1932, Dept. of State, Lat. Am. Ser. No. 6 (Washington, D.C.: Government Printing Office, 1932).

13

United States-Mexican Relations

United States-Mexican relations have not been a model of good neighbor-liness — not that history presents many examples of border nations consistently devoted to the ideas of neighborly tolerance and understanding. But without any attempt to mitigate the United States' share of responsibility for more than a century of diplomatic tensions and occasional conflict with Mexico, we should note that the problems more or less common in the relations of contiguous nations were compounded by the suspicions, arrogance, intolerance, and misunderstandings of two peoples radically different in racial, cultural, social, economic, and historical background. Two civilizations were opposed to each other along a common border of some 1,500 miles.[1] If harmonious relations had resulted this would indeed have been a phenomenon unique in international relationships.

In the nineteenth century the principal disruptive factor in our Mexican relations was the American determination to acquire the northern territories of Mexico in order that the United States might round out its continental boundaries as it felt destined to do. Therefore, until near the end of the century, almost all of the diplomatic problems with Mexico arose from border and territorial issues. Only border Mexico was known to or interested the United States. Few Americans had penetrated into the interior of Mexico, where American economic interests were almost nonexistent. In short, had it not been for these border issues, United States-Mexican relations during the first half century of Mexican independence would have been almost devoid of significant incidents.

[1] "Relations with Mexico . . . are conditioned by many physical and psychological factors peculiar to Mexico, and by the marked and permanent dissimilarities between the two areas and the two peoples . . . Canadians behave like Americans . . . Mexicans do not so behave. [Thus] relations with Mexico cannot be patterned on the easily established and stable relations with Canada." Charles P. Howland, ed., *Survey of American Foreign Relations* (New Haven: Yale University Press, 1931), 1.

During the long dictatorship of Porfirio Díaz the waters of United States-Mexican relations were relatively calm. Border issues receded into the background and disappeared. But another major area of diplomatic conflict was being prepared as a result of the wholesale penetration of Mexico by American capital and business enterprise originally encouraged by the Mexican government. This foreign economic invasion was destined to become a major target of the great socio-economic and nationalistic revolution which began in Mexico in 1910.

1. From Independence to the Fall of Díaz

The inauguration of relations

Although the United States recognized the independence of Mexico from Spain on December 12, 1822, with its acceptance of José Manuel Zozaya as minister appointed by Emperor Agustín Iturbide, it was not until the arrival of Joel R. Poinsett at Mexico City on May 25, 1825, that full diplomatic relations were established. As minister, Poinsett devoted most of his attention to the counteracting of British influence in Mexico, and the encouragement of Mexican federalism as provided by the Constitution of 1824.[2] In promoting the latter, since he seemed to feel that the American model of federalism was on trial, he abused his diplomatic position by actively engaging in Mexican politics, thus arousing resentments which compromised the success of his mission.

Poinsett's meddling in Mexican politics aroused so much opposition that the Mexican government demanded his recall. Since by Poinsett's own admission his continued residence in Mexico had become almost insupportable, Secretary of State Van Buren, in December, 1829, finally ordered his return. His successor, Colonel Anthony Butler, who stayed at his post for seven years (1829–1836) during Andrew Jackson's administration, was an even worse choice than Poinsett, for he was an unscrupulous man who showed practically no interest in Mexico except to attempt by devious means to secure possession of the Texas territory. His efforts to acquire Texas by bribing Mexican officials aroused distrust and suspicions of the United States and led to demands for his recall because of "intrigues unbecoming a diplomatic agent."[3] The undiplomatic behavior of both Poinsett and Butler was an unfortunate inauguration of United States-Mexican relations.

The Texas question

The first problem of any great significance in United States-Mexican relations was a territorial one, that is, possession of the Mexican territory of

[2] For the Poinsett mission to Mexico, see J. Fred Rippy, *Joel R. Poinsett, Versatile American* (Durham: Duke University Press, 1935), 104–134; and James M. Callahan, *American Foreign Policy in Mexican Relations* (New York: The Macmillan Company, 1932), Chap. II.

[3] For Butler's mission, see George L. Rives, *The United States and Mexico, 1821–1848* (2 vols. New York: Charles Scribner's Sons, 1913), I, 234–261.

Texas. Since the 1819 treaty had designated the Sabine River as the eastern boundary between Mexico and the United States, President John Quincy Adams hoped to obtain Mexico's agreement to the Rio Grande or at least the Colorado River as the boundary line, to be compensated by a monetary payment. Minister Poinsett, who had been entrusted with the boundary treaty negotiation, soon abandoned the idea of purchase when he learned of opposition in the Mexican congress.[4] The resultant treaty of 1828 merely confirmed the boundary as fixed by the United States and Spain in 1819. Adams' successor, Andrew Jackson, acting through Anthony Butler, also sought to obtain Texas, but his efforts were just as unsuccessful.

The persistence of the United States in attempting to acquire Texas by diplomatic means aroused Mexican fears that the United States would eventually attempt to incorporate it by fomenting revolution by the numerous American settlers against Mexican rule. In an effort to forestall such a development, the Mexican congress passed a law in April, 1830, which suspended land grants to colonists and prohibited further immigration into Texas from the United States. This law proved impossible of enforcement, however, and only resulted in antagonizing the settlers against Mexican officials. Relations deteriorated until on March 2, 1836, the Texans declared their independence of Mexico. The rout of the Mexicans under Santa Anna by the tiny army of Sam Houston at San Jacinto on April 21, 1836, confirmed independence although the Mexican government stubbornly refused to recognize it and kept hopes alive of reconquering Texas.

Although the struggle of the Texans for independence was viewed with intense interest and sympathy by the American people, the United States government steered an official course of neutrality. This posture seemed, at least to the Mexicans, to be contradicted by Jackson's recognition of Texas on March 3, 1837, the last day of his administration.[5] Although the Texans were desirous of annexation to the United States, the question was temporarily put on the shelf because of the bitter opposition of Mexico on the one hand and of the abolitionists on the other, who opposed the addition of another slaveholding state.

Mexico's lodging of grievances against the United States was countered by United States demands for Mexican acknowledgment of American claims long ignored or evaded by the Mexican government. These claims had arisen principally from irregular and illegal exactions by Mexican customs officials and from seizure and wrongful application of the property of American citizens. At last, on Mexico's suggestion, a claims convention was signed in April, 1839. This convention provided that claims of American citizens against the Mexican government were to be submitted to a commission of two Americans and two Mexicans. Disagreements in the commission were to be referred to the King of Prussia. By the time the commission came to an end in 1842, it had decided 30 of the 84 claims cases presented and awarded

[4] Callahan, *op. cit.,* 52–53.
[5] France recognized Texas in 1839 and Great Britain in 1840.

$2,026,149 of the $6,648,812 demanded.[6] The claims left unsettled, as well as the delays in paying awards because of the depleted Mexican treasury, led to the signing of another claims convention in 1843, but it was not ratified by the Mexican government. Under the terms of the Treaty of Guadalupe Hidalgo in 1848 the United States agreed to pay claims of American citizens against Mexico to an amount not exceeding $3,250,000. To that end Congress provided for a board of commissioners, which finally awarded about $3,200,000 on 198 claims and rejected 70.[7] The foregoing was merely the beginning of the checkered history of claims commissions and other forms of arbitration in the relations between the United States and Mexico.[8]

The annexation of Texas and war with Mexico

The situation which created a sense of urgency in the United States for annexation was apprehension and resentment of European interference in Texas. Anxious to maintain Texas as a buffer between Mexico and the United States, British and French diplomacy sought to mediate for Mexican recognition of Texas independence on condition that Texas should not annex itself to the United States.[9] President Tyler, urged by ex-President Jackson to get Texas before foreign diplomacy blocked annexation, opened negotiations for a treaty. On April 12, 1844, an annexation treaty was signed, but on June 4 it was rejected by the Senate because the treaty had become identified with the defense of slavery.

The Texas question entered prominently into the presidential campaign of 1844, and with the election of the expansionist-minded James K. Polk, who campaigned for annexation, the incorporation of Texas became only a matter of time. A joint resolution, passed by both houses of Congress and approved by President Tyler on March 1, 1845, finally accomplished the annexation of Texas — that is, as far as the United States was concerned, for Texas was yet to be heard from.

The Texas government at that moment was conferring with British and French agents concerning a proposed treaty with Mexico by which the latter would recognize the independence of Texas in return for a promise never to annex itself to another power. It was the confessed objective of both the British and French governments to promote "the continuance of Texas as an Independent Power" for this "must conduce to a more even, and therefore

---

[6] J. B. Moore, *History and Digest of International Arbitration to Which the United States Has Been a Party* (6 vols. Washington, D.C.: Government Printing Office, 1898), II, 1216–1232. See also, A. H. Feller, *The Mexican Claims Commissions, 1923–1934* (New York: The Macmillan Company, 1935), 2–4.

[7] Moore, *Int. Arbit.*, II, 1248–1256.

[8] Although the Treaty of Guadalupe Hidalgo of 1848 provided for the voluntary arbitration of all future disputes between the two countries, the clause was never invoked in any of their many disputes.

[9] For a detailed account of British interests in Texas, see E. D. Adams, *British Interests and Activities in Texas, 1838–1846* (Baltimore: The Johns Hopkins Press, 1910). Also, see Rives, *op. cit.*, I, Chaps. XXIII-XXVII.

a more permanent, balance of interests in the North American Continent."[10] It was this European interference with the relations between two American governments which provoked President Polk, in his first annual message to Congress, on December 2, 1845, to revive the Monroe Doctrine.

Since the Texans preferred annexation to independence, the Franco-British promise of a treaty with Mexico was rejected. The offer of admission to the Union, therefore, was all but unanimously approved by the Texas electorate. On December 29, 1845, President Polk signed a resolution of the Congress admitting Texas as a state.

The consummation of annexation was prelude to war, for Mexico had repeatedly warned that such action would be equivalent to a declaration of war. The Mexican minister at Washington requested his passports and left the country as soon as the joint resolution of annexation had been signed by President Tyler. Since the Mexican government had terminated official relations with the United States minister at Mexico City there was a complete break in diplomatic relations between the two countries. A deaf ear was turned to all efforts by the United States to resume official relations.[11]

In view of the formally declared attitude of the Mexican government, President Polk quite properly sent troops to Texas for the protection of United States territory. But the extent of the territory annexed was in controversy, the United States claiming to the Rio Grande and Mexico contending that Texas had never extended beyond the Nueces River.

Although Polk would have welcomed a war with its promise of conquest of coveted Mexican territories, he was not inclined to go to war if his objectives could be achieved by diplomatic methods. Upon learning that the Mexican government would receive a commissioner to discuss the differences between the two nations, John Slidell was sent by Polk with instructions to offer Mexico $5 million in addition to the assumption by the United States of all claims of American citizens against Mexico, as payment for all of New Mexico. If, however, Mexico was unwilling to cede New Mexico but would recognize the Rio Grande as the western boundary of Texas, the United States would assume the payment of the claims due its own citizens. If Mexico would agree also to cede California, as well as New Mexico, the United States would pay $25 million in addition to the assumption of claims.[12] Mr. Polk's diplomatic effort collapsed. It was then that the President ordered General Zachary Taylor to advance to the Rio Grande.

Shortly after Taylor's arrival at the Rio Grande in late March, 1846, a body of Mexican troops crossed the river on April 25 and attacked one of Taylor's detachments. This was all that President Polk needed to recommend a declaration of war. On May 3, 1846, the Congress declared that a state of war existed.[13]

---

[10] Dexter Perkins, *The Monroe Doctrine, 1826–1867* (Baltimore: The Johns Hopkins Press, 1933), 71, n. 11. For the European mediation, see Rives, *op. cit.,* I, 703–720.

[11] An outstanding work on the Mexican War, with emphasis on military aspects, is Justin H. Smith's, *The War with Mexico* (2 vols. Gloucester, Mass.: Peter Smith, 1963).

[12] *Sen. Exec. Doc.* No. 52, 30th Cong., 1st Sess., 78.

[13] According to Albert K. Weinberg in *Manifest Destiny* (Baltimore: The Johns Hop-

As for the war itself it was both short-lived and one-sided. United States troops quickly and easily penetrated northern Mexico, occupied New Mexico and California, and after the seizure of Vera Cruz fought their way to Mexico City. The actual hostilities were virtually confined to the period from the battle of Palo Alto, near the Rio Grande, on May 8, 1846, to General Winfield Scott's entrance into Mexico City on September 14, 1847. Mexico's chronic internal disorders, or more exactly political anarchy, rendered impossible any effective resistence to the invader.

With the capture of Mexico City imminent, President Polk had appointed Nicholas P. Trist, Chief Clerk of the Department of State, as a special agent to accompany Scott's army overland and arrange a peace settlement. Trist was authorized to offer Mexico a payment of $15 million, plus the assumption of American claims, in return for Mexico's recognition of the United States' right to Texas to the Rio Grande and the cession of New Mexico and Upper California. He was further instructed to offer up to $30 million for the cession of New Mexico, Upper and Lower California, and the right of transit across the Isthmus of Tehuantepec, though the acquisition of Lower California and the transit rights were not to be regarded as indispensable to a settlement.[14]

Although Trist had been ordered recalled by President Polk, he proceeded nevertheless to conclude a peace settlement with the *de facto* Mexican government, the terms of which met essentially the requirements laid down by the President. Known as the Treaty of Guadalupe Hidalgo, signed February 2, 1848, this agreement confirmed the title of the United States to Texas as far as the Rio Grande and provided for the outright cession of New Mexico and Upper California. In return, the United States was to pay $15 million and assume the claims of its own citizens up to $3,250,000.

Although displeased by Trist's insubordination, Polk did not dare repudiate the treaty itself. He promptly sent it to the Senate, which on March 10, 1848, approved it. With the exchange of ratifications on May 30 the terms of the peace settlement became definitive.[15]

Manifest destiny and the Mexican policy of the United States

The Treaty of Guadalupe Hidalgo neither ended the friction between the two countries nor sated the territorial appetite of the United States.[16] In fact,

---

kins Press, 1935), 167, the fundamental cause of the war was "the tension which was created by the annexation of Texas and made critical by the follies of both countries." Americans and Mexicans were equally intolerant and contemptuous of their neighbors.

[14] For extravagant annexationist sentiment in the United States reflective of the nation's destiny to embrace the entire North American continent, see *ibid.*, Chap. VI. Said Carl Schurz, "This republic, being charged with the mission of bearing the banner of freedom over the whole civilized world, could transfer any country, inhabited by any kind of population, into something like itself simply by extending over it the magic charm of its institutions." *Ibid.*, 180. See also John D. P. Fuller, *The Movement for the Acquisition of All Mexico, 1846–1848* (Baltimore: The Johns Hopkins Press., 1936).

[15] Smith, *op. cit.*, II, 233–252.

[16] For the doctrine of "natural growth," which supported aggressive expansionism in the 1850's, see Weinberg, *op. cit.*, Chap. VII.

certain provisions of the treaty of 1848 led to further diplomatic controversy.

The dispute over the southern boundary of New Mexico extending westward from the Rio Grande near El Paso developed from an inaccurate map used in the peace settlement of Guadalupe Hidalgo. A compromise line worked out by the United States and Mexican commissioners was opposed by the United States Congress because it surrendered territory considered to have been ceded to the United States in the treaty of 1848, and particularly because it left the territory south of the Gila River in the possession of Mexico. This would have deprived the United States of the most practicable route for a southern transcontinental railroad. President Pierce therefore rejected the compromise and initiated negotiations with Mexico for acquisition of the desired territory and the release of the United States from the obligation of the treaty of 1848 to prevent Indian raids across the border. James Gadsen, appointed minister to Mexico, was authorized to offer a maximum of $50 million for Lower California and the northern parts of the Mexican states of Coahuila, Chihuahua, and Sonora, as well as release from claims for damages resulting from Indian raids into Mexico. Proportionately lesser amounts were to be offered for smaller cessions by Mexico, though the minimum cession acceptable should provide sufficient territory to accommodate the proposed southern railway route.

Favored by the fact that the Mexican dictator General Santa Anna was in dire need of funds, Mr. Gadsen was able to conclude a treaty of purchase, although only for his minimal territorial objective. The treaty, signed on December 30, 1853, provided for the cession to the United States, for $10 million, of a 19-million-acre triangular area south of the Gila River, called the Mesilla Valley, comprising the southern portions of New Mexico and Arizona. The treaty also released the United States from liability for damages inflicted by Indian raids into Mexico, but no mention was made of claims of American citizens against Mexico.[17]

Although the Gadsen Purchase assured the United States of the territory it needed for the construction of a southern transcontinental railroad, the expansionist elements remained unsatisfied. The Buchanan administration, which like that of Franklin Pierce, was attached to the "doctrine of natural growth," aggressively continued efforts to acquire additional territory in Mexico, particularly northern Sonora and Lower California.[18] The general chaos in Mexican politics resulting from the threat of European intervention for the protection of foreign interests, as well as an increasing accumulation of claims by American citizens against Mexico, seemed to provide the ammunition needed by the American expansionist forces. In December, 1858, after failure to obtain from Mexico indemnity for American claims, President Buchanan appealed unsuccessfully to Congress for authority to assume a "temporary

---

[17] The standard authority on the negotiations and ratification of the Gadsen Treaty is Paul N. Garber, *The Gadsen Treaty* (Philadelphia: University of Pennsylvania Press, 1923); also, J. Fred Rippy, *The United States and Mexico* (New York: Alfred A. Knopf, Inc., 1926), Chaps. VII–VIII.

[18] Callahan, *op. cit.,* 259.

protectorate" over northern Mexico. Undeterred, Buchanan succeeded, in December, 1859, in concluding an agreement — the notorious McLane-Ocampo treaty — with the hard-pressed Benito Juárez government.[19] By it, Mexico was to receive a loan of $4 million and in return the United States was to be granted a perpetual right of way across the Isthmus of Tehuantepec, two railroad routes across northern Mexico to the Gulf of California, the right to protect the transit routes with troops, and the right to intervene in emergencies without the consent of Mexico. Benito Juárez and Mexico were saved from the consequences of such an ill-advised treaty by the refusal of the United States Senate to approve it.

The United States and the French intervention

Shortly after the opening of the American Civil War, the United States was confronted by one of the most serious crises in its relations with Mexico. In July, 1861, President Juárez declared a two-year suspension of payments on Mexico's foreign debt. Angered by this arbitrary action, Great Britain, France, and Spain, all of whom had a variety of grievances against Mexico which had long gone unredeemed, demanded the immediate restoration of payments, and when this demand was not met, they severed relations with Mexico and threatened to send a joint military expedition to force the resumption of payments.

Suspicious of European intentions, Secretary Seward sought to avert intervention by proposing a treaty with Mexico whereby the United States would assume the interest payments on her foreign debt for a five-year period, the money advanced to be secured by a mortgage on the public lands and mineral rights of several states of northern Mexico.[20] Mr. Seward's proposal, had not the United States Senate objected, would probably have led to the absorption of another portion of Mexican territory.

In the meantime, on October 21, 1861, the governments of Great Britain, France, and Spain completed their plans for intervention by concluding a convention at London calling for a joint military demonstration. The tri-power debt-collecting expedition soon resolved into an attempt by the French government alone to overthrow the constitutional government of Mexico under Benito Juárez, and impose Archduke Maximilian of Austria as puppet emperor of Mexico. Since this episode was one of the most flagrant violations of the Monroe Doctrine in its whole history, it has been discussed in Chapter 3.

Border troubles and the advent of Porfirio Díaz

The end of the American Civil War and the withdrawal of the French from Mexico, soon followed by the tragic end of Emperor Maximilian, inaugurated a new era in United States-Mexican relations. The fact that Benito Juárez continued to receive the recognition and support of the Lincoln-Seward ad-

[19] For a full discussion of this agreement, see Rippy, *op. cit.,* 223–227.
[20] *House Exec. Doc.,* No. 100, 37th Cong., 2nd Sess., 22.

ministration throughout his struggle with the French could not fail to arouse a reciprocal friendly disposition.

It was fitting that the new era of amity and peace should be inaugurated by the negotiation of a claims convention on July 4, 1868. This convention provided that all claims by the citizens of either country against the government of the other should be adjudicated by a commission of one member from each state and a neutral umpire, who was to decide cases when there was disagreement. This commission finally completed its work in January, 1876. The United States filed claims for the amount of $470,126,613.40, and Mexico for the amount of $86,661,891.15. Of the American claims the commission awarded $4,125,622.20. Of the Mexican claims it awarded $150,498,412.[21] The enormous discrepancy between the amounts claimed and the amounts awarded is typical, for seldom do awards exceed 10 per cent of the amount claimed, because of fraud and exaggeration of actual damages.

Although the United States seemed to have abandoned the idea of territorial acquisitions at the expense of Mexico, border troubles plagued relations for a number of years.[22] The most serious were invasions of American territory by bands of Mexicans and Indians, mostly cattle thieves, who kept the border area in almost constant turmoil.

Added to the foregoing was the problem of smuggling from the Mexican Free Zone into Texas. The Mexican government had authorized the introduction of foreign goods free of impost duties into the towns along the Rio Grande. This belt six miles wide, called the Free Zone, presented an opportunity to smuggle duty-free goods across the border to the great disadvantage of the merchants of Texas and loss to the United States treasury. The Mexican government turned a deaf ear to United States protests, and instead of abolishing or contracting the Free Zone, actually enlarged it.

The accession of General Porfirio Díaz, a hero of the war of the French intervention, to the Mexican presidency in 1876, via subversion of the established constitutional government, presented the Rutherford B. Hayes administration with an eagerly grasped opportunity to solve the various problems with Mexico by withholding recognition of Díaz until he had agreed to a satisfactory settlement of the various border questions.[23] However, any prospect of a negotiated agreement with Díaz was delayed by the notorious Ord Order of June, 1877.

Because of the difficulty of protecting the long border from marauding incursions, General Ord, commanding in Texas, was authorized by the Secretary of War to cross the Rio Grande in hot pursuit of Mexican border raiders

[21] The work of the Commission under the Convention of 1868 is detailed in Moore, *Int. Arbit.*, II, 1287–1358. See also Feller, *op. cit.*, 6.

[22] For adequate discussions of the border problems, see Rippy, *op. cit.*, 282–311; and Callahan, *op. cit.*, 341–368.

[23] On the problems related to the United States recognition of the Díaz government, see *ibid.*, 369–408; and Stuart A. MacCorkle, *American Policy of Recognition Towards Mexico* (Baltimore: The Johns Hopkins Press, 1933), 67–82.

and to arrest them and punish them on Mexican soil. This order was received with deep indignation in Mexico, and Díaz retaliated by ordering Mexican troops to "repel force with force." A clash was avoided since General Ord and the Mexican commander carefully avoided occasions for a showdown.[24] Soon the crossing of American troops ceased with the better Mexican guarding of the frontier.

The Mexican President's "ace in the hole" was his ability to bring a greater measure of order to Mexico than any preceding Mexican government. Accordingly, responding to the pressure of American merchants and investors, Secretary of State William M. Evarts extended recognition to the Díaz government in May, 1878.[25] President Díaz remained adamant, however, in his insistence that repeal of the Ord Order was a requisite to the resumption of negotiations on pending issues. Finally, after the Ord instructions had been revoked in February, 1880, Díaz was willing to enter into an agreement for reciprocal crossing of the boundary in pursuit of marauders.

A treaty of 1884 created the International (Water) Boundary Commission to exercise exclusive jurisdiction of all differences or questions that might arise along the water boundary, and the land boundary as well. Later treaties and laws added to the functions of the Commission. The United States section has its seat at El Paso and the Mexican section is at Juarez, Chihuahua. Between 1894 and 1911 the Commission was occupied primarily in tracing river changes and in transferring cutoffs or *bancos* along the river to the state to which avulsion added each tract.[26]

A problem of this nature, which the Boundary Commission unfortunately was unable to settle, was the Chamizal controversy. The Chamizal tract was an area of about 600 acres lying on the El Paso side of the Rio Grande and formed by the movement of the river southward, now slowly, now rapidly, particularly in the decade of the 1860's. In 1895 the matter was laid before the Boundary Commission which, however, failed to determine whether the tract should go to the United States under the rule of accretion or to Mexico under the rule of avulsion. Mexico contended that rapid erosion was undistinguishable from avulsion. Finally, in 1910, the two states referred the question to an arbitral commission composed of the two boundary commissioners and a Canadian jurist as umpire. His decision to divide the tract was rejected by the United States on the ground that the tribunal had exceeded its powers.[27] Whatever the legality of the United States position, the rejection of the award became an unfortunate blemish on the arbitral record of the

[24] Rippy, *op. cit.,* 302.

[25] *Ibid.,* 307.

[26] Charles A. Timm, *The International Boundary Commission, United States and Mexico* (Austin: The University of Texas Publications, No. 4134, September 8, 1941), 23 ff.

[27] For a brief and useful survey of the Chamizal controversy to 1912, see Gladys Gregory, "The Chamizal Settlement, A View from El Paso," *Southwest Studies* (Texas Western College), I, No. 2 (Summer, 1963), 3–36; Gordon Ireland, *Boundaries, Possessions, and Conflicts in Central and North America and the Caribbean* (Cambridge: Harvard University Press, 1941), 306–308.

United States[28] and an embarrassment in our Mexican relations for many years after.

It was the tragedy of Porfirio Díaz that, in his efforts to usher Mexico into the world of modern, progressive nations, he neglected the human element — the Mexican masses themselves. The "Díaz system" which was very successful in bringing to Mexico order, stability and unprecedented fiscal solvency — and the great respect and admiration of foreign governments — was based on compacts with foreign capitalists, and with the traditional monopolizers of privilege and power: the army, the Church, and the great landowners. So generous had the dictator been to foreign capital, particularly American, that his government came to be called the mother of foreigners and the stepmother of Mexicans. The Díaz partnership with the land barons marked an ever greater concentration of lands in the hands of the few. By 1910, as a result of the Díaz "agrarian program," most of the occupied lands of the nation belonged to the *hacendados,* and almost 80 per cent of all the farm and plantation laborers of Mexico were landless and virtual slaves. It was the hunger of the peons for their lands which proved to be the most potent force in the revolution.

The miserable state of the peons was a characteristic of the uneven prosperity of Mexico under Díaz. While the rich grew richer the inarticulate body of mestizos and Indians lived in conditions of utter misery and poverty. Social justice seemed to be absent from the lexicon of the dictator.

In September, 1910, Díaz was host to distinguished foreign guests, gathered in Mexico City to celebrate the centenary of independence. That part of the capital city, so reminiscent of the boulevards of Paris, which was restricted for the view of the visitors, was most impressive. But little did they realize that they were looking at a sort of Potemkin city which screened the true Mexico preparing to erupt into revolution in only a matter of days.

2. United States-Mexican Relations, 1910–1940

Francisco Madero

When it became apparent that Porfirio Díaz planned to be "re-elected" in 1910, after earlier promises that he would retire, the indignant opposition rallied around Francisco I. Madero. The young idealist, member of a wealthy landholding family from the northern state of Coahuila, dared to challenge the octogenarian dictator for the presidential election, but was imprisoned for his audacity. Madero escaped, and on October 5, 1910, proclaimed revolution by his Plan of San Luis Potosí. The revolutionary program was essentially political, for Madero failed to see the need of genuine economic

---

[28] The first arbitration case submitted to the Hague Tribunal was the Pious Fund Claims of the Catholic Church of California against the Mexican government. The award was favorable to the United States. *Foreign Relations of the United States,* 1902, 738–785.

and social reform. He did not seem to recognize that his country needed more than free elections. He denounced the election of Díaz (in 1910) as a fraud, and proclaimed his revolution under the banner "effective suffrage, no re-election."[29]

Succeeding events proved that, without his "hand of iron," the dictatorial structure erected by Porfirio Díaz readily collapsed under the impact of the Madero revolt. On May 25, 1911, Díaz resigned the presidency and fled the country. Shortly thereafter Madero was installed as president.

President William Howard Taft, although generally sympathetic with Porfirio Díaz, viewed events in Mexico largely as they concerned Americans living in Mexico and their business interests. The primary objective of the Taft policy was the fostering of conditions favorable to American trade with Mexico and to American interests there. It was a matter of indifference to the United States how these conditions might be achieved by the Mexican nation. After Madero's election and inauguration as president, his government was promptly recognized by President Taft in November, 1911.[30]

With the collapse of the Díaz regime and the beginning of a long period of revolution, diplomatic protection again became a source of controversy between the United States and Mexico. Soon after the fall of Díaz, the American embassy in Mexico City, in charge of Ambassador Henry Lane Wilson, began to receive a volume of complaints of mistreated American citizens. Ambassador Wilson promptly presented these complaints to the Mexican Foreign Office and demanded protection. In view of the failure of the Mexican government seemingly to exert its efforts to extend protection, Mr. Wilson issued a virtual ultimatum demanding the adoption of measures to improve the situation. Then, not satisfied with the Mexican reply denying charges of indifference, the ambassador urged his own government to take vigorous and drastic measures. His experience, he said, had taught him that "these Latin American countries should be dealt with justly and calmly but severely and undeviatingly."[31]

In addition to the more or less natural and unpremeditated circumstance of foreigners suffering injury and damage in an internal uprising in Mexico, the revolt unleashed in 1910, while primarily social and economic, was also marked by a constantly growing spirit of nationalism and antagonism to foreign interests. It was natural that a revolt against the Díaz system, which had favored foreign capital and enterprise, should also be a revolt against foreign interests in Mexico. The revolutionaries' pursuit of the objective of "Mexico for the Mexicans" led to many difficulties in relations with the United States.

[29] Charles C. Cumberland, *Mexican Revolution, Genesis Under Madero* (Austin: University of Texas Press, 1952), 121–122; also, see Stanley R. Ross, *Francisco I. Madero* (New York: Columbia University Press, 1957), for a sympathetic biography of the "Apostle of Mexican Democracy."

[30] For the Mexican policy of President Taft, see Howard F. Cline, *The United States and Mexico* (Cambridge: Harvard University Press, 1953), 128–134.

[31] For. Rel. 1912, 886–887.

Although Madero had been able to provide the spark needed to overthrow Díaz and his dictatorship, he was unable to supply the leadership which the socio-economic revolution he set in motion demanded. He satisfied neither the masses because of his failure to recognize the economic and social needs of the country, nor the more substantial elements of society because of his inability to maintain order and stability. He was soon confronted therefore, with armed opposition, the principal leaders of which were Pascual Orozco in the north, and Emiliano Zapata, the direct actionist agrarian reformer, in the south. A Madero general who quelled the Orozco revolt was Victoriano Huerta, a holdover from the Díaz regime. Following unsuccessful revolts in 1911 and 1912 by Bernardo Reyes and Félix Díaz respectively, both men, the latter a nephew of the fallen dictator, were lodged in prison in Mexico City.[32] There they enjoyed sufficient freedom of communication with conspirator army leaders on the outside to plot the overthrow of Madero.

When Madero was first faced by insurrectionary activities, he appealed to President Taft to stop the flow of arms and munitions across the border to his adversaries. The American President responded by asking Congress for the requisite authority, and, when the executive had been given such discretionary power, Taft on March 14, 1912, proclaimed an arms embargo on all arms shipments to Mexico. Shortly after the embargo was lifted from the Madero government.[33]

Particularly critical of the weak and fumbling Madero was Ambassador Henry Lane Wilson who seemed to believe that Mexico's only salvation rested in a president with a "hand of iron." President Taft was not responsive to Ambassador Wilson's urgings for a strong protective policy. In his message to Congress of December 3, 1912, President Taft defined his Mexican policy: "Throughout this trying period [the past two years] the policy of the United States has been one of patient nonintervention, steadfast recognition of constitutional authority in the neighboring nation, and the exertion of every effort to care for American interests."[34]

Also in view of the coming transfer of presidential powers in March, 1913, President Taft probably preferred to keep the Mexican problem in suspense. This gave rise to charges by Democrats of Republican indifference to American lives and property in Mexico. Before President Taft could turn over his office to President-elect Woodrow Wilson, events in Mexico had taken a turn for the worse.

On February 9, 1913, the first of the *decena trágica* or "tragic ten days,"[35] Bernardo Reyes and Félix Díaz were allowed to escape prison by bribed guards, and took command of troops ready to perform their assigned tasks. After the rebel failure to capture the National Palace, in which assault Reyes lost his life, President Madero made the tragic mistake of entrusting the defense of his government to General Victoriano Huerta. For ten days the

[32] Cumberland, *op. cit.*, Chap. IX.
[33] *For. Rel.*, 1912, 736–750; 1913, 832–875.
[34] *Ibid.*, 1912, xiv.
[35] For the Huerta *coup d'état*, see Cumberland, *op. cit.*, Chap. XI.

civilian population of Mexico City was subjected to great loss of lives and property due to the aimless artillery duel between the rebel batteries in the Ciudadela and the government batteries stationed near the National Palace. Remarkably, the troops on both sides remained in comparative safety, a fact which gave rise to ugly rumors of military deception.

When the Reyes-Díaz revolt broke out on February 9, Ambassador Wilson sought the intervention of the United States to insure Madero's removal, but President Taft rejected his request. Meanwhile, Wilson, though totally without instructions from his own government, urged Madero to resign and led him to believe that the United States was on the verge of military intervention. Moreover, despite being specifically cautioned not to implicate his government in Mexico's internal affairs, the ambassador arranged a meeting[36] between Félix Díaz and Victoriano Huerta, who had decided to take advantage of Madero's distress to promote his own political ambitions.

Since Madero remained adamant in his refusal to leave office, he, his vice-president, Pino Suárez, and a number of his loyal officials were arrested. Before announcing himself to the Mexican nation as their new president, Huerta was careful to give his succession a faint semblance of legality — for Latins have a passion for legalism — by having himself appointed in the line of succession, the way ahead being cleared by convenient resignations. As for the troublesome presence of Francisco Madero and Pino Suárez, that was cleared by convenient assassination.

According to Huerta's version, which was accepted by Henry Lane Wilson, Madero and Pino Suárez were killed while being transferred from one prison to another, during the confusion of an exchange of shots between their guards and a group of partisans attempting to free the prisoners. But the facts seem to be that they were killed by two officers acting under Huerta's orders.[37]

Ambassador Wilson reported optimistically to Secretary of State Philander C. Knox that the change of government would be generally accepted by the Mexican people and that there would be early restoration of peace and prosperity. In urging an immediate recognition of Huerta, he said: "It would be well to note that the Provisional Government takes office in accordance with the Constitution and precedents." Mr. Knox was willing to recognize the new president, but at the price of certain concessions by Huerta, especially his acceptance of a mixed claims commission to award damages.[38] The refusal of Huerta to concede left the problem of recognition to the decision of the incoming Woodrow Wilson administration.

Woodrow Wilson vs. Victoriano Huerta

During the first two years after he became President, Woodrow Wilson was virtually his own Secretary of State for Mexican affairs. A lengthy record of

[36] For Henry Lane Wilson's defense of his mission, see his *Diplomatic Episodes in Mexico, Belgium, and Chile* (New York: Doubleday, Page, and Company, 1927).

[37] Cumberland, *op. cit.,* 240–241.

[38] *For. Rel.,* 1913, 725–734.

discord during the years 1913 and 1914 was the result of the President's essay at being his only policy maker. According to a reliable authority: "Wilson stumbled from crisis to crisis in Mexico with neither clearly formulated objectives nor alternative plans to reach them, and brought the nation to the brink of war as a consequence."[39]

The incoming Democratic President believed, like his Republican predecessor, in order and stability and the protection of American property interests in Mexico, but the Wilson policy differed radically from that of Taft concerning how the desired end might be brought about.[40] Taft had not been disposed to inquire into the origin of a particular Mexican regime or pass judgment on it. His only concern was the ability of the regime to fulfill its international responsibilities. President Wilson, on the other hand, dominated by belief in the democratic ideal, was convinced that permanent order and security could not be achieved in Mexico, or any other country, by a governmental system that did not enjoy formal approval by a majority of the people. Thus, since he believed that all would be well if there were an adherence to constitutionalism, he determined to put the Mexican nation back on the constitutional road. A *sine qua non* was no recognition of the "bloodstained" usurper Victoriano Huerta. Since Henry Lane Wilson was unsympathetic with the new policy at Washington, and scoffed at the prospect of democratic government in Mexico with 80 per cent of the population illiterate,[41] he was finally withdrawn from his post in July.

To force Huerta out of power President Wilson resorted to various means short of armed intervention: withholding of recognition, controlling the supply of arms and munitions to Mexico, and discouraging loans to the Mexican government. On March 11, 1913, Wilson issued a policy statement on Latin America in which he introduced the new principle of *de jure* recognition, that is, of repudiating governments established by unconstitutional methods. In refusing recognition on these grounds, Wilson abandoned the traditional *de facto* recognition policy of the United States.[42] By introducing the element of "constitutional legitimacy" as a requirement of recognition, he rather naively believed that he could exert a decisive influence in restoring constitutional government in Mexico, and in *teaching* Mexicans the ways of democracy. The fact that the principal European powers, as well as Japan and

[39] Cline, *op. cit.*, 162.

[40] President Wilson's "attitude toward the diplomatic protection of existing American interests in Mexico did not differ substantially from that of his predecessors, save in a possibly greater reluctance to resort to forceful measures to back up his demands." Frederick S. Dunn, *The Diplomatic Protection of Americans in Mexico* (New York: Columbia University Press, 1933), 326.

[41] *For. Rel.*, 1913, 776.

[42] *Ibid.*, 7. See also Harley Notter, *The Origins of the Foreign Policy of Woodrow Wilson* (Baltimore: The Johns Hopkins Press, 1937), 223, and D. A. Graber, *Crisis Diplomacy, A History of U.S. Intervention Policies and Practices* (Washington, D.C.: Public Affairs Press, 1959), 167–168, 197–198. Lest his policy be interpreted as a pretext for United States aggrandizement in Latin America, President Wilson stated expressly in a speech at Mobile, Alabama, on October 27, 1913, that "the United States will never again seek one additional foot of territory by conquest."

China, and most of the Latin-American governments, except Argentina, Brazil, and Chile, had extended *de facto* recognition to General Huerta, did not weaken the President in his determination to deny recognition to the "butcher" Huerta.

That Great Britain especially had recognized Huerta greatly annoyed President Wilson, because this made difficult his efforts to deny arms and financial assistance to the Huerta government. The situation was remedied somewhat when, in the latter part of 1913, a tacit understanding seems to have been reached between the British and American governments whereby the British pledged not to interfere with Wilson's Mexican policy, and in return Wilson promised to support nondiscrimination in Panama Canal tolls.[43]

Following his recall of Henry Lane Wilson, President Wilson decided to deal directly with Huerta, and therefore selected as special presidential agent, John Lind, a former governor of Minnesota who was completely unacquainted with Mexico.[44] Lind was instructed to secure: an armistice between Huerta and his adversaries, the "Constitutionalists," headed by "First Chief" Venustiano Carranza; an early and free presidential election in which Huerta would not be a candidate; and an agreement by all parties to abide by the results of the election. If Huerta would agree to this proposal President Wilson would use his influence to secure for the Mexican dictator a loan from American bankers.[45] Huerta would have no part of this proposition.

President Wilson then chose to promote the cause of the Constitutionalists. On February 3, 1914, he lifted the embargo on arms shipments to Mexico, thereby enabling Carranza and Villa to receive munitions across the border from the United States.[46] Although helped by Wilson's action Carranza was suspicious of the American President's motives and denounced United States interference.

President Wilson's self-styled policy of "watchful waiting" announced to the Congress on December 2, 1913, provoked much public criticism of an uncertain President reluctant to give legitimate protection to Americans in Mexico. American public opinion, restive over the continued disorders in Mexico, did not share the President's optimism about a democratic future for that country. This was particularly true of the border population of the United States, which insisted on a strong and active Mexico policy.

A critical battle between the Constitutionalists and the Huerta Federalists at the oil-rich port of Tampico attracted a concentration of foreign warships to protect the interests of their nationals. The commander of the American naval units at Tampico was Admiral Mayo. A smaller force at Vera Cruz was commanded by Admiral Fletcher. On April 9, 1914, some American sailors were arrested by Huerta's men when they went ashore at Tampico to

---

[43] Cline, *op. cit.*, 153.

[44] See *ibid.*, 145–146, for the Lind mission.

[45] *For. Rel.*, 1913, 820–823.

[46] For arms control as an instrument of diplomacy in Mexico, see B. H. Williams, *Economic Foreign Policy of the United States* (New York: McGraw-Hill Book Company, Inc., 1929), 146–150; and Notter, *op. cit.*, 293–294.

load supplies into a whaleboat flying the American flag. On Admiral Mayo's demand the men were released, but he rejected oral apologies as insufficient. In a strong note, or ultimatum, he demanded a formal apology and salute to the American flag. The Mexican commander, backed by President Huerta, refused. President Wilson sustained Mayo's demands, which, considering the trivial nature of the incident, were unreasonable.[47]

Since Huerta could not consent to abject and humiliating apology, there seemed no solution to the impasse except military action. President Wilson was planning to go before the Congress seeking authorization, and Admiral Mayo was perfecting plans for the seizure of Tampico, when the President decided, because of unexpected developments, not to occupy Tampico but Vera Cruz instead.

The pending arrival at Vera Cruz of a German merchant ship the *Ypiranga* with a shipment of arms for the Huertistas seemed to make it imperative that these arms not be landed.[48] Therefore, in order to effect the occupation of Vera Cruz, President Wilson, on April 20, after numbering hostile acts by Huerta's forces, requested Congressional approval to use armed force to secure respect for the dignity and rights of the United States. Congressional delay in enacting the joint resolution did not deter the President from going ahead with armed intervention.

On April 21 Vera Cruz was shelled and occupied. Casualties were suffered by both Americans and Mexicans. The occupation of Vera Cruz was an arrogant and brutal exercise of power, its evils compounded because it all seemed directed to no clear-cut objective. Vera Cruz was occupied ostensibly to prevent the landing of a shipment of arms, yet later the arms were negligently allowed to reach Mexico City. With American forces in command of Vera Cruz President Wilson lost interest in the arms shipment.[49]

The principal effect of the Vera Cruz incident, instead of bringing Huerta to his knees, was to stiffen further his resistance and to cause the Mexican people, including many who otherwise were opposed to his regime, to rally behind him as the stalwart defender of Mexican independence. Wilson himself was distressed over the necessity to occupy Vera Cruz and hoped to withdraw as soon as possible, though not before Huerta had been forced out of power. War seemed imminent until President Wilson accepted the good offices of the diplomatic representatives of Argentina, Brazil, and Chile, though he made it clear to the mediators that the United States would accept no solution that did not include the withdrawal of Huerta from the presidency. Wilson also contended that no provisional government could be successful unless it avowedly and sincerely favored necessary agrarian and political reforms, and that only the Constitutionalists seemed to meet this requisite.

---

[47] Dr. Robert E. Quirk, in *An Affair of Honor, Woodrow Wilson and the Occupation of Veracruz* (Lexington: University of Kentucky Press, 1962), charges the Admiral with a degree of irresponsibility equalled only by that of President Wilson himself.

[48] According to Quirk, in an excellent discussion of the Tampico and Vera Cruz incidents (*ibid.*, 98), "the point of origin of the arms shipment had been New York, not Hamburg."

[49] *Ibid.*, 151.

Notwithstanding, Carranza refused to participate in a conference arranged by the mediatory powers. Huerta, however, reluctantly accepted mediation.[50]

Meeting at Niagara Falls, Ontario, on May 18, 1914, the conference lasted for six weeks. Since the United States insisted on Huerta's resignation, nothing concrete emerged from the conference. Nevertheless, shortly after, on July 14, Victoriano Huerta, faced by military reverses and his government bankrupt, finally resigned the presidency and sailed for Spain. On August 20 the Constitutionalists took over Mexico City. The extent to which Wilson's policy contributed to Huerta's downfall is difficult to assess, although it was not without considerable influence, and the dictator himself was frank to admit this.

Since the American occupation of Vera Cruz had been an act of retaliation against Huerta, there was no longer reason for the continued possession of the port city. But negotiations with Carranza for evacuation of the city proved to be long and difficult. Eventually, when Carranza promised general amnesty for all Mexicans who had served the American occupation government in Vera Cruz, the American withdrawal took place on November 23, 1914.[51]

Woodrow Wilson and Carranza

The fall of Huerta opened the floodgates for violent contest among the revolutionary leaders for the right of succession. On November 14 Villa and Zapata drove Carranza out of Mexico City and a regular civil war set in, with the capital city changing hands several times within one year.[52]

The failure of any Mexican leader to emerge as superior pretender to the presidency caused President Wilson to invite several Latin-American governments to join the United States in agreeing upon a provisional president of Mexico whom they could support and recognize. This effort failed, for, though acceptable to Pancho Villa, Venustiano Carranza would have nothing to do with a conference sponsored by outside "meddlers." Since it appeared that Carranza would be the ultimate military victor, President Wilson decided to recognize him, provided he guarantee protection for the lives and property of foreigners and pledge compliance with the other obligations of international law. When Carranza gave the requested promises, President Wilson, on October 19, 1915, formally extended *de facto* recognition, as did six Latin-American governments.[53]

Angered by Wilson's scuttling him in favor of his former chief, General Villa deliberately attempted to avenge himself on both Carranza and Wilson, by embroiling their countries in war. The first incident in Villa's campaign of vengeance occurred on January 10, 1916, when fifteen American mining engineers, who had been issued safe-conduct passports by the Carranza gov-

[50] For the voluminous correspondence of the United States government on the Mexican problem and the ABC mediation, see *For. Rel.*, 1914, 442–904.

[51] Quirk, *op. cit.*, 169.

[52] See Robert E. Quirk, *The Mexican Revolution, 1914–1915* (Bloomington: Indiana University Press, 1960).

[53] *For. Rel.*, 1915, 771.

ernment, were removed from a train at Santa Ysabel, Sonora, and shot in cold blood. Public indignation in the United States resulting from this foul deed was still at a high pitch, when, on March 9, 1916, about 400 Villa raiders crossed the border and attacked the little town of Columbus, New Mexico, killing sixteen Americans and partly burning the town.[54]

In answer to a clamor by the American press and public for immediate retribution, President Wilson, on March 16, dispatched General John J. Pershing with 6,000 troops into Mexico "to scatter the Villistas and thus end the constant threat of raids."[55] [Although it would seem to be to the interest of Carranza to have Villa captured, the Mexican president strongly resented the move and refused to cooperate with the American forces, though General Pershing had been enjoined by President Wilson to conduct the pursuit "with scrupulous regard to the sovereignty of Mexico." When Wilson accepted restrictions imposed by Carranza on Pershing's operations which condemned them inevitably to futility, the American press and Congress reacted angrily, demanding full-scale military action. But because of the increasing gravity of the European situation, and the possibility that the United States might be drawn into the war against Germany, President Wilson refused to commit his country any deeper in Mexican affairs.

Anxious to extricate himself from the Mexican involvement, President Wilson was actually on the point of withdrawing Pershing's troops, even though no positive objective had been achieved, when Carranza made such a retreat impossible — at least at that time. On April 12, 1916, an American detachment was attacked at Parral, in southern Chihuahua, by civilians and Villistas, and later by Carranza troops, resulting in the death of forty Mexicans and two American troopers. After Wilson had attempted to negotiate for an eventual withdrawal of the American troops, Carranza demanded an immediate exit. Then the intransigent Mexican president compounded the indignities heaped on the American "invaders" by warning General Pershing that if he moved his troops in any direction but north they would be fired on. To prove that this was no bluff, Mexican Federal troops, on June 21, fired on an American scouting party moving eastward at Carrizal. Twelve American soldiers were killed and twenty-three captured.

Political considerations and the increasing gravity of the European war situation could no longer excuse further neglect by President Wilson to adopt a decisive attitude toward the Mexican president. When public opinion in the United States demanded prompt and vigorous action, Wilson immediately demanded the release of the prisoners, and the country was put on a war footing, though the President had no intention of declaring war if it could be avoided. There was Germany to think of.[56]

Nor did Carranza want war. He ordered the release of the American prisoners, and proposed a settlement of differences between the two govern-

[54] *Ibid.,* 1916, 480–481.
[55] "No mention was made in Pershing's orders about capturing that picturesque bandit leader." Cline, *op cit.,* 177. Also, see *For. Rel.,* 1916, 491–492. For an adequate discussion of the Pershing Punitive Expedition, see Callahan, *op. cit.,* 562–571.
[56] Notter, *op. cit.,* 617–618.

ments, either by direct negotiations with the United States, or by Latin-American mediation. A commission composed of representatives of the United States and Mexico met in New London, Connecticut, on September 6, 1916, to wrangle interminably until the following January over the terms of a formula for the withdrawal of Pershing's troops. The negotiations were futile, for it was impossible to reconcile Mexican insistence on the immediate and unconditional withdrawal of the American troops and the American demand that the withdrawal be accompanied by Mexican guarantees against the recurrence of such border incidents as had occasioned the Pershing punitive expedition. On February 5, 1917, Pershing's mission unaccomplished and the border still a security threat, the punitive expeditionary force was withdrawn from Mexico.[57] This was not the only incident which pointed up the unpalatable fact that President Wilson's Mexican policy seemed to lead nowhere. Carranza was rewarded by the resumption of regular diplomatic relations with the United States, when, in February, 1917, Henry P. Fletcher was appointed ambassador to Mexico.

To the irritations caused by Carranza's past intransigence, was now added, after United States entry into World War I, American exasperation with his government because of its apparent sympathy toward Imperial Germany and the failure of Carranza to prevent the use of Mexican territory as a base for German espionage and sabotage against the United States. The German government itself construed Carranza's attitude as sufficiently sympathetic to warrant the promise by the German Foreign Minister, Zimmerman, to return the Mexican territory lost to the United States in 1848 and 1853, in return for Mexican aid. This notorious "Zimmerman note," intercepted and published by the British, was embarrassing to both Germans and Mexicans.[58]

Certain provisions of the new Mexican Constitution of 1917 proved a more important and continuing source of friction with the United States. This constitution, promulgated on February 5, 1917, sought to make effective all of the social and economic gains of the revolution. To this end, elaborate provisions were included in several articles: Article 27 dealt with agrarian reform, nationalization of petroleum deposits, and limitations on the ownership of real property by foreigners in Mexico; Article 123, on labor legislation, carried strong implications of workers' rights against foreign employers; Articles 3 and 130 covered religious and educational reform. It was the celebrated Article 27 which initiated more than a decade of acute diplomatic controversy with the United States.[59]

Article 27 seemed to affect adversely the rights of American landowners and oil companies, for it provided that title of ownership of surface lands did not convey the right to exploit subsoil resources which, belonging to the state, could only be exploited by specific concessions. Only Mexicans and

---

[57] *For. Rel.*, 1917, 905–908, 916–938.

[58] *Ibid.*, 1021; Callahan, *op. cit.*, 572–573.

[59] For an excellent analysis of these constitutional articles, see Frank Tannenbaum, *The Mexican Agrarian Revolution* (New York: The Macmillan Company, 1929), Chap. VIII; also, see Wilfrid H. Callcott, *Liberalism in Mexico, 1857–1929* (Stanford: Stanford University Press, 1931), Chap. XII.

Mexican companies could acquire ownership of lands and waters or obtain concessions to exploit mines or petroleum deposits. Foreigners might be excepted from this restriction if they pledged not to invoke the diplomatic protection of their own governments, but under no circumstances could foreigners acquire ownership of lands or waters within a zone of one hundred kilometers from the frontiers and fifty kilometers from the seacoast. To promote agrarian reform the article also provided that measures should be taken to divide the large landed estates and develop small holdings.

Foreseeing future trouble, Secretary of State Robert Lansing filed protests when the Querétaro Convention was drafting Article 27. The Secretary voiced the concern of American oil companies that their holdings would be confiscated despite the apparent guarantee of Article 14 against retroactive legislation. Despite Carranza's private assurances to Ambassador Fletcher that he would not interfere with the operations of the oil companies, he issued a series of decrees in 1918 which imposed taxes and other restrictive regulations on the companies.[60]

In 1918 and 1919 the situation in Mexico seemed to be slipping back into anarchy; at least this was the view of impatient border Americans as attacks on foreigners at the hands of irresponsible Mexican factions increased. There was little doubt that Carranza's regime was tottering; furthermore, Mexico was not a safe place for Americans, whether they were landowners, mineowners, or oil producers.

Upon the initiative of the Republican majority in the United States Senate, an investigation of Mexican affairs was undertaken by a subcommittee of the Foreign Relations Committee under the chairmanship of Senator Albert B. Fall of New Mexico. This committee, which was charged with determining the extent of damages and outrages suffered by American citizens in Mexico, conducted hearings which lasted from August 8, 1919, until May 28, 1920, and collected voluminous testimony. The investigation, however, was held in an extremely partisan manner; designed to discredit Wilson's conduct of Mexican affairs, as much as to get at the facts of the situation in Mexico, it had a highly inflammatory effect on American public opinion, causing many to advocate armed intervention for the protection of American lives and property.[61] President Wilson still refused to take forcible action against Mexico, and thus the matter rested when Carranza was forced out of office in May, 1920.

The internal opposition to Carranza crystallized in a full-scale revolt led by General Álvaro Obregón of Sonora. Forced to flee Mexico City, Carranza was shot down by a pretended military escort. General Obregón and his allies entered Mexico City on May 8, 1920, but the General did not take the oath of office until late in November of that year. To fill the unexpired term of Carranza, Adolfo de la Huerta, one of the "Sonora Dynasty," was chosen

60 *For. Rel.*, 1917, 1072; Howland, *op. cit.*, 137.

61 U.S. Senate, *Investigation of Mexican Affairs*, Sen. Doc. No. 285, 66th Cong., 2nd Sess., 2 vols.

substitute president by the reorganized congress. He served until November 30, when General Obregón took office, having been elected president on September 8, 1920, by an overwhelming majority.

When de la Huerta and then Álvaro Obregón succeeded to the Mexican presidency over the dead body of Venustiano Carranza, President Wilson was faced once more with the problem of recognition. But as Taft had left him the problem of Victoriano Huerta, he now decided in the last days of his administration, to leave to Warren G. Harding the recognition of Obregón.

Relations with Obregón

Although General Obregón had been chosen president in a duly conducted election, his government was not recognized by the Harding administration for over two years, because he refused to promise, as a condition of American recognition, to sign a treaty guaranteeing American property rights in Mexico acquired prior to the Constitution of 1917.[62] Secretary Hughes asked protection against retroactive legislation in Mexico. He also sought prior understanding on a number of other matters, such as Mexico's default on its public debt and railroad bonds, and claims which extended as far back as 1869, the date of the last claims settlement.

In view of Obregón's refusal to accept conditional recognition, a diplomatic impasse developed between the United States and Mexico which was not broken until August, 1923,[63] when both governments agreed to appoint commissioners to discuss all matters at issue. The result was the Bucareli conference which met in Mexico City from May 15 to August 15, 1923. The outcome of the talks was an "Extra-Official Pact," or gentleman's agreement between the chief executives of the two countries, and two treaties.[64]

In lieu of a formal treaty regarding Article 27, which the Americans wanted, President Obregón subscribed to certain pledges, embodied in an executive agreement, concerning the two outstanding issues: (1) the confiscation of American-owned agricultural lands for the restoration of the *ejidos* or village communal lands, and (2) the confiscation of American-owned oil properties by nationalization of the subsoil deposits.

With respect to the taking of agricultural lands, the State Department had insisted that indemnification should be in cash and according to the just value of the land, and that the Mexican effort to pay in depreciated and inconvertible bonds amounted to confiscation without compensation. The United States

[62] In his message to the Mexican Congress, September 1, 1921, President Obregón said that the signing of such a treaty "would give recognition a conditional character and would injure the sovereignty and dignity of Mexico." *United States Daily,* May 15, 1926, 4.

[63] See Charles W. Hackett, *The Mexican Revolution and the United States, 1910–1926* (Boston: World Peace Foundation, 1926), 351–365, for the diplomatic impasse.

[64] For the Bucareli Conference and agreements, see *ibid.*, 365–375; also, Antonio Gómez Robledo, *The Bucareli Agreements and International Law* (Mexico, D. F.: The National University of Mexico Press, 1940); and *Proceedings of the United States-Mexican Commission Convened in Mexico City,* May 14, 1923 (Washington, D.C.: Government Printing Office, 1925).

government agreed, however, in the "Extra-Official Pact," that out of consideration for the worthy objectives of the agrarian reform in Mexico, it would be willing to accept bonds in payment for the lands provided that each expropriation of surface land did not exceed a given area (i.e., 1,755 hectares, or 4,335 acres).

Regarding the nationalization of the petroleum-bearing subsoil, the Mexican government agreed that the owners of such lands acquired prior to May 1, 1917, who had performed "positive" acts indicating their intention to exploit the oil resources, were to be granted confirmatory concessions. Those owners of surface lands who could not prove the performance of positive acts were to be given priority in filing for drilling concessions.

On the basis of the understanding thus reached in the Bucareli conference, President Obregón was formally recognized on August 31, 1923. Then followed shortly afterwards the signing of two claims conventions; one, a General Claims Convention covering claims dating back to 1868, and the other, a Special Claims Convention, covering all claims arising during the revolutionary period 1910–1920.

United States recognition paid rich dividends almost immediately to President Álvaro Obregón. When the mantle of succession was placed by Obregón on the shoulders of General Plutarco Calles, also of Sonora, Adolfo de la Huerta, the former provisional president, was resentful and launched a revolt. It is believed that the de la Huerta revolution of 1924 might have been successful had it not been for the arms supplied to Obregón by the United States. With de la Huerta out of the way, Calles was easily elected president. For about a year after his inauguration in November, 1924, there was unusual cordiality in relations. This hopeful situation was not to continue into 1926, for beginning in that year, new misunderstandings arose.

Calles and the land and oil controversy

As a matter of fact, hackles began to rise in 1925. Secretary of State Frank B. Kellogg announced publicly, and rather gratuitously, that new revolution was impending in Mexico, and that the government of that country was on trial before the world. Furthermore, he said that United States support of the Mexican government would depend on its compliance with its international obligations. Secretary Kellogg's irritation, which should never have been voiced publicly, probably resulted from the malfunctioning of the Special Claims Commission. The charge that Mexico was on trial was bitterly denied by President Calles.[65]

In December, 1925, relations really took a turn for the worse; the Mexican congress, on the initiative of President Calles, enacted a petroleum law and a land law to implement Article 27 of the Constitution.[66] The former required owners of Mexican oil properties, in order to avoid confiscation, to transfer,

[65] *New York Times,* June 13, 1925; Robledo, *op. cit.,* 111–116.

[66] For an excellent discussion of the Mexican oil and land legislation, see Charles P. Howland, ed., *Survey of American Foreign Relations* (New Haven: Yale University Press, 1931), Chaps. 3 and 4.

before January 1, 1927, their titles of ownership for new concessions terminating in fifty years. Otherwise the petroleum law repeated the pertinent provisions of the Constitution based on the principle of inalienable ownership by the nation of the subsoil deposits. The land law, which also repeated the constitutional restrictions on rights of ownership, required foreign corporations and individuals owning agricultural lands to divest themselves of majority shares. Nor could aliens hold controlling shares in Mexican companies. Sufficient time was conceded to enable foreigners to dispose of their excess holdings. The Mexican government insisted that foreign property owners pledge (Calvo Clause) not to invoke diplomatic protection in disputes over property under penalty of its forfeiture.[67]

The American government protested the new legislation as retroactive, confiscatory, and violative of the solemn pledges of the Bucareli Agreement. Secretary Kellogg, in his famous *Aide Memoire* of November 17, 1925, to the Mexican Foreign Minister, perceived clouds "on the horizon of friendship between the United States and Mexico," and seemed to imply that should the Mexican government be unwilling to amend the sections of the laws deemed harmful to American interests, official recognition would be withdrawn.[68] President Calles vigorously denied Kellogg's charges, and insisted that the "exchange of views" at the Bucareli conference had no binding force.

Once more official United States-Mexican relations were at an impasse. And once again there were insistent demands for forcible intervention in Mexico, but this time those who protested the failure of the Mexican government to respect the property rights of aliens were reinforced by Americans who were scandalized by Calles' attack on the Catholic Church in Mexico. A dangerous socialistic and atheistic infection might not, it was feared, be confined to Mexico. In the heat of the land and oil controversy and the ensuing public clamor, President Coolidge, while predicting a peaceful settlement, contributed to a further deterioration in relations by asserting the duty of the American government to protect its citizens abroad, for "the person and property of a citizen are a part of the general domain of the nation even when abroad."[69]

So vocal and insistent was American public reaction to the apparent insane drift to war with Mexico that the Coolidge administration was forced to give heed. It therefore decided to adopt a more sympathetic and conciliatory attitude in the negotiations for the protection of American interests. Paradoxically, it was a member of the Wall Street House of Morgan, Dwight W. Morrow, a former classmate of President Coolidge at Amherst, whom the President selected to untangle and tranquilize the Mexican situation; his mission launched a new era in United States-Mexican relations.

[67] The Mexican government agreed, in October, 1926, that the United States government had the right to intervene for its nationals, but that they should not seek this protection. Dunn, *op. cit.,* 391–400.

[68] For this document, see *Sen. Doc.* No. 96, 69th Cong., 1st Sess., under the title "Rights of American Citizens in Certain Oil Lands in Mexico."

[69] *New York Times,* March 23, 1927.

The Morrow mission and its aftermath

On assuming his post, Ambassador Morrow immediately inaugurated a new brand of diplomacy characterized by cordial social and official relations on terms of democratic equality. He made it his business, not to please the American colony in Mexico City, but to create an atmosphere of friendly confidence among leading government officials. A feature of the Morrow approach was his ham and eggs breakfasts with President Calles. Soon the new ambassador, because of his democratic habits and real enthusiasm for Mexican culture, won unusual popular favor. The winning of Mexican confidence, respect, and friendship was the basis laid by this Wall Street imperialist for a successful diplomatic mission.[70]

The first step leading to an amicable settlement of the oil question was a decision by the Supreme Court of Mexico on November 17, 1927, that declared unconstitutional those provisions of the petroleum law which required companies to exchange their titles of ownership for fifty-year concessions. Thereupon, the congress, at the suggestion of President Calles, amended the law to validate in perpetuity all titles obtained prior to May 1, 1917, provided, of course, there was evidence of performance of "positive acts." This settlement, a compromise, removed from discussion the most serious cause of contention between the United States and Mexico.

After his settlement of the oil controversy, Ambassador Morrow devoted his official attention to the land question. His efforts to bring about a cessation of land seizures were unsuccessful, as were most of his representations on behalf of individual American claimants. These were problems for the courts and the claims commissions.

Mr. Morrow gave considerable unofficial attention to the Church question. The determination of President Calles to enforce to the letter the religious articles of the Constitution of 1917 resulted in a Catholic strike. Beginning on April 1, 1926, all religious ceremonies were suspended, although the churches were kept open. A state of religious civil war developed in certain parts of Mexico between the fanatical *Cristeros* and the central and state governments. This sad state of affairs was finally ended through the mediatory efforts of the ambassador. However, it was not until June, 1929, that a working agreement was finally reached by Emilio Portes Gil, the new president of Mexico, and the Vatican, which allowed the reopening of churches.[71]

When Ambassador Morrow retired from his post in September, 1930, there were no outstanding controversies or unsettled questions with Mexico, except the problem of the claims commissions.

The two mixed claims commissions, provided by treaties negotiated at the Bucareli conference in 1923, were duly installed in 1924.[72] The General

[70] Cline, *op. cit.,* 210–212.

[71] See J. Lloyd Mecham, *Church and State in Latin America* (Chapel Hill: University of North Carolina Press, 1934), 494–498.

[72] For the work of the two claims commissions, see Feller, *op. cit.* This work contains in the appendix the texts of the pertinent treaties and protocols.

Claims Commission was to consider all claims dating back to 1868, except those for damages suffered through revolutionary acts within the period from November 20, 1910, to May 31, 1920. The latter were to be considered by a Special Claims Commission.

After seven years the General Claims Commission could report, in August, 1931, only the following limited results: *American claims:* filed, 2781, amounting to $513,694,267.17; claims disallowed or dismissed, 50; awards made, 89 amounting to $4,607,926.59. *Mexican claims:* filed, 836, amounting to $246,158,395.32; claims disallowed or dismissed, 4; awards made, 5, amounting to $39,000. Since the progress of the Commission was slow because of constant bickering over the meaning and extent of the responsibility of states for injuries committed against aliens, it was decided in 1934 to conclude a convention providing for all claims to be settled either through a "lump-sum" payment, or through adjudication by an umpire. The convention, however, never materialized, for the work of the Commission in appraising the true value of the claims was never concluded. Thus, there was no settlement of general claims until the problem was merged into the Comprehensive Agreements of November 19, 1941.

The history of the Special Claims Commission was even less satisfactory. The first claim — for the massacre of the American engineers by Villa at Santa Ysabel — amounted to $1,225,000. The Mexican commissioner, supported by the Brazilian umpire, held the Mexican government was not responsible. The United States Commissioner vigorously dissented, and the United States refused to present any further cases to the Special Commission. Finally, in 1934, the two countries agreed, by formal treaty, on a settlement whereby the United States would accept a lump sum, payable in installments, calculated at 2.64 per cent of the total value of United States claims. The ratio of 2.64 per cent was the actual ratio of awards to claims that similar mixed claims commissions adjudicating European claims against Mexico had established.[73] According to this formula the lump sum amounted to $5,448,020.14. The Mexican government agreed to pay annual installments of $500,000 including interest. The final payment for revolutionary claims was made on January 2, 1945.[74]

Cárdenas revives crises

From about 1928 to 1935 the vigor of the Mexican Revolution seemed to have been spent. The "men of the Revolution" were no longer young; more significantly, perhaps, Calles and his satellites had become a new class of capitalists and had taken on economic and social conservatism. Relations between the United States and Mexico, therefore, were not likely to become

[73] U.S. Dept. of State, *U.S. Treaty Series*, No. 883.

[74] A Special Mixed Claims Commission of the United States, created by Act of April 10, 1935, adjudicated the claims of American citizens and awarded from the payments made by Mexico. As a matter of interest, the Santa Ysabel claimants were awarded $92,910. *Special Mexican Claims Commission, Report to the Secretary of State* (Washington, D.C.: Government Printing Office, 1940), 104.

critical. But with the inauguration of President Lázaro Cárdenas on November 30, 1934, the Revolution was revived and relations again became tense.[75]

Under Cárdenas the agrarian reform, which prior to his administration had come almost to a complete stop, entered a new stage of activity. In fact the new program of land distribution resulted in a larger amount of land confiscation than in all the preceding administrations. Of course many American landowners were "expropriated." The Cárdenas program was also directed toward the nationalization of resources and industry. In preparing the way, the Mexican congress enacted in November, 1936, an Expropriation Law which accorded the president almost unlimited powers to take over private property for "public and social welfare."[76]

The Expropriation Law, in conjunction with labor laws, enabled the Mexican government to exert the necessary pressure to create a "labor squeeze," which often made it possible for workers' cooperatives to take over industrial plants and mines. In June, 1937, Cárdenas nationalized the National Railways of Mexico and consolidated its outstanding debts with the general obligations of the Mexican government. These expropriations evoked scarcely a murmur of protest from the Department of State.[77] In March, 1938, President Cárdenas confiscated the foreign-owned oil properties, promising indemnification "in due course."

The expropriation of the vast oil holdings of the British and Americans was not without provocation, for the foreign giants had refused to abide by the award of the Federal Board of Arbitration in favor of rather exorbitant demands by the workers. The oil companies appealed to the Supreme Court, which, on March 1, 1938, confirmed the award of the Board. When the companies hedged on accepting the award in full, President Cárdenas, on March 18, 1938, decreed the expropriation of their properties under the law of 1936. It was the belief of the Mexican president that the arrogant and all-powerful foreign-owned oil industry had challenged constituted authority and that the national honor of Mexico was at stake. The president received the enthusiastic support of the Mexican nation.

Although the oil expropriation was discussed in an earlier chapter in relation to the Good Neighbor policy, additional details are supplied here for a better understanding of the problem.[78] In the first place it should be noted

---

[75] See Charles A. Thomson, "Mexico's Social Revolution," *Foreign Policy Reports,* XIII, No. 10 (August 1, 1937), 114–124.

[76] The law authorized expropriation of private property to promote "the equal distribution of wealth held and monopolized to the exclusive advantage of a few persons." *Diario Oficial,* November 25, 1936. See Charles A. Thomson, "Mexico's Challenge to Foreign Capital," *For. Pol. Rep.,* XIII, No. 11 (August 15, 1937), 126–136.

[77] Wendell C. Gordon, *The Expropriation of Foreign Owned Property in Mexico* (Washington, D.C.: American Council on Public Affairs, 1941), 140–141. Also, see Arthur W. Macmahon, "The Mexican Railways Under Workers' Administration," *Public Administration Review,* I, No. 5 (Autumn, 1941), 458–471.

[78] For the oil expropriations and United States relations, see Gordon, *op. cit.,* 102 ff.; Bryce Wood, *The Making of the Good Neighbor Policy* (New York: Columbia University Press, 1961), 203–259; Charles A. Thomson, "The Mexican Oil Dispute," *For. Pol. Rep.,* XIV, No. 11 (August 15, 1938), 122–132; and Josephus Daniels, *Shirt-Sleeve Diplomat* (Chapel Hill: University of North Carolina Press, 1947), 211–268.

that the companies and the Mexican government were far apart in their estimates of the value of what had been expropriated. The companies placed a value as high as $450 million (United States $200 million; Great Britain $250 million) on their surface installations, other tangible assets, and also the oil underground. The Mexican government, holding that the companies had already recovered several times over on their investments, recognized ownership only of the surface properties. This meant, for example, that the property of the American companies was valued at only about $10 million.

Fearful of jeopardizing the Good Neighbor policy, the State Department refrained from any kind of vigorous action. The oilmen urged the Department to act, but it, breathing the doxology of the Good Neighbor, tried to persuade the companies to settle the matter themselves with Mexico. Repeatedly, the Department acknowledged the right of the Mexican government to expropriate, but insisted — not too vigorously — that the owners of the expropriated properties were entitled to prompt and adequate compensation. President Roosevelt himself, on April 1, undercut the extravagant valuations set by the companies on their holdings, by conceding the Mexican contention that the underground oil should not be counted in the final settlement, i.e., should be confiscated without compensation.[79] Except for urging the Mexican government to make fair recompense, and the companies to come to an agreement with Mexico, the United States government refrained from deeper involvement in the oil controversy.[80]

For the remainder of the Cárdenas administration there was a stalemate between the Mexican government and the expropriated oil companies; refusing to come to terms, the companies exerted themselves, through their international business ramifications, to boycott the nationalized Mexican oil industry both in the sale of its oil and in the purchase of equipment.[81]

In a transparent move to show that the New Deal was more interested in the "little fellow" than in the "large interests," Secretary Cordell Hull began, immediately after the expropriation decree, to direct a series of notes to Mexico, not about oil, but about the seizure of *moderately sized* land holdings that rendered only a *moderate* living to American *farmers* in Mexico. He suggested arbitration of these land seizures extending back to 1927 and amounting to over $10 million.[82] In November, 1938, Mexico agreed to submit the claims for American lands seized since 1927 to a mixed commission. Until commissioners should determine the value of the confiscated properties, Mexico agreed, as proof of its good intentions, to pay $1 million annually.[83] Thus, when the agrarian claims arising subsequent to 1927 were absorbed in a global

---

[79] Cline, *op. cit.*, 244.

[80] In July, 1938, President Cárdenas told the press in Mexico that "the United States Department [of State] had made no demands upon Mexico in regard to the expropriation and had sent no formal note." Wood, *op. cit.*, 214.

[81] *Ibid.*, 227–233. The British Government, uninhibited by a Good Neighbor policy, protested the expropriation too vigorously, with the result that Mexico broke diplomatic relations. In a final settlement, which did not come until 1947, the British companies fared somewhat better than the American companies.

[82] Cline, *op. cit.*, 245–246; Wood, *op. cit.*, 237–247.

[83] *For. Rel.* 1938, V, 714, 717.

settlement of $40 million, contracted in November, 1941, Mexico had paid $6 million for which she was given credit.

In a real sense the revolutionary program as embodied in the Constitution of 1917 attained its culmination in the administration of President Cárdenas. It then remained for his successors to consolidate the gains achieved by 1940 in education, agrarian reform, labor, and economic nationalism. Undoubtedly the crowning achievement of Lázaro Cárdenas was his success in nationalizing the subsoil petroleum resources. By no convenient resort to sophistry is it possible to obscure the fact that the president with the frank acquiescence of the New Deal, was allowed to scrap the Bucareli Agreement of 1923 and confiscate without compensation the underground oil resources belonging to the oil companies by legal acquisition. The plan for compensation worked out later in 1942 was clearly based on the denial of any property rights in the petroleum underground. Those rights had been placed on the sacrificial altar of the Good Neighbor policy.

3. Relations Since 1940

Ávila Camacho and World War II

On December 1, 1940, General Manuel Ávila Camacho was inaugurated President of Mexico, and although he was a Cárdenas designate and therefore an assured victor at the polls, he lacked the revolutionary ardor of his predecessor. In fact, it was the belief of the new president that the Revolution was over and the time had come for rebuilding. With him came an end to the sorties against landowners and the owners of mines and factories. Even the Catholic clergy could relax, for the president confessed that he himself was a "believer." To say that Mexico "moved to the Right" under Camacho and his successors was true only in a relative sense, for the gains of the Revolution were cherished by the new administrations. There was no intention to retreat from any of the established fronts, but, while holding them, to turn attention to the new needs of Mexico, particularly industrialization.

It was not without significance that an "era of good feeling" in United States-Mexican relations was inaugurated following the termination of the Cárdenas administration. It is very doubtful that Cárdenas, who had a congenital dislike for the United States and a strong inclination to the extreme Left, could have managed such a radical departure in Mexican policy as did President Ávila Camacho.

Whereas President Cárdenas had viewed the outbreak of war in Europe in September, 1939, as "an international conflict between ambitious, unscrupulous, and imperialistic interests," and refused to recognize any difference between the war objectives of the Allies and the Axis powers (the Marxist line), President Ávila Camacho denounced fascism and expressed sympathy for the Allies. Whereas Cárdenas had preferred to be a passive spectator, Ávila Camacho and Foreign Minister Ezequiel Padilla gave evidence, long before Pearl Harbor, of a desire to cooperate with the United States.[84]

Probably in anticipation of eventual war involvement, the United States and Mexican administrations proceeded to resolve outstanding differences which might mar their cooperative efforts. The outstanding problems were those created by the Cárdenas expropriations of American-owned lands and oil wells. Other problems related to claims and to Mexico's default on its foreign debt.

On November 19, 1941, the two governments entered into a "global" or "comprehensive" economic pact including the following agreements: (1) Mexico agreed by a special claims convention, to pay the United States a "lump sum" of $40 million in full settlement of the General Claims, and also the agrarian claims since 1927.[85] Since Mexico was credited with $3 million for payments already made, and $3 million to be paid when ratifications of the convention were exchanged, the balance of $34 million was to be liquidated in annual payments of $2.5 million.[86] (2) The United States Treasury agreed to buy each month from the Mexican government up to six million ounces of silver at the world price. (3) The Export-Import Bank opened a line of credit of $30 million to the Mexican government to expedite the completion of the Pan American Highway in Mexico, as well as to build and expand steel factories. Both countries also agreed to begin negotiations for a long-overdue trade pact and signed one on December 23, 1942. Mexico thus became the fifteenth Latin-American country to enter into one of Secretary Hull's reciprocal trade agreements.

As for the expropriated oil properties, the United States and Mexico agreed to the appointment of a mixed commission of experts, one from each government, to determine what a just compensation would be to the American owners for their properties and rights in Mexico.[87] On April 18, 1942, the experts reported their agreement that a total of $23,995,991 was a fair evaluation, and recommended the payment of this sum by the Mexican government. The experts recognized Mexico's chief contention, i.e., that the subsoil wealth belonged to the nation and was inalienable. In other words, the experts reasoned that the taking of the oil wells was not confiscation without compensation, for the subsoil had never belonged to the oil companies.

The State Department advised the companies to accept the award and indicated that this would be its final contribution to a settlement of the issue. Some smaller companies did accept and concluded special settlement agreements with the Mexican government. As a matter of fact, two years earlier, in 1940, the Sinclair Oil Company had broken the united oil front and made

[84] "In a fairly unbroken curve Mexico shifted from a passive spectator in 1939 to a partner in the United States' 'belligerent neutrality' during 1940 and 1941." Cline, *op. cit.,* 265.

[85] For a summary of the accord, see Dept. of State *Bulletin,* XV, No. 126 (November 22, 1941), 399–403; also *For. Pol. Rep.,* XIX, No. 7 (June 15, 1943), 84–85.

[86] Ratifications were exchanged on April 2, 1942. The final installment was paid by Mexico on November 18, 1955.

[87] At that time the Mexican government made a deposit of $9 million on account of the compensation to be paid.

a separate peace with the Mexican government for a cash payment of $8.5 million. The two largest American firms however, refused to accept the sum awarded by the experts, and held out for about a year longer.[88]

In September, 1943, the two governments agreed on a plan of annual installments based on the experts' evaluation of $23,995,991, plus 3 per cent per annum from March 18, 1938, to the date of final settlement of all balances due, a total of $29,137,700.84. The American companies felt compelled to accept, being assured by the Mexican government of release from all pending claims except for unpaid taxes and duties. The Mexican government punctually made the payments agreed upon, and the final installment was paid on September 30, 1947.[89] Thus was written *finis* to the most serious diplomatic issue spawned by the Mexican Revolution.

In November, 1942, another thorn in United States relations with Mexico, i.e., the problem of Mexico's defaulted foreign debt contracted between 1885 and 1913, was extracted, when an agreement was reached by the Mexican government and representatives of the foreign creditors. This agreement, concluded outside direct diplomatic channels, provided for the resumption of partial payments on that part of the debt held by nationals of friendly countries, a large part being held in the United States. A similar agreement concerning the railway debt was concluded in 1946.[90]

Wiping the slate clean of most of the differences between the United States and Mexico facilitated unprecedented cooperation between the two nations during World War II. On December 8, 1941, Mexico broke off relations with Japan, and later with the other Axis nations. At the Rio Meeting of Foreign Ministers, in January, 1942, Foreign Minister Ezequiel Padilla was most eloquent in his endeavor to win support for the United States-sponsored recommendation that all Latin-American governments sever relations with the Axis. On May 30, 1942, following the sinking of a Mexican oil tanker by a German submarine, Mexico formally declared war.

It cannot be said that the Mexican nation was enthusiastically united behind its administration in its momentous decision to cooperate with the United States in resisting Nazi-fascist aggression. It was not a popular war, but was widely known as "Señor Padilla's War," because of the Foreign Minister's well-known pro-United States attitude. But fortunately, since public apathy scarcely ever took the form of opposition,[91] the Ávila Camacho administration was able to furnish a creditable war record for the Mexican nation.

Although Mexico's principal contributions to the war effort were economic, let us first note her politico-military cooperation with the United States. On

[88] *For. Pol. Rep.*, XIX, 85; Cline, *op. cit.*, 249–250.

[89] U.S. Dept. of State *Bulletin*, XVII, No. 432 (October 12, 1947), 747.

[90] Mexico's external debts, state and railroad, were finally liquidated in July, 1960, when the defaulted bonds were paid off in dollars at the rate of 4.5 pesos to the dollar. To enable payments a loan was contracted with the Prudential Life Insurance Company. *Hispanic American Report*, XIII, No. 7 (July, 1960), 438; Cline, *op. cit.*, 287.

[91] Communist, and crypto-Communist opposition ceased in Mexico after Hitler attacked Russia. Vicente Lombardo Toledano, for a time, modified his anti-United States views.

April 2, 1941, a reciprocal Mexican-United States air-transit agreement was announced which opened the air lanes and bases of either country to the military aircraft of the other. This enabled United States planes to fly over Mexico en route to Panama. The United States was not able, however, in the Staff Conversations of 1940 to make base agreements with Mexico. These agreements were not concluded until after Pearl Harbor.

On January 12, 1942, the United States and Mexican governments jointly announced that they had "found it expedient to establish a mixed commission to study the problems relating to the defense of the two countries and to propose to the respective governments the measures which should be adopted."[92] This Joint Mexican-United States Defense Commission also handled the problem of military lend-lease to Mexico. Under the specific provisions of United States-Mexican defense agreements each nation opened its territory and facilities to military use by the other, and pledged its mutual cooperation. The program also called for the advanced training of Mexican military personnel in United States military schools and establishments.

With small craft obtained from the United States, the Mexican navy participated in the antisubmarine patrol in the Gulf of Mexico. Furthermore, it is significant to note that except for Brazil, Mexico was the only Latin-American country which took an active part in the war overseas. A Mexican air squadron of 300 men saw action under General Douglas MacArthur in June, 1945, in the Philippines, and in August, over Formosa. Therefore, next to Brazil, Mexico received the largest lend-lease grants from the United States — $38 million.[93]

In addition to lend-lease, United States economic assistance to Mexico was most generous. Not only were there a number of mutually beneficial agreements between the two countries providing for the purchase of strategic and critical materials, but the United States extended loans, principally through the Exim Bank for the improvement of agriculture, the extension of industry, and rehabilitation of the railways. In April, 1943, a Joint Mexican-American Commission for Economic Cooperation was created following meetings between Presidents Roosevelt and Ávila Camacho in Monterrey, Mexico, and Corpus Christi, Texas. The commission was to consider and make recommendations concerning the most pressing economic problems calling for joint action by the two countries. In a letter from President Roosevelt to President Ávila Camacho, dated February 20, 1944, the American President referred to the fact that the United States, in spite of the demands of war upon all of its resources, met the requirements of Mexico for materials and equipment *on a larger scale than in any of the prewar years.*[94]

For her part Mexico made her greatest contribution to the war effort by stepping up the production of raw materials needed by the United States.

[92] Dept. of State *Bulletin,* VI (January 17, 1942), 67.

[93] Another Mexican contribution to the war effort was the 250,000 Mexicans living in the United States who enlisted in the United States armed forces.

[94] Pan American Union *Bulletin,* LXXIX, No. 4 (April, 1945), 211.

The most vital materials supplied by Mexico were minerals, such as mercury, zinc, lead, copper and antimony. For the period July 1, 1940, to September 30, 1945, United States procurements from Mexico totaled $343 million.[95] It should be noted that Mexico was able to maintain and increase her production of prime materials thanks in part to United States assistance in supplying necessary machinery and equipment.

Mexico also furnished manpower during the war for work on United States farms and railways. For many years prior to the war Mexican workers had swarmed into the United States illegally, both as permanent and seasonal laborers. Although under the terms of the Immigration Law of 1924 citizens of all Latin-American countries were exempt from the quota restrictions, most of the Mexican workers were unable to qualify for immigration visas because they could not meet the employment or self-support requirements of the law. Therefore, because of restricted opportunities in Mexico, and the allure of employment in the United States, hundreds of thousands of Mexicans entered the United States in evasion of the law. So many slipped across the border by wading or swimming the Rio Grande that these illegal migrant workers came to be called "wetbacks." Fearful of detection and deportation, a great number of Mexicans residing in the United States for years — even many who had been born in this country — chose not to risk the naturalization process. This fact helps to explain why, of all aliens resident in the United States, the Mexicans constituted the largest percentage who neglected to become citizens.[96]

With the outbreak of war and the drain of American labor into war industries there was increased demand for Mexican labor to harvest crops and maintain rights-of-way on the railways. The situation called for an organized effort to supply the needed manpower. The first of a number of *bracero,* or labor, agreements, was signed by the United States and Mexican governments on August 4, 1942. According to this war measure the Mexican government agreed to furnish the *braceros,* and the United States agreed to provide officials who would see to it that they were decently housed and paid. The United States government was in effect a guardian of these workers and assumed responsibility for effectuating the protective safeguards established by the work contracts. Mexican *braceros* proved to be a great help during the war in harvesting crops and keeping the trains running.

The exchange of ratifications on November 8, 1945, of the Water Treaty between the United States and Mexico, was indicative of the general spirit of cooperation prevailing at that time. The treaty provided for the equitable allocation to the United States and Mexico of the water available from the Colorado and Tijuana Rivers and of the Rio Grande from Fort Quitman, Texas, to the Gulf of Mexico.[97] Also, the treaty provided that the two gov-

[95] United States Military Academy, *Raw Materials in War and Peace* (West Point, 1947), 110–111, 145–149.
[96] *Fifteenth Census of the United States, 1930. Population.* II, General Report, 405.
[97] U.S. Dept. of State *Bulletin,* X, No. 241 (February 5, 1944), 161–162.

ernments would undertake the construction of storage dams, and other facilities, including flood protection works.[98]

As authorized by the Water Treaty, the International Boundary and Water Commission proceeded with plans for dams and flood-control projects across the Rio Grande. The Falcón Dam, located about seventy-five miles downriver from Laredo, was dedicated on October 19, 1953. This product of international cooperation[99] provided water for a network of irrigation canals on both sides of the river. In October, 1960, an agreement was signed at Ciudad Acuña, Mexico, by Presidents Eisenhower and Adolfo López Mateos, for the construction of Amistad Dam, ten miles up the Rio Grande from Ciudad Acuña, to form part of the system of international storage dams.

President Alemán and postwar relations

The year 1946 brought Miguel Alemán to the presidency of Mexico. The first of a new line of civilian presidents, Alemán's electoral victory, assured because he was the candidate of the official revolutionary party, was doubly assured because his opponent, former Foreign Minister Ezequiel Padilla, had been too ardent a partisan of the United States. Nevertheless, the smooth flow of United States-Mexican relations continued undisturbed during the postwar years of the Truman and Alemán administrations.

In 1947 Presidents Truman and Alemán exchanged ceremonial visits which were prelude to the announcement of further economic cooperation, specifically to help stabilize the peso and to assist the financing of development projects in Mexico. The great bulk of this financing was handled by Nacional Financiera, the financial agency of the Mexican government, to which the Export-Import Bank made loans available.

So rapid was Mexico's economic development that, from 1939 to 1951, its purchases from the United States rose from $83 million to $510 million. Mexico also developed such a thriving tourist industry that in 1951 it was earning for the country more than $150 million in badly needed foreign exchange.[100]

Because of the postwar dollar drain, Mexico had been trying since 1945 to secure United States consent to a revision of the Reciprocal Trade Agreement of 1943, to allow for the protection of infant Mexican industries. Eventually, on December 30, 1950, the agreement was terminated by mutual consent.

One of the most heartening demonstrations of United States-Mexican cooperation was the collaborative effort of the two countries in combatting *aftosa,* the hoof-and-mouth disease which made its appearance in southeastern Mexico in 1946. Because its own great cattle industry was endangered by the highly infectious disease, which was spreading northward in Mexico, the

[98] See C. A. Timm, "Water Treaty Between the United States and Mexico," Dept. of State *Bulletin* X, No. 248 (March 25, 1944), 282–292.

[99] The cost of the dam, $47 million, was borne by the two nations in proportion to the amount of water to be taken by each, i.e., Mexico 41.4 per cent and United States 58.6 per cent.

[100] U.S. Dept. of State *Bulletin,* XXV, No. 650 (December 10, 1951), 960.

United States joined Mexico in various efforts to eradicate it. A Joint American-Mexican *Aftosa* Commission was set up to direct the fight. At first there was a wholesale slaughter of infected animals and the United States assisted in payment of compensation to the owners; later, resistance by owners proved so threatening that the extermination campaign had to give way to the innoculation technique, which in the end proved successful.[101] In March, 1952, five years after the original outbreak of the disease, its definitive eradication was announced, the Joint Commission was dissolved, and the United States quarantine of Mexican cattle was lifted. The eradication campaign had cost the United States $125 million.[102] The successful battle against *aftosa* was only a phase of a widely extended technical cooperation (Point Four) program covering a large number of subjects including agriculture, mining, and public health.

Although Mexico, in the postwar years, indicated a willingness to collaborate with the United States in a variety of economic measures, this willingness did not extend to the military. In 1952 the United States initiated negotiations with most of the Latin-American countries for bilateral Military Assistance Agreements. Twelve Latin-American governments entered into such pacts with the United States, but President Alemán rejected the proposed agreement. To Mexico the terms implied a certain dependence on the United States and a sacrifice of national freedom of decision which could not be accepted.

Braceros and wetbacks

The problem of Mexico's migrant labor, including both *braceros* and "wetbacks," was a troublesome and delicate issue in United States-Mexican relations throughout the postwar period. In April, 1947, the United States Congress enacted legislation providing for the liquidation of the wartime foreign migratory labor program. Henceforward, although other *bracero* agreements were contracted, the United States government no longer subsidized transportation, housing, subsistence, health, and other costs. These were to be assumed by private groups contracting for Mexican labor. This was highly unsatisfactory to the Alemán government, which hoped to secure guarantees against mistreatment of Mexicans in the United States. Finally a temporary compromise agreement was signed which included most of the civil and social guarantees demanded by President Alemán, who reserved the right to restrict *braceros* from areas in the United States where discrimination existed.[103]

The temporary agreement gave way to the Migrant Labor Agreement of August 11, 1951, which was negotiated pursuant to an act of Congress authorizing the Secretary of Labor to recruit agricultural workers from Mexico in order to assist in the harvesting of crops in the United States. Although

---

[101] Cline, *op. cit.*, 394–395.

[102] U.S. Dept. of State *Bulletin*, XXVI (March 31, 1952), 459. *Hisp. Am. Rep.*, V, No. 3 (April, 1952), 10.

[103] U.S. Dept. of State *Bulletin*, XXI, No. 524 (July 18, 1949), 44; Cline, *op. cit.*, 392–393.

due to expire within a year this agreement was periodically amended and extended until eventual termination in 1964.

The *bracero program* had its friends and opponents on both sides of the border. In the United States the truck farmers needed a reliable supply of seasonal "stoop-labor" in view of the inadequate supply of domestic agricultural workers. On the other hand, American organized labor opposed cheap foreign labor which depressed wages. In Mexico there was a large supply of available *braceros,* for the simple truth of the matter was that Mexico's productive land was insufficient to provide food and jobs for its one million per annum population increase. Therefore, there was great pressure in Mexico to hire out as *braceros.* The crowds of men at recruiting stations, often held back at bayonet points, testified to the fact that employment prospects in Mexico were extremely uncertain. Those who did find work as *braceros* (and there were between 200,000 and 400,000 hired every year) were but a fraction of those who were unsuccessful in their attempts to get jobs.[104]

The Mexican government entered into the *bracero* agreements reluctantly, for it felt that Mexican workers were needed for the development of their own country. However, there was the favorable fact that the *braceros'* dollar remittances, averaging about $35 million annually, supplied the foreign exchange needed to maintain a balance of payments equilibrium. Nevertheless, the Mexican government never relaxed its insistence on as favorable terms as possible to assure for its nationals fair wages, good treatment, and freedom from discrimination.

Much less fortunate were the wetbacks, for they enjoyed no contract guarantees. As a result, they were shamefully exploited by border farmers and labor contractors. Notwithstanding, they swarmed into the United States in fantastic numbers, thanks to an undermanned border patrol. The flood reached its peak in the early 1950's. In 1952 it was estimated that 1.5 million crossed the border illegally. The United States Immigration Service reported that 600,000 had been apprehended in 1952 and returned to Mexico. For one caught, one got away. In 1953 over one million wetbacks were caught and deported. In 1954 they were shipped back to Mexico at the rate of 700 to 2,000 daily. At that time a crackdown on illegal entrants, known as "Operation Wetback" was instituted and the border patrol was greatly increased in numbers.[105] The Mexican government also became more cooperative in restraining the exodus of its citizens. Although the crisis was passed in 1955, the flow of wetbacks was never completely stopped.

Relations since 1952

Under Presidents Adolfo Ruíz Cortines (1952–1958) and Adolfo López Mateos (1958–1964), Mexico's policy seemed to be that of seeking to lessen dependence on the United States, politically, militarily, and economically. It

---

[104] The recruiting of *braceros* in Mexico was tainted with graft. Often, worker-applicants had to pay up to $25 each to Mexican officials at the recruiting centers for the privilege of being contracted. *Hisp. Am. Rep.* X, No. 10 (November, 1957), 520.

[105] *Ibid.,* VI, No. 1 (February, 1953), 9; VII, No. 10 (November, 1954), 8.

was in connection with the problems of Communism and the cold war in general, and Castro's Cuba in particular, that the outlines of Mexico's policy trend became more apparent. At the Caracas conference of 1954, the problem of Communism in Guatemala prompted a resolution which declared that the domination or control of an American state by international Communism was a threat to all American states; this resolution also called for appropriate action under existing treaties (i.e., Rio treaty of 1947). Mexico refused to vote on the resolution, pleading that it compromised the sacred principle of nonintervention. On this, as on other occasions, the Mexican position seemed to be that the questionable dangers of Communist aggression did not equal the certain dangers of a United States freed from the restraints of the nonintervention pledge.

It was in connection with the Cuban issue that the positions of the United States and Mexico appeared at greatest variance. Mexicans generally viewed the Castro revolutionary triumph with great enthusiasm, for they saw in it an overdue duplication, on a small scale, of their own great Revolution. This view they were most reluctant to change even in the face of most startling developments in Cuba, for they felt that the Cuban people should be left alone to work out their own destinies without meddling by the OAS. Thus Mexico refused to condemn Cuba at the Seventh Meeting of Foreign Ministers, and refused to suspend Cuba from the OAS at the Eighth Meeting at Punta del Este. Early in 1964 the Mexican government warned the United States that under no circumstances would it agree to an embargo on Cuba. A statement by López Mateos in February, 1964, that the right place to discuss Cuba was the UN and not the OAS was indicative of a growing coolness in Mexico for the regional organization which was believed to be a "colonial office" of the United States.

The decision of the Ninth Meeting of Foreign Ministers, in July, 1964, to require all American governments to suspend diplomatic and economic relations with Cuba was ignored by Mexico, despite its obligations under the Rio treaty. Mexico insisted on maintaining diplomatic relations with Cuba, not only because withdrawing of recognition or breaking off relations would be a form of intervention, but because such measures would mean truckling to the will of the United States.

Mexico's desires to be less dependent politically and economically on the United States are readily understandable, as are the harsh facts which oppose the achievement of this objective. During the past decade between 70 and 80 per cent of Mexico's total trade has been with the United States, the neighbor republic being the best customer of the United States in Latin America. In 1963 American exports to Mexico totaled $826.8 million, and imports amounted to $594 million. American investors, remarkably resilient to expropriation reverses, have returned to Mexico in increased numbers, with the result that in 1962 United States private investments in Mexico amounted to $873 million.[106]

[106] U.S. Dept. of Commerce, *Survey of Current Business,* August, 1963, and April, 1964.

Although the Mexican government has contracted loans with non-United States financial institutions, in order to lessen dependence on this country, the Exim Bank must be cited as by far the principal source of Mexico's foreign credit. Probably the most numerous and substantial loans were for the modernization of Mexico's railways and the expansion of her steel industry.[107] Generally, the loans extended over a wide range of units in Mexico's industrialization program, although agricultural credits must also be mentioned. Under the heading of "economic assistance," loans to Mexico for the period July 1, 1945, through June 30, 1963, amounted to $446 million.[108] Of all the Latin-American countries, Mexico has perhaps made the most gratifying progress in the Alliance for Progress, not only because it enjoyed a considerable head start over the other countries in agrarian and social reform, but because there was greater public and private understanding and acceptance of the program. The Alliance for Progress meant no new departure for Mexico, but rather accelerated progress along lines predetermined many years before.

The long-standing Chamizal controversy with Mexico was finally settled by signature of a convention in August, 1963, and ratification in December. In accordance with the treaty there was virtual acceptance by the United States of the arbitral award of 1912, which divided the territory in dispute — it is located within the city of El Paso. In order to relocate the Rio Grande so that all Mexican territory in that area would be south of a new river channel, the treaty also provided for the transfer to the United States of approximately one-half of Cordova Island, a Mexican enclave north of the present channel of the Rio Grande.[109] Mexicans regarded the Chamizal settlement as a victory of "right and reason" that had been overdue for fifty years.

A relatively slight irritant of the postwar decade was the shrimp fisheries controversy. Beginning in 1952 Mexico began enforcing on United States shrimp boats fishing in Gulf of Mexico waters off the coasts of Campeche and Vera Cruz, a law of 1935 claiming jurisdiction, or "wet sovereignty," out to nine miles. A number of Texas-owned shrimp boats were seized by Mexican patrol craft. Although the United States had never conceded sovereignty beyond the three-mile limit, the State Department instructed the fishermen not to fish in Mexican waters.[110] This appeared to give legal acquiscence to Mexico's claims beyond the three-mile limit. The following years were marked by recurring incidents of American shrimp boats apprehended, and even fired upon, by Mexican patrol craft on the charge of invading the nine-mile limit.

Another problem much too serious to be called an irritant was the so-called Colorado River salinity issue.[111] Under the terms of the Water Treaty of

---

[107] The Exim Bank made no loans to Pemex, for, as the State Department explained, it was not U.S. policy "to lend when private capital was available"; or was it that it was not U.S. policy to subsidize socialization?

[108] *Foreign Grants and Credits by the United States Government.* Fiscal year, 1963, No. 74. U.S. Dept. of Commerce, p. 12.

[109] For the Chamizal Settlement and text of the treaty, see Dept. of State *Bulletin,* XLIX, No. 1265 (September 23, 1963), 480–484. See also Gregory, *op. cit.,* 41–43.

[110] *Hisp. Am. Rep.,* V, No. 3 (April, 1952), 7.

[111] For a good discussion of the salinity problem, see *Hisp. Am. Rep.,* XV, No. 11

1944, Mexico is guaranteed the delivery of 1,500,000 acre feet of water per year. The water is essential for irrigation in Mexico, principally in Mexicali Valley. In November, 1961, the Mexican government filed its first complaint that the water delivered to the Mexican farmers contained such a high content of salt as to be injurious to the crops. The source of the salt was traced to a reclamation project in Arizona where water used to drain the soil of its salt then found its way to the Gila River and the Colorado. Studies undertaken by the International Boundary and Water Commission resulted in no remedial measures. In the meantime Mexican farmers suffered great crop losses, and probable permanent damage to their lands. Their plight became a national issue. Mexicans objected to the United States preoccupation over Mexico's attitude towards Cuba; whereas to them the most important problem in United States-Mexican relations was "salinity" at Mexicali.[112] Fortunately, the issue was settled in March, 1965, by United States agreement to finance construction of a diversion canal to help dispose of the saline waters.

(November, 1962), 989–990. Also, see Dept. of State *Bulletin,* XLVI, No. 1178 (January 22, 1962), 144.

[112] President Lyndon Johnson was so informed by President López Mateos at their Palm Springs, California, meeting. Dept. of State *Bulletin,* L, No. 1290 (March 16, 1964), 398.

SUPPLEMENTARY READING

Bemis, Samuel Flagg, *The Latin American Policy of the United States* (New York: Harcourt Brace and Company, 1943), Chaps. VI, X.

Callahan, James Morton, *American Foreign Policy in Mexican Relations* (New York: The Macmillan Company, 1932).

Cline, Howard F., *Mexico, Revolution to Evolution, 1940–1960* (New York: Oxford University Press, 1963).

Cline, Howard F., *The United States and Mexico* (Cambridge: Harvard University Press, rev. ed., 1963).

Cosío Villegas, Daniel, ed., *Historia moderna de México* (5 vols. Mexico, D.F., 1955–1960).

Daniels, Josephus, *Shirt-Sleeve Diplomat* (Chapel Hill: University of North Carolina Press, 1947).

Dunn, Frederick Sherwood, *The Diplomatic Protection of Americans in Mexico* (New York: Columbia University Press, 1933).

Fabela, Isidro, *Buena y mala vecinidad* (Mexico, D.F., 1958).

Feller, A. H., *The Mexican Claims Commissions, 1923–1934* (New York: The Macmillan Company, 1934).

Gordon, Wendell C., *The Expropriation of Foreign-Owned Property in Mexico* (Washington, D.C.: American Council on Public Affairs, 1941).

Hackett, Charles W., *The Mexican Revolution and the United States, 1910–1926* (Boston: World Peace Foundation, 1926).

Howland, Charles P., ed., *Survey of American Foreign Relations* (New York: Council on Foreign Relations, 1931).

"Investigation of Mexican Affairs," Preliminary Report and Hearings of the Committee on Foreign Relations (the Fall report), *U.S. Sen. Doc.* No. 285, 1920.

Merrill, John C., *"Gringo," The American as Seen by Mexican Journalists.* Latin American Monographs, No. 23, March, 1963 (Gainesville: University of Florida Press, 1963).

Rippy, J. Fred, *The United States and Mexico* (New York: Alfred A. Knopf, Inc., 1926).

Rives, G. L., *The United States and Mexico, 1821–1848* (2 vols. New York: Charles Scribner's Sons, 1913).

Ross, Stanley R., *Francisco I. Madero, Apostle of Mexican Democracy* (New York: Columbia University Press, 1955).

Smith, Justin H., *The War with Mexico* (2 vols. New York: The Macmillan Company, 1919).

Timm, Charles A., *The International Boundary Commission United States and Mexico* (Austin: The University of Texas Publications, No. 4134, September 8, 1941).

Wood, Bryce, *The Making of the Good Neighbor Policy* (New York: Columbia University Press, 1961).

United States Relations with Argentina

United States relations with Argentina until about 1900 were not only unspectacular, but of slight importance to both countries. The far-distant South American country held for the United States no particular political or economic attraction. It was not strategically important and its economic production was not sought by the United States, since it was generally competitive in nature. And Argentina, on the other hand, pursued a policy which, when not isolationist, was oriented toward Europe and certainly not toward the United States. The River Plate nation felt no attraction, economic or political, to the United States. All this was changed however, after the turn of the century, for then the impact of burgeoning American imperialism was felt throughout Latin America — even in Argentina.

Although Argentina was one of the countries least affected directly by the pressures of the northern colossus, its reaction was no less pronounced than that of the other Latin nations. It had also enjoyed phenomenal development and had forged to the front as the wealthiest and most progressive of all the Latin-American nations. Its nationalism thus aroused, Argentina aspired to leadership and regarded the United States as an unwelcome competitor. Hence a basis was laid for growing antagonism between the two countries. But first let us summarize pre-1900 relations.

Nineteenth-century relations

On June 28, 1810, Joel Roberts Poinsett was appointed special agent of the United States to South America, and was ordered to proceed without delay to Buenos Aires. Thus, shortly after the beginning of its independence movement Argentina (then called La Plata) was visited by one of the first official agents sent by the United States to any part of Latin America.

In 1816 Argentina formally declared its independence and sent Manuel H. de Aguirre as its official agent to the United States to seek recognition.[1]

[1] *Supra*, 33–34.

Recognition was delayed however, because of unfavorable reports on the internal situation in La Plata, and because of the pending negotiation of the Florida treaty with Spain. Finally, with the treaty out of the way, and the relative permanence of Argentine independence assured, recognition was forthcoming. The official act of recognition was the appointment, on May 17, 1823, of Caesar A. Rodney as United States minister to Buenos Aires. In his general instructions, Secretary of State John Quincy Adams urged Mr. Rodney to oppose by "friendly counsel . . . a hankering after monarchy" which had "infected the politics of all the successive governing authorities of Buenos Aires." Mr. Rodney was also ordered, while negotiating a commercial treaty, to insist on the most-favored-nation principle.[2] Secretary Adams was greatly concerned about British commercial pre-eminence in the River Plate area.

United States recognition, because it was so long delayed, was received in Argentina with little gratitude. The pronouncement of the Monroe Doctrine was also greeted officially in Buenos Aires with an "unwelcome apathy." Two years later when the American minister was asked whether Monroe's declaration was applicable to a war against Argentina waged by the Emperor of Brazil, he was instructed by Secretary of State Henry Clay to reply that the Monroe Doctrine was not applicable to wars strictly American in origin and object.[3]

A few years later Argentina sought to invoke the Monroe Doctrine in her controversy with Great Britain over possession of the Falkland Islands in the South Atlantic off the coast of Patagonia. The islands originally claimed by Spain were wrested from her by Britain as the result of a dispute in the latter part of the eighteenth century. The British however, neglected to occupy the islands, thus allowing Spain to resume jurisdiction until the end of her colonial rule in the New World.[4] Argentina, claiming the islands as Spain's successor, proceeded to occupy them.

In 1829 Louis Vernet was appointed by Argentina civil and military governor, following a grant to him of a monopoly of the seal fisheries in the waters surrounding the islands. In 1831 Vernet seized three American fishing schooners on charges of violating the fishing regulations and resisting Argentine authority over the islands. The ships were sent as prizes to Buenos Aires where the United States consul entered a strong protest against the seizure. In the meantime a United States warship proceeded to the islands and destroyed the Argentine settlement. This act was made the basis of an Argentine claim against the United States. Since the Argentine government

---

[2] William R. Manning, ed., *Diplomatic Correspondence of the United States Concerning the Independence of the Latin-American Nations* (3 vols. New York: Carnegie Endowment for International Peace, 1925), I, 186–192.

[3] *Ibid.*, 242–243.

[4] According to Julius Goebel, in *The Struggle for the Falkland Islands* (New Haven: Yale University Press, 1927), p. 432, the Spaniards exercised the fullest sovereignty over the islands after 1774, and their acts of sovereignty appear at no time to have been disputed.

refused to recognize the alleged illegal acts of Vernet visited upon American whalers and sealers in the area of the Falklands, diplomatic relations were broken off.[5]

It was at this juncture that Great Britain intervened by sending a warship which took possession of the Falkland Islands on the ground that British rights had never been abandoned. Argentina's contention that the British occupation of the Falkland Islands was a violation of the Monroe Doctrine, a point that has in fact been supported by scholarly authority,[6] went for naught since the State Department refused to see its applicability to the case.

The refusal of the United States to support Argentina in her controversy with Great Britain was disillusioning, because it seemed to prove that the Monroe Doctrine was a selfish policy, which indeed it was, being based in the idea of national self-interest. Since the islands were extremely remote, their possession by the British did not seem to threaten any American interests.

Nor did British and French violations of the Monroe Doctrine in the River Plate area from 1838 to 1850 evoke any protest from Washington. Argentina lay outside the region of vital United States interests. It was no thanks to the United States that dictator Rosas was able to defend the integrity of the Argentina confederation against the efforts of the two great European powers to dismember it.[7]

After the fall of Rosas in 1851, the Argentines paid the United States the high compliment of modeling their new federal constitution of 1853 after our own instrument.[8] This did not mean, however, any improvement of United States position in Argentina. Great Britain continued dominant in the economic picture of the republic.

During the administration of President Domingo Sarmiento (1868–1874), a great admirer of the United States, an attempt was made to divert toward North America some of the full current of Argentine interests that flowed towards Europe. This proved to be only temporary, for by the time that the first Pan American conference met at Washington in 1889 the Argentine representative, Roque Sáenz Peña, frankly declared that it was the policy of his country to give European universalism preference over American regionalism. At Washington in 1889, as in the succeeding Pan American conferences, Argentina was ranged against the United States concept of inter-American cooperation.

This policy conflict, which became a critical issue in United States-Argentine relations in the twentieth century, did not mean, prior to 1900, Argentine hostility toward the United States. This fact was demonstrated by Argentina's acceptance of the United States as arbitrator in three of her international disputes.

---

[5] *Ibid.*, 436–454. Diplomatic relations between the United States and Argentina were not resumed until 1843.

[6] Dexter Perkins, *The Monroe Doctrine, 1826–1867* (Baltimore: The Johns Hopkins Press, 1933), 7.

[7] C. H. Haring, *Argentina and the United States* (Boston: World Peace Foundation, 1942), 21.

[8] With amendments, this is still the Constitution of Argentina.

The first concerned Argentine and Paraguayan claims to the territory between the Rivers Verde and Pilcomayo in the area of the Chaco. The two countries agreed, by treaty in 1876, to submit the dispute to the arbitral judgment of the President of the United States. In November, 1878, President Hayes awarded the disputed territory to Paraguay. Argentina accepted the award, and Paraguay in a gesture of gratitude, renamed the principal town in the region Villa Hayes.[9]

The second case was a dispute between Argentina and Brazil over a portion of the Misiones Territory lying between the Uruguay and Iguassú Rivers. The dispute was arbitrated by President Grover Cleveland, whose award in 1895 was largely favorable to Brazil.

The third arbitration was concerned with disputed territory between Argentina and Chile known as the Puna de Atacama, the northern sector of the international boundary. The dispute, which brought the two South American powers perilously close to war, was settled in 1899 by a mixed commission presided over by W. I. Buchanan, United States minister to Argentina, who, as the neutral member, made the award, a division of the disputed territory between the two countries. The result was an increased measure of good will for the United States, particularly in Buenos Aires.

The United States and Argentina discover each other

It was not until about the turn of the century that the policies of the United States and Argentina began to clash, for only then did the two countries really become aware of each other. We have already noted that politically, the United States and Argentina, for most of the nineteenth century were quite unimportant to each other. Nor did the United States economically cut much of a figure in Argentina. Trade with Argentina at the close of the nineteenth century was as follows: imports into the United States, $8,114,304, and exports from the United States $11,558,237.[10] United States investments were relatively nonexistent. Those of Great Britain, direct and portfolio, were substantial. The era of United States commercial and investment expansion in Argentina was yet to come.

The decade preceding the outbreak of World War I was marked by a significant spurt in United States trade and investments in Argentina. In 1913 United States imports from Argentina amounted to $27 million, and exports to Argentina totaled $53 million. In that year United States investments totaled $40 million.

It was during and following World War I that United States economic relations with Argentina really became important. In 1915 American imports amounted to $74 million, and exports totaled $32 million. In 1927 United States imports had risen to $97 million, and exports to Argentina were $163 million.

[9] John Bassett Moore, *History and Digest of International Arbitration to which the United States has been a Party* (6 vols. Washington, D.C., 1898), II, 1943, V, 4783; William Spence Robertson, *Hispanic American Relations with the United States* (New York: Oxford University Press, 1923), 154.

[10] Robertson, *op. cit.*, 213.

Investment increases were even more remarkable. United States investments in Argentina rose from $40 million in 1913 to $611 million in 1929.[11]
For comparative purposes we note that British investments in Argentina in
1929 amounted to $2,000 million. Until World War II Argentina was so
intimately tied to Britain economically that it was commonly regarded as
an unofficial member of the British empire.

Certainly, by the end of the third decade of the twentieth century there
had developed between the United States and Argentina economic relationships of such great proportions as to profoundly influence their policies —
political and economic. These unfortunately were in conflict. When the
Argentines came to know the *yanquis* it was to mistrust them.

Political relations between the United States and Argentina

The lack of understanding between Argentina and the United States is
easily accounted for. There was first the fact that in Argentina, the remarkable
growth in wealth, well-being, and political status enhanced national self-
consciousness and the desire to play the role of spokesman for all of Latin
America. Excessively proud of their national resources, material developments, "European" culture, and racial superiority, the Argentines were accustomed to call themselves a "white-stock nation," as a mark of distinction
in contrast to their less fortunate sister republics. This belief in their superiority consequently led to a belief in the *right* to leadership in Latin America.[12]

This pretention brought Argentina inevitably into conflict with the pre-
sumed aspirations of the United States to hegemony in the Western Hemisphere. Believing that the Americans were promoting Pan Americanism
merely as a device to impose their primacy upon the Latin nations, Argentina
could always be relied on to take a position in inter-American conferences
opposed to that of the United States. Frequently measures supported by the
United States and most of the other American republics had to be denatured
in order to meet Argentine objections. Then, having succeeded in forcing
the adoption by the conferences of amended and less effective measures,
Argentina consistently failed to ratify or implement these actions. Of the
eighty-seven treaties and conventions negotiated in all of the general and
special Pan American conferences by 1943, Argentina signed sixty-six and
√ ratified but seven. Only two of the ratified treaties dealt with political subjects
of any significance: one was the Argentine Anti-War Pact negotiated by
her Foreign Minister Carlos Saavedra Lamas, and the other was the Convention on European Colonies and Possessions, which Argentina felt she must
ratify because of her claims to the Falkland Islands. By the record, therefore,
Argentina was a conspicuous noncooperating member of the inter-American

[11] Max Winkler, *Investments of United States Capital in Latin America* (Boston:
World Peace Foundation, 1929), 274, 275–278.
[12] For an excellent study of Argentine hostility toward the United States, see S. Walter
Washington, *A Study of the Causes of Hostility Toward the United States in Latin
America: Argentina* (Dept. of State, External Research Staff, Office of Intelligence Re-
search), *External Research Paper*, No. 126.2, May 27, 1957.

system largely because of a lack of sympathetic attachment for a Pan Americanism "made in the U.S.A."

Argentina's attitude toward the United States was one of a deep-seated distrust of American motives. Always fearful of Yankee aggressiveness, Argentina was constantly on the alert against the United States trying to "put something over" on Latin America. However, Argentina was as immune as any nation in Europe from those characteristic manifestations of United States imperialism, which operated as restraints on the sovereign rights of independent states. Situated far outside the geographical area of strategic interest to the United States, Argentina had never been the object of its intervention, diplomatic or armed, political or nonpolitical. Yet, despite this, Argentina had been the Latin-American country most critical of United States motives, with the possible exception of Mexico.

Argentina's official policy of neutrality during World War I reflected its completely uncooperative attitude toward the United States. When the United States severed diplomatic relations with Germany in February, 1917, because of violations of neutral rights, President Wilson called on all remaining neutral states to follow the American example. The Argentine government excused itself on the ground that the South American republic was distant from the scene of the conflict. Fearful of German reaction, President Irigoyen felt it prudent to refrain from any public statement of sympathy for the United States cause "at so critical a juncture."[13] Nevertheless, when on April 6, 1917, the United States declared war on Germany, the Argentine government recognized the justice of this act, "based upon the violation of principles of neutrality made sacred by the rules of international law." Irigoyen however, was determined to remain strictly neutral, although there was considerable popular clamor in the country for a break with Germany. Not even proof that the Count von Luxburg,[14] the German minister at Buenos Aires, had grossly violated Argentina's neutrality swayed Irigoyen from his neutral position.

The attitude of President Irigoyen has been the subject of considerable speculation. Was he pro-German and anti-United States? Immediately following the United States declaration of war, Argentina proposed a conference, to be attended only by the Latin-American states. Irigoyen's plan was to isolate the United States and possibly Brazil from the other American republics and to assert a dominant influence over Latin-American affairs. Although most of the Latin-American governments at first accepted the Argentine invitation, their enthusiasm soon waned when the unwisdom of excluding the United States was realized. In the end it was only Mexico which went so far as to send delegates, who arrived in Buenos Aires only to find that the congress had been postponed indefinitely.[15]

[13] *Foreign Relation of the United States,* 1917, Suppl. 1, 226.
[14] See "The Luxburg Secret Correspondence," *Jour. of Int. Law,* XII, January, 1918.
[15] *For. Rel.,* 1917, Suppl. 1, 388–389; Percy A. Martin, *Latin America and the War* (Baltimore: The Johns Hopkins Press, 1925), 257.

Irigoyen's neutrality policy was severely criticized in the United States, where he was branded pro-German. Evidence does not seem to sustain this view. He apparently was simply "pro-Argentine," his determination being to exploit the war situation to Argentina's advantage.

During the 1920's United States-Argentine relations continued to present the familiar picture of conflicting interests, particularly in the economic area, which aspect of relations will be discussed shortly. Not even the Good Neighbor policy of the New Deal with its scrupulous regard for the rights of small states served to completely dispel Argentina's mistrust of American designs. For example, the proposal of the State Department in 1937, to lease a number of destroyers to Brazil, in order to bolster the Vargas government against totalitarian aggression from abroad, was regarded in Buenos Aires as a nefarious scheme to upset the balance of naval power in South America. In fact there was actually no balance, since Argentina enjoyed a wide margin of naval superiority over both Brazil and Chile. Carlos Saavedra Lamas, the Argentine Foreign Minister, protested that the leasing of destroyers contradicted the Good Neighbor and neutrality policies of the United States, violated the London Naval Treaty of 1930, and threatened to start a naval war in South America.

Secretary Hull replied that the lease of the destroyers did not violate the clause of the naval treaty which prevented transfer, for the ships would not become a part of the Brazilian navy, and were to be used for training purposes only. Furthermore, Argentina's fear that a naval race would be promoted was completely unwarranted, since an equal number of American destroyers was also available to the other South American countries. In the interest of "good neighborliness," however, the American government abandoned its plan to lease destroyers to Brazil.

To further appease Argentina, the United States, late in 1938, abandoned a plan to sell subsidized wheat to Brazil. When the Argentine government heard the rumor that the United States proposed to dump wheat in Brazil, one of Argentina's principal markets, President Ortiz ordered Ambassador Espil at Washington to request information on the matter, and to express the hope that "the United States would act according to President Roosevelt's Good Neighbor policy." This was but one of many instances in which the American government had its obligations under the Good Neighbor policy thrown back at it. The United States dropped the wheat deal for various reasons; not the least of these was its unwillingness to antagonize the Argentines.

President Roosevelt appealed to the American nations, on the eve of the Lima conference in 1938, for mutual solidarity backed by sufficient arms to defend their political independence; this appeal, however, was vigorously criticized in Argentina as a disguised effort to impose an "American peace" on Latin America. At the conference, the Argentine Foreign Minister, Dr. José María Cantillo, was spokesman for the opposition to an armed alliance. When Cordell Hull realized that a defensive pact was out of the question, he hastened to sponsor a strong resolution proclaiming the common purpose of the American republics to defend their liberties and independence against non-American aggressors. Argentina objected that the declaration pointed too directly at the totalitarian states and was fearful of giving offense. She proposed, instead, an affirmation of common allegiance to American ideals and a determination to consult when there was a threat *from any source* — including the United States. Argentina was "not convinced that the United States' Good Neighbor policy would be permanent."[16]

The foregoing illustrations of Argentine jealousy and mistrust of the United States, have been selected from a plentiful store, including the disgraceful Chaco War mediation, in which Saavedra Lamas toyed with the tragedy of two nations to secure advantage and prestige for Argentina over the United States.

Economic relations between the United States and Argentina

Economics as well as nationalism must be considered in a study of the relations between Argentina and the United States; certainly the economic factor was as important as the nationalistic one in determining the Argentine attitude toward its northern neighbor. The problems of United States-Argentine trade relations before World War II, were always difficult. Nearly all of Argentina's eggs were in one basket — a national economy based on a 50 per cent exportation of all national production. Argentina was a leading exporter of wheat, mutton, and wool. In 1937 27.8 per cent of the country's exports went to Great Britain, 12.7 per cent to the United States, 6.4 per cent to Germany, and 6.1 per cent to Italy. In 1938 Argentina was the world's largest exporter of beef and corn, providing three-fourths of the total trade in the former, and one-half of the world's exports of the latter.

To illustrate how vitally the Argentine economy was affected by fluctuations in world prices, in 1928 the quantity of exports was 17,029,000 tons, valued at $1,017,000,000. But in 1931, the greatest volume of exports in Argentine history amounting to 18,477,000 tons, commanded a value of only $427 million. The country depended upon its exports for its very life, and therefore was completely at the mercy of external forces quite beyond its control. Since Argentina was a food-products exporting and debtor country, it had to maintain a "favorable" balance of trade so that, in addition to facilitating the purchase of industrial products from abroad, payments on fixed public and private charges could be made. When there was a decline in the value of exports, the inevitable consequence was a drastic curtailment of imports. If this did not suffice to secure sufficient free exchange, the payments on foreign obligations had to be suspended, as well as all remittances due foreign investors in Argentine enterprises. The economic mechanism of the country was so delicately balanced that it responded automatically to seismic disturbances in the far corners of the economic world.[17]

[16] Washington, *op. cit.*, 34–37. See also J. L. Mecham, *The United States and Inter-American Security* (Austin: University of Texas Press, 1961), Chap. V.
[17] *Foreign Policy Reports*, XX, No. 4 (May 1, 1944), 34–48.

The basic condition which made possible the huge exports of Argentine food products was the need of that country to receive in return imports of manufactured articles from abroad. Great industrial countries, like England and Germany, that imported huge supplies of food products, were ideally situated to dovetail into the Argentine trade scheme. The United States, however, enjoyed no such advantage, since it was a quantity producer of Argentina's principal exports: beef, wheat, and corn. And since its need for other Argentine products — such as flaxseed, quebracho, hides, and casein — was strictly limited, it could not materially increase its purchases. Here then was a well-nigh insuperable obstacle to the development of a greater trade volume with a country which, after the depression, adopted a policy of bilateralism based on the trade slogan, "buy from those who buy from us."[18]

It has been asserted that Argentine relations with the United States "hinge about hard feelings caused by our tariff acts." The Tariff Act of 1867 placed a prohibitive duty upon Argentine wool, which, because of its unwashed state, was heavier with grease than the Australian or New Zealand product. A vigorous campaign was waged by the Argentine minister to the United States to secure a modification of the restrictive clauses, but to no avail. Argentina's suggestion for a reciprocity treaty also fell upon deaf ears.

Nevertheless, a few years later, at the First International Conference of American States, held in Washington in 1889–1890, Secretary of State James G. Blaine proposed a customs union giving all the American countries substantial advantages in their trade with one another. This proposal, which would have given the United States preferences over European nations in the Latin-American markets, without involving any great sacrifice on the part of this country, met fierce opposition, especially on the part of Roque Sáenz Peña, the Argentine delegate, who argued that the system of "belligerent tariffs" would precipitate "the war of one continent against another, eighteen sovereignties allied to exclude from the life of commerce that same Europe which extends to us her hand, sends us her strong arms, and complements our economic existence, after having apportioned us her civilization and culture, her sciences and her arts, industries and customs that have complemented our sociological evolutions."[19] Argentina always opposed any action, economic or political, which would weaken traditional ties with Europe. The Blaine proposal for a customs union was rejected by the Washington conference.

Because of the high duties on wool imposed by the McKinley Tariff Act of 1890, the Argentine government retaliated with higher duties on certain products such as lumber, refined petroleum, agricultural implements, and other iron and steel products.

[18] U.S. Tariff Commission, *The Foreign Trade of Latin America*, Pt. II, Sec. 2, *Argentina* (Washington, D.C.: Government Printing Office, 1940), 17.

[19] First International Conference of American States, *Minutes* (Washington, 1890), 323. See also, T. F. McGann, *Argentina, the United States, and the Inter-American System, 1880–1914* (Cambridge: Harvard University Press, 1957), 130–165.

Under a bargaining provision in the Dingley Tariff Act of 1897,[20] a treaty (one of the so-called Kasson treaties) was negotiated with Argentina whereby the United States made a concession of 20 per cent reduction on wool, and in return Argentina granted a reduction on a number of United States products. The treaty was not ratified by the Senate and thus never became effective. Thenceforward, the United States made no more proposals to Latin America (except Cuba) for trade reciprocity; it ceased to demand or even to desire special tariff rates in Latin-American countries — indeed, it elevated its own tariff schedules to greater and greater heights.

The most serious Argentine opposition to the tariff policy of the United States dates from the passage of the Fordney Tariff Act of 1922. In its general elevation of schedules to unprecedented heights, additional burdens were placed upon certain products of which Argentina was the leading exporter. With or without justification, Argentina felt discriminated against and Argentine businessmen urged their government to make reprisals against the United States. The powerful Argentine Rural Society, composed of the great wheat and cattle barons, urged as a self-defense measure the trade policy of bilateralism. Many urged economic warfare as the only means of forcing the United States to realize how keenly its policy was resented.

Although the investigation of the cost of agricultural production in Argentina by agents of the United States Tariff Commission, as provided by the tariff act, was regarded as unwelcome by the Argentines, no effort was made to bar it. Later, when the Tariff Commission, on the basis of its investigations, recommended that duties on imports of corn and flaxseed be increased, Argentina once more felt discriminated against.

Despite Argentine resentment of the tariff of 1922, there was a considerable gain in American trade. In 1927 the United States exports to Argentina amounted to $144 million, and imports to $88 million. Next to Cuba, no other country in Latin America offered a better market for American goods.

Ignoring all counsels of caution, Congress raised the American protective wall still higher with the Smoot-Hawley Tariff Act of 1930, nearly paralyzing Argentine imports into the United States by placing most of her products in the higher schedules. Popular resentment in Argentina was greater than after the passage of the Fordney Act. The Argentine Rural Society urged its members to boycott American goods. *La Nación,* a leading Buenos Aires newspaper, urged the government to avenge itself on the United States by adopting defensive measures. The government responded immediately with a tariff increase on a wide range of goods customarily imported from the United States. Truly the tariff policy of the United States had to bear a large share of responsibility for clogging the channels of international trade and forcing retaliatory and defensive actions by other countries.

[20] For a survey of the bargaining tariff laws, see Benjamin H. Williams, *Economic Foreign Policy of the United States* (New York: McGraw-Hill Book Company, Inc., 1929), Chap. XIV.

The greatest resentment was created by the American beef quarantine policy. In 1927 the Department of Agriculture prohibited the importation of Argentine fresh meats because of the existence of hoof-and-mouth disease, or *aftosa,* in that country. The Department had the discretion of prohibiting importations either from an entire country or from an infected area. The Tariff Act of 1930 deprived the Department of this discretionary power and required an embargo on such products from a whole country, even though it was known that the disease did not exist in well-defined areas. Since *aftosa* had not been completely eradicated in every part of Argentina, cancellation of the discretionary power was a convenient subterfuge to close the American market to one of Argentina's principal export products. The outcries and resentment were loud and legitimate.

In an effort to appease the Argentines, the Roosevelt administration negoti-ated a Sanitary Convention, signed on May 24, 1935. While affirming the right of either country to prohibit importation of animal or plant products from territories or zones of the other which the importing country found to be affected with or exposed to plant or animal disease, the treaty denied to the importing country the right to prohibit importation from territories or zones within the other country which it found to be free from disease. In short, this treaty would have restored discretionary authority to the Depart-ment of Agriculture.

When at Buenos Aires in 1936 President Roosevelt condemned the use of quarantine or sanitary regulations as disguised tariff measures. In referring to the Sanitary Convention the President promised to urge its early ratifica-tion by the United States Senate. In spite of his assurances, the Convention was never ratified by the Senate, so strong was the lobby of the United States cattle-raisers.[21]

The Argentines lost no opportunity to cite the quarantine as a contradic-tion of the Good Neighbor policy. Refusal to allow Argentina to serve its own fresh beef products in a restaurant in the Argentine pavilion at the New York World's Fair in 1939–1940 did not help matters, nor did the notorious denial of permission for the sale of Argentine corned beef to the United States Navy in the spring of 1939. Despite the fact that the Navy order was insignificant, and canned corned beef was no longer produced commercially in the United States (domestic packers found it more profitable to use the poorer cuts for hamburger and "hot dogs"), an angry storm of protest rose from the American cattle country. Responsive as ever to the political pressure of the stock-raisers, Congress amended the pending Navy appropriation bill by providing that purchases be limited to products produced in the United States and its dependencies, thereby nullifying any Argentine good will created by President Roosevelt's purchase order.[22] The episode lent additional color to the Argentine complaint that the United States

[21] See Percy W. Bidwell, *The Invisible Tariff* (New York: Council on Foreign Rela-tions, 1939).

[22] Haring, *op. cit.,* 28–29.

wished only to sell and not to buy; that it was forcing Argentina to the doctrine of bilateralism, the policy of balancing her international payments by countries.

In October, 1931, foreign exchange in Argentina was put under government control; in order to be eligible to bid for exchange in the official market it was necessary to obtain permits prior to the importation of goods. Those persons who lacked official permits were forced to buy their exchange in the "free market" where the rate was as high as 20 per cent above the official selling rate. By thus guaranteeing the allocation of exchange to pay for imports at the official or most favorable rate, there was formally maintained the policy of favoring products from countries with an import surplus in their trade with Argentina. Under this system, countries like Great Britain encountered no difficulty in buying official, or preferred exchange, whereas Americans, who sold more than they bought from Argentina, received a smaller proportionate share of the official exchange. Thus, by exchange control Argentina pursued a policy of promoting exports by encouraging imports from those countries that bought Argentine products.[23]

Exchange control was supplemented, after 1933, by a series of reciprocal exchange and trade agreements. The first and most notable of these was the Roca-Runciman Exchange Agreement of May 1, 1933. Great Britain undertook not to restrict its market for Argentine products below a certain level, and in return Argentina agreed to tariff reclassification on certain types of products with the intention of favoring Great Britain. Moreover, Argentina agreed to make available for remittance payments to Britain the exchange derived from the sale of Argentine products in the United Kingdom. Thus, under the Roca-Runciman Agreement British surplus purchases from Argentina were balanced by Argentine purchases and remittances on British investments.[24] In other words, the British surplus purchases from Argentina did not help Argentina to buy from the United States, whereas the surplus purchases of the United States in Brazil, for example, helped Brazil to buy from Britain. In this connection the question was asked: Why did not the United States, as had Britain with Argentina, establish a preferential control over dollar exchange arising from its surplus purchases from Brazil, and thus force greater Brazilian purchases from the United States? The answer was, of course, that this would be contrary to the Hull liberal trade policy.

To make more effective her new policy of bilateralism, Argentina negotiated a number of agreements with several European countries. Under the exchange control system, as has been indicated, entry permits were required only on goods entering at the "official exchange" rate. At the same time other goods enjoyed the right of entry, but at the "free exchange" rate. Although this meant higher duties and some delay in securing entry, nevertheless American exporters had access to the Argentine market. However,

[23] See Herbert M. Bratten, "Foreign Exchange Control in Latin America," *For. Pol. Rep.*, XIV, No. 23 (February 15, 1939), 277–281.
[24] *Ibid.*, 277–281.

on January 1, 1939, the Argentine government inaugurated a new system requiring permits even for "free exchange" entry. This resulted in backing up American goods on the wharves and in the warehouses. Shortly after, on February 15, 1939, the Argentine finance minister announced that Argentine imports from the United States would be reduced approximately 40 per cent from the 1938 figure of $71 million to about a $40 million annual level.

The methods employed by Argentina to achieve a reduction of purchases from the United States were patently discriminatory and made Argentina eligible for entry on the United States trade black list according to provision of the Trade Agreement Act of 1934. However, such action was not taken, nor was it seriously contemplated. Instead, Mr. Hull persisted in his efforts to secure Argentina's signature to one of his reciprocal trade agreements. Earlier efforts had failed because of Argentina's refusal to grant the United States equality of treatment with those countries covered by bilateral agreements.

But, after the outbreak of World War II, when Argentina found her former European markets practically closed, she was forced to change her attitude regarding a reciprocal trade agreement with the United States. The agreement, signed in Buenos Aires on October 14, 1941, contained the reciprocal grant by both countries of lowered tariff rates on a number of specific items; most important to the United States, however, was Argentina's guarantee of equality of treatment with respect to her various trade control regulations and devices.[25] Mr. Hull may have won in principle but actually not in substance, for because of exceptions granted by Argentina, notably to Britain, the ideal operation of the old triangular trade principle was not to return. Indeed, the outbreak of World War II was to work a profound change in much more than United States-Argentine economic relations.

Argentina and World War II

As early as the Lima conference of 1938 Argentina gave a preview of its future "neutrality" policy in World War II. On that occasion, when the Declaration of Lima was being considered, the Argentines made it clear that they were not willing to go as far as the other Latin Americans in condemning the Axis. It was President Ramón Castillo who, after his accession to power in July, 1940, converted Argentina's "neutrality" policy into an instrument useful to the Axis. Before the Japanese attack on Pearl Harbor, Ramón Castillo, surrounded by admirers of Hitler and Mussolini, was remarkably tolerant of the activities of German agents and the pro-Axis press propaganda, but he restricted expressions of popular sympathy for the Allied cause.

After the Pearl Harbor attack, Argentina's attitude contrasted rather sharply with that of most of the Latin-American nations which by various

---

[25] *Ibid.*, 229–232. For text of the trade agreement, see Dept. of State *Bulletin*, V (October 18, 1941), 297–301. For an analysis of its provisions, see Dept. of State *Press Releases*, No. 495 (October 14, 1941).

means manifested a strong sense of solidarity with the United States. Although the United States was accorded the status of nonbelligerency by Argentina, it was clear where Castillo's sympathies lay.[26]

At the Rio de Janiero Meeting of Foreign Ministers, in January, 1942, Argentina played its usual role of obstructionism, and forced abandonment of the original project proposed by the United States for the obligatory severance of diplomatic relations with the Axis powers, in favor of a denatured "recommendation" that the American republics break their diplomatic relations with Germany, Italy, and Japan.

The reactionary and dictatorial Castillo government, despite strong moral pressure exerted by the other American republics, and by many influential Argentines themselves, stubbornly refused to sever diplomatic relations. It was later established by evidence found in German archives that the government of the Argentine Republic, from the day of Pearl Harbor, was engaged in grave complicity with Nazi Germany. In May, 1942, President Castillo informed Germany through authorized channels that he not only hoped for an Axis victory, but based his policy on that desired result. Rather than sever relations he was determined, if necessary, "eventually to come out openly on the side of the Axis Powers."[27]

Having assured the Nazis of his purpose not to break relations, Castillo hastened to initiate negotiations for German arms to use against the other American republics if their insistence that Argentina break relations proved to be too strong. The German embassy in December, 1942, at Buenos Aires, urged "practical aid for Argentine armament" as one of the necessities of Germany's campaign "of supporting Castillo's neutrality policy." The German government, however, delayed these negotiations because of its own arms needs.

The military dictatorship

On June 4, 1943, President Ramón S. Castillo was overthrown by a military *junta* headed by General Arturo Rawson. Three days later Rawson was forced out and General Pedro Ramírez, who had been Castillo's Minister of War, became president. Ramírez was granted immediate recognition by the governments of the American republics, including the United States, largely because of the belief that the new regime would sever diplomatic relations with the Axis and take its rightful position beside the United Nations. The error of these assumptions was soon demonstrated.

Not only were relations with the Axis not broken, but the new regime, which began to manifest distinct fascist characteristics, carried to greater extremes the pro-Axis, anti-United States, antidemocratic, and ultranationalistic policies of the preceding administration.[28] Much of the confusion in

26 *For. Pol. Rep.*, XVIII, No. 5 (May 15, 1942), 51–53; XXI, No. 22 (February 1, 1946), 308.
27 U.S. Dept. of State, *Argentine Situation* (Washington, D.C.: Government Printing Office, February, 1946), 5. (Cited hereinafter as the *Blue Book.*)
28 *Ibid.*, 17–65.

American diplomatic and official quarters concerning the aims of the new Argentine regime might have been avoided had anyone been aware of a manifesto circulated secretly among officers of the Argentine army in March, 1943. Leading features of the manifesto were: admiration for Germany which had "given life a heroic meaning" and was "an example" to Argentina; the achievement of national power by a firm dictatorship; and Argentine hegemony in South America "realized by the political genius and the heroism of the Argentine Army."

According to this remarkable document, which must have reflected the aims of the militarist masters of Argentina: "Our government shall be a firm dictatorship, although at the beginning, in order to become firmly established, it will concede the necessary allowances. We shall attract the public, but eventually the people will have to work, make sacrifices and obey. . . . Only thus will it be possible to carry out the armament programme, indispensable for the domination of the continent. With Germany's example, the right spirit will be instilled into the people through the radio, by the controlled press, by literature, by the Church, and by education, and so they will venture upon the heroic road they will be made to travel."[29]

The United States' hasty recognition of President Ramírez was soon regretted. The widening gap between the policies of the two governments was pointed up by the exchange of notes between Secretary of State Hull and the Argentine Foreign Minister, Admiral Segundo Storni. According to the Argentine minister, United States arms aid to Brazil under lend-lease was upsetting the balance of power in South America. Therefore, Storni suggested that the United States, as a gesture of friendship, should send airplanes and arms to Argentina. Mr. Hull, his "Tennessee mountaineer ire aroused," sent Storni a scathing reply declaring that since Argentina had refused to cooperate in hemisphere defense, no arms shipments under lend-lease were possible.[30] Storni, who had laid himself open to a well-deserved rebuff, was forced to resign.

As the days passed it became increasingly clear that the Ramírez government intended no change of the Castillo pro-Axis policy. In fact, German agents reported to Berlin: "As evidence of his government's sincerity, the Argentine President (Ramírez) offered the assurance that repressive measures were being applied only against agents of the United Nations." Furthermore, Ramírez, and Colonel Juan D. Perón, Chief of the Argentine War Ministry, continued negotiations with German agents for the purchase and shipment of arms and for guarantees of protection for Argentine shipping. These efforts failed to materialize, however, largely because one of the agents, Osmar Hellmuth, was apprehended by the British at Trinidad.[31] That the Ramírez regime did not succeed in its efforts to secure German arms was due not

[29] *Political Report*, CI-AA (October 10, 1944), No. SR-121.
[30] Although Mr. Hull's reply was popularly believed to bear the stamp of his Tennessee mountaineer background, it was in fact drafted by the Department's Latin-American expert, Philip Bonsal, a product of Groton and Harvard.
[31] *Blue Book*, 12, 15.

necessarily to lack of desire on the part of the Germans but rather to the effective blockade by the Allies.

One example of the Argentine-Nazi efforts to subvert the governments ✓ of neighboring countries occurred in December, 1943, when a pro-Axis regime was set up in Bolivia with the support of officials of the Argentine and German governments.[32] The United States, on January 24, 1944, and the other American republics refused to recognize the Bolivian *junta* because, as Secretary Hull said, the overthrow of the Bolivian government occurred under circumstances linking the action with subversive groups hostile to the Allied cause. The finger was pointed at Argentine complicity. When Washington threatened to publish evidence of Ramírez's pro-Axis activities in Bolivia and elsewhere unless he severed relations with the Axis, the Argentine president was forced to capitulate. On January 26, 1944, Ramírez ordered severance of official relations with the Axis.[33]

Less than a month later, on February 24, Ramírez himself was forced to retire by a military clique which not only believed that the diplomatic break dragooned by United States pressure had caused Argentina to lose face — members of the clique also feared that Ramírez was about to declare war on the Axis. Vice-President Edelmiro Farrell became acting president, with Perón as vice-president, both under "delegated authority" during the "incapacity" of President Ramírez. Washington, however, announced that recognition would be withheld until Argentina's break with the Axis had been implemented with more than words. Most of the Latin-American governments followed the United States in this respect.

But the Farrell regime refused to implement the break with the Axis; indeed, it showed even more pronounced totalitarian sympathies than had its predecessor. It pushed a steady liquidation of democratic institutions and practices, and promoted the creation of a state and social structure on the Nazi-Fascist-Falangist pattern. Moreover, its failure to clamp down on subversive activities of Axis agents made the diplomatic break meaningless.[34]

Far from moving in the direction of hemisphere solidarity, the Farrell government continued in the opposite direction; thus on June 22 the United States recalled its ambassador from Buenos Aires. Parallel action was taken by most of the other American republics, by Great Britain and by most of the members of the United Nations. In a statement released to the press by the Secretary of State on July 26, Mr. Hull said:

> The injury to the solidarity of the Continent and to the war effort of the United Nations by the continuing acts and utterances of the Farrell regime is abundantly clear. It is the judgment of this Government that the American republics and their associates among the United Nations should firmly adhere to the present policy of non-recognition of the Farrell regime until

[32] *Ibid.*, 20.
[33] Arthur P. Whitaker, *The United States and Argentina* (Cambridge: Harvard University Press, 1954), 127; *Supra*, 148.
[34] *Blue Book*, 27.

by unequivocal acts it is conclusively demonstrated that there has been a
fundamental change of Argentine policy in favor of the cause against the
Axis and in support of inter-American unity and common action.[35]

Mr. Hull employed a number of diplomatic, economic, and moral sanctions
in futile efforts to induce Argentine cooperation. When he proposed drastic
economic sanctions including the embargo of Argentine beef, the British
objected, declaring their preference for Argentine beef to American pork. Ⅴ
Moreover, in the event of a British boycott of Argentine meat supplies,
important not only to British civilians but to Allied troops in Europe, the
United States would have had to make up the deficit. This would have meant
a drastic curtailment of its own domestic meat supplies which the average
American would have found hard to accept in view of the minor issue of
Argentine recalcitrance. The United States had to satisfy itself by forbidding
its ships to call at Argentine ports.

As we have already noted,[36] the Inter-American Conference on Problems
of War and Peace, held at Mexico City in February and March, 1945, from
which Argentina was excluded, ratified a procedure, designed beforehand by a
United States mission to Buenos Aires, to settle the Argentine question. The
face-saving procedure — useful both to the United States as well as to Argentina — provided that Argentina should implement a policy of cooperative
action with the other American states (i.e., declare war) and adhere to the
Final Act of the conference. Argentina complied. On March 27 it declared
a state of war against the Axis countries, thereby becoming eligible, with
Soviet approval, to membership in the San Francisco United Nations Conference.

It soon became evident that Argentine compliance with the Mexico City
resolution was purely opportunistic. There was no change of heart in Buenos
Aires. The Argentine question, so far as the United States was concerned, was
still far from a solution.

Relations with Perón[37]

Having decided to accord its long-delayed recognition of the Farrell-Perón
government, the United States sent Spruille Braden, in May, 1945, as ambassador to Argentina. Braden, the son of a great copper magnate who formerly
owned mines in Chile, came to his Buenos Aires post with considerable
diplomatic experience in Latin America. He had served on the Chaco peace
commission for three years, principally in Buenos Aires, and also as ambassador to Colombia and Cuba. He understood that his mission to Argentina
was not to conciliate the Farrell regime but to stand for democracy; not
directly to criticize or condemn the military dictatorship, but to appeal to the
Argentine people in defense of constitutional representative government.

[35] U.S. Dept. of State *Press Release,* July 26, 1944.   [36] *Supra,* 162.
[37] See Robert J. Alexander, *The Perón Era* (New York: Columbia University Press,
1951), and Whitaker, *The United States and Argentina.* See also, Olive Holmes,
"Perón's 'Greater Argentina' and the United States," *For. Pol. Rep.,* XXIV, No. 14
(December 1, 1948).

Braden was in Argentina only from May to September, 1945, when he was brought back to the State Department as Assistant Secretary of State for Latin-American Affairs. It was during this period that Perón's ascendance was being established, and thus Braden's general allusions to dictatorship were regarded by Perón as direct and personal criticism. He felt obliged therefore, to inaugurate a campaign of lies against the United States Ambassador, and so successful was he that even Americans were misled. It was rather generally accepted that Braden had undiplomatically intervened in the domestic affairs of Argentina. In denying the charge of intervention Braden said: "This is entirely false, since in no speech in Buenos Aires, nor at the University of El Litoral — the one address I made outside Buenos Aires — did I even refer to the government or to Perón. What I did was to defend constitutional representative government as we understand it in the United States. . . . I did not directly criticize or condemn the Perón-Farrell regime or the Argentine police state."[38]

Braden's championship of democracy was received in Argentina with remarkable demonstrations of enthusiastic approval seldom given a foreigner. In fact a competent authority describes him as "the most popular ambassador ever to serve in the most anti-United States nation in Latin America."[39] Since Braden's anti-Perón campaign was not going at all badly it was unfortunate that he was called to Washington before the issue was resolved. Perhaps if he had remained in Buenos Aires he could have swung the balance against Perón in the February presidential election.[40]

Perón won the election, February 24, 1946, but not by a large margin. His campaign slogan, which proved to be very effective, thanks to the technique of the big lie, was *Braden ó Perón*. Braden himself, as Assistant Secretary of State, did not help matters by releasing the *Blue Book* on Argentina only twelve days before the election. Perón seized on this as an act of intervention. Its effect in assuring his election, as is generally claimed, is doubtful. Certainly it did not prevent the election of Perón as was hoped by the State Department. Although the election was publicized as "honest" — and this was probably true — this did not nullify the fact that during the campaign itself Perón's victory was decided by violence and less obvious illegal tactics employed by the government to deny to the opposition opportunity to present its case to the people.

Perón described his victory over Spruille Braden as the disappearance of "the symbol of a routed capitalist domination."[41] The State Department, its Argentine policy a shambles, exhibited nevertheless a remarkable resiliency in accomplishing a complete reversal of policy almost overnight. On February 26, 1946, two days after Perón's victory, President Truman announced that George Messersmith, a career diplomat undistinguished for liberal views, was

---

[38] Thomas F. McGann, "The Ambassador and the Dictator: The Braden Mission to Argentina and its Significance for United States Relations with Latin America," *The Centennial Review*, VI, No. 3, (Sassman, 1962), 351.
[39] *Ibid.*, 350.   [40] Alexander, *op. cit.*, 205.
[41] Whitaker, *op. cit.*, 107.

being appointed ambassador to Buenos Aires to patch up relations with Perón.

The appointment of Messersmith meant victory for those American officials and businessmen who had been belaboring Braden because of his insistence on placing principle above business gain. During the mission of George Messersmith and his immediate successors, James Bruce and Stanton Griffis, both businessmen, the new policy seemed to be to forget the past if this could promote the economic interests of the United States in Argentina. Mr. Bruce succeeded so well in making friends with the Argentines that a Buenos Aires newspaper said he gave the impression of representing Perón's government rather than that of the United States.

Since its objective was "business as usual," the American government was willing to appease Argentina by releasing its gold stocks in the United States, which had been frozen for nearly two years, and by rescinding numerous export restrictions. It even indicated the possibility of making military equipment available to Argentina in order to strengthen inter-American defense. The "permitted" resignation of Spruille Braden as Assistant Secretary of State in June, 1947, may also be regarded as an appeasement sacrifice to Juan D. Perón. Furthermore, the State Department abandoned its opposition to the inclusion of Argentina in a conference to draft a permanent hemisphere defense treaty. The conference, with Perón's representatives present in person, if not in spirit, assembled at Rio de Janeiro in August, 1947. Perón, however, delayed ratification of the Rio treaty until June, 1950.

√The Argentine dictator was not as cooperative as expected. He accepted what the Yankees had to offer, but he made no promises. He declared more than once that he was not to be bought. On the contrary, it seemed to serve his interests to stir up Argentine nationalism occasionally by provoking vitriolic anti-United States propaganda campaigns. These were turned on and off with mechanical precision. Perón found it profitable to resort to the blackmail technique employed by certain other countries that seemed to find the United States to be more generous the more belligerent the tone of their anti-Yankee assault.

Until the end of 1948 Argentina experienced an economic boom due to wartime and postwar demand for its agricultural and meat products. It thus accumulated large balances of dollars and other hard currencies. Confident that the prosperity would never end, the Perón regime embarked on a threefold economic program: (1) rapid industrialization, (2) repatriation of foreign indebtedness, and (3) acquisition of foreign-owned utilities.[42] √

It did not matter that most of the equipment for industrialization had to be bought in the United States when the postwar demand was great, the supplies limited, and the prices high. This unwise policy as well as other aspects of Perón's economic program resulted in the loss of dollar exchange. If Perón intended to continue the emphasis on industrialization, he needed dollars to purchase United States capital goods and machinery. Very likely the Argentine government could obtain a dollar loan if it wished — even

[42] *For. Pol. Rep.* XXIV, No. 14 (December 1, 1948), 160–168.

Secretary of State Dean Acheson made reference to a dollar loan as a "normal outcome" of the situation. But Perón was caught on the horns of a dilemma, for he had rejected the very idea of a loan. In fact, on one occasion he promised that he would shoot himself before asking for Yankee aid.

Because of its failure to promote increased trade with the United States, Argentina was driven to conclude a bilateral trade agreement with Great Britain in June, 1949. British goods were given preferred treatment in exchange for beef and wheat. This agreement shocked Washington, who regarded it as a threat to the United States market in Argentina. Therefore, the United States, seemingly impervious to insults, announced on May 17, 1950, a $125 million loan to Argentina, after receiving vague promises from Perón that foreign capital investments would be fairly treated and that dividends and profits could be transferred to foreign shareholders and firms.

The State Department admitted that its purpose in making the loan was to bail out United States traders who otherwise would have little chance of collecting on Argentina's debts to them because of the scarcity of dollar exchange. Perón claimed that the transaction did not violate his pledge never to accept a foreign loan, since the $125 million was not a "loan" but a "grant" √ to pay off accumulated commercial balances owed to American exporters. At any rate, the charge that it was an "Argentine bail-out" was not far from the truth.[43]

The loan marked the culminating point of the State Department's "about face" in its dealings with Perón. Apparently, expediency dictated that the American government disregard Argentina's unsavory behavior in World War II, and its more recent anti-United States pronouncements, and accept the quasi-fascist government as a full-fledged partner in the hope that it would join the inter-American defense system as designed by the Rio treaty of 1947. Many of our Latin neighbors began to wonder whether a get-tough policy on their part would attract a more favorable Washington attention.

For a brief period following the outbreak of the Korean War Argentina's economy was "riding high." In an Argentine-British bilateral meat pact, April 27, 1951, Britain had to agree to pay more and receive less. Although Perón praised the "superiority" of Argentina's economy over that of hard-currency countries, he overlooked the fact that he was pricing his producers out of the British market for their meat. Economic difficulties were not slow in arriving. By February, 1952, there was a marked decline in Argentina's meat exports. The old problem of dollar shortage reappeared. Perón blamed Argentina's economic ills on a "hostile, imperialistic world." The perennial press campaign against the United States blazed to new intensity. The State Department was compared to "the black hand of the dreaded Mafia."

A favorable attitude toward President Eisenhower at the time of his inauguration was soon dulled by Secretary of State Dulles' remarks about a "fascist

---

[43] See Dept. of State *Bulletin*, XXII, No. 568 (May 22, 1950), 800–803, for the objection of the CIO chairman to the proposed plan, and reply by Asst. Sect. Edward G. Miller, Jr.

movement" in Argentina. This was vigorously denied by Argentine officials and the controlled press. *La Época* of Buenos Aires, declared that not communism or fascism, but Yankee imperialism was the greatest threat to Latin America, which was treated "as if it was a conquered land."[44]

On the occasion of the fact-finding visit to Buenos Aires, in July, 1953, by Dr. Milton Eisenhower, the President's brother, Perón's propaganda machine substituted sweetness and light for its accustomed venom. In welcoming Dr. Eisenhower, Perón himself expressed "complete friendship," and his ambassador in Washington declared that Perón wanted to expand business with the United States to the fullest. This wish was reciprocated by the Eisenhower administration. On October 26, 1953, in commenting on improved relations after the Milton Eisenhower visit, Assistant Secretary of State John M. Cabot said: "I doubt that any good purpose would be served by raking over the dead leaves of the past." Domestic conditions in Argentina, he said, were "none of our business."[45] Mr. Cabot reported that Perón told him Argentine friendship had no price tag on it. Nevertheless, on March 10, 1955, the Export-Import Bank approved a $60 million line of credit to help finance the sale of equipment from the United States for a steel mill in Argentina. This was criticized in the United States as a "financial endorsement" of the Perón government, one of the "worst representatives of totalitarianism."[46]

Post-Perón relations

Since the fall of Perón on September 19, 1955, United States-Argentine relations have presented a picture almost completely at variance with anything in the past. No longer is the South American republic a rival for leadership in Latin America, for even if the desire is still alive, the means of implementing such a policy are absent. Perón's legacy of economic and political bankruptcy afforded the republic slight opportunity to essay more than internal rehabilitation. No longer does Argentine pride scorn United States assistance; on the contrary, over the past ten years, it has been eagerly sought and received.[47] The policy of the United States apparently has been to support economic stability and political order in Argentina, for we seem to feel a compulsion to see democracy vindicated.

Juan Perón left Argentina a looted country. Over and above acts of common pilfering, the dictator wasted the nation's credits. The country was staggering under a multi-billion dollar external debt, and the internal debt was even larger. The government had a gold and monetary reserve amounting to only $450 million, as compared to $1.6 billion in 1945. Certainly large infusions of foreign capital into the economic bloodstream were necessary to

---

[44] *Hispanic American Report*, VI, No. 1 (January, 1953), 34.

[45] U.S. Dept. of State *Bulletin*, XXIX, No. 748 (October 26, 1953), 557.

[46] *Hisp. Am. Rep.*, VIII, No. 3 (March, 1955), 135.

[47] Argentina's traditional international aloofness was largely effaced. Long-delayed ratification of significant inter-American agreements, such as the OAS Charter and the Caracas resolution against Communist encroachment, were forthcoming.

rehabilitate the stricken nation. The new governments of Argentina faced a monumental task.

General Eduardo Lonardi, the first provisional president after Perón's downfall, was recognized by United States Ambassador Albert F. Nufer on September 25, 1955.[48] Because of his alleged clerical leanings and softness toward Peronistas, Lonardi was ousted on November 13 by a military *coup,* and was succeeded in the presidency by General Pedro Eugenio Aramburu. On November 30 there arrived in Buenos Aires Assistant Secretary of State Henry Holland and Samuel Waugh, President of the Export-Import Bank, to discuss a loan then under consideration. On December 2 a $60 million Exim Bank loan was finally approved to help complete an unfinished steel mill. This was the first of a long list of loans and grants by the United States to post-Perón Argentina. Major United States government assistance to Argentina from 1955 to June, 1963, amounted to $361 million.

The inauguration of President Arturo Frondizi, on May 1, 1958, signaled the return of civilian government to Argentina.[49] Unfortunately, there was no return to economic or political stability in the distraught country. The constitutional government of President Frondizi moved from crisis to crisis — riots, strikes, and violence supposedly instigated by the nationalists (Peronistas) and Communists. Then too there was economic crisis marked by balance-of-payment difficulties and spiraling inflation. It was a miracle that Frondizi was able to keep his battered ship of state afloat for four years.

In December, 1958, Argentina received a loan of $329 million from the International Monetary Fund (IMF), the United States Treasury, the Export-Import Bank, the Development Loan Fund, and several United States private banks. This bail-out loan was dubbed by Frondizi's opponents as a sellout to foreign interests.[50] His austerity program, instituted to secure stabilization of the currency, was met by protests and discontent.

It was in the midst of these difficulties that, in January, 1959, Frondizi visited the United States as the guest of President Eisenhower. His was the first visit to the United States by an Argentine president. In an address to the United States Congress, on January 21, 1959, the Argentine president frankly acknowledged his personal satisfaction for United States assistance. He said, "Your country has fully understood its role in this hour in America. Argentina has just been granted important credits by the government and private institutions of the United States."[51] More aid was forthcoming. In June, 1959, a $33 million commodity sales agreement was signed with the United States under Public Law 480 whereby rice and edible oils would be supplied through

[48] Mr. Nufer, a holdover from the Truman administration, continued to serve at Buenos Aires until April, 1956, when he was replaced by another career ambassador, Willard Beaulac.

[49] President Eisenhower was represented at the inauguration ceremonies by Vice-President Nixon.

[50] *Hisp. Am. Rep.,* XI, No. 9 (September, 1958), 574; XI, No. 12 (December, 1958), 693; XII, No. 1 (January, 1959), 49.

[51] U.S. Dept. of State *Bulletin,* XL, No. 1026 (February 23, 1959), 280–283.

an Exim Bank loan. This was followed by more Exim Bank credits. President Frondizi's visit to the United States was reciprocated by President Eisenhower's visit to Buenos Aires in February, 1960.

In an exchange of views between Presidents Frondizi and Kennedy, in April, 1961, concerning the Alliance for Progress, the Argentine president declared his unreserved commitment to the joint cooperative effort. President Kennedy on his part, in September, 1961, pledged all his efforts to consolidate democratic institutions in Argentina, and to speed up the economic development of the country. On the occasion of the grant of a $150 million loan to Argentina for development under the Alliance for Progress, President Kennedy (February 25, 1962) said: "The development of Argentina's economy within a framework of representative democracy is one of the principal goals of the Alliance for Progress.[52]

Only a few days later democracy and constitutional government were dealt a hard blow in Argentina. On March 28, President Frondizi was ousted by the armed forces. The army had long been distrustful of Frondizi, largely because of the President's policy of so-called "national integration" of former Perónistas. There was also opposition to Frondizi's policy of allowing private foreign investors to exploit the petroleum resources of the country. The new military *junta* installed José María Guido as provisional president of the republic. The State Department hesitated to acknowledge the return of military dictatorship, but on April 18 Ambassador Robert McClintock formally recognized the military-directed government of President Guido.

The return, in October, 1963, of civilian constitutional rule to Argentina, in the person of President Arturo Illia, brought new problems for the State Department. These developed because the newly-inaugurated president rescinded some $400 million in petroleum contracts held by American and foreign oil companies. Of thirteen contracts annulled as illegal, nine were with United States companies. The American investments were estimated at about $237 million.[53]

The contracts had been signed between 1958 and 1960 by President Arturo Frondizi's government. In 1958 about 65 per cent of the country's oil needs, amounting to $250 million, had to be imported. This naturally created a heavy drain on the nation's balance of payments. To correct this situation Frondizi announced an oil development program in which foreign oil companies were invited to participate in exploration and development. This reversal of national petroleum policy, which had reserved all oil exploitation to the state petroleum enterprise called Yacimientos Petroliferos Fiscales (Y.P.F.), was generally criticized even by members of Frondizi's Radical Party as a "sellout" to foreign interests. They endeavored to force the president to submit all the contracts to congress for approval, but did not succeed,

---

[52] U.S. Dept. of State *Bulletin*, XLII, No. 1144 (May 29, 1961), 814–815. According to the *New York Times,* December 22, 1963, United States economic aid to Argentina over the preceding two years (1962–1963) totaled $233 million.

[53] *Time*, November 22, 1963, p. 36.

although Frondizi submitted a bill to congress proclaiming the country's petroleum to be the "inalienable" property of the state under the complete control of Y.P.F. The law had no effect on the drilling concessions, and wells were soon discovered, principally in the Rio Negro and Comodoro Rivadavia areas of southern Argentina.[54]

The fact that Argentina was able to free itself of exchange-depleting oil importations would seem to have vindicated Frondizi's policy. Yet this was not the case, for of all issues calculated to raise nationalistic hackles, the foreign exploitation of petroleum reserves tops the list. It was beside the question that the foreign companies, operating under fair contracts with ample safeguards to protect the national interests, were contributing to the economic recovery of the country. The fact of the matter was that, in the popular belief, the great foreign oil companies were the exemplars par excellence of economic imperialism and so could not be allowed to gain a foothold in the country. Argentine nationalism aspired to both political and economic independence.

In the electoral campaign of 1963 Arturo Illia committed himself to annulment of the contracts, arguing that since they had not received congressional approval they were illegal. This pledge he implemented without delay after his inauguration on October 13, 1963.[55]

Washington, dismayed by this turn of events, which could not but adversely affect the Alliance for Progress, attempted to impress on the Illia government the advisability of providing for just compensation. Indications from Buenos Aires that there would be compensation, seemed to abate rising fevers both in Argentina and in the United States. Great damage was done, nevertheless, to the confidence of private investors. This boded ill for the Alliance for Progress, the success of which was largely dependent on attracting more private investors. This is one aspect of the program which has lagged from the very beginning. Argentina has not responded satisfactorily to the challenge of the Alliance program.

[54] *Hisp. Am. Rep.*, XI, No. 8 (August, 1958), 459.
[55] On September 7, 1963, it was announced that Argentina was seeking an Alliance for Progress loan totaling $281,500,000. *New York Times,* September 8, 1963.

SUPPLEMENTARY READING

Alexander, Robert J., *The Perón Era* (New York: Columbia University Press, 1951).

Blanksten, George I., *Perón's Argentina* (Chicago: University of Chicago Press, 1953).

Bruce, James, *Those Perplexing Argentines* (New York: Longmans, Green and Co., 1953).

Consultation Among the American Republics with Respect to the *Argentine Situation*, Dept. of State Publication 2473 (Washington, D.C., 1946). (*The Blue Book*)

Fisk, Ysabel, and Rennie, Robert A., "Argentina in Crisis," *Foreign Policy Reports*, XX, No. 4 (May 1, 1944).

Haring, Clarence H., *Argentina and the United States* (Boston: World Peace Foundation, 1941).

Levene, Ricardo, *A History of Argentina*, W. S. Robertson, trans. (Chapel Hill: University of North Carolina Press, 1937).

Holmes, Olive, "Perón's 'Greater Argentina' and the United States," *Foreign Policy Reports*, XXIV, No. 14 (December 1, 1948).

McGann, Thomas F., *Argentina, the United States, and the Inter-American System, 1880–1914* (Cambridge: Harvard University Press, 1957).

Mecham, J. Lloyd, *The United States and the Inter-American System, 1889–1960* (Austin: University of Texas Press, 1961). (See index for "Argentina.")

Pendle, George, *Argentina* (London and New York: Royal Institute of International Affairs, 1955).

Peterson, Harold F., *Argentina and the United States, 1910–1960* (State University of New York, 1964).

Rennie, Ysabel F., *The Argentine Republic* (New York: The Macmillan Company, 1945).

Smith, Jr., O. Edmund, *Yankee Diplomacy: U.S. Intervention in Argentina* (Dallas: Southern Methodist University Press, 1953).

Stuart, G. H., *Latin America and the United States* (New York: Appleton-Century-Crofts, Inc., 5th ed., 1955), Chap. XVI.

Ugarte, Manuel, *The Destiny of a Continent* (New York: Alfred A. Knopf, Inc., 1925).

Whitaker, Arthur P., *Argentine Upheaval* (New York: Frederick A. Praeger, 1956).

Whitaker, Arthur P., *The United States and Argentina* (Cambridge: Harvard University Press, 1954).

15

United States Relations with Chile

The early record of United States-Chilean relations in the nineteenth century is presented here in some detail as a case study of misadventure in our Latin-American policy. It helps to explain why all has not been well for the United States in Latin America. Few countries have had more occasion than Chile to regard the United States with suspicion, fear, and unfriendliness. This is an anomaly, since there were no fundamental reasons, prior to 1900, for policy conflict with our far-distant Latin-American "neighbor." At the time of those unfortunate incidents there was an almost total absence of political, economic, or ideological basis for the development of critical issues between the two countries. We must assign the major blame to bungling United States diplomacy.

The beginning of relations

Relations between the United States and Chile date from February, 1812, when President Madison's personal agent, Joel Roberts Poinsett, arrived at Santiago, Chile.[1] At that time Chile was in the first phase of its struggle for independence prior to a temporary re-establishment of Spanish authority in 1814. It was the well-advised intention of the Washington government to withhold recognition until the fact of Chilean independence could be more definitely established.

Not only did Poinsett convey to the revolutionaries the sympathy and friendship of the government and people of the United States; he also participated more or less directly in the public and military affairs of Chile. As a result, the British brought pressure on the revolutionary Carrera government to ask the American agent to leave the country. Unfortunately, the

[1] For the Poinsett mission, see J. Fred Rippy, *Joel R. Poinsett, Versatile American* (Durham: Duke University Press, 1935).

favorable impressions made by Poinsett were not destined to persist long in Chile.

The obstructions imposed by the United States government to the efforts of Latin-American agents to secure moral and material support in Washington were interpreted in Chile as lack of sympathy by the United States for their cause. The situation was not necessarily improved by the decision of President Monroe to send a commission of three men to South America to investigate conditions in the new revolutionary governments. Of these, Theodorick Bland alone visited Chile. Arriving in Santiago in May, 1818, he informed Supreme Director Bernardo O'Higgins that the United States was determined to maintain a strict neutrality during Chile's war with Spain. Bland, however, became involved in an internal dispute between Chilean leaders; he also failed to make a good impression on O'Higgins — a view reciprocated by Bland himself. It is not surprising, therefore, that his report did not encourage President Monroe to recognize the Chilean government.[2]

When, in 1819, Admiral Cochrane declared the whole coast of Peru to be in a state of blockade, this meant trouble for the United States, since it refused to recognize the legality of the Admiral's ban. American attempts to run the blockade were not always successful, for Cochrane captured many American vessels as prizes and brought them to Valparaiso.[3]

It devolved on John B. Prevost, United States agent in Chile, to protest these depredations on American commerce, despite the fact that he inclined to sympathize with the Chileans. Although the legality of Cochrane's blockade may have been moot, Prevost believed that consideration should be given to the justice of the Chilean cause, particularly since Chilean ill will was mounting against the United States. But Prevost found no support in Washington, and eventually he was recalled because he allegedly showed no zeal for the protection of American interests.[4]

The inauguration of formal relations

When the Florida treaty of 1821 was finally out of the way, the United States was prepared to recognize the independence of Chile. On January 27, 1823, Heman Allen of Vermont was appointed minister plenipotentiary to Chile, but it was not until April, 1824, that he arrived at Santiago. This act of recognition by the United States was the first of its kind to be taken by any country outside of South America.

It must be confessed that the United States contributed little to the cause of Chilean independence because of its set policy of remaining carefully neutral. Nor did the news of President Monroe's famous pronouncement of

[2] *American State Papers, Foreign Relations* (6 vols. Washington, D.C., 1832–1859), IV, 295, 309; Ricardo Montaner y Bello, *Historia Diplomática de la Independencia de Chile* (Santiago de Chile: Prensas de la Universidad de Chile, 1941), 79–80.

[3] William R. Manning, ed., *Diplomatic Correspondence of the United States Concerning the Independence of the Latin American Nations* (3 vols. New York: Carnegie Endowment for International Peace, 1925), II, 1038–1039.

[4] *Ibid.*, I, 134–135.

December 2, 1823, arouse a grateful response in Chile.[5] On the contrary, thanks to their acquaintance with the Canning-Polignac memorandum, Chileans regarded Canning as "the redeemer of Chile." They well knew that, if any invasion of the American continent had been seriously contemplated by the European alliance, it was Great Britain and not the United States that had interposed an effective veto.

Because of internal political and financial difficulties Chile was not able to send a diplomatic representative to the United States until 1827. In that year, Joaquín Campino was appointed Chile's first minister to the United States. Unsuccessful in his attempts to negotiate a treaty of amity and commerce, or to settle outstanding claims, Campino's mission was terminated in 1829, after which time the post remained vacant for several years.[6]

It remained for Andrés Bello, Chilean Foreign Minister, to successfully negotiate at Santiago, in 1832, a treaty of amity, commerce, and navigation with *Chargé d'Affaires* John Hamm. It was a signal diplomatic victory for Bello, since he obtained for Chile terms the United States had refused to grant other Latin-American nations; to wit, Chile was allowed an exception to the "most-favored-nation" treatment in respect to the other Spanish-American states.[7] Mr. Hamm agreed to this concession because he wanted to clear the way for the settlement of United States claims which had arisen during the war for independence. American claimants were calling for action.

The claims controversy

The claims demands supported by the United States government on behalf of certain of its citizens against the Chilean government, and in disregard of the views of Prevost, originated, as we have noted, from the seizure of American property by Lord Cochrane, and also from the searches and detentions in Chilean ports. The outstanding claim was that of the *Macedonian,* a merchant ship commanded by Captain Eliphalet Smith. The ship reached Peru in 1819 where it disposed of its cargo of goods belonging to Boston merchants for $145,000. Lord Cochrane, who was bombarding Callao at the time, confiscated all of the money. This is known as the "first" *Macedonian* claim.[8]

Another claim arose from the seizure of $70,400 from the same Captain Smith of the *Macedonian* in 1821, by the land forces of Cochrane at a point north of the port of Arica which was not under blockade by the Chilean navy. This is known as the "second" *Macedonian* claim. It is worthy of mention that Captain Smith was reputed to be one of the most noted smugglers on the Pacific coast.

[5] Montaner y Bello, *op. cit.,* 183–184, 283–291.

[6] William R. Manning, *Diplomatic Correspondence of the United States: Inter-American Affairs, 1831–1861* (12 vols. Washington, D.C.: Carnegie Endowment for International Peace, 1932–1939), V, 3.

[7] *Ibid.,* V, 40–41; Henry Clay Evans, *Chile and its Relations with the United States* (Durham: Duke University Press, 1927), 48–51; William R. Sherman, *The Diplomatic and Commercial Relations of the United States and Chile, 1820–1914* (Boston: Richard G. Badger, Publisher, 1926), 27–28.

[8] For discussion of the claims, see Sherman, *op. cit.,* 24–32.

The *Warrior* claim for $15,000 arose from the seizure by the Chileans of the American brig of that name at Coquimbo in April, 1820. The sum total of American claims of a bona fide character, based on illegal seizure of goods or money during the Chilean revolution, aggregated about $160,000.[9]

Heman Allen, our first minister to Santiago, had been instructed to seek a settlement of the *Macedonian* case, which was considered the most important. But neither Mr. Allen nor his successor Samuel Larned, was able to make any progress in the negotiation of a claims settlement. *Chargé* John Hamm, although able to negotiate a commercial treaty, was no more successful than his predecessors in working out a solution of the claims issue. As a result of some pressure by *Chargé* Pollard, Chile agreed in 1840 to pay $15,000 in settlement of the *Warrior* claims. As for the first *Macedonian* claims, Mr. Pollard encountered the usual delaying tactics. Finally, when the American *chargé* threatened to report the matter to his government so that the President could lay it before Congress, the Chilean government agreed to a settlement of $104,000 with interest at 5 per cent from the date of seizure.[10]

Belief that the *Macedonian* claims dispute had finally been resolved was rudely shattered the next year when an entirely new claim, the "second" *Macedonian* claim, *was submitted for the first time.* Although the sum involved was much less than the original *Macedonian* claim, it proved to be the cause of even more serious tensions in our Chilean relations.

Because of the long delay before the United States presented the claim, Chile sought to evade responsibility by the right of prescription. This attempted evasion was rejected by *Chargé* J. S. Pendleton, and a heated exchange of views with the Chilean Foreign Minister followed. Since the claims negotiations at Santiago proved to be unproductive, they were transferred to Washington, where Manuel Carvallo was sent to represent Chile. After several years of fruitless negotiation, Señor Carvallo finally suggested arbitration, but before a definite agreement could be reached he was recalled in December, 1853. It was not until November 10, 1858, that an arbitration convention was signed in Santiago.[11]

The agreement provided that King Leopold of Belgium should be arbitrator. His award was announced on May 15, 1863. Although the claim was found to be valid, the arbitrator decided that, of the amount seized by Admiral Cochrane, only three-fifths belonged to American citizens; the rest was adjudged the property of Peruvian merchants. Therefore, three-fifths of the claim, or $42,000, should be paid the American claimants with interest at 6 per cent dating from 1841.[12]

The ending of the claims dispute did not improve the Chilean attitude toward the United States, for the discovery of gold in California set in motion a chain of developments that resulted in a worsening of relations. A minor factor was the unfavorable impression left in Chile by the rowdyism and

[9] *Ibid.*, 24.

[10] *Ibid.*, 38–40; *Sen. Exec. Doc.* No. 58, 35th Cong., 1st Sess., 4.

[11] *Sen. Exec. Doc.* No. 58, 35th Cong., 1st Sess., 126–409.

[12] J. B. Moore, *History and Digest of International Arbitrations to Which the United States Has Been a Party* (6 vols. Washington, 1898), II, 1449.

disrespect for law by the adventurers who stopped at Chilean ports en route to the California gold fields via Cape Horn. Another factor was the unexpected opportunity for Chile to export foodstuffs to California. A short-lived boom in Chile collapsed by 1855 when Californians were able to raise their own supplies. A resultant financial panic in Chile was blamed, quite unjustifiably, on the Americans.

The most serious aspect of the California problem was the harsh treatment accorded Chileans attracted to the new *El Dorado*. Some who failed to find sudden wealth turned bandits and eventually ran afoul of vigilante committees. Many Chileans, and other Latin youths, suffered unjustly at the hands of the vengeful *Anglos*. Outraged Chile, her protests ignored, could do no more than aid the return home of her nationals. So great was the hostility toward the United States that the American Minister reported in 1855: "An expression of good will towards the United States seems sufficient to seal the political fate of anyone bold enough to utter it." He referred to widespread talk of expelling all Americans from Chile and closing the ports to their commerce.[13]

Because of the incidents we have mentioned, and also because of the United States war on Mexico in 1846, and the filibustering activities of William Walker in Nicaragua, the Chileans developed a fear of United States expansion. Typical of their attitude were the strong words of the firebrand intellectual, Francisco Bilbao, who warned that idealism and human dignity were threatened by the expansionist ambitions of the United States. The Anglo-American colossus, said Bilbao, sought to infest the world with its materialistic individualism, and ultimately all of Latin America would become its protectorate.[14]

American diplomatic representation in Chile has been charged, and perhaps justly, with some of the responsibility for Chilean lack of cordiality, if not downright antagonism, toward the United States. If diplomacy required the withholding of recrimination and anger from negotiation, then the performance of several of our representatives at Santiago proved their diplomatic incompetence.

Of our envoys in this category, Colonel Seth Barton of Louisiana was probably the most notorious. His appointment to the post at Santiago by his old friend, President James K. Polk, was not a happy one. The elderly soldier has been described as "rather sensitive personally and hotheaded," lacking in knowledge of international law, and "wanting in the elements of judiciousness and poise which are essential to such a diplomatic position." It is not surprising, therefore, that Barton's two-year stay in Santiago developed into more of a personal wrangle than a diplomatic mission.[15]

Friction developed when Barton ignored a government order to fly the legation flag on a national holiday, and when his carriage horses were impounded by the municipal authorities after a runaway. Finally, a violent quar-

[13] Manning, *Dipl. Corresp.: Inter-Am. Affairs*, V, 210–211.
[14] Frederick B. Pike, *Chile and the United States, 1880–1962* (Notre Dame: University of Notre Dame Press, 1963), 26.
[15] Sherman, *op. cit.*, 49.

rel developed with the archbishop of Santiago, who opposed the marriage of Barton, a Protestant, to a young Chilean señorita, a Catholic, who belonged to one of the richest and oldest families of the Santiago aristocracy. The prelate's opposition was reinforced when he learned that Barton had been divorced shortly before his departure for Chile. The upshot was that Barton and the señorita were married in the legation by a United States naval chaplain. This event did not still the archbishop's opposition, for he wrote the bride urging her to leave her husband to whom she was not legally married according to the law of the Church.

Barton violently condemned the prelate, and held the government of Chile responsible for the actions of the church dignitary. His undiplomatic outburst resulted in an official demand for his recall. The State Department expressed regret to Chile, but was spared the necessity of recalling its minister by Barton's own decision to leave.[16] The misadventures of Colonel Barton were not untypical of our mediocre representation at Santiago.

United States mediation in the Chilean-Spanish war

In the early 1860's there was an appreciable improvement in our Chilean relations. The Union cause in the American Civil War was popular in Chile because it opposed the institution of slavery, and because the South's desire to extend slavery was believed responsible for imperialistic aggressions by the United States. Chileans who formerly feared the United States became friendly partisans of the Lincoln administration.

Unfortunately, the period of improved relations between Chile and the United States came to an abrupt end in 1865 with the outbreak of war between Spain on the one hand, and Chile in alliance with Peru, Bolivia, and Ecuador, on the other. In 1864 a small naval expedition, sent by Spain to Peru with orders to collect some dubious debts, seized the Chincha Islands with their valuable guano deposits. Chile's vigorous protest against this action, accompanied by various forms of assistance to Peru, brought from the Spanish admiral the charge of unneutral action and a blockade of the Chilean coast. Soon Bolivia and Ecuador joined in the struggle which all regarded as common defense of their independence against a resurgent Spain bent on restoring her colonial empire. In view of the apparent violation of the Monroe Doctrine, and also because the American Civil War was no longer a restraint on the Washington government, the Chileans were confident of American support. Instead, to their astonishment and dismay, President Johnson proclaimed neutrality.[17] Benjamin Vicuña Mackenna, sent to the United States to win support for Chile, and to purchase warships, encountered official opposition and was even arrested for violation of the neutrality laws. In the report of his fruitless mission to the United States the embittered envoy charged that neutral United States helped Spain more than Chile.

16 *Ibid.*, 50–52; Evans, *op. cit.*, 122–125.

17 For Chile's War with Spain, see *Foreign Relations of the United States,* 1862, Pt. 2, 349–413.

The Spanish war was a peculiar affair which dragged on with few encounters and a negligible loss of life. The only serious incident was the bombardment of Valparaiso on March 31, 1866. The efforts of General Kilpatrick, United States minister at Santiago, to restrain the Spanish admiral, or to obtain cooperation from the British and French diplomatic representatives in preventing the bombardment, were fruitless. Since the American minister was unwilling to assume sole responsibility for checking the Spaniards, the American naval squadron withdrew from the harbor of Valparaiso. This was followed immediately by the Spanish bombardment of the town. Only two or three lives were lost, but the property damage was great. Following the senseless bombardment, the Spanish squadron sailed back to Spain after its repulse at Callao by the Peruvians.

Failure of the United States to implement the Monroe Doctrine in support of Chile, and particularly the failure of the American squadron at Valparaiso to prevent the bombardment of the unfortified town, contributed to bitter distrust and dislike. As reported by General Kilpatrick: "Chile looked upon the United States as her best friend, and that friend had failed to assist her in her hour of need." Informed of Chilean disappointment, Secretary of State Seward declared that, whereas the United States would not permit Spain to annex any Chilean territory, it could not "enter as an ally into every war in which a friendly republican state on this continent becomes involved."[18]

The War of the Pacific

The preceding incidents pale into insignificance as examples of Chilean unfriendliness for the United States in contrast to relations during the War of the Pacific. The emergence of Chile at that time into a position of power and prestige in South America seemed to be encountering unsympathetic opposition on the part of the United States. Little wonder that, since the nationalistic emotions of Chileans were at fever heat, there would be violent reaction to the gratuitous interferences by the United States. It was a situation which certainly called for astute diplomacy, but unfortunately little was to be found either in the field or in Washington itself. A brief summary of the war will serve as a frame of reference for our survey of United States diplomatic maneuvers.

The so-called War of the Pacific, which erupted in 1879, was a conflict between Chile on the one side, and Peru and Bolivia on the other. In simple terms Chile was an energetic, economically expanding nation that coveted the great mineral treasures, particularly in nitrates, found in the coastal provinces of her neighbors Bolivia and Peru. Irresistibly tempted by these underdeveloped and sparsely occupied areas, Chile took advantage of the customary political anarchy in the two republics to take the provinces by a war of conquest.

The war originated in a boundary dispute between Chile and Bolivia involving most of the Bolivian province of Antofagasta, rich in nitrates, and

18 *Ibid.,* 408, 414.

Bolivia's only outlet to the sea. Unwisely, Bolivia had allowed the enterprising Chileans to work the deposits. They had even penetrated into the next province to the north, Tarapacá, which was owned by Peru. Bolivian governmental action, allegedly injurious to Chilean mining interests, was the spark which ignited the war.[19] Chile broke off diplomatic relations, and on February 14, 1879, occupied Antofagasta. Bolivia had no choice but to declare war on March 1. Peru attempted mediation, but Chile, accusing Peru of being a secret ally of Bolivia, declared war on Peru on April 5.

The progress of the war was a remarkable demonstration of Chilean military preparation in modern weapons and training. The Bolivians and Peruvians, on the other hand, had difficulty in mobilizing their poorly trained and inadequately equipped troops whose field operations were hampered by political intrigues in their own respective capitals, Lima and La Paz.

The military events of the war may be briefly summarized in four stages. First, there was the Chilean occupation of Antofagasta by forces landed from the fleet stationed for some time in Antofagasta Bay. The Bolivians offered little resistance. The second stage of the war was marked by the naval operations against Peru. A so-called blockade of all the important Peruvian ports was rapidly extended northward until finally, in April, 1880, Callao, the port for Lima, was closed. The blockade created problems for the neutrals engaged in commerce along the west coast. The third stage of the war was a land invasion of Peru by Chilean troops, beginning in the southern provinces. The Peruvians were routed at Tacna, and the port of Arica after long resistance finally surrendered. The fourth and final stage of the war saw the fall of Callao on December 6, 1880, and the occupation of Lima early in 1881. The invaders were then forced to establish a government with which they could make a peace.[20]

United States mediation

The United States viewed the developing war in South America with concern but took no official action to prevent the conflict. Nevertheless, acting without official instructions, Judge Newton D. Pettis, the United States minister to La Paz, made a personal visit to both Lima and Santiago in August, 1879, to urge the warring governments to negotiate a settlement. He received little support from his colleagues at Lima and Santiago; in fact, Thomas A. Osborn, American minister at Santiago, strongly advised against United States mediation because of the war hysteria in Chile.[21]

The State Department, however, while declaring that Mr. Pettis' experiment was unauthorized and even rash, was strongly inclined to a mediatory role.[22]

[19] For causes of the War of the Pacific, see Gonzalo Bulnes, *Las causas de la guerra entre Chile y el Peru* (Santiago de Chile, 1919); V. M. Maurtua, *The Question of the Pacific* (Philadelphia, 1901), 43–51; and Herbert Millington, *American Diplomacy and the War of the Pacific* (New York: Columbia University Press, 1948), 9–32.

[20] For a sketch of the war, see Luis Galdames *A History of Chile*, I. J. Cox, trans. (Chapel Hill: University of North Carolina Press, 1941), 326–336.

[21] Millington, *op. cit.*, 58–60.

[22] For the position of the United States toward the War of the Pacific, see "The War of South America," *Sen. Exec. Doc.* No. 79, 47th Cong., 1st Sess.

The United States not only sincerely desired to see peace maintained in South America; it was concerned over rumored European intervention, and feared a possible violation of the Monroe Doctrine. Accordingly, Secretary of State William Maxwell Evarts instructed our representatives at Lima, La Paz, and Santiago to offer good offices. As a result, the belligerents sent representatives to a peace conference held aboard the U.S.S. *Lackawanna* in the Bay of Arica in October, 1880. By that time Chile's military operations had reached the end of the second stage of the war. The easy and overwhelming success of her arms had whetted an appetite for the spoils of war which could not be easily satisfied. Mr. Osborn, our representative to Santiago, was well aware of this fact. But our representatives to Lima and La Paz, Isaac P. Christiancy and Charles Adams, persisted in the hope that Chile would agree to a "reasonable settlement." Let it be noted that all three American envoys were strongly suspected of bias in support of the particular government to which each was accredited.

At the *Lackawanna* conference all hopes for a fair compromise were quickly dispelled by Chile's demands for the cession not only of Antofagasta, but Tarapacá as well, the payment to Chile of $20 million by Peru and Bolivia jointly, and the occupation of Tacna and Arica by Chilean forces until the obligations of the settlement had been complied with. Since Chile would not modify the conditions laid down, Peru and Bolivia had no choice but to continue the war.[23]

Confidence on the part of the allies that the United States was opposed to conquest by force in South America, may have stimulated their determination to continue the otherwise hopeless struggle. Rumors had circulated that, if the Arica conference failed to end hostilities, the United States would be forced to intervene to forestall European action.

Following the breakdown of the Arica conference, Chile renewed the war with vigor. Callao was captured on December 6, 1880, and Lima was occupied on January 10, 1881. The situation was interpreted by Secretary of State Evarts as a favorable one for the renewal of United States mediation. He was informed, however, by Mr. Osborn, that Chile was opposed to foreign mediation.[24] Such was the situation when the Hayes administration came to an end, and, in March, 1881, Mr. Evarts yielded his duties as Secretary of State to James G. Blaine.

The role of Mr. Blaine

The new Secretary of State not only adopted the Evarts policy of mediating Chile's war with her unfortunate antagonists, thus excluding European interference, but he also played such a forceful role in seeking to end the hostilities, that his name soon became anathema throughout Chile.

As one of his first official acts Mr. Blaine replaced Christiancy and Osborn with two men of his own choice. There can be little doubt that the former

[23] For the Arica conference, see Millington, *op. cit.*, 73–78.
[24] *Ibid.*, 81.

representatives, particularly Christiancy, who ignored instructions and favored forcible intervention, left much to be desired as creditable diplomats, but the men chosen by Blaine himself were of even more questionable ability. They were General Stephen A. Hurlbut, minister to Peru, and General Judson Kilpatrick, minister to Chile. Blaine may have been restricted in his choice by a Congressional resolution recommending the appointment of former Union generals to diplomatic posts.

Both ministers were instructed that it was the policy of the United States to save Peru, if possible, from the loss of territory to Chile.[25] Upon assuming his duties in Lima in August, 1881, General Hurlbut made it clear that the United States government supported peace on the basis of a war indemnity only for Chile. He seemed to believe — as the result of a personal talk with Blaine and President Garfield before his departure for his post — that he was to support Peru against Chile, because Chile was supported by Great Britain.[26] General Hurlbut entered into his role with enthusiasm, with the result that his pronounced pro-Peruvian bias led him into a number of undiplomatic actions.

After the fall of Lima, civil government collapsed in Peru, and it became a problem for the Chileans to find a government with which they could conclude a peace treaty. Eventually, with the approval and support of the Chilean authorities, Francisco García Calderón established a provisional government in Lima, although the legal government under Nicolás Piérola was still in existence, having fled into the hills. Secretary Blaine, realizing Peru's urgent need for a peace settlement, and the need of a government to assume this responsibility, decided to recognize García Calderón.

General Hurlbut urged President García Calderón to resist Chilean demands. He was so successful in stiffening the resistance of Chile's intended puppet president that the occupation authorities were forced to order his arrest and deportation to Chile. Shortly before this action, which was viewed by Hurlbut as a veiled insult to his own country, the American minister sent Admiral Patricio Lynch, the Chilean commander-in-chief in Peru, a memorandum on August 25, 1881, indicating that the United States did not recognize a war for territorial aggrandizement, and therefore Peru should not suffer dismemberment, at least not until she defaulted on a money indemnity.[27]

The publication of the memorandum in Chile created great excitement and a stiffening of anti-American attitude. Although General Hurlbut's action was undiplomatic, that of his counterpart at Santiago, General Kilpatrick, was no less so, for, without consulting the State Department, he assured the Chilean Foreign Minister that his colleague's statements were unauthorized by his government. The Chileans chose to believe General Kilpatrick, who, up to the time of his death very shortly after, had evidenced a pronounced pro-Chilean attitude.[28]

[25] Millington, *op. cit.*, 86.   [26] *Ibid.*, 87.
[27] *Ibid.*   [28] Pike, *op. cit.*, 50–51.

Secretary Blaine's disapproval of General Hurlbut's actions, not the least of which was his signing a compact with a Peruvian faction ceding the port of Chimbote to the United States as a coaling station and the granting of concessions in the nitrate and guano deposits, was not enough to prevent the Secretary's name being dragged into an inquiry by the House Foreign Affairs Committee.[29] Secretary Blaine was charged by his political opponents with being personally and financially interested in a corporation known as the American Nitrate Company, and of using his official position for personal gain. The Secretary was also accused of having an interest in foreign claims of dubious foundation against Peru. However, in spite of these accusations, Blaine was completely absolved of any misconduct by the investigation of the House Committee. If economic motivation was present in his interventionist policies, it was to gain for American capitalists the opportunity to challenge British pre-eminence in the west coast countries of South America.

Following the fiasco of the Lynch memorandum, Mr. Blaine sent William H. Trescott, an experienced diplomat, to the troubled area in South America. Trescott was instructed by Secretary Blaine, with the approval of President Arthur, who had succeeded to the presidency after the assassination of President Garfield, to take a firm stand against the annexation of Tarapacá by Chile if that country did not disavow the arrest and detention of President García Calderón as an act unfriendly to the United States. Some believe that if Blaine's "instructions were carried out and Chile had refused to cooperate, war between the two countries could have resulted easily."[30]

The facts are that before Trescott reached Chile, Blaine had been succeeded as Secretary of State by Frederick T. Frelinghuysen. The American envoy, completely ignorant of the fact that his instructions had been countermanded by the new Secretary, was actually informed of this fact by the Chilean Foreign Minister. Faced by this embarrassing situation, Trescott seemed to have no recourse but to accept, by formal protocol, the Chilean principle that peace depended on territorial transfer.

Imagine Trescott's confusion when Secretary Frelinghuysen informed him that his signed protocol had been repudiated. It seems that whereas the State Department had reluctantly come to the conclusion that Chile's territorial demands could no longer be resisted, the American government would be no party to formal peace negotiations to that end. This did not mean, however, that the United States would abandon its efforts for impartial mediation to secure a moderation of Chile's terms. Active intervention would only be contemplated in case of intrusion by European powers. The policy of Mr. Frelinghuysen did not seem to differ greatly from that of Mr. Blaine.[31] Nor indeed did bungling diplomacy cease when Frelinghuysen's own appointees, James Partridge and Dr. Cornelius Logan, assumed their posts at Lima and

[29] See House Investigating Committee, *House Report*, 1790, 47th Cong., 1st Sess.
[30] Millington, *op. cit.*, 121.
[31] R. H. Bastert, "Diplomatic Reversal: Frelinghuysen's to Blaine's Pan American Policy in 1882," *Mississippi Valley Historical Review*, XLII (March, 1956), 653–671.

Santiago. It is not necessary, fortunately, to recapitulate their misadventures, except to note that both men, like their predecessors, refused to cooperate with each other and manifested a strong bias in favor of the government to which each had been accredited.

The Peruvians, finally convinced of the hopelessness of their cause and of the futility of relying upon the United States, finally decided to deal directly with the Chileans. The Peruvian president reported to his congress: "We have reached the sad conviction that the American Government . . . can do nothing more than it has already done for Peru and Bolivia. . . . You may measure the amount of gratitude we owe to the American Government for its interference on our behalf."[32] Peru and Chile, therefore, signed an agreement, known as the Treaty of Ancón, on October 20, 1883, and exchanged ratifications on March 28, 1884. Peace came without any United States participation.

By terms of the treaty, Tarapacá was ceded outright to Chile. Tacna and Arica were to be held by Chile for ten years; upon the expiration of that period a plebiscite by the inhabitants would decide which should possess the provinces permanently. The victor should pay the loser $10 million for the territory thus acquired. In the Treaty of Ancón Bolivia was ignored completely. By a truce agreed upon between Chile and Bolivia, Chile retained its hold on Antofagasta. By a treaty signed in 1894, Bolivia renounced all claims to the province.

The United States suffered a humiliating loss of prestige by its diplomatic blunders in these negotiations. Although it succeeded in preventing any European mediation, little Chile was able to defy the wishes of the northern colossus at every turn, and in the end negotiated a settlement on its own terms and without the presence of an American representative. Furthermore, by their failure to mediate, the Americans left a legacy of fear, distrust, and hostility in Chile, and bitter disillusion in Peru. This is not the full assessment, for yet another consequence was the Tacna-Arica question which we will discuss shortly.

Problems of the Chilean civil war

A civil war — unusual for politically stable Chile — broke out in 1891 between President Balmaceda and the Congressionalists. Once again the United States became involved in Chilean affairs, and once again damaged its image in that country. In the conflict the Chileans resorted to arms to settle a constitutional issue: the independence of the national presidency or its control by a parliamentary majority. The attempt of President Balmaceda to free the executive of congressional domination led him to acts that aroused the leaders of congress to revolt. Quickly won over to the cause of the Congressionalists, the Chilean navy established a revolutionary base at Tarapacá, and thus denied to Balmaceda the rich revenues from the nitrate mines. The army remained loyal to the president with the result that the struggle became one of army versus navy.

[32] Millington, *op. cit.,* 135.

The superiority of the navy was soon established. Valparaiso was captured, and railroad connections were cut off between Santiago and the coast. The defeat of Balmaceda's army at Viña del Mar was followed by the surrender of Santiago, the abdication of Balmaceda, and his suicide in the Argentine legation where he had sought asylum. The civil war, which established parliamentary supremacy in Chile, lasted only nine months, from January to September, 1891.[33]

The American minister at Santiago during these events was Patrick Egan, a naturalized Irish patriot and rabid Anglophobe. The fact that British interests were sympathetic to the Congressionals may have influenced Egan to side with Balmaceda. At any rate Egan adopted a strong pro-Balmaceda bias, sending dispatches to the State Department that were so favorable to the Balmaceda government they tended to make the Department itself partial to that side of the controversy.[34]

An incident which aroused great public hostility against the United States was the *Itata* affair.[35] Being in need of arms and ammunition, representatives of the Congressional party bought rifles in the United States, and managed to have them put aboard a Chilean steamer, the *Itata,* about forty miles off the coast of San Diego, California. The *Itata* then set out for Chile followed by two United States warships. Although the purchase of the rifles was not a violation of the neutrality laws of the United States, their loading at sea, particularly since the *Itata* had made an illegal departure from San Diego, was a debatable question. Responding to the protest of the Balmaceda representative at Washington, Secretary of State Blaine ordered the return to the United States of the *Itata* and its cargo. Since the guns were badly needed by the Congressionalists this heightened their resentment for the United States which had so clearly identified itself with the Balmacedistas. It is interesting to note that the United States Supreme Court, in 1893, declared that the *Itata* had not violated the neutrality laws of the United States and ordered the ship's return to Chile.

After the fall of the Balmaceda government a number of its former officials sought asylum in the United States legation at Santiago. Mr. Egan was adamant in his rejection of the demand for the surrender of the fugitives unless they were given safe conduct out of the country. The refusal of the Chilean government resulted in a stalemate and the virtual investment of the American legation by Chilean police. Then occurred the notorious *Baltimore* incident in Valparaiso, which caused relations between the United States and Chile to plunge to their nadir.[36]

On October 16, 1891, Captain Winfield S. Schley of the U.S.S. *Baltimore* granted shore leave to more than one hundred of the ship's company. This

---

[33] For the revolution of 1891, see Galdames, *op. cit.,* 345–348.

[34] Pike, *op. cit.,* 67–72.

[35] See Osgood Hardy, "The Itata Incident," *Hispanic American Historical Review* V (May, 1922), 195–226.

[36] For the *Baltimore affair,* see J. M. Barros Franco, *El caso del "Baltimore"* (Santiago de Chile, 1950); and Pike, *op. cit.,* 73–81.

was unwise in view of Chilean animosity toward the Yankees. Inevitably violent fights occurred between members of the crew and Chileans. Two of the sailors were killed, a number were injured, and thirty-six were taken to prison, where they were badly beaten. The Valparaiso police apparently made little or no effort to protect the Americans. The official United States and Chilean versions of the incident were at complete variance.

Captain Schley's report, after "careful investigation," was accepted by the State Department as basis for instructions to Egan to inform Chile that: the conduct of the American sailors was orderly and the attack on them was not only unprovoked but apparently premeditated; the Chilean police, instead of protecting them, were guilty of beating the sailors before and after their arrest; as a result of these actions, two United States sailors had been killed and seventeen wounded. It was the conclusion of the State Department that, since the mob attack was inspired not by hostility to the sailors as individuals, but as representatives of the United States government, whose uniforms they wore, Chile should make a suitable apology and adequate reparations.[37]

Egan's note, embodying the substance of his instructions, was conveyed to Manuel Matta, the Chilean Foreign Minister, on October 26. Matta replied that any decision by his government must await the findings of the criminal court in Valparaiso which was investigating the affair. This investigation, not completed until the end of December, supported the contention of the Chilean government that drunken sailors were responsible for the disorders and that the police had not abused their authority.

Chilean delay in dealing with the refugee situation in the Santiago legation, and the *Baltimore* affair, provoked President Harrison to report the matter to Congress in his message of December 8. He promised to call a special session if Chile did not make a prompt apology and pay an adequate indemnity. The gravity of the situation was heightened by Matta's indiscretion in questioning President Harrison's honesty.

Shortly before the end of December there was a change of government in Santiago, which brought about the retirement of Matta. His successor in the Foreign Office was a man more inclined to be friendly to Egan and the United States. The problem of asylum was soon settled by allowing the refugees to board an American warship, and thus the legation was freed of further police annoyance.

At the very time when it appeared that an amicable settlement was pending, Mr. Blaine and President Harrison launched two bombshells in rapid succession. On January 23, 1892, the Secretary informed the Chilean government, through Mr. Egan, that the United States stood on the Schley version of the *Baltimore* affair and therefore rejected the findings of the Valparaiso court, and demanded adequate satisfaction and reparation. Moreover, a prompt disavowal of the insulting insinuations of Señor Matta against the

[37] For the U.S. case, see "Relations with Chile," *House Exec. Doc.* No. 91, 52nd Cong., 1st Sess., 100 ff.

President of the United States was demanded on pain of a suspension of diplomatic relations.

On January 25 President Harrison sent a special message to Congress in which he laid the whole matter of the *Baltimore* affair and the refugee problem before that body. The President endorsed both Egan's actions and Blaine's ultimatum. While expressing a desire for peace he asked Congress to authorize him to use force to obtain satisfaction of American demands.

Confronted by the threat of war, Chile hastened a reply to the ultimatum. There were expressions of regret for the Valparaiso assault on the American seamen, and for Matta's unfortunate dispatch. As for reparations, the Chilean government expressed willingness to submit the matter to the Supreme Court of the United States or any other arbitration body preferred by President Harrison. Neither of these recourses proved to be necessary, for an offer by Chile to pay $75,000 to families of the dead and injured sailors was acceptable to the State Department.[38]

The coercion of Chile to a full surrender in the *Baltimore* incident left a bad memory in the South American country. Not only was there hurt pride and humiliation, but more perceptive Chileans fearfully foresaw the United States as supreme director of all hemisphere affairs. According to Ambassador Claude Bowers, writing in 1958: "Sixty-five years have come and gone, but the resentment has not entirely died out, and our enemies still use the story of the *Baltimore* to create prejudice against us in a crisis."[39]

The Tacna-Arica question

The long-continued and acrimonious Tacna-Arica dispute, for the origins of which bungling American diplomacy must assume some responsibility, was another heritage of the War of the Pacific. It will be recalled that the Treaty of Ancón left the final disposition of the Peruvian provinces of Tacna and Arica to be decided by a plebiscite to be held ten years after the ratification of the treaty. Since the treaty was ratified in 1884, the plebiscite should have been held in 1894. But it was not held at that time, nor later, because of the failure of Chile and Peru to agree on a satisfactory method of implementing the treaty provisions. In the meantime Chile retained possession of the territory, and promoted its "Chileanization" program. The long-continued stalemate engendered recriminations and bitterness dangerous to peace between the two nations. In fact, the dispute came to be known as "the Alsace-Lorraine question of South America."[40]

[38] Barros Franco, *op. cit.*, 67, 70–72; *For. Rel.*, 1892, 62.

[39] Claude G. Bowers, *Chile Through Embassy Windows, 1939–1953* (New York: Simon and Schuster, 1958), 192.

[40] For the Tacna-Arica question, see W. J. Dennis, *Tacna and Arica, an Account of the Chile-Peru Boundary Dispute and the Arbitration by the United States* (New Haven: Yale University Press, 1931); Graham H. Stuart, *The Tacna-Arica Dispute* (Boston: World Foundation Pamphlet, X, No. 1, 1927).

In the earlier stages of the controversy the United States endeavored to maintain a hands-off attitude. On a number of occasions, in response to Peruvian initiatives, the United States indicated that it had little desire to undertake another mediation. In fact it was not until 1922, when the new Harding administration took over at Washington, that Secretary of State Charles Evans Hughes instructed our representatives in Santiago and Lima to offer the good offices of the United States to facilitate a solution of the Tacna-Arica question. As a result both disputants, with the exclusion of Bolivia, sent delegates to Washington to discuss "the unfulfilled clauses of the Treaty of Ancón."

The Washington conference resulted in a protocol which provided that the question of a plebiscite be submitted to arbitration by the President of the United States. The arbitrator should determine whether in the present circumstances a plebiscite should be held, and if not, he should be allowed to offer the good offices of the United States in seeking a solution. The award was made by President Coolidge on March 4, 1925.[41] It was the decision of the arbitrator that the provisions of the Treaty of Ancón were still in effect and that a plebiscite should be held under United States supervision. A commission of three members — a Chilean, a Peruvian, and an American as presiding officer — should fix the rules for voting and superintend the process. Subsequent events proved that it was an unwise award, for because of the intense "Chileanization" that had taken place in the provinces, it was no longer possible to abide by the original intent of the Treaty of Ancón.

As might be suspected, President Coolidge's award was received with acclaim in Chile and disappointment and protest in Peru. Nevertheless, the President proceeded to set up the plebiscite commission. General John J. Pershing was appointed chairman. The Chileans, fearful of an adverse vote, raised countless obstacles to the General's efforts to insure a fair vote, and finally provoked him to publicly condemn their failure to cooperate. On January 27, 1926, General Pershing returned to the United States on the face-saving plea of ill-health.

General Pershing's successor, General William Lassiter, fared no better in his dealings with the Chileans. Eventually, in June, General Lassiter declared that a plebiscite was impractical, and he placed the blame on the Chilean authorities. The commission suspended its plebiscitary proceedings.

Fortunately, a settlement of the Tacna-Arica dispute was soon forthcoming through direct negotiations between Chile and Peru, with only a minimum contribution by the United States to the final solution. This was Secretary of State Frank B. Kellogg's proffer of good offices, leading to the resumption, in October, 1928, of diplomatic relations between Chile and Peru. With official relations restored the representatives of the two governments quickly negotiated a satisfactory settlement on April 16, 1929. Tacna was returned to Peru together with a Chilean cash settlement of $6 million, and Arica re-

[41] Stuart, *op. cit.*, Appendix I, 74–105.

mained in Chilean hands. Arica was made a free port for the benefit of Peru, as it already had been since 1904, for the benefit of Bolivia.[42]

The Alsop claim

The final of a series of nineteenth-century problems — revolutionary claims, United States mediation in the War of the Pacific, the *Itata* and *Baltimore* affairs, and the Tacna-Arica question — which strained United States-Chilean relations, was the Alsop claim.[43]

Several years before the War of the Pacific, an American commercial firm, Alsop and Company of Valparaiso, had become a creditor of the Bolivian government. Unable to pay its debt, Bolivia assigned to the company certain of her customs receipts collected in the Peruvian port of Arica and a concession to exploit silver mines near the coast. According to the treaty of 1884, which established a truce between Chile and Bolivia, and also by the definitive peace treaty of 1904, Chile agreed to assume responsibility for foreign claims against Bolivia originating in the territory ceded to Chile. Accordingly, the United States, acting on behalf of the Alsop heirs — for the company had long since gone out of business — held Chile responsible for the debt.

A United States-Chilean mixed claims commission, sitting in Washington, decided in 1902, with the United States member dissenting, that the claim was a private matter between the company and the Chilean government, since the company was regarded as strictly a Chilean enterprise. The State Department refused to withdraw its support of its citizens who were Alsop stockholders, and continued to press for a settlement.

In 1903, and again in 1905, Chile offered a lump-sum settlement, which was refused, since it was regarded as grossly inadequate. Chile's offer of 67,000 pounds sterling ($335,000) in 1909 was also rejected. On orders of Secretary of State Knox, the Chilean government was informed it must pay no less than one million dollars in gold or agree to arbitrate. It was the idea of Secretary Knox that the arbitration should be limited to deciding how much money Chile should pay to the Alsop claimants; the Chileans, however, would agree to arbitrate only if the arbiter were allowed to consider whether the United States should have intervened at all, since the Alsop firm was a Chilean company. Secretary Knox reacted violently to the Chilean attitude and gave notice that if Chile did not agree to arbitration on United States terms the American legation at Santiago would be closed at once.

---

[42] For the settlement of the Tacna-Arica question, see Dennis, *op. cit.,* Chap. XIII. The denial to Bolivia of access to the sea was a constant irritant to Chilean-Bolivian relations. President Truman, in a speech in March, 1951, suggested a Bolivian corridor to the sea by grant by Chile in return for the use of waters of Bolivian lakes. The suggestion succeeded only in raising Bolivian hopes and Chilean tempers. *Hispanic American Report,* IV, No. 4 (March, 1951), 36.

[43] For a good discussion of the Alsop claim see Sherman, *op. cit.,* 203–208. Also, see *Foreign Relations of the United States, 1911,* 38–53.

Fortunately, a rupture in relations did not occur, for Secretary Knox and Aníbal Cruz, the Chilean envoy at Washington, were able to agree in a friendly manner to submit the matter to arbitration by the King of England. The award, rendered in 1911, conceded the entire amount of the claim as first admitted by Bolivia. It rejected Chile's contention that the claim was domestic and outside the province of diplomatic intervention.

The Alsop affair was regarded in Chile as just another example of the bullying attitude of the United States which, "at the point of cannons," forced little Chile to abandon its national honor.[44] Fortunately for subsequent United States-Chilean relations this was the last dispute of a critical nature between the two countries.

United States economic penetration of Chile

United States economic penetration of Chile did not occur until during and after World War I. The war interruption of Latin-American access to the goods and money markets of Europe diverted to the United States the commercial and financial relations of the Latin nations, including Chile. The United States far outstripped its nearest rival, Great Britain, in its trade with Chile. In 1910 our imports from Chile amounted to $23 million. In 1929, one-third of Chilean exports, or shipments totaling $71 million, went to the United States. Also, one-third of the total Chilean imports came from the United States.

In 1910 British imports from Chile were five times as much, or about $100 million, as Chile sent to the United States. In 1929 British imports had declined to $37 million. As for exports, Great Britain sent to Chile goods valued at only slightly more than one-half of those obtained by Chile in the United States.[45]

United States investments in Chile also surged ahead of its former European rivals. American investments in Chilean mines, principally copper, date only from the years immediately preceding World War I. In 1913 the Bethlehem Steel Corporation acquired iron mines in Coquimbo, and at about the same time the Braden Copper Mines Company acquired copper holdings near Aconcagua. The Guggenheim interests, for several years a minor operator in Chilean nitrates, in 1915 began copper production at Chuquicamata, the world's largest copper ore deposit. Although there were other American mining companies operating in Chile, the two principal concerns were the Chile Copper Company (controlled by Anaconda) operating the mines at Chuquicamata, and the Braden Copper Mines Company, in the Province of O'Higgins (controlled by the Kennecott Copper Company). The value of

[44] Pike, *op. cit.*, 142–143. According to Pike "as early as September, 1909, Aníbal Cruz had been warned at least by implication that unless Chile yielded in the Alsop matter, the United States might champion the Peruvian cause (over Tacna and Arica)."

[45] The above figures are derived from Max Winkler, *Investment of United States Capital in Latin America* (Boston: World Peace Foundation, 1929), 94–95, and Pike, *op. cit.*, 233–234, 408 (n.112).

American mining investments in Chile in 1928 was $358 million. Chile was the second copper producing country in the world.[46]

In 1912 the total amount of American capital invested in Chile totaled $15 million. In 1928, American investments, direct and portfolio, were estimated at $618 million. Not only had American capital entered into the mining and producing industries, but banks, railroads, steamship lines, and manufacturing plants were created or acquired by Americans. Also, American investments in the public securities of Chile aggregated a considerable size — all this before the Great Depression.[47]

By 1930 the economic penetration of Chile by the United States had become ominous to Chilean nationalists and Yankeephobes. Of the entire capital investment in Chile 52 per cent was foreign, and of this 60 per cent was American; in other words, United States holdings represented 36 per cent of the total capital investment in Chile.[48] Certainly it was a situation which warranted the deep concern of even moderate Chileans. It was understandable therefore, when the depression produced the hardships of unemployment throughout the country, that American capitalists were held responsible. Not only was Wall Street the object of harsh criticism as the symbol of economic imperialism, but the United States government itself, because of the restrictive Smoot-Hawley Tariff Act of 1930, was regarded as selfish and cynically indifferent to the problems of Chile.

Chile's problem: the United States

After the unfortunate series of diplomatic difficulties with the United States, Chile came to regard the northern colossus, after the turn of the century, as a principal adversary in international affairs. More and more Chilean policy and actions were dictated by fear of American imperialism, and particularly fear that the United States would force Chile to relinquish her territorial conquests. Almost the sum total of Chilean policy was concerned with the consolidation and preservation of her war gains. Chile was particularly wary about compulsory arbitration. At the Washington conference in 1889, and again at the Mexico City conference in 1901, the Chileans strongly opposed proposals for general obligatory arbitration. Leading Chilean statesmen were convinced that those who supported arbitration desired to see Chile despoiled of her War of the Pacific gains.[49]

When President Wilson, in 1916, proposed a Pan American pact which called for mutual guarantees of territorial integrity and political independence under the republican form of government, and the arbitration of territorial

[46] Winkler, *op. cit.*, 98–99, 103.

[47] For a listing of U.S. investments in Chile, 1913–1928, see Winkler, *op. cit.*, 103–104. For the status of Chilean bonds in default in 1940, see table on p. 341 in Samuel Flagg Bemis, *The Latin American Policy of the United States* (New York: Harcourt, Brace and Company, 1943).

[48] Pike, *op. cit.*, 233–234.

[49] Luis Orrego Luco, *Los problemas internacionales de Chile; el arbitraje obligatorio* (Santiago de Chile: Impr. Mejia, 1901).

disputes, the opposition of Chile could have been anticipated. With Tacna and Arica in mind, Chile suspected the United States of a plot to coerce a settlement. Chile's opposition was a leading factor in forcing President Wilson to abandon the idea of a pact. It was not until after the settlement of the Tacna-Arica question that Chile felt free to subscribe to arbitration and the other procedures for the peaceful settlement of international disputes.

At the time of United States entry into the war in April, 1917, President Wilson, feeling that the cause of the United States was the cause of all neutral nations, appealed to the Latin-American nations, including Chile, to defend their common rights and validate the principle of continental solidarity. Chile persisted, nevertheless, in her policy of neutrality. It seems that leading Chileans regarded the neutrality of their country "as an essential step toward creating a bloc of truly independent South American nations capable of standing up to the United States in hemisphere relations."[50] Without question Chilean neutrality reflected to some degree a combination of anti-United States and pro-German sentiment in the country.

If Chile counted on a united front of the major South American countries, she was sadly mistaken, for with the exception of Irigoyen's Argentina, Chile was isolated. To make matters worse, both Peru and Bolivia, evidently seeking United States support for their territorial aspirations, quickly rallied to President Wilson's call. It was a situation which, as the war drew to a close, was responsible for a lot of backtracking by Chile and belated efforts to curry the favor of the United States.

A new policy

After the war any attempt by Chile to strengthen ties with Europe to create a counterbalance to the United States was out of the question, since the Yankee giant was capable of vetoing any Old World interference. Also, hopes that the new League of Nations could be the means of putting pressure on the United States were soon dissipated by evidences of League impotence. Therefore, instead of Chile being free of United States influence, there was greater dependence than ever. It was a situation which called for a major reorientation of policy. The earlier policy of isolation, or going it alone, was outmoded. The economic presence of the United States was too patent to be ignored. Resisting United States influence through diplomatic cooperation with the other Latin-American nations had also been tried and failed. The alternative was to cooperate with the United States and work for Chilean security from within an informal alliance.

The decision to adopt a new hemisphere policy seems to have been that of President Carlos Ibañez.[51] Shortly after he seized power in 1927, the dictator, accepting as inevitable the dominance of the United States in inter-American affairs, committed Chile to a new role in the Pan American movement. Chile's

---

[50] Pike, *op. cit.*, 156 (n.192), 366 (n.192).

[51] *Ibid.*, 225. The great Chilean international lawyer Alejandro Alvarez had long been a supporter of the concept of "American" international law.

policy was, in short, to support the inter-American system so that it might be used to impose restraints on the United States by the adoption of new principles of American international law. The success of the new approach, thanks largely to developments independent of Chilean action, must have exceeded the most optimistic expectations.

Although the United States, at Havana in 1928, was able to resist successfully the Latins' demands for nonintervention, Mr. Hughes' victory was short-lived, for at Montevideo in 1933, Mr. Hull capitulated. Thenceforward, during the span of the New Deal, the United States consented to the imposing of various restraints on its own freedom of action.

Chile, and the other Latin-American nations, should then have relaxed their fears and suspicions of the United States. Yet this was not to be, for memories were long and habit could not be easily broken. Moreover, Chilean fears of political intervention by the United States, once relieved, were quickly supplanted by other fears born of no more than the fact of its economic might. But since Chile's commercial relations with the United States during World War II were profitable to the South American nation, there were no immediate unfortunate recriminations or repercussions.

Chile and World War II

As we have noted, Chile at the Rio de Janeiro Meeting of Foreign Ministers in January, 1942, was aligned with Argentina in opposing a strong resolution pledging the suspension of diplomatic relations with the Axis Powers.[52] Ostensibly, Chile was fearful of attack along her 2,500-mile unprotected coastline and discounted the ability of the United States, after the loss of its fleet at Pearl Harbor, to render effective assistance. Additional reasons for Chile's refusal to break off relations with the Axis were nationalistic resentment against the United States pressure and pro-German sentiment in high government circles, particularly in the army.[53]

Although Chile had quickly proclaimed the United States a nonbelligerent, its policy of tolerance toward the Axis Powers after Pearl Harbor represented a break in inter-American solidarity.[54] The question of severing diplomatic relations with the aggressors was shelved indefinitely.

Chile's failure to deny the Axis a diplomatic foothold provoked Under Secretary of State Sumner Welles to declare, in a public address in October, 1942, that the diplomatic immunity enjoyed by the agents of the totalitarian allies in Chile afforded them the means for espionage, sabotage, and subversion, and that, as a result of their reports, United States ships were being

[52] The legal force of Chile's acceptance of a "watered-down resolution" was weakened by a reservation that it was binding only insofar as it did not conflict with the Chilean constitution and was subject to Congressional ratification. Dept. of State *Bulletin,* VI (February 7, 1942), 141.

[53] According to Claude Bowers, U.S. Ambassador to Chile (1939–1953), and regarded by Chileans as *muy simpático,* the principal reason for delay was Chilean insistence on adhering to the democratic process. Bowers, *op. cit.,* 121–122.

[54] See David H. Popper, "Hemisphere Solidarity in the World Crisis," *Foreign Policy Reports,* XVIII, No. 5 (May 15, 1942), 55.

sunk by enemy submarines. This sharp criticism of the Chilean government provoked a cancellation of a proposed visit by President Ríos to Washington.[55] These plain words, however, had a salutary effect in Santiago, for out of a cabinet shuffle came a more vigorous policy to curb Axis operations. On January 29, 1943, Chile severed diplomatic relations with the Axis. Early in 1945, the government, under pressure from the United States, finally declared war. There was another reason for this action — it was the only way Chile could qualify for membership in the San Francisco United Nations Conference.

As a neutral and as a technical belligerent Chile contributed to the war effort of the United States by her production of vital strategic materials. The United States contracted for practically all Chilean copper, and entered into preclusive purchasing agreements covering a long list of other Chilean metals. Subsequently, the United States, through the Office of the Coordinator of Inter-American Affairs, agreed to pay higher prices than those on the world market for copper and some other metals in order to assist the Chilean economy. Chile was also the recipient of United States aid by way of loans by the Export-Import Bank and through lend-lease arrangements. All in all, World War II was not an unprofitable experience for the South American republic, and Chile should have been beholden to the United States. But all too soon the old-time hostilities towards the *yanquis* were rekindled.

Postwar relations

Since World War II there have been no special or unique problems of outstanding importance in United States-Chilean relations. Those that did develop, and there have been many, were merely local manifestations of broad issues affecting most of the Latin-American nations. For example, the recrudescence of anti-Americanism was prevalent throughout the hemisphere and was nourished by factors more or less common in all of the countries, although, as we have noted, Chile had special historical reasons for her attitude toward the United States. It was relatively easy, therefore, for Communists and other enemies of the United States in Chile to oppose cooperation by raising the bogey of American imperialism. This proved to be successful, for example, in withholding Chilean aid in the Korean war, but could not prevent eventual ratification of the Military Assistance Agreement with the United States.[56]

The United States also encouraged resistance to the aggressions of international Communism throughout all of Latin America. Chile presented a special problem because of the exceptional strength of the Communists and their sympathizers. In fact, there were three Communists in the ministry of President Gabriel González Videla (1946–1952), but not for long, because when the actions of these ministers proved to the president that they were taking their orders from Moscow, they were dismissed. Chile broke relations with all of the Communist nations and outlawed the Communist party.

[55] Bowers, *op. cit.*, 110–111.

[56] *Ibid.*, 308–314. The Military Assistance Agreement, which encountered much opposition in the Chilean Congress, was signed on April 9, 1952.

Although outlawed as a party, the Communists were not individually dis-
franchised. Thus, their votes became important in close elections, and their
support was sought by various parties. The Communists of Chile, although
relatively few in numbers, are dangerous because they are militantly led and
seem tireless to a degree amounting to fanaticism. Nevertheless, in the presidential election of 1964, the Marxist, pro-Castro candidate was decisively
defeated and a Communist take-over of the Chilean government was averted.

The abnormal wartime and immediate postwar copper demands had enabled the Chilean economy to maintain a relatively even keel. From about
1948, however, down to the present time, the perennial problems of Chile
have been fluctuations in copper prices and production, strikes, inflation, and
cabinet crises. United States relations with Chile have been influenced by
these factors.

In 1948 Chile produced 446,000 tons of copper, or one-fifth of the world's
production. American-owned mines (Anaconda and Kennecott) produced
all but about 20,000 tons. Copper represented 63 per cent of total Chilean
exports, and therefore was by far the principal source of foreign exchange.
Nitrates, once the great source of national income, represented in 1947 but
13 per cent of the national exports.[57]

In 1955, out of $350 million paid out in Chile by United States companies,
$186 million was paid to the Chilean government as taxes, $90 million was
paid to employees, and $60 million was spent in Chile for materials, equip-
ment, utilities, and other items. The taxes paid by United States companies
accounted for about one-half of all the revenue of the Chilean government.
Of the 44,000 employees who were paid $90 million, only about 260 were
persons sent from the United States.[58]

Chileans looked at the foreign mining companies with mixed feelings.
There were the well-understood nationalistic resentments of foreign capitalistic
concerns extracting irreplaceable national resources, and, on the other hand,
there was the rather general realization that the complexities and vast expense
of the mining operations were beyond the capacity of domestic capital or even
the government itself. The result was a taxation and regulatory policy applied
to the mining companies about as severe as the traffic could bear.

In 1954 the taxation of United States copper interests in Chile amounted
to 85 per cent of their gross operating revenue. This tax burden was "the
largest levied by any copper-producing country." In addition, the companies
were greatly handicapped by complicated exchange regulations and government restrictions on sales. A new copper law, passed in February, 1955,
reduced the tax to 75 per cent on gross operating revenue. This was still by

[57] Wendell C. Gordon, *The Economy of Latin America* (New York: Columbia University Press, 1950), 381; Simon G. Hanson, *Economic Development in Latin America*
(Washington, D.C.: The Inter-American Affairs Press, 1951), 230. From 1920 to 1933
Chilean production of nitrates dropped from 430,000 tons per year to 76,000 tons, and
from $51.88 per ton to $18.80. Before World War II Chile produced 8.5 per cent of the
world's nitrates, and in 1948 only about the same, although the world output had increased 30 per cent.

[58] U.S. Dept. of Commerce, Office of Business Economics, *U.S. Investments in the
Latin-American Economy* (Washington, D.C., 1957), 67.

far the heaviest in the world, and Chilean copper production costs were the world's highest.[59] Since the market price of copper is subject to violent fluctuations, it frequently happened that drops in the price of copper triggered cutback in production and employment — and the inevitable strikes.

These fluctuations of the copper market, and other factors in the economy, plunged Chile into the throes of serious inflation and balance-of-payments difficulties. In short, the country was greatly in need of foreign financial and economic assistance. That the United States was not unheedful of Chile's need is demonstrated by the totals of its grants and credits. Probably the best reason for continuing United States credits to Chile has been to combat inflation by assisting in the stabilization of the currency, and to help overcome the balance-of-payments difficulties.

In the immediate postwar period — that is, July, 1945, to December, 1955, — the total aid to Chile was $85 million. Perhaps there was some justification in the complaint by the Chilean Foreign Minister, in December, 1952, about the "niggardliness of United States economic aid." President Carlos Ibañez, having in mind our Marshall Plan grants to Europe, complained that his country was not treated in the spirit of equality by the United States.[60]

From 1955 to 1962, the latter date being that of the approximate inauguration of the Alliance for Progress, the total grants and credits by the United States to Chile were $253 million. In 1962 and 1963, the first two years of the Alliance for Progress, Chile received from United States government sources $323 million, including $100 million for earthquake relief.[61] Chile is one of the limited number of Latin-American countries with an approved ten-year economic development plan under the Alliance for Progress. It was reported in April, 1963, that "no other country in Latin America is giving more heated attention to reform to meet the growing demands of the masses than Chile."[62]

[59] *Hisp. Am. Rep.*, VIII, No. 1 (January, 1955), 38; No. 2 (February, 1955), 83.

[60] *Ibid.*, V, No. 11 (November, 1952), 31; No. 12 (December, 1952), 28.

[61] *Statistical Abstract of the U.S.* (1963), 863; *New York Times,* December 22, 1963. A disastrous earthquake in southern Chile, May 20, 1960, was responsible for heavy loss of life and property damage. An emergency loan of $100 million was authorized by Congress in August, 1960, and was appropriated the next year on President Kennedy's recommendation.

[62] *New York Times,* April 28, 1963.

SUPPLEMENTARY READING

Bastert, Russell H., "A New Approach to the Origins of Blaine's Pan American Policy," *Hispanic American Historical Review*, XXXIX, No. 3 (August, 1959), 375–412.

Bianchi Barros, Agustín, *Bosquejo histórico de las relaciones Chileno-Norteamericanas durante la independencia* (Santiago de Chile: 1946).

Bowers, Claude, *Chile Through Embassy Windows, 1939–1953* (New York: Simon and Schuster, 1958).

Cohen, Alvin, *Economic Change in Chile, 1929–1950* (Gainesville: University of Florida Press, 1960).

Dennis, W. J., *Tacna and Arica; an Account of the Chile-Peru Boundary Dispute and the Arbitration by the United States* (New Haven: Yale University Press, 1931).

Ellsworth, Paul T., *Chile: An Economy in Transition* (New York: The Macmillan Company, 1945).

Evans, Henry Clay, *Chile and its Relations with the United States* (Durham: Duke University Press, 1927).

Galdames, Luis, *A History of Chile*, I. J. Cox, trans. (Chapel Hill: University of North Carolina Press, 1941).

Hardy, Osgood, "The Itata Incident," *Hispanic American Historical Review*, V (May, 1927), 195–226.

Herring, Hubert, *Good Neighbors* (New Haven: Yale University Press, 1941), 167–244.

Holmes, Olive, "Chile: Microcosm of Modern Conflicts," *Foreign Policy Reports*, XXII, No. 9 (July 15, 1946).

Kiernan, V. G., "Foreign Interests in the War of the Pacific," *Hispanic American Historical Review*, XXXV, No. 1 (February, 1955), 14–36.

McBride, George M., *Chile, Land and Society* (New York: American Geographical Society, 1936).

Millington, Herbert, *American Diplomacy and the War of the Pacific* (New York: Columbia University Press, 1948).

Montaner y Bello, Ricardo, *Historia diplomática de la independencia de Chile* (Santiago de Chile: Ed. Andrés Bello, 1961).

Pike, Frederick B., *Chile and the United States, 1880–1962* (Notre Dame: University of Notre Dame Press, 1963).

Sherman, William Roderick, *The Diplomatic and Commercial Relations of the United States and Chile, 1820–1914* (Boston: Richard G. Badger, Publisher, 1926).

Stevenson, John Reese, *The Chilean Popular Front* (Philadelphia: University of Pennsylvania Press, 1942).

Stuart, Graham H., *Latin America and the United States* (New York: Appleton-Century-Crofts, Inc., 5th ed. 1955), Chap. XVII.

Stuart, Graham H., *The Tacna-Arica Dispute* (Boston: World Peace Foundation Pamphlets, X, 1927, No. 1).

Subercaseaux, Benjamín, *Chile, a Geographic Extravaganza*, Angel Flores, trans. (New York: The Macmillan Company, 1943).

16

United States-Brazilian Relations

Until recently it was generally believed — an assumption we do not dispute — that Brazil was the best friend of the United States in Latin America. The State Department usually could rely on Brazilian support on important international issues. Brazilians certainly were not as suspicious and fearful of the Yankees as were their Spanish-American neighbors. There was evidently in Brazil a huge reservoir of good will toward the United States.

It is not literally true to say that relations between the two countries in the past were altogether friendly. Certain differences made their appearance, particularly in the early years of the Empire, but these fortunately were minor, and often trivial. At no time did there occur incidents comparable to those between the United States and some of the Spanish-American countries. For example, we never fought a war with Brazil and took a lot of her land, nor imposed leaseholds and other limitations on her sovereignty, nor intervened in her internal affairs. Nor for that matter were any of the other countries of South America, except Colombia, the victims of American imperialism; yet even so, their attitude toward the United States was markedly dissimilar from that of Brazil.

Perhaps it was the ties of racial and cultural affinity which caused the Spanish-Americans everywhere to share resentments against the North American colossus. Perhaps Brazilians because of the vastness of their land and its resources and their confidence in their future were resilient to Yankee imperialism. Perhaps Brazil, surrounded by Spanish-speaking nations, felt isolated in South America and so gravitated toward the great Anglo-American republic, another non-Spanish-speaking inhabitant of the hemisphere. At any rate, after the establishment of the Brazilian republic shortly before the beginning of this century, and until World War II, the leaders of Brazil usually agreed that their foreign interests coincided with those of the United States. But after World War II the United States could no longer count on Brazil, or take her for granted, as some Brazilians had complained. Anti-Americanism became quite as pronounced there as in other parts of South America. No longer was the Brazilian government a consistent ally of the United States on foreign policy issues. This startling metamorphosis of national relations challenges our serious concern.

The inauguration of relations[1]

When King John VI left Brazil to return to Portugal, in April, 1821, he left his son, Dom Pedro, in charge of Brazilian affairs with the sound injunction that, if Brazil should demand independence, to grant it, and put the crown on his own head. On September 7, 1822, by the *grito do Ypiranga,* Dom Pedro declared Brazil's independence. On December 1, 1822, he was crowned Pedro I, Emperor of Brazil. In less than a year all evidence of Portuguese control had disappeared. The revolution was almost bloodless. Portuguese recognition, not long in coming, was graciously bestowed on the former colony in 1825. In the meantime however, the United States had recognized Brazilian independence despite Portuguese protest.[2]

The day following the *grito do Ypiranga* Condy Raguet arrived in Rio de Janeiro to assume the duties of American consul. United States consular representation did not constitute recognition. It was not until three years later that the United States government was finally prepared to accord formal recognition to the imperial government of Brazil, despite the fact that it was not republican in form. Secretary John Quincy Adams did not believe that the nature of the Brazilian government should restrain the act of recognition. Therefore, on May 26, 1824, José Silvestre Rebello was presented by Secretary of State Adams to President Monroe as *chargé d'affaires* for the Emperor of Brazil. On March 5, 1825, President Adams appointed Condy Raguet as United States *chargé d'affaires* to Brazil. He was instructed to promote American commercial interests and to prevent England and France from receiving special advantages. The United States government could take pride in the fact that it was the first to recognize the new Brazilian state.[3]

On her part Brazil might be regarded as the first country in South America to recognize the Monroe Doctrine. This was implied by the instructions to Rebello, ordering him to sound out the United States government on the sub-

---

[1] For United States relations with the Portuguese monarchy in Brazil, see Laurence F. Hill, *Diplomatic Relations Between the United States and Brazil* (Durham: Duke University Press, 1932), 3–25.

[2] Secretary Adams assured the Portuguese minister that recognition was not an unfriendly act but merely "recognition of a government existing in fact." W. S. Robertson, "Recognition of Hispanic American Nations," *Hispanic American Historical Review,* I (1918), 268.

[3] Arthur P. Whitaker, "José Silvestre Rebello: the first diplomatic representative of Brazil in the United States," *Ibid.,* XX, No. 3 (August, 1940), 380–401.

ject of an offensive and defensive alliance "since in that message (December 3, 1823) the necessity of our combining and standing shoulder to shoulder for the defense of our rights and of our territory is clearly pointed out."[4] Rebello, having in mind a Portuguese attack on Brazil, raised the matter of an alliance with Adams, and later with Clay when the latter became Secretary of State. Clay replied that there did not seem to be any occasion for an alliance founded on an "improbable contingency," and that if a war were confined to a parent country and its former colony the United States would remain neutral.[5] Thus the United States declined a Brazilian bid for an alliance based on Monroe's famous message.

Within a few months after recognition the United States and Brazil were quarreling with one another. The initiation of friendly relations between the two countries was obstructed because the United States was represented at Rio de Janeiro by impetuous, hot-tempered Condy Raguet.

The outbreak of war in 1825, between Brazil and Argentina (the United Provinces of Rio de la Plata) over possession of Uruguay (the Banda Oriental), created problems for American diplomacy because of Brazil's declaration of a paper blockade.[6] Interference with United States commerce in the estuary of La Plata prompted Raguet to protest vigorously that a blockade to be legal must be effective. The constant infringement of American rights infuriated him to the point where he wrote insulting notes to the Brazilian Foreign Office. Because of his intemperate conduct Raguet was finally forced, in March, 1827, to ask for his passports and withdraw from Brazil.[7] During his mission Raguet had made no progress either in negotiating a commercial treaty or in settling claims.

Raguet's successor, William Tudor, who was *chargé d'affaires* from 1828 to 1830, was remarkably successful in establishing relations on a solid foundation of friendship. He was able to negotiate, in a fair and conciliatory fashion, settlement of most of the outstanding individual claims. Tudor was also able to score a diplomatic triumph by negotiating, in 1828, a commercial treaty with Brazil. This treaty, called "an excellent treaty of commerce," included the most-favored-nation clause, except for relations between Brazil and Portugal.[8] William Tudor, one of the most successful and respected of all United States diplomatic representatives sent to Brazil, died at his post on March 9, 1830.

[4] W. S. Robertson, "South America and the Monroe Doctrine," *Political Science Quarterly*, XXX (1915), 94.

[5] William R. Manning, ed., *Diplomatic Correspondence of the United States Concerning the Independence of the Latin-American Nations* (New York: Oxford University Press, 1925), I, 233–235; II, 808–810, 814–815.

[6] Buenos Aires asked whether the situation did not warrant application of the principles of President Monroe's Message. W. S. Robertson, "South America and the Monroe Doctrine," *op. cit.*, 94 ff.

[7] Hill, *op. cit.*, 49–56; *House Exec. Doc.*, No. 281, 20th Cong., 1st Sess., 15, 30, 103, 108, 141; *American State Papers, Foreign Relations*, VI, 1065–1066.

[8] For text of the treaty, see *Senate Exec. Doc.*, No. 47, 48th Cong., 2nd Sess. 105.

Relations: 1830–1860

The span between the death of Tudor and the outbreak of the American Civil War was not exactly a period of unbroken amity in United States-Brazilian relations, but fortunately the misunderstandings, though irritating were basically trivial.

The treaty of commerce of 1828 expired in 1841. Then followed a scramble for commercial privileges, but Brazil refused to consider another treaty with any nation, for she preferred to have her hands free for the better direction of her commerce.[9]

When David Tod, United States minister to Brazil, proposed, like his predecessors, a new treaty of commerce, the Brazilian government, in 1851, rejected the proposal with the observation that the lack of a treaty with the United States since 1841 had resulted in no harm to the reciprocal relations of the two states. Quite true, the United States was suffering no damage because a treaty was lacking, but it was uncertain how long this condition would continue. With respect to unsettled claims, Minister Tod was able to conclude a claims convention in January, 1849. Brazil placed at the disposition of the President of the United States the sum of $300,000 to meet the claims of American citizens.[10]

Probably the most troublesome of the misunderstandings of the period 1830 to 1860 was the Lieutenant Davis incident. For the sake of brevity we note that in October, 1846, Lt. Alonzo B. Davis of the U.S. frigate *Saratoga,* intervened, as was his duty, in a quarrel in Rio de Janeiro between one of his own men and two other American sailors. When he was attempting to take one of the sailors back to his ship, Brazilian police intervened, beat up the sailors, and imprisoned them. Davis protested and was himself thrown into prison. This was the American version of the affair which was accepted by United States Minister Henry A. Wise and the State Department. The Brazilian version was that Davis interfered after the police had arrested the fighting sailors.[11]

Wise demanded the release of Davis and the sailors, and an apology. Davis was released, merely as a courtesy gesture, but the sailors were kept in prison, and of course there was no apology. The exchange of notes between Wise and the Brazilian foreign minister mounted in acrimony, particularly on the part of Wise, until further intercourse between the United States Minister and the Brazilian government became impossible.

Wise, realizing that his presence in Rio was no longer advantageous to his country, asked to be relieved, but in a manner that would make it clear

9 William R. Manning, ed., *Diplomatic Correspondence of the United States: Inter-American Affairs, 1831–1860* (Washington, D.C.: Carnegie Endowment for International Peace, 1932), II, 122.

10 *House Exec. Doc.,* No. 19, 31st Cong., 1st Sess., 2.

11 *Senate Exec. Doc.,* No. 29, 30th Cong., 1st Sess., 29–33. For a complete statement of the case, see Manning, *Inter-American Affairs,* II, 140–153.

to Brazil that the United States government was not disapproving his acts. Secretary of State Buchanan adopted the minister's suggestion. Perhaps the whole affair, certainly a "tempest in a teapot," would never have attained the importance it did had not Wise been so dogmatic and violent in his protestations. Like Raguet, he was stubborn and determined to defend, often in undiplomatic language, what he conceived to be the honor of his country and his own dignity.

Brazil was the last nation on this continent to abolish the slave trade. Great Britain had persuaded Brazil, by 1831, to cooperate with her in the suppression of the nefarious traffic. But Brazil lent only faint-hearted assistance. The United States, since 1820, had declared the trade to be piracy, but refused to enter into any agreement with Great Britain allowing reciprocal right of search. In 1842 the United States and Britain entered into a treaty providing for joint naval patrol off the African coast, but the Americans were lax in enforcement. The British, however, were vitally interested in the suppression of the traffic and a part of the British fleet was assigned to run down slavers, even to the extent of placing Brazilian vessels caught carrying cargoes of slaves under the jurisdiction of British courts.

Until about 1850 our diplomatic and consular representatives in Brazil usually received little cooperation from Brazilian officials in their efforts to restrain American citizens. Nor were the British able to enforce their law on the pirate ships flying the American flag. The most active period of American participation in the trade was from 1839 to 1949. According to United States Minister Henry A. Wise: "Our flag alone gives the requisite protection against the rights of visit, search, and seizure, and our citizens . . . partake of the profits of the African slave trade, to and from the ports of Brazil, as fully as Brazilians themselves."[12]

In order to terminate the humiliation of British capture of slave ships, even within Brazilian harbors, Emperor Pedro's government in 1850 enacted and enforced measures to stop the traffic. Since the United States, in contrast to the British, had never been particularly zealous in carrying out an anti-slave trade program, the net result was a gain in the favor of the Imperial Government.[13]

United States-Brazilian relations in the 1850's were concentrated upon our unsuccessful endeavors to open the Amazon River to world commerce.[14] United States interest seems to have dated from 1850 when Secretary of State Clayton induced the Navy Department to undertake an exploration of the mighty river. Secretary Clayton alluded to the advantages of free transit on the river. Brazil, suspicious of United States motives, entered into a treaty with Peru restricting use of the Amazon. In 1853, in the administration of President Franklin Pierce, Secretary of State William L. Marcy renewed efforts

[12] *House Exec. Doc.,* No. 61, 30th Cong. 2nd Sess., 70. Over 50,000 new slaves were unloaded in Brazil each year in 1847, 1848, and 1849.

[13] For a discussion of the slave trade issue, see Hill, *op. cit.,* Chap. V.

[14] See P. A. Martin, "The Influence of the United States in the Opening of the Amazon to the World's Commerce," *Hisp. Am. Hist. Rev.,* I (1918), 146 ff.

to secure the opening of the Amazon. On August 8, 1853, Mr. Marcy wrote to William Trousdale, United States minister to Brazil: "The most important object of your mission — an object to which you will devote your early and earnest efforts — is to renew to the citizens of the United States the free use of the Amazon. . . . This restricted policy which it is understood Brazil still persists in maintaining in regard to the navigable rivers passing through her territories is the relic of an age less enlightened than the present."[15] Secretary Marcy's efforts to change Brazil's uncompromising stand failed. In fact, more than a decade was to elapse before the Brazilian government made its own independent decision to alter its policy on the navigation of international rivers. On January 22, 1866, Emperor Pedro II decreed the opening up of the Amazon, San Francisco, and other rivers to the commerce of all nations.[16]

Relations: 1860–1889

Two great wars of the 1860's contributed to diplomatic problems between Brazil and the United States. These were the American Civil War and the Paraguayan War. It was unfortunate that, for most of the period, from 1861 to 1869, the United States minister at Rio de Janiero was General James Watson Webb, whose mission has been described as "distinguished for his disservices."

The government of Pedro II, following the example set by Great Britain, recognized the belligerency of the Confederacy. This meant, among other things, that Confederate cruisers could enjoy certain privileges in Brazilian ports, thus increasing the effectiveness of their raids on Union commerce in the South Atlantic. Minister Webb argued against the recognition of belligerency, and charged that the Southern ships were pirates. Brazil rejected Webb's protests, but gave increasing evidence of desire to be on friendly terms with the United States. The Emperor himself expressed to Webb his hope that the Union would be victorious.[17]

Brazil's efforts to preserve a perfect neutrality were clearly manifested by that government's reaction to General Webb's protests concerning the activities of the Southern cruiser *Alabama*. The notorious commerce raider not only had captured American ships in Brazilian territorial waters, but had been allowed to remain for extended periods in a port on the island Fernando de Noronha, a Brazilian possession lying northeast of Pernambuco. The Brazilian Foreign Office responded promptly saying that the commanding officer at Noronha was guilty of giving aid to the *Alabama*, had been removed from office, and proceedings had been instituted against him.[18] Later when

---

[15] Manning, *Inter-American Affairs*, II, 170.

[16] Martin, *op. cit.*, 159–160. Dom Pedro supported the opening of the river to commerce following the expedition in the Amazon region by the famous American scientist Louis Agassiz.

[17] Mary W. Williams, *Dom Pedro, the Magnanimous* (Chapel Hill: University of North Carolina Press, 1937), 108.

[18] *Diplomatic Correspondence of the United States, 1861–1868*, 1863, Pt. II, 1167–1177.

Webb protested that Confederate vessels had been permitted to use the ports of Bahia and Pernambuco to secure provisions and dispose of their captives, he was again assured of Brazil's earnest endeavor to maintain its neutrality.

The case of the *Wachusett* and the *Florida* resulted from Union violation of Brazil's neutrality. The former, a Union war vessel, entered the port of Bahia and used its guns to capture and tow away a Confederate cruiser, the *Florida*. Brazil demanded reparation and apology. Since the action of the commander of the *Wachusett* was indefensible, Secretary of State William H. Seward, on December 26, 1864, sent a note to the Brazilian government disavowing and regretting what had occurred at Bahia, promising that the commander of the *Wachusett* would be rebuked and dismissed from the service, and the Brazilian flag would receive a salute of twenty-one guns. The salute was fired in the harbor of Bahia in midsummer of 1866. The event created great satisfaction in Brazil and undoubtedly improved the image of the United States.[19]

The diplomatic incidents created by the Paraguayan War arose from the allied blockade of the rivers leading to Paraguay. Brazil, Argentina, and Uruguay had signed a treaty of alliance in May, 1865, to prosecute a common war which had been imposed on them by the Paraguayan dictator Francisco Solano López. In command of the blockading fleet was a Brazilian, and therefore it was to the Brazilian government, principally, that the United States directed its protests when difficulties arose concerning the blockade.

Early in 1866 Charles A. Washburn, the American Minister to Paraguay, returning from a visit to the United States, was prevented from reaching his post because of the blockade of the Paraguay and Paraná rivers. The allied commander pleaded the inconvenience of supplying a military escort, but really opposed Washburn's return because he was believed to be too friendly to López.[20]

General Webb in Rio de Janeiro took up in a most energetic manner the case of Mr. Washburn. He insisted on the long-established precedents of diplomatic right of transit, but the Brazilian government held that the right of blockade included "the right to impede the transit even of the diplomatic agent of a neutral power." When Secretary of State Seward protested vigorously to both Argentina and Brazil, those governments finally ordered their commander-in-chief to allow the American diplomat to pass through their lines. Washburn finally arrived in Asunción in November, 1866.[21]

About a year later Mr. Washburn raised once more the same issue of transit when he sought to return with his family to the United States, only this time the principal question was whether the U.S.S. *Wasp* had the right to go up the Paraguay to Asunción to convey the Minister. The Brazilian commander, the Marquis de Caxias, refused permission to the *Wasp*. Webb reported the whole affair to the Brazilian foreign minister in "plain" language, requesting

[19] Hill, *op. cit.*, 155–159. See also, J. B. Moore, *Digest of International Law* (8 vols. Washington, D.C.: Government Printing Office, 1906), VII, 1090.

[20] Hill, *op. cit.*, 188.

[21] *Dipl. Corresp.*, 1866, Pt. II, 315–323.

an explanation and an apology. When the imperial government endorsed the conduct of Marshal Caxias, Webb wrote an angry response concluding with a threat to ask for his passports.[22]

Although Webb's diplomatic behavior was not endorsed in Washington, it must be conceded that he won his point: the *Wasp* was allowed to pass the allied blockade, and in September, 1868, the Washburns arrived in Buenos Aires on their return to the United States.

General Webb's departure from Rio de Janeiro in the spring of 1869 brought to an end a long mission which has been characterized as "eight busy years of chicanery," and as "an era punctuated too frequently by misunderstanding and buffoonery."[23] These caustic words were provoked principally because Webb allegedly used the threat of suspension of diplomatic relations "as a club to force the imperial government to make a favorable settlement in a monetary-claims case long in negotiation between the two governments." According to an historian of the events, "the $50,000 collected in settlement of the American claim apparently never reached the pockets of the claimants or their heirs, but instead remained in the possession of Minister James Watson Webb."

Fortunately, Webb's successors during the remaining days of the Empire made substantial progress in promoting friendship and understanding with Brazil. The attainment of this objective was facilitated greatly by Emperor Pedro II himself, whose four months' visit to the United States in 1876, on the occasion of the Centennial Exposition in Philadelphia, was taken as evidence of cordiality between the two countries.[24]

Early relations with the Brazilian republic

The break with the Empire was a bloodless *coup* in which the military, led by General Deodoro da Fonseca, took over the power from the civilian government. Although it was announced that the future government would be a federal republic, and a decree was issued convoking a constituent assembly to draft a new constitution, during the interregnum Brazil was actually in the control of a military *junta.*

Announcement of the Brazilian federal republic, on November 15, 1889, was received with favor by the United States government, but recognition was not immediately forthcoming as might have been expected. Secretary Blaine, anxious to escape criticism as an abettor of military dictatorship in Latin America, rather than a champion of popular government, delayed recognition for two and a half months. Finally, on January 29, 1890, formal recognition was extended to Brazilian agents at Washington. On February 19, 1890, the United States Congress, by joint resolution, congratulated "the people of Brazil on their just and peaceful assumption of the powers, duties

[22] *Ibid.,* 1868, 273–299; Hill, *op. cit.,* 187–195.

[23] Laurence F. Hill, ed., *Brazil* (Berkeley and Los Angeles: University of California Press, 1947), 346.

[24] See P. A. Martin, "Causes of the Collapse of the Brazilian Empire," *Hisp. Am. Hist. Rev.,* IV, No. 1 (February, 1921), 1–48.

and responsibilities of self-government, based upon the full consent of the governed, and in their recent adoption of a republican form of government."[25]

United States recognition was tardy compared to actions by many of Brazil's Spanish-American neighbors, but nevertheless there was no lessening of Brazilian appreciation and reciprocation. When the constitutent assembly met in November, 1890, it drafted a constitution which established a federal system of government modeled very closely upon that of the United States. The last act of the constituent assembly was the election, on February 25, 1891, of Fonseca as president, and Marshal Floriano Peixoto as vice-president for the ensuing four years.

Since President Deodoro da Fonseca seemed incapable of functioning as a constitutional executive, his arbitrary methods soon provoked opposition of the congress, some of the army, and all of the navy. Under threat of naval guns on warships in Rio harbor, Deodoro resigned in favor of Floriano Peixoto. The new president, also unacquainted with the meaning of constitutionalism, provoked revolts and then quelled them with dictatorial and praetorian methods. Eventually, on September 6, 1893, almost the entire navy joined the standard of revolt which had been raised by Admiral de Mello.

The revolt which started in Rio Grande do Sul soon spread to Rio de Janeiro. De Mello was in control of the entire harbor and was in a favorable position to render President Floriano Peixoto's position untenable by threatening bombardment of the capital. But unfortunately for the rebels, their naval effectiveness was largely nullified when the commanders of the naval forces of the United States, France, Italy, and Portugal, anchored in the harbor, announced "that they would oppose by force, if necessary, every enterprise against Rio de Janeiro."[26] Thus, failure to obtain recognition of belligerent rights prevented the insurgents from establishing a regular blockade. Unable to make effective use of their strength, the rebel forces began to disintegrate. Those that were cooped up in the harbor of Rio were forced to an unconditional surrender on March 13, 1894. By summer the rebellion was completely checked.

The policy of the United States toward this domestic quarrel in Brazil was presumably that of neutrality, but as carried into execution during the civil war was certainly not impartial. Despite the fact that the revolutionary group had established, and maintained for about six months, a provisional government, Secretary of State Walter Q. Gresham declared, on October 25, 1893, that "recognition by the United States of the insurgents as belligerents would be an unfriendly act toward Brazil and a gratuitous demonstration of moral support of the rebellion."[27] The position of the United States had apparently won the approval of other foreign governments as evidenced by the joint declaration of the commanders of naval forces in Rio harbor.

[25] *Foreign Relations of the United States,* 1890, 21.

[26] *For. Rel.,* 1893, 51.

[27] *Ibid.,* 63. When Commander Stanton, in command of a United States naval squadron, committed "a grave error of judgment" in saluting the flag of the insurgents in Rio harbor, he was immediately transferred to another station. Moore, *op. cit.,* I, 240.

Diplomatic relations: 1894–1914

Certainly, United States policy had been an aid to the titular Peixoto government. It is no surprise, therefore, that there was increased friendship between the Brazilian and American governments. The attitude of friendliness toward the United States indeed became a key feature of Brazilian policy in the years following the inauguration in 1894 of Dr. Prudente de Moraes Barros, Brazil's first civilian president. In fact, on Prudente's inauguration day the cornerstone of a proposed monument to President Monroe was laid in a principal square of the city. This was expressive of Brazil's desire to foster continental solidarity, for it believed that the policy of Monroe signified that all the American states should unite to make sure that European countries would never interfere or intervene in this continent.[28]

Another Brazilian gesture of confidence in the United States was the submission, in April, 1892, of an old and serious dispute between Argentina and Brazil regarding the *Misiones* territory[29] to arbitration by the President of the United States. The main point of dispute was this: which of two river systems marked the boundary between the two countries? Brazil claimed that the boundary should follow the river system on the west, and of course Argentina claimed that the eastern one constituted the boundary line.

The award by President Cleveland, on February 5, 1895, establishing the boundary on the western-most river, was almost wholly in favor of Brazil. The President's decision was a great tribute to the able presentation of Brazil's case by Baron Rio Branco. The evidence furnished by the Baron, as the result of many months of intensive research, has been described as "a monumental work."[30] Undoubtedly President Cleveland was also influenced by the fact, as pointed out by Rio Branco, that of the 6,000 inhabitants of the disputed area all but thirty (and of the thirty not one was Argentinian) were Brazilians. Thus, in application of the principle of *uti possidetis,* the territory should go to Brazil.[31]

So great was President Cleveland's popularity in Brazil it was no surprise that his Venezuelan message flinging defiance at European aggressors in Latin America received hearty endorsement in Brazil. The importance of revising and enforcing the Monroe Doctrine was stressed. In the Spanish-American War Brazil seemed to be very much on the side of the United States.

It was apparent that Brazil did not share the feelings of her Spanish-American neighbors concerning the imperialistic activities of the United States. Although some Brazilians deplored, for example, United States pretentions

---

[28] *For. Rel.,* 1895, 48–52.

[29] In a region where the Jesuit fathers had planted missions the boundary line between the colonial dominions of Spain and Portugal, as provided by the treaty of 1750, had never been definitively established.

[30] Helio Vianna, *Historia Diplomática do Brasil* (São Paulo, n.d.,), 146–147.

[31] J. B. Moore, *History and Digest of International Arbitration to which the United States has been a party* (6 vols. Washington, D.C.: Government Printing Office, 1898), II, 1969–2026.

under the Roosevelt Corollary of the Monroe Doctrine, they realistically appreciated their need of United States friendship. The greatest and most influential exponent of this policy was Baron Rio Branco who, from 1902 to his death in 1912, was Brazil's Foreign Minister.

A two years' (1893–1895) residence in the United States at the time of the *Misiones* arbitration seems to have exercised a most important influence on the attitude of the great Brazilian statesman toward the United States. His intimate friendship with our own great international lawyer, John Bassett Moore, and other important contacts in the United States all contributed to Rio Branco's desire for close relations with this country.[32]

Although Rio Branco looked to Europe for cultural inspiration, he recognized, on a purely practical basis, the value to Brazil of close relations with the United States. He said to the delegates to the Third International Conference of American States at Rio de Janeiro in 1906: "From Europe we come. Europe has been our teacher. . . . But [as for the United States] our interests are the same, they [United States] consume on a large scale most of our important products." He also recognized the utility of the Monroe Doctrine in seeking realization of the dream of American unity. In an attempt to counteract criticism of the United States' Caribbean policy, the Baron wrote a treatise entitled *Brazil, the United States, and Monroeism*.[33] At the Buenos Aires Pan American conference of 1910 the Brazilian delegates, under instructions of Foreign Minister Rio Branco, sought to repudiate anti-Yankee propaganda by conference endorsement of the Monroe Doctrine.[34] Unfortunately, the other Latin members were unwilling to abandon their opposition to the hated doctrine. It is not without significance that the Monroe Palace,[35] originally the official Brazilian building at the St. Louis Exposition, and later reconstructed in Rio de Janeiro, stands at the head of *Avenida do Rio Branco*.

According to a one-time colleague of Rio Branco, the great and good friend of the United States "solidified this policy of approximation [to the United States] to such an extent as to transform it, *without the necessity of a treaty*, into a perfect alliance for the defense of the highest and most sacred destiny of the two Americas."[36]

In 1905 the United States and Brazilian diplomatic posts at Washington and Rio de Janeiro were elevated to the rank of embassies. Joaquim Nabuco, who was selected by Rio Branco as Brazil's first ambassador to the United States, was a distinguished statesman who had been prominent in the anti-slavery and republican movements in the last days of the Empire. Having lived for two years (1876–1877) in the United States, Nabuco once said, "I am a strong Monroista, and thus a partisan of closer relations between Brazil

[32] Delgado de Carvalho, *Historia Diplomático do Brasil* (São Paulo: Companhia Editora Nacional, 1959), 364–365.

[33] Hill, *Dipl. Rel. U.S. and Brazil*, 292.

[34] Pedro Calmon, *Brasil e América* (Rio de Janeiro: José Olympia, Ed., 1943), 90.

[35] This is the only building or monument in Latin America honoring President Monroe.

[36] Dunshee de Abranches, *Brazil and the Monroe Doctrine* (Rio de Janeiro: Impresa Nacional, 1915), 69.

and the United States." He told Elihu Root that he regarded the Monroe Doctrine as "a complete statement of foreign policy."[37]

Joaquim Nabuco's five-year mission in Washington ended with his death in 1910. An eloquent and effective advocate of Rio Branco's policy of "approximation" with the United States,[38] Nabuco contributed greatly to an era of cordial relations between the two countries.

Rio Branco's program of *rapprochement* with the United States was greatly aided by the visit of Secretary of State Elihu Root to Rio de Janeiro in 1906 to head the American delegation to the Third International Conference of American States. In a memorable speech to the conference Mr. Root sought to allay Latin-American suspicions of United States imperialism. In this he achieved encouraging results, at least in Brazil. His visit to Rio, and to other cities of Brazil, proved to be of great material benefit to the political and commercial interests of the United States.[39] It is necessary at this point to take note of the subject of commercial interests as a conditioning factor in the general *rapprochement* between the two republics.

Commercial problems

In 1825, about the time of the inauguration of political relations between the United States and Brazil, the commercial interchange between the two countries was about equal at $2 million for United States imports from Brazil, and $2.3 million for exports to Brazil. By 1850, however, thanks to a developing coffee appetite in the United States, and Brazilian preference for European manufactured products, our imports at $9.3 million exceeded our exports to Brazil by about three to one. The disproportion in trade balance mounted to the colossal proportions of five and even six to one in the last three decades of the nineteenth century.[40]

Secretary of State Blaine had long been concerned about the marked decline in the value of exports from the United States to Brazil. This was one of the reasons why he proposed to the First International Conference of American States at Washington, in 1889, that a kind of American *zollverein* be established by the negotiation of reciprocity treaties among the American nations. The suggestion was vetoed largely because of Argentine objection.

Undeterred by the failure of his reciprocity proposal in the Pan American conference, Secretary Blaine then sought to have included in the pending tariff act a provision to force special concessions from other countries under threat of penalty duties by the United States. The Secretary of State urged the Congress that, since more than 87 per cent of Latin America's products sent to the United States paid no duties, the President should be empowered to use this fact as a leverage to obtain special concessions for American goods.

[37] Calmon, *op. cit.,* 82–83.
[38] Abranches, *op. cit.,* 71–72.
[39] *For. Rel., 1906,* I, 134.
[40] See statistical tables in W. S. Robertson, *Hispanic American Relations with the United States* (New York: Oxford University Press, 1923), Chap. VI.

The upshot of Blaine's propaganda was the incorporation in the McKinley Tariff Act of 1890 of the penalty clause to force concessions. The President was empowered to place a penalty tariff on sugar, molasses, coffee, tea, and hides when these articles, which were admitted free into the United States, were imported from countries whose duties on American products were deemed to be "reciprocally unjust and unequal."[41] Armed with the powers delegated him by Congress, the President proceeded to negotiate agreements for tariff reductions on American goods. Of the several countries which produced articles on the so-called "tropical list," Brazil was probably the most vulnerable to "tariff blackmail" because of its heavy dependence on the American market for its coffee and sugar. Accordingly, in order to escape the reimposition of duties on these articles, the Brazilian minister at Washington was authorized to inform Mr. Blaine that Brazil was prepared to admit either free of duty or with duties greatly reduced, a specified list of articles produced or manufactured in the United States.[42] These concessions were made without any reduction in duties upon Brazilian products imported into the United States, for they were already practically free.

The United States-Brazilian preferential arrangement lasted only until 1894. In 1897, after passage of the Dingley Tariff Act, the Congress returned to penalty tariff bargaining with a somewhat different list of bargaining articles but one that included coffee. After long and persistent negotiations by the Department of State, Brazil, faced by the threat of a penalty tariff on coffee, finally capitulated, and in 1904 agreed to grant a considerable reduction on certain American products. Thenceforward it became the practice, since Brazilian law provided that preferential tariff rates had to be granted annually, for the American ambassador to make annual requests for preferential treatment. In 1922 no request was made by the United States, for in that year the policy of securing concessions by threats of penalties was repudiated as being inconsistent with the general principle of equality of treatment.[43] The United States and Brazil formally agreed to adhere in their mutual relations to the unconditional most-favored-nation treatment.

Coffee, which was responsible for United States efforts to secure preferential trade treatment in Brazil, was also the cause of a minor difficulty between the two countries arising from the so-called "coffee valorization" scheme. The problem was simple: there was an overproduction of coffee. By 1900 Brazil was producing more than four-fifths of the world's coffee, virtually all of this coming from the Brazilian states of Minas Geräes, Espirito Santo, Rio de Janeiro, and São Paulo. São Paulo was by far the largest producer and therefore the one most critically concerned with the fact that Brazil alone

41 *Ibid.,* 214–217.

42 *For. Rel., 1891,* 43–44. For the agreements under the tariff act and their effects, see U.S. Tariff Commission, *Reciprocity and Commercial Treaties* (Washington, D.C.: Government Printing Office, 1919), 145 ff.

43 For a general survey of tariff bargaining for concessions, see Benjamin H. Williams, *Economic Foreign Policy of the United States* (New York: McGraw-Hill Book Company, Inc., 1929), 269–272.

was producing more than the world's annual consumption. São Paulo accordingly took the lead, sometimes acting alone, in various efforts to protect prices because of the enormous coffee surpluses. Finally the valorization plan was adopted in 1906.[44]

The government of the State of São Paulo decided that the most practicable plan was for it to buy the surplus crop in years of overproduction and hold for higher prices until years of underproduction. Since production varied greatly from year to year, such a plan appeared feasible but required a large sum of money. Loans to the extent of $90 million were contracted in London and New York. Thanks to a small coffee crop in 1908 the plan was saved at a critical juncture. It was the practice of the Committee on Coffee Valorization for the State of São Paulo to store and hold coffee off the market until prices rose to a prearranged level. In 1911 the Valorization Committee had stored millions of pounds of coffee in New York warehouses until the price rose to six cents a pound.

It was then that United States Congressman George W. Norris directed public and governmental attention to the activities of the Coffee Valorization Committee. He estimated that the artificially enhanced price of coffee was costing United States consumers millions of dollars a year, and he charged that the committee's work was carried on in the United States in violation of the antitrust law. Thanks to the initiative by Mr. Norris, an investigation by the Department of Justice, in May, 1912, resulted in its filing charges in the Federal District Court of New York against the agents of the valorization committee. The activities of the committee were alleged to be violative of provisions of both the Sherman Antitrust Act and the Wilson Tariff Act, which gave to the United States the right to seize and condemn property imported into the United States and held in restraint of trade.[45]

The Brazilian ambassador protested on the ground that the suit in question was equivalent to the American court's claiming jurisdiction over the acts of a foreign sovereign state. The United States ambassador at Rio reported that there was considerable popular resentment, and he cautioned that since the people of Brazil were "peculiarly sensitive" to the "delicate subject," a continuation of the suit would be embarrassing to American business enterprise in Brazil.[46] To point up this warning there was temporary suspension by Brazil of preferential tariff concessions on American goods which was costly to American exporters.

As a result of the protests, the United States Attorney agreed to drop the suit on condition that the entire stock of valorized coffee in New York be sold immediately in the open market. The State of São Paulo continued its valorization operations, but outside of the United States, of course. Occasionally, when the price of coffee rose, there was caustic criticism in the United States.

---

[44] For the valorization scheme, and also the controversy with the United States, see Hill, *Dipl. Rel. U.S. and Brazil*, 298–300; Williams, *op. cit.*, 400–402: Carvalho, *op. cit.*, 367–369.

[45] *For. Rel.*, 1913, 40–41.

[46] *Ibid.*, 1893, 45, 53.

In 1925, São Paulo approached American bankers for financial assistance to protect the price of coffee, but the bankers declined, having been cautioned by the federal government.[47]

Shortly before World War I (January, 1913) an action not without some influence over future United States-Brazilian relationships was the decision by the Brazilian government to terminate all of its extradition treaties, including that of 1897, with the United States. This was in pursuance of a statute passed by the Brazilian congress in June, 1911. At the time the law was passed the Brazilian Minister of Foreign Affairs stated that notices of denunciation would not be issued until the Supreme Court of Brazil passed upon the constitutionality of the law. When the Court acted favorably, the treaty with the United States was denounced by Brazil on July 25, 1913. The Foreign Minister pointed out that the liberal provisions of the new Brazilian law on extradition were in fact more ample than the treaty.[48] Despite its self-styled liberal extradition law, the refusal of Brazil to be bound by treaty obligation made that country a rather notorious refuge for American fugitives from justice.

World War I

Following the outbreak of the first World War the President of Brazil, on August 4, 1914, decreed the complete neutrality of his country. Although the large German population in Brazil might have been expected to influence the orientation of public attitudes toward Germany, this was not the case. Most of the Brazilians were sympathetic with the cause of the Allies. There were many factors responsible for this — such as British, French, Italian, and Portuguese economic, cultural, and racial influences — but of one thing we can be relatively certain: the influence of the United States, a strict neutral during the first two years of the war, was slight. In fact, the neutrality policy of the United States soon became an object of contempt by many Brazilians, including the distinguished publicist Ruy Barbosa. He attempted to show how despicable was the position of a powerful country that was suffering all manner of insults and yet would not align itself on the side of right, honor, and justice. Barbosa's Brazilian League for the Allies, founded in 1915, included many of the country's most noted writers, publicists, and statesmen.[49]

On January 31, 1917, the Brazilian government was officially informed of German intention to undertake unrestricted submarine warfare, and it promptly declared on February 9 that it could not accept the submarine blockade as effective. When the United States ruptured diplomatic relations with Germany because of the declaration of unrestricted submarine warfare, President Wilson called upon the other neutral powers to do the same. The

[47] Williams, *op. cit.,* 402.

[48] *For. Rel., 1913,* 25 ff.

[49] For a general discussion of Brazil in World War I, see P. A. Martin, *Latin America and the War* (Baltimore: The Johns Hopkins Press, 1925); also, *The Brazilian Green Book* (Ministerio dos Relacões Exteriores), authorized English version with an introduction and notes by Andrew Boyle (London: The Macmillan Company, 1918).

Brazilian government replied that it was standing on its note of February 9 which put responsibility on the Germans. The Brazilians were awaiting the overt act. This came two months later when the Brazilian ship the *Paraná* was torpedoed. On April 11, 1917, Brazil severed diplomatic relations with Germany; this was less than a week after the United States declared war on Germany.

Brazil's position was anomalous until she finally entered the war. On April 25 she declared neutrality in the war between the United States and Germany. This was highly displeasing to many Brazilians, particularly Ruy Barbosa and the Brazilian League for the Allies. Barbosa advocated the ousting of Lauro Muller as Minister of Foreign Affairs on the charge that, being of German origin, he was too complacent toward the Central Powers. On May 3, 1917, Muller was forced to resign and was followed in the foreign ministry by Dr. Nilo Peçanha, who was decidedly pro-Ally. Dr. Peçanha plainly declared that his policy would be favorable to the United States. So also was that of President Braz who suggested to the national congress that it "adopt the attitude that one of the belligerents forms an integral part of the American continent, and that to this belligerent we are bound by traditional friendship and by a similarity of political opinion in the defense of the vital interests of America and the principles accepted by international law."[50]

News that another Brazilian ship had been torpedoed caused President Braz to ask the national congress for authority to undertake necessary defense measures. By virtue of legislative authorization, on June 1, 1917, President Braz revoked the decree of neutrality in the war between the United States and Germany.

In illustration of Brazil's anomalous status, there was cooperation between the American and Brazilian fleets in hunting down German sea raiders in South American waters some months prior to Brazil's formal belligerency. It was not until October 26, 1917, after a Brazilian ship had been torpedoed and her captain taken prisoner, that Brazil declared war.

Once Brazil became a belligerent, her vessels helped the South Atlantic naval patrol; this was the extent of direct military participation. Brazil's economic assistance was greater, adding materially to the food supply of the Allies. In December, 1917, a Brazilian mission was sent to the United States to work for closer military cooperation, and also to purchase equipment and machinery to enable Brazil to increase her war production.

Had the war lasted even a few months longer there would likely have been participation by Brazilian military units in the fighting on the Western Front. Nevertheless, the material contributions of the great South American republic were helpful, but far more important, particularly to the United States, was the moral stimulus of Brazilian formal belligerency. As President Wilson said, Brazil's "action in this moment of crisis, tightens the bonds of friendship which have always held the two republics together."[51]

50 *Ibid.,* 40.
51 *Ibid.,* 90.

Post-World War I relations

By virtue of her declaration of war against the Central Powers, Brazil became one of the signatories of the Treaty of Versailles. Unlike the United States, Brazil ratified the peace treaty and became an original member of the League of Nations, being honored by election to the initial League Council. It was a great disappointment to our Brazilian friends that the United States refrained from membership. Undoubtedly the absence of this country contributed to the cooling of Brazilian enthusiasm for a world body which rather studiously sought to avoid, out of consideration for the United States, any Western Hemisphere involvements. After a time, Brazilian statesmen became impatient with the machinations of European politics and drew their country back into a quasi-isolationism. Thus, with Brazilian withdrawal from the League of Nations in 1926, a possible breach in the wall of United States-Brazilian solidarity failed to develop.

From World War I to 1930 the Brazilian governments continued to adhere faithfully to the Rio Branco policy of "approximation" toward the United States. As before, the United States could usually count on Brazilian support on important issues in inter-American relations. Fortunately, there were no untoward incidents to trouble the smooth flow of the current of United States-Brazilian relations.

Economic relations between the two countries continued to develop on a mutually satisfactory basis. In 1913 Brazilian imports from the United States amounted to $51 million, but her exports to the United States, mostly coffee, totaled $102 million, thereby creating a favorable trade balance of two to one. After the war there was a remarkable increase in United States-Brazilian trade. In return for its great favorable trade balance, Brazil granted a 20 to 30 per cent preferential treatment on major items purchased from the United States. After 1922, however, Brazil was no longer asked for this preference, subject to her acceptance of the unconditional most-favored-nation principle.[52] In 1929, on the eve of the world depression, the amount of trade between the United States and Brazil was over the one-third billion mark, with the balance, of course, in Brazil's favor, because of America's coffee appetite.

The trade increase after World War I was accompanied by an even more spectacular increase of American investments in the Brazilian economy. United States investments in Brazil, in 1913, amounted to about $50 million. In 1929 United States investments amounted to $476 million.[53] On January 1, 1932, United States investments in Brazil amounted to $624 million; of this sum $223 million were direct, and $401 million portfolio.[54] Fortunately for Brazil the American investments were greatly diversified, and no key

[52] See Tables I and III in Max Winkler, *Investments of United States Capital in Latin America* (Boston: World Peace Foundation, 1929), 82, 274–276.

[53] *Ibid.,* Table II, 175, and Table V, 278.

[54] *Foreign Policy Reports,* VII, No. 24 (February 3, 1932), 430.

industry could be said to be under foreign control. Therefore, Brazil was not the "victim" of American imperialism, although her dependence on coffee exports, amounting to about 70 per cent of her total exports, put the country on a so-called "colonial" economic basis.

Financial ties with Brazil were of more recent date. In 1920 almost none of Brazil's national debt was held in the United States, but by 1927 Yankee lenders held $342.4 million, or almost one-third of the foreign debt of Brazil.[55] Brazil's public finance was continually dependent on foreign capital, for since the budgets of the national and state governments were chronically unbalanced, the difference was usually made up by a succession of government loans contracted abroad. These were costly because of the large commissions demanded by the bankers. The Brazilian national government, and its political subdivisions, like the other Latin-American governments, offered their bonds for sale to the American public through the medium of the bankers. The high-water mark, in 1929, of United States investments in Brazilian dollar bonds, subsequently defaulted, amounted to $354 million.[56]

Getulio Vargas

The seizure of the Brazilian government by Getulio Vargas in 1930 by military force, created for the Hoover-Stimson administration a problem of recognition which it muffed. Badly informed by his representatives in Rio de Janeiro concerning the progress of the Vargas revolt, Secretary of State Henry Stimson advised President Hoover to embargo arms shipments to the rebels.[57] This was only two days before Vargas took over the government at Rio. On the basis of faulty information, the State Department had guessed wrong; it therefore hastened to make amends by promptly recognizing the new government.

The fact that the Vargas government developed into a dictatorial regime with fascist coloring, called by Vargas himself "a disciplined democracy," did not create for the United States any direct diplomatic problems. The nature of its government was strictly a Brazilian affair, and was of no concern to the United States so long as it honored its international obligations. The devastating effects of the Great Depression on United States-Brazilian trade relations was however, a matter of serious concern.

In 1929 there was a complete collapse of the price of coffee which had been artificially supported by valorization. It declined from 24.8 cents per pound in March, 1929, to 7.6 cents in October, 1931. This wrought havoc to Brazil's economy, for as the price of coffee dropped, Brazil's means of making payments abroad declined. Furthermore, the sources of foreign loans dried up.[58]

[55] Winkler, *op. cit.*, 86–87.

[56] See tables in Samuel Flagg Bemis, *The Latin American Policy of the United States* (New York: Harcourt Brace and Company, 1943), 336 and 341.

[57] A treaty signed at the Havana Conference of 1928 and ratified by the United States provided that insurgents not recognized as belligerents did not have the right to buy arms in a neutral country.

[58] *For. Pol. Rep.*, XI, No. 1 (March 13, 1935), 9.

The following figures are indicative of the trade disaster that befell both Brazil and the United States. In 1928 the total United States-Brazilian trade amounted to $320.7 million, in 1930 it was $184.6 million, and in 1932 it reached bottom at $110.8 million. The decline was due not so much to a reduction in the quantity of goods and products exchanged, as to a drastic drop in price. Illustrative of Brazil's dependence on the United States, in 1932, 45.8 per cent of all Brazilian exports went to the United States, and 30.2 per cent of all Brazilian imports came from the United States.

The United States-Brazil Trade Agreement which became effective on January 1, 1936, was, except for a unique agreement with Cuba, the first of the many reciprocal trade agreements negotiated by Mr. Hull. Perhaps the relative ease and dispatch with which a trade agreement was negotiated with Brazil was due to the fact that this trade was almost wholly noncompetitive. The United States imported from Brazil 85 per cent of its coffee production, and 96 per cent of our imports from Brazil entered the country free of duty. In exchange the United States sold Brazil industrial and agricultural articles.

According to the terms of the trade agreement[59] the United States undertook to maintain on the free list 90.8 per cent of the imports from Brazil and to reduce duties on 2.5 per cent of other imports. Brazil, in return, pledged to reduce duties on twenty-eight tariff items, and to maintain unchanged rates on thirteen items, in all of which the United States was a principal source of supply.

Brazil, like Argentina, Chile, and other countries of "colonial" economic status, was unable to abandon artificial restraints on trade such as exchange control and barter.[60] In this respect the Hull trade agreements program was not a success. In fact the Export-Import Bank made two loans in 1936 and 1939 to Brazil to unfreeze blocked balances of American exporters which were unpaid because of lack of exchange.

As the war clouds over Europe gathered ominously, and the United States sought to strengthen continental solidarity in view of the pending crisis, the position of Brazil caused considerable uneasiness. It was in 1937 that Getulio Vargas issued his authoritarian constitution establishing a centralized corporative state called *O Estado Novo,* the New State. There was uneasy mistrust in the hearts of democrats that a fascist state was taking form on American soil. Although, after 1937, Vargas' attitude toward inter-American cooperation was in doubt, the State Department refused to interpret the political developments in Brazil as indicative of any change in the traditional friendship between the governments and people of the two countries.

Oswaldo Aranha, who had been a loyal Vargas follower since the uprising of 1930, and who had been rewarded with the post of ambassador to the United States, and then became Foreign Minister, was most influential in

[59] For text of trade agreement, see *For. Pol. Rep.,* XI, No. 6 (May 22, 1935), 63.

[60] From 1934 to 1937 Brazil had a barter agreement with Germany. Eventually, Germany was sending twice as much to Brazil as Great Britain, and half as much as the United States.

orienting Brazilian policy to the side of the United States. In Washington Americans were attracted by the spell of the Brazilian ambassador's personality, and he in turn developed a great admiration for the United States. Thus, when he was called back to Rio de Janeiro to head the Foreign Ministry, he was in strategic position to support cooperation with the United States. His powerful support was needed, since Vargas' sympathies were unclear.

World War II

When it became increasingly evident that inter-American defense cooperation was necessary after the outbreak of war in September, 1939, Brazilian participation was most important. President Vargas, however, held back, apparently straddling the fence until the outcome of the war was less in doubt. This was the situation when, in 1940, Jefferson Caffery, a career diplomat, was sent to Rio de Janeiro as American ambassador. Fortunately, Ambassador Caffery and Foreign Minister Aranha worked out arrangements generally favorable to continental defense and also to the cause of the Allies.

The details of United States negotiations with Brazil, prior to Pearl Harbor, have already been set forth in an earlier chapter.[61] With respect to cooperation for military defense we have noted: the staff agreements, acquisition of base facilities for defense of the "bulge," the joint United States-Brazil Staff Conference, the military missions program, and the lend-lease agreement of October 1, 1941. We have also discussed the more important aspects of economic cooperation. Brazil being an important source of strategic materials, the United States entered into financial arrangements for their production, notably iron, manganese, and rubber. On September 1, 1940, the Exim Bank made a loan of $20 million for a steel mill to be located about 90 miles south of Rio de Janeiro at Volta Redonda. This mill, entirely Brazilian-owned, was destined to be Brazil's greatest steel producer. A general economic arrangement, but one of particular interest to both Brazil and the United States, was the Coffee Marketing Agreement of February, 1941, which allocated among the American coffee-producing countries equitable quotas in the markets of the United States and the rest of the world. Of course Brazil received by far the largest share of the United States market.[62]

As may be implied from the record of United States-Brazilian cooperation, the position of the Vargas government, uncertain some time prior to Pearl Harbor, was no longer in doubt. As a matter of fact, only one month before that fateful event Foreign Minister Aranha pledged 100 per cent cooperation with the United States.

At the Rio de Janeiro meeting of foreign ministers in January, 1942, both Brazil and the United States worked closely together. Immediately after the meeting Brazil severed relations with the Axis Powers. Brazil declared war on the Axis the following August — at the very moment when our fortunes

---

[61] *Supra,* 139–140.
[62] U.S. Dept. of State *Bulletin,* III (November 30, 1940), 483–488.

seemed at their lowest ebb, with the Philippines gone and our fleet sunk at Pearl Harbor.[63]

As in World War I, Brazil declined the role of inactive belligerent in World War II. But in contrast to the first war the record of United States-Brazilian collaboration in the second war, in both the military and economic realms, was far more impressive.

On the military side, the campaigns in Africa and Europe were greatly aided by air bases on the Brazilian "bulge." The Joint Brazil-United States Defense Commission supervised numerous cooperative military measures. The Brazilian navy assumed some responsibility for patrolling the waters of the South Atlantic. The United States made two lend-lease agreements with Brazil which received $154,286,000 or "more than half" of the total shipment of military equipment to all of Latin America.[64] Most of this was for a Brazilian division which was equipped and trained by the United States, and then transported on American ships to the Italian front.

Where economic cooperation for defense was concerned, throughout the war there was a steady flow of essential material from Brazil to the United States. The procurement of strategic materials was facilitated by a master agreement known as the United States-Brazilian Economic Accords of March 3, 1942. These laid the basis for greater production of strategic materials by Brazil, especially rubber and iron ore, while the United States on its part increased the pace of Brazilian rearmament under the terms of lend-lease. A line of credit of $100 million was to be made available by the Exim Bank for this purpose.[65]

For an impressive summary of Brazil's contributions to World War II, we refer to a statement by Secretary of State Cordell Hull in his *Memoirs:*

> Without the air bases Brazil permitted us to construct on her territory, victory either in Europe or in Asia could not have come so soon. These bases, jutting far out into the South Atlantic, permitted us to fly war planes across that ocean in waves to West Africa and hence to the theatres of operation in Europe or on to the Far East. Had it not been for these Brazilian bases we could not have got as much help to the British in Egypt as we did at the crucial battle of El Alamein.
>
> From Brazil, too, we received valuable diplomatic assistance in our negotiations with her mother country, Portugal. That farsighted statesman, Oswaldo Aranha, Brazil's Foreign Minister, never wavered from the cause of the Allies, and neglected no opportunity to give us his backing. In this he

[63] S. Walter Washington, *A Study of the Causes of Hostility Toward the United States in Latin America: Brazil* (Dept. of State, Office of Intelligence Research, External Research Paper No. 120, February 24, 1956), 20.

[64] *Twentieth Report to Congress on Lend-Lease Operations for the period ending June 30, 1945* (Washington, D.C.: Government Printing Office, 1945), 51.

[65] *For. Pol. Rep.*, XVII, No. 24 (March 1, 1942), 307. When in June, 1954, Brazil closed out its World War II lend-lease debt to the United States, it was revealed that Brazil had received lend-lease aid totaling $361 million. *Hispanic American Report*, VII, No. 6 (June, 1954), 44.

had the full support of President Getulio Vargas. Even in the dark days of the first half of 1942 they were willing to assume all the risks that aid to the United Nations comported.

Brazil sent an expeditionary force to Europe. Her small navy played its share in patrolling the Atlantic. She lost an appreciable portion of her merchant marine in her effort to transport supplies to the United States. She assisted us in keeping an eye on Dutch and French Guiana.[66]

Postwar political developments

A brief outline of political developments in Brazil is here presented as a frame of reference for the survey of United States-Brazilian relations since the end of World War II.

President Vargas had promised free elections in 1945, in which he would not be a candidate, but as the time of the election approached it was feared that the dictator was plotting to perpetuate himself in office. Thus, in order to forestall another Vargas *coup d'état,* the military chiefs staged a *coup* of their own. A demonstration of tanks, guns, and troops induced Vargas, on October 29, to resign. The military chiefs set up a provisional government until constitutional government could be re-established. The election held in December, 1945, resulted in the victory of General Erico Dutra, a colorless reactionary. An achievement of the Dutra administration was the adoption of a new national constitution in 1946, a remarkably liberal instrument of government. Nevertheless, the Dutra period was marked by great economic unrest. The result was the dissolution of the Communist party and the mon. The Communists, who were exceptionally strong in Brazil, having received about 800,000 votes in the election of 1947, fomented the general unrest. The result was the dissolution of the Communist Party and the severance of diplomatic relations with the U.S.S.R. Communism, although driven underground, continued to thrive in Brazil.

Proof that the glamor formerly attached to the name "Getulio" had not disappeared, was the substantial victory of Getulio Vargas in the presidential election of 1950. But the ex-dictator, now turned democrat, was no more able than his predecessor to solve Brazil's economic problems. Charged with responsibility for widespread political corruption and reckless handling of the national economy, and probably fearing his removal from office, President Vargas shot himself on August 24, 1954.[67] He was succeeded in the presidency by Vice-President João Café Filho.

Elected in the poll of October, 1955, Juscelino Kubitschek assumed the presidency of Brazil. Although Kubitschek succeeded in his ambition to establish a new national capital at Brasília, both this and other extravagant features of his national development program had serious economic conse-

[66] Cordell Hull, *The Memoirs of Cordell Hull* (2 vols. New York: The Macmillan Company, 1948), II, 1423.

[67] According to Vargas himself, "a river of mud" was running through the presidential palace, and political associates were involved in graft, corruption, and even murder.

quences. It seemed to be the policy of his administration to capitalize on galloping inflation.

When Jânio Quadros, who became president of Brazil on January 31, 1961, advocated an austerity program to solve the country's economic ills, he encountered such strong opposition that he weakly admitted defeat and unexpectedly resigned in August, 1961. The prospect of Vice-President João Goulart's succession to the presidency precipitated a crisis, for his leftist views and affiliations aroused the apprehensions of moderates and conservatives, particularly the military. The upshot of the situation was that the constitutional presidential system was hurriedly replaced by a parliamentary system. Goulart was allowed to succeed to the presidency, but with the powers of the office curbed, as it was hoped, by a ministry responsible to congress. This did not work out as expected; the presidential system was therefore restored, and Goulart had a free hand to attack the multiplying problems of his country, something he did in a thoroughly ineffective manner. He was overthrown by the military in April, 1964. It is on this disquieting note that we turn back to 1945 to pick up our discussion of United States-Brazilian relations.

Post-war relations: 1945–1953

It was during the immediate postwar years, in the administrations of Presidents Dutra and Vargas, that cracks in the former strong wall of United States-Brazilian solidarity began to make their appearance. Fortunately these rifts were confined largely to the area of economic relationships, for in most other matters Brazil did not deviate much from its traditional policy of cooperation with the United States, as was demonstrated at the inter-American conferences held at Rio de Janeiro in 1947 and at Bogotá in 1948. Brazil also adhered to her traditional cooperation in being the first of several Latin-American countries to sign a Military Assistance Agreement with the United States; although this agreement was signed late in 1951, unfortunately it was not ratified until May, 1953. This delay in ratification was caused by nationalist, Communist, and leftist opposition which bitterly assailed an alleged Yankee plot to force the sending of Brazilian troops to Korea.

In October, 1950, the United States and Brazil entered into a cultural agreement, the first of its kind. The pact provided for the exchange of students, teachers, and artists as well as exhibits and other cultural activities between the two countries; it also granted the right to both countries to establish and maintain cultural organizations, such as institutes, information offices, and libraries, in each other's territory.[68]

With Brazil, as with other Latin-American countries, events offered sad proof that economic factors are far more influential than cultural ones in the making and unmaking of international cooperation. The problem facing the United States and Brazil was not only that of providing a more profitable market for Brazilian products, but, more important in the eyes of the Brazilians, United States assistance for their economic development. With the

[68] *Hisp. Am. Rep.*, III (October, 1950), 41.

ending of World War II, Brazilians felt that, since they had been the most helpful and trustworthy of all our allies in Latin America, they were entitled to special consideration — which they complained they did not receive.

The war brought brief prosperity to Brazil. Because of a pronounced favorable balance of trade, at war's end Brazil had a backlog of more than half a billion dollars in balances abroad. Politicians and businessmen were thus encouraged to embark on a reckless spending spree which increased the already serious inflation and exhausted the reserves, and by 1950 the Brazilian economy was demoralized by overspending, corruption, and inflation. This heavy spending induced an unfavorable trade balance which made it difficult for Brazil to meet its foreign obligations.

By the beginning of 1948 Brazil's dollar holdings had been so greatly reduced that the government was forced to adopt the system of import licensing. In order to save dollars, the government also entered into direct barter arrangements with some European countries. These measures were not sufficient, however, to save Brazil from the necessity of negotiating loans from the Export-Import Bank — such as one for $125 million in 1950, and another for $300 million in 1952 — to help cancel dollar debts to United States exporters.

The perennial dollar shortage crises stimulated Brazil's urgent desire to become self-sufficient by industrialization and the diversification of production. In 1948 a Joint United States-Brazilian Technical Commission was established to make a survey of Brazil's economic situation and recommend what was necessary to ensure the nation's future economic development and industrial expansion. The commission made a careful investigation and in a report in February, 1949 — called the "Abbink Report" after the chairman, John Abbink, president of McGraw-Hill Publishing Company — recommended an elaborate program of agricultural, industrial, mineral, and power development. The report emphasized the need for balanced development of the Brazilian economy.[69] Although the report also called attention to the need of American private capital for economic development, this was hardly necessary, for despite the mounting nationalistic campaign in Brazil against any foreign enterprises in the development of the country's resources, after World War II direct American investments had grown faster in Brazil than in any other Latin-American country except Venezuela.

In response to the Abbink Report as well as to Brazilian complaints of United States neglect, in contrast to its multi-billion Marshall Plan assistance to Europe, a Brazil-United States Joint Commission for Economic Development was set up near the end of 1950. Composed of one Brazilian and one United States member, the Commission, located in Rio de Janeiro, was to study the development needs of Brazil and recommend action.[70] Several loans were granted Brazil by the Exim Bank and the World Bank as a result of the work of the Joint Commission. By the end of 1952, $213.3 million had been ap-

[69] *Ibid.,* II, No. 3 (February, 1949), 25.
[70] U.S. Dept. of State *Bulletin,* XXIV, No. 600 (January 1, 1951), 25–26.

proved. From July, 1945, to December, 1955, the total of United States government foreign assistance to Brazil amounted to $470 million.

Despite the foregoing evidence of economic assistance to Brazil there was widespread resentment against what was called "niggardly" treatment by the United States. When the United States made a loan of $125 million to Perón, Brazilians asked if this was the dictator's reward for noncooperation. The United States reacted to this criticism by making a $300 million loan to Brazil on February 21, 1953. Anti-American campaigns against "Yankee imperialism," formerly unusual in Brazil, were encouraged by the propaganda of ultra-nationalists and the outlawed Communist party.[71] By the end of the Truman administration Brazil's relations with the United States had sadly deteriorated.

Relations: 1953–1960

United States public and private economic cooperation with Brazil continued during the Eisenhower administration, although Dr. Milton Eisenhower, on the occasion of his visit in July, 1953, warned the Brazilians that there was a limit to the obligations which a country could assume.

The extent of United States participation in the Brazilian economy, in 1955, was set forth succinctly in a United States Department of Commerce report.[72] United States direct investments in Brazil amounted to $1.2 billion. This total was exceeded only by American investments in Canada, the United Kingdom, and Venezuela. The Brazilian investments were principally in public utilities, trading establishments, and manufacturing. United States companies operating in Brazil spent about $600 million in 1955 for wages, taxes, and materials. Taxes amounted to $80 million, and of about 94,000 persons employed by the companies, only 630 were sent from the United States.

On October 15, 1959, Ambassador John M. Cabot made a notable speech at São Paulo, in which he elaborated on the subject of United States cooperation with Brazil.[73] Through the Exim Bank the United States had extended credits to Brazil for $1.337 billion for 257 projects. These included: the expansion of Volta Redonda, whose steel production had increased eightfold in fourteen years; electric power, which had doubled in seven years; the rehabilitation of Brazil's railroads; and the expansion of the Brazilian merchant marine. A vast technical assistance program, a cooperative work with funds provided by both governments, had been in operation for many years.

With respect to military cooperation, Ambassador Cabot pointed out that Brazil had obtained from the United States two cruisers, four destroyers, eight destroyer escorts, two submarines, and "further destroyers are still to be de-

[71] For example, Senator Guy Gillette's 1950 investigation of the coffee situation, because of the spectacular price rise, caused unfavorable reaction in Brazil, which the Communists whipped up into emotional, outraged indignation.

[72] U.S. Dept. of Commerce, Office of Business Economics, *U.S. Investments in Latin American Economy* (Washington, D.C., 1957), 61–64.

[73] U.S. Dept. of State *Bulletin*, XLI, No. 1065 (November 23, 1959), 753–757.

livered." Brazil had also cooperated by permitting the United States to establish a temporary missile-tracking base on the island of Fernando de Noronha.

Despite the not inconsiderable amount of United States assistance to Brazil, the economic problems of the country seemed to multiply. Brazil finished 1958 with an exchange deficit of over $300 million and sought more United States aid; however, the United States refused to grant further aid without basic reform in Brazil's budget management and credit policy. But President Kubitschek was unwilling to accept economic reforms as demanded by both the International Monetary Fund and the United States government. He seemed confident that the United States would grant new aid without restrictions rather than see Brazil fall into the hands of the extreme nationalists or the Communists. On this gamble Kubitschek won out, for the United States permitted Brazil to postpone its debt payments.[74]

The State Department was quite unhappy because of the excesses of extreme nationalism in Brazil and the apparent softness of the Kubitschek government toward Communism. Nationalism in Brazil, aided and abetted by Communism, was reaching new heights of anti-United States chauvinism.

Relations since 1960

President Kubitschek's successors, Jânio Quadros and João Goulart continued the trend of Brazilian policy which was so disturbing to Washington. Quadros was in office for too short a time to implement what promised to be a policy of independence from United States influence. Goulart, whose leftist views and associations had so frightened the army chiefs of Brazil when he assumed the presidency, did not prove at first as radical as anticipated. But on the other hand his apparent policy of accommodation with Communists, both internal and external, was far from reassuring. It eventually brought about his removal by a military *coup* in April, 1964.

Loans and grants to Brazil, authorized during the first two years of the Alliance for Progress (to August, 1963), totaled over $700 million. According to Secretary Dean Rusk, aid to Brazil under the Alliance for Progress was extremely limited during the calendar year 1962 because the United States had made it clear to Brazil that "assistance could not be effectively applied so long as there was acute inflation and so long as there were lacking economic and financial policies which provided a basis for sound economic growth." Responding to United States pressure Brazil was able by March, 1963, to report a number of major tax reforms and measures to carry forward a development and stabilization program.[75] According to Secretary Rusk, United States assistance would continue to adjust to Brazil's stabilization performance.

A special object of United States assistance has been drought-ridden northeast Brazil. This area of some 600,000 square miles, and 25 million people,

[74] *Hisp. Am. Rep.*, XII, No. 4 (April, 1959), 236, No. 5 (May, 1959), 296.
[75] U.S. Dept. of State *Bulletin*, XLVIII, No. 1242 (April 15, 1963), 557.

is one of South America's most crowded and poverty-stricken regions. An average per capita income is scarcely $100. Northeast Brazil is a crucible of social, economic, and political problems. A Development Agency for Northeast Brazil, or S U D E N E, prepared a five-year plan for the area, envisaging a total cost of $900 million, $500 million to be assumed by Brazil. The program because of its urgency evoked special interest on the part of several agencies of the United States, including the Peace Corps.[76]

[76] U.S. Dept. of State *Bulletin*, XLV, No. 1153 (July 31, 1961), 196–197.

SUPPLEMENTARY READING

Azevedo, Fernando de, *Brazilian Culture: An Introduction to the Study of Culture in Brazil*, William Rex Crawford, trans. (New York: The Macmillan Company, 1950).

Calmon, Pedro, *Brasil e América* (Rio de Janeiro: Livraria José Olympia, Editora, 1943).

Calogeras, João Pandiá, *A History of Brazil*, Percy A. Martin, trans. (Chapel Hill: University of North Carolina Press, 1939).

Freyre, Gilberto, *Brazil: An Interpretation* (New York: Alfred A. Knopf, Inc., 1945).

Ganzert, F. W., "The Baron do Rio Branco, Joaquim Nabuco, and the Growth of Brazilian-American Friendship, 1900–1910," *Hispanic American Historical Review*, 22 (1942), 432–451.

Hill, Laurence F., ed., *Brazil* (Berkeley and Los Angeles: University of California Press, 1947).

Hill, Laurence F., *Diplomatic Relations Between the United States and Brazil* (Durham: Duke University Press, 1932).

Loewenstein, Karl, *Brazil Under Vargas* (New York: The Macmillan Company, 1942).

McClosky, M. B.: "The United States and the Brazilian Naval Revolt, 1893–1894." *Américas*, 2 (1946), 296–321.

Smith, T. Lynn, *Brazil: People and Institutions* (Baton Rouge: Louisiana State University Press, 1954).

Smith, T. Lynn, and Marchant, Alexander, *Brazil: Portrait of Half a Continent* (New York: The Dryden Press, Inc., 1951).

Stuart, Graham H., *Latin America and the United States* (New York: Appleton-Century-Crofts, Inc., 5th ed. 1955), Chap. XVIII.

Tavares de Sa, Hernane, *The Brazilians, People of Tomorrow* (New York: The John Day Company, 1947).

Turner, Charles W. *Ruy Barbosa: Brazilian Crusader for the Essential Freedoms* (Nashville, Tenn.: Abingdon Press, 1945).

Vianna, Helio, *História Diplomática do Brasil* (São Paulo: Edicões Melhoramentos, n.d.).

17

Conclusion

The fundamental objectives of United States policy toward Latin America have been remarkably consistent over the years. From the era of Latin-American emancipation to the present day they have reflected constantly the vital necessities of national security. There has been no deviation, with the recent exception of the case of Castro's Cuba, from the purpose of the United States to capitalize on its hemisphere position as a protection against external threats. It follows naturally, therefore, that the United States in protecting its own security has supported the independence, peace, and stability of the Latin-American nations. No hostile power can be allowed to gain a foothold in the area, for strategically it is our "soft under-belly."

In contrast to pronounced consistency in the fundamental objectives of United States policy toward Latin America, the means employed to attain these ends have not always conformed to a uniform pattern. Varied in nature and application, they comprise the subject matter of this volume. Here we present a brief recapitulation of the evolution of relations, or the implementation of policy, divided into more or less distinct chronological periods.

The initial phase of the long history of United States-Latin American relations, the era of Latin-American emancipation (1810–1824), was marked by realization on the part of the United States that its security was intimately linked with the independence of the new Latin-American states. An early problem created by the outbreak of the wars for Latin-American independence was a territorial issue concerning the Spanish North American borderlands. The Florida no-transfer resolution of 1811 stated the problem succinctly: "the United States cannot without serious inquietude see any part of the said territory pass into the hands of any foreign Power." This has been called "the first significant landmark in the evolution of United States-Latin American policy."

The United States was fortunate in being able to exploit the distresses of a

459

weak and decadent Spain to its own great territorial advantage. The Adams-Onís Transcontinental Treaty of 1821 provided for the definitive cession of the Floridas, and secured the boundary of the Louisiana Purchase from the Gulf of Mexico to the Pacific.

The ratification of the treaty enabled the Monroe-Adams administration finally to heed popular demands for recognition of the Latin-American republics. The United States was in fact the first government outside of the Latin-American area to recognize the new states. This action, taken in defiance of the European governments, has been regarded as a restrained expression of the Western Hemisphere idea "that the peoples of this Hemisphere stand in a special relationship to one another which sets them apart from the rest of the world." This same idea was the basis for Monroe's famous message of 1823 which proclaimed the doctrine of the two spheres.

Despite recognition and the Monroe Doctrine, the United States government was not inclined to closer political relations with Latin America — economic yes, but political no. President John Quincy Adams urged United States participation in the Panama Congress of 1826, not because he favored any political commitments with the Latin Americans, but because he was aware of advantages to our economic interests. President Adams, a typical New Englander, was naturally interested in the foreign commerce of the United States.

We are not able to record, however, that there was a surge in the development of United States commerce with Latin America, as Adams anticipated. Quite to the contrary; for on a comparative basis, trade with Latin America fell behind the pace of our commercial relations with other parts of the world. Not only economically, but politically, the second period of United States-Latin-American relations (1825–1895) was an era of relative inaction and disassociation.

After the pronouncement of the Monroe Doctrine and the recession of the European threat, real or imagined, to Latin-American independence, the United States was concerned with issues other than those of Latin America, particularly the securing of its own continental boundaries. Despite the brave language of President Monroe, Latin-American appeals for defensive alliances were rejected, for there was opposition to any political commitments to the new states. Not only was there a cooling of United States interest in Latin America, but, conversely, enthusiasm for the United States in Latin America also subsided. This mutual inclination to disassociation prevailed for several decades.

The revival of the Monroe Doctrine by President Polk in the 1840's did not necessarily mean a change in American attitude. This revival was more related to the achievement by the United States of its manifest destiny of continental expansion than its concern with the integrity and independence of the Latin-American states. The Mexican War and the great territorial acquisitions by the United States at the expense of a neighboring Latin-American republic also demonstrated expansionism rather than a community of inter-American interests. The development of the canal policy of the United States was likewise quite devoid of any expression of the Western Hemisphere idea.

The Civil War marked a real turn in United States policy and attitude toward Latin America. The expansionism of manifest destiny at the expense of Latin America had run its course. It was no longer supported by majority public opinion. Equally important to the Latins, the Monroe Doctrine became once more a mantle of protection against external aggressors. The determined stand by the United States against the French intervention in Mexico contributed greatly to a restoration of United States prestige throughout the Americas.

The fact that the foreign trade of the United States was increasing in the post-Civil War decades and the Latin-American market was alluring contributed to a new-born desire for cooperation. The decades of the eighties and nineties not only marked the end of the era of inaction and disassociation, but also set the stage for the era of imperialism. James G. Blaine was one of the first to divine the transition about to take place in the world status of the United States and the nature of our future relations with Latin America. He therefore proposed an inter-American conference with the dual objectives of promoting hemispheric peace and trade. So was inaugurated the Pan American movement, the support of which became thereafter a cardinal principle of United States foreign policy.

From the point of view of the United States, inter-American cooperation should be confined largely to those economic, social, and cultural matters concerning which harmonious international agreement was attainable. Political matters, touching as they did sensitive national sovereignty, should be avoided if at all possible. It became the policy of the United States therefore, to avoid extravagant and unrealistic peace commitments, such as general compulsory arbitration, but to favor instead limited and voluntary procedures of peaceful settlement.

The Latin Americans were not attracted to cooperation with the United States by economic lure. They hoped that, through formal association with the rising colossus of the North, they would be able to gain its acceptance of principles safeguarding the rights of small and weak states. The history of Pan Americanism after 1889 was therefore the story of persistent and unremitting advocacy by the Latins for United States recognition of the Calvo Doctrine of absolute and inviolable sovereignty.

A new departure in United States-Latin American relations, the era of imperialism (1895–1932), emerged from the so-called first Venezuelan crisis of 1895. It was the Olney doctrine of paramount interest, which was based on the idea that the safety of the United States required its hegemony on this continent.

It was at the beginning of the brief imperialistic phase of United States-Latin American relations that the meaning of the Monroe Doctrine was modified by the so-called Roosevelt Corollary, or the exercise of an international police power in Latin America. Undoubtedly appeal to the Monroe Doctrine contributed greatly to the self-justification of United States interventions, but it seems that even without the Corollary the trend toward imperialism was too strong to be denied. Following the Spanish-American war the United States was crossing the threshold of world affairs as a new Great Power. It was not only determined to play a more active role in world affairs, but thereby to contribute to the betterment of the world, particularly Latin America. With crusading zeal the superior benefits of American civilization were to be extended to our less fortunate "sister republics." A new form of expansionism, a new kind of manifest destiny, was in the ascendancy in Washington.

The United States attempted to impose its will on the "southern neighbors" in many ways and in many places. Notably there was the imposition of the Platt Amendment on Cuba, the seizure of the Panama Canal Zone, the application of the Roosevelt Corollary to the Dominican Republic, Haiti, and Nicaragua, and other instances too numerous to mention in which the "big stick" was wielded vigorously, not only by Theodore Roosevelt, but also by his successors Taft and Wilson. The methods used to influence the Latins included different kinds of interventions, some direct and forcible, others indirect and nonforcible. The right of intervention had been granted by treaties in some instances, but in other cases it was believed justified by international law.

Apparently the dominant motive for these interventions was not the economic exploitation or dominion over alien peoples, but rather the fostering of their political and economic stability so that there could be no justification or pretext for European intervention. Although the European threat may have been overworked in justification of interventions, we cannot overlook the fact that the existence of the United States created a bulwark against European imperialism in the Western Hemisphere. Had it not been for the United States and its Monroe Doctrine, the Western Hemisphere — divided up as it was into a number of small, feeble, and disorderly states — would have been easy prey to European partition. United States imperialism protected the hemisphere against Old World imperialistic powers. It was a case of our imperialism against their imperialism. But it was a benevolent imperialism that disappeared as soon as the European danger vanished after World War I.

It would be quite unfair to judge United States interventions of the early decades of the century by the standards of later years. That the right of intervention was recognized and widely practiced by the world's great powers must not be overlooked. Moreover, the fact of imperialistic expansion by the European powers was ample justification for the United States to take precautionary measures in the Western Hemisphere. This vigilance could not be relaxed until that threat disappeared.

Of course there was another and very important side to the practice of American imperialism in Latin America. Critics have pointed out that the results of the interventions were ephemeral; that our interference in the Latin-American republics did not result in strengthening democracy; that in this respect we must trust to internal forces rather than external pressures. This is quite true, but to say that the interventions were unjustified since they contributed to Latin America no lasting beneficial results, misses the point, for the prime purpose was not necessarily to establish democratic governments, but merely to forestall the threat, real or imagined, of extracontinental interposition.

The most serious and unfortunate by-product of American imperialism was Latin-American suspicion, resentment, and even hatred for the Yankees. It seemed to them that the United States was fencing off the imperialism of Europe from Latin America in order to appropriate the region for itself: "Hands off Europe, and hands on by the United States." They believed that Yankee imperialism was bent on devouring the liberties of the New World. They also resented the patronizing "civilizing mission" and the self-appointed role of protector. As one Latin put it, "Since there are no longer rain clouds coming up from the east why should a friend, however well-intentioned, insist on holding an umbrella over us?" He added: "We are quite able to do that for ourselves if necessary." This we question.

American imperialism, like the Monroe Doctrine, was confined almost exclusively to the Caribbean area. South America, except the countries of the Spanish Main, was never the victim of United States intervention. Yet, despite this fact, most Latins, particularly the Argentines, joined in the assault on Yankee imperialism, an assault that continued long after our abandonment of the right and the practice of intervention. A ghost of the past is still given reality by Latins who should know better.

In accounting for the retreat from imperialism, anti-Americanism in Latin America had an influence on the conscience of the American people themselves, who had never been happy over the trend of our relations with Latin America after the turn of the century. Much could be abided, however, under guise of support of the Monroe Doctrine and protection of the Panama Canal. But this was no longer true after Versailles, which marked the beginning of an interlude of apparent Western Hemisphere security. Since Latin-American instability in itself was not necessarily a threat to the United States, it was no longer necessary to intervene to maintain order. The result was the abandonment of American imperialism dating from the decade of the 1920's.

The new trend was inaugurated by Charles E. Hughes, Secretary of State under Presidents Harding and Coolidge. Not only did he make a start in withdrawing the Marines from Caribbean countries; in many ways he anticipated the Good Neighbor policy of the next decade.

The activities of Henry Stimson in Nicaragua and Dwight Morrow in Mexico in working out in a conciliatory spirit solutions to difficult problems are usually regarded as further evidences of a new Good Neighbor policy trend in the United States.

President Hoover and Secretary of State Stimson were responsible for final and important steps in liquidating American imperialism and in preparing the way for the Good Neighbor policy. Acts indicative of United States intention to pursue a new course in its Latin-American relations included the following: (1) repudiation of the Roosevelt Corollary of the Monroe Doctrine; (2) return to the traditional Jeffersonian *de facto* recognition policy; (3) withdrawal of our Marines from Nicaragua; (4) notification to American investors in certain Latin-American countries that they must exhaust local remedies before appealing for diplomatic protection; and (5) refusal of the State Department to press for full and punctual settlement of public financial obligations due American citizens.

Despite these considerable concessions to Latin-American nationalistic sensibilities, the Hoover-Stimson policy did not evoke the good will and confidence expected because it omitted one essential ingredient: the unqualified renunciation of intervention. Nevertheless, the retreat from imperialism was well-nigh total; by eradicating most of the vestiges of its power, the United States ended an era of unhappy dominance over Latin America. It remained for the Roosevelt administration to go the full way in tacitly accepting the principles of the Calvo Doctrine. This was the core of the Good Neighbor policy, which guided our Latin-American relations during the long presidency of Franklin D. Roosevelt.

The Good Neighbor era (1933–1945) was inaugurated by the formal renunciation of intervention at the Montevideo conference of 1933. The immediate application of the new policy in our relations with the other American republics left no doubt as to the good faith and sincerity of the New Deal administration. Military occupation of Haiti was terminated. With reference to politically and economically distressed Cuba, the United States refrained from armed intervention and assisted the Cuban people to rehabilitate their nation by negotiating a new reciprocity agreement. A new treaty of relations was also negotiated in which the Platt Amendment was eliminated. With Panama, likewise, a new treaty was made which eliminated sources of friction between the two countries, particularly the right of intervention and the guarantee of Panamanian independence.

Later tangible acts of "good neighborliness" were the withholding by the State Department of diplomatic protection on behalf of the petroleum corporations whose properties had been expropriated by the governments of Bolivia and Mexico. Furthermore, the United States government took no direct action to assist American citizens in recovering their losses on defaulted Latin-American government issues. The bondholders were left to the mercy of the debtor governments. This has been called "dollar diplomacy in reverse." The abandonment by the United States of its rights of protection was an unusual spectacle for a great power. The consequences were far-reaching.

The onslaught of the depression, coupled with the highly protectionist Smoot-Hawley Tariff Act of 1930, precipitated a disastrous decline in both foreign trade and investments. This was the situation inherited by the Roosevelt administration. Its answer was adoption of the Reciprocal Trade Agreements Act and incorporation of the Export-Import Bank. Gradually the New Deal moved from the policy of public loans to stimulate United States trade with Latin America to the general support of Latin-American welfare. This represented the apogee of good neighborliness in the later years of the Roosevelt administration.

As the war clouds gathered over Europe in the late 1930's, the American government urged on its Latin-American associates a strengthening of the hemisphere security system, particularly with respect to meeting external threats. It is encouraging to report that, in contrast to the questionable utility of the intra-American peace pacts, the consultative procedure agreed upon at Buenos Aires and Lima paid off in rich dividends of security action in World War II. In the Consultative Meetings of the Foreign Ministers the American republics proceeded about as far as could be expected in collaborative political, military, and economic action during World War II. Of even greater importance to the war effort were the numerous bilateral agreements (made possible thanks to the Good Neighbor policy) between the United States and most of the Latin-American states covering every aspect of cooperation.

The recalcitrance of Argentina did not detract substantially from the encouraging demonstration of inter-American solidarity in the crisis of World War II. We do not say that the distrust of American hegemony was entirely removed, but Latin-American reverence for Franklin Roosevelt was responsible for the most extraordinary *entente cordiale* ever achieved between the peoples of the hemisphere.

Before the end of the Roosevelt administration there were evidences of cooling interest in the State Department concerning American regionalism. Mr. Hull's "globalism" was in the ascendant. Not a single inter-American consultation occurred from 1942 to 1945. The Latin Americans, however, rose to the defense of the inter-American system, and with the aid of Senator Arthur Vandenberg succeeded at the San Francisco United Nations Conference in safeguarding its autonomous status. Mr. Hull's globalism proved to be only a momentary aberration.

Although we regard United States-Latin American relations since World War II as falling into a new and contemporary period of development — an era of readjustment — this does not mean that there was an abandonment of the Good Neighbor policy by the succeeding administrations. Except for the absence of the magnetic attraction of the Roosevelt personality there was no change. President Truman, on the very day of Roosevelt's death, in a message to the Governing Board of the Pan American Union reassured it that "to the Good Neighbor Policy of which he was the author I wholeheartedly subscribe." Throughout his administration President Truman faithfully and earnestly endeavored to fulfill this pledge. During the Eisenhower administration, too, there was no conscious abandonment of either the spirit or the content of the policy.

The Latin Americans, however, insisted that there was abandonment, and constantly urged "a return" to the policies of the "golden era" of the Roosevelt administration. As a matter of fact, no actual change of policy was responsible for this criticism; rather it was the failure of the postwar administrations to move faster into new economic areas in the spirit of Franklin Roosevelt. It was the belief of the Latin Americans that, whereas President Roosevelt would have responded generously to their appeals for greater economic assistance, Presidents Truman and Eisenhower took them for granted as trusted allies, and put the needs of other areas of the world ahead of theirs.

Our greatest challenge in Latin America since World War II has been that of mobilizing a hemisphere front against the threats posed by international Communism. The United States has been single-minded in this purpose; all else has been subordinated to this objective. The threat is viewed as an external one which must be opposed by political and military means. The adoption of the Rio treaty, the negotiation of military agreements with the Latin-American republics, and a series of significant anti-Communist resolutions urged on the Latins by the United States at various inter-American conferences and meetings of Foreign Ministers were all parts of the pattern of United States policy.

For their part, the Latin Americans have preferred giving priority to inter-American cooperation in economic and social areas in order to combat the poverty, disease, and illiteracy that prevail in their countries. In other words, they have regarded the threat of Communism not as external but as internal, to be handled by remedying those conditions that invite Communism. The United States reluctantly and tardily conceded the validity of the Latin-American argument, but without abandoning its own original position. Thus, while clinging to the belief that international Communism presents an external threat which must be countered by a posture of continental defense, the United States finally embarked upon an aid program of fantastic proportions — the Alliance for Progress — to forestall violent revolution by supporting with billions of dollars far-reaching social reforms and economic development.

Like fighting fire with fire, the United States, with the cooperation of the Latin-American governments, is dedicated to fighting Communist revolution with peaceful socio-economic democratic revolution. The Alliance for Progress is expected to channel the impatient and explosive "rising expectations" of Latin America's degraded masses into programs of basic but manageable reform and thereby immunize them against the contagion of Communism.

Since the demands of the masses are aimed high at fundamental changes in their social and economic institutions, we cannot expect that they will be satisfied with palliatives. If the program of the Alliance for Progress is successful, then truly the United States policy of massive foreign aid will have been vindicated. But if the program fails, will violent revolution — followed perhaps by Communist control — be far behind?

It is ironic to record that after 150 years of relations with Latin America, the area is still the "soft under-belly" of hemisphere defense and a prime security concern of the United States. Since the winning of their independence, most of the Latin-American nations have seemingly made little progress in demonstrating that degree of political maturity essential for the realization of genuine democratic government. It is still a vast area of great instability, poverty, illiteracy, and frustration. In fact, the weakness of the Latin-American portion of the hemisphere to external threats seems to be greater today than ever before.

The balance sheet of our Latin-American relations certainly occasions no optimism, nor on the other hand pessimism; rather it should be regarded as a challenge to move ahead with greater determination and purpose. Though temporary setbacks may occur, there can be little doubt that the challenge will be met both in the United States and in Latin America, for the habit and the value of mutual cooperation has become a part of the way of life of the Americas. It is the heritage of years of intelligent and devoted effort too valuable to be sacrificed.

That the United States will continue to work on behalf of effective and mutually beneficial inter-American relations was the sense of a statement by President Johnson, on December 15, 1963: "Next to keeping peace — and maintaining the strength and vitality which makes freedom secure — no work is more important for our generation of Americans than our work in this hemisphere."

Index

A B C D E F G H I J — R — 7 3 2 1 0 / 6 9 8 7 6 5